MATHEMATICS

Collection of 560+ MCQs based on NCERT

Improves your Score by at least 20%

26 Chapters based on NCERT

DPP
Daily Practice Problems
Chapter-wise Sheets

Date : Start Time : End Time :

MATHEMATICS (Cm10)

SYLLABUS : Limits & Derivatives

Scoring Grid				
DAILY PRACTICE PROBLEM DPP CHAPTERWISE CM10 - MATHEMATICS				
Total Questions	20	Total Marks	72
Attempted		Correct	
Incorrect		Net Score	
Cut-off Score	25	Qualifying Score	36
Success Gap = Net Score – Qualifying Score			
Net Score = (Correct × 4) – (Incorrect × 1)			

• **Corporate Office** : 45, 2nd Floor, Maharishi Dayanand Marg, Corner Market,
Malviya Nagar, New Delhi-110017
Tel. : 011-49842349 / 49842350

Typeset by Disha DTP Team

Printed at : Repro Knowledgecast Limited, Thane

DISHA PUBLICATION

For further information about books from DISHA,
Log on to www.dishapublication.com or email to info@dishapublication.com

INDEX/CHAPTERS

		Page No.
DPP-1	SETS	M-1 – M-4
DPP-2	RELATIONS AND FUNCTIONS	M-5 – M-8
DPP-3	TRIGONOMETRIC FUNCTIONS	M-9 – M-12
DPP-4	COMPLEX NUMBERS AND QUADRATIC EQUATIONS	M-13 – M-16
DPP-5	PERMUTATIONS AND COMBINATIONS	M-17 – M-20
DPP-6	BINOMIAL THEOREM	M-21 – M-24
DPP-7	SEQUENCES AND SERIES	M-25 – M-28
DPP-8	STRAIGHT LINES AND PAIR OF STRAIGHT LINES	M-29 – M-32
DPP-9	CONIC SECTIONS	M-33 – M-36
DPP-10	LIMITS AND DERIVATIVES	M-37 – M-40
DPP-11	MATHEMATICAL REASONING	M-41 – M-44
DPP-12	STATISTICS	M-45 – M-48
DPP-13	PROBABILITY	M-49 – M-52
DPP-14	RELATIONS AND FUNCTIONS	M-53 – M-56
DPP-15	INVERSE TRIGONOMETRIC FUNCTIONS	M-57 – M-60
DPP-16	MATRICES	M-61 – M-64
DPP-17	DETERMINANTS	M-65 – M-68
DPP-18	CONTINUITY AND DIFFERENTIABILITY	M-69 – M-72
DPP-19	APPLICATION OF DERIVATIVES	M-73 – M-76
DPP-20	INTEGRALS	M-77 – M-80
DPP-21	APPLICATION OF INTEGRALS	M-81 – M-84
DPP-22	DIFFERENTIAL EQUATIONS	M-85 – M-88
DPP-23	VECTOR ALGEBRA	M-89 – M-92
DPP-24	THREE DIMENSIONAL GEOMETRY	M-93 – M-96
DPP-25	PROBABILITY	M-97 – M-100
DPP-26	PROPERTIES OF TRIANGLES	M-101 – M-104

Solutions To Chapter-wise DPP Sheets (1-26) S-1 – S-108

MOCK TEST FULL SYLLABUS 1-12

DPP - Daily Practice Problems

Chapter-wise Sheets

Date : ______ Start Time : ______ End Time : ______

MATHEMATICS (CM01)

SYLLABUS : Sets

Max. Marks : 67 **Time : 60 min.**

GENERAL INSTRUCTIONS

- The Daily Practice Problem Sheet contains 20 Questions divided into 5 sections.
  Section I has **6** MCQs with ONLY 1 Correct Option, **3** marks for each correct answer and **–1** for each incorrect answer.
  Section II has **4** MCQs with ONE or MORE THAN ONE Correct options.
  For each question, marks will be awarded in one of the following categories:
  Full marks: **+4** If only the bubble(s) corresponding to all the correct option(s) is (are) darkened.
  Partial marks: **+1** For darkening a bubble corresponding to each correct option provided NO INCORRECT option is darkened.
  Zero marks: If none of the bubbles is darkened.
  Negative marks: **–2** In all other cases.
  Section III has **5** Single Digit Integer Answer Type Questions, **3** marks for each Correct Answer and **0** mark in all other cases.
  Section IV has Comprehension Type Questions having **4** MCQs with ONLY ONE corect option, **3** marks for each Correct Answer and **0** mark in all other cases.
  Section V has **1** Matching Type Question, **2** marks for the correct matching of each row and **0** mark in all other cases.
- You have to evaluate your Response Grids yourself with the help of Solutions.

Section I - Straight Objective Type

This section contains 6 multiple choice questions. Each question has 4 choices (a), (b), (c) and (d), out of which **ONLY ONE** is correct.

1. Consider the following relations:

1. $A - B = A - (A \cap B)$
2. $A = (A \cap B) \cup (A - B)$
3. $A - (B \cup C) = (A - B) \cup (A - C)$

Which of these is/are correct?

(a) (1) and (3) (b) (2) only
(c) (2) and (3) (d) (1) and (2)

2. The value of $(A \cup B \cup C) \cap (A \cap B^c \cap C^c)^c \cap C^c$, is

(a) $B \cap C^c$ (b) $B^c \cap C^c$
(c) $B \cap C$ (d) $A \cap B \cap C$

3. A survey shows that 63% of the Americans like cheese whereas 76% like apples. If x% of the Americans like both cheese and apples, then

(a) $x = 39$ (b) $x = 63$
(c) $39 \le x \le 63$ (d) None of these

RESPONSE GRID	1. ⓐⓑⓒⓓ	2. ⓐⓑⓒⓓ	3. ⓐⓑⓒⓓ

Space for Rough Work

4. Let X and Y be two non-empty sets such that $X \cap A = Y \cap A = \phi$ and $X \cup A = Y \cup A$ for some non-empty set A. Then
   (a) X is a proper subset of Y
   (b) Y is a proper subset of X
   (c) $X = Y$
   (d) X and Y are disjoint sets

5. If $n(A) = 1000$, $n(B) = 500$ and if $n(A \cap B) \geq 1$ and $n(A \cup B) = p$, then
   (a) $500 \leq p \leq 1000$ (b) $1001 \leq p \leq 1498$
   (c) $1000 \leq p \leq 1498$ (d) $1000 \leq p \leq 1499$

6. In a battle 70% of the combatants lost one eye, 80% an ear, 75% an arm, 85% a leg, x % lost all the four limbs. The minimum value of x is
   (a) 10 (b) 12
   (c) 15 (d) None of these

Section II - Multiple Correct Answer Type

This section contains 4 multiple correct answer(s) type questions. Each question has 4 choices (a), (b), (c) and (d), out of which **ONE OR MORE** is/are correct.

7. In a certain town 25% families own a phone and 15% own a car 65% own neither a phone nor a car. 2000 families own both a car and a phone.
   (a) 10% families own both a car and a phone
   (b) 35% families own either a car or a phone.
   (c) 40,000 families live in the town.
   (d) All above are correct

8. At a certain conference of 100 people, there are 29 Indian women and 23 Indian men. Of these Indian people 4 are doctors and 24 are either men or doctors. There are no foreign doctors. If the no. of foreigners and women doctors who are attending the conference are n_1 and n_2.
   (a) $n_1^2 + n_2^2 = 2305$ (b) $n_1 + n_2 - n_1n_2 = 1$
   (c) $n_1^2 - n_2^2 = 2303$ (d) $n_1 + n_2 + n_1n_2 = 98$

9. Let A, B, C be finite sets. Suppose that n (A) = 10, n (B) = 15, n (C) = 20, n $(A \cap B) = 8$ and n $(B \cap C) = 9$. Then the possible value of n $(A \cup B \cup C)$ is
   (a) 26
   (b) 27
   (c) 28
   (d) 29

10. In a class of 60 students, 23 play Hockey 15 Play Basket-ball and 20 play cricket. 7 play Hockey and Basket-ball, 5 play cricket and Basket-ball, 4 play Hockey and Cricket and 15 students do not play any of these games. Then
   (a) 4 play Hockey, Basket-ball and Cricket
   (b) 19 play Hockey but not Cricket
   (c) 1 plays Hockey and Cricket but not Basket-ball
   (d) All above are correct

Section III - Integer Type

This section contains 5 questions. The answer to each of the questions is a single digit integer ranging from 0 to 9.

11. A survey shows that 61%, 46% and 29% of the people watched "3 idiots", "Rajneeti" and "Avatar" respectively. 25% people watched exactly two of the three movies and 3% watched none. What percentage of people watched all the three movies?

RESPONSE GRID	
	4.  5. 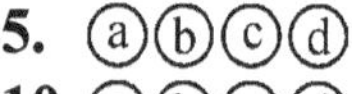 6. ⓐⓑⓒⓓ 7. ⓐⓑⓒⓓ 8. ⓐⓑⓒⓓ
	9. ⓐⓑⓒⓓ 10. ⓐⓑⓒⓓ 11. ⓪①②③④⑤⑥⑦⑧⑨

Space for Rough Work

12. Two finite sets have m and n elements. The number of subsets of the first set is 112 more than that of the second set. The values of $m - n$ is

13. There are 20 students in a chemistry class and 30 students in a physics class. If ten students are to be enrolled in both the courses. Let k be the number of students which are either in physics class or chemistry class if two classes meet at different hours, then find $\frac{k}{8}$.

14. If A is the set of the divisors of the number 15, B is the set of prime numbers smaller than 10 and C is the set of even numbers smaller than 9, then the number of elements in $(A \cup C) \cap B$ is

15. The number of elements in the set

$\{\frac{a}{b} \in I^+ : 2a^2 + 3b^2 = 35, a, b \in Z\}$, where Z is the set of all integers, is

Section IV - Comprehension Type

Based upon the given paragraphs, 4 multiple choice questions have to be answered. Each question has 4 choices (a), (b), (c) and (d), out of which **ONLY ONE** is correct.

PARAGRAPH-1

In a society 60 family read Times Of India (TOI), 70 read Hindustan Times (HT), and 40 read Telegraph (Tel). 10 family read both HT and Tel but not TOI, 18 family read HT & TOI, number of family who read only TOI & Tel but not HT is 10 less than the number of family who read all the three newspaper.

16. What could be the total number of family in the society assuming that each family read at least one news paper?

(a) 114 (b) 126
(c) 129 (d) None of these

17. If number of family who read both TOI and HT but not Tel is more than the number of family who read both TOI and Tel but not HT then what could be the number of family who read only Tel?

(a) 15 (b) 10
(c) 16 (d) None of these

PARAGRAPH-2

In a college student can opt for any one or more available sports, these are Foot Ball (FB), Carom (Cr), Chess (Ch), and Volley Ball (VB), number of students who play FB and any one more game is 10, (I.e FB and Ch is 10, FB and Cr is 10 and so on), similarly number of students who play Cr and any one more game (Except FB as it is already defined as 10) is 8 and number of students who play FB and any two more games is 12. Total count for each of four Game is 100.

18. How many student play Cricket and exactly one more game?

(a) 26 (b) 28
(c) 32 (d) None of these

19. If number of students who play Ch and Exactly one more game is maximum possible then what is the number of students who play only Cr.

(a) 25 (b) 50
(c) 46 (d) None of these

RESPONSE GRID	
12. ⓪①②③④⑤⑥⑦⑧⑨	13. ⓪①②③④⑤⑥⑦⑧⑨
14. ⓪①②③④⑤⑥⑦⑧⑨	15. ⓪①②③④⑤⑥⑦⑧⑨
16. ⓐⓑⓒⓓ 17. ⓐⓑⓒⓓ	18. ⓐⓑⓒⓓ 19. ⓐⓑⓒⓓ

Space for Rough Work

Section V - Matrix-Match Type

This section contains 1 question. It contains statements given in two columns, which have to be matched. Statements in column I are labelled as A, B, C and D whereas statements in column II are labelled as p, q, r and s. The answers to these questions have to be appropriately bubbled as illustrated in the following example. If the correct matches are A-p, A-r, B-p, B-s, C-r, C-s and D-q, then the correctly bubbled matrix will look like the following:

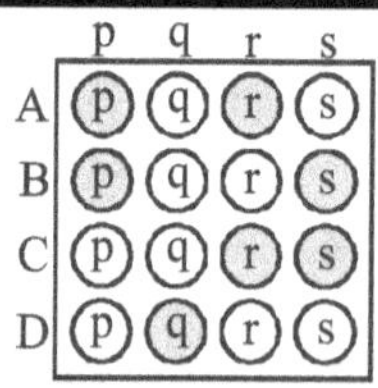

20. The proportion of male students and the proportion of vegetarian students in a school are given below. The school has a total of 800 students, 80% of whom are in the secondary section and rest equally divided between class 11 & 12.

	Male (M)	Vegetarian (V)
Class 12	0.60	
Class 11	0.55	0.55
Secondary Section		0.55
Total	0.475	0.53

Now, Match the columns.

	Column-I		Column-II
(A)	What is the percentage of vegetarian students in class-12	(p)	45
(B)	In class 12, 25% of vegetarians are male. What is the difference between the number of female vegetarians and male non-vegetarians.	(q)	40
(C)	What is the percentage of Male students in the secondary section	(r)	38
		(s)	16

RESPONSE GRID	20. A - ⓟⓠⓡⓢ; B - ⓟⓠⓡⓢ; C - ⓟⓠⓡⓢ

DAILY PRACTICE PROBLEM DPP CM01 - MATHEMATICS			
Total Questions	20	Total Marks	67
Attempted		Correct	
Incorrect		Net Score	
Cut-off Score	27	Qualifying Score	38

$$\text{Net Score} = \sum_{i=1}^{V}\left[(\text{correct}_i \times MM_i) - (In_i - NM_i)\right]$$

Space for Rough Work

DPP - Daily Practice Problems

Chapter-wise Sheets

Date : | Start Time : | End Time :

MATHEMATICS CM02

SYLLABUS : Relations and Functions

Max. Marks : 74 **Time : 60 min.**

GENERAL INSTRUCTIONS

- The Daily Practice Problem Sheet contains 20 Questions divided into 5 sections.
  Section I has **5** MCQs with ONLY 1 Correct Option, **3** marks for each correct answer and **–1** for each incorrect answer.
  Section II has **4** MCQs with ONE or MORE THAN ONE Correct options.
  For each question, marks will be awarded in one of the following categories:
  Full marks: **+4** If only the bubble(s) corresponding to all the correct option(s) is (are) darkened.
  Partial marks: **+1** For darkening a bubble corresponding to each correct option provided NO INCORRECT option is darkened.
  Zero marks: If none of the bubbles is darkened.
  Negative marks: **–2** In all other cases.
  Section III has **4** Single Digit Integer Answer Type Questions, **3** marks for each Correct Answer and **0** mark in all other cases.
  Section IV has Comprehension/Matching Cum-Comprehension Type Questions having **5** MCQs with ONLY ONE correct option, **3** marks for each Correct Answer and **0** mark in all other cases.
  Section V has **2** Matching Type Questions, **2** marks for the correct matching of each row and **0** mark in all other cases.
- You have to evaluate your Response Grids yourself with the help of Solutions.

Section I - Straight Objective Type

This section contains 5 multiple choice questions. Each question has 4 choices (a), (b), (c) and (d), out of which **ONLY ONE** is correct.

1. Let $f : R \to R$ be a periodic function such that

$f(T+x) = 1 + [1 - 3f(x) + 3f(x) + 3(f(x))^2 - (f(x))^3]^{1/3}$

where T is a fixed positive number, then period of $f(x)$ is

(a) T (b) $2T$

(c) $3T$ (d) None of these

2. If $f(x).f(y) = f(x) + f(y) + f(xy) - 2 \; \forall \; x, y \in R$ and if $f(x)$ is not a constant function, then the value of f(a) is –

(a) 1 (b) 2

(c) 0 (d) –1

3. If $f(x)$ is a polynomial function that $f(x).f(-x) = f(2x)$, then–

(a) No such function exists

(b) $f(x)$ is linear

(c) Number of such functions are exactly one

(d) Number of such functions are exactly two

RESPONSE GRID	1. ⓐⓑⓒⓓ	2. ⓐⓑⓒⓓ	3. ⓐⓑⓒⓓ

Space for Rough Work

4. Let $f(x) = \dfrac{x}{1-x}$ and 'a' be a real number.

If $x_0 = a, x_1 = f(x_0), x_2 = f(x_1), x_3 = f(x_2)$.......

and $x_{2009} = 1$, then the value of a is

(a) 0 (b) $\dfrac{2009}{2010}$

(c) $\dfrac{1}{2009}$ (d) $\dfrac{1}{2010}$

5. If { } denotes the fractional part of x, the range of the function $f(x) = \sqrt{\{x\}^2 - 2\{x\}}$ is

(a) ϕ (b) [0, 1/2]

(c) {0, 1/2} (d) {0}

Section II - Multiple Correct Answer Type

This section contains 4 multiple correct answer(s) type questions. Each question has 4 choices (a), (b), (c) and (d), out of which **ONE OR MORE** is/are correct.

6. If A, B and C are three sets, consider

(i) $A \times (B \cap C) = (A \times B) \cap (A \times C)$

(ii) $A \times (B' \cup C')' = (A \times B) \cap (A \times C)$ then :

(a) (i) is correct (b) (i) and (ii) are both correct

(c) (ii) is correct (d) None of these

7. The relation R defined on the set A = {1, 2, 3, 4, 5} by R = $\{(x, y) : |x^2 - y^2| < 16\}$ is not given by

(a) {(1, 1), (2, 1), (3, 1), (4, 1), (2, 3)}

(b) {(2, 2), (3, 2), (4, 2), (2, 4)}

(c) {(3, 3), (4, 3), (5, 4), (3, 4)}

(d) None of these

8. Which of the following function is periodic

(a) $Sgn\,(e^{-x})$

(b) $\sin x + |\sin x|$

(c) $\min(\sin x, |x|)$

(d) $\left[x+\frac{1}{2}\right]+\left[x-\frac{1}{2}\right]+2[-x]$

9. $f(x) = \sqrt{|x|^2 - 5|x| + 6} + \sqrt{8 + 2|x| - |x|^2}$ is real for all x in

(a) [–4, –3] (b) [–3, –2]

(c) [–2, 2] (d) [3, 4]

Section III - Integer Type

This section contains 4 questions. The answer to each of the questions is a single digit integer ranging from 0 to 9.

10. The number of elements in the domain of relation R = $\{(x, y) : x^2 + y^2 = 16, x, y \in Z\}$ is

11. If $2f(xy) = (f(x))^y + (f(y))^x$, for all $x, y \in R$ and $f(1) = 2$, then $f(3) =$

12. Consider $f(x) = \dfrac{4^x}{4^x + 2}$, if $f\left(\dfrac{1}{1997}\right) + f\left(\dfrac{2}{1997}\right) + ... + f\left(\dfrac{1196}{1997}\right) = 499q$, then q is equal to

13. If a, b be two fixed positive integers such that $f(a + x) = b + [b^3 + 1 - 3b^2 f(x) + 3b\{f(x)\}^2 - \{f(x)\}^3]^{1/3}$ for all real x, if period of $f(x)$ is ka, then $k =$

RESPONSE GRID

4. (a)(b)(c)(d) 5. (a)(b)(c)(d) 6. (a)(b)(c)(d) 7. (a)(b)(c)(d) 8. (a)(b)(c)(d)

9. (a)(b)(c)(d) 10. (0)(1)(2)(3)(4)(5)(6)(7)(8)(9) 11. (0)(1)(2)(3)(4)(5)(6)(7)(8)(9)

12. (0)(1)(2)(3)(4)(5)(6)(7)(8)(9) 13. (0)(1)(2)(3)(4)(5)(6)(7)(8)(9)

Space for Rough Work

Section IV - Comprehension/Matching Cum-Comprehension Type

Directions (Qs. 14 and 15) : Based upon the given paragraph, 2 multiple choice questions have to be answered. Each question has 4 choices (a), (b), (c) and (d), out of which **ONLY ONE** is correct.

PARAGRAPH

If $(f(x))^2 \times f\left(\frac{1-x}{1+x}\right) = 64x, x \neq 0,1$, then

14. $f(x)$ is equal to

(a) $4x^{2/3}\left(\frac{1+x}{1-x}\right)^{1/3}$ (b) $x^{1/3}\left(\frac{1-x}{1+x}\right)^{1/3}$ (c) $x^{2/3}\left(\frac{1-x}{1+x}\right)^{1/3}$ (d) $x\left(\frac{1+x}{1-x}\right)^{1/3}$

15. The value of $f(9/7)$ is

(a) $8(7/9)^{2/3}$ (b) $4(9/7)^{1/3}$ (c) $-8(9/7)^{2/3}$ (d) None of these

Directions (Qs. 16-18) : This passage contains a table having 3 columns and 4 rows. Based on the table, there are three questions. Each question has four options (a), (b), (c) and (d) **ONLY ONE** of these four options is correct.

Column 1, 2 and 3 contain informations about functions, domain of the functions and codomain of the functions respectively.

Column 1	Column 2	Column 3
(I) $f(x)=\frac{1}{\log_a x}$, $a>0, a\neq 1$	(i) R– {0}	(P) $(1,\infty)$
(II) $f(x)=\frac{1}{[x]}$	(ii) R–I	(Q) R– {0}
(III) $f(x)=\frac{1}{\{x\}}$	(iii) $R^+ - \{1\}$	(R) R^+
(IV) $f(x)=\frac{1}{\lvert x\rvert}$	(iv) R– [0, 1)	(S) $\left\{\frac{1}{n}, n\in I-\{0\}\right\}$

16. Which of the following options is the only correct combination?

(a) (II) (i) (P) (b) (I) (iv) (R) (c) (III) (ii) (P) (d) (IV) (iii) (Q)

17. Which of the following options is the only in incorrect combination?

(a) (II) (i) (Q) (b) (IV) (iii) (P) (c) (I) (iv) (R) (d) (IV) (ii) (S)

18. Which of the following options is the only incorrect combination?

(a) (III) (iii) (P) (b) (IV) (ii) (S) (c) (II) (i) (S) (d) (I) (iv) (R)

RESPONSE GRID	14. ⓐⓑⓒⓓ	15. ⓐⓑⓒⓓ	16. ⓐⓑⓒⓓ	17. ⓐⓑⓒⓓ	18. ⓐⓑⓒⓓ

Space for Rough Work

Section V - Matrix-Match Type

This section contains 2 questions. It contains statements given in two columns, which have to be matched. Statements in column I are labelled as A, B, C and D whereas statements in column II are labelled as p, q, r and s. The answers to these questions have to be appropriately bubbled as illustrated in the following example. If the correct matches are A-p, A-r, B-p, B-s, C-r, C-s and D-q, then the correctly bubbled matrix will look like the following:

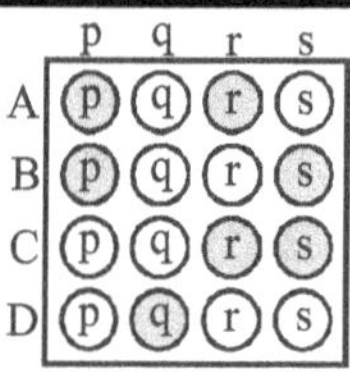

19. **Column-I: Function** | **Column-II: Type of function**

(A) $f(x)=\{(\operatorname{sgn} x)^{\operatorname{sgn} x}\}^n; x \neq 0$, n is an odd integer — (p) odd function

(B) $f(x)=\dfrac{x}{e^x-1}+\dfrac{x}{2}+1$ — (q) even function

(C) $f(x)=\begin{cases}0, & \text{If } x \text{ is rational}\\ 1, & \text{If } x \text{ is irrational}\end{cases}$ — (r) neither odd nor even function

(D) $f(x)=\max\{\tan x, \cot x\}$ — (s) periodic

20. **Column-I** | **Column-II**

(A) Domain of $f(x)=(x^2-1)^{-1/2}$ is — (p) $\left(1,\dfrac{7}{3}\right]$

(B) Range of the function $f(x)=\dfrac{x^2+x+2}{x^2+x+1}$, $x \in R$ is — (q) $(-\infty,-1)\cup(1,\infty)$

(C) The range of $f(x)=\sec\left(\dfrac{\pi}{4}\cos^2 x\right)$, $-\infty < x < \infty$ i is — (r) $(-\infty,5]\cup[9,\infty)$

(D) Range of $f(x)=\dfrac{x^2+34x-71}{x^2+2x-7}$ is — (s) $[1,\sqrt{2}]$

RESPONSE GRID	
	19. A - ⓟⓠⓡⓢ; B - ⓟⓠⓡⓢ; C - ⓟⓠⓡⓢ; D - ⓟⓠⓡⓢ
	20. A - ⓟⓠⓡⓢ; B - ⓟⓠⓡⓢ; C - ⓟⓠⓡⓢ; D - ⓟⓠⓡⓢ

DAILY PRACTICE PROBLEM DPP CM02 - MATHEMATICS			
Total Questions	20	Total Marks	74
Attempted		Correct	
Incorrect		Net Score	
Cut-off Score	26	Qualifying Score	38

$$\text{Net Score} = \sum_{i=I}^{V}\left[(\text{correct}_i \times MM_i) - (In_i - NM_i)\right]$$

Space for Rough Work

DPP - Daily Practice Problems

Chapter-wise Sheets

Date : Start Time : End Time :

MATHEMATICS (CM03)

SYLLABUS : Trigonometric Functions

Max. Marks : 74 **Time : 60 min.**

GENERAL INSTRUCTIONS

- The Daily Practice Problem Sheet contains 20 Questions divided into 5 sections.
  Section I has **6** MCQs with ONLY 1 Correct Option, **3** marks for each correct answer and **–1** for each incorrect answer.
  Section II has **4** MCQs with ONE or MORE THAN ONE Correct options.
  For each question, marks will be awarded in one of the following categories:
  Full marks: **+4** If only the bubble(s) corresponding to all the correct option(s) is (are) darkened.
  Partial marks: **+1** For darkening a bubble corresponding to each correct option provided NO INCORRECT option is darkened.
  Zero marks: If none of the bubbles is darkened.
  Negative marks: **–2** In all other cases.
  Section III has **4** Single Digit Integer Answer Type Questions, **3** marks for each Correct Answer and **0** mark in all other cases.
  Section IV has Comprehension Type Questions having **4** MCQs with ONLY ONE corect option, **3** marks for each Correct Answer and **0** mark in all other cases.
  Section V has **2** Matching Type Questions, **2** marks for the correct matching of each row and **0** mark in all other cases.
- You have to evaluate your Response Grids yourself with the help of Solutions.

Section I - Straight Objective Type

This section contains 6 multiple choice questions. Each question has 4 choices (a), (b), (c) and (d), out of which **ONLY ONE** is correct.

1. If $x\sin a + y\sin 2a + z\sin 3a = \sin 4a$
   $x\sin b + y\sin 2b + z\sin 3b = \sin 4b$
   $x\sin c + y\sin 2c + z\sin 3c = \sin 4c$

   Then, the roots of the equation

   $t^3 - \frac{z}{2}t^2 - \frac{y+2}{4}t + \frac{z-x}{8} = 0$, $a, b, c \neq n\pi$, are

   (a) $\sin a, \sin b, \sin c$ (b) $\cos a, \cos b, \cos c$
   (c) $\sin 2a, \sin 2b, \sin 2c$ (d) $\cos 2a, \cos 2b, \cos 2c$

2. If $u = \sqrt{a^2\cos^2\theta + b^2\sin^2\theta} + \sqrt{a^2\sin^2\theta + b^2\cos^2\theta}$, then the difference between the maximum and minimum values of u^2 is given by

   (a) $(a-b)^2$ (b) $2\sqrt{a^2+b^2}$
   (c) $(a+b)^2$ (d) $2(a^2+b^2)$

RESPONSE GRID	1. ⓐⓑⓒⓓ 2. ⓐⓑⓒⓓ

Space for Rough Work

3. For $0<\theta<\frac{\pi}{2}$, the solution (s) of $\sum_{m=1}^{6} \text{cosec}\left(\theta+\frac{(m-1)\pi}{4}\right)\text{cosec}\left(\theta+\frac{m\pi}{4}\right)=4\sqrt{2}$ is (are)

(a) $\frac{\pi}{4}$ (b) $\frac{\pi}{6}$

(c) $\frac{\pi}{12}$ (d) $\frac{7\pi}{12}$

4. Let $S=\left\{x\in(-\pi,\pi): x\neq 0,\pm\frac{\pi}{2}\right\}$. The sum of all distinct solutions of the equation $\sqrt{3}\sec x+\text{cosec}\, x+2(\tan x-\cot x)=0$ in the set S is equal to

(a) $-\frac{7\pi}{9}$ (b) $-\frac{2\pi}{9}$

(c) 0 (d) $\frac{5\pi}{9}$

5. The maximum value of $(\cos\alpha_1).(\cos\alpha_2)...(\cos\alpha_n)$, under the restrictions $0\le\alpha_1,\alpha_2,...,\alpha_n\le\frac{\pi}{2}$ and $(\cot\alpha_1).(\cot\alpha_2)...(\cot\alpha_n)=1$ is

(a) $1/2^{n/2}$ (b) $1/2^n$

(c) $1/2n$ (d) 1

6. If $\alpha,\beta,\gamma,\delta$ are the smallest positive angles in ascending order of magnitude which have their sines equal to the positive quantity k, then the value of

$4\sin\frac{\alpha}{2}+3\sin\frac{\beta}{2}+2\sin\frac{\gamma}{2}+\sin\frac{\delta}{2}$ is equal to

(a) $2\sqrt{1-k}$ (b) $2\sqrt{1+k}$

(c) $2\sqrt{k}$ (d) None of these

Section II - Multiple Correct Answer Type

This section contains 4 multiple correct answer(s) type questions. Each question has 4 choices (a), (b), (c) and (d), out of which **ONE OR MORE** is/are correct.

7. Let, $f_n(\theta)=\tan\frac{\theta}{2}(1+\sec\theta)(1+\sec 2\theta\quad 1)(\sec 4\theta\quad)$ ......$(1+\sec 2^n\theta)$ then

(a) $f_2\left(\frac{\pi}{16}\right)=1$ (b) $f_3\left(\frac{\pi}{32}\right)=1$

(c) $f_4\left(\frac{\pi}{64}\right)=1$ (d) $f_5\left(\frac{\pi}{128}\right)=1$

8. Given that $\sin\beta=\frac{12}{13}$, $0<\beta<\pi$, then $\{5\sin(\alpha+\beta)-12\cos(\alpha+\beta)\}\text{cosec}\alpha$ is equal to :

(a) $13\sin\alpha$ if $\tan\beta>0$

(b) $13\sin\alpha$ if $\tan\beta<0$

(c) $\frac{119+120\cot\alpha}{13}$ if $\tan\beta<0$

(d) $\frac{119+120\cot\alpha}{13}$ if $\tan\beta>0$

9. If $(a-b)\sin(\theta+\phi)=(a+b)\sin(\theta-\phi)$ and $a\tan\frac{\theta}{2}-b\tan\frac{\phi}{2}=c$, then

(a) $b\tan\phi=a\tan\theta$ (b) $a\tan\phi=b\tan\theta$

(c) $\sin\phi=\frac{2bc}{a^2-b^2-c^2}$ (d) $\sin\theta=\frac{2ac}{a^2-b^2+c^2}$

RESPONSE GRID					
	3. ⓐⓑⓒⓓ	4. ⓐⓑⓒⓓ	5. ⓐⓑⓒⓓ	6. ⓐⓑⓒⓓ	7. ⓐⓑⓒⓓ
	8. ⓐⓑⓒⓓ	9. ⓐⓑⓒⓓ			

Space for Rough Work

10. If $\frac{\tan 3A}{\tan A} = k, (k \neq 1)$, then

(a) $\frac{\cos A}{\cos 3A} = \frac{k^2 - 1}{2k}$ (b) $\frac{\sin 3A}{\sin A} = \frac{2k}{k-1}$

(c) $k < \frac{1}{3}$ (d) $k > 3$

Section III - Integer Type

This section contains 4 questions. The answer to each of the questions is a single digit integer ranging from 0 to 9.

11. If $a \tan\alpha + \sqrt{a^2 - 1}\tan\beta + \sqrt{a^2+1}\tan\gamma = 2a$, where a is constant and α, β, γ are variable angles. Then the least value of $3(\tan^2\alpha + \tan^2\beta + \tan^2\gamma)$ is equal to

12. If $\cos\alpha = \frac{2\cos\beta - 1}{2 - \cos\beta}$ $(0 < \alpha < \beta < \pi)$, then find the value of

$$\sqrt{3}\left(\frac{\tan\frac{\alpha}{2}}{\tan\frac{\beta}{2}}\right)$$

13. If $x\cos\theta = y\cos\left(\theta + \frac{2\pi}{3}\right) = z\cos\left(\theta + \frac{4\pi}{3}\right)$ then find the value of $xy + yz + zx$.

14. Suppose that $\sin^3 x \sin 3x = \sum_{m=0}^{n} c_m \cos mx$ is an identity in x, where $c_0, c_1, c_2, \ldots, c_n$ are constants and $c_n \neq 0$, find the value of n.

Section IV - Comprehension Type

Based upon the given paragraphs, 4 multiple choice questions have to be answered. Each question has 4 choices (a), (b), (c) and (d), out of which **ONLY ONE** is correct.

PARAGRAPH-1

If $P_n = \sin^n\theta + \cos^n\theta$ where $n \in W$ (whole number) and $\theta \in R$ (real number)

15. If $P_1 = m$, then the value of $4(1 - P_6)$ is

(a) $3(m-1)^2$ (b) $3(m^2-1)^2$

(c) $3(m+1)^2$ (d) $3(m^2+1)^2$

16. The value of $6P_{10} - 15P_8 + 10P_6 + 7$ is

(a) 8 (b) 6

(c) 4 (d) 2

PARAGRAPH-2

Consider the equations

$5\sin^2 x + 3\sin x\cos x - 3\cos^2 x = 2$ (1)

$\sin^2 x - \cos 2x = 2 - \sin 2x$ (2)

17. If α is a root of (1) and β is a root of (2) then tan α + tan β can be equal to

(a) $1 + \sqrt{69}/4$ (b) $1 - \sqrt{69}/6$

(c) $\frac{-3+\sqrt{69}}{6}$ (d) $\frac{-3-\sqrt{69}}{3}$

18. If tan α, tan β satisfy (1) and cos γ, cos δ satisfy (2) then tan α tan β + cos γ + cos δ can be equal to

(a) −1 (b) $-\frac{5}{3} + \frac{3}{\sqrt{13}}$

(c) $\frac{5}{3} - \frac{2}{\sqrt{13}}$ (d) $-\frac{5}{3} - \frac{2}{\sqrt{13}}$

RESPONSE GRID	
	10. ⓐⓑⓒⓓ 11. ⓪①②③④⑤⑥⑦⑧⑨ 12. ⓪①②③④⑤⑥⑦⑧⑨
	13. ⓪①②③④⑤⑥⑦⑧⑨ 14. ⓪①②③④⑤⑥⑦⑧⑨
	15. ⓐⓑⓒⓓ 16. ⓐⓑⓒⓓ 17. ⓐⓑⓒⓓ 18. ⓐⓑⓒⓓ

Space for Rough Work

Section V - Matrix-Match Type

This section contains 2 questions. It contains statements given in two columns, which have to be matched. Statements in column I are labelled as A, B, C and D whereas statements in column II are labelled as p, q, r and s. The answers to these questions have to be appropriately bubbled as illustrated in the following example. If the correct matches are A-p, A-r, B-p, B-s, C-r, C-s and D-q, then the correctly bubbled matrix will look like the following:

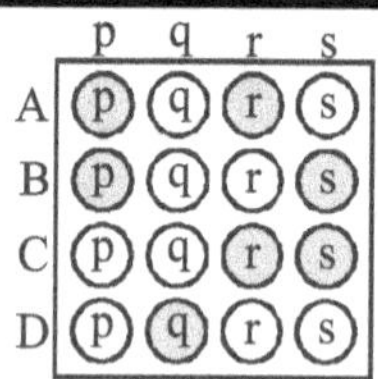

19. **Column-I** **Column-II**

(A) If $f(\theta) = (\sin\theta + \text{cosec}\theta)^2 + (\cos\theta + \sec\theta)^2$, then $f(\theta)$ cannot be less than — p. 1

(B) If $\sin\alpha - \sin\beta = a$ and $\cos\alpha + \cos\beta = b$ then $a^2 + b^2$ cannot exceed — q. 2

(C) If $A + B = \frac{\pi}{2}$, where A and B are positive then $(\sin A + \sin B)\cos\frac{\pi}{4}$ is always less than — r. 4

(D) If $2\cos x + \sin x = 1$, then the value of $7\cos x + 6\sin x$ is equal to — s. 6

20. **Column-I** **Column-II**

(A) The values of $\cos^2\theta + \sin^4\theta$ for all θ — p. belong to (0, 1]

(B) In a ΔABC if $\tan A < 0$ then values of $\tan B \tan C$ — q. belong to $\left[\frac{3}{4}, 1\right]$

(C) For any real $\theta \neq n\pi, n \in I$ then values of $\frac{\cos^2\theta - 1}{\cos^2\theta + \cos\theta}$ — r. are less than 0 or greater than 2

(D) If $A > 0, B > 0$ and $A + B = \frac{\pi}{3}$ then the values of $3\tan A \tan B$ — s. belong to (0, 1)

RESPONSE GRID	
	19. A - (p)(q)(r)(s); B - (p)(q)(r)(s); C - (p)(q)(r)(s); D - (p)(q)(r)(s)
	20. A - (p)(q)(r)(s); B - (p)(q)(r)(s); C - (p)(q)(r)(s); D - (p)(q)(r)(s)

DAILY PRACTICE PROBLEM DPP CM03 - MATHEMATICS			
Total Questions	20	Total Marks	74
Attempted		Correct	
Incorrect		Net Score	
Cut-off Score	26	Qualifying Score	38

$$\text{Net Score} = \sum_{i=1}^{V}\left[(\text{correct}_i \times MM_i) - (In_i - NM_i)\right]$$

Space for Rough Work

DPP - Daily Practice Problems

Chapter-wise Sheets

Date : ______ Start Time : ______ End Time : ______

MATHEMATICS (CM04)

SYLLABUS : Complex Numbers and Quadratic Equations

Max. Marks : 69 **Time : 60 min.**

GENERAL INSTRUCTIONS

- The Daily Practice Problem Sheet contains 20 Questions divided into 5 sections.
  Section I has **6** MCQs with ONLY 1 Correct Option, **3** marks for each correct answer and **–1** for each incorrect answer.
  Section II has **4** MCQs with ONE or MORE THAN ONE Correct options.
  For each question, marks will be awarded in one of the following categories:
  Full marks: **+4** If only the bubble(s) corresponding to all the correct option(s) is (are) darkened.
  Partial marks: **+1** For darkening a bubble corresponding to each correct option provided NO INCORRECT option is darkened.
  Zero marks: If none of the bubbles is darkened.
  Negative marks: **–2** In all other cases.
  Section III has **5** Single Digit Integer Answer Type Questions, **3** marks for each Correct Answer and **0** mark in all other cases.
  Section IV has Comprehension Type Questions having **4** MCQs with ONLY ONE corect option, **3** marks for each Correct Answer and **0** mark in all other cases.
  Section V has **1** Matching Type Question, **2** marks for the correct matching of each row and **0** mark in all other cases.
- You have to evaluate your Response Grids yourself with the help of Solutions.

Section I - Straight Objective Type

This section contains 6 multiple choice questions. Each question has 4 choices (a), (b), (c) and (d), out of which **ONLY ONE** is correct.

1. A complex number z satisfies the equation $|z|^2 - 2iz + 2c(1+i) = 0$, where c is real. The values of c for which the above equation has no solution can be given by

(a) $c \in (-\infty, -1-\sqrt{2})$ (b) $c \in [-1-\sqrt{2}, -1+\sqrt{2}]$

(c) $c \in (-1-\sqrt{2}, \infty)$ (d) $c \in \mathbf{R}$

2. If $z_1 = a + ib$ and $z_2 = c + id$ are complex numbers such that $|z_1| = |z_2| = 1$ and $\text{Re}(z_1\bar{z}_2) = 0$, then the pair of complex numbers $\omega_1 = a + ic$ and $\omega_2 = b + id$ do not satisfy

(a) $|\omega_1| = 1$ (b) $|\omega_2| = 1$

(c) $\text{Re}(\omega_1\bar{\omega}_2) = 0$ (d) $\text{In}\,(\omega_1\bar{\omega}_2) = 0$

RESPONSE GRID	1. ⓐⓑⓒⓓ	2. ⓐⓑⓒⓓ

Space for Rough Work

3. If A, G and H are the Arithmetic mean, Geometric mean and Harmonic mean between two unequal positive integers. Then the equation $Ax^2 - |G|x - H = 0$ does not have
(a) both roots fractions
(b) one negative fraction root
(c) exactly one positive root
(d) no root greater than 2

4. If a, b, c are positive rational numbers such that $a > b > c$ and the quadratic equation $(a+b-2c)x^2 + (b+c-2a)x + (c+a-2b) = 0$ has a root in the interval $(-1, 0)$, then
(a) $c + a > 2b$
(b) Both roots of the given equation are irrational
(c) The equation $ax^2 + 2bx + c = 0$ has both negative real roots
(d) The equation $cx^2 + 2ax + b = 0$ has both positive real roots

5. Let $[a]$ denote the greatest integer less than or equal to a. Given that the quadratic equation $x^2 + [a^2 - 5a + b + 4]x + b = 0$ has roots -5 and 1. Then the set of values of a is
(a) $\left(-1, \frac{5-3\sqrt{5}}{2}\right] \cup \left[\frac{5+3\sqrt{5}}{2}, 6\right)$
(b) $\left(\frac{5-3\sqrt{5}}{2}, \frac{5+3\sqrt{5}}{2}\right)$
(c) $(-\infty, -1] \cup [6, \infty)$
(d) $(-\infty, \infty)$

6. The point of intersection of the curves $\arg(z - 3i) = \frac{3\pi}{4}$ and $\arg(2z + 1 - 2i) = \frac{\pi}{4}$ is
(a) $\frac{1}{4}(3+9i)$
(b) $\frac{1}{4}(3-9i)$
(c) $\frac{1}{2}(3+2i)$
(d) None of these

Section II - Multiple Correct Answer Type

This section contains 4 multiple correct answer(s) type questions. Each question has 4 choices (a), (b), (c) and (d), out of which **ONE OR MORE** is/are correct.

7. Let z_1, z_2, z_3 be complex number such that $|z_1| = |z_2| = |z_3| = 1$ and $\frac{z_1^2}{z_2 z_3} + \frac{z_2^2}{z_3 z_1} + \frac{z_3^2}{z_1 z_2} = -1$, then value of $|z_1 + z_2 + z_3|$ can be
(a) 2
(b) 3
(c) 4
(d) 1

8. Consider the quadratic equation $x^2 - 2px + p^2 - 1 = 0$ where p is parameter, then
(a) Both the roots of the equation are less than 4 if $p \in (-\infty, 3)$
(b) Both the roots of the equation are greater than -2 if $p \in (-\infty, -1)$
(c) Exactly one root of the equation lies in the interval $(-2, 4)$ if $p \in (-1, 3)$
(d) 1 lies between the roots of the equation if $p \in (0, 2)$

9. Equation $\frac{\pi^e}{x-e} + \frac{e^\pi}{x-\pi} + \frac{\pi^\pi + e^e}{x-\pi-e} = 0$ has
(a) one real root in (e, π) and other in $(\pi - e, e)$
(b) one real root in (e, π) and other in $(\pi, \pi + e)$
(c) Two real roots in $(\pi - e, \pi + e)$
(d) No real root

10. If $S = \sum_{k=1}^{10}\left(\sin\frac{2\pi k}{11} - i\cos\frac{2\pi k}{11}\right)$ then
(a) $S + \bar{S} = 0$
(b) $S\bar{S} = 1$
(c) $\sqrt{S} = \pm\frac{1}{\sqrt{2}}(1+i)$
(d) $S - \bar{S} = 0$

RESPONSE GRID					
	3. ⓐⓑⓒⓓ	4. ⓐⓑⓒⓓ	5. ⓐⓑⓒⓓ	6. ⓐⓑⓒⓓ	7. ⓐⓑⓒⓓ
	8. ⓐⓑⓒⓓ	9. ⓐⓑⓒⓓ	10. ⓐⓑⓒⓓ		

Space for Rough Work

Section III - Integer Type

This section contains 5 questions. The answer to each of the questions is a single digit integer ranging from 0 to 9.

11. If $z^2 - z + 1 = 0$, and the value of

$$\left(z+\frac{1}{z}\right)^2+\left(z^2+\frac{1}{z^2}\right)^2+\left(z^3+\frac{1}{z^3}\right)^2+...+\left(z^{24}+\frac{1}{z^{24}}\right)$$

is 8k, then k =

12. Let a and b be the roots of the equation $x^2 - 10cx - 11d = 0$ and those of $x^2 - 10ax - 11b = 0$ are c, d then find the value of $\frac{a+b+c+d}{605}$, when $a \neq b \neq c \neq d \neq 0$

13. If the roots of equation $ax^2+bx+c=0 \quad (a \neq 0)$ are α and β, and the roots of the equation $a^5x^2+ba^2c^2x+c^5=0$ are 4 and 8 then the numerical value of αβ is ________ .

14. If ω and ω^2 be the non-real cube roots of unity and

$$\frac{1}{a+\omega}+\frac{1}{b+\omega}+\frac{1}{c+\omega}=2\omega^2 \text{ and}$$

$$\frac{1}{a+\omega^2}+\frac{1}{b+\omega^2}+\frac{1}{c+\omega^2}=2\omega, \text{ where } a, b, c \text{ are real}$$

then the value of $\frac{1}{a+1}+\frac{1}{b+1}+\frac{1}{c+1}$ is equal to :

15. If $z=\frac{1}{2}(\sqrt{3}-i)$, and the smallest value of positive integer n for which $(z^{89}+i^{97})^{94}=z^n$ is 2k, then k =

Section IV - Comprehension Type

Based upon the given paragraphs, 4 multiple choice questions have to be answered. Each question has 4 choices (a), (b), (c) and (d), out of which **ONLY ONE** is correct.

PARAGRAPH-1

Suppose z and w be two complex numbers such that $|z| \leq 1$, $|w| \leq 1$ and $|z+iw|=|z-iw|=2$. Use the results $|z|^2=z\bar{z}$ and $|z+w| \leq |z|+|w|$, answer the following questions

16. Which of the following is true about $|z|$ and $|\omega|$

(a) $|z|=|w|=\frac{1}{2}$ (b) $|z|=\frac{1}{2}, |w|=\frac{3}{4}$

(c) $|z|=|w|=\frac{3}{4}$ (d) $|z|=|w|=1$

17. Which of the following is true for z and ω

(a) $\text{Re}(z)=\text{Re}(w)$ (b) $I_m(z)=I_m(w)$

(c) $\text{Re}(z)=I_m(w)$ (d) $I_m(z)=\text{Re}(w)$

PARAGRAPH-2

Suppose z_1, z_2 and z_3 represent the vertices A, B and C of an equilateral triangle ABC on the Argand plane.

Then $AB = BC = CA$

$\Rightarrow |z_2 - z_1| = |z_3 - z_2| = |z_1 - z_3|$

Also $\angle CAB = \frac{\pi}{3}$

$\Rightarrow \arg \frac{z_3 - z_1}{z_2 - z_1} = \pm\frac{\pi}{3}$

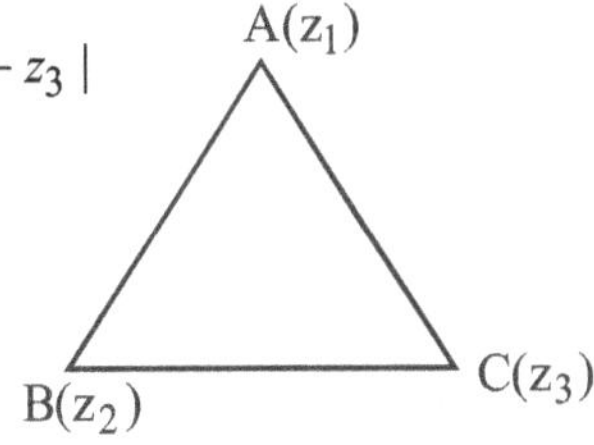

Now solve the following questions :

18. If a and b are two real numbers lying between 0 and 1 such that $z_1 = a + i$, $z_2 = 1 + bi$ and $z_3 = 0$ form an equilateral triangle then

(a) $a=2+\sqrt{3}$ (b) $b=4-\sqrt{3}$

(c) $a=b=2-\sqrt{3}$ (d) $a=2, b=\sqrt{3}$

RESPONSE GRID	
11. ⓪①②③④⑤⑥⑦⑧⑨	12. ⓪①②③④⑤⑥⑦⑧⑨
13. ⓪①②③④⑤⑥⑦⑧⑨	14. ⓪①②③④⑤⑥⑦⑧⑨
15. ⓪①②③④⑤⑥⑦⑧⑨	16. ⓐⓑⓒⓓ 17. ⓐⓑⓒⓓ 18. ⓐⓑⓒⓓ

Space for Rough Work

19. Let the complex numbers z_1, z_2 and z_3 be the vertices of an equilateral triangle. Let z_0 be the circumcentre of the triangle, then $z_1^2+z_2^2+z_3^2=$

(a) z_0^2 (b) $3z_0^2$

(c) $9z_0^2$ (d) 0

Section V - Matrix-Match Type

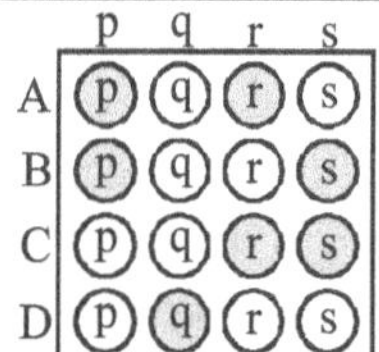

This section contains 1 question. It contains statements given in two columns, which have to be matched. Statements in column I are labelled as A, B, C and D whereas statements in column II are labelled as p, q, r and s. The answers to these questions have to be appropriately bubbled as illustrated in the following example. If the correct matches are A-p, A-r, B-p, B-s, C-r, C-s and D-q, then the correctly bubbled matrix will look like the following:

20.

Column-I		Column-II
(A) The roots of cubic equation $(z+\alpha\beta)^3=\alpha^3\ (\alpha\neq 0, \alpha\in R)$ represent the vertices of a triangle of area equal to	p.	$\lvert\tan\alpha\rvert$
(B) If α is a complex number then the radius of the circle $\left\lvert\dfrac{z-\alpha}{z-\overline{\alpha}}\right\rvert=2$ is equal to	q.	$\dfrac{3\sqrt{3}}{4}\lvert\alpha\rvert^2$
(C) If $\arg z=\alpha$ and $\lvert z-1\rvert=1$ then $\left\lvert\dfrac{z-2}{z}\right\rvert$ is equal to	r.	$\dfrac{2}{3}\lvert\alpha-\overline{\alpha}\rvert$
(D) Let A and B represent complex numbers z_1 and z_2, which are roots of the equation $z^2+pz+q=0$. If $\angle AOB=\alpha\neq 0$ and $OA=OB$, where O is the origin then $\dfrac{p^2}{q}$ is equal to	s.	$4\cos^2\dfrac{\alpha}{2}$

RESPONSE GRID 19. (a)(b)(c)(d) 20. A - (p)(q)(r)(s); B - (p)(q)(r)(s); C - (p)(q)(r)(s); D - (p)(q)(r)(s)

DAILY PRACTICE PROBLEM DPP CM04 - MATHEMATICS			
Total Questions	20	Total Marks	69
Attempted		Correct	
Incorrect		Net Score	
Cut-off Score	22	Qualifying Score	33

$$\text{Net Score}=\sum_{i=I}^{V}\left[(\text{correct}_i\times MM_i)-(In_i-NM_i)\right]$$

Space for Rough Work

DPP - Daily Practice Problems

Chapter-wise Sheets

Date : | Start Time : | End Time :

MATHEMATICS CM05

SYLLABUS : Permutations and Combinations

Max. Marks : 74 **Time : 60 min.**

GENERAL INSTRUCTIONS

- The Daily Practice Problem Sheet contains 20 Questions divided into 5 sections.
  Section I has **5** MCQs with ONLY 1 Correct Option, **3** marks for each correct answer and **–1** for each incorrect answer.
  Section II has **4** MCQs with ONE or MORE THAN ONE Correct options.
  For each question, marks will be awarded in one of the following categories:
  Full marks: **+4** If only the bubble(s) corresponding to all the correct option(s) is (are) darkened.
  Partial marks: **+1** For darkening a bubble corresponding to each correct option provided NO INCORRECT option is darkened.
  Zero marks: If none of the bubbles is darkened.
  Negative marks: **–2** In all other cases.
  Section III has **4** Single Digit Integer Answer Type Questions, **3** marks for each Correct Answer and **0** mark in all other cases.
  Section IV has Comprehension/Matching Cum-Comprehension Type Questions having **5** MCQs with ONLY ONE correct option, **3** marks for each Correct Answer and **0** mark in all other cases.
  Section V has **2** Matching Type Questions, **2** marks for the correct matching of each row and **0** mark in all other cases.
- You have to evaluate your Response Grids yourself with the help of Solutions.

Section I - Straight Objective Type

This section contains 5 multiple choice questions. Each question has 4 choices (a), (b), (c) and (d), out of which **ONLY ONE** is correct.

1. The largest integer 'n' such that 33 ! is divisible by 2^n is

(a) 33 (b) 32
(c) 31 (d) None of these

2. If a, b, c, d are odd natural numbers such that $a+b+c+d=20$ then the number of values of a, b, c, d is

(a) 165 (b) 455
(c) 310 (d) 255

3. The total number of 5-digit numbers of different digits in which the digit in the middle is the largest is

(a) $\sum_{n=4}^{9} {}^{n}p_4$ (b) 4563
(c) 2688 (d) 5292

RESPONSE GRID	1. ⓐⓑⓒⓓ	2. ⓐⓑⓒⓓ	3. ⓐⓑⓒⓓ

Space for Rough Work

4. Two 4-digits numbers are to be formed such that the sum of the number is also a 4-digit number and in no place the addition is with carrying. The number of ways of forming the numbers under above conditions is

(a) 55^4 (b) 220

(c) 45^4 (d) 36×55^3

5. Given that n is odd, the number of ways in which three numbers in A. P. can be selected from 1, 2, 3 ....., n is

(a) $\frac{(n-1)^2}{2}$ (b) $\frac{(n+1)^2}{2}$

(c) $\frac{n^2-1}{4}$ (d) $\frac{(n-1)^2}{4}$

Section II - Multiple Correct Answer Type

This section contains 4 multiple correct answer(s) type questions. Each question has 4 choices (a), (b), (c) and (d), out of which **ONE OR MORE** is/are correct.

6. The number of ways of choosing triplet (x, y, z) such that $z \geq \max\{x, y\}$ and $x, y, z \in \{1, 2, ..., n, n+1\}$ is

(a) ${}^{n+1}C_3 + {}^{n+2}C_3$ (b) ${}^{n+1}C_2 + 2({}^{n+1}C_3)$

(c) $1^2 + 2^2 + ... + n^2$ (d) $2({}^{n+2}C_3) - {}^{n+1}C_2$

7. Number of triangles which can be formed by joining vertices of a regular polygon of n (> 5) sides such that no side is common with the side of polygon is equal to

(a) $\frac{n}{n-3}\,{}^{n-3}C_3$ (b) ${}^{n}C_3 - n - n(n-4)$

(c) ${}^{n-4}C_2 + {}^{n-3}C_3$ (d) ${}^{n+2}C_3$

8. For n > 1, let

$E = (2n+1)(2n+3)(2n+5)...(4n-3)(4n-1)$

Then

(a) 2^n E is divisible by ${}^{4n}C_{2n}$ (b) 2^n E is divisible by n!

(c) $\frac{2^n E}{n!}$ is a positive integer (d) $\frac{2^n E}{(4n)!}$ is not an integer

9. Let A = { 1, 2, 3} and B = { 1, 2, 3, 4, 6, 7}. Among all the functions from A to B, the number of functions f such that

(a) f (i) < f(j) whenever i < j, is 35

(b) f (i) ≤ f(j) whenever i < j, is 84

(c) f(i) > f(j) whenever i < j is 35

(d) none of these

Section III - Integer Type

This section contains 4 questions. The answer to each of the questions is a single digit integer ranging from 0 to 9.

10. If the number of ordered pairs (m, n); m, n Î {1, 2, 3,........., 20} such that $3^m + 7^n$ is a multiple of 10, is equal to 20k, then k =

11. A person has 6 friends and during a certain vacation he met them during several dinners. He found that he dinned with all the 6 exactly on one day, with every 5 of them on 2 days, with every 4 of them on 3 days, with every 3 on 4 days; with every 2 on 5 days. Furthers every friend was present at 7 dinners and every friend was absent at 7 dinners. The number of dinner(s) he had alone is equal to

12. If the number of ordered triplets (a, b, c) such that L.C.M. (a,b) = 1000, L.C.M. (b,c) = 2000 and L.C.M. (c,a) = 2000 is 10q, then q =

13. If all the permutations of the letters of the word TACKLE are written in order as in a dictionary, also if the rank of the word TACKLE is equal to 100 a + b, then a – b =

RESPONSE GRID	
	4. ⓐⓑⓒⓓ 5. ⓐⓑⓒⓓ 6. ⓐⓑⓒⓓ 7. ⓐⓑⓒⓓ 8. ⓐⓑⓒⓓ
	9. ⓐⓑⓒⓓ 10. ⓪①②③④⑤⑥⑦⑧⑨ 11. ⓪①②③④⑤⑥⑦⑧⑨
	12. ⓪①②③④⑤⑥⑦⑧⑨ 13. ⓪①②③④⑤⑥⑦⑧⑨

Space for Rough Work

Section IV - Comprehension/Matching Cum-Comprehension Type

Directions (Qs. 14 and 15) : Based upon the given paragraph, 2 multiple choice questions have to be answered. Each question has 4 choices (a), (b), (c) and (d), out of which **ONLY ONE** is correct.

PARAGRAPH

If p is a prime, then exponent of p in $n!$ equals

$$E_p(\mathrm{n}) = \left[\frac{n}{p}\right] + \left[\frac{n}{p^2}\right] + \left[\frac{n}{p^3}\right] + \ldots$$

14. The largest two digit prime that divides ${}^{200}C_{100}$ is
(a) 59 (b) 53 (c) 47 (d) none of these

15. The number of natural numbers n for n! ends in 26 zeros, is
(a) 4 (b) 5 (c) 6 (d) 7

Directions (Qs. 16-18) : This passage contains a table having 3 columns and 4 rows. Based on the table, there are three questions. Each question has four options (a), (b), (c) and (d) **ONLY ONE** of these four options is correct.

Column-1 contains information about the numbers to be formed.

Column-2 contains digits with condition to be used to form the numbers mentioned in the column-1.

Column-3 contains number of numbers formed mentioned in the column-1 using the digits mentioned in the column-2.

Column 1	Column 2	Column 3
(I) Four digit odd-numbers	(i) 0, 1, 2, 3, 4, 5 (without repetition)	(P) 216
(II) Numbers greater than 1000 but less than 4000	(ii) 0, 1, 2, 3, 5, 7 (with repetition)	(Q) 72
(III) Five digit numbers divisible by 3	(iii) 1, 2, 3 (with repetition)	(R) 77
(IV) Seven digit integers with sum of the digits equal to 10	(iv) 0, 1, 2, 3, 4 (without repetition)	(S) 720

16. Which of the following options is the only correct combination?
(a) (I) (ii) (R) (b) (III) (i) (P) (c) (II) (iv) (S) (d) (IV) (ii) (Q)

17. Which of the following options is the only correct combination?
(a) (IV) (iii) (R) (b) (III) (ii) (Q) (c) (II) (iv) (P) (d) (I) (i) (S)

18. Which of the following options is the only incorrect combination?
(a) (I) (ii) (S) (b) (III) (i) (P) (c) (II) (iv) (R) (d) (IV) (iii) (R)

RESPONSE GRID	14. ⓐⓑⓒⓓ	15. ⓐⓑⓒⓓ	16. ⓐⓑⓒⓓ	17. ⓐⓑⓒⓓ	18. ⓐⓑⓒⓓ

Space for Rough Work

Section V - Matrix-Match Type

This section contains 2 questions. It contains statements given in two columns, which have to be matched. Statements in column I are labelled as A, B, C and D whereas statements in column II are labelled as p, q, r and s. The answers to these questions have to be appropriately bubbled as illustrated in the following example. If the correct matches are A-p, A-r, B-p, B-s, C-r, C-s and D-q, then the correctly bubbled matrix will look like the following:

	p	q	r	s
A	(p)	(q)	(r)	(s)
B	(p)	(q)	(r)	(s)
C	(p)	(q)	(r)	(s)
D	(p)	(q)	(r)	(s)

19. Match the columns :

	Column-I		Column-II
(A)	The number of 6 digit natural numbers, where each digit appears at least twice is	p.	1800
(B)	In how many ways can five different books be tied up in 3 bundles?	q.	677
(C)	In how many ways 5 different subjects can be distributed in 6 periods in a timetable if each subject must occur.	r.	11754
(D)	How many students do you need in a school to guarantee that there are atleast 2 students, who have the same 1st two initials in their 1st names?	s.	25

20. Match the columns :

	Column-I		Column-II
(A)	The total number of three digit numbers, the sum of whose digits is even is equal to	p.	18
(B)	Total number of positive intergal solutions of the equation $xyz = 140$ is equal to	q.	54
(C)	Total number of positive intergal solutions of $x + y + z \leq 10$ is equal to	r.	120
(D)	If the cubic $x^3 + ax^2 + bx + c$ is divisible by $x^2 + 1$, then the number of three digit numbers of the form abc or bca or cab which can be formed is equal to	s.	450

RESPONSE GRID	
	19. A - (p)(q)(r)(s); B - (p)(q)(r)(s); C - (p)(q)(r)(s); D - (p)(q)(r)(s)
	20. A - (p)(q)(r)(s); B - (p)(q)(r)(s); C - (p)(q)(r)(s); D - (p)(q)(r)(s)

DAILY PRACTICE PROBLEM DPP CM05 - MATHEMATICS

Total Questions	20	Total Marks	74
Attempted		Correct	
Incorrect		Net Score	
Cut-off Score	25	Qualifying Score	38

$$\text{Net Score} = \sum_{i=I}^{V} \left[\left(\text{correct}_i \times MM_i \right) - \left(In_i - NM_i \right) \right]$$

Space for Rough Work

DPP - Daily Practice Problems

Chapter-wise Sheets

Date : Start Time : End Time :

MATHEMATICS CM06

SYLLABUS : Binomial Theorem

Max. Marks : 74 **Time : 60 min.**

GENERAL INSTRUCTIONS

- The Daily Practice Problem Sheet contains 20 Questions divided into 5 sections.
  Section I has **6** MCQs with ONLY 1 Correct Option, **3** marks for each correct answer and **–1** for each incorrect answer.
  Section II has **4** MCQs with ONE or MORE THAN ONE Correct options.
  For each question, marks will be awarded in one of the following categories:
  Full marks: **+4** If only the bubble(s) corresponding to all the correct option(s) is (are) darkened.
  Partial marks: **+1** For darkening a bubble corresponding to each correct option provided NO INCORRECT option is darkened.
  Zero marks: If none of the bubbles is darkened.
  Negative marks: **–2** In all other cases.
  Section III has **4** Single Digit Integer Answer Type Questions, **3** marks for each Correct Answer and **0** mark in all other cases.
  Section IV has Comprehension Type Questions having **4** MCQs with ONLY ONE corect option, **3** marks for each Correct Answer and **0** mark in all other cases.
  Section V has **2** Matching Type Questions, **2** marks for the correct matching of each row and **0** mark in all other cases.
- You have to evaluate your Response Grids yourself with the help of Solutions.

Section I - Straight Objective Type

This section contains 6 multiple choice questions. Each question has 4 choices (a), (b), (c) and (d), out of which **ONLY ONE** is correct.

1. If $(1 + x - 2x^2)^6 = 1 + a_1x + a_2x^2 + a_3x^3 + ...$ and $k = a_2 + a_4 + a_6 + ... + a_{12}$ then which one of the following is true about k?

(a) k is a perfect square
(b) k is a prime number
(c) k is a perfect cube
(d) k is more than 64

2. Consider a function $f(x) = \left(1 - \frac{1}{x}\right)$. Then term independent of x in the expansion of $(f(x))^n \cdot \left(f\left(-\frac{1}{x}\right)\right)^n$ is

(a) 0, if n is odd
(b) $(-1)^{\frac{n-1}{2}} \cdot {}^nC_{\frac{n-1}{2}}$, if n is odd
(c) $(-1)^{n/2} \cdot {}^nC_{\frac{n}{2}-1}$, if n is even
(d) None of the above

RESPONSE GRID	1. ⓐⓑⓒⓓ 2. ⓐⓑⓒⓓ

Space for Rough Work

3. If $(1+x)^n = C_0 + C_1x + C_2x^2 + ... + C_nx^n$, then

$\sum\limits_{0 \le i \le j} \sum\limits_{j \le n} (C_i + C_j)^2$ is equal to

(a) $(n-1)\ {}^{2n}C_n + 2^{2n}$
(b) $n\ {}^{2n}C_n + 2^{2n}$
(c) $(n+1)\ {}^{2n}C_n + 2^{2n}$
(d) None of these

4. The number of integral solutions of the equation $x+y+z+w=20$, if $x \ge 1$, $y \ge 2, z \ge 3, w \ge 4$, is

(a) 286 (b) 78
(c) 715 (d) 1001

5. If I is integral part of $(2+\sqrt{3})^n$ and f is its fractional part. Then $(I+f)(1-f)$ is

(a) $I+1$ (b) 1
(c) n (d) 2^n

6. If coefficient of x^n in $(1+x)^{101}(1-x+x^2)^{100}$ is non-zero, then n cannot be of the form

(a) $3r+1$ (b) $3r$
(c) $3r+2$ (d) $4r+1$

Section II - Multiple Correct Answer Type

This section contains 4 multiple correct answer(s) type questions. Each question has 4 choices (a), (b), (c) and (d), out of which **ONE OR MORE** is/are correct.

7. Suppose $x_1, x_2, \ldots, x_n (n > 2)$ are real numbers such that $x_i = -x_{n-i+1}$ for $1 \le i \le n$. Consider the sum $S_n = \sum \sum \sum x_i x_j x_k$ $(1 < i, j, k \le n)$ $(i, j, k\ distinct)$ then which of the following is true?

(a) $S_{10} = 121$ (b) $S_{10} = S_{20}$
(c) $S_{14} = 0$ (d) $S_{30} > S_{31}$

8. Which all statements are correct?

(a) The number of integral terms in the expansion of $(\sqrt{3} + \sqrt[8]{5})^{256}$ is k then $k > 30$
(b) The number of integral terms in the expansion of $(\sqrt{3} + \sqrt[8]{5})^{256}$ is k then $k < 40$
(c) Number of distinct terms in the expansion of $(x+y-z)^{16}$ is k then $k > 140$
(d) Number of distinct terms in the expansion of $(x+y-z)^{16}$ is k then $k < 150$

9. If $f(n) = \sum\limits_{r=1}^{n} [r(n\ {}^{n-1}C_{r-1} - r\ {}^{n}C_{r-1}) + (2r+1)\ {}^{n}C_r]$, then

(a) $f(10) = 120$ (b) $f(20) = 440$
(c) $\sum\limits_{n=1}^{10} f(n) = 495$ (d) $\sum\limits_{n=1}^{10} f(n) = 374$

10. The integer just greater than $(\sqrt{3}+1)^{2m}$ is

(a) divisible by 2^{m+1} (b) divisible by 3^{m+1}
(c) divisible by 2^m (d) divisible by 3^m

Section III - Integer Type

This section contains 4 questions. The answer to each of the questions is a single digit integer ranging from 0 to 9.

11. If $\sum\limits_{r=0}^{n} \left(\frac{r+2}{r+1}\right) C_r = \frac{2^8 - 1}{6}$, then n is equal to

RESPONSE GRID					
	3. ⓐⓑⓒⓓ	4. ⓐⓑⓒⓓ	5. ⓐⓑⓒⓓ	6. ⓐⓑⓒⓓ	7. ⓐⓑⓒⓓ
	8. ⓐⓑⓒⓓ	9. ⓐⓑⓒⓓ	10. ⓐⓑⓒⓓ	11. ⓪①②③④⑤⑥⑦⑧⑨	

Space for Rough Work

12. Given $\left(1-2x+5x^2-10x^3\right)\left(1+x^n\right)=1+a_1x+a_2x^2+\ldots$ and that $a_1^2=2a_2$, then the value of n is

13. If the expansion of $(1 + x + x^2)^n$ be written as $a_0 + a^1x + a_2x^2 + \ldots\ldots + a_{2n}x^{2n}$, then the value of $\dfrac{a_0+a_1+a_3+a_4+a_6+a_7+\ldots}{a_2+a_5+a_8+\ldots}$ if n is a multiple of 3.

14. If $(1+ax)^n=1+8x+24x^2+\ldots\ldots$; then $9\left(\dfrac{n-a}{a+n}\right)$ is equal to (n being a positive Integer)

Section IV - Comprehension Type

Based upon the given paragraphs, 4 multiple choice questions have to be answered. Each question has 4 choices (a), (b), (c) and (d), out of which **ONLY ONE** is correct.

PARAGRAPH-1

If $^nC_0, {}^nC_1, {}^nC_2, \ldots, {}^nC_n$ denote the binomial coefficients in the expansion of $(1+x)^n$ and $a+b=1$, then

15. Find the value of $\sum_{r=0}^{n} r\,{}^nC_r a^r b^{n-r}$ is

(a) na^2 (b) nab
(c) na (d) None of these

16. If $^nC_0, {}^nC_1, {}^nC_2, \ldots, {}^nC_n$ denote the binomial coefficients in the expansion of $(1+x)^n$ and $p+q=1$, then $\sum_{r=0}^{n} r^2\,{}^nC_r p^r q^{n-r}$ is

(a) np (b) npq
(c) n^2p^2+npq (d) None of these

PARAGRAPH-2

The binomial expansion is defined as

$$(x+y^n)=\sum_{r=0}^{n} C_r\, x^{n-r} y^r \text{, where } C_r={}^nC_r.$$

17. The value of $\sum_{0\le i<j\le n}\sum i\cdot {}^nC_j$ is equal to

(a) $n(n+1)2^{n-3}$ (b) $n^2 2^{n-3}$
(c) $n(n-1)2^{n-3}$ (d) None of these

18. The value of $\sum_{0\le i<j\le n}\sum j\cdot {}^nC_i$ is equal to

(a) $n^2 2^{n-3}$ (b) $n(n+3)2^{n-3}$
(c) $(n+3)2^{n-3}$ (d) None of these

RESPONSE GRID	
12. ⓪①②③④⑤⑥⑦⑧⑨	13. ⓪①②③④⑤⑥⑦⑧⑨
14. ⓪①②③④⑤⑥⑦⑧⑨	15. ⓐⓑⓒⓓ 16. ⓐⓑⓒⓓ 17. ⓐⓑⓒⓓ
18. ⓐⓑⓒⓓ	

Space for Rough Work

Section V - Matrix-Match Type

This section contains 2 questions. It contains statements given in two columns, which have to be matched. Statements in column I are labelled as A, B, C and D whereas statements in column II are labelled as p, q, r and s. The answers to these questions have to be appropriately bubbled as illustrated in the following example. If the correct matches are A-p, A-r, B-p, B-s, C-r, C-s and D-q, then the correctly bubbled matrix will look like the following:

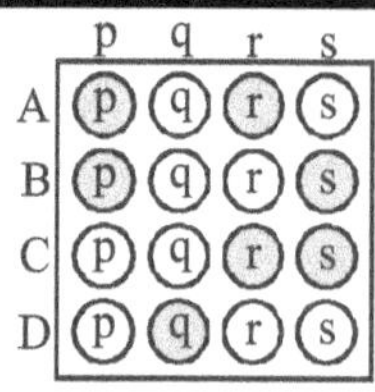

19. Match the statement of Column I with values of Column II.

	Column I		Column II
(A)	If (r + 1)th term is the first negative term in the expansion of $(1+x)^{7/2}$, then the value of r where $\|x\| < 1$ is (x is + ve).	(p)	Divisible by 7
(B)	The coefficient of y in the expansion of $(y^2 + 1/y)^5$ is	(q)	A perfect square
(C)	If the second term in the expansion $\left(a^{\frac{1}{13}} + \frac{a}{\sqrt{a^{-1}}}\right)^n$ is $14a^{5/2}$, then the value of n is	(r)	Divisible by 10
(D)	The sum of coefficient of x^2, x^4, x^6, x^8 in the expression $(1+2x+3x^2+4x^3+\ldots \text{ up to } \infty)^{1/2}$ is (where $\|x\| < 1$) is	(s)	A prime number

20. Match the following.

	Column I		Column II
(A)	Let n be an odd natural number greater than 1. Then the number of zeroes at the end of the sum $99^n + 1$ is	(p)	6
(B)	Let $f(n)=10^n + 3 \cdot 4^{n+2} + 5$, $n \in N$. The greatest value of the integer which divides f(n) for all n is	(q)	0
(C)	If $x + \frac{1}{x} = 1$ and $p = x^{1000} + \frac{1}{x^{1000}}$ and q be the digit at unit place in the number $2^{4n} + 1$, $n \in N$ and $n > 1$, then p + q =	(r)	2
(D)	For integer n > 1, the digit at unit place in the number $\sum_{r=0}^{100} r! + 2^{2n}$ is	(s)	9

RESPONSE GRID	
	19. A - ⓟⓠⓡⓢ; B - ⓟⓠⓡⓢ; C - ⓟⓠⓡⓢ; D - ⓟⓠⓡⓢ
	20. A - ⓟⓠⓡⓢ; B - ⓟⓠⓡⓢ; C - ⓟⓠⓡⓢ; D - ⓟⓠⓡⓢ

DAILY PRACTICE PROBLEM DPP CM06 - MATHEMATICS

Total Questions	20	Total Marks	74
Attempted		Correct	
Incorrect		Net Score	
Cut-off Score	25	Qualifying Score	36

$$\text{Net Score} = \sum_{i=1}^{V}\left[(\text{correct}_i \times MM_i) - (In_i - NM_i)\right]$$

Space for Rough Work

DPP - Daily Practice Problems

Chapter-wise Sheets

Date : | **Start Time :** | **End Time :**

MATHEMATICS (CM07)

SYLLABUS : Sequences and Series

Max. Marks : 74 | **Time : 60 min.**

GENERAL INSTRUCTIONS

- The Daily Practice Problem Sheet contains 20 Questions divided into 5 sections.

  Section I has **6** MCQs with ONLY 1 Correct Option, **3** marks for each correct answer and **–1** for each incorrect answer.

  Section II has **4** MCQs with ONE or MORE THAN ONE Correct options.

  For each question, marks will be awarded in one of the following categories:

  Full marks: **+4** If only the bubble(s) corresponding to all the correct option(s) is (are) darkened.

  Partial marks: **+1** For darkening a bubble corresponding to each correct option provided NO INCORRECT option is darkened.

  Zero marks: If none of the bubbles is darkened.

  Negative marks: **–2** In all other cases.

  Section III has **4** Single Digit Integer Answer Type Questions, **3** marks for each Correct Answer and 0 marks in all other cases.

  Section IV has Comprehension Type Questions having **4** MCQs with ONLY ONE corect option, 3 marks for each Correct Answer and **0** marks in all other cases.

  Section V has **2** Matching Type Questions, **2** mark for the correct matching of each row and 0 marks in all other cases.
- You have to evaluate your Response Grids yourself with the help of Solutions.

Section I - Straight Objective Type

This section contains 6 multiple choice questions. Each question has 4 choices (a), (b), (c) and (d), out of which **ONLY ONE** is correct.

1. If $a_1, a_2, a_3, \ldots$ are in H.P. and $f(k) = \left(\sum_{r=1}^{n} a_r\right) - a_k$, then $\frac{a_1}{f(1)}, \frac{a_2}{f(2)}, \frac{a_3}{f(3)} \ldots \frac{a_n}{f(n)}$ are in

(a) A.P. (b) G.P.

(c) H.P. (d) None of these

2. If a, b, c, d are non–zero real numbers such that $\left(a^2+b^2+c^2\right)\left(b^2+c^2+d^2\right) \le (ab+bc+cd)^2$, then a, b, c, d are in

(a) AP (b) GP

(c) HP (d) None of these

RESPONSE GRID	1. ⓐⓑⓒⓓ 2. ⓐⓑⓒⓓ

Space for Rough Work

3. If $a > 0$, $b > 0$, $c > 0$ and the minimum value of $a(b^2+c^2)+b(c^2+a^2)+c(a^2+b^2)$ is λabc, then find the value of λ
(a) 2 (b) 1
(c) 6 (d) 3

4. If S_r denotes the sum of the first r terms of an AP, and the value of = pr + q then find the value of $p+q$
(a) –1 (b) 1
(c) 3 (d) None of these

5. If $H_1, H_2, ...H_n$ are n harmonic means between a and $b(\neq a)$, then find the value of $\frac{H_1+a}{H_1-a}+\frac{H_n+b}{H_n-b}$
(a) $n+1$ (b) $n-1$
(c) $2n$ (d) $2n+3$

6. If $a_1, a_2, ..., a_n$ are in H.P., then the expression $a_1a_2+a_2a_3+..........+a_{n-1}a_n$ is equal to
(a) $n(a_1-a_n)$ (b) $(n-1)(a_1-a_n)$
(c) na_1a_n (d) $(n-1)a_1a_n$

Section II - Multiple Correct Answer Type

This section contains 4 multiple correct answer(s) type questions. Each question has 4 choices (a), (b), (c) and (d), out of which **ONE OR MORE** is/are correct.

7. If a, b, c are in AP and a^2, b^2, c^2 are in HP, then
(a) $a=b=c$ (b) $a, b, -\frac{1}{2}c$ are in GP
(c) a, b, c are in GP (d) $-\frac{1}{2}a, b, c$ are in GP

8. Sum to n terms of the series $S_n = \frac{1}{(1+x)(1+2x)} + \frac{1}{(1+2x)(1+3x)} + \frac{1}{(1+3x)(1+4x)} + ...$ is
(a) $S_{10} = \frac{10}{(1+x)(1+11x)}$
(b) $S_{10} = \frac{10}{(1+2x)(1+11x)}$
(c) $S_{16} = \frac{16}{(1+x)(1+17x)}$
(d) $S_{18} = \frac{18}{(1+x)(1+17x)}$

9. For $0 < \phi < \pi/2$, if

$$x = \sum_{n=0}^{\infty} \cos^{2n}\phi,\ y = \sum_{n=0}^{\infty} \sin^{2n}\phi,\ z = \sum_{n=0}^{\infty} \cos^{2n}\phi \sin^{2n}\phi \text{ then:}$$

(a) xyz = xz + y (b) xyz = xy + z
(c) xyz = x + y + z (d) xyz = yz + x

10. Given that α, γ are roots of the equation $Ax^2-4x+1=0$ and β, δ the roots of the equation $Bx^2-6x+1=0$, and $\alpha, \beta, \alpha, \gamma$ and δ are in HP, then
(a) A = 3, B = 8 (b) A = 8, B = 3
(c) A = 3, B = –8 (d) A + B = 11

RESPONSE GRID					
	3. ⓐⓑⓒⓓ	4. ⓐⓑⓒⓓ	5. ⓐⓑⓒⓓ	6. ⓐⓑⓒⓓ	7. ⓐⓑⓒⓓ
	8. ⓐⓑⓒⓓ	9. ⓐⓑⓒⓓ	10. ⓐⓑⓒⓓ		

Space for Rough Work

Section III - Integer Type

This section contains 4 questions. The answer to each of the questions is a single digit integer ranging from 0 to 9.

11. Let $a_1, a_2, \ldots, a_{10}$ be in AP and $h_1, h_2, \ldots, h_{10}$ be in HP. If $a_1 = h_1 = 2$ and $a_{10} = h_{10} = 3$, then find the value of a_4h_7

12. If a, b, c are in $G.P.$, x and y be the $A.M.$s between a, b and b, c respectively, then $\left(\frac{a}{x}+\frac{c}{y}\right)\left(\frac{b}{x}+\frac{b}{y}\right)$ is equal to.

13. If $(1+x)(1+x^2)(1+x^4)\ldots(1+x^{128}) = \sum_{r=0}^{n} x^r$, then unit digit of n is

14. Sum to n terms of the series $\frac{1}{5!}+\frac{1!}{6!}+\frac{2!}{7!}+\frac{3!}{8!}+\ldots = \frac{1}{a}\left[\frac{1}{b!}-\frac{(n+c)!}{(n+d)!}\right]$ then $(a + b - c - d)$ is

Section IV - Comprehension Type

Based upon the given paragraphs, 4 multiple choice questions have to be answered. Each question has 4 choices (a), (b), (c) and (d), out of which **ONLY ONE** is correct.

PARAGRAPH-1

If $a_1, a_2, \ldots, a_n$ are in A.P., then $\frac{1}{a_1}, \frac{1}{a_2}, \ldots, \frac{1}{a_n}$, are in H.P. and vice–versa.

If $a_1, a_2, \ldots, a_n$ are in A. P. with common difference d, then for any b (> 0), the number $b^{a_1}, b^{a_2}, b^{a_3} \ldots, b^{a_n}$ are in G.P. with common ratio b^d.

If $a_1, a_2, \ldots a_n$ are positive and in G.P. with common ratio r, then for any base b (b > 0), $\log_b a_1, \log_b a_2, \ldots \log_b a_n$ are in A.P. with common difference $\log_b r$.

15. If a, b, c are in H.P., then $e^{(-a)^{-1}}, e^{(-b)^{-1}}, e^{(-c)^{-1}}$ are in

(a) A.P. (b) GP
(c) H.P. (d) None of these.

16. If x, y, z are respectively the pth, q^{th} and the rth terms of an A.P., as well as of a G.P., then the value of $(x^{y-z}), (y^{z-x}), (z^{x-y})$ is

(a) 1 (b) –1
(c) 0 (d) 2

PARAGRAPH-2

Let V_r denote the sum of first r terms of an arithmetic progression (A.P.) whose first term is r and the common difference is $(2r - 1)$. Let $T_r = V_{r+1} - V_r - 2$ and $Q_r = T_{r+1} - T_r$ for $r = 1, 2, \ldots$

17. The sum $V_1 + V_2 + \ldots + V_n$ is

(a) $\frac{1}{12}n(n+1)(3n^2-n+1)$

(b) $\frac{1}{12}n(n+1)(3n^2+n+2)$

(c) $\frac{1}{2}n(2n^2-n+1)$

(d) $\frac{1}{3}(2n^3-2n+3)$

18. T_r is always

(a) an odd number (b) an even number
(c) a prime number (d) a composite number

RESPONSE GRID	
11. ⓪①②③④⑤⑥⑦⑧⑨	12. ⓪①②③④⑤⑥⑦⑧⑨
13. ⓪①②③④⑤⑥⑦⑧⑨	14. ⓪①②③④⑤⑥⑦⑧⑨
15. ⓐⓑⓒⓓ 16. ⓐⓑⓒⓓ	17. ⓐⓑⓒⓓ 18. ⓐⓑⓒⓓ

Space for Rough Work

Section V - Matrix-Match Type

This section contains 2 questions. It contains statements given in two columns, which have to be matched. Statements in column I are labelled as A, B, C and D whereas statements in column II are labelled as p, q, r and s. The answers to these questions have to be appropriately bubbled as illustrated in the following example. If the correct matches are A-p, A-r, B-p, B-s, C-r, C-s and D-q, then the correctly bubbled matrix will look like the following:

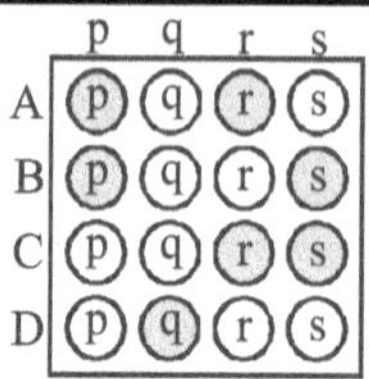

19. Match the columns

	Column I		**Column II**
(A)	The sum of the first n natural number is one – fifth of the sum of their squares, then n is	(p)	4
(B)	The harmonic mean of the roots of the equation $(5+\sqrt{2})x^2 - (4+\sqrt{3})x + 8 + 2\sqrt{3} = 0$ is	(q)	2
(C)	If x, y, z are in HP, $(z > y > x)$. The value of $\frac{(\log(x+z)+\log(x-2y+z))}{\log(z-x\ \ )}$ is	(r)	1
(D)	The nth term of GP is 128 and the sum to its n terms is 255. If its common ratio is 2, the its first term is	(s)	7

20. Match the columns

	Column I		**Column II**
(A)	The arithmetic mean of two positive numbers is 6 and their geometric mean G and harmonic mean H satisfy $G^2 + 3H = 48$ then G^2 is equal to	(p)	308
(B)	$S_n = n^3 - (n-1)^3 + (n-2)^3 - \ldots + (-1)^{n-1} \cdot 1^3$ Then find $\frac{S_{39}}{100}$	(q)	32
(C)	If the first two terms of a harmonic progression be ½ and 1/3, then the harmonic mean of the first four terms is	(r)	$\frac{240}{77}$
(D)	Find the number of numbers lying between 100 and 500 that are divisible by 7 but not by 21.	(s)	38

RESPONSE GRID	
	19. A - ⓟⓠⓡⓢ; **B -** ⓟⓠⓡⓢ; **C -** ⓟⓠⓡⓢ; **D -** ⓟⓠⓡⓢ
	20. A - ⓟⓠⓡⓢ; **B -** ⓟⓠⓡⓢ; **C -** ⓟⓠⓡⓢ; **D -** ⓟⓠⓡⓢ

DAILY PRACTICE PROBLEM DPP CM07 - MATHEMATICS

Total Questions	20	Total Marks	74
Attempted		Correct	
Incorrect		Net Score	
Cut-off Score	26	Qualifying Score	37

$$\text{Net Score} = \sum_{i=1}^{V}\left[(\text{correct}_i \times MM_i) - (In_i - NM_i)\right]$$

Space for Rough Work

DPP - Daily Practice Problems

Chapter-wise Sheets

Date : | Start Time : | End Time :

MATHEMATICS (CM08)

SYLLABUS : Straight Lines and Pair of Straight Lines

Max. Marks : 67 **Time : 60 min.**

GENERAL INSTRUCTIONS

- The Daily Practice Problem Sheet contains 20 Questions divided into 5 sections.
  Section I has **6** MCQs with ONLY 1 Correct Option, **3** marks for each correct answer and **–1** for each incorrect answer.
  Section II has **4** MCQs with ONE or MORE THAN ONE Correct options.
  For each question, marks will be awarded in one of the following categories:
  Full marks: **+4** If only the bubble(s) corresponding to all the correct option(s) is (are) darkened.
  Partial marks: **+1** For darkening a bubble corresponding to each correct option provided NO INCORRECT option is darkened.
  Zero marks: If none of the bubbles is darkened.
  Negative marks: **–2** In all other cases.
  Section III has **5** Single Digit Integer Answer Type Questions, **3** marks for each Correct Answer and **0** mark in all other cases.
  Section IV has Comprehension Type Questions having **4** MCQs with ONLY ONE corect option, **3** marks for each Correct Answer and **0** mark in all other cases.
  Section V has **1** Matching Type Question, **2** marks for the correct matching of each row and **0** mark in all other cases.
- You have to evaluate your Response Grids yourself with the help of Solutions.

Section I - Straight Objective Type

This section contains 6 multiple choice questions. Each question has 4 choices (a), (b), (c) and (d), out of which **ONLY ONE** is correct.

1. If a and b are positive numbers ($a < b$), then the range of values of K for which a real λ can be found such that the equation $ax^2 + 2\lambda xy + by^2 + 2K(x + y + 1) = 0$ represents a pair of straight lines is :

(a) $a < K^2 < b$ (b) $a \le K^2 \le b$

(c) $K^2 \le a$ or $K^2 \ge b$ (d) $K \le 2a$ or $K \ge 2b$

2. Let $ax + by + c = 0$ be a variable straight line, where a, b and c are 1st, 3rd and 7th terms of an increasing A.P. Then the variable straight line always passes through a fixed point which lies on

(a) $x^2 + y^2 = 13$ (b) $x^2 + y^2 = 5$

(c) $y^2 = 4x$ (d) $3x + 4y = 9$.

3. If $5a + 5b + 20c = t$, then the value of t for which the line $ax + by + c - 1 = 0$ always passes through a fixed point is

(a) 0 (b) 20

(c) 30 (d) None on these

RESPONSE GRID 1. ⓐⓑⓒⓓ 2. ⓐⓑⓒⓓ 3. ⓐⓑⓒⓓ

Space for Rough Work

4. The range of values of β such that $(0, \beta)$ lie on or inside the triangle formed by the lines $y+3x+2=0, 3y-2x-5=0, 4y+x-14=0$ is

(a) $5<\beta\le 7$ (b) $\frac{1}{2}\le\beta\le 1$

(c) $\frac{5}{3}\le\beta\le\frac{7}{2}$ (d) None of these

5. If $a^2+b^2-c^2-2ab=0$, then the point of concurrency of family of straight lines $ax+by+c=0$ lies on the line

(a) $y=x$ (b) $y=x+1$

(c) $y=-x$ (d) $x+y=1$

6. If the area of the rhombus enclosed by the lines $lx\pm my\pm n=0$ be 2 square units, then

(a) l,m,n are in G.P. (b) l,n,m are in G.P.

(c) $lm=n$ (d) $ln=m$

Section II - Multiple Correct Answer Type

This section contains 4 multiple correct answer(s) type questions. Each question has 4 choices (a), (b), (c) and (d), out of which **ONE OR MORE** is/are correct.

7. The equation of straight line(s) passing through ordered pairs (a, b) satisfying equation

$\sec^2(a+2)b+a^2-1=0, -\pi<b<\pi$

and haveing slope $\frac{1}{2}$ is

(a) $x-2y=0$ (b) $x-2y=1$

(c) $x-2y=\pi$ (d) $x-2y+\pi=0$

8. Let $0<p<q$ and $a\ne 0$ such that the equation

$$px^2+4\lambda xy+qy^2+4a(x+y+1)=0$$

represents a pair of straight lines, then a can lie in the interval

(a) $(-\infty,\infty)$ (b) $(-\infty,p]$

(c) $[p,q]$ (d) $[q,\infty)$

9. If the points $\left(\frac{a^3}{a-1},\frac{a^2-3}{a-1}\right),\left(\frac{b^3}{b-1},\frac{b^2-3}{b-1}\right)$ and $\left(\frac{c^3}{c-1},\frac{c^2-3}{c-1}\right)$, where a, b, c are different from 1, lie on the line $lx+my+n=0$, then

(a) $a+b+c=-\frac{m}{l}$

(b) $ab+bc+ca=\frac{n}{l}$

(c) $abc=\frac{m+n}{l}$

(d) $abc-(bc+ca+ab)+3(a+b+c)=0$

10. If m_1 and m_2 are the roots of the equation $x^2-ax-a-1=0$, then the area of the triangle formed by the three straight lines $y=m_1x, y=m_2x$ and $y=a\ (a\ne -1)$ is

(a) $\frac{a^2(a+2)}{2(a+1)}$ if $a>-1$

(b) $\frac{-a^2(a+2)}{2(a+1)}$ if $-2<a<-1$

(c) $\frac{a^2(a+2)}{2(a+1)}$ if $a<-2$

(d) 0 for all a

RESPONSE GRID	4. ⓐⓑⓒⓓ	5. ⓐⓑⓒⓓ	6. ⓐⓑⓒⓓ	7. ⓐⓑⓒⓓ	8. ⓐⓑⓒⓓ
	9. ⓐⓑⓒⓓ	10. ⓐⓑⓒⓓ			

Space for Rough Work

Section III - Integer Type

This section contains 5 questions. The answer to each of the questions is a single digit integer ranging from 0 to 9.

11. If $ax^2 + 2hxy + by^2 + 2gx + 2fy + 10 = 0$ represents a pair of straight lines, equidistant from the origin, if $\frac{f^4 - g^4}{bf^2 - ag^2}$ is equal to 2s, then s =

12. Number or integral values of 'b' for which the origin and the point (1, 1) lie on the same side of the straight line $a^2x + aby + 1 = 0$, for all $a \in \mathbf{R} - \{0\}$ is

13. A straight line L with negative slope passes through the points (8, 2) and cuts the positive coordinate axes at points P and Q. As L varies the absolute minimum value of $OP + OQ$ is (O is origin) 9t, then t =

14. If $(\sin\theta, \cos\theta)$, $\theta \in [0, 2\pi]$ and (1, 4) lie on the same side or on the line $\sqrt{3}x - y + 1 = 0$, then the maximum value of $\sin\theta$ will be

15. If the lines $x = a + m$, $y = -2$ and $y = mx$ are concurrent, if the least value of $|a|$ is $\ell\sqrt{k}$, then ℓk =

Section IV - Comprehension Type

Based upon the given paragraphs, 4 multiple choice questions have to be answered. Each question has 4 choices (a), (b), (c) and (d), out of which **ONLY ONE** is correct.

PARAGRAPH-1

A triangle ABC is given where vertex A is (1, 1) and the orthocentre is (2, 4). Also sides AB and BC are members of the family of lines $ax + by + c = 0$ where a, b, c are in $A.P$

16. The vertex B is

(a) (2, 1) (b) (1, –2)
(c) (–1, 2) (d) (1, 2)

17. Triangle ABC is a/an

(a) obtuse angled triangle (b) right angled triangle
(c) acute angled triangle (d) equilateral triangle

PARAGRAPH-2

Let $ABCD$ be a parallelogram the equation of whose diagonals are $AC: x + 2y = 3; BD: 2x + y = 3$. If length of diagonal $AC = 4$ units and area of $ABCD = 8$ sq. units.

18. The length of other diagonal BD is

(a) $\frac{10}{3}$ (b) 2
(c) $\frac{20}{3}$ (d) 5

19. The length of side AB is equal to

(a) $\frac{2\sqrt{58}}{3}$ (b) $\frac{2\sqrt{58}}{9}$
(c) $\frac{3\sqrt{58}}{9}$ (d) $\frac{4\sqrt{58}}{9}$

RESPONSE GRID	
	11. ⓪①②③④⑤⑥⑦⑧⑨ 12. ⓪①②③④⑤⑥⑦⑧⑨
	13. ⓪①②③④⑤⑥⑦⑧⑨ 14. ⓪①②③④⑤⑥⑦⑧⑨
	15. ⓪①②③④⑤⑥⑦⑧⑨ 16. ⓐⓑⓒⓓ 17. ⓐⓑⓒⓓ 18. ⓐⓑⓒⓓ
	19. ⓐⓑⓒⓓ

Space for Rough Work

Section V - Matrix-Match Type

This section contains 1 question. It contains statements given in two columns, which have to be matched. Statements in column I are labelled as A, B, C and D whereas statements in column II are labelled as p, q, r and s. The answers to these questions have to be appropriately bubbled as illustrated in the following example. If the correct matches are A-p, A-r, B-p, B-s, C-r, C-s and D-q, then the correctly bubbled matrix will look like the following:

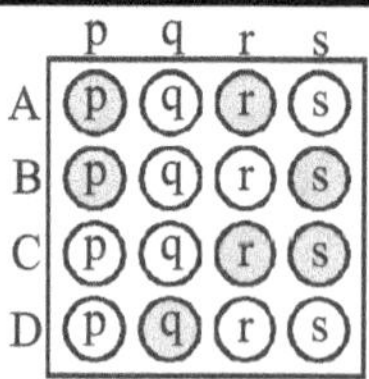

20. Match the following column :

Column-I	Column-II
(A) If the equation $12x^2 - 10xy + 2y^2 + 11x - 5y + c = 0$ represents a pair of straight lines and θ be the angle between them, then $7\|\tan\theta\|$ is equal to	p. –2
(B) If the lines $x^2 + 4xy - 2y^2 + 4x + 2fy + c^2 = 0$ intersect on the x-axis then f is equal to	q. 2
(C) In the equation given in (C) the value of c is equal to	r. 4
	s. 1

RESPONSE GRID 20. A - ⓟⓠⓡⓢ; B - ⓟⓠⓡⓢ; C - ⓟⓠⓡⓢ

DAILY PRACTICE PROBLEM DPP CM08 - MATHEMATICS

Total Questions	20	Total Marks	67
Attempted		Correct	
Incorrect		Net Score	
Cut-off Score	23	Qualifying Score	33

$$\text{Net Score} = \sum_{i=1}^{V}\left[(\text{correct}_i \times MM_i) - (In_i - NM_i)\right]$$

Space for Rough Work

DPP - Daily Practice Problems

Chapter-wise Sheets

Date : Start Time : End Time :

MATHEMATICS CM09

SYLLABUS : Conic Sections

Max. Marks : 69 **Time : 60 min.**

GENERAL INSTRUCTIONS

- The Daily Practice Problem Sheet contains 20 Questions divided into 5 sections.
  Section I has **6** MCQs with ONLY 1 Correct Option, **3** marks for each correct answer and **–1** for each incorrect answer.
  Section II has **4** MCQs with ONE or MORE THAN ONE Correct options.
  For each question, marks will be awarded in one of the following categories:
  Full marks: **+4** If only the bubble(s) corresponding to all the correct option(s) is (are) darkened.
  Partial marks: **+1** For darkening a bubble corresponding to each correct option provided NO INCORRECT option is darkened.
  Zero marks: If none of the bubbles is darkened.
  Negative marks: **–2** In all other cases.
  Section III has **5** Single Digit Integer Answer Type Questions, **3** marks for each Correct Answer and **0** mark in all other cases.
  Section IV has Comprehension Type Questions having **4** MCQs with ONLY ONE corect option, **3** marks for each Correct Answer and **0** mark in all other cases.
  Section V has **1** Matching Type Question, **2** marks for the correct matching of each row and **0** mark in all other cases.
- You have to evaluate your Response Grids yourself with the help of Solutions.

Section I - Straight Objective Type

This section contains 6 multiple choice questions. Each question has 4 choices (a), (b), (c) and (d), out of which **ONLY ONE** is correct.

1. The value of α for which the points $(\alpha, \alpha+2)$ is an interior point of the smaller segment of the circle $x^2+y^2-4=0$ made by the chord whose equation is $3x+4y+12=0$ is

(a) $\left(-\infty, \frac{-20}{7}\right)$ (b) $(-2, 0)$

(c) $\left(-\infty, \frac{-20}{7}\right) \cup (-2, 0)$ (d) None of these

2. If one of two circle $x^2+y^2+\lambda_1(x-y)+c=0$, and $x^2+y^2+\lambda_2(x-y)+c=0$, where $\lambda_1, \lambda_2 \in R$, $\lambda_1 \neq \lambda_2$ lies within the other then

(a) $c<0$ (b) $c=0$ (c) $c>0$ (d) $c \geq 0$

3. The condition that the parabolas $y^2=4ax$ and $y^2=4c(x-b)$ have a common normal other than x -axis (a, b, c being distinct positive real numbers) is

(a) $\frac{b}{a-c}<2$ (b) $\frac{b}{a-c}>2$

(c) $\frac{b}{a-c}<1$ (d) $\frac{b}{a-c}>1$

RESPONSE GRID	1. ⓐⓑⓒⓓ	2. ⓐⓑⓒⓓ	3. ⓐⓑⓒⓓ

Space for Rough Work

4. If the circle $(x+c)^2+y^2=a^2$ and ellipse $\frac{(x-h)^2}{b^2}+\frac{y^2}{a^2}=1$ (a, b, c, h are positive) have common tangent parallel to x-axis only then

(a) $c>b+a-h$ (b) $c<b+a-h$

(c) $c>b+a$ (d) None of these

5. If a rectangular hyperbola $(x-1)(y-2)=4$ cuts a circle $x^2+y^2+2gx+2fy+c=0$ at points (3, 4), (5, 3), (2, 6) and (–1, 0), then the value of $(g+f)$ is equal to

(a) -8 (b) -9 (c) 8 (d) 9

6. A normal to the hyperbola $\frac{x^2}{4}-\frac{y^2}{1}=1$, has equal intercepts on the positive x and y axes. If this normal touches the ellipse $\frac{x^2}{a^2}+\frac{y^2}{b^2}=1$, then a^2+b^2 is equal to

(a) 5 (b) 25 (c) 16 (d) $\frac{25}{3}$

Section II - Multiple Correct Answer Type

This section contains 4 multiple correct answer(s) type questions. Each question has 4 choices (a), (b), (c) and (d), out of which **ONE OR MORE** is/are correct.

7. The value of α in $[0, 2\pi]$ so that $x^2+y^2+2\sqrt{\sin\alpha}x+(\cos\alpha-1)=0$ having intercept on x-axis always greater than 2 is/are

(a) $\left(\frac{\pi}{4},\frac{\pi}{2}\right]$ (b) $\left(\frac{\pi}{4},\pi\right]$

(c) $\left(\frac{\pi}{4},\frac{5\pi}{4}\right)$ (d) $[0,\pi]$

8. The equation $\left|\sqrt{x^2+(y-1)^2}-\sqrt{x^2+(y+1)^2}\right|=K$ will represent a hyperbola for

(a) $K\in(0,2)$ (b) $K\in(0,1)$

(c) $K\in(1,\infty)$ (d) $K\in(0,\infty)$

9. If the circle $x^2+y^2=1$ cuts the rectangular hyperbola $xy=1$ in four points (x_i, y_i) $i=1,2,3,4$ then.

(a) $x_1x_2x_3x_4=-1$ (b) $y_1y_2y_3y_4=1$

(c) $x_1+x_2+x_3+x_4=0$ (d) $y_1+y_2+y_3+y_4=0$

10. If the straight line $3x+4y=24$ intersects the axes at A and B and the straight line $4x+3y=24$ at C and D, then points A, B, C, D lies on

(a) circle (b) parabola

(c) ellipse (d) hyperbola

Section III - Integer Type

This section contains 5 questions. The answer to each of the questions is a single digit integer ranging from 0 to 9.

11. If the circle passing through the distinct points $(1, t)$, $(t, 1)$ and (t, t) for all values of $t\in R$ also passes through fixed point (a, b) then a^2+b^2 is equal to

12. C is the centre of the hyperbola $\frac{x^2}{4}-\frac{y^2}{1}=1$, and '$A$' is any point on it. The tangent at A to the hyperbola meets the line $x-2y=0$ and $x+2y=0$ at Q and R respectively. The value of CQ. CR is equal to

RESPONSE GRID	
	4. ⓐⓑⓒⓓ 5. ⓐⓑⓒⓓ 6. ⓐⓑⓒⓓ 7. ⓐⓑⓒⓓ 8. ⓐⓑⓒⓓ
	9. ⓐⓑⓒⓓ 10. ⓐⓑⓒⓓ 11. ⓪①②③④⑤⑥⑦⑧⑨
	12. ⓪①②③④⑤⑥⑦⑧⑨

Space for Rough Work

13. A chord is drawn from a point $P(1, t)$ to the parabola $y^2 = 4x$ which cuts the parabola at A and B. If $PA.PB = 3|t|$, then the maximum value of t is equal to

14. Maximum number of common normal of $y^2 = 4ax$ and $x^2 = 4by$ may be equal to

15. If the sum of the squares of the lengths of the chords intercepted by the line $x + y = n, n \in \mathbf{N}$ on the circle $x^2 + y^2 = 4$ is 11k, then k=

Section IV - Comprehension Type

Based upon the given paragraphs, 4 multiple choice questions have to be answered. Each question has 4 choices (a), (b), (c) and (d), out of which **ONLY ONE** is correct.

PARAGRAPH-1

The line $x+2y+a=0$ intersects the circle $x^2+y^2-4=0$ at two distinct points A and B. Another line $12x-6y-41=0$ intersects the circle $x^2+y^2-4x-2y+1=0$ at two distinct points C and D.

16. The value for 'a' so that the line $x+2y+a=0$ intersect the circle $x^2+y^2-4=0$ at two distinct points A and B is

(a) $-2\sqrt{5} < a < 2\sqrt{5}$ (b) $0 < a < 2\sqrt{5}$

(c) $-\sqrt{5} < a < \sqrt{5}$ (d) $0 < a < 2\sqrt{5}$

17. The equation of circle passing through the points A, B, C and D is

(a) $5x^2+5y^2+8x+16y-36=0$

(b) $5x^2+5y^2+8x-16y-36=0$

(c) $5x^2+5y^2-8x-16y-36=0$

(d) $5x^2+5y^2+8x-16y+36=0$

PARAGRAPH-2

An ellipse whose major axis is parallel to x-axis such that the segments of a focal chord are 1 and 3 units. The lines $ax+by+c=0$ are the chords of the ellipse such that a, b, c, are in AP and bisected by the point at which they intersent. The equation of its auxiliary circle is

$x^2+y^2+2\alpha x+2\beta y-2\alpha-1=0$ then.

18. Equation of the director circle is

(a) $x^2+y^2-2x+4y+1=0$

(b) $x^2+y^2+2x+2y-3=0$

(c) $x^2+y^2+2x+4y+1=0$

(d) $x^2+y^2-2x+4y-2=0$

19. Eccentricity of ellipse is

(a) $\frac{\sqrt{13}}{4}$ (b) $\frac{1}{2}$ (c) $\frac{\sqrt{3}}{2}$ (d) $\frac{1}{\sqrt{2}}$

RESPONSE GRID	
	13. ⓪①②③④⑤⑥⑦⑧⑨ 14. ⓪①②③④⑤⑥⑦⑧⑨
	15. ⓪①②③④⑤⑥⑦⑧⑨ 16. ⓐⓑⓒⓓ 17. ⓐⓑⓒⓓ 18. ⓐⓑⓒⓓ
	19. ⓐⓑⓒⓓ

Space for Rough Work

Section V - Matrix-Match Type

This section contains 1 question. It contains statements given in two columns, which have to be matched. Statements in column I are labelled as A, B, C and D whereas statements in column II are labelled as p, q, r and s. The answers to these questions have to be appropriately bubbled as illustrated in the following example. If the correct matches are A-p, A-r, B-p, B-s, C-r, C-s and D-q, then the correctly bubbled matrix will look like the following:

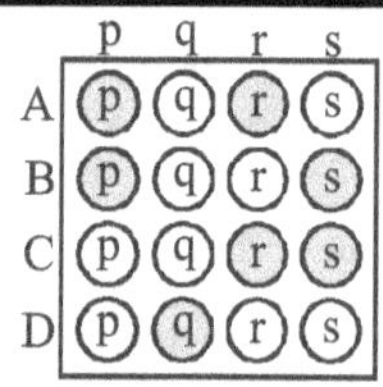

20. Normal to parabola $y^2 = 4x$ at points P and Q of parabola meet at R $(x_2, 0)$ and tangents at P and Q meets at T $(x_1, 0)$. Let $x_2 = 3$

Match the entries of two columns.

Column – I	Column – II
(A) The area of quadrilateral $PTQR$ is	p. 3
(B) If the quadrilateral PTQR can be inscribed in a circle then the value of $\frac{\text{circumferecnce}}{4\pi}$ is	q. 4
(C) The number of nomals that can be drawn to the parabola from R is	r. 1
(D) The square of the length PT is	s. 8

RESPONSE GRID	20. A - ⓟⓠⓡⓢ; B - ⓟⓠⓡⓢ; C - ⓟⓠⓡⓢ; D - ⓟⓠⓡⓢ

DAILY PRACTICE PROBLEM DPP CM09 - MATHEMATICS			
Total Ques! ons	20	Total Marks	69
Attempted		Correct	
Incorrect		Net Score	
Cut-off Score	23	Qualifying Score	32

$$\text{Net Score} = \sum_{i=1}^{V} \left[(\text{correct}_i \times MM_i) - (In_i - NM_i) \right]$$

Space for Rough Work

DPP - Daily Practice Problems

Chapter-wise Sheets

Date : ______ **Start Time :** ______ **End Time :** ______

MATHEMATICS (CM10)

SYLLABUS : Limits and Derivatives

Max. Marks : 72 **Time : 60 min.**

GENERAL INSTRUCTIONS

- The Daily Practice Problem Sheet contains 20 Questions divided into 5 sections.
  Section I has **6** MCQs with ONLY 1 Correct Option, **3** marks for each correct answer and **–1** for each incorrect answer.
  Section II has **4** MCQs with ONE or MORE THAN ONE Correct options.
  For each question, marks will be awarded in one of the following categories:
  Full marks: **+4** If only the bubble(s) corresponding to all the correct option(s) is (are) darkened.
  Partial marks: **+1** For darkening a bubble corresponding to each correct option provided NO INCORRECT option is darkened.
  Zero marks: If none of the bubbles is darkened.
  Negative marks: **–2** In all other cases.
  Section III has **4** Single Digit Integer Answer Type Questions, **3** marks for each Correct Answer and **0** mark in all other cases.
  Section IV has Comprehension Type Questions having **4** MCQs with ONLY ONE corect option, **3** marks for each Correct Answer and **0** mark in all other cases.
  Section V has **2** Matching Type Questions, **2** marks for the correct matching of each row and **0** mark in all other cases.
- You have to evaluate your Response Grids yourself with the help of Solutions.

Section I - Straight Objective Type

This section contains 6 multiple choice questions. Each question has 4 choices (a), (b), (c) and (d), out of which **ONLY ONE** is correct.

1. For $m,\ n \in I^+$, $\lim\limits_{x\to 0}\dfrac{\sin x^n}{(\sin x)^m}$ is equal to

   (a) 1, if $n < m$ (b) 0, if $n > m$
   (c) n/m (d) 0, if $n = m$

2. Let $f(x)$ be a polynomial function of second degree. If $f(a) = f(-1)$ and a, b, c are in AP, then $f'(a), f'(b)$ and $f'(c)$ are in –

   (a) AP (b) GP (c) HP (d) AGP

3. If $S_n = \sum\limits_{k=1}^{n} a_k$ and $\lim\limits_{n\to\infty} a_n = a$, then

   $\lim\limits_{n\to\infty}\dfrac{S_{n+1}-S_n}{\sqrt{\sum\limits_{k=1}^{n} k}}$ is equal to

   (a) 0 (b) a (c) $\sqrt{2}a$ (d) $2a$

4. If A.M. of the products of all distinct pair of positive integers whose sum is n, is denoted by S_n, then the value of $\lim\limits_{n\to\infty}\left(\dfrac{S_n}{n^2}\right)$ is equal to

   (a) 1/6 (b) 1/4

RESPONSE GRID	1. ⓐⓑⓒⓓ	2. ⓐⓑⓒⓓ	3. ⓐⓑⓒⓓ	4. ⓐⓑⓒⓓ

Space for Rough Work

(c) 1/12 (d) None of these

5. If $\phi(x)$ be a polynomial function of the second degree. If $\phi(1) = \phi(-1)$ and a_1, a_2, a_3 are in AP, then $\phi'(a_1), \phi'(a_2), \phi'(a_3)$ are in

(a) AP (b) GP
(c) HP (d) None of these

6. Let $a = \min\{x^2 + 2x + 3, x \in R\}$ and

$b = \lim_{\theta \to 0} \frac{1-\cos\theta}{\theta^2}$. The value of $\sum_{r=0}^{n} a^r . b^{n-r}$ is

(a) $\frac{2^{n+1}-1}{3 \cdot 2^n}$ (b) $\frac{2^{n+1}+1}{3 \cdot 2^n}$

(c) $\frac{4^{n+1}-1}{3 \cdot 2^n}$ (d) None of these

Section II - Multiple Correct Answer Type

This section contains 4 multiple correct answer(s) type questions. Each question has 4 choices (a), (b), (c) and (d), out of which **ONE OR MORE** is/are correct.

7. $f(x) = |x^2 - 3|x| + 2|$, then which of the following is/are true

(a) $f'(x) = 2x - 3$ for $x \in (0, 1) \cup (2, \infty)$
(b) $f'(x) = 2x + 3$ for $x \in (-\infty, -2) \cup (-1, 0)$
(c) $f'(x) = -2x - 3$ for $x \in (-2, -1)$
(d) None of these

8. $f(x) = \lim_{n \to \infty} \frac{x}{x^{2n}+1}$, then

(a) $f(1^+) + f(1^-) = 0$

(b) $f(1^+) + f(1^-) + f(1) = 3/2$

(c) $f(-1^+) + f(-1^{-1}) = -1$

(d) $f(1^+) + f(-1^{-1}) = 0$

9. If $\lim_{x \to 1}(2 - x + a[x-1] + b[1+x])$ exists, then a and b can take the values (where [.] denotes the greatest integer function)

(a) $a = 1/3, b = 1$ (b) $a = 1, b = -1$
(c) $a = 9, b = -9$ (d) $a = 2, b = 2/3$

10. Let $f(x) = \lim_{n \to \infty} \frac{x^{2n}-1}{x^{2n}+1}$, then

(a) $f(x) = 1$ for $|x| > 1$
(b) $f(x) = -1$ for $|x| < 1$
(c) $f(x)$ is not defined for any value of x
(d) $f(x) = 1$ for $|x| = 1$

Section III - Integer Type

This section contains 4 questions. The answer to each of the questions is a single digit integer ranging from 0 to 9.

11. Find the sum of all the values of n for which $f'(x+y) + 1 = f'(x) + f'(y)$ holds where $f(x) = x^n + x$ (n : whole number)

12. Find the value of $\lim_{x \to 0}\left[\frac{\sin(\text{sgn}(x))}{(\text{sgn}(x))}\right]$, where [.] denotes the greatest integer function.

13. Find the value of $\lim_{x \to \infty} \frac{-\ln x^n + [x]}{[x]}$, where $n \in N$ and [.] denotes the greatest integer function.

14. If $y = (1+x)(1+x^2)(1+x^4)..........(1+x^{2^n})$, then find the value of $\frac{dy}{dx}$ at $x = 0$.

RESPONSE GRID	
	5. ⓐⓑⓒⓓ 6. ⓐⓑⓒⓓ 7. ⓐⓑⓒⓓ 8. ⓐⓑⓒⓓ 9. ⓐⓑⓒⓓ
	10. ⓐⓑⓒⓓ 11. ⓪①②③④⑤⑥⑦⑧⑨ 12. ⓪①②③④⑤⑥⑦⑧⑨
	13. ⓪①②③④⑤⑥⑦⑧⑨ 14. ⓪①②③④⑤⑥⑦⑧⑨

Space for Rough Work

Section IV - Comprehension Type

Based upon the given paragraphs, 4 multiple choice questions have to be answered. Each question has 4 choices (a), (b), (c) and (d), out of which **ONLY ONE** is correct.

PARAGRAPH-1

If $L = \lim_{x\to 0} \dfrac{\sin x + ae^x + be^{-x} + c\ln(1+x)}{x^3} \neq \infty$

15. The value of L is
(a) 1/2 (b) – 1/3
(c) –1/6 (d) 3

16. The solution set of $||x+c|-2a| < 4b$ is
(a) $[-2, 2]$ (b) $[0, 2]$
(c) $[-1, 1]$ (d) $[-2, 1]$

PARAGRAPH-2

AP is a diameter of a unit circle with centre at O. Let AC be an arc of this circle, which subtends angle θ radian at centre O. A tangent line is drawn to the circle at the point A and a segment AB on this tangent is laid off whose length is equal to that of the arc AC. A straight line BC is drawn to intersect the extension of the diameter AP at Q. CD is the perpendicular let fall from the point C upon the diameter AP.

17. The area of the trapezoid $ABCD$ is
(a) $\dfrac{1-\cos\theta}{\theta-\sin\theta}$ (b) $(\theta+\sin\theta)\sin^2\dfrac{\theta}{2}$
(c) $2\cos^2\dfrac{\theta}{2}(\theta-\sin\theta)$ (d) $\theta(\theta+\sin\theta)$

18. The value of the limit $\lim_{\theta\to 0^+}(AQ)$ is
(a) 0 (b) 1
(c) 2 (d) 3

Section V - Matrix-Match Type

This section contains 2 questions. It contains statements given in two columns, which have to be matched. Statements in column I are labelled as A, B, C and D whereas statements in column II are labelled as p, q, r and s. The answers to these questions have to be appropriately bubbled as illustrated in the following example. If the correct matches are A-p, A-r, B-p, B-s, C-r, C-s and D-q, then the correctly bubbled matrix will look like the following:

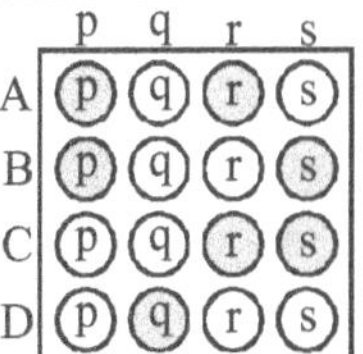

19.

Column-I	Column-II
(A) If $\lim_{x\to\infty}(\sqrt{(x^2-x-1)} - ax - b) = 0$, where $a > 0$, then there exists at least one a and b for which point $(a, 2b)$ lies on the line.	(p) $y = -3$
(B) If $\lim_{x\to\infty} \dfrac{(1+a^3)+8e^{1/x}}{1+(1-b^3)e^{1/x}} = 2$, then there exists at least one a and b for which point (a, b^3) lies on the line	(q) $3x - 2y - 5 = 0$

RESPONSE GRID	15. ⓐⓑⓒⓓ 16. ⓐⓑⓒⓓ 17. ⓐⓑⓒⓓ 18. ⓐⓑⓒⓓ
	19. A - 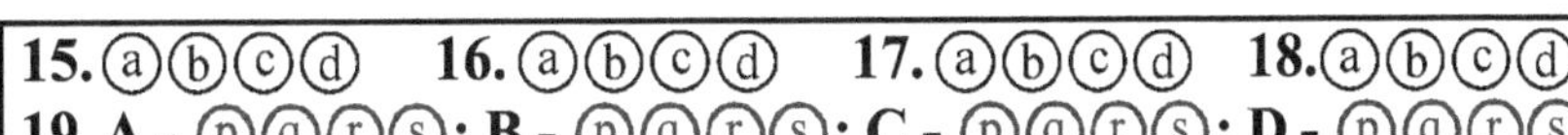

Space for Rough Work

(C) If $\lim_{x\to\infty}(\sqrt{(x^4-x^2+1)}-ax^2-b)=0$, then there exists at least one a and b for which point $(a,-2b)$ lies on the line

(r) $15x-2y-11=0$

(D) If $\lim_{x\to -a}\dfrac{x^7+a^7}{x+a}=7$, where $a<0$, then there exists at least one a for which point $(a, 2)$ lies on the line

(s) $y=2$

20. **Column-I**

(A) If $f(x)=\left(\dfrac{|x|}{|x|+2}\right)^{-x}$, then

(B) If $f(x)=\dfrac{(1+x)^{1/x}-e}{x}$, then

(C) If $f(x)=\left(\dfrac{1+5x^2}{1+3x^2}\right)^{1/x^2}$, then

Column-II

(p) $\lim_{x\to\infty} f(x)=e^2$

(q) $\lim_{x\to 0} f(x)=e^2$

(r) $\lim_{x\to -\infty} f(x)=e^{-2}$

(s) $\lim_{x\to 0} f(x)=-e/2$,

(t) $\lim_{x\to 0} f(x)<-1$

RESPONSE GRID	20. A - ⓟⓠⓡⓢ; B - ⓟⓠⓡⓢ; C - ⓟⓠⓡⓢ; D - ⓟⓠⓡⓢ

DAILY PRACTICE PROBLEM DPP CM10 - MATHEMATICS			
Total Questions	20	Total Marks	72
Attempted		Correct	
Incorrect		Net Score	
Cut-off Score	25	Qualifying Score	36

$$\text{Net Score}=\sum_{i=1}^{V}\left[(\text{correct}_i\times MM_i)-(In_i-NM_i)\right]$$

Space for Rough Work

DPP - Daily Practice Problems

Chapter-wise Sheets

Date : | Start Time : | End Time :

MATHEMATICS (CM11)

SYLLABUS : Mathematical Reasoning

Max. Marks : 76 **Time : 60 min.**

GENERAL INSTRUCTIONS

- The Daily Practice Problem Sheet contains 20 Questions divided into 3 sections.
  Section I has **8** MCQs with ONLY 1 Correct Option, **3** marks for each correct answer and **–1** for each incorrect answer.
  Section II has **11** MCQs with ONE or MORE THAN ONE Correct options.
  For each question, marks will be awarded in one of the following categories:
  Full marks: **+4** If only the bubble(s) corresponding to all the correct option(s) is (are) darkened.
  Partial marks: **+1** For darkening a bubble corresponding to each correct option provided NO INCORRECT option is darkened.
  Zero marks: If none of the bubbles is darkened.
  Negative marks: **–2** In all other cases.
  Section III has **1** Matching Type Question, **2** marks for the correct matching of each row and **0** mark in all other cases.
- You have to evaluate your Response Grids yourself with the help of Solutions.

Section I - Straight Objective Type

This section contains 8 multiple choice questions. Each question has 4 choices (a), (b), (c) and (d), out of which **ONLY ONE** is correct.

1. $\sim(p \Rightarrow q) \Leftrightarrow \sim p \vee \sim q$ is

(a) A tautology

(b) A contradiction

(c) Neither a tautology nor a contradiction

(d) Cannot come to any conclusion

2. The inverse of the statement $(p \wedge \sim q) \to r$ is

(a) $\sim(p \vee \sim q) \to \sim r$ (b) $(\sim p \wedge q) \to \sim r$

(c) $(\sim p \vee q) \to \sim r$ (d) None of these

3. Let f be a function from a set X to a set Y. Consider the following statements:

P: For each $x \in X$, there exists unique $y \in Y$ such that $f(x) = y$

Q: For each $y \in Y$, there exists $x \in X$ such that $f(x) = y$.

R: There exist $x_1, x_2 \in X$ such that $x_1 \neq x_2$ and $f(x_1) = f(x_2)$.

The negation of the statement "f is one-to-one and onto" is

(a) P or not R (b) R or not P

(c) R or not Q (d) P and not R

4. The contrapositive of $p \to (\sim q \to \sim r)$ is –

(a) $(\sim q \wedge r) \to \sim p$ (b) $(q \to r) \to \sim p$

(c) $(q \vee \sim r) \to \sim p$ (d) None of these

RESPONSE GRID	1. ⓐⓑⓒⓓ	2. ⓐⓑⓒⓓ	3. ⓐⓑⓒⓓ	4. ⓐⓑⓒⓓ

Space for Rough Work

5. If $S^*(p, q, r)$ is the dual of the compound statement S(p,q,r) and S $(p,q,r) = \sim p \wedge [\sim (q \vee r)]$ then $S^*(\sim p, \sim q, \sim r)$ is equivalent to –

(a) $S(p, q, r)$ (b) $\sim S(\sim p, \sim q, \sim r)$

(c) $\sim S(p, q, r)$ (d) $S^*(p, q, r)$

6. $\sim(p \rightarrow q) \rightarrow [(\sim p) \vee (\sim q)]$ is

(a) a tautology

(b) a contradiction

(c) neither a tautology nor contradicion

(d) cannot come any conclusion.

7. The statement $p \rightarrow (q \rightarrow p)$ is equivalent to

(a) $p \rightarrow (p \rightarrow q)$ (b) $p \rightarrow (p \vee q)$

(c) $p \rightarrow (p \wedge q)$ (d) $p \rightarrow (p \leftrightarrow q)$

8. In the truth table for the statement $(p \rightarrow q) \leftrightarrow (\sim P \vee q)$, the last column has the truth value in the following order is

(a) TTFF (b) FFFF

(c) TTTT (d) FTFT

Section II - Multiple Correct Answer Type

This section contains 11 multiple correct answer(s) type questions. Each question has 4 choices (a), (b), (c) and (d), out of which **ONE OR MORE** is/are correct.

9. Let p, q and r be any three logical statements. Which of the following are not correct?

(a) $\sim [p \wedge (\sim q)] \equiv (\sim p) \wedge q$

(b) $\sim [(p \vee q) \wedge (\sim r) \equiv (\sim p) \vee (\sim q) \vee (\sim r)$

(c) $\sim [p \vee (\sim q)] \equiv (\sim p) \wedge q$

(d) $\sim [p \vee (\sim q)] \equiv (\sim p) \wedge \sim q$

10. If p and q are two statement then $(p \leftrightarrow \sim q)$ is true when –

(a) p and q both are true

(b) p and q both are false

(c) p is false and q is true

(d) p is true and q is flase

11. Identify the correct statements

(a) $\sim [p \vee (\sim q)] \equiv (\sim p) \vee q$

(b) $[p \vee q] \vee (\sim p)$ is a tautology

(c) $[p \wedge q) \wedge (\sim p)$ is a contradiction

(d) $\sim [p \vee q] \equiv (\sim p) \vee (\sim q)$

12. Which of the following statements are tautology?

(a) $(\sim p \vee \sim q) \vee (p \vee \sim q)$ (b) $(p \rightarrow q) \vee (p \wedge \sim q)$

(c) $(\sim p \wedge q) \wedge (\sim q)$ (d) $(\sim p \wedge q) \vee (\sim q)$

RESPONSE GRID					
	5. ⓐⓑⓒⓓ	6. ⓐⓑⓒⓓ	7. ⓐⓑⓒⓓ	8. ⓐⓑⓒⓓ	9. ⓐⓑⓒⓓ
	10. ⓐⓑⓒⓓ	11. ⓐⓑⓒⓓ	12. ⓐⓑⓒⓓ		

Space for Rough Work

13. Which of the following are correct?

(a) $p \vee \sim p$ is a tautology

(b) $\sim(\sim p) \leftrightarrow$ p is a tautology

(c) $p \wedge \sim p$ is a contradiction

(d) $((p \wedge q) \rightarrow q) \rightarrow p$ is a tautology

14. If p is any statement, t is tautology and c is a contradiction, then which of the following are correct?

(a) $p \vee (\sim p) = c$ (b) $p \vee t = t$

(c) $p \wedge t = p$ (d) $p \wedge c = c$.

15. Dual of following statement are given which are correct?

(a) $(p \vee q) \wedge (r \vee s)$, $(p \wedge q) \vee (r \wedge s)$

(b) $[p \vee (\sim q) \wedge (\sim p)$,$[p \wedge (\sim q)] \vee (\sim p)$

(c) $(p \wedge q) \vee r$, $(p \vee q) \wedge r$

(d) $(p \vee q) \vee s$, $\wedge (p \wedge q) \vee s$.

16. Which of the following are incorrect?

(a) $(\sim p \Rightarrow q) = \sim q \Rightarrow \sim p$

(b) $(\sim p \vee q) \equiv \vee p \vee \sim q$

(c) $\sim(p \Rightarrow q) \equiv p \wedge \sim q$

(d) $\sim(p \vee q) \equiv \sim p \wedge \sim q$

17. Which of the following is not true for the statements p and q ?

(a) $p \wedge q$ is true when at least one of p and q is true

(b) $p \rightarrow q$ is true when p is true and q is false

(c) $p \leftrightarrow q$ is true only when both p and q are true

(d) $\sim(p \vee q)$ is true only when both p and q are false

18. Which of the following are correct?

(a) $p \rightarrow q$ is logically equivalent to $\sim p \vee q$

(b) If the truth values of p, q, r are T, F, T respectively, then the truth value of $(p \vee q) \wedge (q \vee r)$ is T

(c) $\sim(p \vee q \vee r) \cong \sim p \wedge \sim q \wedge \sim r$

(d) The truth value of $p \wedge \sim(p \vee q)$ is always T.

19. Which of the following are not true?

(a) $(\sim p \vee \sim q) \equiv (p \wedge q)$

(b) $(p \rightarrow q) \equiv (\sim q \rightarrow \sim p)$

(c) $\sim(p \rightarrow \sim q) \equiv (p \wedge \sim q)$

(d) $\sim(p \leftrightarrow q) \equiv (p \rightarrow q) \rightarrow (q \rightarrow p)$

RESPONSE GRID					
	13. 	14. ⓐⓑⓒⓓ	15. ⓐⓑⓒⓓ	16. ⓐⓑⓒⓓ	17. ⓐⓑⓒⓓ
	18. ⓐⓑⓒⓓ	19. ⓐⓑⓒⓓ			

Space for Rough Work

Section III - Matrix-Match Type

This section contains 1 question. It contains statements given in two columns, which have to be matched. Statements in column I are labelled as A, B, C and D whereas statements in column II are labelled as p, q, r and s. The answers to these questions have to be appropriately bubbled as illustrated in the following example. If the correct matches are A-p, A-r, B-p, B-s, C-r, C-s and D-q, then the correctly bubbled matrix will look like the following:

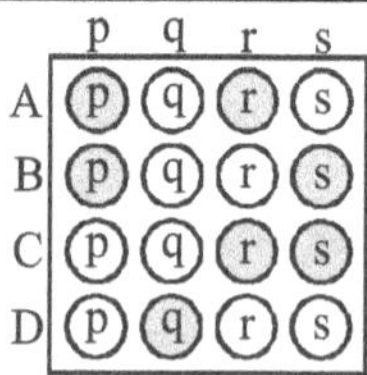

20. Match the followings:

	Column-I		**Column-II**
(A)	Dual of statement $[(p \vee q) \wedge (\sim q)] \vee (\sim p)$	p.	$[p \wedge \sim q] \vee (\sim p)$
(B)	Logically equivalent of $[(p \vee q) \wedge (\sim q)] \vee (\sim p)$	q.	$[(\sim p \wedge \sim q) \vee q] \wedge p$
(C)	Negation of $[(p \vee q) \wedge (\sim q)] \vee (\sim p)$	r.	$[(\sim p \wedge \sim q) \vee q] \vee (\sim p)$
(D)	Contrapositive of $[(p \vee q) \wedge (\sim q)] \rightarrow (\sim p)$	s.	$[(p \wedge q) \vee \sim q] \wedge (\sim p)$

RESPONSE GRID	20. A - ⓟⓠⓡⓢ; B - ⓟⓠⓡⓢ; C - ⓟⓠⓡⓢ; D - ⓟⓠⓡⓢ

DAILY PRACTICE PROBLEM DPP CM11 - MATHEMATICS			
Total Questions	20	Total Marks	76
Attempted		Correct	
Incorrect		Net Score	
Cut-off Score	27	Qualifying Score	38

$$\text{Net Score} = \sum_{i=1}^{V}\left[(\text{correct}_i \times MM_i) - (In_i - NM_i)\right]$$

Space for Rough Work

DPP - Daily Practice Problems

Chapter-wise Sheets

Date : | Start Time : | End Time :

MATHEMATICS CM12

SYLLABUS : Statistics

Max. Marks : 69 **Time : 60 min.**

GENERAL INSTRUCTIONS

- The Daily Practice Problem Sheet contains 20 Questions divided into 5 sections.
  Section I has **7** MCQs with ONLY 1 Correct Option, **3** marks for each correct answer and **–1** for each incorrect answer.
  Section II has **4** MCQs with ONE or MORE THAN ONE Correct options.
  For each question, marks will be awarded in one of the following categories:
  Full marks: **+4** If only the bubble(s) corresponding to all the correct option(s) is (are) darkened.
  Partial marks: **+1** For darkening a bubble corresponding to each correct option provided NO INCORRECT option is darkened.
  Zero marks: If none of the bubbles is darkened.
  Negative marks: **–2** In all other cases.
  Section III has **6** Single Digit Integer Answer Type Questions, **3** marks for each Correct Answer and **0** mark in all other cases.
  Section IV has Comprehension Type Questions having **2** MCQs with ONLY ONE corect option, **3** marks for each Correct Answer and **0** marks in all other cases.
  Section V has **1** Matching Type Question, **2** marks for the correct matching of each row and **0** mark in all other cases.
- You have to evaluate your Response Grids yourself with the help of Solutions.

Section I - Straight Objective Type

This section contains 7 multiple choice questions. Each question has 4 choices (a), (b), (c) and (d), out of which **ONLY ONE** is correct.

1. In a series of $2n$ observations, half of them equals 'a' and remaining equals '$-a$'. If S.D. is 2, then $|a|$ equals

(a) $\frac{1}{n}$ (b) $\sqrt{2}$

(c) 2 (d) $\frac{\sqrt{2}}{n}$

2. For (2n + 1) observations $x_1, -x_1, x_2, -x_2, \ldots\ldots x_n, -x_n$ and 0 where x's are all distinct. Let S.D. and M.D. denote the standard deviation and median respectively.Then which of the following is always true?

(a) S.D < M.D.

(b) S.D.> M.D.

(c) S.D. = M.D.

(d) Nothing can be said in general about the relationship of S.D. and M.D.

RESPONSE GRID	1. ⓐⓑⓒⓓ	2. ⓐⓑⓒⓓ

Space for Rough Work

3. The standard deviation of 25 numbers is 40. If each of the number is increased by 5, then the new standard deviation is

(a) 40 (b) 45

(c) $40+\frac{21}{25}$ (d) $40-\frac{21}{25}$

4. If $\sum_{i=1}^{9}(x_i-5)=9$ and $\sum_{i=1}^{9}(x_i-5)^2=45$, then the standard deviation of the 9 items $x_1, x_2, ..., x_9$ is

(a) 9 (b) 4

(c) 3 (d) 2

5. Two variables X and U are related by the relationship $X=5+2U$. The mean and the coefficient of variation of X are 10 and 2.6 respectively. The coefficient of variation of the variable U is

(a) 5.2 (b) 2.6

(c) 1.3 (d) 52

6. The mean deviation from the mean of the A.P.

$a, a+d, a+2d, ... a, a+2nd$ is

(a) $n(n+1)d$ (b) $\frac{n(n+1)d}{2n+1}$

(c) $\frac{n(n+1)d}{2n}$ (d) $\frac{n(n-1)d}{2n+1}$

7. The variance of first n natural numbers is

(a) $\frac{n^2+1}{12}$ (b) $\frac{n^2-1}{12}$

(c) $\frac{(n+1)(2n+1)}{6}$ (d) $\left[\frac{n(n+1}{2}\right]^2$

Section II - Multiple Correct Answer Type

This section contains 4 multiple correct answer(s) type questions. Each question has 4 choices (a), (b), (c) and (d), out of which **ONE OR MORE** is/are correct.

8. The mean of the numbers a, b, 8, 5, 10 is 6 and the variance is 6.80. Then which one of the following gives possible values of a and b ?

(a) $a=0, b=7$ (b) $a=4, b=3$

(c) $a=1, b=6$ (d) $a=3, b=4$

9. The mean of five observations is 4 and their variance is 5·2. If three of these observations are 2, 4 and 6, then the other two observations are

(a) 3 and 5 (b) 2 and 6

(c) 5 and 5 (d) 1 and 7

10. Let x_1, x_2, ... x_n be n observations such that $\sum x_i^2 = 400$ and $\sum x_i = 80$. Then the possible value of n among the following is

(a) 15 (b) 18

(c) 20 (d) 12

RESPONSE GRID					
	3. ⓐⓑⓒⓓ	4. ⓐⓑⓒⓓ	5. ⓐⓑⓒⓓ	6. ⓐⓑⓒⓓ	7. ⓐⓑⓒⓓ
	8. ⓐⓑⓒⓓ	9. ⓐⓑⓒⓓ	10. ⓐⓑⓒⓓ		

Space for Rough Work

11. If the standard deviation of the numbers 2, 3, a and 11 is 3.5, then which of the following is true?

(a) Sum of possible values of a is less than 11.

(b) Difference of possible values of a is greater than 1.

(c) Product of possible values of a is 28.

(d) Each possible value of a is less than or equal to 6.

Section III - Integer Type

This section contains 6 questions. The answer to each of the questions is a single digit integer ranging from 0 to 9.

12. The standard deviation of 9, 16, 23, 30, 37, 44, 51 is k + 10 where k =

13. If the variance of 1, 2, 3, 4, 5, ..., 10 is $\frac{99}{12}$, then the standard deviation of 3, 6, 9, 12, ..., 30 is $\frac{3}{2}\sqrt{30+m}$ where m =

14. Let a, b, c, d and e be the observations with mean m and standard deviation s. The standard deviation of the observations a + k, b + k, c + k, d + k and e + k is s+ k α where α=

15. If M. D. is 12, the value of S.D. will be 20 – p where, p =

16. Consider the following frequency distribution

x	A	2A	3A	4A	5A	6A
f	2	1	1	1	1	1

where, A is a positive integer and has variance 160. Then the value of A is

17. Consider the following data.
36, 72, 46, 42, 60, 45, 53, 46, 51, 49
Then the mean deviation about the median for the data is

Section IV - Comprehension Type

Based upon the given paragraph, 2 multiple choice questions have to be answered. Each question has 4 choices (a), (b), (c) and (d), out of which **ONLY ONE** is correct.

PARAGRAPH

Let $\bar{x}$ and σ^2 be respectively the mean and variance of n observations $x_1, x_2, ..., x_n$ and $d_i = -x_i - a$, i = 1, 2,....n, where a is any numbers.

18. Variance of $d_1, d_2, ... d_n$ is :

(a) $\sigma^2 - a$ (b) σ^2

(c) $\sigma^2 + a$ (d) $2\sigma^2$

19. variance of first n even natural numbers is :

(a) n^2 (b) $n^2 - 1$

(c) $\frac{n^2-1}{3}$ (d) $\frac{n^2-1}{4}$

RESPONSE GRID	
	11. ⓐⓑⓒⓓ 12. ⓐⓑⓒⓓ 13. ⓐⓑⓒⓓ 14. ⓐⓑⓒⓓ
	15. ⓪①②③④⑤⑥⑦⑧⑨ 16. ⓪①②③④⑤⑥⑦⑧⑨
	17. ⓪①②③④⑤⑥⑦⑧⑨ 18. ⓐⓑⓒⓓ 19. ⓐⓑⓒⓓ

Space for Rough Work

Section V - Matrix-Match Type

This section contains 1 question. It contains statements given in two columns, which have to be matched. Statements in column I are labelled as A, B, C and D whereas statements in column II are labelled as p, q, r and s. The answers to these questions have to be appropriately bubbled as illustrated in the following example. If the correct matches are A-p, A-r, B-p, B-s, C-r, C-s and D-q, then the correctly bubbled matrix will look like the following:

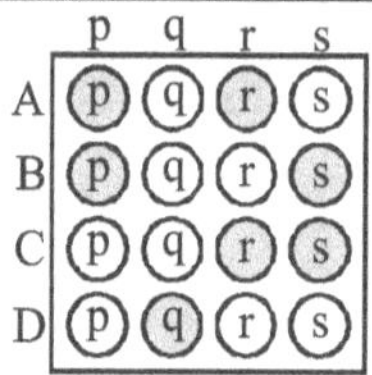

20.

Column - I	Column - II
(A) Mean deviation about the median for the data 3, 9, 5, 3, 12, 10, 18, 4, 7, 19, 21, is	p. $\frac{\sigma}{\bar{x}} \times 100$
(B) Mean deviation about the median for the data 13, 17, 16, 14, 11, 13, 10, 16, 11, 18, 12, 17, is	q. $\sqrt{\frac{1}{n}\sum_{i=1}^{n}(x_i - \bar{x}^{\,2})}$
(C) The standard deviation of n observations $x_1, x_2, \ldots, x_n$ is given by	r. 2.33
(D) The coefficient of variation (CV) is defined as	s. 5.27

RESPONSE GRID	20. A - ⓟⓠⓡⓢ; B - ⓟⓠⓡⓢ; C - ⓟⓠⓡⓢ; D - ⓟⓠⓡⓢ

DAILY PRACTICE PROBLEM DPP CM12 - MATHEMATICS			
Total Questions	20	Total Marks	67
Attempted		Correct	
Incorrect		Net Score	
Cut-off Score	27	Qualifying Score	38

$$\text{Net Score} = \sum_{i=I}^{V}\left[(\text{correct}_i \times MM_i) - (In_i - NM_i)\right]$$

Space for Rough Work

DPP - Daily Practice Problems

Chapter-wise Sheets

Date : ______ Start Time : ______ End Time : ______

MATHEMATICS (CM13)

SYLLABUS : Probability

Max. Marks : 69 **Time : 60 min.**

GENERAL INSTRUCTIONS

- The Daily Practice Problem Sheet contains 20 Questions divided into 5 sections.
  Section I has **6** MCQs with ONLY 1 Correct Option, **3** marks for each correct answer and **–1** for each incorrect answer.
  Section II has **4** MCQs with ONE or MORE THAN ONE Correct options.
  For each question, marks will be awarded in one of the following categories:
  Full marks: **+4** If only the bubble(s) corresponding to all the correct option(s) is (are) darkened.
  Partial marks: **+1** For darkening a bubble corresponding to each correct option provided NO INCORRECT option is darkened.
  Zero marks: If none of the bubbles is darkened.
  Negative marks: **–2** In all other cases.
  Section III has **5** Single Digit Integer Answer Type Questions, **3** marks for each Correct Answer and **0** marks in all other cases.
  Section IV has Comprehension Type Questions having **4** MCQs with ONLY ONE corect option, **3** marks for each Correct Answer and **0** mark in all other cases.
  Section V has **1** Matching Type Question, **2** marks for the correct matching of each row and **0** mark in all other cases.
- You have to evaluate your Response Grids yourself with the help of Solutions.

Section I - Straight Objective Type

This section contains 6 multiple choice questions. Each question has 4 choices (a), (b), (c) and (d), out of which **ONLY ONE** is correct.

1. A die is rolled three times, the probability of getting a larger number than the previous number is :

(a) $\frac{5}{216}$ (b) $\frac{5}{54}$ (c) $\frac{1}{6}$ (d) $\frac{5}{36}$

2. A natural number x is chosen at random from the first 100 natural numbers. The probability that $\frac{x^2-60x+800}{x-30}<0$ is

(a) $\frac{3}{25}$ (b) $\frac{1}{50}$ (c) $\frac{7}{25}$ (d) $\frac{3}{50}$

3. If p is chosen at random in the closed interval [0, 5], then the pobability that the equation $x^2+px+\frac{1}{4}(p+2)=0$ has real roots is

(a) $\frac{1}{2}$ (b) $\frac{1}{4}$ (c) $\frac{3}{5}$ (d) $\frac{2}{5}$

4. Out of $3n$ consecutive integers, three are selected at random. The chance that their sum is divisible by 3 is

(a) $\frac{3n^2-3n+2}{(3n-1)(3n-2)}$ (b) $\frac{3n^2-3n+2}{n(3n-1)(3n-2)}$

(c) $\frac{n^3}{(3n-1)(n-2)(n-3)}$ (d) None of these

RESPONSE GRID	1. ⓐⓑⓒⓓ	2. ⓐⓑⓒⓓ	3. ⓐⓑⓒⓓ	4. ⓐⓑⓒⓓ

Space for Rough Work

5. The probablilty that the length of a randomly chosen chord of a circle lies between $\frac{2}{3}$ and $\frac{5}{6}$ of its diameter is

(a) $\frac{5}{16}$ (b) $\frac{1}{16}$

(c) $\frac{1}{4}$ (d) $\frac{5}{12}$

6. 10 persons sit around a circular table with 10 numbered chairs. The probability that the two particular persons A and B are always together is

(a) $\frac{2}{9}$ (b) $\frac{1}{5}$

(c) $\frac{1}{9}$ (d) $\frac{2}{5}$

Section II - Multiple Correct Answer Type

This section contains 4 multiple correct answer(s) type questions. Each question has 4 choices (a), (b), (c) and (d), out of which **ONE OR MORE** is/are correct.

7. A square in inscribed in a circle. If p_1 is the probability that a randomly chosen point of the circle lies within the square and p_2 is the probability that the point lies outside the square, then

(a) $p_1 = p_2$ (b) $p_1 > p_2$

(c) $p_1 < p_2$ (d) $p_1^2 - p_2^2 < \frac{1}{3}$

8. If $\frac{1+4p}{4}, \frac{1-p}{4}, \frac{1-2p}{4}$ are probabilities of three mutually exclusive and exhaustive events, then the possible values of p belong to the set

(a) $\left(0, \frac{2}{3}\right)$ (b) $\left[0, \frac{1}{2}\right]$

(c) $\left[-\frac{1}{4}, \frac{1}{2}\right]$ (d) $\left[-\frac{2}{3}, \frac{2}{3}\right]$

9. The probabilities of three events A, B and C are $P(A) = 0.6$, $P(B) = 0.4$ and $P(C) = 0.5$. If $P(A \cup B) = 0.8$, $P(A \cap C) = 0.3$, $P(A \cap B \cap C) = 0.2$ and $P(A \cup B \cup C) \geq 0.85$. Then

(a) $P(A \cap B) < 0.35$ (b) $P(B \cap C) \geq 0.2$

(c) $P(B \cap C) \leq 0.35$ (d) $P(A \cap B) > 0.25$

10. There is a key-ring which has 'n' keys of which only one is the right key of the lock. A person tries to open the lock at random. If he discards the key already tried, and the probability that he opens the lock at k^{th} trial is P then which all statements are correct?

(a) P is less than k/n (b) P is independent of k

(c) $1/n \leq P \leq k/n$ (d) $P = k/2n$

RESPONSE GRID	
	5. ⓐⓑⓒⓓ 6. ⓐⓑⓒⓓ 7. ⓐⓑⓒⓓ 8. ⓐⓑⓒⓓ 9. ⓐⓑⓒⓓ
	10. ⓐⓑⓒⓓ

Space for Rough Work

Section III - Integer Type

This section contains 5 questions. The answer to each of the questions is a single digit integer ranging from 0 to 9.

11. Two friends Ankur and Rahul have equal number of sons. There are only 3 mangoes which are to be distributed among the sons. The probability that 2 mangoes go to the sons of the one friend and one mango to the son of the other is 6/7. Find how many sons each of the two friends have

12. A bag contains four tickets with numbers 00, 01, 10, 11. A ticket is drawn and replaced. In this way five tickets are drawn. If the probability that the sum of the number on the ticket drawn is 23 is P. then find $[\frac{1}{10p}]$ here [.] is greatest integer function.

13. Arti and Bharti are two candidates seeking admission in I.I.T. The probability that Arti is selected is 0.5 and the probability that both Arti and Bharti are selected is at most 0.3. If probability of Bharti getting selected P then find the maximum possible value of 10P.

14. 5 girls and 10 boys sit at random in a row having 15 chairs numbered as 1 to 15. If the probability that the end seats are occupied by the girls and between any two girls odd number of boys take seat is $\frac{20}{n}$, then $\frac{n}{1001}$ is equal to

15. A fair coin is tossed 15 times. If the probability of getting head as many times in the first ten throw as in the last five is k, then $\frac{32768k}{1001}$ is equal to.

Section IV - Comprehension Type

Based upon the given paragraphs, 4 multiple choice questions have to be answered. Each question has 4 choices (a), (b), (c) and (d), out of which **ONLY ONE** is correct.

PARAGRAPH-1

There are two dice A and B both having six faces. Die A has 3 faces marked with 1, 2 faces marked with 2 and 1 face marked with 3. Die B has 1 face marked with 1, 2 faces marked with 2 and 3 faces marked with 3. Both dice are thrown randomly once. If E be the event of getting sum of the numbers appearing on top faces equal to x and let $P(E)$ be the probability of event E, then

16. $P(E)$ is maximum when x equals to

(a) 5 (b) 3
(c) 4 (d) 6

17. $P(E)$ is minimun when x equals to

(a) 3 (b) 4
(c) 5 (d) 6

PARAGRAPH-2

If the squares of a 8×8 chess board are painted either red or black at random.

18. The probability that not all squares is any column are alternating in colour is

(a) $\left(1-\frac{1}{2^7}\right)^8$ (b) $\frac{1}{2^{56}}$

(c) $1-\frac{1}{2^7}$ (d) none of these

RESPONSE GRID	
11. ⓪①②③④⑤⑥⑦⑧⑨	12. ⓪①②③④⑤⑥⑦⑧⑨
13. ⓪①②③④⑤⑥⑦⑧⑨	14. ⓪①②③④⑤⑥⑦⑧⑨
15. ⓪①②③④⑤⑥⑦⑧⑨	16. ⓐⓑⓒⓓ 17. ⓐⓑⓒⓓ 18. ⓐⓑⓒⓓ

Space for Rough Work

19. The probability that the chess board contains equal number of red and black squares is

(a) $\frac{^{64}C_{32}}{2^{64}}$ (b) $\frac{\lfloor 64}{2^{64}.\lfloor 32}$ (c) $\frac{2^{32}-1}{2^{64}}$ (d) None of these

Section V - Matrix-Match Type

This section contains 1 question. It contains statements given in two columns, which have to be matched. Statements in column I are labelled as A, B, C and D whereas statements in column II are labelled as p, q, r and s. The answers to these questions have to be appropriately bubbled as illustrated in the following example. If the correct matches are A-p, A-r, B-p, B-s, C-r, C-s and D-q, then the correctly bubbled matrix will look like the following:

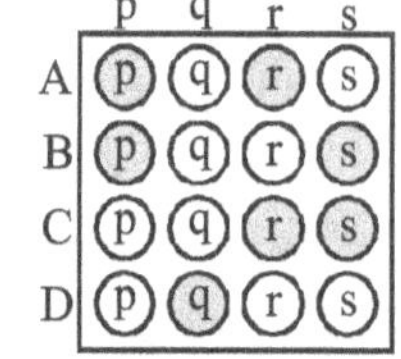

20.

	Column 1		**Column 2**
(A)	A bag contains 4 red, & 6 white. Two balls are drawn at random. What is the probability that one of them is red and other is white	**(p)**	31/32
(B)	A bag contains 6 apples, 4 bananas and 8 mangoes. If three fruits are drawn at random, then what is the probability that all the three are apples	**(q)**	8/15
(C)	Five coins are tossed together. What is the probability that at least one tail will appear?	**(r)**	75/198
(D)	Team of 5 is to be constituted out of 6 girls and 6 boys then what is probability that team has 3 girls 2 boys	**(s)**	5/204

RESPONSE GRID	19. ⓐⓑⓒⓓ 20. A - ⓟⓠⓡⓢ; B - ⓟⓠⓡⓢ; C - ⓟⓠⓡⓢ; D - ⓟⓠⓡⓢ

DAILY PRACTICE PROBLEM DPP CM13 - MATHEMATICS			
Total Questions	20	Total Marks	69
Attempted		Correct	
Incorrect		Net Score	
Cut-off Score	22	Qualifying Score	33

$$\text{Net Score} = \sum_{i=I}^{V}\left[(\text{correct}_i \times MM_i) - (In_i - NM_i)\right]$$

Space for Rough Work

DPP - Daily Practice Problems

Chapter-wise Sheets

Date : Start Time : End Time :

MATHEMATICS (CM14)

SYLLABUS : Relation and Functions

Max. Marks : 72 **Time : 60 min.**

GENERAL INSTRUCTIONS

- The Daily Practice Problem Sheet contains 20 Questions divided into 5 sections.
  Section I has **5** MCQs with ONLY 1 Correct Option, **3** marks for each correct answer and **–1** for each incorrect answer.
  Section II has **4** MCQs with ONE or MORE THAN ONE Correct options.
  For each question, marks will be awarded in one of the following categories:
  Full marks: **+4** If only the bubble(s) corresponding to all the correct option(s) is (are) darkened.
  Partial marks: **+1** For darkening a bubble corresponding to each correct option provided NO INCORRECT option is darkened.
  Zero marks: If none of the bubbles is darkened.
  Negative marks: **–2** In all other cases.
  Section III has **4** Single Digit Integer Answer Type Questions, **3** marks for each Correct Answer and **0** mark in all other cases.
  Section IV has Comprehension/Matching Cum-Comprehension Type Questions having **5** MCQs with ONLY ONE corect option, **3** marks for each Correct Answer and **0** mark in all other cases.
  Section V has **2** Matching Type Questions, **2** mark for the correct matching of each row and **0** mark in all other cases.
- You have to evaluate your Response Grids yourself with the help of Solutions.

Section I - Straight Objective Type

This section contains 5 multiple choice questions. Each question has 4 choices (a), (b), (c) and (d), out of which **ONLY ONE** is correct.

1. Let $f(x)=\dfrac{2}{x+1}$, $g(x)=\cos x$ and $h(x)=\sqrt{x+3}$ then the range of the composite function fogoh, is

(a) R^+ (b) $R-\{0\}$

(c) $[1,\infty)$ (d) $R^+-\{1\}$

2. Let R be the relation on the set R of all real numbers defined by aRb iff $|a-b|\le 1$. Then R is

(a) reflexive and symmetric

(b) symmetric and transitive

(c) transitive and reflexive

(d) Equivalence Relation

3. Let $g:\ R\to R$ be given by $g(x)=3+4x$.

If $g^n(x)=gogo.......og\ (x)$, then $g^{-n}(x)=$(where $g^{-n}(x)$ denotes inverse of $g^n(x)$)

(a) $(4^n-1)+4^n x$ (b) $(x+1)4^{-n}-1$

(c) $(x+1)4^n-1$ (d) $(4^{-n}-1)x+4^n$

RESPONSE GRID	1. ⓐⓑⓒⓓ	2. ⓐⓑⓒⓓ	3. ⓐⓑⓒⓓ

Space for Rough Work

4. $x^2 = xy$ is a relation which is
(a) symmetric and reflexive
(b) reflexive only
(c) transitive and reflexive
(d) Equivalence Relation

5. Let $f : R \to R$ be a function defined by

$f(x) = \dfrac{e^{|x|} - e^{-x}}{e^x + e^{-x}}$. Then

(a) f is both one-one and onto
(b) f is one-one but not onto
(c) f is onto but not one-one
(d) f is neither one-one nor onto.

Section II - Multiple Correct Answer Type

This section contains 4 multiple correct answer(s) type questions. Each question has 4 choices (a), (b), (c) and (d), out of which **ONE OR MORE** is/are correct.

6. Let $f : A \to B$ and $g : B \to C$ be functions and $gof : A \to C$. Which of the following statement is true
(a) If gof is one-one then f and g both are one-one
(b) If gof is one-one then f is one-one
(c) If gof is bijection then f is one-one and g is onto
(d) If f and g are both one-one then gof is one-one.

7. Let f : D ® R be defined by $f(x) = ln\ (ln\ (ln\ (ln\ x)))$ then
(a) $f(x)$ is into
(b) $f(x)$ is one-one
(c) $f(x)$ is onto
(d) $D = (e^e, \infty)$

8. $f : R \to [-1, \infty)$ and $f(x) = \ln([\,|\sin 2x| + |\cos 2x|\,])$ (where [.] is the greatest integer function).
(a) Z
(b) $f(x)$ is periodic with fundamental period $\pi/4$
(c) $f(x)$ is invertible in $\left[0, \dfrac{\pi}{4}\right]$
(d) $f(x)$ is into function

9. Let $f(x) = \max\{1 + \sin x, 1, 1 - \cos x\}$, $x \in [0, 2\pi]$ and $g(x) = \max\{1, |x - 1|\}$ $x \in R$, then
(a) $g(f(0)) = 1$
(b) $g(f(0)) = 1$
(c) $f(g(1)) = 1$
(d) $f(g(0)) = 1 + \sin 1$

Section III - Integer Type

This section contains 4 questions. The answer to each of the questions is a single digit integer ranging from 0 to 9.

10. If the function $f(x) = \dfrac{x-1}{c - x^2 + 1}$ does not take any value in the internal $\left[-1, -\dfrac{1}{3}\right]$, then the largest integral value that c can attain is equal to

11. Let f be a function such that $f(x + f(y)) = f(x) + y$, $\forall\ x, y \in R$, if $f(1000)$ is equal to 200k, then k =

12. Let f: [0, 1] → [0, 1] defined by $f(x) = \dfrac{1-x}{1+x}$, for $0 \le x \le 1$ and let $g : [0, 1] \to [0, 1]$ defined by $g(x) = 4x(1 - x), 0 \le x \le 1$. If range of $fog\ (x)$ is $[\alpha, \beta]$, then $\alpha + \beta =$

13. If $f : R - \{2\} \to R$ satisfying

$2f(x) + 3f\left(\dfrac{2x+29}{x-2}\right) = 100x + 80$, then unit digit of $f(3)$ is

RESPONSE GRID	
	4. ⓐⓑⓒⓓ 5. ⓐⓑⓒⓓ 6. ⓐⓑⓒⓓ 7. ⓐⓑⓒⓓ 8. ⓐⓑⓒⓓ
	9. ⓐⓑⓒⓓ 10. ⓪①②③④⑤⑥⑦⑧⑨ 11. ⓪①②③④⑤⑥⑦⑧⑨
	12. ⓪①②③④⑤⑥⑦⑧⑨ 13. ⓪①②③④⑤⑥⑦⑧⑨

Space for Rough Work

Section IV - Comprehension/Matching Cum-Comprehension Type

Directions (Qs. 14 and 15) : Based upon the given paragraph, 2 multiple choice questions have to be answered. Each question has 4 choices (a), (b), (c) and (d), out of which **ONLY ONE** is correct.

PARAGRAPH

Consider to functions

$$f(x)=\begin{cases}[x], & -2\le x\le -1\\ |x|+1, & -1<x\le 2\end{cases}\text{ and}$$

$$g(x)=\begin{cases}[x], & -\pi\le x<0\\ |x|+1, & 0\le x\le \pi\end{cases},$$

where [.] denotes the greatest integer function.

14. The exhaustive domain of $g(f(x))$ is
(a) $[0,2]$ (b) $[-2,0]$
(c) $[-2,2]$ (d) $[-1,2]$

15. The range of $g(f(x))$ is
(a) $[\sin 3, \sin 1]$
(b) $[\sin 3, 1]\cup\{-2,-1,0\}$
(c) $[\sin 3, 1]\cup\{-2,-1\}$
(d) $[\sin 1, 1]$

Directions (Qs. 16-18) : This passage contains a table having 3 columns and 4 rows. Based on the table, there are 3 questions. Each question has four options (a), (b), (c) and (d) **ONLY ONE** of these four options is correct.

By appropriately matching the information given in the three columns of the following table, give the answer of the questions that follows.

Column 1	Column 2	Column 3
(I) $x^2=2y+1$ is	(i) Not injective but surjective for	(P) $R\to[0,\infty)$
(II) $y=\|x\|+2$ is	(ii) Neither injective nor surjective for	(Q) $R\to\left[-\frac{1}{2},\infty\right)$
(III) $y=x+\frac{1}{x}$ is	(iii) Injective and surjective for	(R) $R\to R$
(IV) $y^2=2x-4$ is	(iv) Injective but not surjective for	(S) $R-\{0\}\to R\sim(-2,2)$

16. Which of the following options is the only correct combination?
(a) (I) (ii) (P) (b) (II) (iii) (S)
(c) (III) (i) (S) (d) (IV) (iv) (Q)

17. Which of the following options is the only correct combination?
(a) (I) (iii) (S) (b) (II) (ii) (R)
(c) (III) (iv) (P) (d) (IV) (i) (Q)

18. Which of the following options is the only incorrect combination?
(a) (I) (i) (Q) (b) (II) (ii) (R)
(c) (III) (i) (S) (d) (IV) (i) (P)

RESPONSE GRID	
	14. ⓐⓑⓒⓓ 15. ⓐⓑⓒⓓ 16. ⓐⓑⓒⓓ 17. ⓐⓑⓒⓓ
	18. ⓐⓑⓒⓓ

Space for Rough Work

Section V - Matrix-Match Type

This section contains 2 questions. It contains statements given in two columns, which have to be matched. Statements in column I are labelled as A, B, C and D whereas statements in column II are labelled as p, q, r and s. The answers to these questions have to be appropriately bubbled as illustrated in the following example. If the correct matches are A-p, A-r, B-p, B-s, C-r, C-s and D-q, then the correctly bubbled matrix will look like the following:

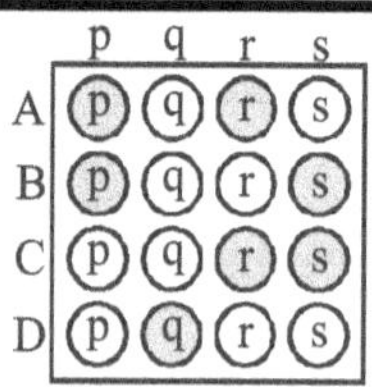

19. Let $f: R \to R$ and $g: R \to R$ be functions such that $f(g(x))$ is a one-one function.

Column-I	Column-II
(A) Then $g(x)$	(p) must be one-one
(B) Then $f(x)$	(q) may not be one-one
(C) If $g(x)$ is onto then $f(x)$	(r) may be many-one
(D) If $g(x)$ is into then $f(x)$	(s) must be many-one

20.

Column-I	Column-II
(A) Let $f(x) = \max\{1+\sin x, 1, 1-\cos x\}, x \in [0, 2\pi]$ and $g(x) = \max, \{1, \lvert x-1\rvert\}, x \in R$, then	(p) $g(f(a)) = 1$
	(q) $f(g(0)) = 0$
(B) Let $f(x) = \ell n\left(\frac{1+x}{1-x}\right) \forall x \in (-1,1)$ and $g(x) = \left(\frac{3x+x^3}{1+3x^2}\right)$, then	(r) $f(g(0)) = 1$
(C) Let $f(x) = 1 + x^2$ and $g(x) = x - x^2$, then	(s) $g(f(0)) = 1$
	(t) $g\left(f\left(\frac{e-1}{e+1}\right)\right) = 1$

RESPONSE GRID	
	19. A - (p)(q)(r)(s); B - (p)(q)(r)(s); C - (p)(q)(r)(s); D - (p)(q)(r)(s)
	20. A - (p)(q)(r)(s); B - (p)(q)(r)(s); C - (p)(q)(r)(s); D - (p)(q)(r)(s)

DAILY PRACTICE PROBLEM DPP CM14 - MATHEMATICS			
Total Questions	20	Total Marks	72
Attempted		Correct	
Incorrect		Net Score	
Cut-off Score	24	Qualifying Score	35

$$\text{Net Score} = \sum_{i=I}^{V}\left[(\text{correct}_i \times MM_i) - (In_i - NM_i)\right]$$

Space for Rough Work

DPP - Daily Practice Problems

Chapter-wise Sheets

Date : ______ **Start Time :** ______ **End Time :** ______

MATHEMATICS (CM15)

SYLLABUS : Inverse Trigonometric Functions

Max. Marks : 69 **Time : 60 min.**

GENERAL INSTRUCTIONS

- The Daily Practice Problem Sheet contains 20 Questions divided into 5 sections.
  Section I has **5** MCQs with ONLY 1 Correct Option, **3** marks for each correct answer and **–1** for each incorrect answer.
  Section II has **4** MCQs with ONE or MORE THAN ONE Correct options.
  For each question, marks will be awarded in one of the following categories:
  Full marks: **+4** If only the bubble(s) corresponding to all the correct option(s) is (are) darkened.
  Partial marks: **+1** For darkening a bubble corresponding to each correct option provided NO INCORRECT option is darkened.
  Zero marks: If none of the bubbles is darkened.
  Negative marks: **–2** In all other cases.
  Section III has **5** Single Digit Integer Answer Type Questions, **3** marks for each Correct Answer and **0** mark in all other cases.
  Section IV has Comprehension/Matching cum-comprehension Type Questions having **5** MCQs with ONLY ONE corect option, **3** marks for each Correct Answer and **0** mark in all other cases.
  Section V has **1** Matching Type Question, **2** marks for the correct matching of each row and **0** mark in all other cases.
- You have to evaluate your Response Grids yourself with the help of Solutions.

Section I - Straight Objective Type

This section contains 5 multiple choice questions. Each question has 4 choices (a), (b), (c) and (d), out of which **ONLY ONE** is correct.

1. The set of values of x for which the identity

$$\cos^{-1}x+\cos^{-1}\left(\frac{x}{2}+\frac{1}{2}\sqrt{3-3x^2}\right)=\frac{\pi}{3}$$ holds good, is

(a) $[0,1]$ (b) $\left[0,\frac{1}{2}\right]$

(c) $\left[\frac{1}{2},1\right]$ (d) $\{-1,0,1\}$

2. $\sin^{-1}\left(a-\frac{a^2}{3}+\frac{a^3}{9}+....\right)+\cos^{-1}(1+b+b^2+...)=\frac{\pi}{2}$ when

(a) $a=-3$ & $b=1$ (b) $a=1$ & $b=-\frac{1}{3}$

(c) $a=\frac{1}{6}$ & $b=\frac{1}{2}$ (d) none of these

3. The number of all possible 5-tuples $(a_1, a_2, a_3, a_4, a_5)$ such that $a_1+a_2\sin x+a_3\cos x+a_4\sin 2x+a_5\cos 2x=0$ holds for all x is

(a) zero (b) 1

(c) 2 (d) infinite

RESPONSE GRID	1. ⓐⓑⓒⓓ	2. ⓐⓑⓒⓓ	3. ⓐⓑⓒⓓ

Space for Rough Work

4. $x = n\pi - \tan^{-1} 3$ is a solution of the equation

$$12\tan 2x + \frac{\sqrt{10}}{\cos x} + 1 = 0 \text{ for}$$

(a) no value of n (b) all integral values of n
(c) even values of n (d) odd values of n

5. If S_n denotes the sum to n terms of the series

$$\cot^{-1}\frac{7}{4} + \cot^{-1}\frac{19}{4} + \cot^{-1}\frac{39}{4} + \ldots\text{ then}$$

(a) $S_n = \tan^{-1}\frac{n}{2n+5}$ (b) $S_n = \cot^{-1}\frac{n+5}{2n}$

(c) $S_n = \cot^{-1}\frac{4n}{2n+5}$ (d) $S_\infty = \cot^{-1}\frac{1}{2}$

Section II - Multiple Correct Answer Type

This section contains 4 multiple correct answer(s) type questions. Each question has 4 choices (a), (b), (c) and (d), out of which **ONE OR MORE** is/are correct.

6. If $\tan^{-1}y = 4\tan^{-1}x$, then y is not finite if

(a) $x^2 = 3 + 2\sqrt{2}$ (b) $x^2 = 3 - 2\sqrt{2}$

(c) $x^4 = 6x^2 - 1$ (d) $x^4 = 6x^2 + 1$

7. If the equation $\sin^{-1}(x^2 + x + 1) + \cos^{-1}(ax + 1) = \frac{\pi}{2}$ has exactly two solutions then a can not have the integral value

(a) –1 (b) 0 (c) 1 (d) 2

8. If $\tan^{-1}(\sin^2\theta + 2\sin\theta + 2) + \cot^{-1}(4^{\sec^2\phi} + 1) = \frac{\pi}{2}$ has solution for some θ and ϕ then

(a) $\sin\theta = -1$ (b) $\sin\theta = 1$

(c) $\cos\phi = 1$ (d) $\cos\phi = -1$

9. If α, β, γ are the roots of $\tan^{-1}(x-1) + \tan^{-1}x + \tan^{-1}(x+1) = \tan^{-1}3x$, then

(a) $\alpha + \beta + \gamma = 0$ (b) $\alpha\beta + \beta\gamma + \gamma\alpha = -1/4$

(c) $\alpha\beta\gamma = 1$ (d) $|\alpha - \beta|_{max} = 1$

Section III - Integer Type

This section contains 5 questions. The answer to each of the questions is a single digit integer ranging from 0 to 9.

10. The sum of the solutions of the equation

$2\sin^{-1}\sqrt{x^2 + x + 1} + \cos^{-1}\sqrt{x^2 + x} = \frac{3\pi}{2}$ is –p. The value of p is –

11. Find the value of $-\cos\left[\cos^{-1}\left(-\frac{\sqrt{3}}{2}\right) + \frac{\pi}{6}\right]$.

12. If $\sin^{-1}\left(x - \frac{x^2}{2} + \frac{x^3}{4} - \ldots\right) + \cos^{-1}\left(x^2 - \frac{x^4}{2} + \frac{x^6}{4} - \ldots\right) = \frac{\pi}{2}$ for $0 < |x| < \sqrt{2}$, then find the value of x.

13. If $\sin^{-1}\left(\frac{x}{5}\right) + \operatorname{cosec}^{-1}\left(\frac{5}{4}\right) = \frac{\pi}{2}$, then find the value of x.

14. If $\cos^{-1}x - \cos^{-1}\frac{y}{2} = a$ then $4x^2 - 4xy\cos\alpha + y^2$ is equal to $k\sin^2\alpha$. The value of k is –

RESPONSE GRID	
	4. ⓐⓑⓒⓓ 5. ⓐⓑⓒⓓ 6. ⓐⓑⓒⓓ 7. ⓐⓑⓒⓓ 8. ⓐⓑⓒⓓ
	9. ⓐⓑⓒⓓ 10. ⓪①②③④⑤⑥⑦⑧⑨ 11. ⓪①②③④⑤⑥⑦⑧⑨
	12. ⓪①②③④⑤⑥⑦⑧⑨ 13. ⓪①②③④⑤⑥⑦⑧⑨
	14. ⓪①②③④⑤⑥⑦⑧⑨

Space for Rough Work

Section IV - Comprehension/Matching Cum-Comprehension Type

Directions (Qs. 15 and 16) : Based upon the given paragraph, 2 multiple choice questions have to be answered. Each question has 4 choices (a), (b), (c) and (d), out of which **ONLY ONE** is correct.

PARAGRAPH

The function $\sin^{-1}x$, $\cos^{-1}x$, $\tan^{-1}x$, $\cot^{-1}x$, $\text{cosec}^{-1}x$ and $\sec^{-1}x$ are called inverse circular functions. Each of the inverse circular function is multivalued. To make each inverse circular function single valued let us define the principal values as follow.

$\sin^{-1}x \in \left[\frac{3\pi}{2}, \frac{5\pi}{2}\right], \cos^{-1}x \in [2\pi, 3\pi]$ (in both cases $x \in [-1, -1]$)and $\tan^{-1}x \in \left(\frac{3\pi}{2}, \frac{5\pi}{2}\right), x\,(-\infty, \infty)$.

15. Number of possible solutions for the equation $\sin^{-1}x + \cos^{-1}y = \frac{11\pi}{2}$ is /are

(a) 0 (b) 1

(c) 2 (d) infinite

16. Range of values of x for which $2\sin^{-1}x = \sin^{-1}\left(2x\sqrt{1-x^2}\right)$ holds, is

(a) $\left[-\frac{1}{2}, \frac{1}{2}\right]$ (b) $\left[-\frac{1}{\sqrt{2}}, \frac{1}{\sqrt{2}}\right]$

(c) $[-1, 1]$ (d) $\left[-\infty, -\frac{1}{\sqrt{2}}\right]$

Directions (Qs. 16-17) : This passage contains a table having 3 columns and 4 rows. Based on the table, there are three questions. Each question has four options (a), (b), (c) and (d) **ONLY ONE** of these four options is correct.

Column 1 contains information about inverse trigonometric equations.

Column 2 contains information about constraints on x.

Column 3 contains information about the value of x.

Column 1	Column 2	Column 3
(I) $\tan^{-1}\sqrt{x(x+1)} + \sin^{-1}\sqrt{x^2+x+1} = \frac{\pi}{2}$	(i) $0 < \lvert x \rvert < \sqrt{2}$	(P) 1
(II) $\sin[\cot^{-1}(1+x)] = \cos(\tan^{-1}x)$	(ii) $-\infty < x < \infty$	(Q) -1
(III) $\sin^{-1}\left(x - \frac{x^2}{2} + \frac{x^3}{3} \ldots\right) + \cos^{-1}\left(x^2 - \frac{x^4}{2} + \frac{x^6}{4} \ldots\right) = \frac{\pi}{2}$	(iii) $-\infty < x < 0$	(R) $\frac{25}{23}$
(IV) $\sum_{n=1}^{23}\left[\cot^{-1}\left(1 + \sum_{k=1}^{n} 2k\right)\right] = x$	(iv) $1 < x < 2$	(S) $\frac{-1}{2}$

RESPONSE GRID	15. ⓐⓑⓒⓓ 16. ⓐⓑⓒⓓ

Space for Rough Work

17. Which of the following is the only correct option?

(a) (III) (i) (P) (b) (II) (iv) (S)

(c) (IV) (iii) (R) (d) (I) (ii) (Q)

18. Which of the following is the only correct combination?

(a) (I) (iii) (P) (b) (IV) (i) (Q)

(c) (II) (ii) (S) (d) (III) (iv) (R)

19. Which of the following is the only incorrect option?

(a) (I) (iii) (Q) (b) (II) (ii) (S)

(c) (III) (i) (P) (d) (IV) (iv) (S)

Section V - Matrix-Match Type

This section contains 1 question. It contains statements given in two columns, which have to be matched. Statements in column I are labelled as A, B, C and D whereas statements in column II are labelled as p, q, r and s. The answers to these questions have to be appropriately bubbled as illustrated in the following example. If the correct matches are A-p, A-r, B-p, B-s, C-r, C-s and D-q, then the correctly bubbled matrix will look like the following:

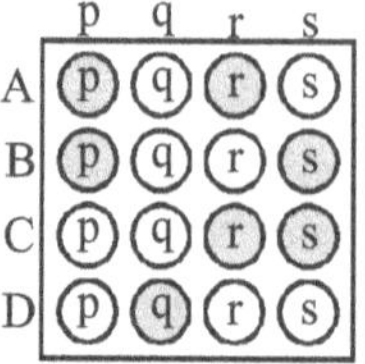

20.

Column-I	Column-II
(A) $(\sin^{-1}x)^2+(\sin^{-1}y)^2=\frac{\pi^2}{2}\Rightarrow x^3+y^3=$	p. 1
(B) $(\cos^{-1}x)^2+(\cos^{-1}y)^2=2\pi^2\Rightarrow x^5+y^5=$	q. –2
(C) $(\sin^{-1}x)^2(\cos^{-1}y)^2=\frac{\pi^4}{4}\Rightarrow \lvert x-y\rvert=$	r. 0
(D) $\lvert\sin^{-1}x-\sin^{-1}y\rvert=\pi\Rightarrow x^y=$	s. 2

RESPONSE GRID	
	17. ⓐⓑⓒⓓ 18. ⓐⓑⓒⓓ 19. ⓐⓑⓒⓓ
	20. A - ⓟⓠⓡⓢ; B - ⓟⓠⓡⓢ; C - ⓟⓠⓡⓢ; D - ⓟⓠⓡⓢ

DAILY PRACTICE PROBLEM DPP CM15 - MATHEMATICS

Total Questions	20	Total Marks	69
Attempted		Correct	
Incorrect		Net Score	
Cut-off Score	22	Qualifying Score	31

$$\text{Net Score}=\sum_{i=I}^{V}\left[(\text{correct}_i\times MM_i)-(In_i - NM_i)\right]$$

Space for Rough Work

DPP - Daily Practice Problems

Chapter-wise Sheets

Date : | Start Time : | End Time :

MATHEMATICS CM16

SYLLABUS : Matrices

Max. Marks : 69 **Time : 60 min.**

GENERAL INSTRUCTIONS

- The Daily Practice Problem Sheet contains 20 Questions divided into 5 sections.
  Section I has **6** MCQs with ONLY 1 Correct Option, **3** marks for each correct answer and **–1** for each incorrect answer.
  Section II has **4** MCQs with ONE or MORE THAN ONE Correct options.
  For each question, marks will be awarded in one of the following categories:
  Full marks: **+4** If only the bubble(s) corresponding to all the correct option(s) is (are) darkened.
  Partial marks: **+1** For darkening a bubble corresponding to each correct option provided NO INCORRECT option is darkened.
  Zero marks: If none of the bubbles is darkened.
  Negative marks: **–2** In all other cases.
  Section III has **5** Single Digit Integer Answer Type Questions, **3** marks for each Correct Answer and **0** mark in all other cases.
  Section IV has Comprehension Type Questions having **4** MCQs with ONLY ONE corect option, **3** marks for each Correct Answer and **0** mark in all other cases.
  Section V has **1** Matching Type Question, **2** marks for the correct matching of each row and **0** mark in all other cases.
- You have to evaluate your Response Grids yourself with the help of Solutions.

Section I - Straight Objective Type

This section contains 6 multiple choice questions. Each question has 4 choices (a), (b), (c) and (d), out of which **ONLY ONE** is correct.

1. If $A_1, A_3, ..., A_{2n-1}$ are n skew – symmetric matrices of same order, then

$$X = \sum_{r=1}^{n} (2r-1)(A_{2r-1})^{2r-1} \text{ will be}$$

(a) symmetric
(b) skew – symmetric
(c) neither symmetric nor skew symmetric
(d) depends on 'n' is even or odd

2. If B, C are square matrices of order n and if $A = B + C$, $BC = CB$, $C^2 = 0$, then for any positive integer N, $A^{N+1} = B^K[B + (N+1)C]$, then K/N is

(a) 1 (b) $\frac{1}{2}$
(c) 2 (d) None of these

RESPONSE GRID	1. ⓐⓑⓒⓓ	2. ⓐⓑⓒⓓ

Space for Rough Work

3. Consider $A=\begin{bmatrix} a & b & c \\ c & a & b \\ b & c & a \end{bmatrix}$ and AA' = I if and only if a, b, c are the roots of the equation

(a) $x^3+abc=0$ (b) $x^3+x^2-abc=0$

(c) $x^3-2x^2+abc=0$ (d) $x^3\pm x^2+abc=0$

4. If A and B are symmetric matrices and A B = BA, then $A^{-1}B$ is a

(a) symmetric matrix

(b) skew–symmetric matrix

(c) unit matrix

(d) None of these

5. If A and B are two matrices such that AB = B and BA = A, then $A^2 + B^2$ is equal to

(a) 2AB (b) 2BA

(c) A + B (d) AB

6. If $A=\begin{bmatrix} \alpha & 0 \\ 1 & 1 \end{bmatrix}$ and $B=\begin{bmatrix} 9 & a \\ b & c \end{bmatrix}$ and $A^2 = B$, then the value of a + b + c is

(a) 1 or –1 (b) 5 or –1

(c) 5 or 1 (d) No real values

Section II - Multiple Correct Answer Type

This section contains 4 multiple correct answer(s) type questions. Each question has 4 choices (a), (b), (c) and (d), out of which **ONE OR MORE** is/are correct.

7. Let $A=\begin{bmatrix} 2 & 3 \\ -1 & 2 \end{bmatrix}$ and $f(x)=x^2-4x+7$. Then

(a) $f(A)=0$ (b) $f(A)=\begin{bmatrix} 1 & 2 \\ -1 & 3 \end{bmatrix}$

(c) $A^5=\begin{bmatrix} 118 & -93 \\ 31 & -118 \end{bmatrix}$ (d) $A^5=\begin{bmatrix} -118 & -93 \\ 31 & -118 \end{bmatrix}$

8. For $k=\frac{1}{\sqrt{50}}$ and PP′ = I, where $P=\begin{bmatrix} 2/3 & 3k & a \\ -1/3 & -4k & b \\ 2/3 & -5k & c \end{bmatrix}$, then

(a) $a=\frac{\pm 13}{2\sqrt{5}}$ (b) $b=\frac{\pm 16}{5\sqrt{2}}$

(c) $a=\frac{\pm 13}{5\sqrt{2}}$ (d) $c=\frac{\pm 1}{2\sqrt{3}}$

9. If $A=\begin{bmatrix} i & 0 \\ 0 & i \end{bmatrix}$, n ∈ N, then A^{75} is not equal to

(a) $\begin{bmatrix} 0 & i \\ i & 0 \end{bmatrix}$ (b) $\begin{bmatrix} 1 & i \\ i & 1 \end{bmatrix}$

(c) $\begin{bmatrix} 1 & 0 \\ 0 & 1 \end{bmatrix}$ (d) None of these

10. If the matrix $\begin{bmatrix} 0 & 2\beta & \gamma \\ \alpha & \beta & -\gamma \\ \alpha & -\beta & \gamma \end{bmatrix}$ is orthogonal, then

(a) $\alpha=\pm\frac{1}{\sqrt{2}}$ (b) $\beta=\pm\frac{1}{\sqrt{3}}$

(c) $\gamma=\pm\frac{1}{\sqrt{2}}$ (d) $\beta=\pm\frac{1}{\sqrt{6}}$

RESPONSE GRID	
	3. ⓐⓑⓒⓓ 4. ⓐⓑⓒⓓ 5. ⓐⓑⓒⓓ 6. ⓐⓑⓒⓓ 7. ⓐⓑⓒⓓ
	8. ⓐⓑⓒⓓ 9. ⓐⓑⓒⓓ 10. ⓐⓑⓒⓓ

Space for Rough Work

Section III - Integer Type

This section contains 5 questions. The answer to each of the questions is a single digit integer ranging from 0 to 9.

11. Let $A = \begin{bmatrix} 0 & \alpha \\ 0 & 0 \end{bmatrix}$ and $(A + I)^{50} - 50A = \begin{bmatrix} a & b \\ c & d \end{bmatrix}$, find $abc + abd + bcd + acd$

12. If matrix $A = \begin{bmatrix} -5 & -8 & 0 \\ 3 & 5 & 0 \\ 1 & 2 & -1 \end{bmatrix}$ then find sum of digits of $tr(A) + tr(A^2) + tr(A^3) + ... + tr(A^{100})$

13. If matrix $A = \begin{bmatrix} a & b & c \\ b & c & a \\ c & a & b \end{bmatrix}$ where a, b c are real positive numbers, abc = 1 and $A^T A = I$. Then the value of $a^3 + b^3 + c^3$ is

14. Consider a matrix $A = \begin{bmatrix} a_{11} & a_{12} \\ a_{21} & a_{22} \end{bmatrix}$ and another matrix $B = \begin{bmatrix} 1 & 1 \\ 2 & 1 \end{bmatrix}$ such that AB = BA then find the value of $\left(\dfrac{a_{11}}{a_{12}}\right)^2$

15. Consider a 2×2 matrix $A = \begin{bmatrix} 1 & 1 \\ -1 & 1 \end{bmatrix}$ and then find the value of matrix

$$B = A^{10} - A^9 + 2A^8 - A^7 + 4A^6 - 2A^5$$

$$+4A^4 + A^3 - A^2 + A + I = \begin{bmatrix} a & b \\ c & d \end{bmatrix}$$

find $(a + b + c + d)$

Section IV - Comprehension Type

Based upon the given paragraphs, 4 multiple choice questions have to be answered. Each question has 4 choices (a), (b), (c) and (d), out of which **ONLY ONE** is correct.

PARAGRAPH-1

If $(x+a)^n = \sum_{k=0}^{n} \left(C_r^n\right) x^k a^{n-k}$

Let $a_k = k(^{10}C_k)$, $b_k = (10 - k)(^{10}C_k)$ and

$$A_k = \begin{bmatrix} a_k & 0 \\ 0 & b_k \end{bmatrix}$$

If $A = \sum_{k=1}^{9} A_k = \begin{bmatrix} a & 0 \\ 0 & b \end{bmatrix}$.

16. Find the sum of digits of trace of the matrix A

(a) 5 (b) 14

(c) 8 (d) None of these

17. Which of the following is correct about 'ab'

(a) 'ab' has 4 prime factors

(b) Largest prime factor of 'ab' is a three digit prime number

(c) 'ab' is a 5 digit number

(d) None of these

PARAGRAPH-2

Let $a_k = {}^nC_k$ for $0 \le k \le n$ and $A_k = \begin{bmatrix} a_{k-1} & 0 \\ 0 & a_k \end{bmatrix}$ for $0 \le k \le n$ and

$\sum_{k=1}^{n-1} A_k \cdot A_{k+1} = \begin{bmatrix} a & 0 \\ 0 & b \end{bmatrix}$,

RESPONSE GRID	
	11. ⓪①②③④⑤⑥⑦⑧⑨ 12. ⓪①②③④⑤⑥⑦⑧⑨
	13. ⓪①②③④⑤⑥⑦⑧⑨ 14. ⓪①②③④⑤⑥⑦⑧⑨
	15. ⓪①②③④⑤⑥⑦⑧⑨ 16. ⓐⓑⓒⓓ 17. ⓐⓑⓒⓓ

Space for Rough Work

18. Find 'a'

(a) ${}^{2n}C_{n+1}$ (b) ${}^{2n}C_n$

(c) ${}^{2n-1}C_n$ (d) None of these

19. Find 'b'

(a) ${}^{2n}C_{n+1}$ (b) ${}^{2n}C_n$

(c) ${}^{2n-1}C_n$ (d) None of these

Section V - Matrix-Match Type

This section contains 1 question. It contains statements given in two columns, which have to be matched. Statements in column I are labelled as A, B, C and D whereas statements in column II are labelled as p, q, r and s. The answers to these questions have to be appropriately bubbled as illustrated in the following example. If the correct matches are A-p, A-r, B-p, B-s, C-r, C-s and D-q, then the correctly bubbled matrix will look like the following:

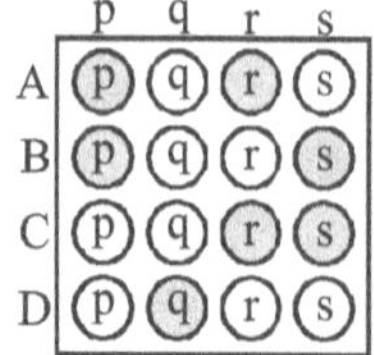

20. **Column - I** **Column - II**

(A) Find the trace of the matrix X for which

$$\begin{bmatrix} 1 & -4 \\ 3 & -2 \end{bmatrix} X = \begin{bmatrix} -16 & -6 \\ 7 & 2 \end{bmatrix}$$

(p) 2

(B) If $\begin{bmatrix} 2 & -1 \\ 1 & 0 \\ -3 & 4 \end{bmatrix} \begin{bmatrix} 1 & m & n \\ x & y & z \end{bmatrix} = \begin{bmatrix} -1 & -8 & -10 \\ 1 & -2 & -5 \\ 9 & 22 & 15 \end{bmatrix}$, then the value of $l + m + n + x + y + z$ is?

(q) 0

(C) Find the number of rational values of X which satisfy

$$[|x|] \begin{bmatrix} 1 & 3 & 2 \\ 0 & 5 & 1 \\ 0 & 3 & 2 \end{bmatrix} \begin{bmatrix} 1 \\ 1 \\ x \end{bmatrix} = 0$$

(r) 1

(D) If $\begin{bmatrix} 1/25 & 0 \\ x & 1/25 \end{bmatrix} = \begin{bmatrix} 5 & 0 \\ -a & 5 \end{bmatrix}^{-2}$, then the value of $\frac{125x}{a}$ is

(s) 8

RESPONSE GRID	18. ⓐⓑⓒⓓ 19. ⓐⓑⓒⓓ 20. A - ⓟⓠⓡⓢ; B - ⓟⓠⓡⓢ; C - ⓟⓠⓡⓢ; D - ⓟⓠⓡⓢ

DAILY PRACTICE PROBLEM DPP CM16 - MATHEMATICS			
Total Questions	20	Total Marks	69
Attempted		Correct	
Incorrect		Net Score	
Cut-off Score	21	Qualifying Score	32

$$\text{Net Score} = \sum_{i=1}^{V} \left[(\text{correct}_i \times MM_i) - (In_i - NM_i) \right]$$

Space for Rough Work

DPP - Daily Practice Problems

Chapter-wise Sheets

Date : | Start Time : | End Time :

MATHEMATICS CM17

SYLLABUS : Determinants

Max. Marks : 69 **Time : 60 min.**

GENERAL INSTRUCTIONS

- The Daily Practice Problem Sheet contains 20 Questions divided into 5 sections.
  Section I has **6** MCQs with ONLY 1 Correct Option, **3** marks for each correct answer and **–1** for each incorrect answer.
  Section II has **4** MCQs with ONE or MORE THAN ONE Correct options.
  For each question, marks will be awarded in one of the following categories:
  Full marks: **+4** If only the bubble(s) corresponding to all the correct option(s) is (are) darkened.
  Partial marks: **+1** For darkening a bubble corresponding to each correct option provided NO INCORRECT option is darkened.
  Zero marks: If none of the bubbles is darkened.
  Negative marks: **–2** In all other cases.
  Section III has **5** Single Digit Integer Answer Type Questions, **3** marks for each Correct Answer and **0** mark in all other cases.
  Section IV has Comprehension Type Questions having **4** MCQs with ONLY ONE corect option, **3** marks for each Correct Answer and **0** mark in all other cases.
  Section V has **1** Matching Type Question, **2** marks for the correct matching of each row and **0** mark in all other cases.
- You have to evaluate your Response Grids yourself with the help of Solutions.

Section I - Straight Objective Type

This section contains 6 multiple choice questions. Each question has 4 choices (a), (b), (c) and (d), out of which **ONLY ONE** is correct.

1. If $x \neq 0,\ y \neq 0,\ z \neq 0$ and $\begin{vmatrix} 1+x & 1 & 1 \\ 1+y & 1+2y & 1 \\ 1+z & 1+z & 1+3z \end{vmatrix}$

$= pxyz\left(q + \frac{1}{x} + \frac{1}{y} + \frac{1}{z}\right)$, then, $(p+q)$ is equal to

(a) 7 (b) 5
(c) 9 (d) None of these

2. The system of equations $(a\alpha + b)x + ay + bz = 0$

$$(b\alpha + c)x + by + cz = 0$$

$$(a\alpha + b)y + (b\alpha + c)z = 0$$

has a non-trivial solution, if

(a) a, b, c are in A.P
(b) a, b, c are in G.P
(c) a, b, c are in H.P
(d) α is a root of $ax^2 - 2bx + c = 0$

RESPONSE GRID 1. ⓐⓑⓒⓓ 2. ⓐⓑⓒⓓ

Space for Rough Work

3. If a, b, c, d > 0 and $(a^2 + b^2 + c^2)^2 x^2 - 2(ab + bc + cd)x + b^2 + c^2 + d^2 \le 0$.

Then, $\begin{vmatrix} p & x & \log a \\ q & y & \log b \\ r & z & \log c \end{vmatrix}$ is equal to, here p, q, r, x, y, and z are in AP

(a) 1 (b) −1 (c) 2 (d) 0

4. If $U_n = \begin{vmatrix} 1 & k & k \\ 2n & k^2+k+1 & k^2+k \\ 2n-1 & k^2 & k^2+k+1 \end{vmatrix}$ and $\sum_{n=1}^{k} U_n = 110$, then k is equal to

(a) 10 (b) 9
(c) 6 (d) None of these

5. Let $f(n) = \begin{vmatrix} n & n+1 & n+2 \\ {}^nP_n & {}^{n+1}P_{n+1} & {}^{n+2}P_{n+2} \\ {}^nC_n & {}^{n+1}C_{n+1} & {}^{n+2}C_{n+2} \end{vmatrix}$ where the symbols have their usual meanings. Then $f(n)$

(a) $f(5) = 3720$ (b) $f(5) = 2040$
(c) $f(4) = 5040$ (d) None of these

6. The value of the determinant of nth order $\begin{vmatrix} x & 1 & 1 & \dots \\ 1 & x & 1 & \dots \\ 1 & 1 & x & \dots \\ \dots & \dots & \dots & \dots \end{vmatrix}$, is

(a) $(x-1)^{n-1}(x+n-1)$ (b) $(x-1)^n(x+n-1)$
(c) $(1-x)^{n-1}(x+n-1)$ (d) None of these.

Section II - Multiple Correct Answer Type

This section contains 4 multiple correct answer(s) type questions. Each question has 4 choices (a), (b), (c) and (d), out of which **ONE OR MORE** is/are correct.

7. If f(x) satisfies the equation

$$\begin{vmatrix} f(x-3) & f(x+6) & f[(x+1)(x-2)-(x-1)^3] \\ 5 & 4 & -5 \\ 5 & 6 & 15 \end{vmatrix} = 0$$

for all real x, then:

(a) $f(13) = f(53)$ (b) $f(7) = f(127)$
(c) $f(9) = f(25)$ (d) $f(-4) = f = (4)$

8. If $f(x) = \begin{vmatrix} x & a & a & a \\ a & x & a & a \\ a & a & x & a \\ a & a & a & x \end{vmatrix}$ then

(a) $f(2a) = 5a^4$ (b) $f(3a) = 48a^4$
(c) $f(4a) = 64a^4$ (d) $f(-a) = -16a^4$

9. If $\Delta = \begin{vmatrix} my+nz & mq+nr & mb+nc \\ kz-mx & kr-mp & kb-ma \\ -nx-ky & -np-kq & -na-kb \end{vmatrix}$

(a) Δ is independent of a, b, c
(b) Δ is independent of x, y, z
(c) Δ is independent of p, q, r.
(d) Δ is independent of x, y, z but dependent on a, b, c

10. If a point (x, y) moves on a curve and satisfies the equation $\begin{vmatrix} a & b & ax+by \\ b & c & bx+cy \\ ax+by & bx+ay & 0 \end{vmatrix} = 0$. Then,

(a) a, b, c form a GP
(b) a, b, c form an HP
(c) the point (x, y) lies on a curve that passes through the origin
(d) the point (x, y) lies on a curve that does not pass through the origin

RESPONSE GRID					
	3. ⓐⓑⓒⓓ	4. ⓐⓑⓒⓓ	5. ⓐⓑⓒⓓ	6. ⓐⓑⓒⓓ	7. ⓐⓑⓒⓓ
	8. ⓐⓑⓒⓓ	9. ⓐⓑⓒⓓ	10. ⓐⓑⓒⓓ		

Space for Rough Work

Section III - Integer Type

This section contains 5 questions. The answer to each of the questions is a single digit integer ranging from 0 to 9.

11. For a non–zero, real a, b and c $\begin{vmatrix} \frac{a^2+b^2}{c} & c & c \\ a & \frac{b^2+c^2}{a} & a \\ b & b & \frac{c^2+a^2}{b} \end{vmatrix} = (\alpha abc)$

then the values of $[\alpha]+3$ is, where $[x]$ is greatest integer less than or equal to x.

12. If A and B are two matrices of order 3×3 where $|A| = -2$, $|B| = 2$ then $|(A^{-1}\text{adj}(B^{-1})\text{adj}(2A^{-1})|$ is equal to

13. If $a_1, a_2, \ldots\ldots a_{12}$ are in AP, and $A = \begin{vmatrix} a_1a_5 & a_1 & a_2 \\ a_2a_6 & a_2 & a_3 \\ a_3a_7 & a_3 & a_4 \end{vmatrix}, B = \begin{vmatrix} a_2a_{10} & a_2 & a_3 \\ a_3a_{11} & a_3 & a_4 \\ a_4a_{12} & a_4 & a_5 \end{vmatrix}$

Find the sum of the digits AB if common difference of AP is 2

14. If $a^2 + b^2 + c^2 = -2$ and then the equation $\begin{vmatrix} 1+a^2x & (1+b^2)x & (1+c^2)x \\ (1+a^2)x & 1+b^2x & (1+c^2)x \\ (1+a^2)x & (1+b^2)x & 1+c^2x \end{vmatrix} = 0$ has how many distinct roots?

15. a and b are real and

$ax + (\sin b)y + (\cos b)z = 0$; $x + (\cos b)y + (\sin b)z = 0$

$-x + (\sin b)y - (\cos b)z = 0$

Find the number of integral values of 'a' for which the system of linear equations has a non-trivial solution

Section IV - Comprehension Type

Based upon the given paragraphs, 4 multiple choice questions have to be answered. Each question has 4 choices (a), (b), (c) and (d), out of which **ONLY ONE** is correct.

PARAGRAPH-1

Read the paragraph carefully and answer the following questions:

A determinant is called cyclic if it follows the arrangement symmetrically with a, b, c for example $\begin{vmatrix} 1 & 1 & 1 \\ a & b & c \\ a^2 & b^2 & c^2 \end{vmatrix}$ is a cyclic determinant

Now, if we increase the degree of any row in this determinant symmetrically its value will be multiplied by expression which is also cyclic and increases the degree of the value of determinant,

16. The value of $\begin{vmatrix} 1 & 1 & 1 \\ a^2 & b^2 & c^2 \\ bc & ca & ab \end{vmatrix}$ is equal to

(a) $(a-b)(b-c)(c-a)$
(b) $(a-b)(b-c)(c-a)(a+b+c)$
(c) $(a-b)(b-c)(c-a)\ (ab+bc+ca)$
(d) $(a-b)(b-c)(c-a)\ abc$

17. The value of $\begin{vmatrix} a & b & c \\ a^2 & b^2 & c^2 \\ bc & ca & ab \end{vmatrix}$ is equal to

(a) $(a-b)(b-c)(c-a)\ (a+b+c)^2$
(b) $(a-b)(b-c)(c-a)\ (a+b+c)$
(c) $(a-b)(b-c)(c-a)\ (ab+bc+ca)$
(d) $(a-b)(b-c)(c-a)\ \left(a^2+b^2+c^2+ab+bc+ca\right)$

RESPONSE GRID	
11. ⓪①②③④⑤⑥⑦⑧⑨	12. ⓪①②③④⑤⑥⑦⑧⑨
13. ⓪①②③④⑤⑥⑦⑧⑨	14. ⓪①②③④⑤⑥⑦⑧⑨
15. ⓪①②③④⑤⑥⑦⑧⑨	16. ⓐⓑⓒⓓ 17. ⓐⓑⓒⓓ

Space for Rough Work

PARAGRAPH-2

The system of equations $a_1x + b_1y + c_1z = d_1$, $a_2x+b_2y+c_2z = d_2$, $a_3x + b_3y + c_3z = d_3$ can be written as

$AX = B$ where $A = \begin{bmatrix} a_1 & b_1 & c_1 \\ a_2 & b_2 & c_2 \\ a_3 & b_3 & c_3 \end{bmatrix}, X = \begin{bmatrix} x \\ y \\ z \end{bmatrix}$ and $B = \begin{bmatrix} d_1 \\ d_2 \\ d_3 \end{bmatrix}$ the system is

(i) consistent with unique solution iff $|A| \neq 0$

(ii) either inconsistent or consistent with infinite solutions if $|A| = 0$ and $(\text{adj.} A)B = 0$

(iii) Inconsistent iff $|A| = 0$ and $(\text{adj } A)B \neq 0$

18. The system of equations $x + y + z = 3$, $2x + y + 2z = 5$, $x - y + 3z = 3$ has

(a) only solution $x = 1, y = 1, z = 1$

(b) Infinite solutions

(c) no solution

(d) None of these

19. The system of equations $x + y + z = 3$, $2x + 2y + 2z = 7$, $x - y + 3z = 3$ has

(a) only solution $x = 1, y = 1, z = 1$

(b) Infinite solution

(c) no solution

(d) None of these

Section V - Matrix-Match Type

This section contains 1 question. It contains statements given in two columns, which have to be matched. Statements in column I are labelled as A, B, C and D whereas statements in column II are labelled as p, q, r and s. The answers to these questions have to be appropriately bubbled as illustrated in the following example. If the correct matches are A-p, A-r, B-p, B-s, C-r, C-s and D-q, then the correctly bubbled matrix will look like the following:

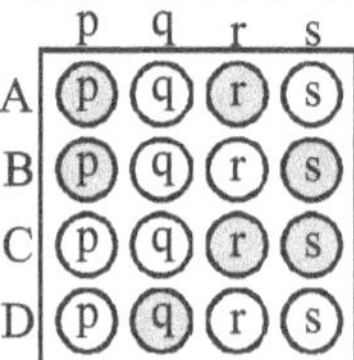

20. **Column - I** | **Column - II**

(A) Simplify $\begin{vmatrix} 1+\sin^2\theta & \cos^2\theta & \sin 2\theta \\ \sin^2\theta & 1+\cos^2\theta & \sin 2\theta \\ \sin^2\theta & \cos^2\theta & 1+\sin 2\theta \end{vmatrix}$ — (p) $(3\cos\theta - \sin\theta)2$

(B) If $\begin{bmatrix} 1 & -\tan\theta \\ \tan\theta & 1 \end{bmatrix}\begin{bmatrix} 1 & \tan\theta \\ -\tan\theta & 1 \end{bmatrix}^{-1} = \begin{bmatrix} a & -b \\ b & a \end{bmatrix}$ then a = — (q) $2 + \sin 2\theta$

(C) If $\begin{bmatrix} 1 & -\tan\theta \\ \tan\theta & 1 \end{bmatrix}\begin{bmatrix} 1 & \tan\theta \\ -\tan\theta & 1 \end{bmatrix}^{-1} = \begin{bmatrix} a & -b \\ b & a \end{bmatrix}$ then b = — (r) $\cos 2\theta$

(D) $\begin{vmatrix} 1 & 3\cos\theta & 1 \\ \sin\theta & 1 & 3\cos\theta \\ 1 & \sin\theta & 1 \end{vmatrix}$ equals — (s) $\sin 2\theta$

RESPONSE GRID	18. ⓐⓑⓒⓓ 19. ⓐⓑⓒⓓ 20. A - ⓟⓠⓡⓢ; B - ⓟⓠⓡⓢ; C - ⓟⓠⓡⓢ; D - ⓟⓠⓡⓢ

DAILY PRACTICE PROBLEM DPP CM17 - MATHEMATICS

Total Questions	20	Total Marks	69
Attempted		Correct	
Incorrect		Net Score	
Cut-off Score	23	Qualifying Score	34

$$\text{Net Score} = \sum_{i=1}^{V}\left[(\text{correct}_i \times MM_i) - (In_i - NM_i)\right]$$

Space for Rough Work

DPP - Daily Practice Problems

Chapter-wise Sheets

Date : Start Time : End Time :

MATHEMATICS CM18

SYLLABUS : Continuity and Differentiability

Max. Marks : 74 **Time : 60 min.**

GENERAL INSTRUCTIONS

- The Daily Practice Problem Sheet contains 20 Questions divided into 5 sections.

  Section I has **5** MCQs with ONLY 1 Correct Option, **3** marks for each correct answer and **–1** for each incorrect answer.

  Section II has **4** MCQs with ONE or MORE THAN ONE Correct options.

  For each question, marks will be awarded in one of the following categories:

  Full marks: **+4** If only the bubble(s) corresponding to all the correct option(s) is (are) darkened.

  Partial marks: **+1** For darkening a bubble corresponding to each correct option provided NO INCORRECT option is darkened.

  Zero marks: If none of the bubbles is darkened.

  Negative marks: **–2** In all other cases.

  Section III has **4** Single Digit Integer Answer Type Questions, **3** marks for each Correct Answer and **0** mark in all other cases.

  Section IV has Comprehension/Matching Cum-Comprehension Type Questions having **5** MCQs with ONLY ONE correct option, **3** marks for each Correct Answer and **0** mark in all other cases.

  Section V has **2** Matching Type Questions, **2** marks for the correct matching of each row and **0** mark in all other cases.
- You have to evaluate your Response Grids yourself with the help of Solutions.

Section I - Straight Objective Type

This section contains 5 multiple choice questions. Each question has 4 choices (a), (b), (c) and (d), out of which **ONLY ONE** is correct.

1. If $f(x)=\begin{cases} \dfrac{e^{[x]+|x|}-2}{[x]+|x|}, & x \neq 0 \\ -1, & x=0 \end{cases}$ ([.]denotes the greatest integer function) then

(a) $f(x)$ is continuous at $x=0$

(b) $\lim\limits_{x\to 0^+} f(x)=-1$

(c) $\lim\limits_{x\to 0^-} f(x)=1$

(d) None of these

2. If $f''(x)=-f(x)$ and $g(x)=f'(x)$ and

$F(x)=\left(f\left(\frac{x}{2}\right)\right)^2+\left(g\left(\frac{x}{2}\right)\right)^2$ and given that $F(5)=5$, then $F(10)$ is equal to

(a) 5 (b) 10

(c) 0 (d) 15

RESPONSE GRID	1. ⓐⓑⓒⓓ	2. ⓐⓑⓒⓓ

Space for Rough Work

3. Given $f:[-2a,2a]\to R$ is an odd function such that the left hand derivative at x = a is zero and $f(x)=f(2a-x)\ \forall\ x\in(a,2a)$, then its left had derivative at $x=-a$ is

(a) 0 (b) a
(c) $-a$ (d) does not exist

4. If $f(x)=\cos x\cos 2x\cos 2^2x\cos 2^3x\ .....\cos 2^{n-1}x$ and $n>1$, then $f'\left(\frac{\pi}{2}\right)$ is

(a) 1 (b) 0
(c) -1 (d) None of these

5. Let f be a differentiable function satisfying $[f(x)]^n=f(nx)$ for all $x\in R$.
Then, $f'(x)f(nx)=$

(a) $f(x)$ (b) 0
(c) $f(x)f'(nx)$ (d) None of these

Section II - Multiple Correct Answer Type

This section contains 4 multiple correct answer(s) type questions. Each question has 4 choices (a), (b), (c) and (d), out of which **ONE OR MORE** is/are correct.

6. If $f(x)=\begin{vmatrix} x^n & \sin x & \cos x \\ n! & \sin(n\pi/2) & \cos(n\pi/2) \\ a & a^2 & a^3 \end{vmatrix}$, then the value of $\frac{d^n}{dx^n}(f(x))$ at $x=0$ for $n=2m+1$, is

(a) -1 (b) 0
(c) a (d) independent of a

7. If $f(x)=x+|x|+\cos([\pi^2]x)$ and $g(x)=\sin x$, where [.] denotes the greatest integer function, then

(a) $f(x)+g(x)$ is continuous everywhere
(b) $f(x)+g(x)$ is differentiable everywhere
(c) $f(x)\times g(x)$ is differentiable everywhere
(d) $f(x)\times g(x)$ is continuous but not differentiable at $x=0$

8. Let $f(x)=x^3+3x^2-33x-33$ for $x>0$ and 'g' be its inverse, then the value of 'k' such that $kg'(2)=1$, is equal to

(a) -36 (b) 51
(c) 72 (d) 42

9. If $f(x)=\begin{cases}(\sin^{-1}x)^2\cos(1/x), & x\neq 0\\ 0, & x=0\end{cases}$ then

(a) $f(x)$ is continuous everywhere in $x\in(-1,1)$
(b) $f(x)$ is discontinuous in $x\in[-1,1]$
(c) $f(x)$ is differentiable everywhere in $x\in(-1,1)$
(d) $f(x)$ is non-differentiable anywhere in $x\in[-1,1]$

Section III - Integer Type

This section contains 4 questions. The answer to each of the questions is a single digit integer ranging from 0 to 9.

10. If the number of points of non-differentiability of $f(x)=\max\{\sin x,\cos x,0\}$ in $(0, 2n\pi)$ is pn, then find the value of p.

11. If $\frac{d^2x}{dy^2}\left(\frac{dy}{dx}\right)^3+\frac{d^2y}{dx^2}=k$, then find the value of k.

12. Let $f(x)=\begin{cases}\frac{1-\cos 4x}{x^2}, & x<0\\ a, & x=0\\ \frac{\sqrt{x}}{\sqrt{16+\sqrt{x}}-4}, & x>0\end{cases}$

Determine the value of 'a' if possible, so that the function is continuous at $x=0$.

13. Let $f(x)$ and $g(x)$ be differentiable for $0\le x\le 1$, such that $f(0)=0, g(0)=0, f(1)=6$. Let there exist a real number c in (0, 1) such that $f'(c)=2g'(c)$, then find the value of $g(1)$

RESPONSE GRID	
	3. ⓐⓑⓒⓓ 4. ⓐⓑⓒⓓ 5. ⓐⓑⓒⓓ 6. ⓐⓑⓒⓓ 7. ⓐⓑⓒⓓ
	8. ⓐⓑⓒⓓ 9. ⓐⓑⓒⓓ 10. ⓪①②③④⑤⑥⑦⑧⑨
	11. ⓪①②③④⑤⑥⑦⑧⑨ 12. ⓪①②③④⑤⑥⑦⑧⑨
	13. ⓪①②③④⑤⑥⑦⑧⑨

Space for Rough Work

Section IV - Comprehension/Matching Cum-Comprehension Type

Directions (Qs. 14 and 15) : Based upon the given paragraph, 2 multiple choice questions have to be answered. Each question has 4 choices (a), (b), (c) and (d), out of which **ONLY ONE** is correct.

PARAGRAPH

If $y = f(x)$ be a differentiable function of x such that whose second, third, ..., nth derivatives exist. *i.e.*, nth derivative of y is denoted by

$$y_n, \frac{d^n y}{dx^n}, D^n y, y^n, f^n(x)$$

$$\Rightarrow \quad \frac{d^n y}{dx^n} = \lim_{h\to 0} \frac{f^{n-1}(x+h) - f^{n-1}(x)}{h}$$

On the basis of above information, answer the following questions :

14. If $y = e^{3x+7}$, then the value of y_n (0) is

(a) 1 (b) 3^n

(c) $3^n . e^7$ (d) $3^n . e^7 . 7!$

15. If $y = \dfrac{\ln x}{2-3x}$, then the value of y_n (1) is

(a) 0 (b) $(-1)^n . 3^n$

(c) $(-1)^n . 3^n . n!$ (d) None of these

Directions (Qs. 16-18) : This passage contains a table having 3 columns and 4 rows. Based on the table, there are three questions. Each question has four options (a), (b), (c) and (d) **ONLY ONE** of these four options is correct.

Column 1 contains information about the functions.

Column 2 contains information about continuity and differentiability of functions given in column I.

Column 3 contains information about points/intervals where given function is either continuous or differentiable.

Column I	Column II	Column III
(I) $f(x) = \begin{cases} x^p \sin\frac{1}{x} & x \neq 0 \\ 0 & x = 0 \end{cases}$	(i) Neither continuous nor derivable	(P) {2}
(II) $f(x) = \begin{cases} 4x^2 + [2x]\,x, & -\frac{1}{2} \le x < 0 \\ ax^2 - bx, & 0 \le x < \frac{1}{2} \end{cases}$	(ii) Continuous but not differentiable	(Q) $(-1, 0)$
(III) $f(x) = [x^2] + [-x]^2$	(iii) Continuous and differentiable	(R) {0}
(IV) $f(x) = \cos\pi(\lvert x\rvert + [x])$	(iv) Differentiable but not continuous	(S) $\left(\frac{-1}{2}, \frac{1}{2}\right)$

RESPONSE GRID	14. ⓐⓑⓒⓓ 15. ⓐⓑⓒⓓ

Space for Rough Work

16. Which of the following options is the only correct combination?

(a) (II) (i) (S) (b) (III) (i) (P)

(c) (I) (ii) (Q) (d) (IV) (iv) (R)

17. For $0 < p \le 1$, check the continuity and differentiability at $x = 0$ of the function $f(x) = \begin{cases} x^p \sin\frac{1}{x} & x \neq 0 \\ 0 & x = 0 \end{cases}$

(a) Continuous but not differentiable

(b) Continuous and differentiable

(c) Differentiable but not continuous

(d) Neither continuous nor derivable

18. Which of the following options is the only incorrect combination?

(a) (I) (ii) (R) (b) (II) (iii) (S)

(c) (III) (i) (P) (d) (IV) (ii) (Q)

Section V - Matrix-Match Type

This section contains 2 questions. It contains statements given in two columns, which have to be matched. Statements in column I are labelled as A, B, C and D whereas statements in column II are labelled as p, q, r and s. The answers to these questions have to be appropriately bubbled as illustrated in the following example. If the correct matches are A-p, A-r, B-p, B-s, C-r, C-s and D-q, then the correctly bubbled matrix will look like the following:

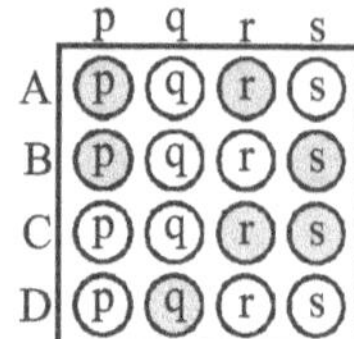

19. Let $f(x) = \begin{cases} \dfrac{5e^{1/x}+2}{3-e^{1/x}}, & x \neq 0 \\ 0, & x = 0 \end{cases}$

Column I	Column II
(A) $y = f(x)$ is	(p) continuous at $x = 0$
(B) $y = xf(x)$ is	(q) discontinuous at $x = 0$
(C) $y = x^2 f(x)$ is	(r) differentiable at $x = 0$
(D) $y = x^{-1} f(x)$ is	(s) non-differentiable at $x = 0$

20.

Column I	Column II
(A) $f(x) = \lvert x^3 \rvert$ is	(p) continuous in (–1, 1)
(B) $f(x) = \sqrt{\lvert x \rvert}$ is	(q) differentiable in (–1, 1)
(C) $f(x) = \lvert \sin^{-1} x \rvert$ is	(r) differentiable in (0, 1)
(D) $f(x) = \cos^{-1} \lvert x \rvert$	(s) not differentiable at least one point in (–1, 1)

RESPONSE GRID

16. ⓐⓑⓒⓓ 17. ⓐⓑⓒⓓ 18. ⓐⓑⓒⓓ

19. A - ⓟⓠⓡⓢ; B - ⓟⓠⓡⓢ; C - ⓟⓠⓡⓢ; D - ⓟⓠⓡⓢ

20. A - ⓟⓠⓡⓢ; B - ⓟⓠⓡⓢ; C - ⓟⓠⓡⓢ; D - ⓟⓠⓡⓢ

DAILY PRACTICE PROBLEM DPP CM18 - MATHEMATICS

Total Questions	20	Total Marks	74
Attempted		Correct	
Incorrect		Net Score	
Cut-off Score	23	Qualifying Score	34

$$\text{Net Score} = \sum_{i=1}^{V} \left[(\text{correct}_i \times MM_i) - (In_i - NM_i) \right]$$

Space for Rough Work

DPP - Daily Practice Problems

Chapter-wise Sheets

Date : | Start Time : | End Time :

MATHEMATICS CM19

SYLLABUS : Application of Derivatives

Max. Marks : 74 | **Time : 60 min.**

GENERAL INSTRUCTIONS

- The Daily Practice Problem Sheet contains 20 Questions divided into 5 sections.
  Section I has **6** MCQs with ONLY 1 Correct Option, **3** marks for each correct answer and **–1** for each incorrect answer.
  Section II has **4** MCQs with ONE or MORE THAN ONE Correct options.
  For each question, marks will be awarded in one of the following categories:
  Full marks: **+4** If only the bubble(s) corresponding to all the correct option(s) is (are) darkened.
  Partial marks: **+1** For darkening a bubble corresponding to each correct option provided NO INCORRECT option is darkened.
  Zero marks: If none of the bubbles is darkened.
  Negative marks: **–2** In all other cases.
  Section III has **4** Single Digit Integer Answer Type Questions, **3** marks for each Correct Answer and **0** mark in all other cases.
  Section IV has Comprehension Type Questions having **4** MCQs with ONLY ONE corect option, **3** marks for each Correct Answer and **0** mark in all other cases.
  Section V has **2** Matching Type Questions, **2** marks for the correct matching of each row and **0** mark in all other cases.
- You have to evaluate your Response Grids yourself with the help of Solutions.

Section I - Straight Objective Type

This section contains 6 multiple choice questions. Each question has 4 choices (a), (b), (c) and (d), out of which **ONLY ONE** is correct.

1. The value of θ, $\theta \in [0, \pi/2]$ for which the sum of intercepts on co-ordinate axes by tangent at point $(3\sqrt{3}\cos\theta, \sin\theta)$ of ellipse $\frac{x^2}{27} + y^2 = 1$ is minimum, is :

(a) $\frac{\pi}{6}$ (b) $\frac{\pi}{4}$ (c) $\frac{\pi}{3}$ (d) $\frac{\pi}{2}$

2. Function $f(x) = \tan^{-1}(\sin x + \cos x)$ is monotonic increasing when

(a) $x < 0$ (b) $x > 0$
(c) $0 < x < \pi/2$ (d) $0 < x < \pi/4$

3. The equation of one of the tangents to the curve $y = \cos(x + y), -2\pi \le x \le 2\pi$ that is parallel to the line $x + 2y = 0$ is

(a) $x + 2y = 1$ (b) $x + 2y = \pi/2$
(c) $x + 2y = \pi/4$ (d) None of these

RESPONSE GRID	1. ⓐⓑⓒⓓ	2. ⓐⓑⓒⓓ	3. ⓐⓑⓒⓓ

Space for Rough Work

4. The ratio of the altitude of the cone of greatest volume which can be inscribed in a given sphere to the diameter of the sphere is
(a) 2/3 (b) 3/4
(c) 1/3 (d) 1/4

5. Let $y = f(x)$ be the equation of a parabola which is touched by the line $y = x$ at the point where $x = 1$. Then,
(a) $f'(0) = f'(1)$
(b) $f'(1) = -1$
(c) $f(0) + f'(0) + f'(0) = 1$
(d) $2f(0) = 1 - f'(0)$

6. In a ΔABC, $B = 90^\circ$ and $a + b = 4$. The area of the triangle is maximum when C is
(a) $\frac{\pi}{4}$ (b) $\frac{\pi}{6}$
(c) $\frac{\pi}{3}$ (d) None of these

Section II - Multiple Correct Answer Type

This section contains 4 multiple correct answer(s) type questions. Each question has 4 choices (a), (b), (c) and (d), out of which **ONE OR MORE** is/are correct.

7. The point on the curve $9y^2 = x^3$, where the normal to the curve makes equal intercepts with the axes is
(a) $\left(4, \frac{8}{3}\right)$ (b) $\left(-4, \frac{8}{3}\right)$
(c) $\left(4, -\frac{8}{3}\right)$ (d) None of these

8. If $f(x)$ is defined in $[-3, 3]$ by
$$f(x) = \max.\left\{\sqrt{9-x^2}, \sqrt{1+x^2}\right\}, -3 \le x \le 0$$
$$= \min.\left\{\sqrt{9-x^2}, \sqrt{1+x^2}\right\}, 0 \le x \le 3,$$ then $f(x)$ has
(a) a point of discontinuity at $x = 0$
(b) a point of maximum at $x = -2$ and a point of minimum at $x = 2$
(c) a point of minimum at $x = -2$ and a point of maximum at $x = 2$
(d) no turning point

9. Let the function $f(x) = \sin x + \cos x$, be defined in $[0, 2\pi]$, then $f(x)$
(a) increases in $\left(\frac{\pi}{4}, \frac{\pi}{2}\right)$
(b) decreases in $\left(\frac{\pi}{4}, \frac{5\pi}{4}\right)$
(c) increases in $\left[0, \frac{\pi}{4}\right) \cup \left(\frac{5\pi}{4}, \frac{7\pi}{4}\right]$
(d) decreases in $\left[0, \frac{\pi}{4}\right) \cup \left(\frac{\pi}{2}, 2\pi\right]$

10. The normal to the curve represented parametrically by $x = a(\cos\theta + \theta\sin\theta)$ and $y = a(\sin\theta - \theta\cos\theta)$ at any point θ, is such that it
(a) makes a constant angle with the x-axis
(b) is at a constant distance from the origin
(c) touches a fixed circle
(d) passes through the origin

RESPONSE GRID					
	4. ⓐⓑⓒⓓ	5. ⓐⓑⓒⓓ	6. ⓐⓑⓒⓓ	7. ⓐⓑⓒⓓ	8. ⓐⓑⓒⓓ
	9. ⓐⓑⓒⓓ	10. ⓐⓑⓒⓓ			

Space for Rough Work

Section III - Integer Type

This section contains 4 questions. The answer to each of the questions is a single digit integer ranging from 0 to 9.

11. Find the point of inflexion of $(x-5)^{55}(x-6)^{66}$.

12. If θ be the angle of intersection of curves $y=[|\sin x|+|\cos x|]$ and $x^2+y^2=5$, where [.] denotes the greatest integer function, then find the value of $\tan^2\theta$.

13. Find the greatest value of $f(x)=(x+1)^{1/3}-(x-1)^{1/3}$ on [0, 1].

14. The altitude of a cone is 20 cm and its semi-vertical angle is 30°. If the semi-vertical angle is increasing at the rate of 2° per second, if the radius of the base is increasing at the rate of $\frac{160}{b}$, then b =

Section IV - Comprehension Type

Based upon the given paragraphs, 4 multiple choice questions have to be answered. Each question has 4 choices (a), (b), (c) and (d), out of which **ONLY ONE** is correct.

PARAGRAPH-1

A conical vessel is to be prepared out of a circular sheet of copper of unit radius as shown in the figure where α be the angle of the sector removed (i.e. ∠AOB), then

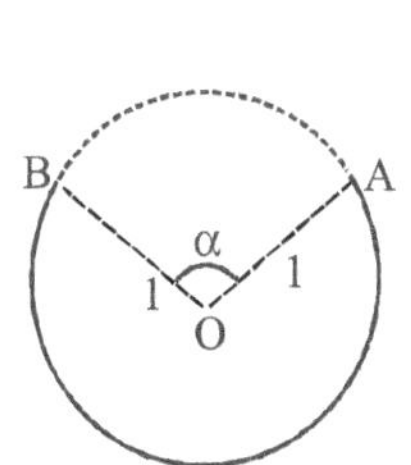

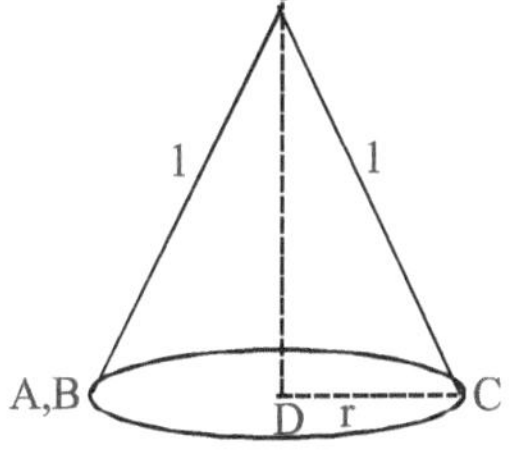

Then, $\alpha=\frac{AB}{1}$

$\Rightarrow AB=\alpha \Rightarrow ABC=2\pi-\alpha$

Circumference of the base of the cone $=2\pi-\alpha$

Let r be the radius of the base of the cone then

$2\pi r=2\pi-\alpha \Rightarrow r=1-\frac{\alpha}{2\pi}$

15. The volume of the vessel. (If $\alpha=\pi$)

(a) $\frac{\pi}{24}$ (b) $\frac{\sqrt{3}\pi^2}{6}$

(c) $\frac{\sqrt{3}\pi}{24}$ (d) None of these

16. The value of 'r' for which volume is maximum (when α is variable)

(a) $\sqrt{2}/3$ (b) $2/\sqrt{3}$

(c) $\sqrt{2/3}$ (d) None of these

PARAGRAPH-2

Analyse the following graph of derivative of a function $f(x)$, i.e. $y=g(x)$, where $g(x)=f'(x)$ and answer the following questions : $(a \le x \le b)$. Given $f(c)=0$.

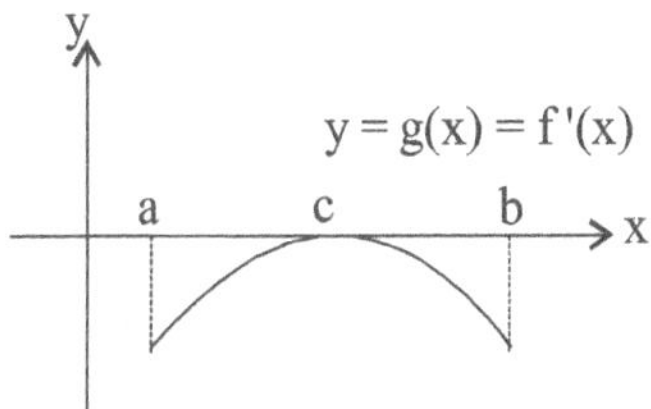

17. The graph of $y=f(x)$ will intersect x-axis

(a) never (b) once

(c) twice (d) cannot be determined

18. The equation $f(x)=0$, $a \le x \le b$ has

(a) no real roots

(b) two distinct real roots

(c) two repeated roots

(d) at least three repeated roots

RESPONSE GRID	
	11. ⓪①②③④⑤⑥⑦⑧⑨ 12. ⓪①②③④⑤⑥⑦⑧⑨
	13. ⓪①②③④⑤⑥⑦⑧⑨ 14. ⓪①②③④⑤⑥⑦⑧⑨
	15. ⓐⓑⓒⓓ 16. ⓐⓑⓒⓓ 17. ⓐⓑⓒⓓ 18. ⓐⓑⓒⓓ

Space for Rough Work

Section V - Matrix-Match Type

This section contains 2 questions. It contains statements given in two columns, which have to be matched. Statements in column I are labelled as A, B, C and D whereas statements in column II are labelled as p, q, r and s. The answers to these questions have to be appropriately bubbled as illustrated in the following example. If the correct matches are A-p, A-r, B-p, B-s, C-r, C-s and D-q, then the correctly bubbled matrix will look like the following:

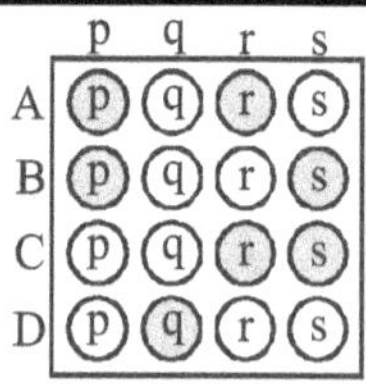

19. **Column-I** **Column-II**

(A) The normal line to $y = be^{-x/a}$ where it crosses y-axis, has slope equal to (p) $\frac{a^2}{b^2}$

(B) Subnormal length to $xy = a^2 b^2$ at any point (x, y) is p then $\frac{1}{p}|y^3|$ is equal to (q) $\frac{a}{b}$

(C) The length of subtangent at any point (x, y) on the ellipse $\frac{x^2}{a^2}+\frac{y^2}{b^2}=1$ is p then $\frac{p|x|}{y^2}$ is equal to (r) $a^2 b^2$

(D) If m be slope of tangent at any point (x, y) on the curve $\frac{x^2}{a^2}-\frac{y^2}{b^2}=1$ then $\frac{my}{x}$ is equal to (s) $\frac{b^2}{a^2}$

20. **Column-I** **Column-II**

(A) A circular plate is expanded by heat from radius 6 cm to 6.06 cm. Approximate increase in the area is (p) 5

(B) If an edge of a cube increases by 2%, then percentage increase in the volume is (q) 0.72π

(C) If the rate of decrease of $\frac{x^2}{2}-2x+5$ is thrice the rate of decrease of x, then x is equal to (rate of decrease is non zero) (r) 6

(D) The rate of increase in the area of an equailateral triangle of side 30 cm, when each side increases at the rate of 0.1 cm/s is (s) $\frac{3\sqrt{3}}{2}$

RESPONSE GRID	
	19. A - ⓟⓠⓡⓢ; B - ⓟⓠⓡⓢ; C - ⓟⓠⓡⓢ; D - ⓟⓠⓡⓢ
	20. A - ⓟⓠⓡⓢ; B - ⓟⓠⓡⓢ; C - ⓟⓠⓡⓢ; D - ⓟⓠⓡⓢ

DAILY PRACTICE PROBLEM DPP CM19 - MATHEMATICS

Total Questions	20	Total Marks	74
Attempted		Correct	
Incorrect		Net Score	
Cut-off Score	23	Qualifying Score	34

$$\text{Net Score} = \sum_{i=1}^{V}\left[(\text{correct}_i \times MM_i) - (In_i - NM_i)\right]$$

Space for Rough Work

DPP - Daily Practice Problems

Chapter-wise Sheets

Date : | Start Time : | End Time :

MATHEMATICS (CM20)

SYLLABUS : Integrals

Max. Marks : 74 | **Time : 60 min.**

GENERAL INSTRUCTIONS

- The Daily Practice Problem Sheet contains 20 Questions divided into 5 sections.
  Section I has **6** MCQs with ONLY 1 Correct Option, **3** marks for each correct answer and **–1** for each incorrect answer.
  Section II has **4** MCQs with ONE or MORE THAN ONE Correct options.
  For each question, marks will be awarded in one of the following categories:
  Full marks: **+4** If only the bubble(s) corresponding to all the correct option(s) is (are) darkened.
  Partial marks: **+1** For darkening a bubble corresponding to each correct option provided NO INCORRECT option is darkened.
  Zero marks: If none of the bubbles is darkened.
  Negative marks: **–2** In all other cases.
  Section III has **4** Single Digit Integer Answer Type Questions, **3** marks for each Correct Answer and **0** mark in all other cases.
  Section IV has Comprehension Type Questions having **4** MCQs with ONLY ONE corect option, **3** marks for each Correct Answer and **0** mark in all other cases.
  Section V has **2** Matching Type Questions, **2** marks for the correct matching of each row and **0** mark in all other cases.
- You have to evaluate your Response Grids yourself with the help of Solutions.

Section I - Straight Objective Type

This section contains 6 multiple choice questions. Each question has 4 choices (a), (b), (c) and (d), out of which **ONLY ONE** is correct.

1. $\int \frac{dx}{3\sin^2 x + 4\cos^2 x} =$

(a) $\frac{1}{2\sqrt{3}}\tan^{-1}\left(\frac{1}{2}\tan x\right)+c$

(b) $\frac{1}{2}\tan^{-1}\left(\frac{\sqrt{3}}{2}\tan x\right)+c$

(c) $\frac{1}{2\sqrt{3}}\tan^{-1}\left(\frac{\sqrt{3}}{2}\tan x\right)+c$

(d) None of these

2. $\int |x|\ln|x|\, dx$ equals $(x \neq 0)$

(a) $\frac{x^2}{2}\ln|x| - \frac{x^2}{4} + c$

(b) $\frac{1}{2}x|x|\ln x + \frac{1}{4}x|x| + c$

(c) $-\frac{x^2}{2}\ln|x| + \frac{x^2}{4} + c$

(d) $\frac{1}{2}x|x|\ln|x| - \frac{1}{4}x|x| + c$

RESPONSE GRID	1. ⓐⓑⓒⓓ	2. ⓐⓑⓒⓓ

Space for Rough Work

3. If $\int \frac{(\sqrt{x})^5}{(\sqrt{x})^7 + x^6} dx = \lambda \ln\left(\frac{x^a}{x^a+1}\right) + c$, then $a + \lambda$ is

(a) $=2$ (b) >2
(c) <2 (d) $=1$

4. A student evaluate $\int_0^\infty \frac{\tan^{-1} x}{\sqrt{x}(1+x)} dx$ by substituting $x = 1/t$ and obtains the correct answer equal $\frac{502\pi^2}{k}$. Using the same substitution or otherwise, find the value of k.

(a) 2008 (b) 1008
(c) 880 (d) 750

5. $\lim_{n\to\infty}\left(\tan\frac{\pi}{2n}\cdot\tan\frac{2\pi}{2n}\cdot\tan\frac{3\pi}{2n}\ldots\tan\frac{n\pi}{2n}\right)^{\frac{1}{n}} =$

(a) 0 (b) 1
(c) e (d) $1/e$

6. If p, q, r, s are in arithmetic progression and

$$f(x) = \begin{vmatrix} p+\sin x & q+\sin x & p-r+\sin x \\ q+\sin x & r+\sin x & -1+\sin x \\ r+\sin x & s+\sin x & s-q+\sin x \end{vmatrix}$$ such that

$\int_0^2 f(x)\,dx = -4$, then the common difference of the progession is

(a) ± 1 (b) $\frac{1}{2}$
(c) ± 2 (d) None of these

Section II - Multiple Correct Answer Type

This section contains 4 multiple correct answer(s) type questions. Each question has 4 choices (a), (b), (c) and (d), out of which **ONE OR MORE** is/are correct.

7. If $I = \int \frac{\sin^3(\theta/2)}{\cos(\theta/2)\sqrt{\cos^3\theta + \cos^2\theta + \cos\theta}} d\theta$ then I equals

(a) $\cot^{-1}(\tan\theta + \sec\theta) + c$
(b) $\cot^{-1}(\cos\theta + \sec\theta + 1) + c$
(c) $\tan^{-1}\left(\tan\frac{\theta}{2} + \sec\frac{\theta}{2} + 1\right) + c$
(d) $\tan^{-1}(\cos\theta + \sec\theta + 1) + c$

8. If $I = \int \frac{(x^2+n)(n-1)x^{2n-1}}{(x\sin x + n\cos x)^2} dx$

$= f(x) + g(x) + c$, then

(a) $f(x) = \frac{x^n}{x^n \sin x + n\cos x}$

(b) $f(x) = -\frac{x^n \sec x}{x^n \sin x + nx^{n-1}\cos x}$

(c) $g(x) = \tan x$

(d) $g(x) = \sec x$

9. If $\int \sin^{-1} x \cos^{-1} x\, dx = f^{-1}(x)$

$\left[Ax - x f^{-1}(x) - 2\sqrt{1-x^2}\right] + 2x + c$, then

(a) $f(x) = \sin x$ (b) $f(x) = \cos x$
(c) $A = \frac{\pi}{4}$ (d) $A = \frac{\pi}{2}$

10. Let e be the eccentricity of a hyperbola and $f(e)$ be the eccentricity of its conjugate hyperbola then $\int_1^3 \underbrace{fff\ldots\ldots f}_{n \text{ times}}(e)\,de$ is equal to

(a) 4, if n is even (b) 4, if n is odd
(c) 2, if n is even (d) $2\sqrt{2}$, if n is odd

RESPONSE GRID	
	3. ⓐⓑⓒⓓ 4. ⓐⓑⓒⓓ 5. ⓐⓑⓒⓓ 6. ⓐⓑⓒⓓ 7. ⓐⓑⓒⓓ
	8. ⓐⓑⓒⓓ 9. ⓐⓑⓒⓓ 10. ⓐⓑⓒⓓ

Space for Rough Work

Section III - Integer Type

This section contains 4 questions. The answer to each of the questions is a single digit integer ranging from 0 to 9.

11. If the value of $\int_0^{100\pi}([\cot^{-1}x]+[\tan^{-1}x])\,dx$ is $100\pi+p\cot p$, then the value of p is (where [.] denotes greatest integer function).

12. Let $f:(0,\infty)\to R$ be a differentiable function such that $x\int_0^x(1-t)f(t)dt=\int_0^x t\,f(t)dt\ \forall x\in(0,\infty)$ and $f(1)=1$. The value of $\lim_{x\to\infty} f(x)$ is equal to

13. If $I(n)=\int_0^{\pi/2}\theta\sin^n\theta\,d\theta,\ n\in N,\ n>3$, and $[2010\,I(2010)-2009\,I(2008)]^{-1}$ is equal to $1005\,a$ then $a=$

14. If $\int \operatorname{cosec}^2 x\,ln\left(\cos x+\sqrt{\cos 2x}\right)dx$

$= f(x)\,ln\left(\cos x+\sqrt{\cos 2x}\right)+g(x)+f(x)-x+c,$

then $f^2(x)-g^2(x)$ is equal to $\left(0<x\le\frac{\pi}{2}\right)$.

Section IV - Comprehension Type

Based upon the given paragraphs, 4 multiple choice questions have to be answered. Each question has 4 choices (a), (b), (c) and (d), out of which **ONLY ONE** is correct.

PARAGRAPH-1

Let $f(x)$ and $\phi(x)$ are two continuous functions on R satisfying $\phi(x)=\int_a^x f(t)\,dt,\ a\ne 0$ and another continuous function $g(x)$ satisfying $g(x+\alpha)+g(x)=0\ \forall x\in R, \alpha>0$ and $\int_b^{2k} g(t)\,dt$ is independent of b.

15. If $f(x)$ is an even function, then
(a) $\phi(x)$ is also an even function
(b) $\phi(x)$ is an odd function
(c) If $f(a-x)=-f(x)$, then $\phi(x)$ is an even function
(d) If $f(a-x)=-f(x)$, then $\phi(x)$ is an odd function

16. Least positive value of c if c, k, b are in A.P., is
(a) 0 (b) 1
(c) α (d) 2α

PARAGRAPH-2

If A is square matrix and e^A is defined as

$$e^A=I+A+\frac{A^2}{2!}+\frac{A^3}{3!}+\ldots=\frac{1}{2}\begin{bmatrix} f(x) & g(x)\\ g(x) & f(x)\end{bmatrix},\ \text{where } A=\begin{bmatrix} x & x\\ x & x\end{bmatrix}$$

and $0<x<1$, I is an identity matrix.

17. $\int\frac{g(x)}{f(x)}dx$ is equal to
(a) $\log(e^x+e^{-x})+c$ (b) $\log(e^x-e^{-x})+c$
(c) $\log(e^{2x}-1)+c$ (d) none of these

18. $\int(g(x)+1)\,\sin x\,dx$ is equal to
(a) $\frac{e^x}{2}(\sin x-\cos x)$ (b) $\frac{e^{2x}}{5}(2\sin x-\cos x)$
(c) $\frac{e^x}{5}(\sin 2x-\cos 2x)$ (d) none of these

RESPONSE GRID	
	11. ⓪①②③④⑤⑥⑦⑧⑨ 12. ⓪①②③④⑤⑥⑦⑧⑨
	13. ⓪①②③④⑤⑥⑦⑧⑨ 14. ⓪①②③④⑤⑥⑦⑧⑨
	15. ⓐⓑⓒⓓ 16. ⓐⓑⓒⓓ 17. ⓐⓑⓒⓓ 18. ⓐⓑⓒⓓ

Space for Rough Work

Section V - Matrix-Match Type

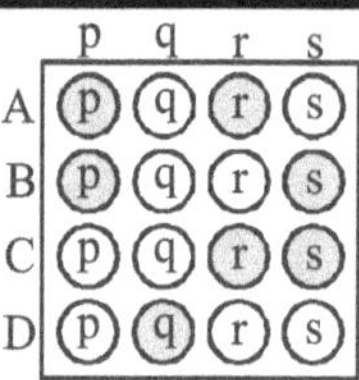

This section contains 2 questions. It contains statements given in two columns, which have to be matched. Statements in column I are labelled as A, B, C and D whereas statements in column II are labelled as p, q, r and s. The answers to these questions have to be appropriately bubbled as illustrated in the following example. If the correct matches are A-p, A-r, B-p, B-s, C-r, C-s and D-q, then the correctly bubbled matrix will look like the following:

19. If $\int \frac{\log_e(x+\sqrt{1+x^2})}{\sqrt{1+x^2}}dx = fog(x) + c$, Now match the entries from the following two columns:

Column-I	Column-II
(A) $f(2)$ is equal to	(p) 0
(B) $g(0)$ is equal to	(q) 1
(C) If $\int f(x)g(x)dx = ax^3g(x)+b(1+x^2)^{3/2}+c(1+x^2)^{1/2}+d$, then $a+c$ is equal to	(r) 2
(D) If $\int e^{g(x)}dx = ax(x+\sqrt{1+x^2}+ag(x)+c)$ then a is equal to	(s) $\frac{1}{2}$
	(t) $\frac{1}{3}$

20.

Column-I	Column-II
(A) $\sqrt{2}\int_0^{\infty}\left[\frac{3}{x^2+1}\right]dx$ is equal to	(p) 1
(B) $\ln 3\int_{-10}^{10}\frac{3^x}{3^{[x]}}dx$ is equal to	(q) 2
(C) $\int_{-1}^{1}[x[1+\sin\pi x]+1]dx$ is equal to	(r) 3
(D) If $\int_0^{\pi/3}\left\{a^2\left(\frac{\cos 3x}{4}+\frac{3}{4}\cos x\right)a\sin x - 20\cos x\, dx \le -\frac{a^2}{3}\right\}$, then a can be equal to	(s) 4
(In all of the above, [.] represents the greatest integer function)	(t) 40

RESPONSE GRID	
	19. A - (p)(q)(r)(s); B - (p)(q)(r)(s); C - (p)(q)(r)(s); D - (p)(q)(r)(s)
	20. A - (p)(q)(r)(s); B - (p)(q)(r)(s); C - (p)(q)(r)(s); D - (p)(q)(r)(s)

DAILY PRACTICE PROBLEM DPP CM20 - MATHEMATICS			
Total Questions	20	Total Marks	74
Attempted		Correct	
Incorrect		Net Score	
Cut-off Score	24	Qualifying Score	35

Net Score = $\sum_{i=I}^{V}$[(correct × MM) − (In × NM)]

Space for Rough Work

DPP - Daily Practice Problems

Chapter-wise Sheets

Date : | **Start Time :** | **End Time :**

MATHEMATICS CM21

SYLLABUS : Application of Integrals

Max. Marks : 69 **Time : 60 min.**

GENERAL INSTRUCTIONS

- The Daily Practice Problem Sheet contains 20 Questions divided into 5 sections.
  Section I has **5** MCQs with ONLY 1 Correct Option, **3** marks for each correct answer and **–1** for each incorrect answer.
  Section II has **4** MCQs with ONE or MORE THAN ONE Correct options.
  For each question, marks will be awarded in one of the following categories:
  Full marks: **+4** If only the bubble(s) corresponding to all the correct option(s) is (are) darkened.
  Partial marks: **+1** For darkening a bubble corresponding to each correct option provided NO INCORRECT option is darkened.
  Zero marks: If none of the bubbles is darkened.
  Negative marks: **–2** In all other cases.
  Section III has **5** Single Digit Integer Answer Type Questions, **3** marks for each Correct Answer and **0** mark in all other cases.
  Section IV has Comprehension/Matching Cum-Comprehension Type Questions having **5** MCQs with ONLY ONE corect option, **3** marks for each Correct Answer and **0** mark in all other cases.
  Section V has **1** Matching Type Questions, **2** marks for the correct matching of each row and **0** mark in all other cases.
- You have to evaluate your Response Grids yourself with the help of Solutions.

Section I - Straight Objective Type

This section contains 5 multiple choice questions. Each question has 4 choices (a), (b), (c) and (d), out of which **ONLY ONE** is correct.

1. The area bounded by $y = \sec^{-1} x$, $y = \operatorname{cosec}^{-1} x$ and line $x - 1 = 0$ is

(a) $\left(\log(3+2\sqrt{2}) - \frac{\pi}{2}\right)$ sq.units

(b) $\left(\frac{\pi}{2} - \log(3+2\sqrt{2})\right)$ sq.units

(c) $(\pi - \log_e 3)$ sq. units

(d) None of these

2. The area of the loop of the curve, $ay^2 = x^2(a-x)$ is

(a) $4a^2$ sq. units (b) $\frac{8a^2}{15}$ sq.units

(c) $\frac{16a^2}{9}$ sq.units (d) None of these

RESPONSE GRID 1. ⓐⓑⓒⓓ 2. ⓐⓑⓒⓓ

Space for Rough Work

3. The area enclosed by the curves, $xy^2 = a^2(a-x)$ and $(a-x)y^2 = a^2x$ is

(a) $(\pi-2)a^2$ sq. units (b) $(4-\pi)a^2$ sq. units

(c) $\pi a^2/3$ sq. units (d) None of these

4. If $f(x) = \begin{cases} \sqrt{\{x\}}, & x \notin z \\ 1, & x \in z \end{cases}$ and $g(x) = \{x\}^2$, (where {.} denotes fractional part of x), then area bounded by $f(x)$ and $g(x)$ for $x \in [0,10]$ is

(a) 5/3 (b) 5

(c) 10/3 (d) None of these

5. The area bounded by $y = 2-|2-x|, y = \frac{3}{|x|}$ is

(a) $\left(\frac{5-4\ln 2}{3}\right)$ sq. units

(b) $\left(\frac{2-\ln 3}{2}\right)$ sq. units

(c) $\left(\frac{4-3\ln 3}{2}\right)$ sq. units

(d) None of these

Section II - Multiple Correct Answer Type

This section contains 4 multiple correct answer(s) type questions. Each question has 4 choices (a), (b), (c) and (d), out of which **ONE OR MORE** is/are correct.

6. $y = f(x)$ and $y = g(x)$ are two continuous positive functions intersecting only at three points (0, 1), (3, 4) and (5, 6). A function $h(x) = \max.(f(x),$ $g(x))$ is defined as $h(x) = \begin{cases} f(x), 0 \le x < 3 \\ g(x), 3 \le x \le 5 \end{cases}$.

If $\int_0^5 f(x)\,dx = a,$ $\int_0^5 g(x)\,dx = b, \int_3^5 f(x)\,dx = c, \int_0^3 g(x)\,dx = d,$ then area of region bounded between $f(x)$ and $g(x)$ from $x = 0$ to $x = 5$ is

(a) $a - 2c + b - d$

(b) $a + b - 2c - 2d$

(c) $\int_0^3 f(x)\,dx + \int_5^3 f(x)\,dx + \int_3^0 g(x)\,dx + \int_3^5 g(x)\,dx$

(d) $\int_0^3 (g(x) - f(x))\,dx + \int_3^5 (f(x) - g(x))\,dx$

7. Which of the following have the same bounded area ?

(a) $f(x) = \sin x, g(x) = \sin^2 x$, where $0 \le x \le 10\pi$

(b) $f(x) = \sin x, g(x) = |\sin x|$, where $0 \le x \le 20\pi$

(c) $f(x) = |\sin x|, g(x) = \sin^3 x$, where $0 \le x \le 10\pi$

(d) $f(x) = \sin x, g(x) = \sin^4 x$, where $0 \le x \le 10\pi$

8. Let f and g be continuous function on $a \le x \le b$ and $p(x) = \max\{f(x), g(x)\}$ and $q(x) = \min\{f(x), g(x)\}$. The area bounded by the curves $y = p(x)$, $y = q(x)$ and the ordinates $x = a$ and $x = b$ is given by

(a) $\int_a^b (f(x) - g(x))dx$ (b) $\int_a^b (p(x) - q(x))dx$

(c) $\int_a^b |p(x) - q(x)|dx$ (d) $\int_a^b |f(x) - g(x)|dx$

9. Let S be the area of the region enclosed by $y = e^{-x^2}$, $y = 0, x = 0$ and $x = 1$; then

(a) $S \ge \frac{1}{e}$ (b) $S \ge 1 - \frac{1}{e}$

(c) $S \le \frac{1}{4}\left(1 + \frac{1}{\sqrt{e}}\right)$ (d) $S \le \frac{1}{\sqrt{2}} + \frac{1}{\sqrt{e}}\left(1 - \frac{1}{\sqrt{2}}\right)$

RESPONSE GRID	
	3. (a)(b)(c)(d) 4. (a)(b)(c)(d) 5. (a)(b)(c)(d) 6. (a)(b)(c)(d) 7. (a)(b)(c)(d)
	8. (a)(b)(c)(d) 9. (a)(b)(c)(d)

Space for Rough Work

Section III - Integer Type

This section contains 5 questions. The answer to each of the questions is a single digit integer ranging from 0 to 9.

10. The area of the region bounded between the curves $|y|-|\sin x|\geq 0$ and $x^2+y^2-\pi^2\leq 0$ is π^3-A. Find the value of A.

11. Area of the region bounded by the curve $y=\{x^2\}$, where $\{.\}$ denotes fractional part function $\forall\ x\in[-2, 2]$ is $p\left(\sqrt{q}+\sqrt{r}-\frac{7}{3}\right)$. Find the value of $p+q+r$.

12. If the area of the region bounded by the curves $|y+x|\leq 1$, $|y-x|\leq 1$ and $3x^2+3y^2=1$ is $\left(p-\frac{\pi}{p+1}\right)$ square unit then p is equal to

13. If $14+1nk$ be the area bounded by the curves $|y|=e^{-|x|}-\frac{1}{2}$ and $\frac{|x|+|y|}{2}+\left|\frac{|x|-|y|}{2}\right|\leq 2$ then k is equal to

14. If the total area between the curves $f(x)=\cos^{-1}(\sin x)$ and $g(x)=\sin^{-1}(\cos x)$ on the interval $[0, 98\pi]$ is A, then find the last digit of A (Given $\pi=22/7$).

Section IV - Comprehension/Matching Cum-Comprehension Type

Directions (Qs. 15 and 16) : Based upon the given paragraph, 2 multiple choice questions have to be answered. Each question has 4 choices (a), (b), (c) and (d), out of which **ONLY ONE** is correct.

PARAGRAPH

Consider the areas S_0, S_1, S_2, ... bounded by the x-axis and half- waves of the curve $y=e^{-x}\sin x$, where $x\geq 0$.

15. The value of S_0 is

(a) $\frac{1}{2}(1+e^{\pi})$ sq. units

(b) $\frac{1}{2}(1+e^{-\pi})$ sq. units

(c) $\frac{1}{2}(1-e^{-\pi})$ sq. units

(d) $\frac{1}{2}(e^{\pi}-1)$ sq. units

16. The sequence S_0, S_1, S_2, ... forms a G.P. with common ratio

(a) $\frac{e^{\pi}}{2}$ (b) $e^{-\pi}$

(c) e^{π} (d) $\frac{e^{-\pi}}{2}$

Directions (Qs. 17-19) : This passage contains a table having 3 columns and 4 rows. Based on the table, there are three questions. Each question has four options (a), (b), (c) and (d) **ONLY ONE** of these four options is correct.

Column 1 contains information about equations in two variables x and y where p, q and k are arbitrary constants.

Column 2 contains information about shape of the graphs of given equations in column-1.

Column 3 contains information about the area of the regions bounded by the graphs in column-2.

RESPONSE GRID	
10. ⓪①②③④⑤⑥⑦⑧⑨	11. ⓪①②③④⑤⑥⑦⑧⑨
12. ⓪①②③④⑤⑥⑦⑧⑨	13. ⓪①②③④⑤⑥⑦⑧⑨
14. ⓪①②③④⑤⑥⑦⑧⑨	15. ⓐⓑⓒⓓ 16. ⓐⓑⓒⓓ

Space for Rough Work

Column 1	Column 2	Column 3
(I) $\|x-p\|+\|y-q\|=k$	(i) Rectangle	(P) $\frac{2k^2}{pq}$
(II) $\|x-p\|-\|y-q\|=k$	(ii) Rhombus	(Q) $2k^2$
(III) $p\|x\|+q\|y\|=k$	(iii) Square	(R) Undetermined
(IV) $\|x+y\|=p$ and $\|x-y\|=q$	(iv) Non-quadrilateral	(S) $2pq$

17. Which of the following options is the only correct combination?
(a) (II) (i) (S) (b) (III) (ii) (P) (c) (I) (iii) (S) (d) (IV) (ii) (P)

18. For $\left|x-\frac{1}{p}\right|+\left|y-\frac{1}{q}\right|=k,$ the area bounded by region is similar to
(a) (I) (iii) (Q) (b) (II) (iv) (R) (c) (III) (ii) (P) (d) (IV) (i) (S)

19. Which of the following options is the only incorrect combination?
(a) (I) (iii) (Q) (b) (III) (ii) (P) (c) (II) (iv) (R) (d) (IV) (i) (Q)

Section V - Matrix-Match Type

This section contains 1 questions. It contains statements given in two columns, which have to be matched. Statements in column I are labelled as A, B, C and D whereas statements in column II are labelled as p, q, r and s. The answers to these questions have to be appropriately bubbled as illustrated in the following example. If the correct matches are A-p, A-r, B-p, B-s, C-r, C-s and D-q, then the correctly bubbled matrix will look like the following:

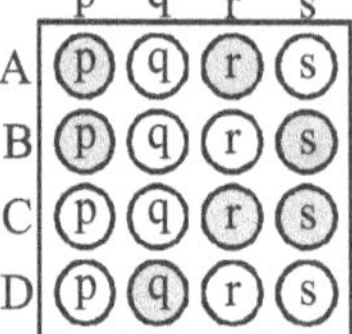

20.

Column - I	Column - II
(A) Area enclosed by $y=[x]$ and $y=\{x\}$, where [.] and {.} represent greatest integer and fractional part functions, is	(p) 16/5 sq. units
(B) The area bounded by the curves $y^2=x^3$ and $\|y\|=2x$, is	(q) 1 sq. units
(C) The smaller area included between the curves $\sqrt{x}+\sqrt{\|y\|}=1$ and $\|x\|+\|y\|=1$, is	(r) 4 sq. units
(D) Area bounded by the curves $y=\left[\frac{x^2}{64}+2\right]$ (where [.] denotes the greatest integer function), $y=x-1$ and $x=0$ above the x-axis, is	(s) 2/3 sq. units

RESPONSE GRID	
	17. ⓐⓑⓒⓓ 18. ⓐⓑⓒⓓ 19. ⓐⓑⓒⓓ
	20. A - ⓟⓠⓡⓢ; B - ⓟⓠⓡⓢ; C - ⓟⓠⓡⓢ; D - ⓟⓠⓡⓢ

DAILY PRACTICE PROBLEM DPP CM21 - MATHEMATICS			
Total Questions	20	Total Marks	69
Attempted		Correct	
Incorrect		Net Score	
Cut-off Score	22	Qualifying Score	33

$$\text{Net Score}=\sum_{i=I}^{V}\left[\left(\text{correct}_i \times MM_i\right)-\left(In_i - NM_i\right)\right]$$

Space for Rough Work

DPP - Daily Practice Problems

Chapter-wise Sheets

Date : ______ **Start Time :** ______ **End Time :** ______

MATHEMATICS (CM22)

SYLLABUS : Differential Equations

Max. Marks : 74 **Time : 60 min.**

GENERAL INSTRUCTIONS

- The Daily Practice Problem Sheet contains 20 Questions divided into 5 sections.
  Section I has **5** MCQs with ONLY 1 Correct Option, **3** marks for each correct answer and **–1** for each incorrect answer.
  Section II has **4** MCQs with ONE or MORE THAN ONE Correct options.
  For each question, marks will be awarded in one of the following categories:
  Full marks: **+4** If only the bubble(s) corresponding to all the correct option(s) is (are) darkened.
  Partial marks: **+1** For darkening a bubble corresponding to each correct option provided NO INCORRECT option is darkened.
  Zero marks: If none of the bubbles is darkened.
  Negative marks: **–2** In all other cases.
  Section III has **4** Single Digit Integer Answer Type Questions, **3** marks for each Correct Answer and **0** mark in all other cases.
  Section IV has Comprehension/Matching Cum–Comprehension Type Questions having **5** MCQs with ONLY ONE corect option, **3** marks for each Correct Answer and **0** mark in all other cases.
  Section V has **2** Matching Type Questions, **2** marks for the correct matching of each row and **0** mark in all other cases.
- You have to evaluate your Response Grids yourself with the help of Solutions.

Section I - Straight Objective Type

This section contains 5 multiple choice questions. Each question has 4 choices (a), (b), (c) and (d), out of which **ONLY ONE** is correct.

1. The gradient of the curve passing through the point (4, 0) is given by $\frac{dy}{dx}-\frac{y}{x}+\frac{5x}{(x+2)(x-3)}=0$. If the point $(5, a)$ lies on the curve, then the value of 'a', is

(a) $5\ln\frac{7}{12}$ (b) $\frac{67}{12}$

(c) $5\sin\frac{7}{12}$ (d) None of these

2. If for the differential equation $y'=\frac{y}{x}+\phi\left(\frac{x}{y}\right)$, the general solution is $y=\frac{x}{\log|Cx|}$, then $\phi(x/y)$ is given by

(a) $-x^2/y^2$ (b) y^2/x^2

(c) x^2/y^2 (d) $-y^2/x^2$

RESPONSE GRID	1. ⓐⓑⓒⓓ	2. ⓐⓑⓒⓓ

Space for Rough Work

3. If $\phi(x)$ is a differentiable function, then the solution of the differential equation $dy + \{y\phi'(x) - \phi(x)\phi'(x)\}\, dx = 0$ is
(a) $y = \{\phi(x) - 1\} + ce^{-\phi(x)}$
(b) $y\phi(x) = \{\phi(x)\}^2 + c$
(c) $ye^{\phi(x)} = \phi(x)e^{\phi(x)} + c$
(d) $y - \phi(x) = \phi(x)\, e^{-\phi(x)}$

4. Choose the incorrect statements
(a) The order of differential equation $\sqrt{1+\frac{d^2y}{dx^2}} = x$ is 1.
(b) The solution of differential equation
$x\,dy - y\,dx = \sqrt{x^2+y^2}\,dx$ is
$y + \sqrt{x^2+y^2} = cx^2$.
(c) $\frac{d^2y}{dx^2} = 2\left(\frac{dy}{dx} - y\right)$ is differential equation of family curves $y = e^x (A\cos x + B\sin x)$.
(d) The solution of differential equation
$(1+y^2) + (x - 2e^{\tan^{-1}y})\frac{dy}{dx} = 0$ is
$xe^{\tan^{-1}y} = e^{2\tan^{-1}y} + k$

5. The solution of $\frac{xdx + ydy}{xdy - ydx} = \sqrt{\frac{a^2 - x^2 - y^2}{x^2+y^2}}$ is
(a) $\sqrt{x^2+y^2} = a\left\{\sin\left(\tan^{-1}\frac{y}{x} + c\right)\right\}$
(b) $\sqrt{x^2+y^2} = a\cos\left\{\left(\tan^{-1}\frac{y}{x} + c\right)\right\}$
(c) $\sqrt{x^2+y^2} = a\left\{\tan\left(\sin^{-1}\frac{y}{x} + c\right)\right\}$
(d) None of these

6. The differential equation $\frac{d^2x}{dy^2} + y + \cot^2 x = 0$ must be satisfied by
(a) $2 + c_1\cos x + \sqrt{c_2}\sin x$
(b) $\cos x.\ln\left(\tan\frac{x}{2}\right) + 2$
(c) $2 + c_1\cos x + c_2\sin x + \cos x\log\left(\tan\frac{x}{2}\right)$
(d) all the above

7. The curve for which the area of the triangle formed by the x-axis, the tangent line and radius vector of the point of tangency is equal to a^2 is
(a) $x = cy + \frac{a^2}{y}$
(b) $y = x - cx^2$
(c) $y = cx + \frac{a^2}{x}$
(d) $x = cy - \frac{a^2}{y}$
(where c is arbitrary constant)

8. Which one of the following functions is / are homogeneous ?
(a) $f(x,y) = \frac{x-y}{x^2+y^2}$
(b) $f(x,y) = x^{\frac{1}{3}}y^{-\frac{2}{3}}\tan^{-1}\frac{x}{y}$
(c) $f(x,y) = x\,(\ln\sqrt{x^2+y^2} - \ln y) + ye^{x/y}$
(d) $f(x,y) = x\left[\ln\frac{2x^2+y^2}{x} - \ln(x+y)\right] + y^2\tan\frac{x+2y}{3x-y}$

9. The orthogonal trajectories of the family of coaxial circle $x^2+y^2+2gx+c=0$, where g is a parameter are
(a) family of circles with center on y-axis
(b) system of coaxial parabolas
(c) $x^2+y^2-c'x-cy=0$, where c' is an arbitrary constant
(d) system of coaxial circles with radical axis along x-axis

Section II - Multiple Correct Answer Type

This section contains 4 multiple correct answer(s) type questions. Each question has 4 choices (a), (b), (c) and (d), out of which **ONE OR MORE** is/are correct.

Section III - Integer Type

This section contains 4 questions. The answer to each of the questions is a single digit integer ranging from 0 to 9.

10. If the equation of a curve $y = y(x)$ satisfies the differential equation
$x\int_0^x y(t)dt = (x+1)\int_0^x ty(t)dt,\ x > 0$, and $y(1) = e$, then $y\left(\frac{1}{2}\right)$ is equal to

RESPONSE GRID	
3. ⓐⓑⓒⓓ 4. ⓐⓑⓒⓓ 5. ⓐⓑⓒⓓ 6. ⓐⓑⓒⓓ 7. ⓐⓑⓒⓓ	
8. ⓐⓑⓒⓓ 9. ⓐⓑⓒⓓ 10. ⓪①②③④⑤⑥⑦⑧⑨	

11. The population of a country increases at a rate proportional to the number of inhabitants. If the population doubles in 30 years then the number of years in the nearest integer when the population will triple is equal to 6 m, where m equals,

12. If the differential equation corresponding to $y=\sum_{i=1}^{3} C_i e^{m_i x}$ where C_i's are arbitrary constants and m_1, m_2, m_3 are roots of $m^3-7m+6=0$ is $\frac{d^3y}{dx^3}-7\frac{dy}{dx}+ky=0$ then k is equal to

13. Find the degree of the following differential equations:

$$\left(\frac{dy}{dx}\right)^4-2x\left(\frac{d^3y}{dx^3}\right)^2=x^2y\frac{d^2y}{dx^2}-\frac{d^3y}{dx^3}$$

Section IV - Comprehension/Matching Cum-Comprehension Type

Directions (Qs. 14 and 15) : Based upon the given paragraph, 2 multiple choice questions have to be answered. Each question has 4 choices (a), (b), (c) and (d), out of which **ONLY ONE** is correct.

PARAGRAPH

For certain curves $y=f(x)$ satisfying $\frac{d^2y}{dx^2}=6x-4$, $f(x)$ has local minimum value 5 when $x=1$.

14. Number of critical point for $y=f(x)$ for $x\in[0,2]$ is
(a) 0 (b) 1
(c) 2 (d) 3

15. Global minimum value of $y=f(x)$ for $x\in[0,2]$ is
(a) 5 (b) 7
(c) 8 (d) 9

Directions (Qs. 16-18) : This passage contains a table having 3 columns and 4 rows. Based on the table, there are two questions. Each question has four options (a), (b), (c) and (d) **ONLY ONE** of these four options is correct.

PARAGRAPH

Appropriately match the information given in the three columns of the given table.

	Column 1 [Differential Equations]		Column 2 [Integrating factors (I.F.)]		Column 3 [Solutions of Differential equations]
(I)	$(1+x^2)\frac{dy}{dx}+2xy-4x^2=0$	(i)	$e^{x/\sqrt{1-x^2}}$	(P)	$x=y^3+cy$
(II)	$(x+2y^3)\frac{dy}{dx}=y$	(ii)	$e^{-x}(1+x)$	(Q)	$y(1+x^2)=\frac{4}{3}x^3+c$
(III)	$(1+x)\frac{dy}{dx}-xy=1-x$	(iii)	$2y^2$	(R)	$y=\frac{x}{\sqrt{1-x^2}}+ce^{-x/\sqrt{1-x^2}}$
(IV)	$\frac{dy}{dx}+\frac{y}{(1-x^2)^{3/2}}=\frac{x+\sqrt{1-x^2}}{(1-x^2)^2}$	(iv)	$1+x^2$	(S)	$y(1+x)=x+ce^x$

16. Which of the following options is the only correct combination?
(a) (I) (i) (R) (b) (II) (ii) (S)
(c) (III) (iv) (P) (d) (IV) (i) (R)

17. Which of the following options is the only correct combination?
(a) (IV) (iii) (R) (b) (II) (iv) (P)
(c) (III) (ii) (S) (d) (I) (i) (S)

18. Which of the following options is the only incorrect combination?
(a) (II) (iv) (R) (b) (III) (ii) (S)
(c) (I) (iv) (Q) (d) (IV) (i) (R)

RESPONSE GRID	
	11. ⓪①②③④⑤⑥⑦⑧⑨ 12. ⓪①②③④⑤⑥⑦⑧⑨
	13. ⓪①②③④⑤⑥⑦⑧⑨ 14. ⓐⓑⓒⓓ 15. ⓐⓑⓒⓓ
	16. ⓐⓑⓒⓓ 17. ⓐⓑⓒⓓ 18. ⓐⓑⓒⓓ

Space for Rough Work

Section V - Matrix-Match Type

This section contains 2 questions. It contains statements given in two columns, which have to be matched. Statements in column I are labelled as A, B, C and D whereas statements in column II are labelled as p, q, r and s. The answers to these questions have to be appropriately bubbled as illustrated in the following example. If the correct matches are A-p, A-r, B-p, B-s, C-r, C-s and D-q, then the correctly bubbled matrix will look like the following:

	p	q	r	s
A	(p)	(q)	(r)	(s)
B	(p)	(q)	(r)	(s)
C	(p)	(q)	(r)	(s)
D	(p)	(q)	(r)	(s)

19. Let a function $y = f(x)$ satisfies the following conditions

1. $\frac{dy}{dx} = y + \int_0^1 y\,dx$ 2. $f(0) = 1$

Column-I	Column-II
A. $f''(0)$ is equal to	(p) $f(0)$
B. $f(1)$ is equal to	(q) $\frac{2}{3-e}$
C. $\lim_{x \to 0} \frac{f(x)-1}{x}$ is equal to	(r) $\frac{e+1}{3-e}$
D. $\frac{1}{2}f'(\ln(3\text{-}e))$ is equal to	(s) $f'(0)$
	(t) 1

20.

Column-I	Column-II
(A) Let $f(x)$ is a derivable function satisfying $f(x) = \int_0^x e^t \sin(x-t)\,dt$ and $g(x) = f''(x) - f(x)$ then the possible integers in the range of $g(x)$ is	(p) -1
(B) If the substitution $x = \tan^{-1}(t)$ transforms the differential equation $\frac{d^2y}{dx^2} + xy\frac{dy}{dx} + \sec^2 x = 0$ into a differential equation $(1+t^2)\frac{d^2y}{dt^2} + (2t + y\tan^{-1}(t))\frac{dy}{dt} = k$ then k is equal to	(q) 0
(C) If $a^2 + b^2 = 1$ then $(a^3b - ab^3)$ can be equal to	(r) 1
(D) If the system of equations $\left.\begin{matrix} x - \lambda y - z = 0 \\ \lambda x - y - z = 0 \\ x + y - z = 0 \end{matrix}\right\}$ has a unique solution, then the value of λ can be	(s) 2

RESPONSE GRID	
	19. A - (p)(q)(r)(s); B - (p)(q)(r)(s); C - (p)(q)(r)(s); D - (p)(q)(r)(s)
	20. A - (p)(q)(r)(s); B - (p)(q)(r)(s); C - (p)(q)(r)(s); D - (p)(q)(r)(s)

DAILY PRACTICE PROBLEM DPP CM22 - MATHEMATICS			
Total Questions	20	Total Marks	74
Attempted		Correct	
Incorrect		Net Score	
Cut-off Score	22	Qualifying Score	32

$$\text{Net Score} = \sum_{i=1}^{V}\left[(\text{correct}_i \times MM_i) - (In_i - NM_i)\right]$$

Space for Rough Work

DPP - Daily Practice Problems

Chapter-wise Sheets

Date :   Start Time :   End Time :

MATHEMATICS (CM23)

SYLLABUS : Vector Algebra

Max. Marks : 69   **Time : 60 min.**

GENERAL INSTRUCTIONS

- The Daily Practice Problem Sheet contains 20 Questions divided into 5 sections.
  Section I has **6** MCQs with ONLY 1 Correct Option, **3** marks for each correct answer and **–1** for each incorrect answer.
  Section II has **4** MCQs with ONE or MORE THAN ONE Correct options.
  For each question, marks will be awarded in one of the following categories:
  Full marks: **+4** If only the bubble(s) corresponding to all the correct option(s) is (are) darkened.
  Partial marks: **+1** For darkening a bubble corresponding to each correct option provided NO INCORRECT option is darkened.
  Zero marks: If none of the bubbles is darkened.
  Negative marks: **–2** In all other cases.
  Section III has **5** Single Digit Integer Answer Type Questions, **3** marks for each Correct Answer and **0** mark in all other cases.
  Section IV has Comprehension Type Questions having **4** MCQs with ONLY ONE corect option, **3** marks for each Correct Answer and **0** mark in all other cases.
  Section V has **1** Matching Type Question, **2** marks for the correct matching of each row and **0** mark in all other cases.
- You have to evaluate your Response Grids yourself with the help of Solutions.

Section I - Straight Objective Type

This section contains 6 multiple choice questions. Each question has 4 choices (a), (b), (c) and (d), out of which **ONLY ONE** is correct.

1. Let $\vec{a} = 2\hat{i} + \hat{j} - 2\hat{k}, \vec{b} = \hat{i} + \hat{j}$. If $\vec{c}$ is a vector such that $\vec{a} \bullet \vec{c} = |\vec{c}|, |\vec{c} - \vec{a}| = 2\sqrt{2}$ and the angle between $\vec{a} \times \vec{b}$ and $\vec{c}$ is 30°, then $|(\vec{a} \times \vec{b}) \times \vec{c}|$ equals:

(a) $\frac{1}{2}$ (b) $\frac{3\sqrt{3}}{2}$

(c) 3   (d) $\frac{3}{2}$

2. If $\hat{x}, \hat{y}$ and $\hat{z}$ are three unit vectors in three-dimensional space, then the minimum value of $|\hat{x} + \hat{y}|^2 + |\hat{y} + \hat{z}|^2 + |\hat{z} + \hat{x}|^2$

(a) $\frac{3}{2}$ (b) 3

(c) $3\sqrt{3}$ (d) 6

3. $ABCD$ is parallelogram. The position vectors of A and C are respectively, $3\hat{i} + 3\hat{j} + 5\hat{k}$ and $\hat{i} - 5\hat{j} - 5\hat{k}$. If M is the midpoint of the diagonal DB, then the magnitude of the projection of $\overrightarrow{OM}$ on $\overrightarrow{OC}$, where O is the origin, is

(a) $7\sqrt{51}$ (b) $\frac{7}{\sqrt{50}}$

(c) $7\sqrt{50}$ (d) $\frac{7}{\sqrt{51}}$

RESPONSE GRID	1. ⓐⓑⓒⓓ	2. ⓐⓑⓒⓓ	3. ⓐⓑⓒⓓ

Space for Rough Work

4. Let $\vec{p} = a\hat{i} + b\hat{j} + c\hat{k}$ and $\vec{q} = b\hat{i} + c\hat{j} + a\hat{k}$, where a, b, $c \in R$. If 'θ' be the angle between $\vec{p}$ and $\vec{q}$ then,

(a) $\theta \in (0, \pi/2)$ (b) $\theta \in [0, 2\pi/3]$

(c) $\theta \in (2\pi/3, \pi]$ (d) $\theta \in [\pi/2, \pi]$

5. If $\cos\alpha \neq 1, \cos\beta \neq 1$ and $\cos\gamma \neq 1$, then the vector $\vec{a} = \hat{i}\cos\alpha + \hat{j} + \hat{k}, \vec{b} = \hat{i} + \hat{j}\cos\beta + \hat{k}$, $\vec{c} = \hat{i} + \hat{j} + \hat{k}\cos\gamma$ are

(a) Coplanar vectors

(b) Coplanar vectors if $\cos\alpha = \cos\beta = \cos\gamma \neq 1$

(c) Coplanar vectors if $\cos\alpha \neq \cos\beta \neq \cos\gamma$

(d) Never coplanar

6. If the vector $\vec{b} = (\tan\alpha, -1, 2\sqrt{\sin\alpha/2})$ and $\vec{c} = \left(\tan\alpha, \tan\alpha, -\frac{3}{\sqrt{\sin\alpha/2}}\right)$ are orthogonal and a vector $\vec{a} = (1, 3, \sin 2\alpha)$ makes an obtuse angle with the z-axis then the value of α is

(a) $\alpha = (4n+1)\pi - \tan^{-1}2$

(b) $\alpha = (4n+2)\pi - \tan^{-1}2$

(c) $\alpha = (4n+1)\pi + \tan^{-1}2$

(d) $\alpha = (4n+2)\pi + \tan^{-1}2$

Section II - Multiple Correct Answer Type

This section contains 4 multiple correct answer(s) type questions. Each question has 4 choices (a), (b), (c) and (d), out of which **ONE OR MORE** is/are correct.

7. If $\vec{b}$ is vector whose initial point divides the join of $5\hat{i}$ and $5\hat{j}$ in the ratio $k:1$ and terminal point is origin and $|\vec{b}| \leq \sqrt{37}$, then k belongs to

(a) $\left[-6, -\frac{1}{6}\right]$ (b) $(-\infty, -6) \cup \left[-\frac{1}{6}, \infty\right)$

(c) $[0, 6]$ (d) $\left[-\frac{1}{6}, \infty\right)$

8. Let $\vec{a} = \alpha\hat{i} + 2\hat{j} - 3\hat{k}, \vec{b} = \hat{i} + 2\alpha\hat{j} - 2\hat{k}, \vec{c} = 2\hat{i} - \alpha\hat{j} + \hat{k}$ and $(\vec{a} \times \vec{b}) \times (\vec{b} \times \vec{c})\} \times (\vec{c} \times \vec{a}) = \vec{0}$, then

(a) $\alpha = \frac{2}{3}$

(b) if $\alpha = 0$, then given vectors product is $-60(2\hat{i} + \hat{k})$

(c) $(\vec{a}.\vec{b})\vec{c} - (\vec{b}.\vec{c})\vec{a} = 0$ will give no real value of α

(d) none of these

9. Let ΔPQR be a triangle. Let $\vec{a} = \overline{QR}, \vec{b} = \overline{RP}$ and $\vec{c} = \overline{PQ}$. If $|\vec{a}| = 12$, $|\vec{b}| = 4\sqrt{3}$, $\vec{b}.\vec{c} = 24$, then which of the following is (are) true?

(a) $\frac{|\vec{c}|^2}{2} - |\vec{a}| = 12$ (b) $\frac{|\vec{c}|^2}{2} + |\vec{a}| = 30$

(c) $|\vec{a} \times \vec{b} + \vec{c} \times \vec{a}| = 48\sqrt{3}$ (d) $\vec{a}.\vec{b} = -72$

10. Let $\vec{x}$, $\vec{y}$ and $\vec{z}$ be three vectors each of magnitude $\sqrt{2}$ and the angle between each pair of them is $\frac{\pi}{3}$. If $\vec{a}$ is a non-zero vector perpendicular to $\vec{x}$ and $\vec{y} \times \vec{z}$ and $\vec{b}$ is a non-zero vector perpendicular to $\vec{y}$ and $\vec{z} \times \vec{x}$, then

(a) $\vec{b} = \left(\vec{b}.\vec{z}\right)\left(\vec{z} - \vec{x}\right)$

(b) $\vec{a} = \left(\vec{a}.\vec{y}\right)\left(\vec{y} - \vec{z}\right)$

(c) $\vec{a}.\vec{b} = -\left(\vec{a}.\vec{y}\right)\left(\vec{b}.\vec{z}\right)$

(d) $\vec{a} = -\left(\vec{a}.\vec{y}\right)\left(\vec{z} - \vec{y}\right)$

RESPONSE GRID	
	4. ⓐⓑⓒⓓ 5. ⓐⓑⓒⓓ 6. ⓐⓑⓒⓓ 7. ⓐⓑⓒⓓ 8. ⓐⓑⓒⓓ
	9. ⓐⓑⓒⓓ 10. ⓐⓑⓒⓓ

Space for Rough Work

Section III - Integer Type

This section contains 5 questions. The answer to each of the questions is a single digit integer ranging from 0 to 9.

11. $ABCD$ is a regular tetrahedron; A is the origin; AB is the x-axis; ABC lies in the xy-plane; $AB = d$. Under these conditions the number of possible tetrahedra is

12. Let $\vec{u}$ and $\vec{v}$ be two unit vectors. If $\vec{w}$ be any vector such that $\vec{w}+(\vec{w}\times\vec{u})=\vec{v}$, then the least value of $|(\vec{u}\times\vec{v}).\vec{w}|^{-1}$ is equal to

13. Let $\vec{a}=\hat{i}+\hat{j}+\hat{k}, \vec{b}=x_1\hat{i}+x_2\hat{j}+x_3\hat{k}$, where $x_1, x_2, x_3 \in \{-3,-2,-1,0,1,2\}$.

Number of possible vectors $\vec{b}$ such that $\vec{a}$ and $\vec{b}$ are mutually perpendicular is 5k, where k equals.

14. Two points P and Q are given in the rectangular cartesian co-ordinates on the curve $y=2^{x+2}$, such that $\overrightarrow{OP}.\hat{i}=-1$ and $\overrightarrow{OQ}.\hat{i}=2$, where $\hat{i}$ is a unit vector along the x-axis. The magnitude of the vector $\overrightarrow{OQ}-4\overrightarrow{OP}$, is 2k, where k equal.

15. Let $\vec{a}$, $\vec{b}$ and $\vec{c}$ be three non-coplanar unit vectors such that the angle between every pair of them is $\frac{\pi}{3}$. If $\vec{a}\times\vec{b}+\vec{b}\times\vec{c}=p\vec{a}+q\vec{b}+r\vec{c}$, where p, q and r are scalars, then the value of $\frac{p^2+2q^2+r^2}{q^2}$ is

Section IV - Comprehension Type

Based upon the given paragraphs, 4 multiple choice questions have to be answered. Each question has 4 choices (a), (b), (c) and (d), out of which **ONLY ONE** is correct.

PARAGRAPH-1

The vertices of a ΔABC are A (2, 0, 2), B (– 1, 1, 1) and C (1, –2, 4). The points D and E divide the sides AB and AC in the ratio 1 : 2 respectively. Another point F is taken in space such that perpendicular drawn from F on ΔABC meet the Δ at the point of intersection of line segment CD and BE at P. If distance of F from plane of ΔABC is $\sqrt{2}$ units, then

16. The position vector of P is

(a) $\hat{i}-\hat{j}+3\hat{k}$ (b) $\hat{i}-\hat{j}$

(c) $2\hat{i}-\hat{j}-3\hat{k}$ (d) $\hat{i}+\hat{j}+3\hat{k}$

17. The volume of tetrahedron $ABCF$ is

(a) $\frac{7}{3}$ cubic units (b) $\frac{7}{5}$ cubic units

(c) $\frac{3}{5}$ cubic units (d) 7cubic units

PARAGRAPH-2

Let $\vec{a}_1$ be projection of $\vec{a}$ on $\vec{b}$ and $\vec{a}_2$ be the projection of $\vec{a}_1$ on $\vec{c}$, then

18. $\vec{a}_2 =$

(a) $\frac{943}{49}(2\hat{i}-3\hat{j}-6\hat{k})$ (b) $\frac{943}{49^2}(2\hat{i}-3\hat{j}-6\hat{k})$

(c) $\frac{943}{49}(-2\hat{i}+3\hat{j}+6\hat{k})$ (d) $\frac{943}{49^2}(-2\hat{i}+3\hat{j}+6\hat{k})$

19. $\vec{a}_1.\vec{b} =$

(a) -41 (b) $-\frac{41}{7}$

(c) 41 (d) 287

RESPONSE GRID	
	11. ⓪①②③④⑤⑥⑦⑧⑨ 12. ⓪①②③④⑤⑥⑦⑧⑨
	13. ⓪①②③④⑤⑥⑦⑧⑨ 14. ⓪①②③④⑤⑥⑦⑧⑨
	15. ⓪①②③④⑤⑥⑦⑧⑨ 16. ⓐⓑⓒⓓ 17. ⓐⓑⓒⓓ 18. ⓐⓑⓒⓓ
	19. ⓐⓑⓒⓓ

Space for Rough Work

Section V - Matrix-Match Type

This section contains 1 question. It contains statements given in two columns, which have to be matched. Statements in column I are labelled as A, B, C and D whereas statements in column II are labelled as p, q, r and s. The answers to these questions have to be appropriately bubbled as illustrated in the following example. If the correct matches are A-p, A-r, B-p, B-s, C-r, C-s and D-q, then the correctly bubbled matrix will look like the following:

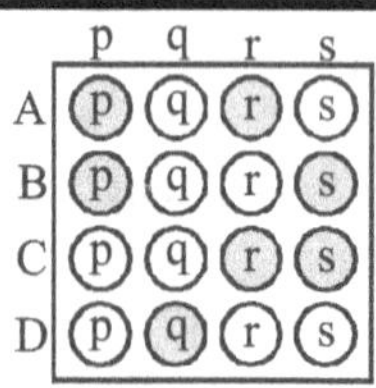

20. **Column-I** / **Column-II**

Column-I	Column-II
(A) If $\vec{a}+\vec{b}+\vec{c}=\alpha\vec{d}, \vec{b}+\vec{c}+\vec{d}=\beta\vec{a}$ and $\vec{a}, \vec{b}, \vec{c}$ are non-coplanar then the $\lvert\vec{a}+\vec{b}+\vec{c}+\vec{d}\rvert$ is	p. $\frac{2\pi}{3}$
(B) If $\vec{a}$ and $\vec{b}$ are unit vectors inclined at an angle θ to each other and $\left\lvert\vec{a}+\vec{b}\right\rvert < 1$, then θ can be equal to	q. $\frac{3\pi}{4}$
(C) If $\vec{a}$ is unit vector perpendicular to another unit vector $\vec{b}$ then $\lvert\vec{a}\times[\vec{a}\times\{\vec{a}\times(\vec{a}\times\vec{b})\}]\rvert$ is equal to	r. $\frac{5\pi}{6}$
(D) Let $\vec{a}, \vec{b}, \vec{c}$ be three unit vectors such that $\vec{a}+\vec{b}+\vec{c}=\vec{0}$, then the angle between $\vec{a}$ and $\vec{b}$ is equal to	s. 0
	t. 1

RESPONSE GRID	20. A - ⓟⓠⓡⓢ; B - ⓟⓠⓡⓢ; C - ⓟⓠⓡⓢ; D - ⓟⓠⓡⓢ

DAILY PRACTICE PROBLEM DPP CM23 - MATHEMATICS			
Total Questions	20	Total Marks	69
Attempted		Correct	
Incorrect		Net Score	
Cut-off Score	21	Qualifying Score	32

$$\text{Net Score} = \sum_{i=1}^{V}\left[(\text{correct}_i \times MM_i) - (In_i - NM_i)\right]$$

Space for Rough Work

DPP - Daily Practice Problems

Chapter-wise Sheets

Date : | Start Time : | End Time :

MATHEMATICS CM24

SYLLABUS : Three Dimensional Geometry

Max. Marks : 74 **Time : 60 min.**

GENERAL INSTRUCTIONS

- The Daily Practice Problem Sheet contains 20 Questions divided into 5 sections.
  Section I has **5** MCQs with ONLY 1 Correct Option, **3** marks for each correct answer and **–1** for each incorrect answer.
  Section II has **4** MCQs with ONE or MORE THAN ONE Correct options.
  For each question, marks will be awarded in one of the following categories:
  Full marks: **+4** If only the bubble(s) corresponding to all the correct option(s) is (are) darkened.
  Partial marks: **+1** For darkening a bubble corresponding to each correct option provided NO INCORRECT option is darkened.
  Zero marks: If none of the bubbles is darkened.
  Negative marks: **–2** In all other cases.
  Section III has **4** Single Digit Integer Answer Type Questions, **3** marks for each Correct Answer and **0** mark in all other cases.
  Section IV has Comprehension/Matching Cum-Comprehension Type Questions having **5** MCQs with ONLY ONE corect option, **3** marks for each Correct Answer and **0** mark in all other cases.
  Section V has **2** Matching Type Questions, **2** marks for the correct matching of each row and **0** mark in all other cases.
- You have to evaluate your Response Grids yourself with the help of Solutions.

Section I - Straight Objective Type

This section contains 5 multiple choice questions. Each question has 4 choices (a), (b), (c) and (d), out of which **ONLY ONE** is correct.

1. A rectangle $ABCD$ of dimension r and $2r$ is folded along diagonal BD such that planes ABD and CBD are perpendicular to each other, then the distance AC' (in new position is)

(a) $\sqrt{3}\,r$ (b) $\sqrt{85}\,r$ (c) $\frac{\sqrt{85}}{5}r$ (d) $\sqrt{\frac{17}{5}}\,r$

2. Let Q be the foot of perpendicular from the origin to the plane $4x-3y+z+13=0$ and R be a point $(-1,-6)$ on the plane. Then length QR is :

(a) $\sqrt{14}$ (b) $\sqrt{\frac{19}{2}}$

(c) $3\sqrt{\frac{7}{2}}$ (d) $\frac{3}{\sqrt{2}}$

3. Equation of the line of the shortest distance between the lines $\frac{x}{1}=\frac{y}{-1}=\frac{z}{1}$ and $\frac{x-1}{0}=\frac{y+1}{-2}=\frac{z}{1}$ is:

(a) $\frac{x}{1}=\frac{y}{-1}=\frac{z}{-2}$ (b) $\frac{x-1}{1}=\frac{y+1}{-1}=\frac{z}{-2}$

(c) $\frac{x-1}{1}=\frac{y+1}{-1}=\frac{z}{1}$ (d) $\frac{x}{-2}=\frac{y}{1}=\frac{z}{2}$

RESPONSE GRID 1. ⓐⓑⓒⓓ 2. ⓐⓑⓒⓓ 3. ⓐⓑⓒⓓ

Space for Rough Work

4. Consider the triangle AOB in the x-y plane where A ≡ (1, 0, 0); B ≡ (0,2, 0) ; and O ≡ (0, 0, 0). The new position of O, when triangle is rotated about side AB by 90° can be

(a) $\left(\frac{4}{5},\frac{3}{5},\frac{2}{\sqrt{5}}\right)$ (b) $\left(\frac{-3}{5},\frac{\sqrt{2}}{5},\frac{2}{\sqrt{5}}\right)$

(c) $\left(\frac{4}{5},\frac{2}{5},\frac{2}{\sqrt{5}}\right)$ (d) $\left(\frac{4}{5},\frac{2}{5},\frac{1}{\sqrt{5}}\right)$

5. The median AD of the triangle ABC is bisected at E, BE meets AC in F, then AF: AC =

(a) 3:4 (b) 1:3 (c) 1:2 (d) 1:4

Section II - Multiple Correct Answer Type

This section contains 4 multiple correct answer(s) type questions. Each question has 4 choices (a), (b), (c) and (d), out of which **ONE OR MORE** is/are correct.

6. If $OABC$ is a tetrahedron such that $OA^2 + BC^2 = OB^2 + CA^2 = OC^2 + AB^2$ then
   (a) OA is perpendicular to BC
   (b) OB is perpendicular to CA
   (c) OC is perpendicular to AB
   (d) AB is perpendicular to BC
7. The x-y plane in rotated about its line of intersection with the y-z plane by 45°, then the equation of the new plane is/are
   (a) z + x = 0 (b) z – y = 0
   (c) x + y + z = 0 (d) z – x = 0
8. The equation of the plane which is equally inclined to the lines $\frac{x-1}{2}=\frac{y}{-2}=\frac{z+2}{1}$ and $\frac{x+3}{8}=\frac{y-4}{1}=\frac{z}{-4}$
   (a) 14x – 5y – 7z = 0 (b) 2x + 7y – z = 0
   (c) 3x – 4y – z = 0 (d) x + 2y – 5z = 0
9. A rod of length 2 units whose one end is (1, 0 –1) and other end touches the plane x – 2y + 2z + 4 = 0, then
   (a) The rod sweeps the figure whose volume is 3π cubic units.
   (b) The area of the region which the rod traces on the plane is 2π.
   (c) The length of the projection of the rod on the plane is $\sqrt{3}$ units.
   (d) The centre of the region which the rod traces on the plane is (4/3, –2/3, 1/3).

Section III - Integer Type

This section contains 4 questions. The answer to each of the questions is a single digit integer ranging from 0 to 9.

10. P is a point and PM, PN are perpendiculars from P to the ZX and XY planes respectively. If OP makes angles θ, α, β, γ with the plane OMN and the XY, YZ, ZX plane respectively then $\sin^2\theta(\text{cosec}^2\alpha+\text{cosec}^2\beta+\text{cosec}^2\gamma)$ is equal to
11. A plane passing through (1 1, 1) cuts positive direction of co-ordinate axes at A, B and C the volume of tetrahedron OABC satisfies $V \ge \frac{k}{l}$, then $(k-l)$ equals.
12. If the ratio in which the plane $\vec{r}.(\vec{i}-2\vec{j}+3\vec{k})=17$ divides the line joining the points $-2\vec{i}+4\vec{j}+7\vec{k}$ and $3\vec{i}-5\vec{j}+8\vec{k}$ is $\frac{a}{b}$, then $|a-b|=$
13. L_1 and L_2 are two lines whose vector equations are $L_1:\vec{r}=\lambda\left((\cos\theta+\sqrt{3})\hat{i}+(\sqrt{2}\sin\theta)\hat{j}+(\cos\theta-\sqrt{3})\hat{k}\right)$
    $L_2:\vec{r}=\mu\left(a\hat{i}+b\hat{j}+c\hat{k}\right)$, where λ and μ are scalars and α is the acute angle between L_1 and L_2. If the angle 'α' (independent of θ) is equal to $\frac{\pi}{k}$, then $k=$

Section IV - Comprehension/Matching Cum-Comprehension Type

Directions (Qs. 14 and 15) : Based upon the given paragraph, 2 multiple choice questions have to be answered. Each question has 4 choices (a), (b), (c) and (d), out of which **ONLY ONE** is correct.

PARAGRAPH

If the projections of three points A, B, C on a given plane are A', B', C', then $\Delta A'B'C' = \cos\theta(\Delta ABC)$, where θ is the angle between the planes ABC and A'B'C' (i.e., the angle that the positive direction of a normal to one makes with the positive direction of a normal to the other). In general, if A_0 is the area of any plane curve and A is the area of its projection on any given plane, then $A = \cos\theta\, A_0$.

14. Suppose AB is a diameter of a circle and P is a plane through AB making an angle θ with the plane of the circle. If diameter of the circle be $2a$, then the eccentricity of the curve of projection of the circle on P is
    (a) sin θ (b) $\frac{2a\sin\theta}{1+a}$
    (c) $\frac{a\cos\theta}{1+a}$ (d) $1+\sin^2\theta$

RESPONSE GRID	
	4. ⓐⓑⓒⓓ 5. ⓐⓑⓒⓓ 6. ⓐⓑⓒⓓ 7. ⓐⓑⓒⓓ 8. ⓐⓑⓒⓓ
	9. ⓐⓑⓒⓓ 10. ⓪①②③④⑤⑥⑦⑧⑨ 11. ⓪①②③④⑤⑥⑦⑧⑨
	12. ⓪①②③④⑤⑥⑦⑧⑨ 13. ⓪①②③④⑤⑥⑦⑧⑨ 14. ⓐⓑⓒⓓ

Space for Rough Work

15. A plane makes intercepts OA, OB, OC whose measures are a, b, c on the axes OX, OY, OZ. The area of the triangle ABC is

(a) $\sqrt{a^4+b^4+c^4-a^2b^2-b^2c^2-c^2a^2}$

(b) $\frac{1}{2}\sqrt{a^2b^2+b^2c^2+c^2a^2}$

(c) $a^2+b^2+c^2-bc-ca-ab$

(d) $\frac{1}{4}\sqrt{(a+b+c)(b+c-a)(c+a-b)(a+b-c)}$

Directions (Qs. 16-18) : This passage contains a table having 3 columns and 4 rows. Based on the table, there are three questions. Each question has four options (a), (b), (c) and (d) **ONLY ONE** of these four options is correct.

Consider the lines L_1, L_2 and the planes P_1, P_2. Let $ax+by+cz=d$ be the equation of the plane passing through the point of intersection of lines L_1 and L_2, and perpendicular to planes P_1 and P_2.

Column 1, 2 and 3 contains equation of lines, equation of planes and values of a, b, c & d respectively.

Column 1	Column 2	Column 3
(I) $L_1: \frac{x-1}{2}=\frac{y}{-1}=\frac{z+3}{1}$,	(i) $P_1: 7x+y+2z=3$	(P) $a=5; b=4$
$L_2: \frac{x-4}{1}=\frac{y+3}{1}=\frac{z+3}{2}$	$P_2: 3x+5y-6z=4$	$c=-7; d=1$
(II) $L_1: \frac{x-2}{3}=\frac{y-3}{4}=\frac{z-1}{5}$,	(ii) $P_1: 2x+5y+3z=4$	(Q) $a=1; b=-2$
$L_2: \frac{x-4}{1}=\frac{y-2}{3}=\frac{z-1}{2}$	$P_2: 5x+3y+7z=3$	$c=1; d=0$
(III) $L_1: \frac{x-1}{1}=\frac{y-0}{0}=\frac{z-0}{0}$	(iii) $P_1: x+2y+3z=2$	(R) $a=1; b=-3$
$L_2: \frac{x-0}{0}=\frac{y-1}{1}=\frac{z-0}{0}$	$P_2: 2x+3y+4z=4$	$c=-2; d=13$
(IV) $L_1: \frac{x-2}{5}=\frac{y-3}{4}=\frac{z-1}{3}$	(iv) $P_1: 5x+4y+z=2$	(S) $a=2; b=3$
$L_2: \frac{x-3}{3}=\frac{y-4}{2}=\frac{z-2}{5}$	$P_2: 3x+2y+5z=4$	$c=3; d=-4$

16. Which of the following options is the only correct combination?

(a) (I) (i) (R) (b) (II) (ii) (Q) (c) (III) (iii) (P) (d) (IV) (iv) (S)

17. Which of the following options is the only correct combination?

(a) (II) (iii) (S) (b) (IV) (i) (Q) (c) (III) (iv) (P) (d) None of these

18. Which of the following options is the only correct combination?

(a) (I) (iv) (R) (b) (II) (i) (S) (c) (III) (iii) (Q) (d) (IV) (ii) (P)

RESPONSE GRID	15. ⓐⓑⓒⓓ	16. ⓐⓑⓒⓓ	17. ⓐⓑⓒⓓ	18. ⓐⓑⓒⓓ

Space for Rough Work

Section V - Matrix-Match Type

This section contains 2 questions. It contains statements given in two columns, which have to be matched. Statements in column I are labelled as A, B, C and D whereas statements in column II are labelled as p, q, r and s. The answers to these questions have to be appropriately bubbled as illustrated in the following example. If the correct matches are A-p, A-r, B-p, B-s, C-r, C-s and D-q, then the correctly bubbled matrix will look like the following:

	p	q	r	s
A	(p)	(q)	(r)	(s)
B	(p)	(q)	(r)	(s)
C	(p)	(q)	(r)	(s)
D	(p)	(q)	(r)	(s)

19. **Column I** / **Column II**

(A) If the coordinates of the mid-points of the sides BC, CA, AB of ΔABC are $(a, 0, 0), (0, b, 0), (0, 0, c)$ respectively then $\frac{AB^2+BC^2+CA^2}{a^2+b^2+c^2}$ is equal to

(B) The distance of the image of the point $(1, -2, 3)$ in the plane $x-y+z=5$ from the origin is equal to

(C) If θ be the angle between a diagonal of a cube and an edge of the cube intersecting the diagonal then $\tan\theta$ is equal to

(D) If the equation $px^2+y^2+qz^2+2yz+zx+3xy=0$ represents a pair of mutually perpendicular planes then q is equal to

p. 3/4

q. –3

r. 8

s. $\sqrt{2}$

t. $5\sqrt{2}$

20. **Column I** / **Column II**

(A) If the plane $ax-by+cz=d$ contains the line $\frac{x-a}{a}=\frac{y-2d}{b}=\frac{z-c}{c}$, then $\frac{b}{d}$ is equal to

(B) The distance of the point $(1, -2, 3)$ from the plane $x-y+z-5=0$ measured parallel to $\frac{x}{2}=\frac{y}{3}=\frac{z-1}{-6}$ is equal to

(C) If the straight lines $\frac{x-2}{1}=\frac{y-3}{1}=\frac{4-z}{k}$ and $\frac{x-1}{k}=\frac{y-4}{2}=\frac{z-5}{1}$ intersect then k is equal to

(D) If a line makes an angle θ with x and y-axis then $\cot\theta$ can be equal to

p. 0

q. 1

r. 2

s. $\frac{1}{3}$

t. –3

RESPONSE GRID	
	19. A - (p)(q)(r)(s); B - (p)(q)(r)(s); C - (p)(q)(r)(s); D - (p)(q)(r)(s)
	20. A - (p)(q)(r)(s); B - (p)(q)(r)(s); C - (p)(q)(r)(s); D - (p)(q)(r)(s)

DAILY PRACTICE PROBLEM DPP CM24 - MATHEMATICS			
Total Questions	20	Total Marks	74
Attempted		Correct	
Incorrect		Net Score	
Cut-off Score	26	Qualifying Score	36

$$\text{Net Score} = \sum_{i=I}^{V}\left[(\text{correct}_i \times MM_i) - (In_i - NM_i)\right]$$

DPP - Daily Practice Problems

Chapter-wise Sheets

Date : ☐ Start Time : ☐ End Time : ☐

MATHEMATICS (CM25)

SYLLABUS : Probability

Max. Marks : 74 **Time : 60 min.**

GENERAL INSTRUCTIONS

- The Daily Practice Problem Sheet contains 20 Questions divided into 5 sections.
  Section I has **5** MCQs with ONLY 1 Correct Option, **3** marks for each correct answer and **–1** for each incorrect answer.
  Section II has **4** MCQs with ONE or MORE THAN ONE Correct options.
  For each question, marks will be awarded in one of the following categories:
  Full marks: **+4** If only the bubble(s) corresponding to all the correct option(s) is (are) darkened.
  Partial marks: **+1** For darkening a bubble corresponding to each correct option provided NO INCORRECT option is darkened.
  Zero marks: If none of the bubbles is darkened.
  Negative marks: **–2** In all other cases.
  Section III has **4** Single Digit Integer Answer Type Questions, **3** marks for each Correct Answer and **0** mark in all other cases.
  Section IV has Comprehension/Matching Cum-Comprehension Type Questions having **5** MCQs with ONLY ONE correct option, **3** marks for each Correct Answer and **0** mark in all other cases.
  Section V has **2** Matching Type Questions, **2** marks for the correct matching of each row and **0** mark in all other cases.
- You have to evaluate your Response Grids yourself with the help of Solutions.

Section I - Straight Objective Type

This section contains 5 multiple choice questions. Each question has 4 choices (a), (b), (c) and (d), out of which **ONLY ONE** is correct.

1. The probabilities that a student passes in Mathematics, physics and chemistry are m, p and c, respectively. Of these subjects, the student has a 75% chance of passing in at least one, a 50% chance of passing in exactly two. Which of the following relations are true?

(a) $p+m+c=19/20$ (b) $p+m+c=27/20$

(c) $pmc=1/10$ (d) $pmc=1/4$

2. Raj and Sanchita are playing game in which they throw two dice alternately till one of them gets 9. Which one of the following could be the probability that Sanchita win the game?

(a) 7/15 or 8/15 (b) 6/11 or 5/11

(c) 8/17 or 9/17 (d) None of these

RESPONSE GRID	1. ⓐⓑⓒⓓ	2. ⓐⓑⓒⓓ

Space for Rough Work

3. Suppose A and B shoot independently until each hits his target. They have probabilities $\frac{3}{5}$ and $\frac{5}{7}$ of hitting the targets at each shot. The probability that B will require more shots than A is

(a) $\frac{6}{31}$ (b) $\frac{7}{31}$ (c) $\frac{8}{31}$ (d) $\frac{1}{2}$

4. Two persons A and B agree to meet at a place between 5 to 6 p.m. The first one to arrive waits for 20 minutes and then leaves. If the time of their arrival be independent and at random, then the probability that A and B meet is

(a) $\frac{1}{3}$ (b) $\frac{4}{9}$ (c) $\frac{5}{9}$ (d) $\frac{2}{3}$

5. If X has a binomial distribution, B(n, p) with parameters n and p such that $P(X=2)=P(X=3)$, then E(X), the mean of variable X, is

(a) $2-p$ (b) $3-p$

(c) $\frac{p}{2}$ (d) $\frac{p}{3}$

Section II - Multiple Correct Answer Type

This section contains 4 multiple correct answer(s) type questions. Each question has 4 choices (a), (b), (c) and (d), out of which **ONE OR MORE** is/are correct.

6. Let $P(X=r)=pq^r$ and $P(Y=r)=pq^r$, where $r=1, 2, \ldots\ldots\ldots$, $0<p<1, q=1-p$. Suppose X and Y are independent. Let $Z=\max(X, Y)$. Then

(a) $P(Z \le m)=(1-q^m)^2$

(b) $P(Z=m)=2pq^{m-1}-p(1+q)q^{2m-2}$

(c) $\sum_{m\ge 1} P(Z=m)=\frac{1}{p}$

(d) $P(X \le m)=1-q^m$

7. n letters to each of which corresponds an addressed envelope are placed in the envelopes at random. What is the probability that no letter is placed in the right envelope?

(a) first $n-2$ terms in the expansion of e^{-1}.

(b) first n-1 terms in the expansion of e^{-1}.

(c) $=\frac{1}{2!}-\frac{1}{3!}+\frac{1}{4!}-\ldots..+(-1)^n.\frac{1}{n!}$

(d) first n-3 terms in the expansion of e^{-1}.

8. There is 30% chance that it rains on any particular day. Then in a period of 7 days

(a) The probability that there is at least one rainy day within a period of 7 days is $1-\left(\frac{7}{10}\right)^6$

(b) The probability that there is at least one rainy day within a period of 7 days is $1-\left(\frac{7}{10}\right)^7$

(c) Given that there is at least one rainy day, what is the probability that there are at least two rainy days is

$$\frac{1-\left(\frac{7}{10}\right)^7-7\left(\frac{3}{10}\right)\left(\frac{7}{10}\right)^7}{1-\left(\frac{7}{10}\right)^7}$$

(d) Given that there is at least one rainy day, what is the probability that there are at least two rainy days is

$$\frac{1-\left(\frac{7}{10}\right)^7-7\left(\frac{3}{10}\right)\left(\frac{7}{10}\right)^6}{1-\left(\frac{7}{10}\right)^7}$$

9. An urn contains four tickets with numbers 112, 121, 211, 222 and one ticket is drawn. Let A_i $(i=1, 2, 3)$ be the event that the ith digit of the number of tickets drawn is 1. Then

(a) $P(A_1)=P(A_2)=P(A_3)$

(b) A_1, A_2, A_3 are pairwise independent.

(c) A_1, A_2, A_3 are the not mutually independent although they are pairwise independent.

(d) $P(A_1)=1/2$

Section III - Integer Type

This section contains 4 questions. The answer to each of the questions is a single digit integer ranging from 0 to 9.

10. Rahul has to write a project, Probability that he will get a project copy is 'p', probability that he will get a blue pen is 'q' and probability that he will get a black pen is ½. If he can complete the project either with blue or with black pen or with both and probability that he completed the project is ½ then find $p(1+q)$.

RESPONSE GRID	
	3. ⓐⓑⓒⓓ 4. ⓐⓑⓒⓓ 5. ⓐⓑⓒⓓ 6. ⓐⓑⓒⓓ 7. ⓐⓑⓒⓓ
	8. ⓐⓑⓒⓓ 9. ⓐⓑⓒⓓ 10. ⓪①②③④⑤⑥⑦⑧⑨

11. An urn contains five balls. Two balls are drawn and are found to be white. If P is the probability that all the balls are white and P = a/b in simplest form then find a + b.

12. A fair coin is tossed n times. Let X denote the number of heads appeared. If P(X = 4), P(X = 5) and P(X = 6) are in AP, then the smallest values of n is ___________.

13. An artillery target may be either at point I with probability $\frac{8}{9}$ or at the point (II) with probability $\frac{1}{9}$. There are 21 shells each of which can be fired either at point I or II. Each shell may hit the target independently of the other shell with probability $\frac{1}{2}$. Minimum number of shells that must be fired at point I to hit the target with maximum probability is equal to 2k. Then value of k is.

Section IV - Comprehension/Matching Cum-Comprehension Type

Directions (Qs. 14 and 15) : Based upon the given paragraph, 2 multiple choice questions have to be answered. Each question has 4 choices (a), (b), (c) and (d), out of which **ONLY ONE** is correct.

PARAGRAPH

Suppose there are three urns 1st containing 2 white and 3 black balls 2nd contain 3 white and 2 black balls, and 3rd contain 4 white and one black ball respectively. There is equal probability of each urn being chosen.

14. One ball is drawn from an urn chosen at random. What is the probability that a white ball is drawn?
(a) 2/5 (b) 3/5
(c) 2/9 (d) None of these

15. If it is known that a white ball has been drawn, find the probability that it was drawn from the first urn.
(a) 2/5 (b) 3/5
(c) 2/9 (d) None of these

Directions (Qs. 16-18) : This passage contains a table having 3 columns and 4 rows. Based on the table, there are three questions. Each question has four options (a), (b), (c) and (d) **ONLY ONE** of these four options is correct.

Column 1	Column 2	Column 3
(I) $P(A^C) = 0.3, P(b) = 0.4$, $P(A \cap B^C) = 0.5$	(i) $P(A \cap B \cap C^C) + P(A \cap B^C \cap C) + P(A^C \cap B \cap C) + P(A \cap B \cap C)$	(P) $\frac{26}{31}$
(II) $P(A) = \frac{1}{5}, P(B) = \frac{4}{5}, P(C) = \frac{7}{100}$	(ii) $P[B/(A \cap B^C)]$	(Q) $\frac{3}{4}$
(III) $P(A) = \frac{1}{2}; P(B) = \frac{1}{4} = P(C)$	(iii) $P(B/\bar{C})$	(R) $\frac{1}{4}$
(IV) If A, B, C are pairwise independent events and $P(A) = \frac{1}{2}, P(B) = \frac{1}{3}, P(C) = \frac{1}{4}$	(iv) $P(A \cup B \cup C)$	(S) $\frac{5}{31}$

16. Which of the following options is the only correct combination?
(a) (I) (ii) (R) (b) (II) (iii) (P)
(c) (III) (iv) (S) (d) (IV) (i) (Q)

RESPONSE GRID

11. ⓪①②③④⑤⑥⑦⑧⑨ 12. ⓪①②③④⑤⑥⑦⑧⑨
13. ⓪①②③④⑤⑥⑦⑧⑨ 14. ⓐⓑⓒⓓ 15. ⓐⓑⓒⓓ 16. ⓐⓑⓒⓓ

Space for Rough Work

17. Which of the following options is the only correct combination?
(a) (I) (iii) (R) (b) (II) (ii) (Q)
(c) (III) (i) (S) (d) (II) (iii) (P)

18. Which of the following options is the only incorrect combination?
(a) (I) (ii) (R) (b) (III) (i) (S)
(c) (II) (iii) (P) (d) (IV) (iv) (Q)

Section V - Matrix-Match Type

This section contains 2 questions. It contains statements given in two columns, which have to be matched. Statements in column I are labelled as A, B, C and D whereas statements in column II are labelled as p, q, r and s. The answers to these questions have to be appropriately bubbled as illustrated in the following example. If the correct matches are A-p, A-r, B-p, B-s, C-r, C-s and D-q, then the correctly bubbled matrix will look like the following:

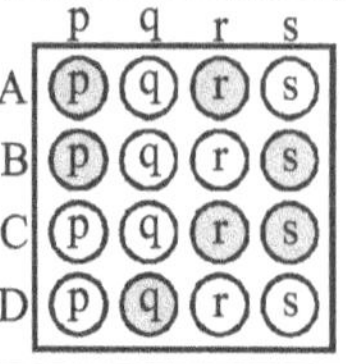

19. Match the columns.

	Column-I		Column-II
(A)	Aman and Binay are playing dart game and it is known that Aman can hit the target 4 out of 5 shots while Binay can hit the target 3 out of 4 shots, what is the probability that target will be hit if both of them try	(p)	5/11
(B)	Kushal and Karina are playing with a dice wherein they throw a dice alternately. Kushal wins if he throws a prime number and Karina wins if she throws a composite number. Kushal starts the game and game continues till one of them win. What is the probability that Kushal will win the game	(q)	1/4
(C)	In the above question (B) what is the probability that Karina wins the game	(r)	19/20
(D)	Raj and Sanchita are playing game in which they throw a die alternately till one of them gets a six. Which one of the following could be the probability that Sanchita win the game	(s)	3/4

20. In a tournament there are twelve players $S_1, S_2, ..., S_{12}$ and divided into six pairs at random. From each game a winner is decided on the basis of a game played between the two players of the pair. Assuming all the pairs are of equal strength, then match the following :

	Column-I		Column-II
(A)	Probability that S_2 is among the losers is	p.	$\frac{5}{22}$
(B)	Probability that exactly one of S_3 and S_4 is among the losers, is	q.	$\frac{10}{11}$
(C)	Probability that both S_2 and S_4 are among the winners is	r.	$\frac{1}{2}$
(D)	Probability of S_4 and S_5 not playing against each other is	s.	$\frac{6}{11}$

RESPONSE GRID	17. ⓐⓑⓒⓓ 18. ⓐⓑⓒⓓ 19. A - ⓟⓠⓡⓢ; B - ⓟⓠⓡⓢ; C - ⓟⓠⓡⓢ; D - ⓟⓠⓡⓢ 20. A - ⓟⓠⓡⓢ; B - ⓟⓠⓡⓢ; C - ⓟⓠⓡⓢ; D - ⓟⓠⓡⓢ

DAILY PRACTICE PROBLEM DPP CM25 - MATHEMATICS

Total Questions	20	Total Marks	74
Attempted		Correct	
Incorrect		Net Score	
Cut-off Score	26	Qualifying Score	36

$$\text{Net Score} = \sum_{i=I}^{V}\left[(\text{correct}_i \times MM_i) - (In_i - NM_i)\right]$$

Space for Rough Work

DPP - Daily Practice Problems

Chapter-wise Sheets

Date : | Start Time : | End Time :

MATHEMATICS CM26

SYLLABUS : Properties of Triangles

Max. Marks : 74 **Time : 60 min.**

GENERAL INSTRUCTIONS

- The Daily Practice Problem Sheet contains 20 Questions divided into 5 sections.
  Section I has **6** MCQs with ONLY 1 Correct Option, **3** marks for each correct answer and **–1** for each incorrect answer.
  Section II has **4** MCQs with ONE or MORE THAN ONE Correct options.
  For each question, marks will be awarded in one of the following categories:
  Full marks: **+4** If only the bubble(s) corresponding to all the correct option(s) is (are) darkened.
  Partial marks: **+1** For darkening a bubble corresponding to each correct option provided NO INCORRECT option is darkened.
  Zero marks: If none of the bubbles is darkened.
  Negative marks: **–2** In all other cases.
  Section III has **4** Single Digit Integer Answer Type Questions, **3** marks for each Correct Answer and **0** mark in all other cases.
  Section IV has Comprehension Type Questions having **4** MCQs with ONLY ONE corect option, **3** marks for each Correct Answer and **0** mark in all other cases.
  Section V has **2** Matching Type Questions, **2** marks for the correct matching of each row and **0** mark in all other cases.
- You have to evaluate your Response Grids yourself with the help of Solutions.

Section I - Straight Objective Type

This section contains 6 multiple choice questions. Each question has 4 choices (a), (b), (c) and (d), out of which **ONLY ONE** is correct.

1. In ΔABC, if $\cot\theta = \cot A + \cot B + \cot C$, then $\sin(A-\theta).\sin(B-\theta).\sin(C-\theta) =$

(a) $\sin^3\theta$ (b) $\sin A\sin B\sin C$
(c) $3\sin\theta$ (d) 1

2. If $A+B+C = \pi$, then the greatest value of $\cos A + \cos B + \cos C$ is

(a) 2 (b) 3
(c) $\frac{3}{2}$ (d) 1

3. If a, b, c be the sides of a triangle and $P = \frac{(a+b+c)^2}{ab+bc+ca}$, then

(a) $P \in [1, 2]$ (b) $P \in [3, 4)$
(c) $P \in (2, 4]$ (d) None of these

RESPONSE GRID	1. ⓐⓑⓒⓓ	2. ⓐⓑⓒⓓ	3. ⓐⓑⓒⓓ

Space for Rough Work

4. In a triangle ABC, if $\frac{a^2+b^2}{a^2-b^2}\sin(A-B)=1$, and C is not a right angle, then $\cos(A-B)=$

(a) $\tan\left(\frac{C}{2}+\frac{\pi}{4}\right)$ (b) $\tan\left(\frac{C}{2}-\frac{\pi}{4}\right)$

(c) $\cos\left(\frac{C}{2}+\frac{\pi}{4}\right)$ (d) $\sin\left(\frac{C}{2}-\frac{\pi}{4}\right)$

5. The angle of elevation of the top of a tower from a point A due south of it is $\tan^{-1}0.6$, and that from B due east of it is $\tan^{-1}0.75$. If h is the height of the tower, and AB = λh, then $\lambda^2=$

(a) $\frac{41}{9}$ (b) $\frac{40}{9}$

(c) $\frac{41}{2}$ (d) None

6. The angle of elevation of the top C of a vertical tower CD of height h from a point A in the horizontal plane is 45° and from a point B at a distance a from A on the line making an angle 30° with AD in the vertical plane, it is 60°, then

(a) $a=h(\sqrt{3}+1)$ (b) $h=a(\sqrt{3}+1)$

(c) $a=h(\sqrt{3}-1)$ (d) $h=a(\sqrt{3}-1)$

Section II - Multiple Correct Answer Type

This section contains 4 multiple correct answer(s) type questions. Each question has 4 choices (a), (b), (c) and (d), out of which **ONE OR MORE** is/are correct.

7. If in a triangle ABC, $b\cos^2\frac{A}{2}+a\cos^2\frac{B}{2}=\frac{3c}{2}$, then

(a) $c^2\ge ab$ (b) $2c>\sqrt{ab}$

(c) $\frac{a+c}{2c-a}+\frac{b+c}{2c-b}\le 4$ (d) $\frac{a}{c}+\frac{c}{b}+\frac{b}{a}\ge 3$

8. If the sides a, b, c of a triangle ABC form successive terms of $G.P.$ with common ratio r (>1), then which of the following is / are correct

(a) $r<\frac{\sqrt{5}+1}{2}$ (b) $A<B<\frac{\pi}{3}$

(c) $B>\frac{\pi}{3}$ (d) $C>\frac{\pi}{3}$

9. In a ΔABC, the incircle touches the sides BC, CA, and AB at P, Q and R respectively and its radius is 4 units. If the lengths BP, CQ and AR are consecutive integers then

(a) sides are also consecutive integers

(b) Sides are in $A.P.$

(c) Perimeter of the triangle is 42 unit

(d) diameter of the circumcircle is 65 unit

10. In a triangle ABC, if $\sec A$, $\sec B$, $\sec C$ are in H.P. then

(a) a, b, c are in H.P.

(b) $\cot\frac{A}{2}, \cot\frac{B}{2}, \cot\frac{C}{2}$ are in H.P.

(c) r_1, r_2, r_3 are in A.P.

(d) $\cot\frac{A}{2}, \cot\frac{B}{2}, \cot\frac{C}{2}$ are in A.P.

Section III - Integer Type

This section contains 4 questions. The answer to each of the questions is a single digit integer ranging from 0 to 9.

11. For a triangle ABC, with altitudes h_1, h_2, h_3 and in radius r, the minimum value of $\frac{h_1+r}{h_1-r}+\frac{h_2+r}{h_2-r}+\frac{h_3+r}{h_3-r}$ is

RESPONSE GRID	
	4. ⓐⓑⓒⓓ 5. ⓐⓑⓒⓓ 6. ⓐⓑⓒⓓ 7. ⓐⓑⓒⓓ 8. ⓐⓑⓒⓓ
	9. ⓐⓑⓒⓓ 10. ⓐⓑⓒⓓ 11. ⓪①②③④⑤⑥⑦⑧⑨

Space for Rough Work

12. If in the triangle ABC, $\tan\frac{A}{2}$, $\tan\frac{B}{2}$ and $\tan\frac{C}{2}$ are in harmonic progression then the least value of $\cot^2\frac{B}{2}$ is equal to

13. Let ABC be a triangle of area Δ and $A'B'C'$ be the triangle formed by the altitudes of ΔABC as its sides with area Δ' and $A''B''C''$ be the triangle formed by the altitudes of $\Delta A'B'C'$ as its sides with area Δ''. If $\Delta' = 30$ and $\Delta'' = 20$ then the value of $\frac{\Delta}{9}$ is

14. If p_1, p_2, p_3 are the altitudes of a triangle which circumscribes a circle of diameter $\frac{4}{3}$ units, then the least value of $p_1 + p_2 + p_3$ is equal to

Section IV - Comprehension Type

Based upon the given paragraphs, 4 multiple choice questions have to be answered. Each question has 4 choices (a), (b), (c) and (d), out of which **ONLY ONE** is correct.

PARAGRAPH–1

Let r and R represent the inradius and circum radius of a triangle ABC of which r_1, r_2, r_3 are respectively the radii of excircles opposite to vertices A, B and C. Perimeter of triangle is $2s$.

15. The cubic equation with r_1, r_2, r_3 as three roots is given by
(a) $x^3 - x^2(R + r) + sx - rs^2 = 0$
(b) $x^3 - x^2(R - 2r) + s^2x - rs^2 = 0$
(c) $x^3 - x^2(4R + r) + s^2x - rs^2 = 0$
(d) $x^3 - 4x^2(R + r) + s^2x - rs^2 = 0$

16. The expression $(s + r_1)(s + r_2)(s + r_3)$ equals to
(a) $2s^2(s + r + 2R)$ (b) $2s^2(s + 2R)$
(c) $R(s^2 + r^2)$ (d) None of these

PARAGRAPH–2

When any two sides and the angle opposite to one of them are given then either no triangle, or one triangle or two triangles are possible. Let the sides a, b and the angle A be given

Then, $\cos A = \dfrac{b^2 + c^2 - a^2}{2bc}$

$\Rightarrow c^2 - (2b\cos A)c + b^2 - a^2 = 0$

This is a quadratic equation in c. So, two values of c will be obtained real, coincident or imaginary. Values of c from the above equation are given by $c_1 = b\cos A \pm \sqrt{a^2 - b^2\sin^2 A}$, say c_1 and c_2

The discriminant of the above equation is

$D = 4b^2\cos^2 A - 4(b^2 - a^2) = 4(a^2 - b^2\sin^2 A)$

We can have following cases :

(i) If $D < 0$, i.e. $a < b\sin A$, then no triangle is possible

(ii) If $D = 0$, i..e., $a = b\sin A$, then only one triangle is possible provided A is acute. In case A is obtuse then no triangle is possible as then c_1 and c_2 will be negative.

(iii) If $D > 0$, i.e., $a > b\sin A$, then two triangles are possible provided c_1 and c_2 are both positive.

17. If A is acute then two different triangles are possible if and only if
(a) $a < b\sin A$ (b) $a > b\sin A$ and $a < b$
(c) $a > b\sin A$ and $a > b$ (d) $a > b\sin A$ and $a = b$

18. If $a > b\sin A$ and $a = b$ then
(a) No triangle is possible
(b) Only one triangle is possible
(c) Two distinct triangles are possible
(d) Any of the (a), (b), (c) may be true

RESPONSE GRID	
	12. ⓪①②③④⑤⑥⑦⑧⑨ 13. ⓪①②③④⑤⑥⑦⑧⑨
	14. ⓪①②③④⑤⑥⑦⑧⑨ 15. ⓐⓑⓒⓓ 16. ⓐⓑⓒⓓ 17. ⓐⓑⓒⓓ
	18. ⓐⓑⓒⓓ

Space for Rough Work

Section V - Matrix-Match Type

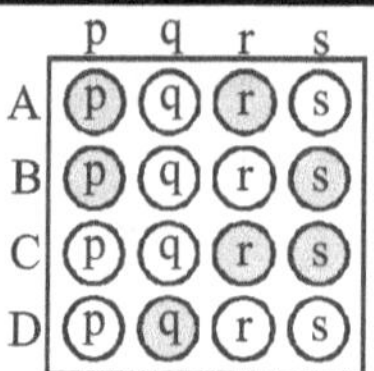

This section contains 2 questions. It contains statements given in two columns, which have to be matched. Statements in column I are labelled as A, B, C and D whereas statements in column II are labelled as p, q, r and s. The answers to these questions have to be appropriately bubbled as illustrated in the following example. If the correct matches are A-p, A-r, B-p, B-s, C-r, C-s and D-q, then the correctly bubbled matrix will look like the following:

19.

Column-I	Column-II
(A) If in a triangle ABC, $\frac{r}{r_1}=\frac{1}{4}$, then the value of $\tan\frac{A}{2}\left(\tan\frac{B}{2}+\tan\frac{C}{2}\right)$ is equal to	p. $\frac{3}{4}$
(B) In a triangle the least value of $\frac{r_1r_2r_3}{r^3}$ is	q. 1
(C) If the sides a, b, c of a triangle ABC are in A.P. then the ratio $\frac{b}{c}$ can be equal to	r. 3
(D) Let P be an interior point of the triangle ABC and the lines AP, BP and CP when produced meet the opposite sides in D, E and F respectively then $\frac{PD}{AD}+\frac{PE}{BE}+\frac{PE}{CF}$ is equal to	s. 27

20.

Column-I	Column-II
(A) If α, β, γ be the lengths of medians of triangle ABC then $\frac{\alpha^2+\beta^2+\gamma^2}{a^2+b^2+c^2}$ is equal to	p. 1
(B) Let the point P lies interior of an equilateral triangle ABC of side length 2 and its distances from the sides BC, CA and AB are respectively x, y and z, then $x+y+z$ is equal to	q. $\sqrt{3}$
(C) In a triangle ABC. A, B, C are in A.P. and a, b, c are in G.P. then $\frac{a^2b+b^2c+c^2a}{a^3+b^3+c^3}$ is equal to	r. $\frac{3}{4}$
(D) In triangle ABC, the least value of $\sqrt{\frac{abc(a+b+c)}{\Delta}}$ is	s. 4

RESPONSE GRID	
	19. A - ⓟⓠⓡⓢ; B - ⓟⓠⓡⓢ; C - ⓟⓠⓡⓢ
	20. A - ⓟⓠⓡⓢ; B - ⓟⓠⓡⓢ; C - ⓟⓠⓡⓢ

DAILY PRACTICE PROBLEM DPP CM26 - MATHEMATICS

Total Questions	20	Total Marks	74
Attempted		Correct	
Incorrect		Net Score	
Cut-off Score	28	Qualifying Score	39

$$\text{Net Score} = \sum_{i=I}^{V}\left[(\text{correct}_i \times MM_i) - (In_i - NM_i)\right]$$

Space for Rough Work

1. **(d)** Statement (1) and (2) are correct. Hence, option (d) is correct.

2. **(b)**

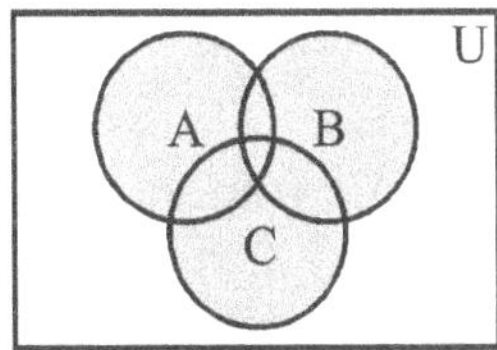

(i) $A \cup B \cup C$

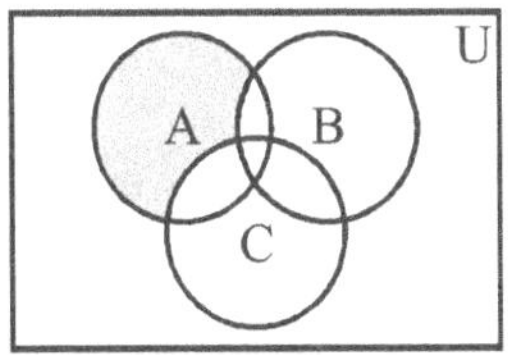

(ii) $(A \cap B^c \cap C^c)$

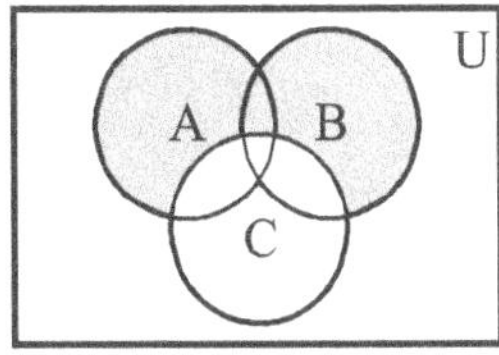

(iii) C^c

From Fig. (i), (ii) and (iii), we get
$(A \cup B \cup C) \cap (A \cap B^c \cap C^c)^c \cap C^c = (B^c \cap C^c)$

3. **(c)** Let C represents the set of Americans like cheese and A represents the set of Americans like apples.
$C \cap A$ represents the set of Americans like both cheese and apples.
$\therefore\ n(C) = 63, n(A) = 76$, and $n(C \cap A) = x$
We know that,
$n(C \cup A) = n(C) + n(A) - n(C \cap A)$
$100 = 63 + 76 - x$
$\Rightarrow x = 139 - 100 = 39$ and $n(C \cap A) \le n(C)$
$\Rightarrow x \le 63$
$\therefore\ 39 \le x \le 63.$

4. **(c)** Suppose $a \in X$ and $a \in A$
$\Rightarrow a \in X \cup A \Rightarrow a \in Y \cup A$
$\Rightarrow a \in Y$ and $a \in A \cap (\because X \cup A = Y \cup A)$
$\Rightarrow a \in Y \cap A \Rightarrow Y \cap A$ is non-empty
This contradicts that $Y \cap A = \phi$
So, $X = Y$

5. **(d)** $n(A) = 1000, n(B) = 500, n(A \cap B) \ge 1,$
$n(A \cup B) = p$
$n(A \cup B) = n(A) + n(B) - n(A \cap B)$
$p = 1000 + 500 - n(A \cap B)$
$1 \le n(A \cap B) \le 500$
Hence $p \le 1499$ and $p \ge 1000$
$1000 \le p \le 1499$

6. **(a)** Minimum value of $x = 100 - (30 + 20 + 25 + 15)$
$= 100 - 90 = 10$

7. **(b, c)** Let there are x families

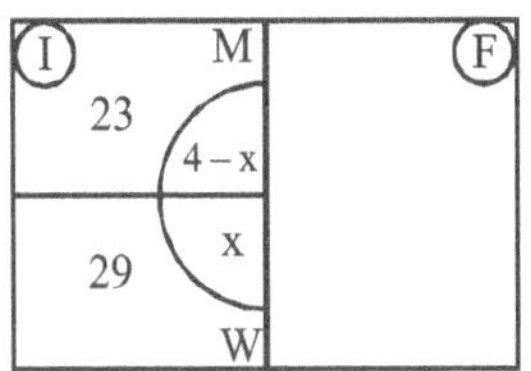

$a + b + c + d = x$
$a + c = 2.5x,\ b + c = 0.15x$
$d = 0.65x, c = 2000$
$\therefore a + b + 2c + d = 1.05x$
$x + c = 1.05x$
$\therefore 0.05x = c = 2000 \Rightarrow x = 40{,}000$
So $a = 8000, b = 4000\ d = 26000$
$c = 2000 \Rightarrow$ 5% families own both a car and a phone
$a + b + c = 14000$
$\Rightarrow$ 35% families own either a car or a phone

8. **(a, b, c)** See the following Venn diagram

$n(I) = 29 + 23 = 52$
$n(F) = 100 - 52 = 48 = n_1$
$n(m \cup D) = n(m) + n(D) - n(m \cap D)$
$24 = 23 + 4 - n(m \cap D)$
$\therefore n(m \cap D) = 3$
$\therefore n(W \cap D) = 4 - 3 = 1 = n_2$

9. **(a, b, c)** We have
$n(A \cup B \cup C) = n(A) + n(B) + n(C) -$
$n(A \cap B) - n(B \cap C) - n(C \cap A) + n(A \cap B \cap C)$
$= 10 + 15 + 20 - 8 - 9 - n(C \cap A) + n(A \cap B \cap C)$
$= 28 - \{n(C \cap A) - n(A \cap B \cap C)\}$ ...(i)
Since $n(C \cap A) \ge n(A \cap B \cap C)$
We have $n(C \cap A) - n(A \cap B \cap C) \ge 0$...(ii)
From (i) and (ii)
$n(A \cup B \cup C) \le 28$ ...(iii)
Now, $n(A \cup B) = n(A) + n(B) - n(A \cap B)$
$= 10 + 15 - 8 = 17$
and $n(B \cup C) = n(B) + n(C) - n(B \cap C)$
$= 15 + 20 - 9 = 26$
Since, $n(A \cup B \cup C) \ge n(A \cup C)$ and
$n(A \cup B \cup C) \ge n(B \cup C)$, we have
$n(A \cup B \cup C) \ge 17$ and $n(A \cup B \cup C) \ge 26$
Hence $n(A \cup B \cup C) \ge 26$ ...(iv)
From (iii) and (iv) we obtain
$26 \le n(A \cup B \cup C) \le 28$
Also $n(A \cup B \cup C)$ is a positive integer
$\therefore n(A \cup B \cup C) = 26$ or 27 or 28

10. **(b, c)** $a+e+f+g=23$
$b+d+f+g=15$
$c+d+e+g=20$
$f+g=7;\ d+g=5$
$e+g=4$
$a+b+c+d+e+f+g=60-15=45$
By substitutions,
$a+e=16,\ b+d=8,\ b+f=10, c+e=15,\ c+d=16$
Also, $b+c+d=22$
$a+c+e=30,\ a+b+f=25$
From these, we get
$b=6, a=15, c=14\ e=1, d=2, f=4$ and $g=3$
Clearly(a) is not correct
for (b) $a+f=19 \Rightarrow$ (b)is correct
for (c) $e=1 \Rightarrow$ (c) is correct

11. **(7)** The given condition is as follows-

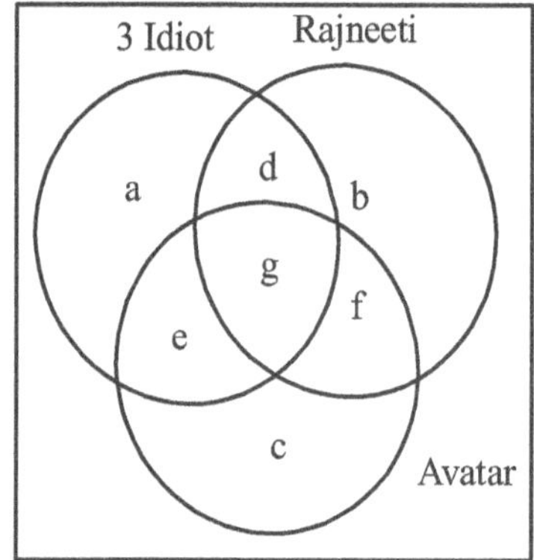

We know that $\{(a+d+e+g)+(b+d+f+g)+(c+e+f+g)\}-(d+e+f)-2g$
$=a+b+c+d+e+f+g$
or $61x+46x+29x-25x-2g=97x$
or $2g=14x$ or $g=7x$

12. **(3)** $2^m-2^n=112 \Rightarrow 2^n(2^{m-n}-1)=16.7$
$\therefore\ 2^n(2^{m-n}-1)=2^4(2^3-1)$
Comparing we get $n=4$ and $m-n=3$
$\Rightarrow n=4$ and $m=7 \Rightarrow m-n=3$

13. **(5)** Let C be the set of students in chemistry class and P be the set of students in physics class.
Given n (C) = 20, n (P) = 30 and n $(C\cap P)=10$. We have to find n $(C\cup P)$
If two classes meet at different hours, then
n $(C\cap P)=10$ (given)
So, n $(C\cup P)=n(C)+\cap(P)-(C\cap P)=40$

14. **(3)** $A=\{1,3,5,15\}, B=\{2,3,5,7\}\ C=\{2,4,6,8\}$
$\therefore A\cup C=\{1,2,3,4,5,6,7,8,15\}$
$(A\cup C)\cap B=\{2, 3, 5\}$

15. **(2)** Given set is $\{\frac{a}{b}\in I^+ : 2a^2+3b^2=35, a,b\in Z\}$
We can see that, $2(\pm2)^2+3(\pm3)^2=35$
and $2(\pm4)^2+3(\pm1)^2=35$
$\therefore$ (2, 3), (2, – 3), (–2, – 3), (–2, 3), (4, 1), (4, – 1), (– 4, –1), (–4, 1)

For 16-17

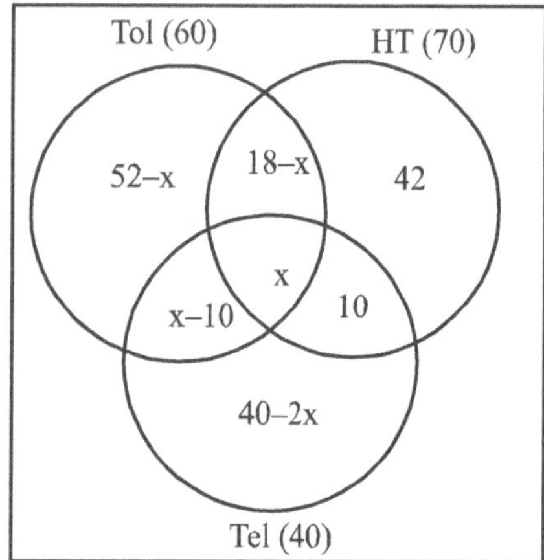

Let us assume that the number of family who read all the news paper is x, then remaining is as given the venn diagram.

16. **(b)** Total number of family is $152-2x$
From venn diagram $10\le x\le 18$
So minimum total number of family
$=152-2\times18=152-36=116$
And maximum number of family
$=152-2\times10=152-20=132$
So total number of family must be between 132 and 116 and an even number hence 126 is a possible option.

17. **(c)** From the given condition $18-x>x-10$
or $28>2x$ or $x<14$
But we have seen that $x\ge10$ hence range of x is $10\le x<14$
Number of family who read only Tel is
$40-2x$ whose minimum value is 12 and maximum value is 20 with even number.

For 18-19

From the given condition number of students who play FB and any one more game is 10 we can conclude $e=g=i=10$,
From the given condition number of students who play Cr and any one more game is 8 we can conclude, $h=j=8$.
From the given condition number of students who play FB and any two more games is 12 we can conclude $k=n=l=12$
Hence the Venn diagram will be as follows -
Since total number of students who play FB is 100 hence
$a+e+g+k+l+o+i+n=100$
or $a+o=34$
Similarly $o+m+b=50$
$o+m+c+f=58$

$o + m + d + f = 58$

Or $c + f = 8 + b$

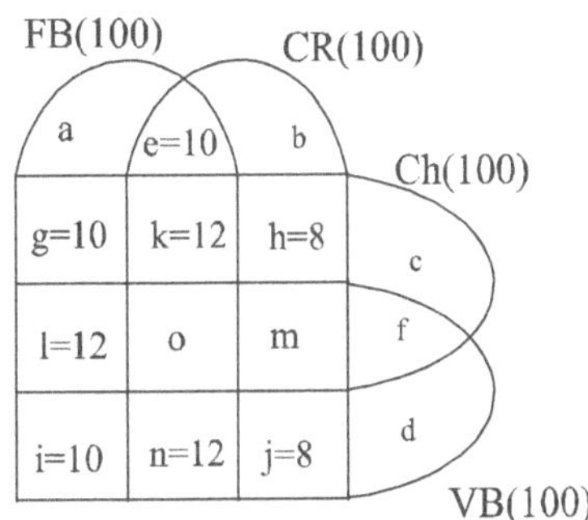

18. **(a)** From the Venn Diagram we have to find the value of Cr + FB, Cr + Ch , and Cr + VB or we have to find the value of $e + h + j = 10 + 8 + 8 = 26$

19. **(b)** Since number of students who play Chess and exactly 1 more game is $g + h + f = 18 + f$ is maximum when f is maximum and since $c + f = 8 + b$ hence for f is maximum b has to be maximum and maximum value of b is 50 when $o = m = 0$.

20. **(A)** → **(q)**; **(B)** → **(s)**; **(C)** → **(p)**

(A) Total no. of male students = $0.475 \times 800 = 380$,

Total no. of veg. students = $0.53 \times 800 = 424$

Total number of students in secondary section $= 0.80 \times 800 = 640$, out of these $0.55 \times 640 = 352$ are vegetarian, so we can re-write and complete the table as follows

	Male (M)	Vegetarian (V)
Class12	48	32
Class 11	44	40
Secondary Section	288	352
Total	380	424

Hence % of vegetarian students in class 12

$= 32/80 \times 100 = 40\%$

(B) The number of vegetarian male in class $12 = 0.25 \times 32 = 8$, since total number of males in class 12 is 48, hence the number of non-vegetarian males in this class $= 48 - 8 = 40$.

The number of vegetarian female $= 32 - 8 = 24$

Hence required difference $= 40 - 24 = 16$

(C) Total number of male students in secondary section = 288, and total number of students in this section is 640, hence required %

$= 288/640 \times 100 = 45\%$

1. **(b)** Given :

$$f(T+x)=1+\left[\{1-f(x)^3\}\right]^{1/3}$$

$$=1+(1-f(x))$$

$\Rightarrow f(T+x)+f(x)=2$ .....(1)

$\Rightarrow f(2T+x)+f(T+x)=2$ .....(2)

$(2)-(1)\Rightarrow f(2T+x)-f(x)=0$

$\Rightarrow f(2T+x)=f(x)$

Also T is positive and least therefore period of $f(x)=2T$

2. **(b)** Put $x=y=1$, $(f(1))^2=3f(1)-2$

$\Rightarrow f(1)=1$ or 2

Let $f(1)=1$, then put $y-1$

$f(x).f(1)=f(x)+f(1)+f(x)-2$

$\Rightarrow f(x)=1$ constant function

$\therefore f(1)\neq 1$, hence $f(1)=2$

3. **(d)** Let degree of $f(x)$ is n

Equating the degree of LHS and RHS, we get

$n+n=n\Rightarrow n=0$

$\Rightarrow f(x)=c\Rightarrow c^2=c$

$\Rightarrow c=0,1\Rightarrow f(x)=0,1$

4. **(d)** $x_0=a,\ x_1=f(x)=\dfrac{x_0}{1-x_0}=\dfrac{a}{1-a}$;

$$x_2=f(x_1)=\frac{x_1}{1-x_1}=\frac{\frac{a}{1-a}}{1-\frac{a}{1-a}}=\frac{a}{1-2a}$$

$$\therefore\ x_{2009}=\frac{a}{1-2009\,a}=1\ \Rightarrow 1-2009\,a=a$$

$$\Rightarrow a=\frac{1}{2010}$$

5. **(d)** $\{x^2\}-2\{x\}\geq 0$

$\Rightarrow \{x\}(\{x\}-2\}\geq 0$

$\Rightarrow \{x\}\leq 0$ or $\{x\}\geq 2$

Second case is not possible. Hence $\{x\}=0$, as $\{x\}\leq$ [0, 1) Hence range of $f(x)$ contains only one element 0.

6. **(a, b, c)** Let (a, b) ∈ A × (B ∩ C)

⇒ a ∈ A and b ∈ (B ∩ C)

⇒ a ∈ A and (b ∈ B and b ∈ C)

⇒ (a ∈ A and b ∈ B) and (a ∈ A and b ∈ C)

⇒ (a, b) ∈ A × B and (a, b) ∈ (A × C)

(a, b) ∈ (A × B) ∩ (A × C)

⇒ A × (B ∩ C) ⊂ (A × B) ∩ (A × C) … (i)

Again, let (x, y) ∈ (A × B) ∩ (A × C)

(x, y) ∈ A × B and (x, y) ∈ A × C

⇒ (x ∈ A and y ∈ B) and (x ∈ A and y ∈ C)

⇒ x ∈ A and (y ∈ B and y ∈ C)

⇒ x ∈ A and y ∈ (B ∩ C)

⇒ (x, y) ∈ A × (B ∩ C)

⇒ (A × B) ∩ (A × C) ⊂ A × (B ∩ C) … (ii)

From equations (i) and (ii), we get

A × (B ∩ C) = (A × B) ∩ (A × C) … (iii)

Now, $A\times(B'\cup C')'=A\times\left[(B')'\cap(C')'\right]$

[by De-Morgan's law]

$=A\times(B\cap C)$ $\left[\because (A')'=A\right]$

$=(A\times B)\cap(A\times C)$ [by equation (iii)]

7. **(a, b, c)** We have $R=\{(x,y):|x^2-y^2|<16\}$

Let x = 1,

$|x^2-y^2|<16\Rightarrow|1-y^2|<16$

$\Rightarrow |y^2-1|<16\Rightarrow y=1,2,3,4$

Let x = 2,

$|x^2-y^2|<16\Rightarrow|4-y^2|<16$

$\Rightarrow |y^2-4|<16\Rightarrow y=1,2,3,4$

Let x = 3,

$|x^2-y^2|<16\Rightarrow|9-y^2|<16$

$\Rightarrow |y^2-9|<16\Rightarrow y=1,2,3,4$

Let x = 4,

$|x^2-y^2|<16\Rightarrow|16-y^2|<16$

$\Rightarrow |y^2-16|<16\Rightarrow y=1,2,3,4,5$

Let x = 5,

$|x^2-y^2|<16\Rightarrow|25-y^2|<16$

$\Rightarrow |y^2-25|<16\Rightarrow y=4,5$

∴ R = {(1, 1), (1, 2), (1, 3), (1, 4), (2, 1), (2, 2), (2, 3), (2, 4), (3, 1), (3, 2), (3, 3), (3, 4), (4, 1), (4, 2), (4, 3), (4, 4), (4, 5), (5, 4), (5, 5)}.

8. **(a, b, c, d)**

Option (a) : $Sgn\,(x)=\begin{cases}1, & x>0\\ 0, & x=0\\ -1, & x<0\end{cases}$

$\therefore\ Sgn\,(e^{-x})=1\quad(\because e^{-x}>0)$

$Sgn\,(e^{-x})$ is constant function. Hence, it is periodic.

Option (b) : $\because$ Period of $\sin x$ is 2π

and period of $|\sin x|$ is π

$\therefore$ Period of $\sin x+|\sin x|$ is LCM $\{2\pi,\pi\}$

Option (c) : Let $f(x)=\min\{\sin x,|x|\}=\sin x$

$[\because \sin x<|x|]$

$\sin x$ is periodic with period 2π.

Option (d) :

$$f(x)=\left[x+\frac{1}{2}\right]+\left[x-\frac{1}{2}\right]+2[-x]$$

$$=\left(x+\frac{1}{2}\right)-\left\{x+\frac{1}{2}\right\}+\left(x-\frac{1}{2}\right)-\left\{x-\frac{1}{2}\right\}$$
$$+2\,(-x\ \{-x\})$$

$$=-\left\{x+\frac{1}{2}\right\}-\left\{x-\frac{1}{2}\right\}-2\,\{-x\}$$

Hence, $f(x)$ is periodic.

9. **(a, c, d)** $\sqrt{|x^2|-5|x|+6}=\sqrt{(|x|-2)\,(|x|-3)}$
is real for $0\le|x|\le 4$
$\therefore f(x)$ is real for all $0\le|x|\le 2$ or $3\le|x|\le 4$.

10. **(3)** We have, (x, y) ∈ R, if $x^2+y^2=16$

i.e., $y=\pm\sqrt{16-x^2}$

For, x = 0, y = ± 4

For, x = ± 4, y = 0

We observe that no other values of x, y ∈ Z, which satisfy $x^2+y^2=16$

R = {(0, 4), (0, – 4), (4, 0), (– 4, 0)}

∴ Domain of R = {0, 4, – 4}.

11. **(8)** Given $2f(xy)=(f(x))^{y}+(f(y))^{x}$ ...(1)

Putting $y=1$, we get $2f(x)=f(x)+(f(1))^{x}$

$\Rightarrow f(x)=(f(1))^{x}=2^{x}$ $[\because f(1)=2]$

$\Rightarrow f(3)=2^3=8$

12. **(2)** Given, $f(x)=\dfrac{4^x}{4^x+2}$ ...(1)

We observe that $f\left(\dfrac{1}{1997}\right)$ and $f\left(\dfrac{1996}{1997}\right)$ are s uch that

$$\frac{1}{1997}+\frac{1996}{1997}=1$$

$\therefore$ If $x=\dfrac{1}{1997},\dfrac{1996}{1997}=1-x$

Also, $f\left(\dfrac{2}{1997}\right)$ and $f\left(\dfrac{1995}{1997}\right)$ are such that

$\dfrac{2}{1997}+\dfrac{1995}{1997}=1\ \therefore$

If $x=\dfrac{2}{1997}$, then $\dfrac{1995}{1997}=1-x$

Now, $f(x)+f(1-x)=\dfrac{4^x}{4^x+2}+\dfrac{4^{1-x}}{4^{1-x}+2}$

$$=\frac{4^x}{4^x+2}+\frac{4}{4+2.4^x}=\frac{4^x}{4^x+2}$$
$$+\frac{2}{2+4^x}=\frac{4^x+2}{4^x+2}=1$$

Thus, $f(x)+f(1-x)=1$

Now, $f\left(\dfrac{1}{1997}\right)+f\left(\dfrac{2}{1997}\right)+f\left(\dfrac{3}{1997}\right)$
$+\ldots.+f\left(\dfrac{1995}{1997}\right)+f\left(\dfrac{1996}{1997}\right)$

$$=\left[f\left(\frac{1}{1997}\right)+f\left(\frac{1996}{1997}\right)\right]+$$
$$\left[f\left(\frac{2}{1997}\right)+f\left(\frac{1995}{1997}\right)\right]+\ldots \text{ to 998 terms}$$

$=1+1+1+\ldots$ to 998 terms $=998$

13. **(2)** $f(a+x)=b+[1+b^3-3b^2f(x)+3b\,\{f(x)\}^2-\{f(x)\}^3]^{1/3}$

$=b+[1+\{b-f(x)\}^3]^{1/3}$

$\Rightarrow f(a+x)-b=[1-\{f(x)-b\}^3]^{1/3}$

$\Rightarrow \phi(a+x)=[1-\{\phi(x)\}^3]^{1/3}$ ...(1)

where $\phi(x)=f(x)-b$

$\Rightarrow \phi(2a+x)=[1-\{\phi(x+a)\}^3]^{1/3}=\phi(x)$ form (1)

$\Rightarrow f(x+2a)-b=f(x)-b$

$\Rightarrow f(x+2a)=f(x)$

$\therefore$ $f(x)$ is periodic with period $2a$.

14. (a), 15. (c)

$$(f(x))^2 f\left(\frac{1-x}{1+x}\right)=64x$$

$$\Rightarrow (f(x))^4\left\{f\left(\frac{1-x}{1+x}\right)\right\}^2 \quad \text{....(1)}$$

Putting $\dfrac{1-x}{1+x}=y$, and $x=\dfrac{1-y}{1+y}$, we get

$$\left\{f\left(\frac{1-y}{1+y}\right)\right\}^2.f(y)=64\left(\frac{1-y}{1+y}\right)$$

$$\Rightarrow f(x).\left\{f\left(\frac{1-x}{1+x}\right)\right\}^2=64\left(\frac{1-x}{1+x}\right)\ldots(2)$$

Equation (1) by (2), we get

$$\frac{\{f(x)\}^4\left\{f\left(\frac{1-x}{1+x}\right)\right\}^2}{f(x)\left\{f\left(\frac{1-x}{1+x}\right)\right\}^2}=\frac{(64x)^2}{64\left(\frac{1-x}{1+x}\right)}$$

$\Rightarrow \quad \{f(x)\}^3 = 64x^2\left(\frac{1+x}{1-x}\right)$

$\Rightarrow \quad f(x) = 4x^{2/3}\left(\frac{1+x}{1-x}\right)^{1/3}$

$f(9/7) = -8(9/7)^{2/3}$

16. **(b)**
17. **(b)**
18. **(c)**

Sol. (I) $f(x) = \frac{1}{\log_a x}, a > 0, \ a \neq 1$

Domain = R – [0, 1)
Co-domain = R^+

(II) $f(x) = \frac{1}{[x]}$

Domain = R – {0}
Co-domain = R – {0}

(III) $f(x) = \frac{1}{\{x\}}$

Domain = $R^+ - \{1\}$
Co-domain = $(1, \infty)$

(IV) $f(x) = \frac{1}{|x|}$

Domain = R – I

Co-domain = $\left\{\frac{1}{n}, n \in I - \{0\}\right\}$

19. **(A)–(p); (B)–(q); (C)–(q, s);**

(A) $f(x) = \{(\text{sgn}\, x)^{\text{sgn}\, x}\}^n = \begin{cases} [(x)^1]^n, x > 0 \\ [(-1)^{-1}]^n, x < 0 \end{cases}$

$= \begin{cases} 1, x > 0 \\ -1, x < 0 \end{cases}$

Hence, $f(x)$ is an odd function.

(B) $f(x) = \frac{x}{e^x - 1} + \frac{x}{2} + 1$

$\Rightarrow \quad f(-x) = \frac{-x}{e^{-x} - 1} - \frac{x}{2} + 1 = \frac{xe^x}{e^x - 1} - \frac{x}{2} + 1$

$= \frac{xe^x - x + x}{e^x - 1} - \frac{x}{2} + 1$

$= x + \frac{x}{e^x - 1} - \frac{x}{2} + 1 = \frac{x}{e^x - 1} + \frac{x}{2} + 1$

$= f(x)$

(C) $f(x) = \begin{cases} 0, & \text{if } x \text{ is rational} \\ 1, & \text{if } x \text{ is irrational} \end{cases}$

$f(-x) = \begin{cases} 0, & \text{if } -x \text{ is rational} \\ 1, & \text{if } -x \text{ is irrational} \end{cases}$

20. (A) $\rightarrow$ (q); (B) $\rightarrow$ (p); (C) $\rightarrow$ (s); (D) $\rightarrow$ (r)

1. (b) The first equation can be written as

$$x\sin a + y\times 2\sin a\cos a + z\sin a(3-4\sin^2 a)$$
$$= 2\times 2\sin a\cos a\cos 2a$$
$$\Rightarrow x+2y\cos a+z(3+4\cos^2 a-4)$$
$$= 4\cos a(2\cos^2 a-1)\ as \sin a\neq 0$$
$$\Rightarrow 8\cos^3 a-4z\cos^2 a-(2y+4)\cos a+(z-x)=0$$
$$\Rightarrow \cos^3 a-\frac{z}{2}\cos^2 a-\frac{y+2}{4}\cos a+\frac{z-x}{8}=0$$

which shows that cos a is root of the equation

$$t^3-\frac{z}{2}t^2-\frac{y+2}{4}t+\frac{z-x}{8}=0$$

Similarly from second and third equations we can varify that $\cos b$ and $\cos c$ are the roots of the above equation

2. (a) $$u^2 = a^2+b^2+2\sqrt{\begin{matrix}(a^4+b^4)\cos^2\theta\sin^2\theta\\ +a^2b^2(\cos^4\theta+\sin^4\theta)\end{matrix}} \quad \ldots(i)$$

Now $(a^4+b^4)\cos^2\theta\sin^2\theta+a^2b^2(\cos^4\theta+\sin^4\theta)$

$$=(a^4+b^4)\cos^2\theta\sin^2\theta+a^2b^2(1-2\cos^2\theta\sin^2\theta)$$
$$=(a^4+b^4-2a^2b^2)\cos^2\theta\sin^2\theta+a^2b^2$$
$$=(a^2-b^2)^2.\frac{\sin^2 2\theta}{4}+a^2b^2 \quad \ldots(ii)$$
$$\because 0\le\sin^2 2\theta\le 1$$
$$\Rightarrow 0\le(a^2-b^2)^2\frac{\sin^2 2\theta}{4}\le\frac{(a^2-b^2)^2}{4}$$
$$\Rightarrow a^2b^2\le(a^2-b^2)^2\frac{\sin^2 2\theta}{4}+a^2b^2$$
$$\le(a^2-b^2)^2.\frac{1}{4}+a^2b^2 \quad \ldots(iii)$$

$\therefore$ from (i), (ii) and (iii)

Minimum value of $u^2 = a^2+b^2+2\sqrt{a^2b^2}=(a+b)^2$

Maximum value of u^2

$$=a^2+b^2+2\sqrt{(a^2-b^2)^2.\frac{1}{4}+a^2b^2}$$
$$=a^2+b^2+\frac{2}{2}\sqrt{(a^2+b^2)^2}=2(a^2+b^2)$$

$\therefore$ Max value – Min value

$$=2(a^2+b^2)-(a+b^2)=(a-b)^2$$

3. (c) We have

$$\sum_{m=1}^{6}\operatorname{cosec}\left[\theta+\frac{(m-1)\pi}{4}\right]\operatorname{cosec}\left[\theta+\frac{m\pi}{4}\right]=4\sqrt{2}$$

$$\Rightarrow \sum_{m=1}^{6}\frac{\sin\frac{\pi}{4}}{\sin\left[\theta+\frac{(m-1)\pi}{4}\right]\sin\left[\theta+\frac{m\pi}{4}\right]}=4$$

$$\Rightarrow \sum_{m=1}^{6}\frac{\sin\left[\left(\theta+\frac{m\pi}{4}\right)-\left(\theta+\frac{(m-1)\pi}{4}\right)\right]}{\sin\left(\theta+\frac{(m-1)\pi}{4}\right)\sin\left(\theta+\frac{m\pi}{4}\right)}=4$$

$$\Rightarrow \sum_{m=1}^{6}\frac{\left[\begin{matrix}\sin\left(\theta+\frac{m\pi}{4}\right)\cos\left(\theta+\frac{(m-1)\pi}{4}\right)\\ -\cos\left(\theta+\frac{m\pi}{4}\right)\sin\left(\theta+\frac{(m-1)\pi}{4}\right)\end{matrix}\right]}{\sin\left(\theta+\frac{(m-1)\pi}{4}\right)\sin\left(\theta+\frac{m\pi}{4}\right)}=4$$

$$\Rightarrow \sum_{m=1}^{6}\left[\cot\left(\theta+\frac{(m-1)\pi}{4}\right)-\cot\left(\theta+\frac{m\pi}{4}\right)\right]=4$$

$$\Rightarrow \left[\cot\theta-\cot\left(\theta+\frac{\pi}{4}\right)\right]+\left[\cot\left(\theta+\frac{\pi}{4}\right)-\cot\left(\theta+\frac{2\pi}{4}\right)\right]$$
$$+\ldots+\left[\cot\left(\theta+\frac{5\pi}{4}\right)-\cot\left(\theta+\frac{6\pi}{4}\right)\right]=4$$

$$\Rightarrow \cot\theta-\cot\left(\theta+\frac{3\pi}{2}\right)=4\Rightarrow\cot\theta+\tan\theta=4$$

$$\Rightarrow \cos^2\theta+\sin^2\theta=4\sin\theta\cos\theta$$

$$\Rightarrow \sin 2\theta=\frac{1}{2}\Rightarrow 2\theta=\frac{\pi}{6}\text{or}\frac{5\pi}{6}\quad\Rightarrow\theta=\frac{\pi}{12}\text{or}\frac{5\pi}{12}$$

4. (c) $\sqrt{3}\ \sec x+\operatorname{cosec} x+2(\tan x-\cot x)=0$

$$\Rightarrow \frac{\sqrt{3}}{2}\sin x+\frac{1}{2}\cos x=\cos^2 x\ \sin^2 x$$

$$\Rightarrow \cos\left(x-\frac{\pi}{3}\right)=\cos 2x$$

$$\Rightarrow x-\frac{\pi}{3}=2n\pi\pm 2x$$

$$\Rightarrow x=\frac{2n\pi}{3}+\frac{\pi}{9}\ \text{or}\ x=-2n\pi-\frac{\pi}{3}$$

For $x \in S, n=0 \Rightarrow x=\frac{\pi}{9},-\frac{\pi}{3}$

$n=1 \Rightarrow x=\frac{7\pi}{9}$

$n=-1 \Rightarrow x=\frac{-5\pi}{9}$

$\therefore$ Sum of all values of $x=\frac{\pi}{9}-\frac{\pi}{3}+\frac{7\pi}{9}-\frac{5\pi}{9}=0$

5. **(a)** We are given that

$(\cot\alpha_1).(\cot\alpha_2)\ldots.(\cot\alpha_n)=1$

$\Rightarrow (\cos\alpha_1)(\cos\alpha_2)\ldots.(\cos\alpha_n)$

$=(\sin\alpha_1)(\sin\alpha_2)\ldots.(\sin\alpha_n)$ ....(i)

Let $y=(\cos\alpha_1)(\cos\alpha_2)\ldots.(\cos\alpha_n)$ (to be max.)

Squaring both sides, we get

$y^2=(\cos^2\alpha_1)(\cos^2\alpha_2)\ldots.(\cos^2\alpha_n)$

$=\cos\alpha_1\sin\alpha_1\cos\alpha_2\sin\alpha_2\ldots.\cos\alpha_n\sin\alpha_n$ (Using (i))

$=\frac{1}{2^n}[\sin 2\alpha_1\sin 2\alpha_2\ldots.\sin 2\alpha_n]$

As $0\le\alpha_1,\alpha_2,\ldots..\alpha_n\le\pi/2$

$\therefore 0\le 2\alpha_1, 2\alpha_2,\ldots..2\alpha_n\le\pi$

$\Rightarrow 0\le\sin 2\alpha_1,\sin 2\alpha_2,\ldots..\sin 2\alpha_n\le 1$

$\therefore y^2\le\frac{1}{2^n}.1\Rightarrow y\le\frac{1}{2^{n/2}}$

$\therefore$ Max. value of y is $1/2^{n/2}$.

6. **(b)** $\alpha<\beta<\gamma<\delta$ and $\sin\alpha=\sin\beta=\sin\gamma=\sin\delta=k$

$\Rightarrow\beta=\pi-\alpha,\ \gamma=2\pi+\alpha,\ \delta=3\pi-\alpha$

So that the given expression is equal to

$$4\sin\frac{\alpha}{2}+3\sin\left(\frac{\pi-\alpha}{2}\right)+2\sin\frac{2\pi+\alpha}{2}+\sin\frac{3\pi-\alpha}{2}$$

$$=4\sin\frac{\alpha}{2}+3\cos\frac{\alpha}{2}-2\sin\frac{\alpha}{2}-\cos\frac{\alpha}{2}$$

$$=2\left(\sin\frac{\alpha}{2}+\cos\frac{\alpha}{2}\right)=2\sqrt{1+2\sin\frac{\alpha}{2}\cos\frac{\alpha}{2}}=2\sqrt{1+k}$$

7. **(a,b,c,d)** We have, $1+\sec\theta=\frac{1+\cos\theta}{\cos\theta}=\frac{2\cos^2\frac{\theta}{2}}{\cos\theta}$,

similarly for others.

$$f_n(\theta)=\tan\frac{\theta}{2}.\frac{2\cos^2\frac{\theta}{2}}{\cos\theta}.\frac{2\cos^2\theta}{\cos 2\theta}\ldots..\frac{2\cos^2 2^{n-1}\theta}{\cos 2^n\theta}$$

$$=\tan\frac{\theta}{2}.2^{n+1}\frac{[\cos\theta.\cos 2\theta\ldots\ldots.\cos 2^{n-1}\theta]\cos^2\frac{\theta}{2}}{\cos 2^n\theta}$$

$$=\frac{\sin\theta}{\cos 2^n\theta}.2^n.\frac{\sin 2^n\theta}{2^n\sin\theta}=\tan 2^n\theta$$

$$\therefore f_2\left(\frac{\pi}{16}\right)=\tan\left(4.\frac{\pi}{16}\right)=1,.$$

$$f_3\left(\frac{\pi}{32}\right)=\tan\left(8.\frac{\pi}{32}\right)=1$$

Similarly others are also true.

8. **(a,c)** $\sin\beta=\frac{12}{13}\Rightarrow\cos\beta=\pm\frac{5}{13}$

according as $\tan\beta>0$ or <0

$\therefore 5\sin(\alpha+\beta)-12\cos(\alpha+\beta)$

$=5[\sin\alpha\cos\beta+\cos\alpha\sin\beta]$

$-12[\cos\alpha\cos\beta-\sin\alpha\sin\beta]$

$=(5\cos\beta+12\sin\beta)\sin\alpha$

$+(5\sin\beta-12\cos\beta)\cos\alpha$

$$=\left(\frac{25}{13}+\frac{144}{13}\right)\sin\alpha+\left(\frac{60}{13}-\frac{60}{13}\right)\cos\alpha$$

$=13\sin\alpha$ if $\tan\beta>0$

$\Rightarrow\{(5\sin(\alpha+\beta)-12\cos(\alpha+\beta)\}\operatorname{cosec}\alpha=13$

If $\tan\beta<0$ then $5\sin(\alpha+\beta)-12\cos(\alpha+\beta)$

$$=\frac{119}{13}\sin\alpha+\frac{120}{13}\cos\alpha$$

$\Rightarrow[5\sin(\alpha+\beta)-12\cos(\alpha+\beta)]\operatorname{cosec}\alpha$

$$=\frac{119}{13}+\frac{120}{13}\cot\alpha$$

9. **(b, c, d)** From the first relation we have

$a[\sin(\theta+\phi)-\sin(\theta-\phi)]=b[\sin(\theta-\phi)+\sin(\theta+\phi)]$

$\Rightarrow 2a\sin\phi\cos\theta=2b\sin\theta\cos\phi$

$\Rightarrow a\tan\phi=b\tan\theta\Rightarrow$ (b) is correct

$$\Rightarrow \frac{2a\tan\frac{\phi}{2}}{1-\tan^2\frac{\phi}{2}} = \frac{2b\tan\frac{\theta}{2}}{1-\tan^2\frac{\theta}{2}}$$

From the second relation replacing

$\tan\frac{\theta}{2} = \frac{1}{a}[b\tan\frac{\phi}{2}+c]$ we have

$$\frac{a\tan\frac{\phi}{2}}{1-\tan^2\frac{\phi}{2}} = \frac{\left(b(b\tan\frac{\phi}{2}+c)\right)}{a\left[1-\left\{\frac{1}{a}(b\tan\frac{\phi}{2}+c\right\}^2\right]}$$

$$\Rightarrow \tan\frac{\phi}{2}\left[a^2-(b\tan\frac{\phi}{2}+c)^2\right]$$

$$= b\left(b\tan\frac{\phi}{2}+c\right)\left(1-\tan^2\frac{\phi}{2}\right)$$

$$\Rightarrow \tan\frac{\phi}{2}(a^2-b^2-c^2) = bc\left(1+\tan^2\frac{\phi}{2}\right)$$

$$\Rightarrow \frac{2\tan\frac{\phi}{2}}{1+\tan^2\frac{\phi}{2}} = \frac{2bc}{a^2-b^2-c^2}$$

$$\Rightarrow \sin\phi = \frac{2bc}{a^2-b^2-c^2}$$

Similarly we get $\sin\theta = \frac{2ac}{a^2-b^2+c^2}$

10. (b,c,d) Given : $\frac{\tan 3A}{\tan A} = k$ ...(1)

$$\Rightarrow \frac{\tan 3A - \tan A}{\tan A} = k-1 \Rightarrow \frac{\sin 2A}{\cos 3A \sin A} = k-1$$

$$\Rightarrow \frac{2\cos A}{\cos 3A} = k-1 \Rightarrow \frac{\cos A}{\cos 3A} = \frac{k-1}{2}$$

$\Rightarrow$ (a) is incorrect

Again $\frac{\tan 3A}{\tan A} = k \Rightarrow \frac{\sin 3A}{\cos 3A}.\frac{\cos A}{\sin A} = k$

$$\Rightarrow \frac{\sin 3A}{\sin A} = k.\frac{2}{k-1} = \frac{2k}{k-1}$$

$$\Rightarrow \frac{3\sin A - 4\sin^3 A}{\sin A} = \frac{2k}{k-1}$$

$$\Rightarrow 3-4\sin^2 A = \frac{2k}{k-1} \text{ or } 4\sin^2 A = \frac{k-3}{k-1}$$

$$\Rightarrow 0 < \frac{k-3}{k-1} < 4 \ [\sin A \neq 0 \text{ or } 1]$$

Now, $\frac{k-3}{k-1} > 0$ is $k<1$ or $k>3$ ...(ii)

and $\frac{k-3}{k-1} < 4$

$\Rightarrow \frac{3k-1}{k-1} > 0 \Rightarrow k < \frac{1}{3}$ or $k > 1$ ...(iii)

(ii) and (iii) simultaneously hold if $k < \frac{1}{3}$ or $k > 3$

11. (4)

We have

$$\left(a\tan\beta - \sqrt{a^2-1}\tan\alpha\right)^2 + \left(\sqrt{a^2+1}\tan\beta - \sqrt{a^2-1}\tan\gamma\right)^2$$

$$+\left(a\tan\gamma - \sqrt{a^2+1}\tan\alpha\right)^2 \geq 0$$

$$\Rightarrow \{a^2+a^2-1+a^2+1\}(\tan^2\alpha+\tan^2\beta+\tan^2\gamma)$$

$$-\left\{a\tan\alpha + \sqrt{a^2-1}\tan\beta + \sqrt{a^2+1}\tan\gamma\right\}^2 \geq 0$$

$$\Rightarrow \tan^2\alpha + \tan^2\beta + \tan^2\gamma \geq \frac{4a^2}{3a^2} \Rightarrow 3\sum\tan^2\alpha \geq 4$$

12. (3)

$$1+\cos\alpha = 1+\frac{2\cos\beta-1}{2-\cos\beta}$$

$$= \frac{2-\cos\beta+2\cos\beta-1}{2-\cos\beta} = \frac{1+\cos\beta}{2-\cos\beta}$$

$$\Rightarrow 2\cos^2\frac{\alpha}{2} = \frac{2\cos^2(\beta/2)}{1+2\sin^2(\beta/2)}$$

$$\Rightarrow \cos^2\frac{\alpha}{2} = \frac{\cos^2(\beta/2)}{1+2\sin^2(\beta/2)} \quad ...(1)$$

$$\Rightarrow 1-\cos^2\frac{\alpha}{2} = 1-\frac{\cos^2(\beta/2)}{1+2\sin^2(\beta/2)}$$

$$= \frac{1+2\sin^2(\beta/2)-\cos^2(\beta/2)}{1+2\sin^2(\beta/2)} = \frac{3\sin^2\frac{\beta}{2}}{1+2\sin^2\frac{\beta}{2}}$$

$$\Rightarrow \sin^2\frac{\alpha}{2} = \frac{3\sin^2(\beta/2)}{1+2\sin^2(\beta/2)} \quad ...(2)$$

Divide eqs. (2) by (1), we get

$$\tan^2\frac{\alpha}{2} = 3\tan^2\frac{\beta}{2} \Rightarrow \frac{\tan(\alpha/2)}{\tan(\beta/2)} = \sqrt{3}$$

$$\Rightarrow \sqrt{3}\frac{\tan(\alpha/2)}{\tan(\beta/2)} = 3$$

13. (0)

We have $xy + yz + zx = xyz\left(\frac{1}{x}+\frac{1}{y}+\frac{1}{z}\right)$

Now, $x\cos\theta = y\cos\left(\theta+\frac{2\pi}{3}\right) = z\cos\left(\theta+\frac{4\pi}{3}\right) = k$ (say)

then $x = \frac{k}{\cos\theta}, y = \frac{k}{\cos\left(\theta+\frac{2\pi}{3}\right)}$ and $z = \frac{k}{\cos\left(\theta+\frac{4\pi}{3}\right)}$

$$\Rightarrow \frac{1}{x}+\frac{1}{y}+\frac{1}{z} = \frac{1}{k}\left[\cos\theta+\cos\left(\theta+\frac{2\pi}{3}\right)+\cos\left(\theta+\frac{4\pi}{3}\right)\right]$$

$$= \frac{1}{k}\left[\cos\theta+\cos\theta\left(\frac{-1}{2}\right)-\sin\theta\left(\frac{\sqrt{3}}{2}\right)+\cos\theta\left(-\frac{1}{2}\right)-\sin\theta\left(-\frac{\sqrt{3}}{2}\right)\right]$$

$$= \frac{1}{k}\left[\cos\theta-\cos\theta-\frac{\sqrt{3}}{2}\sin\theta-\frac{\sqrt{3}}{2}\sin\theta\right] = 0$$

$\therefore\ xy + yz + zx = 0$

14. (6)

Given that $\sin^3 x\sin 3x = \sum_{m=0}^{n} c_m\cos mx$

or $\left(\frac{3\sin x-\sin 3x}{4}\right).\sin x = \sum_{m=0}^{n} c_m\cos mx$

or $\frac{3}{8}.(2\sin 3x\sin x)-\frac{1}{8}.2\sin^2 3x = \sum_{m=0}^{n} c_m\cos mx$

or $\frac{3}{8}.[\cos 2x-\cos 4x]-\frac{1}{8}[1-\cos 6x] = \sum_{m=0}^{n} c_m\cos mx$

or $-\frac{1}{8}+\frac{3}{8}\cos 2x-\frac{3}{8}\cos 4x+\frac{1}{8}\cos 6x = \sum_{m=0}^{n} c_m\cos mx$.

Comparing, we get n = 6.

15. (b) $\because\ P_1 = m$

$P_1^2 = m^2$

$\sin^2\theta + \cos^2\theta + 2\sin\theta\cos\theta = m^2$

$\Rightarrow\ \sin\theta\cos\theta = \frac{(m^2-1)}{2}$

Now, from eq. (iii), we get

$P_6 = 1 - 3\sin^2\theta\cos^2\theta$

$\Rightarrow\ (1-P_6) = 3(\sin\theta\cos\theta)^2 = \frac{3(m^2-1)^2}{4}$

$\Rightarrow\ 4(1-P_6) = 3(m^2-1)^2$

16. (a) Let $\sin^2\theta\cos^2\theta = k$, then from eq. (i), we get

$P_n - P_{n-2} = -kP_{n-4}$.

From eq. (ii), $P_4 = 1-2k$

and from eq. (iii), $P_6 = 1-3k$

Put $n = 10$,

then $P_{10} - P_8 = -kP_6 = -k(1-3k)$

$\therefore\ P_{10} - P_8 = 3k^2 - k \quad ...(iv)$

and put $n = 8$, then $P_8 - P_6 - kP_4 = -k(1-2k)$

$P_8 = P_6 + 2k^2 - k$

$= 1 - 3k + 2k^2 - k$

$\Rightarrow\ P_8 = 2k^2 - 4k + 1$

From eq. (iv), $P_{10} = 5k^2 - 5k + 1$

$\therefore\ 6P_{10} - 15P_8 + 10P_6 + 7$

$= 6(5k^2-5k+1) - 15(2k^2-4k+1) + 10(1-3k) + 7$

$= 8$

17. (b) $5\sin^2 x + 3\sin x\cos x - 3\cos^2 x = 2(\sin^2 x + \cos^2 x)$

$\Rightarrow\ 3\tan^2 x + 3\tan x - 5 = 0$

$\Rightarrow\ \tan x = \frac{-3\pm\sqrt{69}}{6}$

and $\sin^2 x - \cos 2x = 2 - \sin 2x$

$3\sin^2 x + 2\sin x\cos x = 3(\sin^2 x + \cos^2 x)$

$\Rightarrow\ \cos x(2\sin x - 3\cos x) = 0$

Either $\cos x = 0$ or $\tan x = \frac{3}{2} \Rightarrow \cos x = \pm\frac{2}{\sqrt{13}}$

Taking $= \alpha = \frac{-3\pm\sqrt{69}}{6}$, $\tan\beta = \frac{3}{2}$

we get $\tan\alpha + \tan\beta = 1\pm\sqrt{69}/6$

18. (d) Taking $\tan\alpha = \frac{-3+\sqrt{69}}{6}$, $\tan\beta = \frac{-3-\sqrt{69}}{6}$

$\cos\gamma = 0, \cos\delta = \pm\frac{2}{\sqrt{13}}$

we get $\tan\alpha\tan\beta + \cos\gamma + \cos\delta = -\frac{5}{3}\pm\frac{2}{\sqrt{13}}$

19. A - p,q,r,s; B - r,s; C - q,r,s; D - q, s

(A) $f(\theta) = (\sin\theta + \operatorname{cosec}\theta)^2 + (\cos\theta + \sec\theta)^2$

$$= \sin^2\theta + \cos^2\theta + \sec^2\theta + \operatorname{cosec}^2\theta + 4$$

$$= 5 + 1 + \cot^2\theta + 1 + \tan^2\theta = 9 + (\tan\theta - \cot\theta)^2 \geq 9$$

(B) $\sin\alpha - \sin\beta = a,\ \cos\alpha + \cos\beta = b$

$$\Rightarrow a^2 + b^2 = 2 + 2\cos(\alpha+\beta) = 4\cos^2\frac{\alpha+\beta}{2} \leq 4$$

(C) $\dfrac{\sin A + \sin B}{2} \leq \sin\left(\dfrac{A+B}{2}\right)$

$\therefore \sin A + \sin B \leq 2\sin\frac{\pi}{4}$

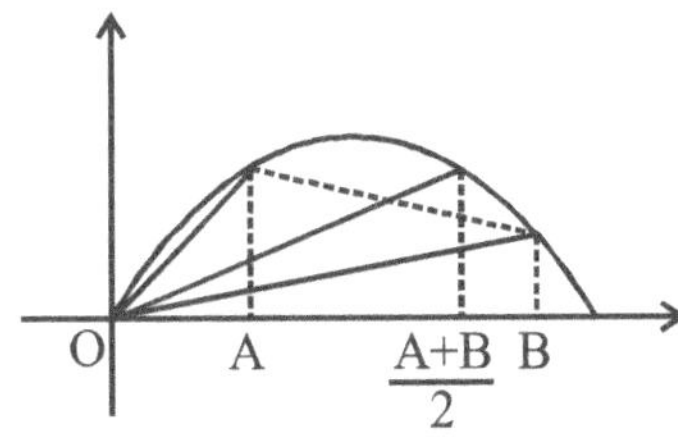

or $\frac{1}{\sqrt{2}}(\sin A + \sin B) \leq 1$

(D) Let $A = 7\cos x + 6\sin x = 6(2\cos x + \sin x) - 5\cos x$
$= 6 - 5\cos x$
Now, $2\cos x + \sin x = 1 \Rightarrow \sin x = 1 - 2\cos x$
$\Rightarrow \sin^2 x = 1 - \cos^2 x = 1 - 4\cos x + 4\cos^2 x$

$\therefore \cos x = 0$ or $\frac{4}{5}$. So, $A = 6$ or 2

20. A - q; B - p, s; C - r; D - p

(A) $y = \cos^2\theta + \sin^4\theta = \cos^2\theta + \sin^2\theta(1 - \cos^2\theta)$

$$= 1 - \frac{1}{4}\sin^2 2\theta \Rightarrow \frac{3}{4} \leq A \leq 1$$

(B) $\tan A < 0 \Rightarrow A > \frac{\pi}{2} \Rightarrow 0 < B + C < \frac{\pi}{2}$

$$\Rightarrow \tan(B+C) > 0 \Rightarrow \frac{\tan B + \tan C}{1 - \tan B\tan C} > 0$$

$$\Rightarrow 0 < \tan B\tan C < 1$$

(C) Let $y = \dfrac{\cos^2\theta - 1}{\cos^2 + \cos\theta}$

$$\Rightarrow (y-1)\cos^2\theta + y\cos\theta + 1 = 0$$

$$\Rightarrow \cos\theta = -1 \text{ or } \cos\theta = \frac{1}{1-y}$$

$$-1 < \frac{1}{1-y} < 1$$

$$\Rightarrow y < 0 \text{ or } y > 2$$

(D) $y = \tan A\tan B = \tan A\tan\left(\frac{\pi}{3} - A\right)$

$= x\left(\dfrac{\sqrt{3} - x}{1 + \sqrt{3}x}\right)$, where $x = \tan A$

$$\Rightarrow x^2 + \sqrt{3}x(y-1) + y = 0$$

$$\because x \in R \Rightarrow 3(y-1)^2 - 4y \geq 0 \Rightarrow y \leq \frac{1}{3} \text{ or } y \geq 3$$

Also, $0 < A, B < \frac{\pi}{3} \Rightarrow 0 < \tan A, \tan B < \sqrt{3}$

$$\Rightarrow 0 < \tan A\tan B < 3$$

$$\therefore 0 < y \leq \frac{1}{3}$$

1. **(a)** Let $z = x + iy$, then the equation is

$$x^2 + y^2 - 2i(x+iy) + 2c(1+i) = 0$$

$$\Rightarrow (x^2 + y^2 + 2y + 2c) + i(2c - 2x) = 0$$

$$\Rightarrow x^2 + y^2 + 2y + 2c = 0 \text{ and } x = c$$

$$\Rightarrow c^2 + y^2 + 2y + 2c = 0$$

$$\Rightarrow y = -1 \pm \sqrt{1-2c-c^2}$$

$$\because y \in \mathbf{R} \Rightarrow 1 - 2c - c^2 \geq 0$$

$$\Rightarrow c^2 + 2c - 1 \leq 0 \Rightarrow -1-\sqrt{2} \leq c \leq -1+\sqrt{2}$$

$\therefore$ The equation has a solution, if

$c \in [-1-\sqrt{2}, -1+\sqrt{2}]$ and the solution is given by

$$z = c + i(-1 \pm \sqrt{1-2c-c^2})$$

The equation has no solution, if

$$c \in (-\infty, -1-\sqrt{2}) \cup (-1+\sqrt{2}, \infty)$$

2. **(d)** $|z_1| = |z_2| = 1 \Rightarrow a^2 + b^2 = c^2 + d^2 = 1$ ...(1)

and Re $(z_1\bar{z}_2) = 0 \Rightarrow$ Re$\{(a+ib)(c-id)\} = 0$

$\Rightarrow ac + bd = 0$ ...(2)

Now from (1) and (2), $a^2 + b^2 = 1$

$\Rightarrow a^2 + \dfrac{a^2c^2}{d^2} = 1 \Rightarrow a^2 = d^2$ ...(3)

Also $c^2 + d^2 = 1 \Rightarrow c^2 + \dfrac{a^2c^2}{b^2} = 1$

$\Rightarrow b^2 = c^2$ ...(4)

$|\omega_1| = \sqrt{a^2+c^2} = \sqrt{a^2+b^2} = 1$ [From (1) and (4)]

and $|\omega_2| = \sqrt{b^2+d^2} = \sqrt{c^2+d^2} = 1$ [from (1) and (4)]

Further Re $(\omega_1\bar{\omega}_2) =$ Re$\{(a+ic)(b-id)\}$

$= ab + cd = ab + \left(-\dfrac{ac}{b}\right)c$ [From (2)]

$= \dfrac{ab^2 - ac^2}{b} = 0$ [from (4)].

Also, $\text{Im}(\omega_1\overline{\omega_2}) = bc - ad = bc - a\left(-\dfrac{ac}{b}\right)$

$$= \frac{(a^2+b^2)c}{b} = \frac{c}{b} = \pm 1 \neq 0$$

$\therefore |\omega_1| = 1, |\omega_2| = 1$ and Re$(\omega_1\bar{\omega}_2) = 0$

3. **(a)** If $f(x) = Ax^2 - |G|x - H$, then $f(0) = -H < 0$ and $f(-1) = A + |G| - H > 0$. So, $f(x) = 0$ has one root in $(-1, 0)$ hence the equation has a negative fraction root. Also,

$f(2) = 4A - 2|G| - H = 2(A - |G|) + (A - H) + A > 0$.

So, $f(x) = 0$ has one root in $(0, 2)$, hence the equation has a positive root, which cannot exceed 2.

4. **(c)** $a > b > c$ ...(1)

and given equation is

$(a+b-2c)x^2 + (b+c-2a)x + (c+a-2b) = 0$ ...(2)

$\because$ Equation (2) has a root in the interval $(-1, 0)$

$\therefore f(-1)f(0) < 0$

$\Rightarrow (2a-b-c)(c+a-2b) < 0$ ...(3)

From (1), $a > b \Rightarrow a - b > 0$ and

$a > c \Rightarrow a - c > 0 \therefore 2a - b - c > 0$ ...(4)

From (3) and (4), $c + a - 2b < 0$ or $c + a < 2b$. Option (a) is wrong. Again, the sum of coefficients of the equation $= 0$, that is one root is 1 and the other root is $\dfrac{c+a-2b}{a+b-2c}$, which is a rational number as a, b, c are rational. Hence, both the roots of the equation are rational .

$\Rightarrow$ (b) is wrong. Further, the discriminate of equation $ax^2 + 2bx + c = 0$ is $D = 4b^2 - 4ac$.

As deduced earlier, $c + a < 2b$

$$\Rightarrow 4b^2 > (c+a)^2$$

$$\Rightarrow 4b^2 > c^2 + a^2 + 2ac$$

$$\Rightarrow 4b^2 - 4ac > c^2 + a^2 - 2ac$$

$= (c-a)^2 \Rightarrow 4b^2 - 4ac > 0 \Rightarrow D > 0$. Also, each of a,b,c are positive.

$\therefore$ The equation $ax^2 + 2bx + c = 0$ has real and negative roots. So (c) is correct.

5. **(a)** Since -5 and 1 are the roots. Product of roots $= -5 \times 1 = b \Rightarrow b = -5$ and

Sum of roots $= -5 + 1 = -[a^2 - 5a + b + 4]$

$\Rightarrow [a^2 - 5a - 1] = 4 \Rightarrow 4 \le a^2 - 5a - 1 < 5$

$[\because [x] = n \Rightarrow n \le x < n+1]$

$\Rightarrow a^2 - 5a - 5 \ge 0$ and $a^2 - 5a - 6 < 0$

$\Rightarrow a \le \frac{5-\sqrt{45}}{2}$ or $a \ge \frac{5+\sqrt{45}}{2}$ and $-1 < a < 6$

$\Rightarrow -1 < a \le \frac{5-3\sqrt{5}}{2}$ or $\frac{5+3\sqrt{5}}{2} \le a < 6$

$\Rightarrow a \in \left(-1, \frac{5-3\sqrt{5}}{2}\right] \cup \left[\frac{5+3\sqrt{5}}{2}, 6\right)$

6. **(d)** Let $z = x + iy$, then $\arg(z - 3i) = \arg(x + iy - 3i) = \frac{3\pi}{4}$

$\Rightarrow x < 0, y - 3 > 0$ $\quad (\because \frac{3\pi}{4}$ is in II quadrant)

and $\frac{y-3}{x} = \tan\frac{3\pi}{4} = -1$

$\Rightarrow y = -x + 3 \ \forall x < 0$ and $y > 3$ ...(1)

and $\arg(2z + 1 - 2i) = \arg[(2x+1) + i(2y-2)] = \frac{\pi}{4}$

$\Rightarrow 2x + 1 > 0, 2y - 2 > 0$ $\quad (\because \frac{\pi}{4}$ is in I quadrant)

and $\frac{2y-2}{2x+1} = \tan\frac{\pi}{4} = 1 \Rightarrow 2y - 2 = 2x + 1$

$\Rightarrow y = x + \frac{3}{2} \ \forall x > -\frac{1}{2}, y > 1$ .....(2)

From equations (1) and (2), we get graph

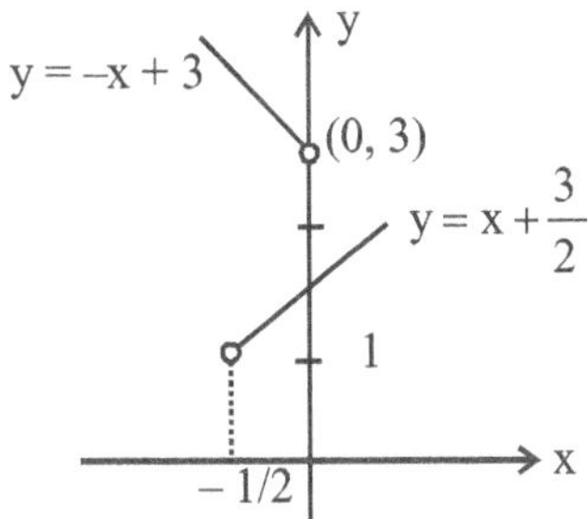

It is clear from the graph that two lines do not intersect.

$\therefore$ No point of intersection.

Caution : *It is most likely that the students after getting two straight lines, solve them to get the point of intersection* $\left(\frac{3}{4}, \frac{9}{4}\right)$*. Clearly the principal values of arguments must be considered.*

7. **(a, d)**

We have $z_1^3 + z_2^3 + z_3^3 = -z_1z_2z_3$.

$\Rightarrow -4z_1z_2z_3 = z_1^3 + z_2^3 + z_3^3 - 3z_1z_2z_3$

$= (z_1 + z_2 + z_3)(z_1^2 + z_2^2 + z_3^2 - z_2z_3 - z_3z_1 - z_1z_2)$

$= (z_1 + z_2 + z_3)[(z_1 + z_2 + z_3)^2 - 3(z_2z_3 + z_3z_1 + z_1z_2)]$

$\Rightarrow z^3 - 3z(z_2z_3 + z_3z_1 + z_1z_2) + 4z_1z_2z_3 = 0$

where $z = z_1 + z_2 + z_3$

$\Rightarrow z^3 = z_1 z_2 z_3 \left[3z\left(\frac{1}{z_1} + \frac{1}{z_2} + \frac{1}{z_3}\right) - 4\right]$

$= z_1z_2z_3\left[3z\left(\bar{z}_1 + \bar{z}_2 + \bar{z}_3\right) - 4\right]$ $\quad [\because |z_1| = |z_2| = |z_3| = 1]$

$= z_1z_2z_3\left[3z\bar{z} - 4\right]$

$\Rightarrow |z|^3 = |z_1||z_2||z_3| \ |3|z|^2 - 4|$

$\Rightarrow |z|^3 - |3|z|^2 - 4| = 0$

If $|z| \ge 2/\sqrt{3}$, we get

$|z|^3 - |3|z|^2 + 4| = 0$

$\Rightarrow (|z| - 2)(|z|^2 - |z| - 2) = 0$

$\Rightarrow (|z| - 2)^2(|z| + 1) = 0$

$\Rightarrow |z| - 2 = 0$ or $|z| = 2$

If $|z| < 2/3$, we get

$|z|^3 + 3|z|^2 - 4 = 0$

$\Rightarrow (|z| - 1)(|z|^2 + 4|z| + 4) = 0$

$\Rightarrow |z| - 1 = 0 \Rightarrow |z| = 1$

8. **(a,d)** Discriminant $D = 4p^2 - 4(p^2 - 1) = 4 > 0$

$\because$ Roots of the equation are real and distinct

Now both the roots are less than 4 if

$D \ge 0$, $f(4) > 0$ and $4 > -\frac{-2p}{2}$

$\Rightarrow 16 - 8p + p^2 - 1 > 0$ and

$4 > p \Rightarrow (p-3)(p-5) > 0$ and $p < 4$

$\Rightarrow p < 3$ or $p > 5$ and $p < 4 \Rightarrow p \in (-\infty, 3)$

Again both the roots are greater than

-2 if $D \ge 0$, $f(-2) > 0$ and $-2 < -\frac{-2p}{2}$

$\Rightarrow (4 + 4p + p^2 + 1) > 0$ and

$3 < p \Rightarrow (p+3)(p+1) > 0$ and $p > -3$

$\Rightarrow p < -3$ or $p > -1$ and $p > -3 \Rightarrow p \in (-1, \infty)$

Further exactly one root lies in the interval $(-2, 4)$ if

$D > 0$ and $f(-2)f(4) < 0$

$\Rightarrow (p+3)(p+1)(p-3)(p-5) < 0$

$\Rightarrow p \in (-3, -1) \cup (3, 5)$

Finally, 1 lies between the roots if $D > 0$ and $f(1) < 0$

$\Rightarrow 1 - 2p + p^2 - 1 < 0 \Rightarrow p(p-2) < 0$

$\Rightarrow 0 < p < 2 \Rightarrow p \in (0, 2)$

Alternatively :

$x^2 - 2px + p^2 - 1 = 0 \Rightarrow (x-p)^2 = 1$

$\therefore x = p \pm 1$

Both the roots are less than 4 if $p+1 < 4$ and $p-1 < 4 \Rightarrow p < 3$

Both the roots are greater than –2 if $p+1 > -2$ and $p-1 > -2 \Rightarrow p > -1$

Exactly one root lies in (–2, 4) if $-2 < p+1 < 4$ or $-2 < p-1 < 4$ but not both

$\Rightarrow p \in (-3, -1) \cup (3, 5)$

One root is less than 1 and other greater than 1 if $p+1 < 1 < p-1$ or $p-1 < 1 < p+1 \Rightarrow 0 < p < 2$

NOTE : *The alternate method is easier than the general method, so if the roots of quadratic in terms of parameter come out to be free of radical the alternative method is better.*

9. **(b,c)** The given equation is,

$$\pi^e (x-\pi)(x-\pi-e) + e^\pi (x-e)(x-\pi-e) + (\pi^\pi + e^e)(x-e)(x-\pi) = 0$$

Let $f(x) = \pi^e (x-\pi)(x-\pi-e) + e^\pi (x-e)(x-\pi-e) + (\pi^\pi + e^e)(x-e)(x-\pi)$

Then $f(e) = \pi^e (e-\pi)(-\pi) > 0 \quad [\because e < \pi]$

and $f(\pi) = e^\pi (\pi - e)(-e) < 0$

$\therefore$ Equation $f(x) = 0$ has a real root in (e, π).

Again $f(\pi + e) = (\pi^\pi + e^e)(\pi)(e) > 0$.

$\therefore$ Equation $f(x) = 0$ has a real root in $(\pi, e + \pi)$.

$\therefore$ $f(x) = 0$ has a real roots in (e, π)

and other in $(\pi, \pi + e)$

Also, $\pi - e < e$

$\therefore$ Equation $f(x) = 0$ has two real roots in $(\pi - e, \pi + e)$.

10. **(a,b,c)**

Put $\omega = \cos\frac{2\pi}{11} + i\sin\frac{2\pi}{11}$,

so that for $1 \le k \le 10$

$$\sin\frac{2\pi}{11} - i\cos\frac{2\pi k}{11}$$

$$= -i\left(\cos\frac{2\pi k}{11} + i\sin\frac{2\pi k}{11}\right)$$

$= -i\omega^k$ [De Moivre's theorem]

Thus,

$$S = -i\sum_{k=1}^{10} \omega^k = -\frac{i\omega(1-\omega^{10})}{1-\omega} = \frac{i\omega(1-\omega^{11})}{1-\omega}$$

But $\omega^{11} = \cos 2\pi + i\sin 2\pi = 1 + i0 = 1$

$\therefore \quad S = i$

$\Rightarrow \quad S + \bar{S} = 0, \; S\bar{S} = 1$

and $\sqrt{S} = \pm\frac{1}{\sqrt{2}}(1+i)$

11. **(6)**

Solving $z^2 - z + 1 = 0 \Rightarrow z = \frac{1 \pm i\sqrt{3}}{2}$

Taking $z = \frac{1 + i\sqrt{3}}{2} = \cos\frac{\pi}{3} + i\sin\frac{\pi}{3}$

$\Rightarrow z^n = \cos\frac{n\pi}{3} + i\sin\frac{n\pi}{3}$, $n = 1, 2, \ldots, 24$

$\therefore \quad z^n + \frac{1}{z^n} = 2\cos\frac{n\pi}{3}$

$$\therefore \quad \left(z + \frac{1}{z}\right)^2 + \left(z^2 + \frac{1}{z^2}\right)^2 + \left(z^3 + \frac{1}{z^3}\right)^2 + \ldots\ldots + \left(z^{24} + \frac{1}{z^{24}}\right)^2$$

$$= 2^2\cos^2\frac{\pi}{3} + 2^2\cos^2\frac{2\pi}{3} + 2^2\cos^2\frac{3\pi}{3} + 2^2\cos^2\frac{24\pi}{3}$$

$$= 2\left[\left(1 + \cos\frac{2\pi}{3}\right) + \left(1 + \cos\frac{4\pi}{3}\right) + \left(1 + \cos\frac{6\pi}{3}\right) + \ldots\ldots + \left(1 + \cos\frac{48\pi}{3}\right)\right]$$

$$=2\left[24+\frac{\cos\left\{\frac{2\pi}{3}+\frac{23\pi}{3}\right\}\sin\frac{24\pi}{3}}{\sin\frac{\pi}{3}}\right]=2(24+0)=48$$

Using the formula,

$\cos\alpha+\cos(\alpha+\beta)+\cos(\alpha+2\beta)+.......+$

$$\cos\{\alpha+(n-1)\beta\}=\frac{\cos\left\{\alpha+\frac{(n-1)\beta}{2}\right\}\sin\frac{n\beta}{2}}{\sin\frac{\beta}{2}}$$

12. **(2)** Roots of $x^2-10cx-11d=0$ are a and $b \Rightarrow a+b=10c$ and $ab=-11d$
Similarly c and d are the roots of
$x^2-10ax-11b=0 \Rightarrow c+d=10a$ and $cd=-11b$
$\Rightarrow a+b+c+d=10(a+c)$ and $abcd=121bd$
$\Rightarrow b+d=9(a+c)$ and $ac=121$
Also we have $a^2-10ac-11d=0$ & $c^2-10ac-11b=0$
$\Rightarrow a^2+c^2-20ac-11(b+d)=0$
$\Rightarrow (a+c)^2-22\times121-99(a+c)=0 \Rightarrow a+c=121$ or -22
For $a+c=-22$ we get $a=c$
$\therefore$ rejecting this value we have $a+c=121$
$\therefore a+b+c+d=10(a+c)=1210$

13. **(2)** $ax^2+bx+c=0$ has roots α and β

$$\Rightarrow \alpha+\beta=-\frac{b}{a},\ \alpha\beta=\frac{c}{a}.$$

If the roots of equation $a^5x^2+ba^2c^2x+c^5=0$ are γ and δ, then

$$\gamma+\delta=-\frac{b}{a}\left(\frac{c}{a}\right)^2=(\alpha+\beta)\alpha^2\beta^2=\alpha^3\beta^2+\alpha^2\beta^3$$

Clearly roots are $\alpha^3\beta^2$ and $\alpha^2\beta^3$

$$\Rightarrow \alpha^5\beta^5=32 \Rightarrow \alpha\beta=2$$

14. **(2)** The given relation can be rewritten as

$$\frac{1}{a+\omega}+\frac{1}{b+\omega}+\frac{1}{c+\omega}=\frac{2}{\omega}$$

and $$\frac{1}{a+\omega^2}+\frac{1}{b+\omega^2}+\frac{1}{c+\omega^2}=\frac{2}{\omega^2}$$

$\Rightarrow$ ω and ω^2 are roots of $\frac{1}{a+x}+\frac{1}{b+x}+\frac{1}{c+x}=\frac{2}{x}$

$$\Rightarrow \frac{3x^2+2(a+b+c)x+bc+ca+ab}{(a+x)(b+x)(c+x)}=\frac{2}{x}$$

$$\Rightarrow x^3-(bc+ca+ab)x-2abc=0 \qquad ...(1)$$

Two roots of the equation (1) are ω and ω^2. Let the third root be α, then

$\alpha+\omega+\omega^2=0 \Rightarrow \alpha=-\omega-\omega^2=1.$

$\therefore$ $\alpha=1$ will satisfy equation (1)

$$\Rightarrow \frac{1}{a+1}+\frac{1}{b+1}+\frac{1}{c+1}=2$$

15. **(5)** We have $z=\frac{1}{2}\left(\sqrt{3}-i\right)$

$=-\frac{1}{2}i\left(1+i\sqrt{3}\right)=i\omega$

where $\omega\neq1$ is a cube of unity.

$\therefore$ $z^{89}=(i\omega^2)^{89}=i^{89}\,\omega^{178}=i\omega$

Also, $i^{97}=i^{96}\,i=i$

Thus, $(z^{89}+i^{97})^{94}=(i\omega+i)^{94}=[i(-\omega^2)]^{94}=-\omega^2$

Also, $z^n=i^n\,\omega^{2n}$

$\therefore$ The given equation becomes

$-\omega^2=i^n\,\omega^{2n} \Rightarrow i^n\,\omega^{2n-2}=-1$

This is possible if n is of the type 4k + 2 and 2n – 2 is a multiple of 3.

That is $2(4k+2)-2=8k+2$ is multiple of 3.

The least value of k for which this is possible is 2.

Therefore, n = 10.

16. **(d)** $\because |z+i\omega|\leq|z|+|i\omega|=|z|+|i||\omega|\leq2$
$\therefore |z+i\omega|=2 \Leftrightarrow |z|=|\omega|=1.$

17. **(d)** Let $z=x+iy$ and $\omega=\alpha+i\beta$

Now $|z+i\omega|=2 \Rightarrow (z+i\omega)(\bar{z}-i\bar{\omega})=4$

$\Rightarrow |z|^2+|\omega|^2+i\omega\bar{z}-i\bar{\omega}z=4$

$\Rightarrow i\omega\bar{z}-i\bar{\omega}z=2 \qquad ...(1)$

and $|z-i\bar{\omega}|=2 \Rightarrow (z-i\bar{\omega})(\bar{z}+i\omega)=4$

$\Rightarrow |z|^2+|\omega|^2+i\omega z-i\bar{\omega}\bar{z}=4$

$\Rightarrow i\omega z-i\bar{\omega}\bar{z}=2 \qquad ...(2)$

Add (1) and (2), $\Rightarrow i(\omega-\bar{\omega})(z+\bar{z})=4$

$\Rightarrow i(2i\beta)(2x)=4 \Rightarrow \beta x=-1 \qquad ...(3)$

Subtract (1) from (2),

$\Rightarrow i(\omega+\bar{\omega})(z-\bar{z})=0 \Rightarrow \alpha y=0 \qquad ...(4)$

From (4), either $\alpha=0$ or $y=0$.

If $y=0$, then $x^2+y^2=1 \Rightarrow x=\pm1 \Rightarrow z=1$ or -1

If $\alpha=0$, then $\alpha^2+\beta^2=1 \Rightarrow \beta=\pm1 \Rightarrow w=\pm i.$

So, $I_m(z)=\text{Re}(w)=0$

18. (c) Using the result

$z_1^2+z_2^2+z_3^2-z_1z_2-z_2z_3-z_3z_1=0$, we get

$a^2-1+2ai+1-b^2+2bi+0-a+b-i-abi=0$

$\therefore\ a^2-b^2-a+b=0$ and $2a+2b-ab-1=0$

$\Rightarrow a=b$ and $2a+2b-ab-1=0$

($\because\ a+b=1$ does not give real solution)

$\therefore\ a=b$ and $a^2-4a+1=0$

$a=b=2-\sqrt{3}$ $\qquad(\because\ a<1, b<1)$

19. (b) $z_0=\dfrac{z_1+z_2+z_3}{3}$

$\Rightarrow\ z_1^2+z_2^2+z_3^2-2z_1z_2-2z_2z_3-2z_3z_1=9z_0^2$

$\Rightarrow\ 3(z_1^2+z_2^2+z_3^2)=9z_0^2\ \Rightarrow\ z_1^2+z_2^2+z_3^2=3z_0^2$

$(\because\ z_1^2+z_2^2+z_3^2=z_1z_2+z_2z_3+z_3z_1)$

20. A - q; B - r; C - p; D - s

(A) $(z+\alpha\beta)^3=\alpha^3\Rightarrow z+\alpha\beta=\alpha,\omega\alpha,\omega^2\alpha$

$\Rightarrow z=\alpha-\alpha\beta,\ \omega\alpha-\alpha\beta,\ \omega^2\alpha-\alpha\beta$, say z_1, z_2, z_3 respectively

Now, $|z_1-z_2|=|z_2-z_3|=|z_3-z_1|=\sqrt{3}|\alpha|$

So, the triangle is equilateral and has area

$=\dfrac{\sqrt{3}}{4}|z_1-z_2|^2$

(B) $|z-\alpha|^2=4|z-\bar{\alpha}|^2$

$\Rightarrow z\bar{z}-\alpha\bar{z}-\bar{\alpha}z+\alpha\bar{\alpha}=4(z\bar{z}-\alpha z-\bar{\alpha}\bar{z}+\alpha\bar{\alpha})$

$\Rightarrow 3z\bar{z}+(\alpha-4\bar{\alpha})\bar{z}+(\bar{\alpha}-4\alpha)z+3\alpha\bar{\alpha}=0$

or $z\bar{z}+\dfrac{\alpha-4\bar{\alpha}}{3}\bar{z}+\dfrac{\bar{\alpha}-4\alpha}{3}z+\alpha\bar{\alpha}=0$

which is a circle of radius

$=\sqrt{\left|\dfrac{\alpha-4\bar{\alpha}}{3}\right|^2-\alpha\bar{\alpha}}=\sqrt{-\dfrac{4}{9}(\alpha-\bar{\alpha})^2}=\dfrac{2}{3}|\alpha-\bar{\alpha}|$

(C) z lies on a circle of radius 1 and centre at (1, 0)

$\angle OPA=\pm\dfrac{\pi}{2}\Rightarrow\dfrac{2-z}{0-z}=\dfrac{|2-z|}{|z|}e^{\pm i\frac{\pi}{2}}$

$\Rightarrow\dfrac{z-2}{z}=\dfrac{AP}{OP}(\pm i)=\pm i\tan\alpha$

$\therefore\left|\dfrac{z-2}{z}\right|=|\tan\alpha|$

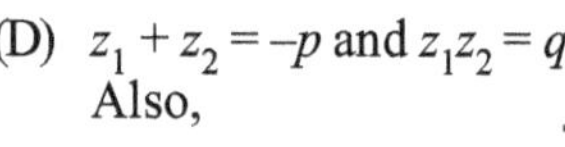

(D) $z_1+z_2=-p$ and $z_1z_2=q$

Also,

$\dfrac{z_2}{z_1}=\cos\alpha\pm i\sin\alpha$

$\Rightarrow\dfrac{z_2-z_1\cos\alpha}{z_1}=\pm i\sin\alpha$

or $z_2^2-2z_2z_1\cos\alpha+z_1^2\cos^2\alpha=-z_1^2\sin^2\alpha$

$\Rightarrow z_1^2+z_2^2=2z_1z_2\cos\alpha$

or $(z_1+z_2)^2=2z_1z_2(1+\cos\alpha)\Rightarrow\dfrac{p^2}{q}=4\cos^2\dfrac{\alpha}{2}$

1. **(c)** $33! = 1.2.3.5 \ldots\ldots 33$

$= (2.4.6 \ldots\ldots 32)(1.3.5 \ldots\ldots 33)$

$= 2^{16}(1.2.3.4 \ldots\ldots 16)(1.3.5 \ldots\ldots 33)$

$= 2^{16}(2.4.6 \ldots\ldots 16)(1.3.5 \ldots\ldots 15)(1.3.5 \ldots\ldots 33)$

$= 2^{16}.2^{8}(1.2.3 \ldots\ldots 8)(1.3.5 \ldots\ldots 15)(1.3.5 \ldots\ldots 33)$

$= 2^{24}(2.4.6.8)(1.3.5.7)(1.3.5 \ldots\ldots 15)(1.3.5 \ldots\ldots 33)$

$= 2^{24}.2^{4}(1.2.3.4)(1.3.5.7)(1.3.5 \ldots\ldots 15)(1.3.5 \ldots\ldots 33)$

$= 2^{28}(2.4)(1.3)(1.3.5.7)(1.3.5 \ldots\ldots 15)(1.3.5 \ldots\ldots 33)$

$= 2^{28}.2^{2}(1.2)(1.3)(1.3.5.7)(1.3.5 \ldots\ldots 15)(1.3.5 \ldots\ldots 33)$

$= 2^{31}(1.3)(1.3.5.7)(1.3.5 \ldots\ldots 15)(1.3.5 \ldots\ldots 33)$

Thus the maximum value of 'n' for which 33 ! is divisible by 2^n is 31.

ALTERNATIVELY, the exponent of 2 in 33 ! is given by

$$E_2(33!) = \left[\frac{33}{2}\right] + \left[\frac{33}{2^2}\right] + \left[\frac{33}{2^3}\right] + \left[\frac{33}{2^4}\right] + \left[\frac{33}{2^5}\right]$$

$$= 16 + 8 + 4 + 2 + 1 = 31.$$

NOTE : If p is a prime number then largest-power k of p such that p^k divides $n!$ is given by

$$\left[\frac{n}{p}\right] + \left[\frac{n}{p^2}\right] + \left[\frac{n}{p^3}\right] + \ldots\ldots$$

It is also called exponent of p in $n!$ and we write $E_p(n!)$

Where $[x]$ represents integral part of x

2. **(a)** Let $a = 2p + 1, b = 2q + 1, c = 2r + 1, d = 2s + 1$ where p, q, r and s are non-negative integers.

$\therefore\ 2p + 1 + 2q + 1 + 2r + 1 + 2s + 1 = 20$ or $p + q + r + s = 8$

The required number of solutions = The number of non-negative integral solutions of $(p + q + r + s = 8)$.

$= {}^{8+4-1}C_{4-1} = {}^{11}C_3$

$= 165.$

3. **(d)** The smallest number, which can occur in the middle is 4.

The number of numbers with 4 in the middle

$= {}^4P_4 - {}^3P_3$

($\because$ The other four places are to be filled by 0, 1, 2 and 3, and a number cannot begin with 0)

Similarly, the number of numbers with 5 in the middle

$= {}^5P_4 - {}^4P_3$, etc.

$\therefore$ The required number of numbers

$= ({}^4P_4 - {}^3P_3) + ({}^5P_4 - {}^4P_3) + ({}^6P_4 - {}^5P_3) + \ldots\ldots + ({}^9P_4 - {}^8P_3) = \sum_{n=4}^{9} ({}^nP_4 - {}^{n-1}P_3)$

4. **(d)** We may consider the problem as filling the digits in boxes of the figure :

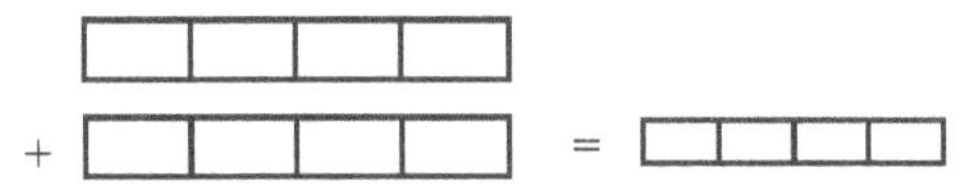

If 0 is placed in the units place of the upper number then the units place of the lower number can be filled in 9 ways (filling by any one of 0, 1, 2 ...., 9).

If 1 is placed in the units place of the upper number then the units place of the lower number can be filled in 9 ways (filling by any one of 0, 1, 2, ..., 8), etc.

$\therefore$ The units column can be filled in $10 + 9 + 8 + \ldots\ldots + 1$, i.e., 55 ways. Similarly for the second and the third columns. The number of ways for the fourth column $= 8 + 7 + \ldots\ldots + 1 = 36$.

$\therefore$ The required number of ways $= 55 \times 55 \times 55 \times 36$.

5. **(d)** Let $n = 2m + 1$

For the three numbers in A. P., we have the following pattern, Common Numbers Ways difference

1	$(1, 2, 3), (2, 3, 4), \ldots\ldots (n-2, n-1, n)$	$(n-2)$
2	$(1, 3, 5), (2, 4, 6), \ldots\ldots (n-4, n-2, n)$	$(n-4)$
3	$(1, 4, 7), (2, 5, 8), \ldots\ldots (n-6, n-3, n)$	$(n-6)$
4	....	
5	....	
.	....	
.	....	
.	....	
m	$(1, m+1, 2m+1)$	1

$\therefore$ Favourable number of ways

$= (n-2) + (n-4) + (n-6) + \ldots\ldots + 3 + 1$

m terms $= \frac{m}{2}(n - 2 + 1) = \frac{n-1}{2} \cdot \frac{n-1}{2} = \frac{(n-1)^2}{4}$

Alternatively, if a, b, c are in A. P., then $a + c = 2b$

$\therefore$ Sum of terminal digits is even.

$\therefore$ Terminal digits must be either both even or both odd.

$\therefore$ Required number of selections = number of ways of selecting 2 odd numbers from $\frac{n+1}{2}$ odd numbers + number of ways of selecting 2 even numbers from $\frac{n-1}{2}$ even number [$\because$ n is odd]

$$= {}^{\frac{n+1}{2}}C_2 + {}^{\frac{n-1}{2}}C_2 = \frac{\frac{n+1}{2}\times\frac{n-1}{2}}{2} + \frac{\frac{n-1}{2}\times\frac{n-3}{2}}{2}$$

$$= \frac{(n-1)^2}{4}.$$

6. **(b,c,d)** When $z=n+1$ we can choose x, y from $\{1,2,...,n\}$

$\therefore$ when $z=n+1, x, y$ can be chosen in n^2 ways and if $z=n, x, y$ can be chosen in $(n-1)^2$ ways and so on

$$\therefore n^2+(n-1)^2+...+1^2=\frac{1}{6}n(n+1)(2n+1)$$

ways of choosing triplets

ALTERNATIVELY triplets with $x=y<z, x<y<z, y<z<x$

can be chosen in ${}^{n+1}C_2, {}^{n+1}C_3, {}^{n+1}C_3$ ways.

There are ${}^{n+1}C_2+2({}^{n+1}C_3)={}^{n+2}C_2+{}^{n+1}C_3$

$$=2({}^{n+2}C_3)-{}^{n+1}C_2.$$

7. **(a, b, c)** Number of all possible triangles = ${}^nC_3$

Out of these n triangles have two sides common with polygon and $n(n-4)$ triangles have exactly one side common with polygon.

So, desired number of triangles

$$={}^nC_3-n-n(n-4)$$

$$=\frac{n(n-1)(n-2)}{6}-n-n(n-4)$$

$$=\frac{n}{6}(n-4)(n-5)=\frac{n}{n-3}\,{}^{n-3}C_3$$

ALTERNATIVELY:

If we consider a particular vertex, say A_i. If A_i is not included in the selection then we have to select 3 vertices from remaining $(n-1)$ vertices on a circle such that no two are consecutive, which can be done in ${}^{(n-1)-3+1}C_3$ ways = ${}^{n-3}C_3$ ways.

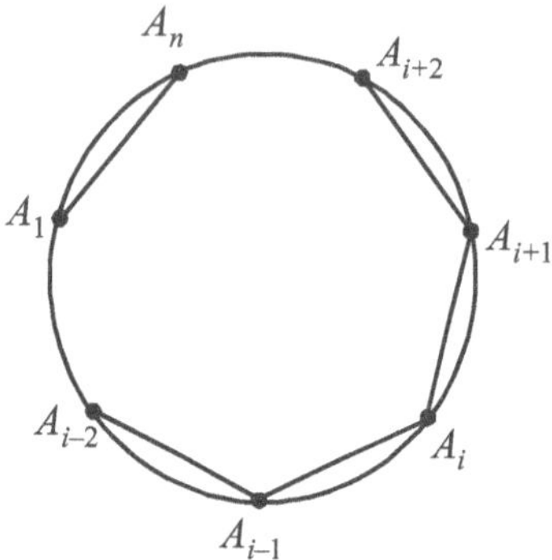

If A_i is included, then A_{i-1} and A_{i+1} can not be included, so we can choose 2 points from remaining $n-3$ points such that they are not adjacent in ${}^{n-3-2+1}C_2={}^{n-4}C_2$ ways. So, desired number of triangles $={}^{n-3}C_3+{}^{n-4}C_2$

8. **(a, b, c, d)**

We have

E = (2n + 1) (2n + 3) (2n + 5) ... (4n –3) (4n –1)

$$=\frac{(2n)!(2n+1)(2n+2)(2n+3)(2n+4)...(4n-1)(4n)}{(2n)(2n+2)(2n+4)...(4n)}$$

$$=\frac{(4n)!n!}{(2n)!2^n n!\,n(+1)(n+2)...(2n)}=\frac{1}{2^n}\cdot\frac{(4n)!n!}{(2n)!(2n)!}$$

$\Rightarrow 2^n E = ({}^{4n}C_{2n})(n!)$

This shows that 2^n E is divisible by ${}^{4n}C_{2n}$ and also by n!

$$\Rightarrow\frac{2^n E}{n!}={}^{4n}C_{2n}\text{, a positive integer.}$$

Also, note that

$$\frac{2^n E}{(4n)!}=\frac{n!}{(2n)!(2n)!}\text{ is not an integer as n > 1.}$$

9. **(a, b, c)** For f(i) < f(j) whenever i<j, is equivalent to choose 3 numbers out of {1, 2, 3, 4, 5, 6, 7} in ${}^7C_3$. For f (i) ≤ f (j) whenever i <j, the number of ways is ${}^7C_3+2({}^7C_2)+{}^7C_1=84$

For (c), see (a).

10. **(5)** The terminal digit in the different powers of 3 and 7 are as follows :

$$\begin{cases} 3^1=3 & 3^2=9 & 3^3=.........7 & 3^4=.........1 \\ 3^5=......3 & 3^6=.......9 & 3^7=......... & 3^8=.........1 \\ 3^9=......3 \end{cases}$$

$$\begin{cases} 7^1=7 & 7^2=9 & 7^3=.........3 \\ 7^5=......7 & 7^6=.......9 & 7^7=.........3 \\ 7^9=......7 \end{cases}$$

$7^4=..........1$

$7^8=..........1$

$$\begin{cases} m = 1;\ n = 1, 5, 9, 13, 17,\}\ 5 \text{ pairs} \\ m = 2;\ n = 4, 8, 12, 16, 20,\}\ 5 \text{ pairs} \\ m = 3;\ n = 3, 7, 11, 15, 19,\}\ 5 \text{ pairs} \\ m = 4;\ n = 2, 6, 10, 14, 18,\}\ 5 \text{ pairs} \\ \ldots\ldots\ldots\ldots \\ m = 20;\ n = 2, 6, 10, 14, 18,\}\ 5 \text{ pairs} \end{cases}$$

$\therefore$ required (m, n) pairs $= 20 \times 5 = 100$ pairs

ALTERNATIVELY:

End digits in power of 3 and 7 repeat in cycle of 4

$3^m \to 3^{4k} = 1\ \ 3^{4k+1} = 3 \qquad 3^{4k+2} = 9\ \ 3^{4k+3} = 7$

$7^n \to 7^{4k} = 1 \qquad 7^{4k+1} = 7 \qquad 7^{4k+2} = 9\ \ 7^{4k+3} = 3$

So the numbers $\{1, 2, 3, \ldots, 20\}$ can be divided into 4 sets

$4k$ type $\{4, 8, 12, 16, 20\} = A$

$4k + 1$ type $\{1, 5, 9, 13, 17\} = B$

$4k + 2$ type $\{2, 6, 10, 14, 18\} = C$

$4k + 3$ type $\{3, 7, 11, 15, 19\} = D$

Now $3^m + 7^n$ is divisible by 10, if end digit of the number is 0.

Thus if $m \in A$ then $n \in C$, if $m \in B$ then $n \in B$

if $m \in C$ then $n \in A$, if $m \in D$ then $n \in D$

So, desired number of ordered pairs (m, n)

$= 5 \times 5 + 5 \times 5 + 5 \times 5 + 5 \times 5 = 100$

11. **(1)** Let A_t, $t = 1, 2, \ldots\ldots 6$ be the set of days on which the friend is present at dinner and B_t be the set of days on which the friend is absent at dinner. Then $|A_t| = |B_t| = 7$

Also $|A_i \cap A_j| = 7$, $|A_i \cap A_j \cap A_k| = 4$

$|A_i \cap A_j \cap A_k \cap A_l| = 3$, $|A_i \cap A_j \cap A_k \cap A_l \cap A_m| = 2$

and

$|A_1 \cap A_2 \cap A_3 \cap A_4 \cap A_5 \cap A_6| = 1$

Where i, j, k, l, m, vary from 1 to 6 and are distinct. Now the number of dinners at which at least one friend was present

$$= |A_1 \cup A_2 \cup \ldots\ldots \cup A_6| = \sum |A_i| - \sum |A_i \cap A_j| + \sum |A_i \cap A_j \cap A_k|$$

$$- \sum |A_i \cap A_j \cap A_k \cap A_l| + \sum |A_i \cap A_j \cap A_k \cap A_l \cap A_m| - |A_1 \cap A_2 \cap \ldots\ldots \cap A_6|$$

$$= {}^6C_1 \times 7 - {}^6C_2 \times 5 + {}^6C_3 \times 4 - {}^6C_4 \times 3 + {}^6C_5 \times 2 - {}^6C_6 \times 1 = 13$$

Total number of dinners is $|A_t| + |B_t| = 7 + 7 = 14$

$\therefore$ Number of dinners the person had alone $= 14 - 13 = 1$

12. **(7)**

$1000 = 2^3.5^3, 2000 = 2^4.5^3$

So, $a = 2^A.5^R, b = 2^B.5^S, c = 2^C.5^T$,

$\max(A, B) = 3, \max(A, C) = \max(B, C) = 4$

$\max(R, S) = \max(R, T) = \max(S, T) = 3$.

We can choose R, S, T in following ways

(1) $R = S = T = 3$ in 1 ways

(2) Two of R, S and T are 3 and one is 2 in 3 ways

(3) Two of R, S and T are 3 and one is 1 in 3 ways

(4) Two of R, S and T are 3 and one is 0 in 3 ways

So, R, S and T can be selected in 10 ways

Now, we can choose A, B, C in following ways

(1) C is necessarily 4

(2) One of A and B is 3 and other 2 in two ways

(3) One of A and B is 3 and other 1 in two ways

(4) One of A and B is 3 and other 0 in two ways

(5) $A = B = 3$ in one way

So, A, B, and C can be selected in 7 ways

So, the required number $= 10 \times 7 = 70$.

13. **(2)**

Dictionary will have first the words starting with the letter A, then by C, E, K, L and finally the words starting with T.

Number of words starting with $A = 5! = 120$ [Since there are 5 letters other than A, and position of A is fixed]

Number of words starting with $C = 5! = 120$

Number of words starting with $E = 5! = 120$

Number of words starting with $K = 5! = 120$

Number of words starting with $L = 5! = 120$

Now, we consider the words starting with T. Before the word TACKLE occurs, there will be the words TACEKL, TACELK, TACKEL then TACKLE.

$\therefore$ Rank of TACKLE $= 120 + 120 + 120 + 120 + 120 + 4 = 604$.

14. **(d)** ${}^{200}C_{100} = \dfrac{(200)(199)\ldots\ldots(101)}{(1)\,(2)\ldots(100)}$

All the two digit numbers occur in the denominator. Thus, the exponent of the largest two digit prime must at least 3 in (200)!. Since $[200/3] = 66$, we find the required largest two digit prime is 61.

15. **(b)** $E_5(n) = \sum_{k=1}^{\infty}\left[\dfrac{n}{5^k}\right] < \sum_{k=1}^{\infty}\left(\dfrac{n}{5^k}\right) = \dfrac{n}{4}$

$\Rightarrow n > 4E_5(n) = 104$

But for $n \le 109$, $E_5(n) < 26$

$\therefore n \ge 110$

The desired numbers are 110, 111, 112, 113, 114.

Solution For 16 - 18

- Number of four digit odd-number which are formed by using 0, 1, 2, 3, 5, 7 (with repetition)
  $= 5 \times 6 \times 6 \times 4 = 36 \times 20 = 720$
- Number of numbers greater than 1000 but less than 4000 which are formed by using the digits 0, 1, 2, 3, 4, 5 (without repetition)
  $= 3 \times 4 \times 3 \times 2 = 72$
- We know that a number is divisible by 3 only when the sum of the digits is divisible by 3.
  Now the possible number of combinations of 5 digits out of 6 different digits 0, 1, 2, 3, 4, 5 (without repetition) are ${}^6C_5 = 6$, which are as follows–

$1+2+3+4+5=15=3\times 5$ (divisible by 3)
$0+2+3+4+5=14$ (not divisible by 3)
$0+1+3+4+5=13$ (not divisible by 3)
$0+1+2+4+5=12=3\times 4$ (divisible by 3)
$0+1+2+3+5=11$ (not divisible by 3)
$0+1+2+3+4=10$ (not divisible by 3)

Thus the number should certain the digits 1, 2, 3, 4, 5 or the digits 0, 1, 2, 4, 5.

Taking 1, 2, 3, 4, 5, the 5 digit numbers are $= \lfloor 5 = 120$

Taking 0, 1, 2, 4, 5, the 5 digit numbers are $= \lfloor 5 - \lfloor 4$
$=96$

$\therefore$ Total number of numbers $= 120+96=216$

- Now the 7 digit numbers using the digits 1, 2 and 3 only such that the sum of digits in a number is 10
This can be done by taking 2, 2, 2, 1, 1, 1, 1 or by taking 2, 3, 1, 1, 1, 1, 1.

$\therefore$ Number of ways $= \dfrac{\lfloor 7}{\lfloor 3\ \lfloor 4} + \dfrac{\lfloor 7}{\lfloor 5} = 77$

16. **(b)**
17. **(a)**
18. **(c)**

19. **A - r; B - s; C - p; D - q**

(A) Number of 6 digit numbers which can be formed using only 1 digit = 9

Number of 6 digit numbers can be formed using 2 digits

Case 1 : When zero is included

$$= {}^9C_6\left[\frac{\lfloor 5}{\lfloor 3\lfloor 2}+\frac{\lfloor 5}{\lfloor 3\lfloor 2}+\frac{\lfloor 5}{\lfloor 4}\right]=225$$

Case 2 : When zero is not included

$$= {}^9C_2\left[\frac{\lfloor 6}{\lfloor 2\lfloor 4}+\frac{\lfloor 6}{\lfloor 3\lfloor 3}+\frac{\lfloor 6}{\lfloor 2\lfloor 4}\right]=1800$$

Number of such numbers using 3 digits

Case 1 : When zero is included

$$= {}^9C_2\left[\frac{\lfloor 5}{\lfloor 2\lfloor 2}+\frac{\lfloor 5}{\lfloor 2\lfloor 2}\right]=2160$$

Case 2 : When zero is excluded

$$= {}^9C_3\left[\frac{\lfloor 6}{\lfloor 2\lfloor 2\lfloor 2}\right]=7560$$

Total number $=9+225+1800+2160+7560=11754.$

(B) Since books are to be tied up in a bundle so that books are to be kept in a group or set and hence required number of ways

$$= \frac{1}{\lfloor 3}[3^5 - {}^3C_1 2^5 + {}^3C_2] = 25.$$

(C) One subject must be repeated in two periods. So the required number of ways $= 5\times\dfrac{6!}{2!}=1800$

(D) There are $26\times 26 = 676$ different possible set of two initials possible. So there are to be minimum $676+1=677$ students to guarantee.

20. **A - s; B - q; C - r; D - p**

(A) Total number of three digit numbers $= 9\times 10\times 10$
Half of which will have sum of digits even.

(B) $xyz = 140 = 2^2 . 5 . 7$
Therefore number of positive integral solutions
$= 3\times 3\times {}^4C_2 = 54.$

(C) $x+y+z+t = 10$, where $1\le x, y, z \le 8,\ 0\le t\le 7$
Therefore desired number of solutions = coeff. of x^{10} in $(x+x^2+ \ldots + x^8)^3 \times (1+x+x^2+\ldots+x^7)$
$= {}^{10}C_7 = {}^{10}C_3 = 120.$

(D) We must have $i^3 + ai^2 + bi + c = 0$ and
$(-i)^3 + a(-i)^2 + b(-i) + c = 0$
$\Rightarrow b = 1$ and $a = c$
Therefore number of numbers of type *abc* or *cba* is ${}^9C_1 = 9$
Number of numbers of type bac or *bca* is ${}^{10}C_1 = 10$
But 111 is included in both the counting.

1. (b) Given, $(1+x-2x^2)^6 = 1 + a_1x + a_2x^2 + ...$
Putting x = 1, we get $0 = 1 + a_1 + a_2 + a_3 + ... a_{12}$ ...(i)
Putting x = – 1, we get 64
$= 1 - a_1 + a_2 - a_3 + \ldots + a_{12}$ ...(ii)
On adding Eqs. (i) and (ii), we get
$64 = 2 + 2a_2 + 2a_4 + 2a_6 + ... + 2a_{12}$
$\Rightarrow a_2 + a_4 + a_6 + \ldots + a_{12} = 31.$

2. (a) The given question is same as to find the term independent of x in the expansion of

$$(1+x^n)\cdot\left(1-\frac{1}{x}\right)^n$$

The given expression can be written as

$$= (-1)^n \cdot \frac{(1-x^2)^n}{x^n}$$

$\therefore$ The term independent of x in the above expansion is same as the coefficient of x^n in $(-1)^n \cdot (1-x^2)^n$ which in turn is equal to the coefficient of x^n in

$$(-1)^n\left\{{}^nC_0 + {}^nC_1(-x)^2 + {}^nC_2(-x^2)^2 + \ldots + {}^nC_n(-x^2)^n\right\},$$

and the expansion contains only even powers of x. So, if n is odd
$\Rightarrow$ Coefficient is zero.

3. (a) Given expression is $\sum\sum_{0\le i\le j\le n}(C_i + C_j)^2$

$= n\left(C_0^2 + C_1^2 + \ldots + C_n^2\right) + 2\sum\sum_{0\le i\le j\le n} C_iC_j$

$= n \bullet {}^{2n}C_n + [(C_0 + C_1 + ... + C_n)^2 - (C_0^2 + C_1^2 + ... + C_n^2)]$

$= n \cdot {}^{2n}C_n + (2^n)^2 - {}^{2n}C_n = (n-1)\,{}^{2n}C_n + 2^{2n}$

4. (a) Required number of positive integral solutions
= coefficient of α^{20} in $(\alpha + \alpha^2 + ...)(\alpha^2 + \alpha^3 + ...)(\alpha^3 + \alpha^4 + ...)(\alpha^4 + \alpha^5 + ...)$
= coefficient of α^{20} in $\alpha^4 . \alpha^3 . \alpha^2 . \alpha$
$(1 + \alpha + \alpha^2 + ...)$
= coefficient of α^{10} in $(1-\alpha)^{-4} = {}^{10+4-1}C_{10}$
$= {}^{13}C_{10} = 286$

5. (b) Given $(2+\sqrt{3})^n = I + f$, where I is integer and $0 \le f < 1$. We note that $(2+\sqrt{3})(2-\sqrt{3}) = 1$. So let us assume that

$F = (2-\sqrt{3})^n$. Clearly $0 < F < 1$. Now,

$I + f + F = (2+\sqrt{3})^n + (2-\sqrt{3})^n$

$= 2[{}^nC_0 2^n + {}^nC_2 2^{n-2}.3 + {}^nC_4.2^{n-4}.3^2 + ...]$
$= 2 \times$ Integer = Integer
$\because I + f + F$ is integer $\Rightarrow f + F$ must be integer.
$\therefore 0 \le f < 1$ and $0 < F < 1 \Rightarrow 0 < f + F < 2$
$\Rightarrow f + F = 1 \Rightarrow F = 1 - f$
$\therefore (I+f)(1-f) = (I+f)F = (2+\sqrt{3})^n\ (2-\sqrt{3})^n = 1$

6. (c) The expression is $(1+x)^{101}(1-x+x^2)^{100}$

$= (1+x)((1+x)(1-x+x^2))^{100}$

$= (1+x)(1+x^3)^{100}$

$= (1+x)\{C_0 + C_1x^3 + C_2x^6 + \ldots + C_{100}x^{300}\}$

$$= (1+x)\sum_{r=0}^{100} {}^nC_r x^{3r} = \sum_{r=0}^{100} {}^nC_r x^{3r} + \sum_{r=0}^{100} {}^nC_r x^{3r+1}$$

Hence there will be no term containing $3r + 2$.

7. (b, c) Since i, j, k are distinct, $n-i+1, n-j+1, n-k+1$ are also distinct and they all lie from 1 to n. Now,

$$S = \sum\sum\sum(-x_{n-i+1})(-x_{n-j+1})(-x_{n-k+1})$$

$$= -\sum\sum\sum x_i x_j x_k = -S$$

$\Rightarrow$ S = 0 for all n

8. (a, b, c) Consider option (a) and (b) we get

$$T_{r+1} = {}^{256}C_r\,(3)^{\frac{256-r}{2}}.5^{r/8}$$

for $r = 0, 8, 16, 24 \ldots.., 256$ are rational, thus 33 terms are rational

So option (a) and (b) are correct.

Consider option (c) and (d) we get

Number of distinct terms is ${}^{(16+3-1)}C_{3-1} = {}^{18}C_2$

$= \frac{18\times 17}{2} = 9 \times 17 = 153$

Option (c) is correct but (d) is wrong.

9. **(a, b, c)** $f(n)=\sum_{r=1}^{n}\left(r(r+1)^{2}\,{}^{n}C_r - r^2\,{}^{n}C_{r-1}\right)$

$=(n+1)^2-1$

Now,

$$\sum_{n=1}^{n} f(n)=\left(2^2-1\right)+\left(3^2-1\right)+\left(4^2-1\right)+\left(5^2-1\right)$$

$$+\left(6^2-1\right)+\left(7^2-1\right)+\left(8^2-1\right)+\left(9^2-1\right)$$

$$+\left(10^2-1\right)$$

So $f(10)=11^2-1=120$

$f(20)=21^2-1=440$

10. **(a, c)** Let $\left(\sqrt{3}+1\right)^{2m}=I+F$, where $I\in N$ and $0<F<1$

Let $G=\left(\sqrt{3}-1\right)^{2m}$ then,

$$I+F+G=\left(\sqrt{3}+1\right)^{2m}+\left(\sqrt{3}-1\right)^{2m}$$

$$=2^m\left(2+\sqrt{3}\right)^m+2^m\left(2-\sqrt{3}\right)^m=2^{m+1}\times$$

an integer .... (i)

$\Rightarrow$ $I+F+G=$ an even integer

$\Rightarrow$ $F+G=$ an even integer $-I$

$\Rightarrow$ $F+G=$ an integer

$\Rightarrow$ $F+G=1$ [since $0<F<1, 0<G<1$]

Putting $F+G=1$ in Eq.(i), we get

$I+1=2^{m+1}\times$ an integer

$\Rightarrow$ 2^{m+1} is a factor of the integer just greater than $\left(\sqrt{3}+1\right)^{2m}$

11. **(5)** Now, $\sum_{r=0}^{n}\left(\frac{r+1+1}{r+1}\right){}^{n}C_r$

$$=\sum_{r=0}^{n}{}^{n}C_r+\frac{1}{(n+1)}\sum_{r=0}^{n}{}^{n+1}C_{r+1}$$

$$=2^n+\frac{1}{(n+1)}\left(2^{n+1}-1\right)$$

Since, $\sum_{r=0}^{n}\left(\frac{r+2}{r+1}\right){}^{n}C_r=\frac{2^8-1}{6}$ (given)

$\therefore 2^n+\frac{2^{n+1}-1}{n+1}=\frac{2^8-1}{6}$ therefore, n = 5

12. **(6)** $(1-2x+5x^2-10x^3)[C_0+C_1x+C_2x^2+\ldots]$

$=1+a_1x+a_2x^2+\ldots$

$a_1=n-2$ and $a_2=\frac{n(n-1)}{2}-2n+5$

Put $a_1^2=2a_2$

$(n-2)^2=n(n-1)-4n+10$

$n^2-4n+4=n^2-5n+10 \quad n=6$

13. **(2)** Since, $\left(1+x+x^2\right)^n=a_0+a_1x+a_2x^2+\ldots+a_{2n}x^{2n}$ ....(i)

Substituting $x=\omega$, ω^2 and 1 and then, adding them together $a_0+a_3+a_6+\ldots=3^{n-1}$

Multiplying Eq. (i) by x^2 and then repeating the same process again $a_1+a_4+a_7+\ldots=3^{n-1}$

$\Rightarrow a_0+a_3+a_6+\ldots=a_1+a_4+a_7+\ldots$

$=a_2+a_5+a_8+\ldots$

Since the required ratio is $\frac{2\cdot 3^{n-1}}{3^{n-1}}=2$

14. **(3)** We know that

$(1+ax)^n={}^{n}C_0+{}^{n}C_1(ax)^1+{}^{n}C_2(ax)^2+\ldots\ldots=$

$1+8x+24x^2+\ldots$ ....(i)

Now comparing coefficients of x^0, x^1, x^2 we get

${}^{n}C_0=1 \Rightarrow 1=1$

${}^{n}C_1=8 \Rightarrow na=8$

and ${}^{n}C_2\,.\,a^2=24\Rightarrow\frac{n(n-1)}{2}a^2=24$

Put $n=\frac{8}{a}$ we get

$$\Rightarrow\left[\left(\frac{8}{a}\right)^2-\frac{8}{a}\right]a^2=48$$

$\Rightarrow 64-8a=48 \Rightarrow a=2$

$\therefore n=4$

$$\therefore \frac{n-a}{a+n}=\frac{4-2}{2+4}=\frac{1}{3}$$

$$9\left(\frac{n-a}{a+n}\right)=3$$

15. **(c)** We have,

$$\sum_{r=0}^{n} r\,{}^{n}C_r a^r b^{n-r}$$

$$=\sum_{r=0}^{n} r.\frac{n}{r}\,{}^{n-1}C_{r-1}a.\,a^{r-1}b^{(n-1)-(r-1)}$$

$= na\left\{\sum_{r=0}^{n} {}^{n-1}C_{r-1}a^{r-1}\, b^{(n-1)-(r-1)}\right\}$

$= na(a+b)^{n-1}$

16. **(c)** We have, $\sum_{r=0}^{n} r^2\ {}^nC_r p^r q^{n-r}$

$= \sum_{r=0}^{n}\left[r(r-1)+r\right]{}^nC_r p^r q^{n-r}$

$= \sum_{r=0}^{n} r(r-1)\ {}^nC_r p^r q^{n-r} + \sum_{r=0}^{n} r.\ {}^nC_r p^r q^{n-r}$

$= \sum_{r=0}^{n} r(r-1)\frac{n}{r}.\frac{n-1}{r-1}\ {}^{n-2}C_{r-2}p^r q^{n-r}$

$+\sum_{r=0}^{n} r.\frac{n}{r}\ {}^{n-1}C_{r-1}p^r q^{n-r}$

$= n(n-1)p^2(p+q)^{n-2} + np(p+q)^{n-1}$

$= n(n-1)p^2 + np$ [since $p+q=1$]

$= n^2p^2 - np^2 + np$

$= n^2p^2 + npq$ [since $p+q=1$]

17. **(c)** $\sum_{0\le i<j\le n}\sum i.\ {}^nC_j = \sum_{r=1}^{n} {}^nC_r(0+1+2+\ldots r-1)$

$= \frac{1}{2}\left\{n(n-1)2^{n-2} + n.\,2^{n-1} - n.\,2^{n-1}\right\}$

$= n(n-1)2^{n-3}$

18. **(b)** $\sum_{0\le i<j\le n}\sum j.\ {}^nC_i$

$= \sum_{r=0}^{n-1} {}^nC_r\left[(r+1)+(r+2)+\ldots(n)\right]$

$= \sum_{r=0}^{n-1} {}^nC_r\left(\frac{n-r}{2}(r+1+n)\right)$

$= \sum_{r=0}^{n-1} {}^nC_r\left(\frac{n+1}{2}(n-r)+\frac{r(n-r)}{2}\right)$

$= \frac{n+1}{2}.\sum_{r=0}^{n}(n-r)\ {}^nC_r + \frac{n}{2}\sum_{r=0}^{n} r.\ {}^nC_r$

$-\frac{1}{2}\sum_{r=0}^{n} r^2.\ {}^nC_r$

$= \frac{n+1}{2}\sum_{r=0}^{n} r.\ {}^nC_r - \frac{n}{2}\sum_{r=0}^{n} r.\ {}^nC_r + \frac{1}{2}\sum_{r=0}^{n} r^2.\ {}^nC_r$

$= \frac{1}{2}\left(\sum_{r=0}^{n} r.\ {}^nC_r + \sum_{r=0}^{n} r^2.\ {}^nC_r\right)$

$= n(n+3).\,2^{n-3}$

19. **(A) → (s); (B) → (r); (C) → (p); (D) → (q)**

(A) $T_{r+1} = \dfrac{\frac{7}{2}\left(\frac{7}{2}-1\right)\left(\frac{7}{2}-2\right)\ldots\left(\frac{7}{2}-r+1\right)x^r}{r!}$

First negative term, if $\frac{7}{2}-r+1<0$ *i.e.*, $r>\frac{9}{2}$.

Hence, $r=5$

(B) $T_{r+1} = {}^5C_r\left(y^2\right)^{5-r}\left(\frac{1}{y}\right)^r = {}^5C_r y^{10-3r}$

$\therefore 10 = 3r+1 \Rightarrow r=3.$

So, coefficient of $y = {}^5C_3 = 10$

(C) $T_2 = 14a^{5/2}$

$\Rightarrow\ {}^nC_1\left(a^{\frac{1}{13}}\right)^{n-1}(a^{3/2})^1 = 14a^{5/2}$

$\Rightarrow\ na^{\frac{n-1}{13}} = 14a$

$\Rightarrow\ n=14$

(D) $\left(1+2x+3x^2+4x^3+\ldots\right)^{1/2}$

$= \left[(1-x)^{-2}\right]^{1/2}$

$= (1-x)^{-1} = 1+x+x^2+\ldots+x^n+\ldots$

Required sum is $1+1+1+1=4$

20. **(A) → (r); (B) → (s); (C) → (p); (D) → (q)**

(A) $1+99^n = 1+(100-1)^n = 1+\{{}^nC_0\,100^n - {}^nC_1\,100^{n-1} + \ldots - {}^nC_n\}$

Since n is odd

$= 100\{C_0\,100^{n-1} - {}^nC_1\,100^{n-2} + \ldots - {}^nC_{n-2}\,100 + {}^nC_{n-1}\}$

= 100 × integer whose unit place is different from 0

there are two zeroes at the end of the sum 99^n+1.

(B) $f(n) = 10^n + 3.4^{n+2} + 5$

$= 10^n - 1 + 3.4^{n+2} + 6 = (10^n-1) + 6\left(2^{2n+3}+1\right)$

$= (10-1)\{10^{n-1}+10^{n-2}+\ldots\ldots+10+1\} + 6(2+1)\{2^{2n+2} - 2^{2n+1} + \ldots\ldots - 2+1\}$

Which is divisible by 9

(C) $x+\frac{1}{x} = 1 \Rightarrow x^2-x+1=0 \Rightarrow x = \frac{1\pm\sqrt{3}i}{2}$

$\Rightarrow x = -\omega, -\omega^2$

$\Rightarrow$ Now , $p = \omega^{1000} + \frac{1}{\omega^{1000}} = = (\omega^3)^{333}.\ \omega +$

$\frac{1}{(\omega^3)^{333}.\omega} = \omega + \frac{1}{\omega} + = \omega + \omega^2 = -1$

Similarly, for $x = -\omega^2$, also $p = -1$

For $n > 1, 2^n = 4k,\ k \in N$

$\therefore$ q = (the digit at unit place in 2^n) + 1 = 6 + 1 = 7

$\therefore$ $p + q = 7 + (-1) = 6$

(D) We know that the digit at unit place in each of 5!, 6! ,.........,100! is 0 and

$0! + 1! + 2! + 3! + 4! = 34$

$\therefore$ Digit at unit place in $\sum_{r=0}^{100} r!$ is 4. Now

$2^{2n} = 2^{4k}$

$(k \in N, = 2^n$ is multiple of 4 $n > 1)$,

$\therefore$ The digit at unit place in $2^{2n} = 2^{4k} = (16)^k$ is 6.

$\therefore$ The digit at unit place in $\sum_{r=0}^{100} r! + 2^{2n} = 0$

1. **(c)** We have

$$f(k)=\left(\sum_{r=1}^{n}a_r\right)-a_k=S_n-a_k$$

$$\Rightarrow \frac{f(k)}{a_k}=\frac{S_n}{a_k}-1\,\forall k=1,2,\ldots,n$$

Given $a_1,a_2,\ldots,a_n$ are in H.P.

$\Rightarrow \frac{1}{a_1},\frac{1}{a_2},\ldots\ldots\ldots\ldots,\frac{1}{a_n}$ are in A.P.

$\Rightarrow \frac{S_n}{a_1}-1,\frac{S_n}{a_2}-1\ldots\ldots\ldots\ldots,\frac{S_n}{a_n}-1$ are in A.P.

$\Rightarrow \frac{f(1)}{a_1},\frac{f(2)}{a_2},\ldots\ldots\ldots\ldots,\frac{f(n)}{a_n}$ are in A.P.

2. **(b)** On simplification,

$$(b^2-ac)^2+(c^2-bd)^2+(ad-bc)^2\not>0,$$

which is possible iff; each of

$$(b^2-ac)=(c^2-bd)=(ad-bc)=0$$

$$\Rightarrow b^2=ac,c^2=bd,ad=bc\Rightarrow \frac{b}{a}=\frac{c}{b}=\frac{d}{c}$$

3. **(c)** We know that AM $\geq$ GM

$$\frac{ab^2+ac^2+bc^2+ba^2+ca^2+cb^2}{6}\geq\left(a^6b^6c^6\right)^{1/6}$$

$$\Rightarrow\quad a(b^2+c^2)+b(c^2+a^2)+c(a^2+b^2)\geq 6abc$$

4. **(c)** $\frac{S_{3r}-S_{r-1}}{S_{2r}-S_{2r-1}}$

$$=\frac{\frac{3r}{2}[2a+(3r-1)d]-\frac{(r-1)}{2}[2a+(r-2)d]}{\frac{2r}{2}[2a+(2r-1)d]-\frac{(2r-1)}{2}[2a+(2r-2)d]}$$

$$\Rightarrow\quad \frac{2a(2r+1)+d(8r^2-2)}{2a+d(4r-2)}$$

$$=\frac{(2r+1)[2a+2(2r-1)d]}{[2a+2(2r-1)d]}$$

$=(2x+1)=(pr+q)$
so $p=2$ and $q=1$

$p+q=2+1=3$

5. **(c)** As a, H_1, H_2, ..., H_n, b are in HP.

$\frac{1}{a},\frac{1}{H_1},\frac{1}{H_2},\ldots,\frac{1}{H_n},\frac{1}{b}$ are in AP

Let d be the common difference of the AP, then

$$\frac{1}{b}=\frac{1}{a}+(n+1)d\Rightarrow d=\frac{1}{n+1}\frac{a-b}{ab}$$

Thus, $\frac{1}{H_1}=\frac{1}{a}+d$ and $\frac{1}{H_n}=\frac{1}{b}-d$

$$\Rightarrow\quad \frac{a}{H_1}=1+ad \text{ and } \frac{b}{H_n}=1-bd$$

Now, $\frac{H_1+a}{H_1-a}+\frac{H_n+b}{H_n-b}=\frac{1+\frac{a}{H_1}}{1-\frac{a}{H_1}}+\frac{1+\frac{b}{H_n}}{1-\frac{b}{H_n}}$

$$=\frac{1+1+ad}{1-1-ad}+\frac{1+1-ba}{1-1+bd}$$

$$=\frac{2+ad}{-ad}+\frac{2-bd}{bd}=\frac{2a-abd-2b-abd}{abd}$$

$$=\frac{2[(a-b)-abd]}{abd}$$

$$=\frac{2[(n+1)dab-abd]}{abd}=2n$$

6. **(d)** $\frac{1}{a_2}-\frac{1}{a_1}=\frac{1}{a_3}-\frac{1}{a_2}=\ldots\ldots\ldots=\frac{1}{a_n}-\frac{1}{a_{n-1}}=d$ (say)

Then $a_1a_2=\frac{a_1-a_2}{d}$, $a_2a_3=\frac{a_2-a_3}{d}$,

$\ldots\ldots\ldots, a_{n-1}a_n=\frac{a_{n-1}-a_n}{d}$

$\therefore\quad a_1a_2+a_2a_3+\ldots\ldots\ldots+a_{n-1}a_n$

$$=\frac{a_1-a_2}{d}+\frac{a_2-a_3}{d}+\ldots+\frac{a_{n-1}-a_n}{d}$$

$$=\frac{1}{d}[a_1-a_2+a_2-a_3+\ldots+a_{n-1}-a_n]$$

$$=\frac{a_1-a_n}{d}$$

Also, $\frac{1}{a_n}=\frac{1}{a_1}+(n-1)d$

$$\Rightarrow \frac{a_1-a_n}{a_1a_n}=(n-1)d\Rightarrow \frac{a_1-a_n}{d}=(n-1)a_1a_n$$

Which is the required result.

7. **(a, b, d)** Since three numbers in AP so $2b = a + c$ and

$$b^2 = \frac{2a^2c^2}{a^2+c^2}$$

Eliminating b, we get $\left(\frac{a+c}{2}\right)^2 = \frac{2a^2c^2}{a^2+c^2}$

$$\Rightarrow \left(a^2+c^2\right)^2 + 2ac\left(a^2+c^2\right) - 8a^2c^2 = 0$$

$$\Rightarrow \left(a^2+c^2+4ac\right)\left(a^2+c^2-2ac\right) = 0$$

$$\Rightarrow \left[(a+c)^2 + 2ac\right](a-c)^2 = 0$$

$$\Rightarrow 4\left(b^2+\frac{1}{2}ac\right)(a-c)^2 = 0$$

$$\Rightarrow a-c=0 \quad or \quad b^2 = -\frac{1}{2}ac$$

If $a = c$, we get $a = b = c$

If $b^2 = -\frac{1}{2}ac$, then either $a, b, -\frac{1}{2}c$ are in GP

or $-\frac{1}{2}a, b, c$ are in GP

8. **(a, c)** If t_r denotes the rth term of the series, then

$$xt_r = \frac{x}{(1+rx)(1+(r+1)x)}$$

$$= \frac{1}{1+rx} - \frac{1}{1+(r+1)x}$$

$$\Rightarrow x\sum_{r=1}^{n} t_r = \sum_{r=1}^{n}\left[\frac{1}{1+rx} - \frac{1}{1+(r+1)x}\right]$$

$$= \frac{1}{1+x} - \frac{1}{1+(n+1)x} = \frac{nx}{(1+x)(1+(n+1)x)}$$

$$\Rightarrow S_n = \sum_{r=1}^{n} t_r = \frac{n}{(1+x)[1+(n+1)x]}$$

9. **(b, c)** We have for $0 < \phi < \frac{\pi}{2}$

$$x = \sum_{n=0}^{\infty} \cos^{2n}\phi = 1 + \cos^2\phi + \cos^4\phi + ...\infty$$

$$\frac{1}{1-\cos^2\phi} = \frac{1}{\sin^2\phi} \qquad ....(1)$$

[Using sum of infinite G.P. $\cos^2\alpha$ being < 1]

$$y = \sum_{n=0}^{\infty} \sin^{2n}\phi = 1 + \sin^2\phi + \sin^4\phi + ...\infty$$

$$= \frac{1}{1-\sin^2\phi} = \frac{1}{\cos^2\phi} \qquad ....(2)$$

$$z = \sum_{n=0}^{\infty} \cos^{2n}\phi \sin^{2n}\phi$$

$$= 1 + \cos^2\phi\sin^2\phi + \cos^4\phi\sin^4\phi + ...\infty$$

$$= \frac{1}{1-\cos^2\phi\sin^2\phi} \qquad ....(3)$$

Substituting the values of $\cos^2\phi$ and $\sin^2\phi$ in (3), from (1) and (2), we get

$$z = \frac{1}{1-\frac{1}{x}.\frac{1}{y}} \Rightarrow z = \frac{xy}{xy-1}$$

$$\Rightarrow xyz - z = xy \Rightarrow xyz = xy + z.$$

Also, $x + y + z = \frac{1}{\cos^2\phi} + \frac{1}{\sin^2\phi} + \frac{1}{1-\cos^2\phi\sin^2\phi}$

$$\frac{[\sin^2\phi(1-\cos^2\phi\sin^2\phi) + \cos^2\phi(1-\cos^2\phi\sin^2\phi) + \cos^2\phi\sin^2\phi]}{\cos^2\phi\sin^2\phi\,(1-\cos^2\phi\sin^2\phi)}$$

$$= \frac{(\sin^2\phi+\cos^2\phi)\,(1-\cos^2\phi\sin^2\phi) + \cos^2\phi\sin^2\phi}{\cos^2\phi\sin^2\phi\,(1-\cos^2\phi\sin^2\phi)}$$

$$= \frac{1}{\cos^2\phi\sin^2\phi\,(1-\cos^2\phi\sin^2\phi)} = xyz$$

Thus (b) and (c) both are correct.

10. **(a, d)** α, β, γ and δ are in HP

$\Rightarrow \frac{1}{\alpha}, \frac{1}{\beta}, \frac{1}{\gamma}, \frac{1}{\delta}$ are in AP

Let d be the common difference of this AP.

Now, a, γ are roots of $Ax^2 - 4x + 1 = 0$

$$\therefore \frac{\alpha+\gamma}{\alpha\gamma} = \frac{\frac{4}{A}}{\frac{1}{A}} = 4$$

or $\frac{1}{\alpha} + \frac{1}{\gamma} = 4 ie, \frac{1}{\alpha} + \frac{1}{\alpha} + 2d = 4$

or $\frac{1}{\alpha} + d = 2$ ...(i)

β, δ are roots of $Bx^2 - 6x + 1 = 0$

$$\therefore \frac{\beta+\delta}{\beta\delta} = \frac{1}{\beta} + \frac{1}{\delta} = \frac{6/B}{1/B} = 6$$

or $\frac{1}{\alpha} + d + \frac{1}{\alpha} + 3d = 6$

or $\frac{1}{\alpha} + 2d = 3$ ...(ii)

From Eqs. (i) and (ii), on solving, we get

$\frac{1}{\alpha}=1, d=1 \therefore \frac{1}{\alpha}=1, \frac{1}{\beta}=2, \frac{1}{\gamma}=3, \frac{1}{\delta}=4$

Since, $\frac{1}{\alpha\gamma}=A \Rightarrow A=3$

Also, $\frac{1}{\beta\delta}=B, \Rightarrow B=8$

Hence, A = 3 and B = 8.

11. **(6)** Given that $a_{10}=3 \Rightarrow a_1+9d=3$

$\Rightarrow 2+9d = 3 \ [a_1=2]$

$\Rightarrow d=\frac{1}{9}$

$\therefore a_4=a_1+3d=2+\frac{3}{9}=\frac{7}{3}$

$h_{10}=3$

$\Rightarrow \frac{1}{h_{10}}=\frac{1}{3}$

$\Rightarrow$ Common difference of corresponding AP is $D=-\frac{1}{54}$

$\therefore \frac{1}{h_7}=\frac{1}{h_1}+6D=\frac{1}{2}-\frac{1}{9}=\frac{7}{18}$

$\Rightarrow h_7=\frac{18}{7}$

so, $a_4h_7=\frac{7}{3}\times\frac{18}{7}=6$

12. **(4)** Given $b^2=ac, x=\frac{a+b}{2}, y=\frac{b+c}{2}$

Now, $\frac{a}{x}+\frac{c}{y}=\frac{2a}{a+b}+\frac{2c}{b+c}$

$=\frac{2(ab+ac+ac+bc)}{ab+ac+b^2+bc}=2 \quad [\because b^2=ac]$

Again $\frac{b}{x}+\frac{b}{y}=2b\left[\frac{1}{a+b}+\frac{1}{b+c}\right]$

$=\frac{2b(b+c+a+b)}{ab+ac+b^2+bc}=2$

$\therefore \left(\frac{a}{x}+\frac{c}{y}\right)\left(\frac{b}{x}+\frac{b}{y}\right)=4.$

13. **(5)** $(1+x)(1+x^2)(1+x^4)\ldots(1+x^{128})$

$=1+x+x^2+\ldots+x^n$

$\Rightarrow (1-x)\{(1+x)(1+x^2)(1+x^4)\ldots(1+x^{128})\}$

$=1-x^{n+1}$

$\Rightarrow (1-x^2)\{(1+x^2)\ldots(1+x^{128})\}=1-x^{n+1}$

$\Rightarrow (1-x^4)(1+x^4)\ldots(1+x^{128})=1-x^{n+1}$

$\Rightarrow 1-x^{256}=1-x^{n+1}$

$\therefore n+1=256$ or $n=255$

14. **(4)** We have $t_r=\frac{(r-1)!}{(r+4)!}$

And $t_{r+1}=\frac{r!}{(r+5)!}$

Now, $rt_r-(r+5)t_{r+1}=\frac{r!}{(r+4)!}-\frac{r!}{(r+4)!}=0$

$\Rightarrow rt_r-(r+1)t_{r+1}=4t_{r+1}$

$\Rightarrow 4\sum_{r=1}^{n-1}t_{r+1}=\sum_{r=1}^{n-1}\left[rt_r-(r+1)t_{r+1}\right]$

$\Rightarrow 4(t_2+t_3+\ldots+t_n)=1t_1-nt_n$

$\Rightarrow 4(t_1+t_2+\ldots+t_n)=5t_1-nt_n$

$=5\left(\frac{0!}{5!}\right)-\frac{n(n-1)!}{(n+4)!}=\frac{1}{4!}-\frac{n!}{(n+4)!}$

$\Rightarrow t_1+t_2+\ldots+t_n=\frac{1}{4}\left[\frac{1}{4!}-\frac{n!}{(n+4)!}\right]$

So a = 4, b = 4, c = 0 and d = 4 and a + b – c – d = 4

15. **(b)** Here a, b, c, are in H.P.

$\Rightarrow a^{-1}, b^{-1}, c^{-1}$ are in A.P.

$\Rightarrow e^{(-a)^{-1}}, e^{(-b)^{-1}}, e^{(-c)^{-1}}$ are in G.P.

16. **(a)** Since x, y, z are respectively the pth, q^{th} and the rth terms of a G.P so $\ell n\,x$, $\ell n\,y$, $\ell n\,z$ are in A.P. with common difference ℓnt. Here t is the common ratio

Also, x, y, z are in A.P.(say with common difference d.)

Hence, $x-y=(p-q)d$ etc.

and $\ell n\,x-\ell n\,y=(p-q)\ell n\,t$.

Let $S=(x^{y-z}), (y^{z-x}), (z^{x-y})$

so that $\ell n\,S=(y-z)\ell n\,x+(z-x)\ell n\,y+(x-y)\ell n\,z$

$=(q-r)d\ell n\,x+(r-p)d\ell n\,y+(p-q)d\ell n\,z$

$=d[p(\ell n\,z-\ell n\,y)+q(\ell n\,x-\ell n\,z)+r(\ell n\,y-\ell n\,x)]$

$=d\ell nt\,[p(r-q)+q(p-r)+r(q-p)]=0$

$\Rightarrow S=1$

17. **(b)** $V_1+V_2+\ldots..+V_n=\sum_{r=1}^{n}V_r=\sum_{r=1}^{n}\left(r^3-\frac{r^2}{2}+\frac{r}{2}\right)$

$=\sum n^3-\frac{\sum n^2}{2}+\frac{\sum n}{2}$

$$=\frac{n^2(n+1)^2}{4}-\frac{n(n+1)(2n+1)}{12}+\frac{n(n+1)}{4}$$

$$=\frac{n(n+1)}{4}\left[n(n+1)-\frac{2n+1}{3}+1\right]$$

$$=\frac{n(n+1)(3n^2+n+2)}{12}$$

18. **(d)** $T_r = V_{r+1} - V_r - 2$

$$=\left[(r+1)^3-\frac{(r+1)^2}{2}+\frac{r+1}{2}\right]-\left[r^3-\frac{r^2}{2}+\frac{r}{2}\right]-2$$

$= 3r^2 + 2r + 1$

$T_r = (r + 1)(3r - 1)$

For each r, T_r has two different factors other than 1 and itself.

$\therefore$ T is always a composite number.

19. **(A) → (s), (B) → (p), (C) → (q), (D) → (r)**

(A) Given, $\Sigma n = \frac{1}{5}\left(\sum n^2\right)$

or $\quad \frac{n(n+1)}{2}=\frac{1}{5}\frac{n(n+1)(2n+1)}{6}$

$\Rightarrow$ $2n + 1 = 15$

$\Rightarrow$ $2n = 14$

$\Rightarrow$ $n = 7$

(B) Let α and β be the roots of the given equation,

$\alpha+\beta=\frac{4+\sqrt{3}}{5+\sqrt{2}}$ and $\alpha\beta=\frac{8+2\sqrt{3}}{5+\sqrt{2}}$

Hence, required harmonic mean

$$=\frac{2\alpha\beta}{\alpha+\beta}=\frac{2\left(\frac{8+2\sqrt{3}}{5+\sqrt{2}}\right)}{\frac{4+\sqrt{3}}{5+\sqrt{2}}}=4$$

(C) x, y, z are in HP.

$$y=\frac{2xz}{x+z}$$

$\Rightarrow$ $x-2y+z=x+z-\frac{4xz}{x+z}$

$$=\frac{(x+z)^2-4xz}{x+z}=\frac{(z-x)^2}{x+z}$$

$\Rightarrow$ $(x+z)(x-2y+z)=(z-x)^2$

$\Rightarrow$ $\log(x+z)+\log(x-2y+z)=2\log(z-x)$

(D) $\frac{128r-a}{r-1}=255$

$\Rightarrow$ $\frac{256-a}{2-1}=255$ [since $r = 2$]

$\Rightarrow$ $256 - a = 225$

$\Rightarrow$ $a = 1$

20. **(A) → (q); (B) → (p); (C) → (r); (D) → (s)**

(A) $a+b=12$

$$ab+\frac{6ab}{a+b}=48$$

$$ab+\frac{ab}{2}=48$$

$\therefore ab = 32$

(B) As $n = 39$ is odd, the value of the given expression

$=1^3-2^3+3^3-\ldots+n^3$

$=\left(1^3+2^3+3^3+\ldots+n^3\right)-2\left\{2^3+4^3+\ldots+(n-1)^3\right\}$

$$=\left\{\frac{n(n+1)}{2}\right\}^2-16\left\{1^3+2^3+\ldots+\left(\frac{n-1}{2}\right)^3\right\}$$

$$=\frac{n^2(n+1)^2}{4}-16\cdot\left\{\frac{\frac{n-1}{2}\cdot\frac{n+1}{2}}{2}\right\}^2$$

$$=\frac{(n+1)^2\cdot(2n-1)}{4}$$

On putting the value we get $\frac{S_{39}}{100}=\frac{30800}{100}=308$

(C) HM of $\frac{1}{2},\frac{1}{3},\frac{1}{4},\frac{1}{5}$ is

$$\frac{4}{\frac{1}{2}+\frac{1}{3}+\frac{1}{4}+\frac{1}{5}}=\frac{240}{77}$$

(D) The numbers between 100 and 500 that are divisible by 7 are 105, 112, 119, 126, 133, 140, 147, ..., 483, 490, 497.

Let such numbers be n.

Then, $497 = 105 + (n - 1) \times 7$ or $n = 57$

So there are 57 number of numbers lying between 100 and 500 that are divisible by 7

The number between 100 and 500 that are divisible by 21 are 105, 126, 147, ..., 483.

Let such number be m.

Then, $483 = 105 + (m - 1) \times 21$ or $n = 19$

So there are 19 number of numbers lying between 100 and 500 that are divisible by 21

Hence, the required number $= n - m = 57 - 19 = 38$

1. (d) We have $ax^2+2\lambda xy+by^2+2Kx+2Ky+2K=0$

$h=\lambda, g=K, c=2K, f=K$

$=abc+2fgh-af^2-bg^2-ch^2=0$

$ab.(2K)+2\lambda K^2+aK^2-bK^2-2\lambda^2K=0$

$2K\lambda^2-2K^2\lambda+(a+b)K^2-2abK=0$

For real λ, $B^2-4AC\geq 0$

$4K^4-4\,2K[(a+b)K^2-2aK]\geq 0$

$K^2-2(a+b)K+4ab\geq 0, (K-2a)(K-2b)\geq 0$

$K\leq 2a$ or $K\geq 2b$.

2. (a) Let d be common difference of A.P, then $b=a+2d$ and $c=a+6d$. Clearly $(b-a)\times 3=c-a$

$\Rightarrow\ 2a-3b+c=0.$

So, the straight line $ax+by+c=0$, passes through $(2,-3)$, which also satisfies $x^2+y^2=13$.

3. (b) Equation of line $\frac{ax}{c-1}+\frac{by}{c-1}+1=0$ has two independent parameters. It can pass through a fixed point if it contains only one independent parameter.

So, there must be one relation between $\frac{a}{c-1}$ and $\frac{b}{c-1}$ indepentent of a, b and c so that $\frac{a}{c-1}$ can be expressed in terms of $\frac{b}{c-1}$ and straight line contains only one independent parameter. The given relation can be expressed as $\frac{5a}{c-1}+\frac{4b}{c-1}=\frac{t-20c}{c-1}$. Now RHS be independent of c if $t=20$.

4. (c)

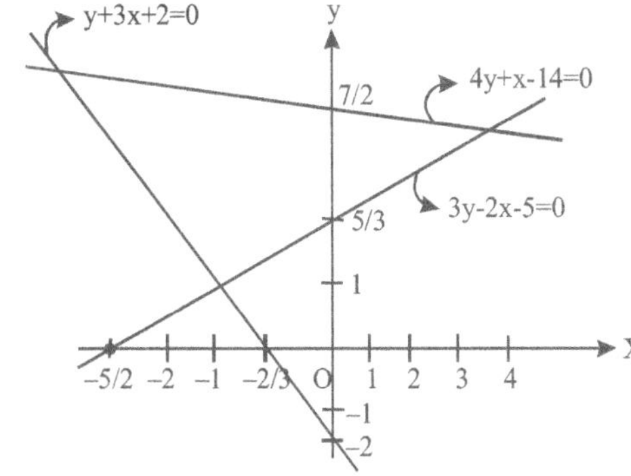

From diagram it is clear that $\frac{5}{3}\leq\beta\leq\frac{7}{2}$.

5. (c) We have, $(a-b)^2-c^2=0$

$\Rightarrow\ (a-b+c)(a-b-c)=0.$

$\Rightarrow$ Line $ax+by+c=0$ passes through either of two points $(1,-1)$ and $(-1,1)$.

6. (b) By solving the sides of the rhombus, its vertices are

$\left(0,-\frac{n}{m}\right), \left(-\frac{n}{\ell},0\right),\left(0,\frac{n}{m}\right)$ and $\left(\frac{n}{\ell},0\right)$

$\therefore$ area $=\frac{1}{2}\times\frac{2n}{m}\times\frac{2n}{1}=2$

$\Rightarrow\ n^2=lm$ or l, n, m are in G.P.

7. (a,c,d) The given equation is

$\sec^2(a+2)b+a^2-1=0$

$\Rightarrow \tan^2(a+2)b+a^2=0$, which holds if and only if

$a=0, \tan^2(a+2)b=0$

$\Rightarrow\ \tan^2 2b=0$

$\Rightarrow\ b=0,\frac{\pi}{2},-\frac{\pi}{2}$

$(a,b)=(0,0),\left(0,\frac{\pi}{2}\right),\left(0,-\frac{\pi}{2}\right)$

$y-0=\frac{1}{2}(x-0), y-\frac{\pi}{2}=\frac{1}{2}(x-0)$

and $y+\frac{\pi}{2}=\frac{1}{2}(x-0)$

$2y=x, 2y-\pi=x, 2y+\pi=x.$

8. (b,d) $p.q.4a+2.2a.2a.2\lambda-p.4a^2-q.4a^2-4a.4\lambda^2=0$

$\Rightarrow\ 4\lambda^2-4a\lambda+\{(p+q)a-pq\}=0 \quad (\because a\neq 0)$

$\because\ \lambda\in R,\ 16a^2-4.4\{(p+q)a-pq\}\geq 0$

or $(a-p(a-q)\geq 0$

$\therefore\ a\leq p$ or $a\geq q$

9. (a,b,d) Since the given points lie on the line $lx+my+n=0$, a, b, c are the roots of the equation

$$l\left(\frac{t^3}{t-1}\right)+m\left(\frac{t^2-3}{t-1}\right)+n=0$$

Or $\quad lt^3+mt^2+nt-(3m+n)=0 \qquad$ ...(i)

$\Rightarrow \quad a+b+c=-\frac{m}{l}$; $ab+bc+ca=\frac{n}{l}$ ...(ii)

and $abc=\frac{3m+n}{l}$ ...(iii)

So, that from (i), (ii) and (iii) we get
$abc-(bc+ca+ab)+3(a+b+c)=0.$

10. (a,b,c) Verticles of the given triangle are (0, 0), $\left(\frac{a}{m_1}, a\right)$ and $\left(\frac{a}{m_2}, a\right)$ so that the area of the triangle is equal to $=\frac{a^2(m_2-m_1)}{2m_1m_2}$

Since m_1, m_2 are the roots of $x^2-ax-a-1=0$
so $m_1+m_2=a,\ m_1m_2=-(a+1)$

$\Rightarrow (m_1-m_2)^2=a^2+4(a+1)=(a+2)^2$

$\Rightarrow m_1-m_2=\pm(a+2)$

So the required area is

$$\Delta=\pm\frac{a^2(a+2)}{-2(a+1)}=\pm\frac{a^2(a+2)}{2(a+1)}$$

Since the area Δ is a positive quantity.

$\Delta=\frac{a^2(a+2)}{2(a+1)}$ if $a>-1$.

or $a<-2$ and $\Delta=-\frac{a^2(a+2)}{2(a+1)}$ if $-2<a<-1$.

11. (5) We have $ax^2+2hxy+by^2+2gx+2fy+c=0$, where $c=10$
Let $ax^2+2hxy+by^2+2gx+2fy+c\equiv(l_1x+m_1y+n_1)(l_2x+m_2y+n_2)$
Comparing the coefficient of similar terms, we get
$l_1l_2=a,\ m_1m_2=b,\ n_1n_2=c$
$l_1m_2+l_2m_1=2h,\ l_1n_2+l_2n_1=2g,\ m_1n_2+m_2n_1=2f$
Now, the two lines are equidistant from origin

$$\therefore \frac{0.l_1+0m_1+n_1}{\sqrt{l_1^2+m_1^2}}=\frac{0.l_2+0.m_2+n_2}{\sqrt{l_1^2+m_2^2}}$$

$\Rightarrow n_1^2(l_2^2-m_2^2)=n_2^2(l_1^2-m_1^2)$

$\Rightarrow n_1^2l_2^2-n_2^2l_1^2=n_2^2m_1^2-n_1^2m_2^2$. On squaring, we get

$(n_1l_2+n_2l_1)^2[(n_1l_2+n_2l_1)^2-4n_1n_2l_1l_2]$

$=(m_1n_2+m_2n_1)^2.[(m_1n_2+m_2n_1)^2-4m_1m_2n_1n_2]$

$\therefore \quad 4g^2[4g^2-4ac]=4f^2[4f^2-4bc]$

$\Rightarrow f^4-g^4=c(bf^2-ag^2)\Rightarrow\frac{f^4-g^4}{bf^2-ag^2}=c=10$

12. (3) Since (0, 0) and (1, 1) lie on the same side, so

$a^2+ab+1>0$

$\because a\in\mathbf{R}\Rightarrow D<0\Rightarrow b^2-4<0$

$\Rightarrow -2<b<2\Rightarrow b=-1,0,1$

13. (2) Let the equation of the line L be $y-2=m(x-8), m<0$

Coordinates of P and Q are $P\left(8-\frac{2}{m},0\right)$ and $Q(0,2-8m)$

So, $OP+OQ=8-\frac{2}{m}+2-8m=10+\frac{2}{-m}+8(-m)$

$\geq 10+2\sqrt{\frac{2}{-m}\times 8(-m)}\geq 18$

So, absolute minimum value of $OP+OQ=18$

14. (0) Since $\sqrt{3}.1-4+1<0$, so $\sqrt{3}\sin\theta-\cos\theta+1\leq 0$

$\Rightarrow \frac{\sqrt{3}}{2}\sin\theta-\frac{1}{2}\cos\theta\leq-\frac{1}{2}$

$\Rightarrow \sin\left(\theta-\frac{\pi}{6}\right)\leq-\frac{1}{2}$

$\Rightarrow \frac{7\pi}{6}\leq\theta-\frac{\pi}{6}\leq\frac{11\pi}{6}\Rightarrow\frac{4\pi}{3}\leq\theta\leq 2\pi$

$\Rightarrow$ maximum value of $\sin\theta$ is 0.

15. (4) Eliminating x and y from three equations, we get

$-2=m(a+m)\Rightarrow m^2+am+2=0$.

Since $m\in\mathbf{R}\Rightarrow$ discriminant ≥ 0

$\therefore a^2-8\geq 0\Rightarrow |a|\geq 2\sqrt{2}$.

16. (b) Slope of AH, is $\frac{4-1}{2-1}=3$

$\Rightarrow \left(-\frac{a}{b}\right)3=-1$

$\Rightarrow 3a=b$

$b-3a=0$

Also, $a+c=2b$

$\Rightarrow a-2b+c=0$

$a(1)+b(-2)+c=0$

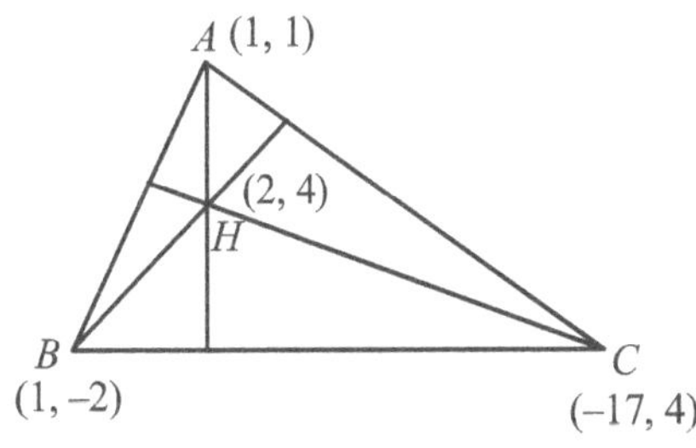

$\Rightarrow$ Lines are concurrent at $(1, -2)$. So, B is $(1, -2)$

17. (a) Slope of $AC(m_1) = \frac{1-4}{1+17} = -\frac{3}{18} = -\frac{1}{6}$

Slope of $BC(m_2) = \frac{-2-4}{1+17} = -\frac{6}{18} = -\frac{1}{3}$

$$\therefore \tan C = \frac{m_2 - m_1}{1 + m_1 m_2} = \frac{-\frac{1}{3} + \frac{1}{6}}{1 + \left(-\frac{1}{6}\right)\left(-\frac{1}{3}\right)} < 0$$

$\Rightarrow \angle BCA$ is obtuse.

18. (c) $\tan\theta = \left|\frac{-\frac{1}{2} + 2}{1+1}\right| = \frac{3}{4}$

$\Rightarrow \sin\theta = \frac{3}{5}$

$\therefore$ area of $\Delta CPD = \frac{1}{2} \times PC \times PD \sin\theta = 2$

$\Rightarrow \frac{1}{2} \times 2 \times PD \times \frac{3}{5} = 2$

$\Rightarrow PD = \frac{10}{3} \Rightarrow BD = \frac{20}{3}$

19. (a) $\cos(\pi - \theta) = \frac{PB^2 + PC^2 - BC^2}{2PB.PC}$

$$\Rightarrow -\frac{4}{5} = \frac{4 + \frac{100}{9} - BC^2}{2 \times 2 \times \frac{10}{3}} \Rightarrow BC = \frac{2\sqrt{58}}{3}.$$

20. (A) → (s); (B) → (r); (C) → (p, q)

(A) $|\tan\theta| = \frac{2\sqrt{25-24}}{12+2} = \frac{1}{7}$

(B) Put $y = 0$, we get $x^2 + 4x + c^2 = 0$, which gives equal roots if $c^2 = 4$, then equation becomes $x^2 + 4xy - 2y^2 + 4x + 2fy + 4 = 0$ which pepresents a pair of st. lines if $f = 4$

(C) As obtained in (C) $c^2 = 4$

1. **(d)** Since point $(\alpha, \alpha+2)$ lies inside the circle

$\Rightarrow \quad \alpha^2+(\alpha+2)^2-4<0$

$\Rightarrow \quad -2<\alpha<0 \quad$ ....(1)

and also point $(\alpha, \alpha+2)$ lies in the smaller segment made by the line so that

$\Rightarrow \quad 3\alpha+4(\alpha+2)+12<0$

$\Rightarrow \quad \alpha<-\dfrac{20}{7} \quad$ ...(2)

(since centre of circle (0, 0) and point $(\alpha, \alpha+2)$ lies in the opposite sides of the given line)

From (1) and (2), $\alpha \in \phi$.

2. **(c)** $x^2+y^2+\lambda_1(x-y)+c=0$ ...(1)

$x^2+y^2+\lambda_2(x-y)+c=0$

Radical axes $(\lambda_1-\lambda_2)(x-y)=0 \Rightarrow x=y$.

Putting in (1) $\quad 2x^2+c=0$

$\Rightarrow \quad c>0$ for non real x.

3. **(b)** For y^2+4ax, Normal : $y=mx-2am-am^3$ ... (i)

For $y^2=4c(x-b)$, normal : $y=m(x-b)-2cm-cm^3$ ... (ii)

If two parabolas have common normal :
Then (i) & (ii) must be identical
After comparing the coeffecients we get

$m=\pm\sqrt{\dfrac{2(a-c)-b}{(c-a)}}$

which is real of $-2-\dfrac{b}{c-a}>0 \Rightarrow \dfrac{b}{a-c}>2$.

4. **(b)** The given circle and ellipse have common tangent parallel to x-axis only.

$\Rightarrow$ the circle and the ellipse intersect at 2 distinct points.

$\Rightarrow \quad h+c<a+b$

$\Rightarrow \quad c<a+b-h$.

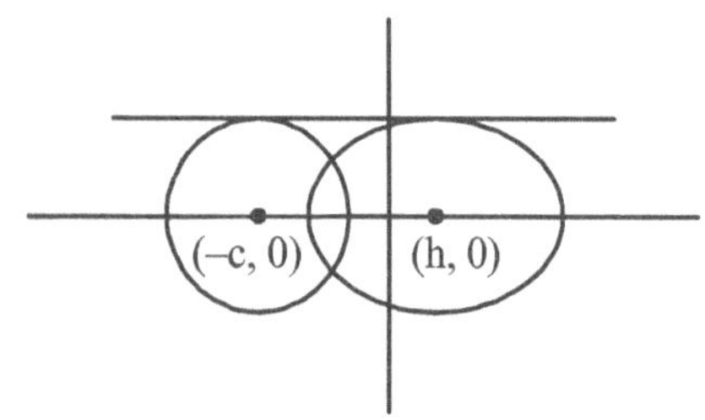

5. **(a)** We know that if a circle cuts a rectangular hyperbola then arithmetic mean of points of intersection is the mid-point of centre of hyperbola and circle.

So, $\dfrac{3+5+2+(-1)}{4}=\dfrac{-g+1}{2}, \dfrac{4+3+6+0}{4}=\dfrac{-f+2}{2}$

$\Rightarrow \quad g+f=\left(-\dfrac{7}{2}\right)+\left(-\dfrac{9}{2}\right)=-8.$

6. **(d)** The equation of the normal to the hyperbola $\dfrac{x^2}{4}-\dfrac{y^2}{1}=1$ at $(2\sec\theta, \tan\theta)$ is

$2x\cos\theta+y\cot\theta=5 \quad$ ...(1)

Slope of the normal $=-2\sin\theta=-1 \Rightarrow \sin\theta=\dfrac{1}{2}$

$\Rightarrow \quad \theta=\dfrac{\pi}{6}.$

Y–intercept of the normal $=\dfrac{5}{\cot\theta}=\dfrac{5}{\sqrt{3}}$

Since it touches the ellipse $\dfrac{x^2}{a^2}+\dfrac{y^2}{b^2}=1$

$\therefore \quad \left(\dfrac{5}{\sqrt{3}}\right)^2=a^2(-1)^2+b^2 \Rightarrow a^2+b^2=\dfrac{25}{3}$

7. **(a, b)** Here circle equation is

$x^2+y^2+2\sqrt{\sin\alpha}\,x+(\cos\alpha-1)=0$

so $\sqrt{\sin\alpha}$ will be defined for $\sin\alpha \geq 0$

$\Rightarrow \alpha \in [0, \pi] \quad$ ...(1)

also, Length of intercept on x-axis

$=2\sqrt{g^2-c}=2\sqrt{\sin\alpha-\cos\alpha+1}>2$

$\Rightarrow \sin\alpha-\cos\alpha>0$

$\dfrac{\pi}{4}<\alpha<\dfrac{5\pi}{4} \quad$ ...(2)

from (1) and (2)

$\alpha \in \left(\dfrac{\pi}{4}, \pi\right]$

8. **(a,b)** We have $\left|\sqrt{x^2+(y-1)^2}-\sqrt{x^2+(y+1)^2}\right|=K$

Which is equivalent to $|S_1P-S_2P|=$ Const.

Where $S_1 \equiv (0, 1)$, $S_2 \equiv (0, -1)$ and $P \equiv (x, y)$.

Using properties of a hyperbola, the above equation represents a hyperbola, then we have.

$2a = K$

[where 2a is the transverse axis and e is the eccentricity]

and $2ae = S_1 S_2 = 2$

Dividing, we have $e = \frac{2}{K}$

Since, $e > 1$ for a hyperbola, therefore $K < 2$.

Also, K must be a positive quantity. Hence, we have, $K \in (0, 2)$.

9. **(b,c,d)** Let $(x_i, y_i) = \left(t_i, \frac{1}{t_i}\right)$ $i = 1, 2, 3, 4.$

Any point on the rectangular hyperbola $xy = 1$ is $\left(t, \frac{1}{t}\right)$ which lies on the circle

$$x^2 + y^2 = 1 \text{ if } t^2 + \frac{1}{t^2} = 1 \Rightarrow t^4 - t^2 + 1 = 0$$

The roots of this equation are t_1, t_2, t_3, t_4 where

$t_1 + t_2 + t_3 + t_4 = 0 \Rightarrow x_1 + x_2 + x_3 + x_4 = 0$

$$\sum t_1 t_2 = -1, \sum t_1 t_2 t_3 = 0$$

$t_1\, t_2\, t_3\, t_4 = 1 \Rightarrow x_1 x_2 x_3 x_4 = y_1 y_2 y_3 y_4 = 1$

and $y_1 + y_2 + y_3 + y_4 = \frac{1}{t_1} + \frac{1}{t_2} + \frac{1}{t_3} + \frac{1}{t_4}$

$$= \frac{\sum t_1 t_2 t_3}{t_1 t_2 t_3 t_4} = 0.$$

10. **(a, b, c, d)**

Equation of the curve passing through all four points A, B, C, D can be written as

$(3x + 4y - 24)(4x + 3y - 24) + \lambda xy = 0.$

$\Rightarrow 12x^2 + 12y^2 + (25 + \lambda)xy - 168x - 168y + 576 = 0$

Clearly for $\lambda = -25$, it represents a circle for different values of λ, it can represent other curves

11. **(2)**

Let circle $x^2 + y^2 + 2gx + 2fy + c = 0$......(A)

it is passing through $(1, t)$, $(t, 1)$ and (t, t)

then $1 + t^2 + 2g + 2ft + c = 0$ ......(i)

$t^2 + 1 + 2gt + 2f + c = 0$ ......(ii)

$2t^2 + 2gt + 2ft + c = 0$ .....(iii)

(ii) – (i) and (iii) – (ii),

Then $2g\,(t - 1) + 2f\,(1 - t) = 0$ or $g - f = 0$ and $t^2 - 1 + 2f(t - 1) = 0$

$\therefore\ f = -\frac{(t+1)}{2} = g$

From (iii), $2t^2 - t(t+1) - t(t+1) + c = 0 \Rightarrow c = 2t$

From (A), $x^2 + y^2 - (t+1)x - (t+1)y + 2t = 0 \Rightarrow (x^2 + y^2 - x - y) - t(x + y - 2) = 0,$

Which is of the form $S + \lambda L = 0$. Hence always pass through points of intersection of

$x^2 + y^2 - x - y = 0$ and $x + y - 2 = 0$. On solving we get $x = 1$ and $y = 1$. So, $a = 1, b = 1$

12. **(5)**

The tangent at any point $A(2\sec\theta, \tan\theta)$ is given by

$$\frac{x\sec\theta}{2} - \frac{y\tan\theta}{1} = 1.$$

It meets the line $x - 2y = 0$

$$\Rightarrow \frac{x\sec\theta}{2} - \frac{x\tan\theta}{2} = 1 \Rightarrow x = \frac{2}{\sec\theta - \tan\theta}$$

$$\Rightarrow Q \equiv \left(\frac{2}{\sec\theta - \tan\theta}, \frac{1}{\sec\theta - \tan\theta}\right) \quad ...(1)$$

Also, the tangent meets the line $x + 2y = 0$ at R, so

$$\Rightarrow \frac{x}{2}\sec\theta + \frac{x}{2}\tan\theta = 1 \Rightarrow x = \frac{2}{\sec\theta + \tan\theta}$$

$$\Rightarrow R \equiv \left(\frac{2}{\sec\theta + \tan\theta}, \frac{-1}{\sec\theta + \tan\theta}\right) \quad ...(2)$$

$$\text{Now, } CQ.CR = \sqrt{\frac{2^2 + 1^2}{(\sec\theta - \tan\theta)^2}}\sqrt{\frac{2^2 + 1^2}{(\sec\theta + \tan\theta)^2}}$$

$$= 2^2 + 1^2$$

$\Rightarrow CQ.CR = 5$

13. **(4)**

Let equation of line passing through $P(1, t)$ be

$$\frac{x-1}{\cos\theta} = \frac{y-t}{\sin\theta} = r$$

$\Rightarrow x = r\cos\theta + 1$ and $y = r\sin\theta + t.$

Line meets the parabola at A and B

$\Rightarrow (r\sin\theta + t)^2 = 4(r\cos\theta + 1)$

$\Rightarrow r^2\sin^2\theta + 2r(t\sin\theta - 2\cos\theta) + t^2 - 4 = 0$

$$\therefore\ PA.PB = \left|\frac{t^2 - 4}{\sin^2\theta}\right| = 3|t|$$

$$\Rightarrow \frac{|t^2 - 4|}{3|t|} = \sin^2\theta \le 1$$

$\Rightarrow\ t^2-3|t|-4\le 0$

$\Rightarrow\ (|t|+1)(|t|-4)\le 0$

$\Rightarrow\ |t|\le 4$

Hence the maximum value of t is 4.

14. (5) Equation of normal to $y^2=4ax$ and $x^2=4by$ in terms of m are given by

$$y = mx-2am-am^3 \text{ and } y = mx+2b+\frac{b}{m^2}$$

For common normal $2b+\frac{b}{m^2}+2am+am^3=0$

$\Rightarrow am^5+2am^3+2bm^2+b=0.$

So, a maximum of 5 normals are possible.

15. (2) $AB^2=4AM^2$ (See figure)

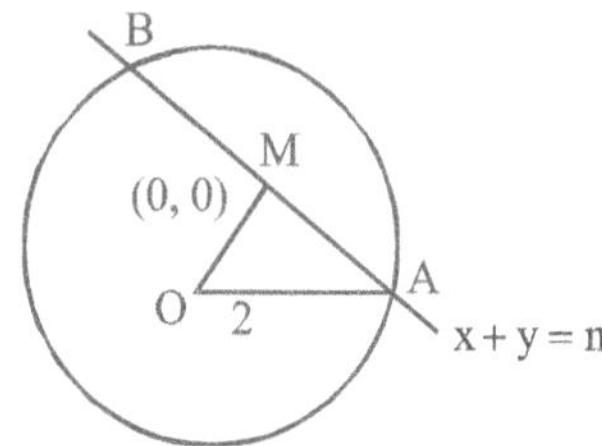

$$4\left(4-\frac{n^2}{2}\right)=2(8-n^2), n\in \mathbf{N}\Rightarrow n=1 \text{ or } 2$$

Hence required sum $=2(8-1^2+8-2^2)=2\times 11$

16. (a) Line $x+2y+a=0$ intersects the circle

$$x^2+y^2-4=0 \text{ if } \left|\frac{0+0+a}{\sqrt{1+4}}\right|<2$$

$\Rightarrow\ -2\sqrt{5}<a<2\sqrt{5}.$

17. (c) Equation of circle passing through point of intersection of circle $x^2+y^2-4=0$ and $x+2y+2=0$ is given by

$x^2+y^2-4+\lambda(x+2y+2)=0$ ...(1)

again common chord of circle represented by equation (1) and circle $x^2+y^2-4x-2y+1=0$ is

$(\lambda+4)x+2(\lambda+1)y+2\lambda-5=0$ ...(2)

since equation (2) and $12x-6y-41=0$ represent the same line

$$\therefore \frac{\lambda+4}{14}=\frac{2(\lambda+1}{-6}=\frac{2\lambda-5}{-41}\ \Rightarrow\ \lambda=-\frac{8}{5}.$$

Hence equation of required circle is

$5x^2+5y^2-8x-16y-36=0.$

For (18-19) $a-2b+c=0$

$\Rightarrow\ ax+by+c=0$

passes through $(1,-2)$

So, the centre of the ellipse is $(1,-2)$, which is also the centre of the auxiliary circle, so, $-\alpha=1,-\beta=-2$

$\Rightarrow \alpha=-1, \beta=2.$

Radius of auxiliary circle $=\sqrt{1+4-1}=2$

$\therefore$ Major axis of ellipse = 4. Also if segments of focal chord are l_1 and l_2 then $\frac{1}{l_1}+\frac{1}{l_2}=\frac{2}{(b^2/a)}$

$$\therefore \frac{1}{1}+\frac{1}{3}=\frac{4}{b^2}\Rightarrow b^2=3$$

$\therefore$ Equation of director circle is

$(x-1)^2+(y+2)^2=4+3$

Eccentricity $=\sqrt{1-\frac{3}{4}}=\frac{1}{2}$

18. (d)

19. (b)

20. (A)→(s); (B)→(r); (C)→(p), (D)→(s)

(A) $y^2=4x$ .....(1)

Clearly, if $P(at^2,2at)$ then by symmetry,

$Q(at^2,-2at)$

Equation of tangent is $ty=x+at^2$

For T, $y=0$, $x_1=-at^2$

and equation of normal is

$y=-tx+2at+at^3$

For R, $y=0$, $x_2=(2at+at^2)$ .....(2)

Here, $a=1\Rightarrow x_1=-t^2$ and $x_2=(2+t^2)$

$x_2=3=2+t^2\Rightarrow t^2=1\Rightarrow t=\pm 1$

Take $t=1$, then $x_1=-1$,

$\therefore\ PM=2at=2\times 1\times 1=2$

$RT=x_1+x_2=(1+3)=4$

$\therefore$ Area of quadrilateral $PTQR$

$=2\times\left(\frac{1}{2}\times 4\times 2\right)=8$ sq. units

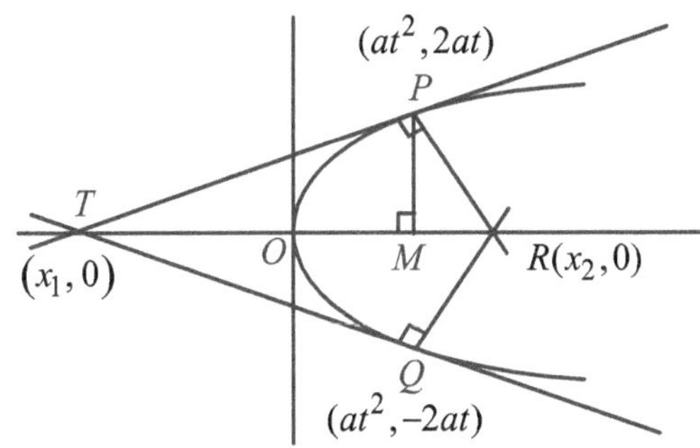

(B) Clearly, RT will be the diameter of circle
$\therefore$ Circumference $= (\pi \times \text{diameter})$

$= \pi \times RT = \dfrac{\pi \times 4}{4\pi} = 1.$

(C) Since in the part (1), we have found $x_2 \left(2a + at^2\right) > 2a,$

$(\text{ if } t \neq 0)$

$\therefore$ For three real normals, $x_2 > 2a = 2 \times 1 = 2$

i.e. $x_2 > 2.$

(D) Equation of PT is $y = x + a \Rightarrow \angle PTM = \dfrac{\pi}{4}$

$\Rightarrow \sin\dfrac{\pi}{4} = \dfrac{PM}{PT} = \dfrac{2}{PT}$

$\therefore PT = 2\sqrt{2}$

1. **(b)** Writing the given expression in the form $\left(\frac{\sin x^n}{x^n}\right)\left(\frac{x^n}{x^m}\right)\left(\frac{x}{\sin x}\right)^m$ and noting that the $\lim_{\theta\to 0}\frac{\sin\theta}{\theta}=1$, we see that the required limit equals to 1 if $n=m$, and 0 if $n>m$.

2. **(a)** Let $f(x)=ax^2+bx+c$
Then, $f(1)=a+b+c$
and $f(-1)=a-b+c$
Since $f(1)=f(-1)$
$\Rightarrow a+b+c=a-b+c$
$\Rightarrow 2b=0$ or $b=0$
i.e., $f(x)=ax^2+c$
$\therefore f'(x)=2ax$
$f'(a)=2a^2, f'(b)=2ab, f'(c)=2ac$
Now, $2f'(b)=f'(a)+f'(c)$
If $2.2ab=2a^2+2ac$
If $2b=a+c$
If a, b, c are in AP, which is given.
$\therefore f'(a), f'(b), f'(c)$ are in AP.

3. **(a)** $\lim_{n\to\infty}\frac{S_{n+1}-S_n}{\sqrt{\sum_{k=1}^{n}k}}=\lim_{n\to\infty}\frac{a_{n+1}}{\sqrt{\frac{n(n+1)}{2}}}=0$ $(\because a_{n+1}=a)$

4. **(a)** It can be easily shown that,

$$S_n=\begin{cases}\frac{n}{6}\left(n+\frac{1}{2}\right), & \text{when } n \text{ is even}\\ \frac{n}{6}(n+1), & \text{when } n \text{ is odd}\end{cases}$$

Thus $\frac{S_n}{n^2}=\begin{cases}\frac{1}{6}\left(1+\frac{1}{2n}\right), & \text{when } n \text{ is even}\\ \frac{1}{6}\left(1+\frac{1}{n}\right), & \text{when } n \text{ is odd}\end{cases}$

$\Rightarrow \lim_{n\to\infty}\frac{S_n}{n^2}=\frac{1}{6}$

5. **(a)** $\phi(x)=ax^2+bx+c$
$\because \phi(1)=\phi(-1)\Rightarrow a+b+c=a-b+c$
$\Rightarrow b=0$
$\therefore \phi(x)=ax^2+c$
$\Rightarrow \phi'(x)=2ax$
$\therefore \phi'(a_1)=2aa_1, \phi'(a_2)=2aa_2, \phi'(a_3)=2aa_3$
$\because a_1, a_2, a_3$ are in AP
$\therefore \phi'(a_1), \phi'(a_2), \phi'(a_3)$ are also in AP.

6. **(c)** $a=\min\{x^2+2x+3, x\in R\}$

$=\min\{(x+1)^2+2, x\in R\}$
$=2$

and $b=\lim_{\theta\to 0}\frac{1-\cos\theta}{\theta^2}$

$=\lim_{\theta\to 0}\frac{(1-\cos\theta)(1+\cos\theta)}{\theta^2(1+\cos\theta)}=\frac{1}{2}$

$\therefore \sum_{r=0}^{n}a^r\cdot b^{n-r}=b^n\sum_{r=0}^{n}\left(\frac{a}{b}\right)^r$

$=\left(\frac{1}{2}\right)^n\sum_{r=0}^{n}(4)^r$

$=\frac{1}{2^n}(1+4+4^2+...+4^n)$

$=\frac{1}{2n}.1.\left(\frac{4^{n+1}-1}{4-1}\right)$

$=\frac{4^{n+1}-1}{3\cdot 2^n}$

7. **(a, b, c)**
$f(x)=|x^2-3|x|+2|$

$$=\begin{cases}|x^2-3x+2|, & x\ge 0\\ |x^2+3x+2|, & x<0\end{cases}$$

$$=\begin{cases}x^2-3x+2, & x^2-3x+2\ge 0,\ x\ge 0\\ -x^2+3x-2, & x^2-3x+2<0,\ x\ge 0\\ x^2+3x+2, & x^2+3x+2\ge 0,\ x<0\\ -x^2-3x-2, & x^2+3x+2<0,\ x<0\end{cases}$$

$$=\begin{cases}x^2-3x+2, & x\in[0,1]\cup[2,\infty)\\ -x^2+3x-2, & x\in(1,2)\\ x^2+3x+2, & x\in(-\infty,-2]\cup[-1,0)\\ -x^2-3x+2, & x\in(-2,-1)\end{cases}$$

$$\Rightarrow f'(x)=\begin{cases}2x-3, & x\in(0,1)\cup(2,\infty)\\ -2x+3, & x\in((1,2)\\ 2x+3, & x\in(-\infty,-2)\cup(-1,0)\\ -2x-3, & x\in(-2,-1)\end{cases}$$

8. **(b,c,d)** $f(x)=\lim\limits_{x\to\infty}\frac{x}{x^{2n}+1}$

$$=\begin{cases} x, x^2<1 \\ 0, x^2>1 \\ 1/2, x=1 \\ -1/2, x=-1 \end{cases}$$

$\Rightarrow\ f(1^+)=f(-1^-)=0$

$f(1^-)=1, f(-1^+)=-1$

$f(1)=1/2$

9. **(b, c)** Since the greatest integer function is discontinuous (sensitive) at integral values of x, then for a given limit to exist both left- and right-hand limit must be equal.

L.H.L. $=\lim\limits_{x\to 1^-}(2-x+a[x-1]+b[1+x])$

$=2-1+a(-1)+b(1)=1-a+b$

R.H.L. $=\lim\limits_{x\to 1^+}(2-x+a[x-1]+b[1+x])$

$=2-1+a(0)+b(2)=1+2b$

On comparing, we have $-a=b$

10. **(a, b, c)**

$f(x)=\lim\limits_{n\to\infty}\frac{x^{2n}-1}{x^{2n}+1}$

Option (a) : $|x|>1$

Then $f(x)=\lim\limits_{n\to\infty}\frac{1-\frac{1}{x^{2n}}}{1+\frac{1}{x^{2n}}}=\frac{1-0}{1+0}=1$

Option (b) : $|x|<1$

Then $f(x)=\lim\limits_{n\to\infty}\frac{x^{2n}-1}{x^{2n}+1}=\frac{0-1}{0+1}=-1$

Option (c) : From alternate (a) and (b),

$f(x)=1$, for $|x|>1$

$f(x)=-1$, for $|x|<1$

But $1\neq -1$

$\therefore f(x)$ is not defined for any value of x.

Option (d) : $|x|=1$

Then $f(x)=0$

11. **(2)** $f'(x)=nx^{n-1}+1$; $f'(y)=ny^{n-1}+1$;

$f'(x+y)=n(x+y)^{n-1}+1$

by given equation we get,

$n(x+y)^{n-1}+2=n(x)^{n-1}+n(y)^{n-1}+2$

$\Rightarrow\ (x+y)^{n-1}=x^{n-1}+y^{n-1}$ ....(1)

For $n-1\le 1$, $\therefore\ n=0,2$; since for $n=1$ equation (1) does not holds.

12. **(0)** $\lim\limits_{x\to 0^+}\left[\frac{\sin(\operatorname{sgn} x)}{\operatorname{sgn}(x)}\right]$

$=\lim\limits_{x\to 0^+}\left[\frac{\sin 1}{1}\right]$

$=0$

And $\lim\limits_{x\to 0^-}\left[\frac{\sin(\operatorname{sgn} x)}{\operatorname{sgn}(x)}\right]$

$=\lim\limits_{x\to 0^-}\left[\frac{\sin(-1)}{-1}\right]$

$=\lim\limits_{x\to 0^-}[\sin 1]$

$=0$

13. **(1)** $\lim\limits_{x\to\infty}\frac{-\ln x^n+[x]}{[x]}=\lim\limits_{x\to\infty}\frac{-n\ln x+[x]}{[x]}$

$=1-n\lim\limits_{x\to\infty}\frac{\ln x}{[x]}$ ....(1)

$0<x-1<[x]\le x$

$\Rightarrow\frac{1}{x}\le\frac{1}{[x]}<\frac{1}{x-1}\Rightarrow\frac{\ln x}{x}\le\frac{\ln x}{[x]}<\frac{\ln x}{x-1}$

$\Rightarrow\ \lim\limits_{x\to\infty}\frac{\ln x}{x}\le\lim\limits_{x\to\infty}\frac{\ln x}{[x]}<\lim\limits_{x\to\infty}\frac{\ln x}{x-1}$

$\Rightarrow 0\le\lim\limits_{x\to\infty}\frac{\ln x}{[x]}$

$\therefore\ \lim\limits_{x\to\infty}\frac{\ln x}{[x]}=0$ ....(2)

From (1) and (2) we get, $\lim\limits_{x\to\infty}\frac{-\ln x^n+[x]}{[x]}=1$

14. **(1)** Here,

$y=(1+x)(1+x^2)(1+x^4).......(1+x^{2^n})$

$=\frac{1}{1-x}\{(1-x)(1+x)(1+x^2)(1+x^4)$ ......$(1+x^{2^n})\}$

$=\frac{1}{1-x}\{(1-x^2)(1+x^2)(1+x^4).......(1+x^{2^n})\}$

$=\frac{1}{1-x}\{(1-x^4)(1+x^4)..........(1+x^{2^n})\}$

$\therefore\ y=\dfrac{(1-x^{2^{n+1}})}{(1-x)}$

$\therefore\ \dfrac{dy}{dx}=\dfrac{-2^{n+1}.(x^{2^{n+1}-1})\ (1-x)-(1-x^{2^{n+1}}).(-1)}{(1-x)^2}$

Now, $\dfrac{dy}{dx}$ at $x=0$;

$$\left(\frac{dy}{dx}\right)_{x=0}=\frac{-2^{n+1}.(0).(1)+(1-0)}{(1-0)^2}=1.$$

For 15–16.

$$L=\lim_{x\to0}\frac{\sin x+ae^x+be^{-x}+c\ln(1+x)}{x^3}$$

$$=\lim_{x\to0}\left[\frac{\left(x-\frac{x^3}{3!}\right)+a\left(1+\frac{x}{1!}+\frac{x^2}{2!}+\frac{x^3}{3!}\right)}{x^3}+\frac{b\left(1-\frac{x}{1!}+\frac{x^2}{2!}-\frac{x^3}{3!}\right)+c\left(x-\frac{x^2}{2}+\frac{x^3}{3}\right)}{x^3}\right]$$

$$=\lim_{x\to0}\left[\frac{(a+b)+(1+a-b+c)x+\left(\frac{a}{2}+\frac{b}{2}-\frac{c}{a}\right)x^2}{x^3}+\frac{\left(-\frac{1}{3!}+\frac{a}{3!}-\frac{b}{3!}+\frac{c}{3}\right)x^3}{x^3}\right]$$

$$\Rightarrow a+b=0,1+a-b+c=0,\ \frac{a}{2}+\frac{b}{2}-\frac{c}{2}=0$$

and $L=-\dfrac{1}{3!}+\dfrac{a}{3!}-\dfrac{b}{3!}+\dfrac{c}{3}$

Solving first three equations,
we get $c=0$, $a=-1/2$, $b=1/2$.
Then, $L=-1/3$

Equation $ax^2+bx+c=0$ reduces to

$x^2-x=0\Rightarrow x=0,1$

$||x+c|-2a|<4b$

reduces to $||x|+1|<2$

$\Rightarrow -2<|x|+1<2$

$\Rightarrow 0\le|x|<1$

$\Rightarrow x\in[-1,1]$

15. **(b)** **16. (c)**

17. **(b)** $\widehat{AC}=\theta=AB$

$CD=\sin\theta$ and $OD=\cos\theta$

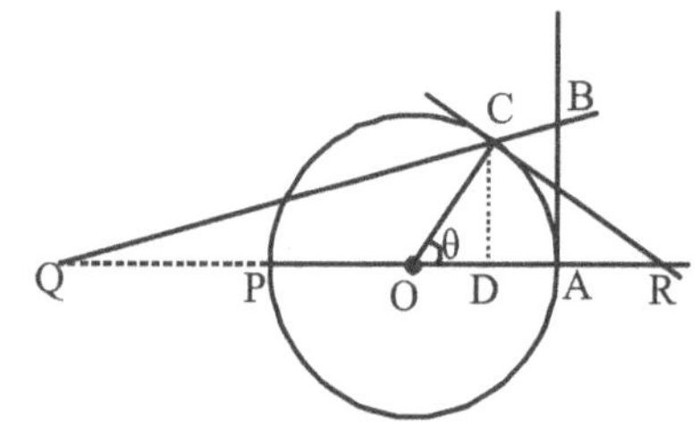

Therefore $AD=1-\cos\theta$

Therefore area of trapezoid,

$$ABCD=\frac{1}{2}(AB+CD)\times AD$$

$$=\frac{(\theta+\sin\theta)(1-\cos\theta)}{2}=(\theta+\sin\theta)\sin^2\frac{\theta}{2}$$

18. **(d)** ΔABQ and DCQ are similar, so

$$\frac{AB}{CD}=\frac{AQ}{DQ}=\frac{AQ}{AQ-AD}$$

$$\Rightarrow\frac{\theta}{\sin\theta}=\frac{AQ}{AQ-(1-\cos\theta)}$$

or, $AQ=\dfrac{\theta(1-\cos\theta)}{\theta-\sin\theta}$

$$\therefore\ \lim_{\theta\to0^+}AQ=\lim_{\theta\to0^+}\frac{\theta(1-\cos\theta)}{\theta-\sin\theta}$$

$$=\lim_{\theta\to0^+}\frac{1-\cos\theta+\theta\sin\theta}{1-\cos\theta}$$

$$=\lim_{\theta\to0^+}\frac{2\sin\theta+\theta\cos\theta}{\sin\theta}=3$$

19. **(A) → (q); (B) → (p, q, r); (C) → (r, s); D → (s)**

(A) Here, $a>0$, if $a\le0$, then limit $=\infty$

$$\therefore\ \lim_{x\to\infty}\frac{(\sqrt{x^2-x+1})-ax-b)(\sqrt{x^2-x+1})+ax+b)}{(\sqrt{x^2-x+1})+ax+b)}$$

$$=\lim_{x\to\infty}\frac{(x^2-x+1)-(ax+b)^2}{\sqrt{(x^2-x+1)}+ax+b}$$

$$= \lim_{x\to\infty} \frac{(1-a^2)x^2-(1+2ab)x+(1-b^2)}{\sqrt{(x^2-x+1)}+ax+b}$$

This is possible only when $1-a^2=0$ and $1+2ab=0$

$\therefore\ a=\pm 1$

$\Rightarrow a=1 \qquad (\because a>0)$

$\Rightarrow b=-1/2$

$\Rightarrow$ (a, 2b) = (1, –1)

(B) Divide numerator and denominator by $e^{1/x}$, then

$$\lim_{x\to\infty} \frac{(1+a^3)e^{\frac{1}{x}}+8}{e^{\frac{1}{x}}+(1-b^3)}=2$$

$$\Rightarrow \frac{0+8}{0+1-b^3}=2$$

$$\Rightarrow 1-b^3=4$$

$\therefore\ b^3=-3 \Rightarrow b=-3^{1/3}$

Then, $a\in R$

$\Rightarrow (a,b^3)=(a,-3)$

(C) $\lim_{x\to\infty}(\sqrt{(x^4-x^2+1)}-ax^2-b)=0$

Put $x=\frac{1}{t}$

$$\therefore\ \lim_{t\to 0}\left(\sqrt{\left(\frac{1}{t^4}-\frac{1}{t^2}+1\right)}-\frac{a}{t^2}-b\right)=0$$

$$\Rightarrow \lim_{t\to 0}\frac{\sqrt{(1-t^2+t^4)}-a-bt^2}{t^2}=0 \text{ ...(1)}$$

Since R.H.S. is finite, numerator must be equal to 0 at $t\to 0$.

$\therefore 1-a=0, \therefore a=1$

From equation (1),

$$\lim_{t\to 0}\frac{\sqrt{(1-t^2+t^4)}-1-bt^2}{t^2}=0$$

$$\lim_{t\to 0}(-1+t^2)\left(\frac{(1-t^2+t^4)^{1/2}-(1)^{1/2}}{(1-t^2+t^4)-1}\right)=b$$

$$\Rightarrow (-1)\left(\frac{1}{2}\right)=b \Rightarrow a=1, b=-\frac{1}{2}$$

$\Rightarrow (a,-2b)=(1,2)$

(D) $\lim_{x\to -a}\frac{a^7-(-x)^7}{a-(-x)}=7$

$\Rightarrow\ 7a^6=7 \Rightarrow a^6=1 \Rightarrow a=-1$

20. A→(p, r) ; B→(s, t) ; C→(q)

(A) For $x\to\infty, |x|=x$

$$\therefore\ f(x)=\left(\frac{x}{x+2}\right)^{-x}=\left(\frac{x+2}{x}\right)^{x}=\left(1+\frac{2}{x}\right)^{x}$$

$$\Rightarrow \lim_{x\to\infty} f(x)=\lim_{x\to\infty}\left(1+\frac{2}{x}\right)^x=e^2$$

and for $x\to -\infty, |x|=-x$

$$\therefore\ f(x)=\left(\frac{-x}{-x+2}\right)^{-x}=\left(\frac{-x+2}{-x}\right)^{x}=\left(1-\frac{2}{x}\right)^{x}$$

$$\Rightarrow \lim_{x\to -\infty} f(x)=\lim_{x\to -\infty}\left(1-\frac{2}{x}\right)^x=e^{-2}$$

(B) $\because f(x)=\frac{(1+x)^{1/x}-e}{x}$

$$=\frac{e\left\{1-\frac{x}{2}+\frac{11}{24}x^2+...\right\}-e}{x}$$

$$=\frac{e\left(-\frac{x}{2}+\frac{11}{24}x^2+...\right)}{x}$$

$$=e\left(-\frac{1}{2}+\frac{11}{24}x+...\right)$$

$$\Rightarrow \lim_{x\to 0} f(x)=-\frac{e}{2}<-1$$

(C) $f(x)=\left(\frac{1+5x^2}{1+3x^2}\right)^{1/x^2}$

$$\therefore\ \lim_{x\to 0} f(x)=\lim_{x\to 0}\left(\frac{1+5x^2}{1+3x^2}\right)^{1/x^2}$$

$$=e^{\lim_{x\to 0}\left(\frac{1+5x^2}{1+3x^2}-1\right)\frac{1}{x^2}}$$

$$=e^{\lim_{x\to 0}\left(\frac{2}{1+3x^2}\right)}=e^2$$

1. (c)

p	q	$p \Rightarrow q$	$\sim(p \Rightarrow q)$	$\sim p$	$\sim q$	$\sim p \vee \sim q$	$\sim(p \Rightarrow q) \Leftrightarrow \sim p \vee \sim q$
T	T	T	F	F	F	F	T
T	F	F	T	F	T	T	T
F	T	T	F	T	F	T	F
F	F	T	F	T	T	T	F

Last column shows that result is neither a tautology nor a contradiction.

2. (c) The inverse of the proposition $(p \wedge \sim q) \to r$ is
$\sim (p \wedge \sim q) \to \sim r$
$\equiv \sim p \vee \sim (\sim q) \to \sim r$
$\equiv \sim p \vee q \to \sim r$

3. (c) Negation of 'f is one to one and onto' is R or not Q.

4. (a) We know that the contropositive of $p \to q$ is $\sim q \to \sim p$. So contra positive of $p \to (\sim q \to \sim r)$ is
$\sim (\sim q \to \sim r) \to \sim p$
$\equiv \sim q \wedge [\sim (\sim r)] \sim p$
$\because \sim (p \to q) \equiv p \wedge \sim q$
$\equiv \sim q \wedge r \to \sim p$

5. (c) $S(p, q, r) = \sim p \wedge [\sim (q \vee r)]$
So, $S(\sim p, \sim q, \sim r) \equiv \sim(\sim p) \wedge [\sim(\sim q \vee \sim r)] \equiv p \wedge (q \vee r)$
$S^*(p, q, r) \equiv \sim p \vee [\sim (q \wedge r)]$
$S^*(\sim p, \sim q, \sim r) \equiv p \vee (q \vee r)$
Clearly, $S^*(\sim p, \sim q, \sim r) \equiv \sim S(p, q, r)$

6. (a)

7. (b) Let us make the truth table for the given statements, as follows :

p	q	$p \vee q$	$q \to p$	$p \to (q \to p)$	$p \to (p \vee q)$
T	T	T	T	T	T
T	F	T	T	T	T
F	T	T	F	T	T
F	F	F	T	T	T

From table we observe
$p \to (q \to p)$ is equivalent to $p \to (p \vee q)$

8. (c)

p	q	$p \to q$	$\sim p$	$\sim p \vee q$	$(p \to q) \leftrightarrow \sim(p \vee q)$
T	T	T	F	T	T
T	F	F	F	F	T
F	T	T	T	T	T
F	F	T	T	T	T

9. (a, b, d) Statement given in option (c) is only correct.
$\sim [p \vee (\sim q)] = (\sim p) \wedge \sim (\sim q)$
$= (\sim p) \wedge q$

10. (c, d) We know that $p \leftrightarrow q$ is true if p and q both are true or false.
so $p \leftrightarrow \sim q$ is true when if p and $\sim q$ is true.
i.e., p is true and q is false.
or p and $\sim q$ is false, i.e. p is false and q is true.
Hence, options (c) and (d) are correct

11. (a, b, c) Since $\sim (p \vee q) \equiv \sim p \wedge \sim q$
(By De-Morgans' law)
$\therefore \sim (p \vee q) \not\equiv \sim p \vee \sim q$
$\therefore$ (d) is the false statement

12. (a, b, d) We consider following truth table.

p	q	$\sim p$	$\sim q$	$p \wedge q$	$p \vee q$	$(\sim(p \vee q))$	$(p \wedge q) \wedge (\sim(p \vee q))$
T	T	F	F	T	T	F	F
T	F	F	T	F	T	F	F
F	T	T	F	F	T	F	F
F	F	T	T	F	F	T	F

Clearly last column of the above truth table contains only F. Hence $(p \wedge q) \wedge (\sim(p \vee q))$ is a contradiction

13. (a, b, c) The truth value of $\sim(\sim p) \leftrightarrow p$ as follow

p	$\sim p$	$\sim(\sim p)$	$\sim(\sim p) \to p$	$p \to \sim(\sim p)$	$\sim(\sim p) \leftrightarrow p$
T	F	T	T	T	T
F	T	F	T	T	T

Since last column of above truth table contains only T.
Hence $\sim (\sim p) \to p$ is a tautology.

14. (b, c, d)

15. (a, b, c)

16. (a, b, d) $p \Rightarrow q \equiv \sim p \vee q \therefore \sim (p \Rightarrow q) \equiv p \wedge \sim q$.

17. (a, b, c) We know that $p \wedge q$ is true when both p and q are true.
So, option (a) is not true.
We know that $p \to q$ is false when p is true and q is false.
So, option (b) is not true.
We know that $p \leftrightarrow q$ is true when either both p and q are true or both are false. So, option (c) is not true.
If p and q both are false, then
$p \vee q$ is false $\Rightarrow \sim (p \vee q)$ is true.
Hence, option (d) is true.

18. (a, b, c) The truth tables of $p \to q$ and $\sim p \vee q$ are given below:

p	q	$\sim p$	$p \to q$	$\sim(p \vee q)$
T	T	F	T	T
T	F	F	F	F
F	T	T	T	T
F	F	T	T	T

Clearly, truth tables of $p \to q$ and $\sim p \vee q$ are same.
So, $p \to q$ is logically equivalent to $\sim p \vee q$.
Hence, option (a) is correct.

If the truth value of p, q, r are T, F, T respectively, then the truth values of $p \vee q$ and $q \vee r$ are each equal to T. Therefore, the truth value of $(p \vee q) \wedge (q \vee r)$ is T.
Hence, option (b) is correct.
We have, $\sim (p \vee q \vee r) \cong (\sim p \wedge \sim q \wedge \sim r)$
So, option, (c) is correct.
If p is true and q is false, then $p \vee q$ is true. Consequently,
$\sim (p \vee q)$ is false and hence $p \wedge \sim (p \vee q)$ is false.
Hence, option (d) is wrong.

19. **(a, c, d)** Since $\sim(p \vee q) \equiv (\sim p \wedge \sim q)$ and $\sim (p \wedge q) \equiv (\sim p \vee q)$

So option (b) and (d) are not true.

$(p \rightarrow q) \equiv p \wedge \sim q)$, so option (c) is not true.

Now $p \rightarrow q \sim p \vee q$

$\sim q \rightarrow \sim p \equiv [\sim (\sim q) \vee \sim p] \equiv q \vee \sim p \equiv \sim p \vee q$

$p \rightarrow q \equiv \sim q \rightarrow \sim p$

20. **(A) → (s); (B) → (p); (C) → (q); (D) → (r)**

(A) Dual of statement $[(p \vee q) \wedge (\sim q)] \vee (\sim p)$ is $[(p \wedge q) \vee (\sim q)] \wedge (\sim p)$

(B) Logically equivalent of $[(p \vee q) \wedge (\sim q)] \vee \sim p$ is $[(p \wedge \sim q) \vee (q \wedge \sim q)] \vee \sim p$ or $[p \wedge \sim q] \vee \sim p$

(C) Negation of $[(p \vee q) \wedge (\sim q)] \vee (\sim p)$ is $\sim[(p \vee q) \wedge (\sim q)] \wedge \sim(\sim p)$ or $[(\sim p \wedge \sim q) \vee q)] \wedge p$

(D) Contrapositive of $[(p \vee q) \wedge (\sim q)] \rightarrow (\sim p)$ is $\sim (\sim p) \rightarrow \sim[(p \vee q) \wedge (\sim q)]$ or $p \rightarrow [\sim(p \vee q) \vee q]$ or $(\sim p) \vee [(\sim p \wedge \sim q) \vee q]$

1. (c) $\because\ \sigma=\sqrt{\frac{\Sigma xi^2}{N}-\left(\frac{\Sigma x_i}{N}\right)^2}$

$\therefore\ 2=\sqrt{\frac{(a^2+a^2.....'2n'\text{ times})}{2n}-0}$

$\Rightarrow\ 4=\frac{2na^2}{2n}\Rightarrow a^2=4\Rightarrow|a|=2$

2. (b) On arranging the given observations in ascending order, we get

All negative terms $\underbrace{0}_{(n+1)^{th}\text{ term}}$ All positive terms

The median of given observations = $(n+1)^{th}$term = 0

$\therefore$ S.D.>M.D.

3. (a) If each item of a data is increased or decreased by the same constant, then the standard deviation of the data remains unchanged.

4. (d) Let $\sum_{i=1}^{9}(x_i-5)=9$

$\Rightarrow\ \sum_{i=1}^{9}x_i-\sum_{i=1}^{9}5=9$

$\Rightarrow\ \sum_{i=1}^{9}x_i-(9\times5)=9$

$\sum x_i-45=\Rightarrow\sum x_i=54$

Similarly,

$\sum x_i^2-10\times54+25\times9=45$

$\Rightarrow\ \sum x_i^2=360$

$\Rightarrow\ \sigma=\sqrt{\frac{360}{9}-\left(\frac{54}{9}\right)^2}=\sqrt{\frac{324}{81}}=2$

5. (c) Two distributions are linerarly related

6. (b) The mean of the series

$$\bar{X}=\frac{1}{2n+1}\{a+(a+d)+(a+2d)+.....+(a+2nd)\}$$

$$=\frac{1}{2n+1}\left\{\frac{2n+1}{2}(2a+2nd)\right\}=a+nd$$

Therefore, mean deviation from mean

$$\frac{1}{2n+1}\sum_{r=0}^{2n}|(a+rd)-(a+nd)|=\frac{1}{2n+1}\sum_{r=0}^{2n}|r-n|d$$

$$=\frac{[2(1+2+...+n)+0]d}{2n+1}=\frac{n(n+1)d}{2n+1}$$

7. (b) We know that variance $(\sigma^2)=\frac{\sum x_i^2}{n}-\left(\frac{\sum x_i}{n}\right)^2$

First n natural numbers are:

x_i	x_i^2
1	1^2
2	2^2
3	3^2
4	4^2
5	5^2
⋮	⋮
n	n^2

$\therefore\ \sum x_i^2=\frac{n(n+1)(2n+1)}{6}$ and $\sum x_i=\frac{n(n+1)}{2}$

$\therefore\ \sigma^2=\frac{\sum x_i^2}{n}-\left(\frac{\sum x_i}{n}\right)^2$

$$=\frac{n(n+1)(2n+1)}{6n}-\left[\frac{n(n+1)}{2n}\right]^2$$

$$=\frac{(2n^2+3n+1)}{6}-\left(\frac{n+1}{2}\right)^2$$

$$=\frac{2[2n^2+3n+1]-3(n^2+1+2n)}{12}$$

$$=\frac{4n^2+6n+2-3n^2-3-6n}{12}=\frac{n^2-1}{12}.$$

8. (b,d) Mean of $a, b, 8, 5, 10$ is 6

$\Rightarrow\ \frac{a+b+8+5+10}{5}=6\Rightarrow a+b=7$ ...(i)

Variance of $a, b, 8, 5, 10$ is 6.80

$\Rightarrow\ \frac{(a-6)^2+(b-6)^2+(8-6)^2+(5-6)^2+(10-6)^2}{5}=6.80$

$\Rightarrow\ a^2-12a+36+(1-a)^2+21=34$ [using eq. (i)]

$\Rightarrow\ 2a^2-14a+24=0\Rightarrow a^2-7a+12=0$

$\Rightarrow$ $a = 3$ or 4

$\Rightarrow$ $b = 4$ or 3

$\therefore$ The possible values of a and b are $a = 3$ and $b = 4$

or, $a = 4$ and $b = 3$

9. **(c, d)** Let the other two observations be 'a' and 'b'

$$\therefore \text{mean} = \frac{2+4+6+a+b}{5}$$

$$\Rightarrow 4 = \frac{12+a+b}{5} \Rightarrow a+b=8$$

$$\text{Variance} = \frac{1}{n}\sum x^2 - \bar{x}^2 = 5.2$$

$$\Rightarrow \frac{1}{5}\left(4+16+36+a^2+b^2\right)-16=5.2$$

$$\Rightarrow a^2+b^2=50$$

10. **(b, c)** We know that for positive real numbers $x_1, x_2, ..., x_n$, we have

$$\frac{\sum x_i^2}{n} \geq \left(\frac{\sum x_i}{n}\right)^2 \Rightarrow \frac{400}{n} \geq \left(\frac{80}{n}\right)^2$$

$\Rightarrow n \geq 16$. So only possible value for $n = 18, 20$

11. **(a, b, c, d)** $\bar{x} = \frac{2+3+a+11}{4} = \frac{a}{4}+4$

$$\sigma = \sqrt{\sum \frac{x_i^2}{n} - (\bar{x})^2}$$

$$\Rightarrow 3.5 = \sqrt{\frac{4+9+a^2+121}{4} - \left(\frac{a}{4}+4\right)^2}$$

$$\Rightarrow \frac{49}{4} = \frac{4(134+a^2)-(a^2+256+32a)}{16}$$

$$\Rightarrow 3a^2 - 32a + 84 = 0$$

12. **(4)** Standard deviation $= \sigma = d\sqrt{\frac{n^2-1}{12}}$

d = size between each observation = 7

n = total number of observation = 7

$$\therefore \quad \sigma = 7\sqrt{\frac{(7)^2-1}{12}} = 7\sqrt{\frac{49-1}{12}}$$

$$= 7\sqrt{\frac{48}{12}} = 7 \times 2 = 14$$

13. **(3)** Variance of $1, 2, 3, 4, 5, ... 10$ is $\frac{99}{12}$

$\therefore$ variance of $3, 6, 9, 12, ... 30$ is $9 \times \frac{99}{12}$

$\therefore$ S.D. of $3, 6, 9, 12, ... 30 = \sqrt{9 \times \frac{99}{12}} = \frac{3}{2}\sqrt{33}$

14. **(0)** We know that, if any constant is added in each observation, then standard deviation remains same.

$\therefore$ The standard deviation of the observations $a+k, b+k, c+k, d+k, e+k$ is s.

15. **(5)** We know that Q.D $= \frac{5}{6} \times M.D. = \frac{5}{6} \times 12 = 10$

$$\therefore \text{S.D} = \frac{3}{2} \times Q.D. = \frac{3}{2} \times 10 \Rightarrow S.D. = 15.$$

16. **(7)**

x_i	f_i	$f_i x_i$	$f_i x_i^2$
A	2	2A	$2A^2$
2A	1	2A	$4A^2$
3A	1	3A	$9A^2$
4A	1	4A	$16A^2$
5A	1	5A	$25A^2$
6A	1	6A	$36A^2$
Total	**7**	**22A**	$\mathbf{92A^2}$

$$\because \sigma^2 = \frac{\sum f_i x_i^2}{\sum f_i} - \left(\frac{\sum f_i x_i}{\sum f_i}\right)^2$$

$$\Rightarrow 160 = \frac{92A^2}{7} - \left(\frac{22A}{7}\right)^2$$

$$\Rightarrow 160 = \frac{92A^2}{7} - \frac{484A^2}{49} \Rightarrow 160 = \frac{92 \times 7A^2 - 484A^2}{49}$$

$$\Rightarrow 160 \times 49 = 644A^2 - 484A^2 \Rightarrow 160A^2 = 7840$$

$$\Rightarrow A^2 = \frac{7840}{160} \Rightarrow A^2 = 49 \Rightarrow A = \pm 7$$

$A = 7$ as A is a positive integer.

17. **(7)** The given data is 36, 72, 46, 42, 60, 45, 53, 46, 51, 49

Arranging the data in ascending order,

36, 42, 45, 46, 46, 49, 51, 53, 60, 72

Number of observation = 10 (even)

Median (M)

$$= \frac{\left(\frac{N}{2}\right)^{th} \text{observation} + \left(\frac{N}{2}+1\right)^{th} \text{observation}}{2}$$

$$= \frac{\left(\frac{10}{2}\right)^{th} \text{observation} + \left(\frac{10}{2}+1\right)^{th} \text{observation}}{2}$$

$$= \frac{5^{th}\text{observation} + 6^{th}\text{observation}}{2} = \frac{46+49}{2} = 47.5$$

x_i	$\lvert x_i - M \rvert$
36	$\lvert 36-47.5 \rvert = 11.5$
42	$\lvert 42-47.5 \rvert = 5.5$
45	$\lvert 45-47.5 \rvert = 2.5$
46	$\lvert 46-47.5 \rvert = 1.5$
46	$\lvert 46-47.5 \rvert = 1.5$
49	$\lvert 49-47.5 \rvert = 1.5$
51	$\lvert 51-47.5 \rvert = 3.5$
53	$\lvert 53-47.5 \rvert = 5.5$
60	$\lvert 60-47.5 \rvert = 12.5$
72	$\lvert 72-47.5 \rvert = 24.5$
	$\mathbf{\Sigma \lvert x_i - M \rvert = 70}$

$\therefore$ Mean deviation about median

$$= \frac{\sum |x_i - M|}{n} = \frac{70}{10} = 7$$

18. **(b)** $\bar{x} = \dfrac{x_1 + x_2 + x_3 + ... + x_n}{n}$

$$\sigma^2 = \frac{1}{n}\sum_{i=1}^{n}(x_i - \bar{x})^2$$

Mean of $d_1, d_2, d_3, ..., d_n$

$$= \frac{d_1 + d_2 + d_3 + ... + d_n}{n}$$

$$= \frac{(-x_1 - a) + (-x_2 - a) + (-x_3 - a) + ... + (-x_n - a)}{n}$$

$$= -\left[\frac{x_1 + x_2 + x_3 + ... + x_n}{n}\right] - \frac{na}{n}$$

$$= -\bar{x} - a$$

Since, $d_i = -x_i - a$ and we multiply or subtract each observation by any number the mode remains the same. Hence mode of $-x_i - a$ i.e. d_i and x_i are same.

Now variance of $d_1, d_2, ..., d_n$

$$= \frac{1}{n}\sum_{i=1}^{n}\,[d_i - (-\bar{x} - a)]^2$$

$$= \frac{1}{n}\sum_{i=1}^{n}\,[-x_i - a + \bar{x} + a]^2$$

$$= \frac{1}{n}\sum_{i=1}^{n}\,(-x_i + \bar{x})^2$$

$$= \frac{1}{n}\sum_{i=1}^{n}\,(\bar{x} - x_i)^2 = \sigma^2$$

19. **(c)** For the numbers 2, 4, 6, 8, ..., $2n$

$$\bar{x} = \frac{2[n(n+1)]}{2n} = (n+1)$$

And $Var = \dfrac{\Sigma(x - \bar{x})^2}{2n} = \dfrac{\Sigma x^2}{n} - (\bar{x})^2$

$$= \frac{4\Sigma n^2}{n} - (n+1)^2$$

$$= \frac{4n(n+1)(2n+1)}{6n} - (n+1)^2$$

$$= \frac{2(2n+1)(n+1)}{3} - (n+1)^2$$

$$= (n+1)\left[\frac{4n + 2 - 3n - 3}{3}\right]$$

$$= \frac{(n+1)(n-1)}{3} = \frac{n^2 - 1}{3}$$

$\therefore$ Statement-1 is false. Clearly, statement - 2 is true.

20. **(A)$\to$ s; (B) $\to$ r; (C)$\to$ q; (D)$\to$ p**

(A) Given data is
3, 3, 4, 5, 7, 9, 10, 12, 18, 19, 21.
Median (M) = 6th obs = 9
$|x_i - M|$ are 6, 6, 5, 4, 2, 0, 1, 3, 9, 10, 12

$$\therefore \sum_{i=1}^{11}|x_i - M| = 58$$

$$M.D(M) = \frac{1}{11} \times 58 = 5.27$$

(B) Data in ascending order is
10, 11, 11, 12, 13, 13, 14, 16, 16, 17, 17, 18

$$\text{Median} = \frac{6^{th}\text{ obs} + 7^{th}\text{ obs}}{2} = \frac{13 + 14}{2} = \frac{27}{2}$$

$$= 13.5$$

Now, $\sum|x_i - M| = 28$

$$\therefore \quad M.D(M) = \frac{28}{12} = 2.33$$

1. (b) Total number of cases $= 6 \times 6 \times 6 = 216$

Let the second number is i (clearly $1 < i < 6$), then first number can be chosen in $i - 1$, ways and third number can be chosen in $6 - i$ ways.

Hence number of ways $= (i - 1)(6 - i)$.

$\therefore$ i can take values 2 to 5.

$\therefore$ Favourable no. of cases

$$= \sum_{i=2}^{5} (i-1)(6-i) = 1 \times 4 + 2 \times 3 + 3 \times 2 + 4 \times 1 = 20$$

$\therefore$ Required probability $= \dfrac{20}{216} = \dfrac{5}{54}$

2. (c) $\dfrac{x^2 - 60x + 800}{x - 30} < 0 \Rightarrow \dfrac{(x-20)(x-40)}{x-30} < 0$

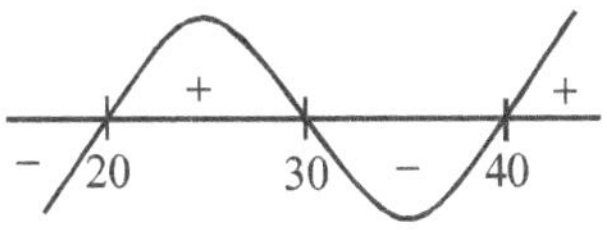

$\therefore$ $x \in \{1, 2, ..., 19\} \cup \{31, 32, ..., 39\}$ $[\because x \in N]$

$\therefore$ Number of favourable cases $= 19 + 9 = 28$. Total no. of cases $= 100$

$\therefore$ Required probability $= \dfrac{28}{100} = \dfrac{7}{25}$

3. (c) Here, $n(S) =$ length of the interval $[0, 5] = 5$

$n(E) =$ length of the interval $\subseteq [0, 5]$ in which p belongs such that the given equation has real roots.

Now, $x^2 + px + \dfrac{1}{4}(p+2) = 0$ will have real roots if

$$p^2 - 4.1.\frac{1}{4}(p+2) \ge 0 \quad \Rightarrow p^2 - p - 2 \ge 0$$

$\Rightarrow (p+1)(p-2) \ge 0$

$\Rightarrow p \le -1$ or $p \ge 2$

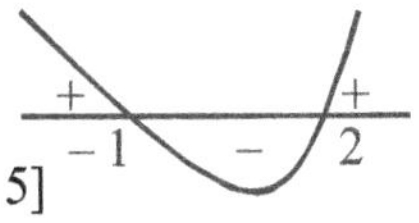

But $p \in [0, 5]$. So, $E = [2, 5]$

$\therefore$ $n(E) =$ length of the interval $[2, 5] = 3$

$\therefore$ Required probability $= \dfrac{3}{5}$

4. (a) Let $3n$ consecutive integers be

$N+1, N+2, N+3, ..., N+3n$ (starting with the integer N)

We write these $3n$ numbers in 3 rows as following;

$N+1, N+4, N+7, ..., N+3n-2$

$N+2, N+5, N+8, ..., N+3n-1$

$N+3, N+6, N+9, ..., N+3n$

The sum of three selected number will be divisible by 3 it either all three belong to the same row or all three belong to different rows. So, the favourable no. of cases

$$= 3({}^nC_3) + ({}^nC_1)({}^nC_1)({}^nC_1)$$

$$= \frac{3n(n-1)(n-2)}{3!} + n^3 = \frac{3n^3 - 3n^2 + 2n}{2}$$

Also, the total no of cases

$$= {}^{3n}C_3 = \frac{3n(3n-1)(3n-2)}{3!} = \frac{n(3n-1)(3n-2)}{2!}$$

$\therefore$ Required probability

$$= \frac{\dfrac{3n^3 - 3n^2 + 2n}{2}}{\dfrac{n(3n-1)(3n-2)}{2}} = \frac{3n^2 - 3n + 2}{(3n-1)(3n-2)}$$

5. (c) Let l be the length of the chord AB of the given circle of radius a and r be the distance of the mid point D of the chord from the centre C, then $r = a\cos\theta$ and $l = 2a\sin\theta$.

According to given condition :

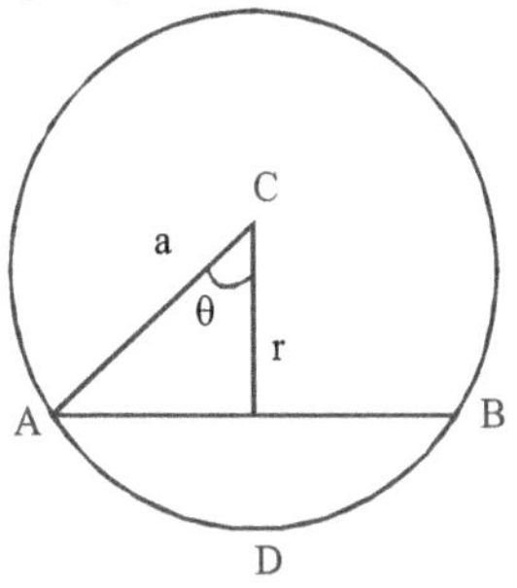

$$\frac{2}{3}(2a) < 2a\sin\theta < \frac{5}{6}(2a) \Rightarrow \frac{2}{3} < \sin\theta < \frac{5}{6}$$

$$\Rightarrow \frac{\sqrt{11}}{6} < \cos\theta < \frac{\sqrt{5}}{3} \Rightarrow \frac{\sqrt{11}}{6}a < r < \frac{\sqrt{5}}{3}a$$

$\therefore$ The given condition is satisfied if the mid point of the chord lies within the region between the concentric circles of radii $\dfrac{\sqrt{11}}{6}a$ and $\dfrac{\sqrt{5}}{3}a$.

Hence, the required probability

$$= \frac{\pi\left(\dfrac{\sqrt{5}}{3}a\right)^2 - \pi\left(\dfrac{\sqrt{11}}{6}a\right)^2}{\pi a^2} = \frac{1}{4}$$

6. (a) Since the chairs are numbered, so for counting of total number of cases it is equivalent to linear permutation. Hence, total number of cases = 10!

If two particular persons A and B sit together then the total number of linear arrangements =2! 9!. Consider one of such arrangements in which the arrangement started at chair 1 (C_1) and ends at chair 10 (C_{10}).

$C_1 - C_2 - C_3 - .... - C_9 - C_{10}$

If two persons sit at C_1 and C_{10} then it will lead to 2! 8! new arrangements. So the favourable number of cases = 2! 9! + 2! 8! = 2!8! (10)

$\therefore$ Probability $= \frac{2!8!(10)}{10!} = \frac{2}{9}$

7. **(b, d)** If a be the radius of the circle, the area of the inscribed sqrare $= 2a^2$

$\therefore p_1 = \frac{2a^2}{\pi a^2} = \frac{2}{\pi}$ and $p_2 = 1 - p, = \frac{\pi - 2}{\pi}$

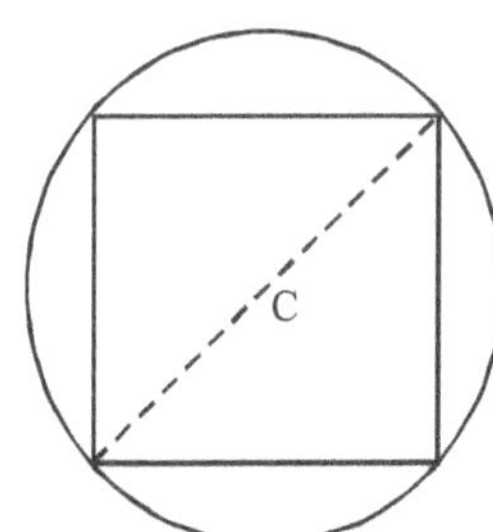

$\because \pi - 2 < 2 \Rightarrow \frac{\pi-2}{\pi} < \frac{2}{\pi} \Rightarrow p_2 < p_1$

Again, $p_1^2 - p_2^2 = (p_1 + p_2)(p_1 - p_2) = \frac{4-\pi}{\pi} < \frac{1}{3}$

$[\therefore 3 < \pi < 4]$

8. **(b, c)** We must have, $0 \le \frac{1+4p}{4} \le 1,\ 0 \le \frac{1-p}{4} \le 1$ and $0 \le \frac{1-2p}{4} \le 1,$

$\Rightarrow -\frac{1}{4} \le p \le \frac{3}{4},\ -3 \le p \le 1,\ -\frac{3}{2} \le p \le \frac{1}{2}$

Again the events are mutually exclusive and exhaustive, so $0 \le \frac{1+4p}{4} + \frac{1-p}{4} + \frac{1-2p}{4} \le 1$

$\Rightarrow -3 \le p \le 1$

Taking intersection of all four intervals of p, we get

$-\frac{1}{4} \le p \le \frac{1}{2}$

9. **(a, b, c)** $P(A \cup B) = P(A) + P(B) - P(A \cap B)$

$0.8 = 0.6 + 0.4 - P(A \cap B)$

$\therefore\ P(A \cap B) = 0.2$

$P(A \cup B \cup C) = (0.6 + 0.4 + 0.5)$

$-(0.2 + P(B \cap C) + 0.3) + 0.2$

$= 1.5 - 0.3 - P(B \cap C)$

We know $0.85 \le P(A \cup B \cup X) \le 1$

or $0.85 \le 1.2 - P(B \cap X) \le 1$

$\therefore\ 0.2 \le P(B \cap X) \le 0.35.$

10. **(a, b, c)** We have to find the probability that the person unlocks the lock at k^{th} trial. It means that he fails in first $(k-1)$ trials.

$= P(\text{he fails in } k-1 \text{ trials}) \times P(\text{he succeeds in } k^{th} \text{ trial})$

$= \left[\frac{n-1}{n} \cdot \frac{n-2}{n-1} \cdot \frac{n-3}{n-2} \cdots\cdots \frac{n-(k-1)}{n-(k-2)}\right]$

$\times \left[\frac{1}{n-(k-1)}\right] = \frac{1}{n}$

11. **(4)** Let each of them have n sons. Hence we have to distribute 3 mangoes amongst the sons of Ankur and Rahul, in such a manner that one mango goes to the sons of one and two mango to the sons of other.

1 to Ankur's sons and 2 to Rahul's son + 2 to Ankur's son and 1 to Rahul's son

= Total number of ways of distributing

$= {}^nC_1 \cdot {}^nC_2 + {}^nC_2\, {}^nC_1 = 2 \cdot {}^nC_1\, {}^nC_2 = m$

And total number of ways is ${}^{2n}C_3 = n.$

$\therefore\ 2 \cdot \frac{{}^nC_1\, {}^nC_2}{{}^{2n}C_3} = \frac{6}{7}$

$7 \cdot \frac{n(n-1)}{2} \cdot n = 3 \cdot \frac{2n(2n-1)(2n-2)}{6}$

$\Rightarrow n = 4.$

12. **(1)** Consider one combination 01, 01, 01, 10, 10.

In each case numbers can come in different orders.

Hence the required probability

$= \frac{5!}{2!\,2!\,1!}\left(\frac{1}{4}\right)^5 + \frac{5!}{2!\,1!\,1!\,1!}\left(\frac{1}{4}\right)^5 + \frac{5!}{3!\,2!}\left(\frac{1}{4}\right)^5$

$= 5!\left(\frac{1}{4}\right)^5 \left[\frac{1}{4} + \frac{1}{2} + \frac{1}{12}\right] = \frac{1}{4^5} \cdot 120 \left[\frac{10}{12}\right] = \frac{100}{4^5}$

$= \left[\frac{1}{10p}\right] = \left[\frac{1024}{1000}\right] = 1$

13. **(8)** Let A denote the event that he candidate A is selected and B the event that B is selected. It is given that

$P(A) = .5$

$P(A \cap B) \le .3$

Now $P(A) + P(B) - P(A \cap B) = (A \cup B) \le 1$

or $0.5 + P(B) - P(A \cap B) \le 1$, by (1)

or $P(B) \le .5 + P(A \cap B) \le 0.5 + .3,$

by (2) or $P(B) \le .8$

So maximum possible value of 10P is 8.

14. **(3)** Total no. of arrangements = 15!

Extreme chairs are occupied by girls, thus there are

four gaps among 5 girls where boys can be seated. Let the number of boys in these four gaps be $2x+1, 2y+1, 2z+1$ and $2t+1$, then

$2x+1+2y+1+2z+1+2t+1=10 \Rightarrow x+y+z+t=3$

Where x, y, z, t are integers and

$0 \le x \le 3,\ 0 \le y \le 3,\ 0 \le z \le 3,\ 0 \le t \le 3$

$\therefore$ The number of ways of selecting positions for boys = coefficient of x^3 in $(1+x+x^2+x^3)^4$

$$= \text{coefficient of } x^3 \text{ in } \left(\frac{1-x^4}{1-x}\right)^4$$

$=$ coefficent of x^3 in $(1-x^4)^4(1-x)^{-4} = {}^6C_3 = 20$

$\therefore$ Number of arrangements of boys and girls with given condition $= 20 \times 10! \times 5!$

$$\therefore \text{ Required probability } = \frac{20 \times 10! \times 5!}{15!} = \frac{20}{3003}$$

$$\Rightarrow \frac{n}{1001} = \frac{3003}{1001} = 3$$

15. **(3)** In the last five throws there can be 0, 1, 2, 3, 4 or 5 heads and the same should be the case in the first ten throws.

$n(E)$ = number of favourable cases

$$= {}^5C_0{}^{10}C_0 + {}^5C_1{}^{10}C_1 + {}^5C_2{}^{10}C_2 + {}^5C_3{}^{10}C_3 + {}^5C_4{}^{10}C_4 + {}^5C_5{}^{10}C_5 = 3003$$

and $n(S)$ = total number of ways $= 2^{15} = 32768$

$$k = \frac{n(E)}{n(S)} = \frac{3003}{32768} \Rightarrow \frac{32768k}{1001} = 3$$

16. **(c)** x can be 2, 3, 4, 5, 6.

The number of ways in which sum 2, 3, 4, 5, 6 can occur are the coefficients of x^2, x^3, x^4, x^5, x^6, in

$$\left(3x+2x^2+x^3\right)\left(x+2x^2+3x^3\right)$$

$= 3x^2+8x^3+14x^4+8x^5+3x^6$.

The greatest coefficient of 14 occurs with x^4, so $P(E)$ is maximum when $x=4$

This shows that sum that occurs most often is 4.

17. **(d)** Sum that occurs minimum times is 2 or 6.

18. **(a)** Total number of ways of painting first column when colours are not alternating is 2^8-2.

$\Rightarrow$ The probability when no column has alternating

$$\text{colours is } \left(\frac{2^8-2}{2^8}\right)^8 = \left(1-\frac{1}{2^7}\right)^8.$$

19. **(a)** The number of ways the square has equal number of red and black squares is ${}^{64}C_{32}$

$$\Rightarrow \text{probability} = \frac{{}^{64}C_{32}}{2^{64}}$$

20. **(A) → (q); (B) → (s); (C) → (p); (D) → (r)**

(A) Here sample space is selecting 2 out of 10 i.e ${}^{10}C_2$ and 2 balls can be selected in ${}^4C_1 \times {}^6C_1$ ways such that one of them is red and the other is white hence required probability is

$$\frac{4 \times 6 \times 2}{10 \times 9} = \frac{8}{15}$$

(B) Total number of fruits is $6+4+8=18$, so three fruits can be selected in ${}^{18}C_3$ ways and that represents the sample space.

3 apples can be selected out of 6 in ${}^6C_3$ ways so required

$$\text{probability is } = \frac{6C_3}{18C_3} = \frac{6 \times 5 \times 4}{18 \times 17 \times 16} = \frac{5}{204}$$

Alternately: Probability that 1st one is apple is 6/18, 2nd one apple is 5/17 and 3rd one apple is 4/16 so required

$$\text{probability is } \frac{6 \times 5 \times 4}{18 \times 17 \times 16} = \frac{5}{204}$$

(C) Probability that none of them will appear tail is $(1/2)^5 = 1/32$

So required probability that at least one tail will appear is $1 - 1/32 = 31/32$

(D) Out of 12 students 5 can be selected in ${}^{12}C_5 = (12 \times 11 \times 10 \times 9 \times 8)/120 = 792$ ways and the number of ways of selecting 3 girls and 2 boys is ${}^6C_3 \times {}^6C_2 = 20 \times 15 = 300$.

So required probability is $300/792 = 75/198$

DAILY PRACTICE PROBLEMS

MATHEMATICS SOLUTIONS

DPP/CM14

1. (c) f image of goh image

Let fogoh = F (x) = f[goh (x)]

$= f[g(\sqrt{x+3})] = f(\cos\sqrt{x+3})$

$$F(x) = \frac{2}{\cos\sqrt{x+3}+1}$$

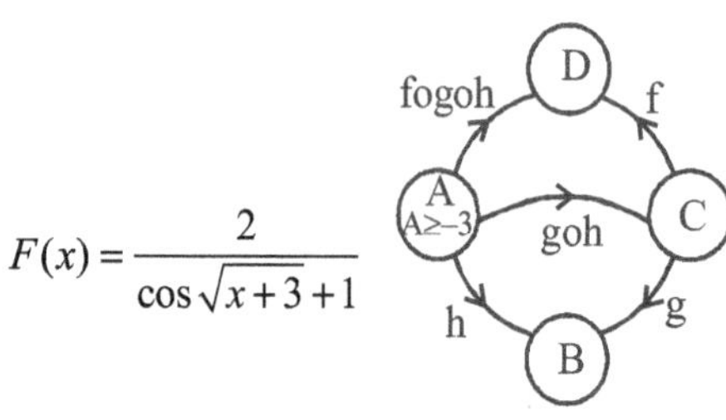

Domain : $x+3 \ge 0$

now $-1 < \cos\sqrt{x+3} \le 1$

$\sqrt{x+3} \ne (2n-1)\pi, n \in N$

2. (a) a R b $\Rightarrow$ $|a-b| \le 1$

$\therefore$ a R b as $|a-a| = 0 \le 1$

$\Rightarrow$ R is reflexive.

Let a = 2, b = 2.5, c = 3.4, then $|a-b| = 0.5 < 1$ and $|b-c| = 0.9 < 1$

But $|a-c| = |2-3.4| = 1.4 \not\le 1$

$\Rightarrow$ (a, c) $\notin$ R

$\Rightarrow$ R is not transitive.

Clearly $|a-b| \le 1$

$\Rightarrow$ $|b-a| \le 1$

$\Rightarrow$ R is symmetric.

3. (b) Here

$g^2(x) = gog(x) = g\{g(x)\} = g(3+4x)$

$= 15 + 4^2x = (4^2-1) + 4^2x$

$g^3(x) = gogog(x)$

$= g(15+4^2x) = 3 + 4(15+4^2x)$

$= 63 + 4^3x = (4^3-1) + 4^3x$

Generalizing, we get

$g^n(x) = (4^n-1) + 4^n x = y$ (say)

then $x = (y+1-4^n)4^{-n}$

$\Rightarrow g^{-n}(y) = (y+1)4^{-n} - 1$

$\therefore g^{-n}(x) = (x+1)4^{-n} - 1$

4. (b) $\because$ $x^2 = xy$ $\Rightarrow x(x-y) = 0$

$\Rightarrow$ x = 0 or x = y

$\because$ x = x $\forall$ x $\in$ A $\Rightarrow$ R is reflexive

Also x R y $\Rightarrow$ x = 0 or x = y

When x = 0, then $x^2 = xy$; $y \ne 0$, then $y^2 \ne yx$ as L.H.S $\ne 0$, R.H.S = 0

$\Rightarrow$ R is not symmetric.

Let x R y and y R z

$\Rightarrow$ Either x = 0 or x = y and y = 0 or y = z

Case (i) : x = 0, y = 0 and z $\ne$ 0, then $x^2 = xz$

$\Rightarrow$ xRz

Case (ii) : x = 0, y = z $\ne$ = 0, then $x^2 = xz$

$\Rightarrow$ x = z $\Rightarrow$ xRz

Case (iii) : x = y $\ne$ 0; y = z

$\Rightarrow$ R is transitive.

5. (d) f is not one-one as $f(0) = 0$ and $f(-1) = 0$.

f is also not onto a for $y = 1$ there is no $x \in$ R such that $f(x) = 1$. If there is such an $x \in$ R, then $e^{|x|} - e^{-x} = e^x + e^{-x}$.

Clearly $x \ne 0$. For $x > 0$, this equation gives

$e^{-x} = 0$ which is not possible and for $x < 0$, $\frac{e^{2x}+1}{e^x} = 0$, which is also not possible.

6. (b,c,d) As shown gof is one-one but g is many-one

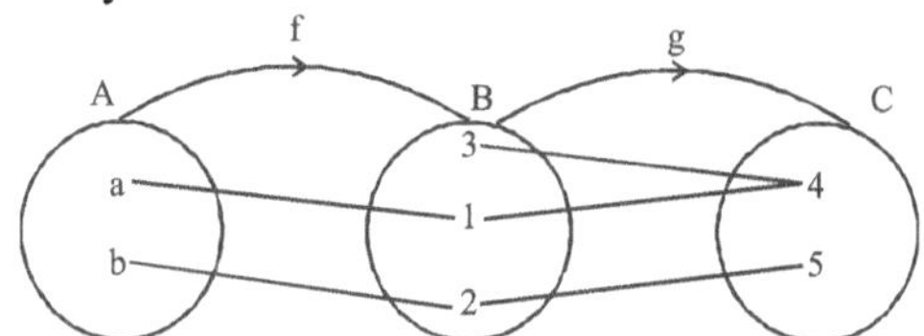

$\Rightarrow$ (A) is not correct.

(b) If gof is one-one then f is also one-one,

If f is many-one then gof can not be one-one

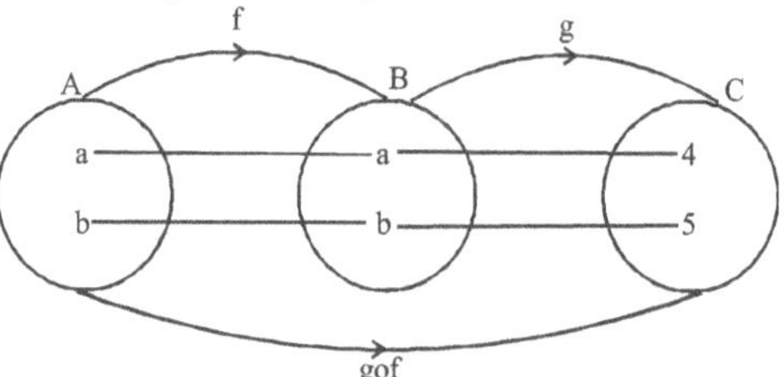

(c) and (d) are obviously true.

7. (b, c, d)

For $f(x)$ to be real

$x > 0$, $\ln x > 0$, $\ln(\ln x) > 0$ and

$\ln(\ln(\ln x)) > 0$

$\Rightarrow$ $x > 0, x > 1, x > e$ and $x > e^e$

$\Rightarrow$ $D = (e^e, \infty)$

Clearly range of $f(x) = R \Rightarrow f(x)$ is onto

Also, $f'(x) = \frac{1}{x\ln(x)\ln(\ln x)} > 0$ if $x > e^e$

$\therefore f(x)$ is one -one in its domain.

8. (b, d)

The period of $f(x) = |\sin 2x| + |\cos 2x|$ is $\pi/4$

$\Rightarrow$ $[f(x)]$ is also periodic with period $\pi/4$.

Also $1 \le f(x) \le \sqrt{2}$

$\Rightarrow$ $[f(x)] = 1 f(x)$ is a many-one and into function.

9. (a, b, d)

$$f(x) = \max\{1+\sin x, 1, 1-\cos x\} = \begin{cases} 1+\sin x, & 0 \le x \le \frac{3\pi}{4} \\ 1-\cos x, & \frac{3\pi}{4} \le x \le \frac{3\pi}{2} \\ 1, & \frac{3\pi}{2} \le x \le 2\pi \end{cases}$$

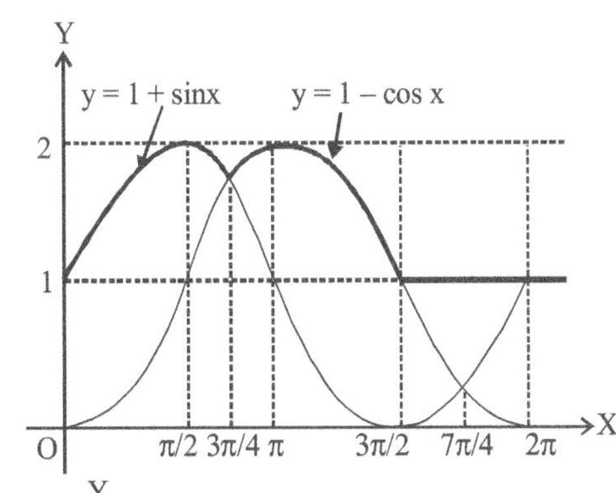

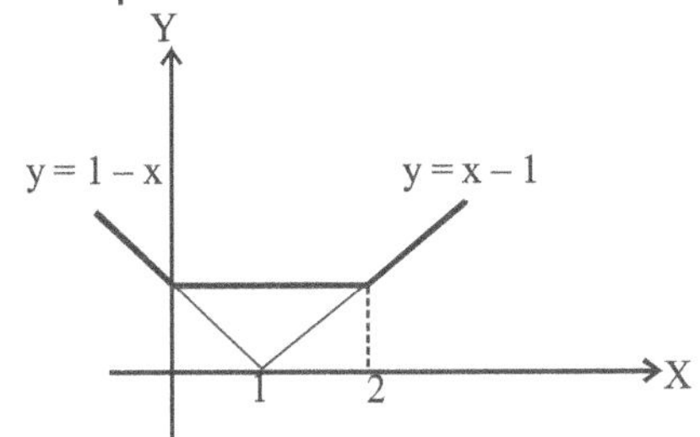

$$g(x) = \max\{1, |x-1|\} = \begin{cases} 1-x, & x \le 0 \\ 1, & 0 \le x \le 2 \\ x-1, & x \ge 2 \end{cases}$$

$\therefore f(0) = 1 \Rightarrow g(f(0)) = 1$ and $f(1) = 1 + \sin 1$

$\left(\because 0 < 1 < \frac{3\pi}{4}\right)$

$\Rightarrow g(f(1)) = 1$ $\qquad (\because 1 < 1 + \sin 1 < 2)$

Again $g(1) = 1 \Rightarrow f(g(1)) = 1 + \sin 1$ and

$g(0) = 1 \Rightarrow f(g(0)) = 1 + \sin 1$

10. (0)

Let $y = f(x) = \dfrac{x-1}{c-x^2+1}$

Take $y = -t$, where $t \in \left[\frac{1}{3}, 1\right]$,

$\therefore \quad -t = \dfrac{x-1}{c-x^2+1}$

$\Rightarrow \quad x^2 - c - 1 = \dfrac{x-1}{t} \Rightarrow x^2 - \dfrac{1}{t}x + \dfrac{1}{t} - c - 1 = 0$

As $-t \in \left[-1, -\frac{1}{3}\right]$, hence the above must not possess real solution

$\therefore \quad \left(\dfrac{1}{t}\right)^2 - 4\left(\dfrac{1}{t} - c - 1\right) < 0 \Rightarrow \dfrac{1}{t^2} - \dfrac{4}{t} + 4 < -4c$

$\Rightarrow c < -\dfrac{1}{4}\left(\dfrac{1}{t} - 2\right)^2$

Now, $\dfrac{1}{3} \le t \le l \Rightarrow 1 \le \dfrac{1}{t} - 2 \le 1 \Rightarrow -\dfrac{1}{4} \le \dfrac{1}{4}\left(\dfrac{1}{t} - 2\right)^2 \le 0$

Hence, $c \in \left(-\infty, -\frac{1}{4}\right]$

11. (5)

Given $f(x + f(y)) = f(x) + y, \forall\, x, y \in R$

Putting $y = x$, we get $f(x + f(x)) = f(x) + x$

$\Rightarrow \quad f(x + f(x)) = x + f(x)$

$\Rightarrow f(t) = t \quad$ [Putting t in place of $x + f(x)$]

$\Rightarrow f(x) = x \;\forall\, x \in R$

$\Rightarrow f(1000) = 1000$

12. (1)

$fog(x) = f(g(x)) = f(4x(1-x))$

$\Rightarrow \dfrac{1-4x(1-x)}{1+4x(1-x)}$ when $0 \le 4x(1-x) \le 1$ and $0 \le x \le 1$

But $4x - 4x^2 \ge 0 \Rightarrow 0 \le x \le 1$

$4x - 4x^2 \le 1 \Rightarrow (2x-1)^2 \ge 0 \Rightarrow x \in R$

Hence $fog(x) = \dfrac{1-4x+4x^2}{1+4x-4x^2}$, $0 \le x \le 1$

Let $y = \dfrac{4x^2-4x+1}{-(4x^2-4x)+1}$, $\qquad 0 \le x \le 1$

Put $4x^2 - 4x = t \qquad t \in [-1, 0]$

$y = \dfrac{1+t}{1-t}, \dfrac{dy}{dt} = \dfrac{1-t+1+t}{(1-t)^2} > 0$

Range of $fog(x) = [0, 1]$

$\Rightarrow \alpha + \beta = 1$

13. (6)

Given, $2f(x) + 3f\left(\dfrac{2x+29}{x-2}\right) = 100x + 80$

Putting $\dfrac{2x+29}{x-2}$ in place of x, we get

$$2f\left(\frac{2x+29}{x-2}\right) + 3f\left(\frac{\frac{2(2x+29)}{x-2} + 29}{\frac{2x+29}{x-2} - 2}\right) = 100\left(\frac{2x+29}{x-2}\right) + 80$$

or $2f\left(\frac{2x+29}{x-2}\right)+3f(x)=100\frac{(2x+29)}{x-2}+80$

$2.(1)-3.(2)\Rightarrow -5f(x)$

$=200x+160-300\frac{(2x+29)}{x-2}-240$

$=-300\frac{(2x+29)}{x-2}+200x-80$

$\therefore\ f(x)=60\left(\frac{2x+29}{x-2}\right)-40x+16$

$\therefore\ f(3)=60\times 35-120+16=1996$

For Qs. 14 & 15

$$g(f(x))=\begin{cases}[f(x)] & -\pi\le f(x)<0\\ \sin f(x), & 0\le f(x)\le\pi\end{cases}$$

$$=\begin{cases}[[x]], & -\pi\le[x]<0,\ -2\le x\le -1\\ [|x|+1], & -\pi\le|x|+1<0,\ -1<x\le 2\\ \sin[x], & 0\le[x]\le\pi,\ -2\le x\le -1\\ \sin(|x|+1), & 0\le|x|+1\le\pi,\ -1<x\le 2\end{cases}$$

$$=\begin{cases}[x], & -2\le x\le -1\\ \sin(|x|+1), & -1<x\le 2\end{cases}$$

Hence, the domain is $[-2, 2]$.
Also for $-2\le x\le -1$, $[x]=-2,-1$
and for $-1<x\le 2$, $|x|+1\in[1,3]$
$\Rightarrow\ \sin(|x|+1)\in[\sin 3, 1]$
Hence, the range is $\{-2,-1\}\cup[\sin 3, 1]$
Also for $y\in[\sin 3,1],[y]=0.1$
Hence, the number of integral points in the range is 4.

14. (c) 15. (c)

16. (c) Since $y=x+\frac{1}{x}$
Clearly the given relation is many one and therefore not an injective relation with domain R ~ {0} and range R ~ (–2, 2)

17. (b) Since, $y=|x|+2$
Clearly, this relation is many-one and so not injective. Here, domain of this solution is $(-\infty,\infty)$ and range is $(2,\infty)$. Hence, this solution is not surjective from R to R whereas it is surjective from R to $[2,\infty)$.

18. (d) Since $y^2=2x-4=2(x-2)$
Clearly there are infinitely many pairs of points having same abscissa in $(2,\infty)$
So, the given relation is one-many relation.
Here, domain of $y^2=2x-4$ is $[2,\infty)$ and range is $(-\infty,\infty)$.
Hence, this relation is surjective from $R\to R$ and also in $R\to[0,\infty)$

19. (A)–(p); (B)–(q, r); (C)–(p); (D)–(q, r)
Since $f(g(x))$ is a one-one function.
$f(g(x_1))\ne f(g(x_2))$ whenever $g(x_1)=g(x_2)$
$\Rightarrow\ f(g(x_1))\ne(g(x_2))$ whenever $x_1\ne x_2$
$\Rightarrow\ (g(x_1))\ne(g(x_2))$ whenever $x_1\ne x_2$
$\Rightarrow\ g(x)$ is one-one.
If $f(x)$ is not one-one, then $f(x)=y$ is satisfied by $x=x_1$, x_2
$\Rightarrow\ f(x_1)=f(x_2)=y$ also if $g(x)$ is onto, then let $g(x_1)=x_1$ and $g(x_2)=x_2$
$\Rightarrow\ f(g(x_1))=f(g(x_2))$
$\Rightarrow\ f(g(x))$ cannot be one-one.

20. A – (s, p); (B) – (q, t); (C)–(r)
(A) $\because f(x)=\max\{1+\sin x, 1, 1-\cos x\}$

$$=\begin{cases}1+\sin x, & 0\le x\le\frac{3\pi}{4}\\ 1-\cos x, & \frac{3\pi}{4}\le x\le\frac{3\pi}{2}\\ 1, & \frac{3\pi}{2}\le x\le 2\pi\end{cases}$$

$$g(x)=\max\{1,|x-1|\}=\begin{cases}1-x, & x\le 0\\ 1, & 0\le x\le 2\\ x-1, & x\ge 2\end{cases}$$

$\therefore\ f(0)=1\Rightarrow g(f(0)=g(1)=1$
$\therefore\ g(f(0))=1$ (S)

and $f(1)=1+\sin 1$ $\left(\because 0<1<\frac{3\pi}{4}\right)$

$\therefore\ g(f(1))=g(1+\sin 1)=1$ $(\because 1<1+\sin 1<2)$

$\therefore\ g(f(1))=1$ (p)

(B) $\because\ f(g(x))=\ell n\left(\frac{1+g(x)}{1-g(x)}\right)$

$\therefore\ f(g(0))=\ell n\left(\frac{1+g(0)}{1-g(0)}\right)$

$=\ell n\left(\frac{1+0}{1-0}\right)=\ell n\ 1=0$ (q)

and $g\left(f\left(\frac{e-1}{e+1}\right)\right)=g\left(\ell n\left(\frac{1+\frac{e-1}{e+1}}{1-\frac{e-1}{e+1}}\right)\right)$

$=g(\ell n(e))=g(1)$

$=\frac{3+1}{1+3}=\frac{4}{4}=1$ (t)

(C) $f(g(0))=f(0)=1+0^2=1$ (r)
$gf(0)=g(1)=1-1^2=0$
$gf((1))=g(2)=2-2^2=-2$

1. (c) **Case 1 :** If $0 \le x \le \frac{1}{2}$, then

$$\cos^{-1}\left(\frac{x}{2}+\frac{1}{2}\sqrt{3-3x^2}\right)=\cos^{-1}\left(x.\frac{1}{2}+\sqrt{1-x^2}.\frac{\sqrt{3}}{2}\right)$$

$$=\cos^{-1}x-\cos^{-1}\frac{1}{2}$$

$\therefore$ Equation is

$$\cos^{-1}x+\cos^{-1}x-\cos^{-1}\frac{1}{2}=\frac{\pi}{3}\Rightarrow x=\frac{1}{2}$$

Case 2 : If $\frac{1}{2}\le x\le 1$, then

$$\cos^{-1}\left(\frac{x}{2}+\frac{1}{2}\sqrt{3-3x^2}\right)=\cos^{-1}\frac{1}{2}-\cos^{-1}x$$

$\therefore$ Equation is $\cos^{-1}x+\cos^{-1}\frac{1}{2}-\cos^{-1}x=\frac{\pi}{3}$,

which is identity

Hence the identity holds good for $x\in\left[\frac{1}{2},1\right]$.

2. (b) The given relation is possible when

$$a-\frac{a^2}{3}+\frac{a^3}{9}+...=1+b+b^2+...$$

Also

$$-1\le a-\frac{a^2}{3}+\frac{a^3}{9}+...\le 1\ \&\ -1\le 1+b+b^2+...\le 1$$

$$\Rightarrow |b|<1\Rightarrow |a|<3 \text{ and } \frac{a}{1+\frac{a}{3}}=\frac{1}{1-b}$$

$\Rightarrow \frac{3a}{a+3}=\frac{1}{1-b}$, there are infinitely many solution.

But in given options it is satisfied only when $a = 1$ and $b=-\frac{1}{3}$.

3. (b) Since the equation

$a_1+a_2\sin x+a_3\cos x+a_4\sin 2x+a_5\cos 2x=0$ holds for all values of x,

$a_1+a_3+a_5=0$ (on putting $x=0$)

$a_1-a_3+a_5=0$ (on putting $x=\pi$)

$\Rightarrow\ a_3=0$ and $a_1+a_5=0$ ...(1)

Putting $x=\frac{\pi}{2}$ and $\frac{3\pi}{2}$, we get

$a_1+a_2-a_5=0$ and $a_1-a_2-a_5=0$ ...(2)

$\Rightarrow a_2=0$ and $a_1-a_5=0$ (1) and (2) give

$a_1=a_2=a_3=a_5=0$

The given equation reduces to $a_4\sin 2x=0$. This is true for all values of x, therefore $a_4=0$

Hence, $a_1=a_2=a_3=a_4=a_5=0$

Thus the number of 5-tuples is one.

4. (d) $x=n\pi-\tan^{-1}3\Rightarrow\tan^{-1}3=n\pi-x$

$\Rightarrow\ \tan(n\pi-x)=3\Rightarrow -\tan x=3$

$$\Rightarrow\ \tan 2x=\frac{2\tan x}{1-\tan^2 x}=\frac{3}{4} \text{ and}$$

$$\cos x=\pm\frac{1}{\sqrt{1+\tan^2 x}}=\pm\frac{1}{\sqrt{10}}$$

on substituting these value in the given equation we find only $\cos x=-\frac{1}{\sqrt{10}}$ satisfies the equation, so that the given equation holds for values of x for which $\tan x=-3$ and $\cos x=-\frac{1}{\sqrt{10}}$ which is possible if x lies in the second quadrant only and so n must be an odd integer.

5. (d) $T_r=\cot^{-1}\left(\frac{4r^2+3}{4}\right)=\tan^{-1}\frac{1}{1+r^2-\frac{1}{4}}$

$$=\tan^{-1}\frac{\left(r+\frac{1}{2}\right)-\left(r-\frac{1}{2}\right)}{1+\left(r+\frac{1}{2}\right)\left(r-\frac{1}{2}\right)}$$

$$=\tan^{-1}\left(r+\frac{1}{2}\right)-\tan^{-1}\left(r-\frac{1}{2}\right)$$

$$S_n=\sum T_r=\tan^{-1}\left(n+\frac{1}{2}\right)-\tan^{-1}\frac{1}{2}=\tan^{-1}\left(\frac{4n}{2n+5}\right)$$

$$S_\infty=\lim_{n\to\infty}S_n=\tan^{-1}2=\cot^{-1}\frac{1}{2}.$$

6. (a,b,c) If we put $x=\tan\theta$, the given equality becomes

$\tan^{-1}y=4\theta$

$$\Rightarrow y=\tan 4\theta=\frac{2\tan 2\theta}{1-\tan^2 2\theta}=\frac{2\left[\frac{2\tan\theta}{1-\tan^2\theta}\right]}{1-\left(\frac{2\tan\theta}{1-\tan^2\theta}\right)^2}$$

$$= \frac{2 \times 2x(1-x^2)}{(1-x^2)^2 - 4x^2} = \frac{4x(1-x^2)}{1-6x^2+x^4}$$

so that y is finite if $x^4 - 6x^2 + 1 \neq 0$

$$\Rightarrow x^2 \neq \frac{6 \pm \sqrt{36-4}}{2} \neq 3 \pm 2\sqrt{2}$$

7. **(a, c, d)** The given equation holds if $x^2 + x + 1 = ax + 1$ and $-1 \le x^2 + x + 1 \le 1$

$\Rightarrow x(x+1+a) = 0$ and $-1 \le x \le 0$

$\Rightarrow x = 0$ or $a - 1$ and $-1 \le x \le 0$

$\therefore x = 0$ is one solution and for another different solution $-1 \le a - 1 < 0$

$\Rightarrow 0 \le a < 1$. So only integral value a can have is 0.

8. **(a,c,d)** The equation holds if

$$\sin^2\theta + 2\sin\theta + 2 = 4^{\sec^2\phi} + 1$$

Now LHS $= (\sin\theta + 1)^2 + 1 \le 5$ and RHS ≥ 5

$(\because \sec^2\phi \ge 1)$

So, LHS = RHS $\Rightarrow \sin\theta = -1$ and $\sec^2\phi = 1$

9. **(a, b, d)**

$\tan^{-1}(x-1) + \tan^{-1}(x) + \tan^{-1}(x+1) = \tan^{-1} 3x$

$\Rightarrow \tan^{-1}(x-1) + \tan^{-1}(x) = \tan^{-1} 3x - \tan^{-1}(x+1)$

$$\Rightarrow \tan^{-1}\left[\frac{(x-1)+x}{1-(x-1)(x)}\right] = \tan^{-1}\left[\frac{3x-(x+1)}{1+3x(x+1)}\right]$$

$$\Rightarrow \frac{2x-1}{1-x^2+x} = \frac{2x-1}{1+3x^2+3x}$$

$\Rightarrow (1-x^2+x)(2x-1) = (1+3x^2+3x)(2x-1)$

$$\Rightarrow x = 0, \pm\frac{1}{2}$$

10. **(1)** $0 \le x^2 + x + 1 \le 1$ and $0 \le x^2 + x \le 1$

$\therefore x = -1, 0$

for $x = -1$

$$\text{L.H.S} = 2\sin^{-1} 1 + \cos^{-1} 1 + 0 = \frac{3\pi}{2}$$

$\therefore x = -1$ is a solution.

For $x = 0$, L.H.S. $= 2\sin^{-1} 1 + \cos^{-1} 0 = \dfrac{3\pi}{2}$

$\therefore x = 0$ is a solution.

$\therefore$ sum of the solutions $= -1$.

11. **(1)**

$$-\cos\left[\cos^{-1}\left(-\frac{\sqrt{3}}{2}\right) + \frac{\pi}{6}\right] = -\cos\left[\pi - \cos^{-1}\left(\frac{\sqrt{3}}{2}\right) + \frac{\pi}{6}\right]$$

$[\because \cos^{-1}(-x) = \pi - \cos^{-1} x]$

$$= -\cos\left(\pi - \frac{\pi}{6} + \frac{\pi}{6}\right) = -1\cos\pi = -(-1) = 1$$

12. **(1)** We know that, $\sin^{-1} y + \cos^{-1} y = \dfrac{\pi}{2}, |y| \le 1$

$\therefore$ According to question

$$x - \frac{x^2}{2} + \frac{x^3}{3} - ...... = x^2 - \frac{x^4}{2} + \frac{x^6}{4} .....$$

$$\Rightarrow \frac{x}{1+\frac{x}{2}} = \frac{x}{1+\frac{x^2}{2}},\ (\because 0 < |x| < \sqrt{2}) \Rightarrow \frac{x}{2+x} = \frac{x^2}{2+x^2}$$

$\Rightarrow 2x + x^3 = 2x^2 + x^3 \Rightarrow x = x^2$

But $x \neq 0$, hence $x = 1$

13. **(3)** $\sin^{-1}\left(\dfrac{x}{5}\right) + \text{cosec}^{-1}\left(\dfrac{5}{4}\right) = \dfrac{\pi}{2}$ ...(i)

Let $\theta = \text{cosec}^{-1}\left(\dfrac{5}{4}\right)$; $\text{cosec}\,\theta = \dfrac{5}{4}$

$$\therefore \sin\theta = \frac{1}{\text{cosec}\,\theta} = \frac{4}{5} \Rightarrow \theta = \sin^{-1}\left(\frac{4}{5}\right) \quad ...(ii)$$

We know that $\sin\dfrac{\pi}{2} = 1$ $\quad \therefore \dfrac{\pi}{2} = \sin^{-1}(1)$ ... (iii)

From eq. (i), $\sin^{-1}\left(\dfrac{x}{5}\right) = \dfrac{\pi}{2} - \text{cosec}^{-1}\left(\dfrac{5}{4}\right) = \dfrac{\pi}{2} - \theta$

Using eq. (ii) and eq. (iii)

$$\sin^{-1}\left(\frac{x}{5}\right) = \sin^{-1}(1) - \sin^{-1}\left(\frac{4}{5}\right) = \sin^{-1}\left(\sqrt{1-\frac{16}{25}} - \frac{4}{5}\sqrt{1-1}\right)$$

(Using Formula of $\sin^{-1} A - \sin^{-1} B$)

$$\Rightarrow \sin^{-1}\frac{x}{5} = \sin^{-1}\left(\frac{3}{5} - 0\right)$$

$$\Rightarrow \sin^{-1}\frac{x}{5} = \sin^{-1}\frac{3}{5} \Rightarrow x = 3$$

14. **(4)** We have $\cos^{-1} x - \cos^{-1}\dfrac{y}{2} = \alpha$

$$\Rightarrow x = \cos\left(\cos^{-1}\frac{y}{2} + \alpha\right)$$

$$= \cos\left(\cos^{-1}\frac{y}{2}\right)\cos\alpha - \sin\left(\cos^{-1}\frac{y}{2}\right)\sin\alpha$$

$$\Rightarrow 2x = y\cos\alpha - \sin\alpha\sqrt{4-y^2}$$

$$\Rightarrow 2x - y\cos\alpha = -\sin\alpha\sqrt{4-y^2}$$

Squaring, we get

$4x^2 + y^2\cos^2\alpha - 4xy\cos\alpha = 4\sin^2\alpha - y^2\sin^2\alpha$

$\Rightarrow 4x^2 - 4xy\cos\alpha + y^2 = 4\sin^2\alpha$

15. **(b)** Extreme value of $\sin^{-1} x = \dfrac{5\pi}{2}$ and $\cos^{-1} y = 3\pi$

$$\Rightarrow \sin^{-1} x + \cos^{-1} y \le \frac{11\pi}{2}$$

$\therefore$ Only 1 possible ordered pairs $(1, -1)$.

16. **(b)** We have $2\theta = \sin^{-1}(\sin 2\theta)$ [let $\sin^{-1}x = \theta$].

$$\Rightarrow \frac{3\pi}{2} \le 2\theta \le \frac{5\pi}{2} \Rightarrow \frac{3\pi}{4} \le \theta \le \frac{5\pi}{4}$$

$$\Rightarrow -\frac{1}{\sqrt{2}} \le x \le \frac{1}{\sqrt{2}}.$$

17. **(a)** $\sin^{-1}\left(x - \frac{x^2}{2} + \frac{x^3}{3} ...\right) + \cos^{-1}\left(x^2 - \frac{x^4}{2} + \frac{x^6}{4} ...\right)$

$$= \frac{\pi}{2}$$

$$\Rightarrow \cos^{-1}\left(x^2 - \frac{x^4}{2} + \frac{x^6}{4} ...\right)$$

$$= \frac{\pi}{2} - \sin^{-1}\left(x - \frac{x^2}{2} + \frac{x^3}{4} ...\right)$$

$$\Rightarrow \cos^{-1}\left(x^2 - \frac{x^4}{2} + \frac{x^6}{4} ...\right)$$

$$= \cos^{-1}\left(x - \frac{x^2}{2} + \frac{x^3}{4} ...\right)$$

$$\Rightarrow x^2 - \frac{x^4}{2} + \frac{x^6}{4} ... = x - \frac{x^2}{2} + \frac{x^3}{4} ...$$

On both sides we have G.P. of infinite terms

$$\therefore \frac{x^2}{1 - \left(\frac{-x^2}{2}\right)} = \frac{x}{1 - \left(\frac{-x}{2}\right)} \Rightarrow \frac{2x^2}{2 + x^2} = \frac{2x}{2 + x}$$

$$\Rightarrow 2x + x^3 = 2x^2 + x^3 \Rightarrow x(x - 1) = 0$$

$$\Rightarrow x = 0, 1 \text{ but } 0 < |x| < \sqrt{2} \Rightarrow x = 1$$

18. (c) $\sin[\cot^{-1}(1 + x)] = \cos(\tan^{-1}x)$

$$\Rightarrow \sin\left[\sin^{-1}\left(\frac{1}{\sqrt{1 + (1 + x)^2}}\right)\right]$$

$$= \cos\left[\cos^{-1}\left(\frac{1}{\sqrt{1 + x^2}}\right)\right]$$

$$\Rightarrow \frac{1}{\sqrt{1 + (1 + x)^2}} = \frac{1}{\sqrt{1 + x^2}}$$

$$\Rightarrow 1 + 1 + 2x + x^2 = 1 + x^2$$

$$\Rightarrow 2x + 1 = 0$$

$$\Rightarrow x = \frac{-1}{2}$$

19. **(d)** $\cot^{-1}\left(1 + \sum_{k=1}^{n} 2k\right) = \cot^{-1}[1 + n(n + 1)]$

$$= \tan^{-1}\left[\frac{(n + 1) - n}{1 + (n + 1)n}\right] = \tan^{-1}(n + 1) - \tan^{-1}n$$

$$\therefore \sum_{n=1}^{23} [\tan^{-1}(n + 1) - \tan^{-1}n]$$

$$= \tan^{-1}24 - \tan^{-1}1$$

$$= \tan^{-1}\frac{23}{25}$$

$$\therefore \cot\left[\sum_{n=1}^{23} \cot^{-1}\left(1 + \sum_{k=1}^{n} 2k\right)\right]$$

$$= \cot\left[\tan^{-1}\frac{23}{25}\right] = \frac{25}{23} > 1$$

20. **A → (q, r, s); (B) → (q); (C) → (r, s); (D) → (p)**

(A) $(\sin^{-1}x)^2 + (\sin^{-1}y)^2 = \frac{\pi^2}{2}$

$$\Rightarrow (\sin^{-1}x)^2 = (\sin^{-1}y)^2 = \frac{\pi}{4}$$

$$\Rightarrow \sin^{-1}x = \pm\frac{\pi}{2}, \sin^{-1}y = \pm\frac{\pi}{2}$$

$\Rightarrow x = \pm 1$ and $y = \pm 1$

$\Rightarrow x^3 + y^3 = -2, 0, 2$

(B) $(\cos^{-1}x)^2 + (\cos^{-1}y)^2 = 2\pi^2$

$\Rightarrow (\cos^{-1}x)^2 = (\cos^{-1}y)^2 = \pi$

$\Rightarrow x = y = -1$

$\Rightarrow x^5 + y^5 = -2$

(C) $(\sin^{-1}x)^2 (\cos^{-1}y)^2 = \frac{\pi^4}{4}$

$\Rightarrow (\sin^{-1}x)^2 = \frac{\pi^2}{4}$ and $(\cos^{-1}y)^2 = \pi^2$

$\Rightarrow (\sin^{-1}x) = \pm\frac{\pi}{2}$ and $(\cos^{-1}y) = \pi$

$\Rightarrow x = \pm 1$ and $y = -1$

$\Rightarrow |x - y| = 0, 2$

(D) $|\sin^{-1}x - \sin^{-1}y| = \pi$

$\Rightarrow \sin^{-1}x = -\frac{\pi}{2}$ and $\sin^{-1}y = \frac{\pi}{2}$

or $\sin^{-1}x = \frac{\pi}{2}$ and $\sin^{-1}y = -\frac{\pi}{2}$

$\Rightarrow x^y = 1^{(-1)}$ or $(-1)^1 = 1$ or -1

1. **(b)** Given that $X = A_1 + 3$

$A_3^2 + ... (2n-1)(A_{2n-1})^{2n-1}$

We know that if A is a skew-symmetric matrix then $A^T = -A$

$X^T = -[A_1 + 3A_3^3 + ... (2n-1)(A_{2n-1})^{2n-1}]$

$= -X$, so skew-symmetric

2. **(a)** We have, BC = CB, and

$A^{N+1} = (B+C)^{N+1}$

$= {}^{N+1}C_0 B^{N+1} + {}^{N+1}C_1 B^N C + {}^{N+1}C_2 B^{N-1} C^2 + ... + {}^{N+1}C_r B^{N+1-r} C^r + ...$

But given that $C^2 = 0 \Rightarrow C^3 = C^4 = ... = C^r = 0$

Hence, $A^{N+1} = {}^{N+1}C_N B^{N+1} + {}^{N+1}C_1 B^N C$

$= B^{N+1} + (N+1) B^N C$

$= B^N[B + (N+1)C]$

Thus K = N

3. **(d)** Consider $AA' = \begin{bmatrix} a & b & c \\ c & a & b \\ b & c & a \end{bmatrix}\begin{bmatrix} a & c & b \\ b & a & c \\ c & b & a \end{bmatrix}$

$$= \begin{bmatrix} a^2+b^2+c^2 & ac+ab+bc & ab+bc+ca \\ ca+ab+bc & a^2+b^2+c^2 & cb+ba+ac \\ ab+cb+ac & bc+ca+ab & a^2+b^2+c^2 \end{bmatrix} = I$$

$\therefore$ $a^2 + b^2 + c^2 = 1$ and $ab + bc + ca = 0$.

$\Rightarrow$ $a + b + c = \pm 1$

So a, b, c are the roots of the equation

$x^2 \pm x^2 + abc = 0$

4. **(a)** We have,

$AB = BA \Rightarrow B'A' = (AB)' \Rightarrow AB$ is symmetric

Also, $ABA^{-1} = BAA^{-1} = B$

$\Rightarrow$ $A^{-1}ABA^{-1} = A^{-1}B \Rightarrow BA^{-1} = A^{-1}B$

$\Rightarrow$ $(A^{-1}B)' = (BA^{-1})' \Rightarrow (A^{-1})'B' = A^{-1}B$

(Since, A^{-1} is symmetric)

So $A^{-1}B$ is a symmetric matrix.

5. **(c)** We have,

$A^2 + B^2 = AA + BB = A(BA) + B(AB)$

$(\therefore AB = B$ and $BA + A)$

$= (AB)A + (BA)B$

$= BA + AB = A + B$ $(\therefore AB = B$ and $BA = A)$

6. **(b)** We have

$$A^2 = \begin{bmatrix} \alpha & 0 \\ 1 & 1 \end{bmatrix}\begin{bmatrix} \alpha & 0 \\ 1 & 1 \end{bmatrix} = \begin{bmatrix} \alpha^2 & 0 \\ \alpha+1 & 1 \end{bmatrix} = \begin{bmatrix} 9 & a \\ b & c \end{bmatrix}$$

$\Rightarrow$ we get $\alpha^2 = 9$

$\Rightarrow$ $\alpha = \pm 3$ and $a = 0, c = 1, b = a + 1 = 3 + 1 = 4$

or $b = -3 + 1 = -2$

So $a + b + c = (0 + 4 + 1) = 5$ or $(0 - 2 + 1) = -1$

7. **(a, d)** $A = \begin{bmatrix} 2 & 3 \\ -1 & 2 \end{bmatrix}$, $f(x) = x^2 - 4x + 7$

$f(A) = A^2 - 4A + 7I_2$

$$= \begin{bmatrix} 2 & 3 \\ -1 & 2 \end{bmatrix}\begin{bmatrix} 2 & 3 \\ -1 & 2 \end{bmatrix} - 4\begin{bmatrix} 2 & 3 \\ -1 & 2 \end{bmatrix} + 7\begin{bmatrix} 1 & 0 \\ 0 & 1 \end{bmatrix}$$

$$= \begin{bmatrix} (4-3) & (6+6) \\ (-2-2) & (-3+4) \end{bmatrix} + \begin{bmatrix} -8 & -12 \\ 4 & -8 \end{bmatrix} + \begin{bmatrix} 7 & 0 \\ 0 & 7 \end{bmatrix}$$

$$= \begin{bmatrix} 0 & 0 \\ 0 & 0 \end{bmatrix} = 0$$

Thus, $A^2 - 4A + 7I_2 = 0$

$\Rightarrow A^2 = 4A - 7I_2$

$A^3 = A(4A - 7I_2) = 4A^2 - 7A = 4(4A - 7I_2) - 7A$

$= 16A - 28I_2 - 7A = 9A - 28I_2$

$A^4 = A(9A - 28I_2) = 9A^2 - 28A$

$= 9(4A - 7I_2) - 28A = 8A - 63I_2$

$A^5 = A(8A - 63I_2) = 8A^2 - 63A = 8(4A - 7I_2) - 63A$

$= -31A - 56I_2$

Put, $A = \begin{bmatrix} 2 & 3 \\ -1 & 2 \end{bmatrix}$, $I_2 = \begin{bmatrix} 1 & 0 \\ 0 & 1 \end{bmatrix}$

$$A^5 = -31\begin{bmatrix} 2 & 3 \\ -1 & 2 \end{bmatrix} - 56\begin{bmatrix} 1 & 0 \\ 0 & 1 \end{bmatrix}$$

$$= \begin{bmatrix} -62 & -93 \\ 31 & -62 \end{bmatrix} + \begin{bmatrix} -56 & 0 \\ 0 & -56 \end{bmatrix}$$

$$= \begin{bmatrix} -118 & -93 \\ 31 & -118 \end{bmatrix}$$

8. **(b, c)** For PP' = I

$$\begin{bmatrix} 2/3 & 3k & a \\ -1/3 & -4k & b \\ 2/3 & -5k & c \end{bmatrix}\begin{bmatrix} 2/3 & -1/3 & 2/3 \\ 3k & -4k & -5k \\ a & b & c \end{bmatrix}$$

$$= \begin{bmatrix} \frac{4}{9}+9k^2+a^2 & -\frac{2}{9}-12k^2+ab & \frac{4}{9}-15k^2+ac \\ -\frac{2}{9}-12k^2+ab & \frac{1}{9}+16k^2+b^2 & -\frac{2}{9}+20k^2+bc \\ \frac{4}{9}-15k^2+ac & -\frac{2}{9}+20k^2+bc & \frac{4}{9}+25k^2+c^2 \end{bmatrix}$$

$$= \begin{bmatrix} 1 & 0 & 0 \\ 0 & 1 & 0 \\ 0 & 0 & 1 \end{bmatrix}$$

$$\frac{4}{9}+9k^2+a^2=1$$

$$-\frac{2}{9}-12k^2+ab=0$$

$$\frac{4}{9}-15k^2+ac=0$$

$$\frac{1}{9}+16k^2+b^2=1$$

$$-\frac{2}{9}+20k^2+bc=0$$

$$\frac{4}{9}+25k^2+c^2=1$$

On solving these equations we get

$$ab=\frac{208}{450},\ bc=-\frac{80}{450},\ ac=\frac{-65}{450}$$

$$\text{and } a^2=\frac{169}{450},\ b^2=\frac{256}{450},\ c^2=\frac{25}{450}$$

$$\text{Hence, } a=\pm\frac{13}{5\sqrt{2}},\ b=\pm\frac{16}{5\sqrt{2}},\ c=\pm\frac{1}{3\sqrt{2}}$$

9. **(a, b, c)** We have,

$$A^2=\begin{bmatrix} i & 0 \\ 0 & i \end{bmatrix}\begin{bmatrix} i & 0 \\ 0 & i \end{bmatrix}=\begin{bmatrix} i^2 & 0 \\ 0 & i^2 \end{bmatrix}=\begin{bmatrix} -1 & 0 \\ 0 & -1 \end{bmatrix}$$

$$A^3=\begin{bmatrix} -1 & 0 \\ 0 & -1 \end{bmatrix}\begin{bmatrix} i & 0 \\ 0 & i \end{bmatrix}=\begin{bmatrix} -i & 0 \\ 0 & -i \end{bmatrix}$$

$$A^4=\begin{bmatrix} -1 & 0 \\ 0 & -1 \end{bmatrix}\begin{bmatrix} -i & 0 \\ 0 & -i \end{bmatrix}=\begin{bmatrix} 1 & 0 \\ 0 & 1 \end{bmatrix}$$

$$A^{75}=A^3=\begin{bmatrix} -i & 0 \\ 0 & -i \end{bmatrix}$$

10. **(a, d)** Let $A=\begin{bmatrix} 0 & 2\beta & \gamma \\ \alpha & \beta & -\gamma \\ \alpha & -\beta & \gamma \end{bmatrix}$

Then $A'=\begin{bmatrix} 0 & \alpha & \alpha \\ 2\beta & \beta & -\beta \\ \gamma & -\gamma & \gamma \end{bmatrix}$

Given that, A is orthogonal. $\therefore AA'=I$

$$\Rightarrow \begin{bmatrix} 0 & 2\beta & \gamma \\ \alpha & \beta & -\gamma \\ \alpha & -\beta & \gamma \end{bmatrix}\begin{bmatrix} 0 & \alpha & \alpha \\ 2\beta & \beta & -\beta \\ \gamma & -\gamma & \gamma \end{bmatrix}=\begin{bmatrix} 1 & 0 & 0 \\ 0 & 1 & 0 \\ 0 & 0 & 1 \end{bmatrix}$$

$$\Rightarrow \begin{bmatrix} 4\beta^2+\gamma^2 & 2\beta^2-\gamma^2 & -2\beta^2+\gamma^2 \\ 2\beta^2-\gamma^2 & \alpha^2+\beta^2+\gamma^2 & \alpha^2-\beta^2-\gamma^2 \\ -2\beta^2+\gamma^2 & \alpha^2-\beta^2-\gamma^2 & \alpha^2+\beta^2+\gamma^2 \end{bmatrix}$$

$$= \begin{bmatrix} 1 & 0 & 0 \\ 0 & 1 & 0 \\ 0 & 0 & 1 \end{bmatrix}$$

Equating the corresponding elements, we have

$$\left.\begin{matrix} 4\beta^2+\gamma^2 & =1 \\ 2\beta^2-\gamma^2 & =0 \end{matrix}\right\} \Rightarrow \beta=\pm\frac{1}{\sqrt{6}},\ \gamma=\pm\frac{1}{\sqrt{3}}$$

$$\alpha^2+\beta^2+\gamma^2=1 \ \Rightarrow \alpha^2+\frac{1}{6}+\frac{1}{3}=1$$

$$\Rightarrow \alpha=\pm\frac{1}{\sqrt{2}}$$

11. **(0)** As $A^2=0, A^k=0\ \forall\, k\ge 2$.

Thus, $(A+I)^{50}=I+50A$

$\Rightarrow (A+I)^{50}-50A=I$

$\therefore a=1, b=0, c=0, d=1$

abc + abd + bcd + acd = 0

12. (2) Consider $A2=\begin{bmatrix}-5 & -8 & 0\\ 3 & 5 & 0\\ 1 & 2 & -1\end{bmatrix}\begin{bmatrix}-5 & -8 & 0\\ 3 & 5 & 0\\ 1 & 2 & -1\end{bmatrix}$

$$=\begin{bmatrix}25-24+0 & 40-40+0 & 0+0+0\\ -15+15+0 & -24+25+0 & 0+0+0\\ -5+6-1 & -8+10-2 & 0+0+1\end{bmatrix}$$

$$=\begin{bmatrix}1 & 0 & 0\\ 0 & 1 & 0\\ 0 & 0 & 1\end{bmatrix}=I$$

So $A^3=\begin{bmatrix}-5 & -8 & 0\\ 3 & 5 & 0\\ 1 & 2 & -1\end{bmatrix}$ and so on

$tr(A)+tr(A^2)\,tr(A^3)+...+tr(A^{100})$

$=(-1)+(3)+(-1)+(3)+...+(-1)+(3)=200$

13. (4) Given that $A^TA=I$ so

$$\begin{bmatrix}a & b & c\\ b & c & a\\ c & a & b\end{bmatrix}\begin{bmatrix}a & b & c\\ b & c & a\\ c & a & b\end{bmatrix}=\begin{bmatrix}1 & 0 & 0\\ 0 & 1 & 0\\ 0 & 0 & 1\end{bmatrix}$$

$$\Rightarrow\begin{bmatrix}a^2+b^2+c^2 & ab+bc+ca & ab+bc+ca\\ ab+bc+ca & a^2+b^2+c^2 & ab+bc+ca\\ ab+bc+ca & ab+bc+ca & a^2+b^2+c^2\end{bmatrix}$$

$$=\begin{bmatrix}1 & 0 & 0\\ 0 & 1 & 0\\ 0 & 0 & 1\end{bmatrix}$$

$\Rightarrow\ a^2+b^2+c^2=1$ ... (i)

And $ab+bc+ca=0$ ..(ii)

We know

$a^3+b^3+c^3=(a+b+c)$

$(a^2+b^2+c^2-ab-bc-ca)+3abc$

$=(a+b+c)+3$ ...(iii)

Now, $(a+b+c)^2=a^2+b^2+c^2+2(ab+bc+ca)$

$=1+2.0=1$

$\Rightarrow$ $a+b+c=1$ (Since, a, b, c are real positive number)

Now, From Eq. (iii), $a^3+b^3+c^3=4$

14. (2) Given that AB = BA

So $\begin{bmatrix}a_{11} & a_{12}\\ a_{21} & a_{22}\end{bmatrix}\begin{bmatrix}1 & 1\\ 2 & 1\end{bmatrix}=\begin{bmatrix}1 & 1\\ 2 & 1\end{bmatrix}\begin{bmatrix}a_{11} & a_{12}\\ a_{21} & a_{22}\end{bmatrix}$

So $a_{11}+2a_{12}=a_{11}+a_{21}$ ...(i)

$a_{11}+a_{12}=a_{12}+a_{22}$ ...(ii)

$a_{21}+2a_{22}=2a_{11}+a_{21}$ ...(iii)

$a_{21}+a_{22}=2a_{12}+a_{22}$ ...(iv)

On solving these we get

$$\frac{a_{11}}{a_{12}}=\frac{\sqrt{2}}{1}$$

$$\left(\frac{a_{11}}{a_{12}}\right)^2=2$$

15. (0) Since $A=\begin{bmatrix}1 & 1\\ -1 & 1\end{bmatrix}$ so $A^2-2A+2I=0$

$B=A^{10}-A^9+2A^8-A^7+4A^6-2A^5+4A^4$

$+A^3-A^2+A+I=(A^2-2A+2I)\,f(A)+(A-I)$

so $B=A-1$

$$=\begin{bmatrix}1 & 1\\ -1 & 1\end{bmatrix}-\begin{bmatrix}1 & 0\\ 0 & 1\end{bmatrix}=\begin{bmatrix}0 & 1\\ -1 & 0\end{bmatrix}=\begin{bmatrix}a & b\\ c & d\end{bmatrix}$$

So $a+b+c+d=0$

16. (a) Trace of the matrix A is a + b

$$=\sum_{k=1}^{9}(a_k+b_k)=10\sum_{k=1}^{9}C_k^{10}=10(2^{10}-2)$$

$=10220$

Sum of digits is 5

17. (b) $a=\sum_{k=1}^{9}k\,({}^{10}C_k)=\sum_{k=1}^{10}k\,({}^{10}C_k)$

$-10({}^{10}C_{10})=10(2^9)-10=10(2^9-1)$

Similarly, $b=10(2^9-1)$

Thus, $ab=100(2^9-1)^2$

Largest prime factor is 511

For Questions 18 & 19

Consider

$$A_1.A_2=\begin{bmatrix}a_0 & 0\\ 0 & a_1\end{bmatrix}\begin{bmatrix}a_1 & 0\\ 0 & a_2\end{bmatrix}=\begin{bmatrix}a_0a_1 & 0\\ 0 & a_1a_2\end{bmatrix}$$

And so on.

Given that $\sum_{k=1}^{n-1} A_k.A_{k+1} = \begin{bmatrix} a & 0 \\ 0 & b \end{bmatrix}$

$a = a_0a_1 + a_1a_2 + ... + a_{n-2}a_{n-1} = a_na_1 + a_{n-1}a_2 + ... + a_2\,a_{n-1}$
= number of ways of selecting (n + 1) persons out of n men and n women = ${}^{2n}C_{n+1}$

Similarly $b = {}^{2n}C_{n+1}$

18. **(a)** **19.** **(a)**

20. **(A) → (*s*); (B) → (*r*); (C) → (*q*); (D) → (*p*)**

(A) Let $X = \begin{bmatrix} a & b \\ c & d \end{bmatrix}$ then

$$\begin{bmatrix} 1 & -4 \\ 3 & -2 \end{bmatrix}\begin{bmatrix} a & b \\ c & d \end{bmatrix} = \begin{bmatrix} -16 & -6 \\ 7 & 2 \end{bmatrix}$$

Or $\begin{bmatrix} a-4c & b-4d \\ 3a-2c & 3b-2d \end{bmatrix} = \begin{bmatrix} -16 & -6 \\ 7 & 2 \end{bmatrix}$

On equating we get a = 6, b = 2, c = 11/2 and d = 2

So trace of the matrix = 6 + 2 = 8

(B) Given

$$\begin{bmatrix} 2 & -1 \\ 1 & 0 \\ -3 & 4 \end{bmatrix}\begin{bmatrix} l & m & n \\ x & y & z \end{bmatrix} = \begin{bmatrix} -1 & -8 & -10 \\ 1 & -2 & -5 \\ 9 & 22 & 15 \end{bmatrix}$$

$$\begin{bmatrix} 2l-x & 2m-y & 2n-z \\ l & m & n \\ -3l+4x & -3m+4y & -3n+4z \end{bmatrix} = \begin{bmatrix} -1 & -8 & -10 \\ 1 & -2 & -5 \\ 9 & 22 & 15 \end{bmatrix}$$

$\Rightarrow$ 2l − x = −1, 2m − y = -8, 2n − z = −10, l = 1, m = −2, n = −5

$\Rightarrow$ x = 3, y = 4, z = 0, l = 1, m = −2, n = −5

$$\Rightarrow \begin{bmatrix} l & m & n \\ x & y & z \end{bmatrix} = \begin{bmatrix} 1 & -2 & -5 \\ 3 & 4 & 0 \end{bmatrix}$$

So l + m + n + x + y + z = 1 − 2 − 5 + 3 + 4 + 0 = 1

(C) We have $\begin{bmatrix} 1 & x & 1 \end{bmatrix}\begin{bmatrix} 1 & 3 & 2 \\ 0 & 5 & 1 \\ 0 & 3 & 2 \end{bmatrix}\begin{bmatrix} 1 \\ 1 \\ x \end{bmatrix} = 0$

$$\Rightarrow \begin{bmatrix} 1 & 5x+6 & x+4 \end{bmatrix}\begin{bmatrix} 1 \\ 1 \\ x \end{bmatrix} = 0$$

$$\Rightarrow \begin{bmatrix} 1+5x+6+x^2+4x \end{bmatrix} = 0$$

$$\Rightarrow x^2 + 9x + 7 = 0$$

$$\Rightarrow x = \frac{-9 \pm \sqrt{53}}{2}$$

(D) We multiply both sides by $\begin{bmatrix} 5 & 0 \\ -a & 5 \end{bmatrix}$ then

$$\begin{bmatrix} 1/5 & 0 \\ -a/25+5x & 1/5 \end{bmatrix} = \begin{bmatrix} 5 & 0 \\ -a & 5 \end{bmatrix}^{-1}$$

Again multiply both sides by $\begin{bmatrix} 5 & 0 \\ -a & 5 \end{bmatrix}$,

$$\begin{bmatrix} 1/5 & 0 \\ -a/25+5x & 1/5 \end{bmatrix}\begin{bmatrix} 5 & 0 \\ -a & 5 \end{bmatrix} = \begin{bmatrix} 1 & 0 \\ 0 & 1 \end{bmatrix}$$

Or $\frac{-2a}{5} + 25x = 0$

Or $\frac{125x}{a} = 2$

DAILY PRACTICE PROBLEMS

MATHEMATICS SOLUTIONS

DPP/CM17

1. **(b)** Given $\begin{vmatrix} 1+x & 1 & 1 \\ 1+y & 1+2y & 1 \\ 1+z & 1+z & 1+3z \end{vmatrix}$

$$= xyz \begin{vmatrix} 1+\frac{1}{x} & \frac{1}{x} & \frac{1}{x} \\ 1+\frac{1}{y} & 2+\frac{1}{y} & \frac{1}{y} \\ 1+\frac{1}{z} & 1+\frac{1}{z} & 3+\frac{1}{z} \end{vmatrix}$$

$$= xyz\left(3+\frac{1}{x}+\frac{1}{y}+\frac{1}{z}\right) \begin{vmatrix} 1+\frac{1}{x} & \frac{1}{x} & \frac{1}{x} \\ 1+\frac{1}{y} & 2+\frac{1}{y} & \frac{1}{y} \\ 1+\frac{1}{z} & 1+\frac{1}{z} & 3+\frac{1}{z} \end{vmatrix}$$

$(R_1 \to R_1 + R_2 + R_3)$

$$= xyz\left(3+\frac{1}{x}+\frac{1}{y}+\frac{1}{z}\right) \begin{vmatrix} 1 & 0 & 0 \\ 1+\frac{1}{y} & 1 & -1 \\ 1+\frac{1}{z} & 0 & 2 \end{vmatrix}$$

$$= 2xyz\left(3+\frac{1}{x}+\frac{1}{y}+\frac{1}{z}\right)$$

$(p+q) = 5$

2. **(b)** The given system of equations will have a non-trivial solution if

$$\Delta = \begin{vmatrix} a\alpha+b & a & b \\ b\alpha+c & b & c \\ 0 & a\alpha+b & b\alpha+c \end{vmatrix} = 0$$

Applying $R_3 \to R_3 - \alpha R_1 - R_2$, we get

$$\Delta = \begin{vmatrix} a\alpha+b & a & b \\ b\alpha+c & b & c \\ -\left(a\alpha^2+2b\alpha+c\right) & 0 & 0 \end{vmatrix} = 0$$

$\Rightarrow \; -(a\alpha^2 + 2b\alpha + c)(ac - b^2) = 0$

$\Rightarrow \; a\alpha^2 + 2b\alpha + c = 0$ or $(ac - b^2) = 0$

$\Rightarrow \; \alpha$ is a root of $ax^2 + 2bx + c = 0$ or a, b, c are in G.P.

3. **(d)** Given

$(a^2 + b^2 + c^2)^2 x^2 - 2(ab + bc + cd)x + b^2 + c^2 + d^2 \le 0$

$\Rightarrow \; (ax - b)^2 + (bx - c)^2 + (cx - d)^2 \le 0$

$\Rightarrow \; (ax - b)^2 + (bx - c)^2 + (cx - d)^2 = 0$

$\Rightarrow \; \frac{b}{a} = \frac{c}{b} = \frac{d}{c} = x \Rightarrow$ or $2 \log b = \log a + \log c$

Now, $\Delta = \begin{vmatrix} p & x & \log a \\ q & y & \log b \\ r & z & \log c \end{vmatrix}$

In each row, terms are in AP so $\Delta = 0$

4. **(a)** We have,

$$\sum_{n=1}^{k} U_n = \begin{vmatrix} \sum_{n=1}^{k} 1 & k & k \\ 2\sum_{n=1}^{k} n & k^2+k+1 & k^2+k \\ 2\sum_{n=1}^{k} n - \sum_{n=1}^{k} 1 & k^2 & k^2+k+1 \end{vmatrix}$$

$$= \begin{vmatrix} k & k & k \\ k(k+1) & k^2+k+1 & k^2+k \\ k^2 & k^2 & k^2+k+1 \end{vmatrix}$$

$$= \begin{vmatrix} k & 0 & k \\ k^2+k & 1 & k^2+k \\ k^2 & 0 & k^2+k+1 \end{vmatrix}$$

[Applying $C_2 \to C_2 - C_1$]

$= k(k^2 + k + 1) - k^3 = k(k + 1) = 110$

$\Rightarrow \; k = 10$

5. **(a)** $f(n) = \begin{vmatrix} n & n+1 & n+2 \\ n! & (n+1)! & (n+2) \\ 1 & 1 & 1 \end{vmatrix}$

$$\begin{vmatrix} n & 1 & 1 \\ n! & nn! & (n+1)(n+1)! \\ 1 & 0 & 0 \end{vmatrix}$$

= Using $C_3 \to C_3 - C_2,\ C_2 \to C_2 - C_1$

$= (n + 1)(n + 1)! - nn! = n![(n + 1)^2 - n]$

$= n!(n^2 + n + 1)$

$f(5) = 3720$

6. **(a)** We have, $\begin{vmatrix} x & 1 & 1 & \dots \\ 1 & x & 1 & \dots \\ 1 & 1 & x & \dots \\ \dots & \dots & \dots & \dots \end{vmatrix}$

$$= \begin{vmatrix} x & 1 & 1 & \dots \\ (1-x) & (x-1) & 0 & \dots \\ (1-x) & 0 & x-(1 & ..) \\ \dots & \dots & \dots & \dots \end{vmatrix}$$

[Applying $R_2 \to R_2 - R_1, R_3 \to R_3 - R_1$ $\vdots\vdots\vdots\; R_n \to R_n - R_1$]

$$x(x-1)^{n-1} + \underbrace{(x-1)^{n-1} + (x-1)^{n-1} + \dots + (x-1)^{n-1}}_{(n-1)\text{ times}}$$

[Expanding along R_1]

$= x(x-1)^{n-1} + (x-1)^{n-1}[1 + 1 + \dots + (n-1)\text{ times}]$

$= (x-1)^{n-1}(x+n-1)$.

7. **(a, b, c, d)** The determinant of L.H.S on expansion = 0

$= 90f(x-3) - 100f(x+5) + 10f(x-3) = 0$

$100f(x-3) = 100f(x+5)$

So, f(x) satisfies the equation $f(x+5) = f(x-3)$.

Hence f (x) is periodic with period 8.

8. **(a, b, d)** We have,

$$f(x)\begin{vmatrix} x & a & a & a \\ a & x & a & a \\ a & a & x & a \\ a & a & a & x \end{vmatrix} = (x+3a)\begin{vmatrix} 1 & a & a & a \\ 1 & x & a & a \\ 1 & a & x & a \\ 1 & a & a & x \end{vmatrix}$$

[Applying $C_1 \to C_1 + C_2 + C_3 + C_4$ and taking $(x+3a)$ common from C_1]

$$= (x+3a)\begin{vmatrix} 1 & a & a & a \\ 0 & x-a & 0 & 0 \\ 0 & 0 & x-a & 0 \\ 0 & 0 & 0 & x-a \end{vmatrix}$$

[Applying $R_2 \to R_2 - R_1$, $R_3 \to R_3 - R_1$ and $R_4 \to R_4 - R_1$] $f(x) = (x+3a)(x-a)^3$

[Expanding along C_1]

9. **(a, b, c)** $\Delta = \begin{vmatrix} x & y & z \\ p & q & r \\ a & b & c \end{vmatrix}\begin{vmatrix} 0 & m & n \\ -m & 0 & k \\ -n & -k & 0 \end{vmatrix}$.

where $\begin{vmatrix} 0 & m & n \\ -m & 0 & k \\ -n & -k & 0 \end{vmatrix}$ is skew-symmetric

$\therefore \Delta = 0$

10. **(a, c)** Apply $C_3 \to C_3 - xC_1 - yC_2$

$$\Delta = \begin{vmatrix} a & b & 0 \\ b & c & 0 \\ ax+by & bx+ay & -(ax^2+ay^2+2bxy) \end{vmatrix} = 0$$

$$\Rightarrow (b^2 - ac)(ax^2 + 2bxy + ay^2) = 0$$

$\Rightarrow$ Either $b^2 = ac$ or $ax^2 + 2bxy + ay^2 = 0$

Thus, the point (x, y) lies on a curve through the origin.

11. **(7)** $R_1 \to cR_1, R_2 \to aR_2, R_3 \to bR_3$

$$\Rightarrow \frac{1}{abc}\begin{vmatrix} a^2+b^2 & c^2 & c^2 \\ a^2 & b^2+c^2 & a^2 \\ b^2 & b^2 & c^2+a^2 \end{vmatrix}$$

Use $R_1 \to R_1 - (R_2 + R_3)$

$$\Rightarrow \frac{1}{abc}\begin{vmatrix} 0 & -2b^2 & -2a^2 \\ a^2 & b^2+c^2 & a^2 \\ b^2 & b^2 & c^2+a^2 \end{vmatrix}$$

$R_2 \to R_2 + 1/2\,R_1$ and $R_3 \to R_3 + 1/2\,R_1$

$$\Rightarrow \frac{1}{abc}\begin{vmatrix} 0 & -2b^2 & -2a^2 \\ a^2 & c^2 & 0 \\ b^2 & 0 & c^2 \end{vmatrix}$$

$$\Rightarrow \frac{1}{abc} \Rightarrow [2b^2(a^2c^2) - 2a^2(-b^2c^2)]$$

$$= \frac{4a^2b^2c^2}{abc} = 4abc$$

So $[\alpha] + 3 = 7$

12. **(2)** We know that $|A^{-1}| = \frac{1}{|A|}$ and $|\text{adj } B| = |B|^{n-1}$ here 'n' is the order of matrix

Now consider

$$\left|\left(A^{-1}adj\left(B^{-1}\ adj\right)2A^{-1}\right|\right| = \left|\frac{1}{|A|}\frac{1}{|B|^2}\frac{64}{|A|^2}\right|$$

$$= \left|\frac{64}{(-2)(4)(4)}\right| = |-2| = 2$$

13. **(7)** Consider

$$A=\begin{vmatrix} a_1a_5 & a_1 & a_2 \\ a_2a_6 & a_2 & a_3 \\ a_3a_7 & a_3 & a_4 \end{vmatrix}$$

$$=\begin{vmatrix} a_1a_5-a_3a_7 & a_1-a_3 & a_2-a_4 \\ a_2a_6-a_3a_7 & a_2-a_3 & a_3-a_4 \\ a_3a_7 & a_3 & a_4 \end{vmatrix}$$

$= d(a_1 - a_2)(a_2 - a_3)(a_3 - a_1) = -2d^4$

Similarly $B = -2d^4$

So $AB = 4d^8 = 1024$

14. **(1)** $C_1 \to C_1 + C_2 + C_3$

$$\begin{vmatrix} 1+2x+x(a^2+b^2+c^2) & (1+b^2)x & (1+c^2)x \\ 1+2x+x(a^2+b^2+c^2) & 1+b^2x & (1+c^2\ x) \\ 1+2x+x(a^2+b^2+c^2) & (1+b^2\ x) & 1+c^2x \end{vmatrix}=0$$

Since $a^2 + b^2 + c^2 = -2$

$$\begin{vmatrix} 1 & (1+b^2)x & (1+c^2)x \\ 1 & 1+b^2x & (1+c^2\ x) \\ 1 & (1+b^2\ x) & 1+c^2x \end{vmatrix}=0$$

$R_2 \to R_2 - R_1$ and $R_3 \to R_3 - R_1$

$$\begin{vmatrix} 1 & (1+b^2)x & (1+c^2)x \\ 0 & 1-x & 0 \\ 0 & 0 & 1-x \end{vmatrix}=0$$

On expanding we get $(1 - x)^2 = 1 - 2x + x^2 = 0$

It has only one root.

15. **(3)** For non-trivial solution,

$$\Delta=\begin{vmatrix} a & \sin b & \cos b \\ 1 & \cos b & \sin b \\ -1 & \sin b & -\cos b \end{vmatrix}=0$$

$\Rightarrow$ $a[-\cos^2 b - \sin^2 b] - \sin b\,[-\cos b + \sin b] + \cos b[\sin b + \cos b] = 0$

$\Rightarrow$ $-a + \sin 2b + \cos 2b = 0$

$\Rightarrow$ $a = \cos 2b + \sin 2b = \sqrt{2}\cos\left(2b - \frac{\pi}{4}\right)$,

since, $-1 \le \cos\left(2b - \frac{\pi}{4}\right) \le 1$

$\Rightarrow$ $-\sqrt{2} \le \sqrt{2}\cos\left(2b - \frac{\pi}{4}\right) \le \sqrt{2}$

$\Rightarrow$ $-\sqrt{2} \le a \le \sqrt{2}$

$\Rightarrow$ $a \in [-\sqrt{2}, \sqrt{2}]$

Possible integral values are –1, 0 and 1

(For Q. 16 – Q.17)

Let $\Delta=\begin{vmatrix} 1 & 1 & 1 \\ a & b & c \\ a^2 & b^2 & c^2 \end{vmatrix}$

$$=\begin{vmatrix} 1 & 0 & 0 \\ a & b-a & c-a \\ a^2 & b^2-a^2 & c^2-a^2 \end{vmatrix}$$

$(C_2 \to C_2 - C_1, C_3 \to C_3 - C_1)$

$$=(b-a)(c-a)\begin{vmatrix} 1 & 0 & 0 \\ a & 1 & 1 \\ a^2 & b+a & c+a \end{vmatrix}$$

$= (b-a)(c-a)(c-b) = (a-b)(b-c)(c-a)$

16. **(b)** $\Delta_1=\begin{vmatrix} 1 & 1 & 1 \\ a^2 & b^2 & c^2 \\ bc & ca & ab \end{vmatrix}=\frac{1}{abc}\begin{vmatrix} a & b & c \\ a^3 & b^3 & c^3 \\ abc & abc & abc \end{vmatrix}$

$$=\begin{vmatrix} a & b & c \\ a^3 & b^3 & c^3 \\ 1 & 1 & 1 \end{vmatrix}=\begin{vmatrix} 1 & 1 & 1 \\ a & b & c \\ a^3 & b^3 & c^3 \end{vmatrix}$$

$\because$ Δ_1 is cyclic and obtained by increasing the degree of third row of Δ by unity (1), so the value of Δ will be multiplied by a linear cyclic expression, i.e. $(a + b + c)$, so, $\Delta_1 = \Delta\ (a + b + c)$

17. **(c)** $\Delta_2=\begin{vmatrix} a & b & c \\ a^2 & b^2 & c^2 \\ bc & ca & ca \end{vmatrix}=\begin{vmatrix} 1 & 1 & 1 \\ a^2 & b^2 & c^2 \\ a^3 & b^3 & c^3 \end{vmatrix}$

Now Δ_2 is obtained by increasing the degree of second row and third row by unity each, so the value of Δ will be multiplied by a quadratic cyclic expression, say, $\{k_1(a^2 + b^2 + c^2) + k_2(bc + ca + ab)\}$

So, $\Delta_2 = \Delta\,[k_1(a^2 + b^2 + c^2) + k_2(bc + ca + ab)]$

The values of k_1 and k_2 can be obtained by substituting suitable unequal values of k_1 and k_2. For example.

Put $a = 0, b = 1, c = -1$ then we get $2k_1 - k_2 = -1$

Put $a = 0, b = 1, c = 2$ then we get $5k_1 + 2k_2 = 2$

Thus $k_1 = 0$ and $k_2 = 1$

Thus $\Delta_2 = \Delta\,(bc + ca + ab)$

18. **(a)** $\Delta=\begin{vmatrix} 1 & 1 & 1 \\ 2 & 1 & 2 \\ 1 & -1 & 3 \end{vmatrix}=\begin{vmatrix} 1 & 2 & 0 \\ 2 & 3 & 0 \\ 1 & 0 & 2 \end{vmatrix}=-2$

$\therefore$ System of equation has unique solution

Now $A=\begin{vmatrix} 1 & 1 & 1 \\ 2 & 1 & 2 \\ 1 & -1 & 3 \end{vmatrix} \Rightarrow \text{adj}\,A=\begin{bmatrix} 5 & -4 & 1 \\ -4 & 2 & 0 \\ -3 & 2 & -1 \end{bmatrix}$

$$B=\begin{bmatrix}3\\5\\3\end{bmatrix}\Rightarrow(\text{adj }A)B=\begin{bmatrix}-2\\-2\\-2\end{bmatrix}$$

$$\therefore\quad A^{-1}B=\frac{1}{\Delta}(\text{adj }A)B=-\frac{1}{2}\begin{bmatrix}-2\\-2\\-2\end{bmatrix}=\begin{bmatrix}1\\1\\1\end{bmatrix}$$

$$\therefore\quad X=\begin{bmatrix}x\\y\\z\end{bmatrix}=\begin{bmatrix}1\\1\\1\end{bmatrix}\Rightarrow x=y=z=1$$

ALTERNATIVELY:

After finding $\Delta \neq 0$, we can check the option (a) which satisfies the given equation. [If it do not satisfy the system of equations. (d) will be the answer]

19. (c) $A=\begin{bmatrix}1&1&1\\2&2&2\\1&-1&3\end{bmatrix}\Rightarrow|A|=0\ \text{adj}A=\begin{bmatrix}8&-4&0\\-4&2&0\\-4&2&0\end{bmatrix}$

$$\therefore(\text{adj }A)B=\begin{bmatrix}8&-4&0\\-4&2&0\\-4&2&0\end{bmatrix}\begin{bmatrix}3\\7\\3\end{bmatrix}=\begin{bmatrix}-4\\2\\2\end{bmatrix}\neq 0$$

$\therefore$ The system has no solution.

20. (A)→(q); (B)→(r); (C)→(s); (D)→(p)

(A) Applying $C_1 \to C_1 + C_2$, we get

$$\begin{vmatrix}2&\cos^2\theta&\sin 2\theta\\2&1+\cos^2\theta&\sin 2\theta\\1&\cos^2\theta&1+\sin 2\theta\end{vmatrix}$$

Applying $R_2 \to R_2 - R_1$ and $R_3 \to R_3 - R_1$,

$$\text{we get}\begin{vmatrix}2&\cos^2\theta&\sin 2\theta\\0&1&0\\-1&0&1\end{vmatrix}=2+\sin^2 2\theta$$

(B) $\begin{bmatrix}1&-\tan\theta\\\tan\theta&1\end{bmatrix}\begin{bmatrix}1&\tan\theta\\-\tan\theta&1\end{bmatrix}^{-1}$

$$=\begin{bmatrix}1&-\tan\theta\\\tan\theta&1\end{bmatrix}\left(\frac{1}{1+\tan^2\theta}\right)\begin{bmatrix}1&-\tan\theta\\\tan\theta&1\end{bmatrix}$$

$$=\frac{1}{1+\tan^2\theta}\begin{bmatrix}1-\tan^2\theta&-2\tan\theta\\2\tan\theta&1-\tan^2\theta\end{bmatrix}$$

$$=\begin{bmatrix}\cos 2\theta&-\sin 2\theta\\\sin 2\theta&\cos 2\theta\end{bmatrix}\quad\therefore a=\cos 2\theta,\ b=\sin 2\theta$$

$\therefore$ a = cos 2θ, b = sin 2θ

(D) we have,

$$=\begin{vmatrix}1&3\cos\theta&1\\\sin\theta&1&3\cos\theta\\0&\sin\theta-3\cos\theta&0\end{vmatrix}$$

[Applying $R_3 \to R_3 - R_1$]

$$=\begin{vmatrix}1&3\cos\theta&1\\\sin\theta&1&3\cos\theta\\0&\sin\theta-3\cos\theta&0\end{vmatrix}$$

$= -(\sin\theta - 3\cos\theta)(3\cos - \sin\theta)$

$= (3\cos\theta - \sin\theta)^2$

1. **(d)** $f(x)=\begin{cases}\dfrac{e^{[x]+|x|}-2}{[x]+|x|}, & x\neq 0\\ -1, & x=0\end{cases}$

$\underset{x\to 0^-}{\text{Lt}}\ f(x)=\underset{x\to 0^-}{\text{Lt}}\ \dfrac{e^{[x]+|x|}}{[x]+|x|}=\dfrac{e^{-1}-2}{-1}$

$\underset{x\to 0^+}{\text{Lt}}\ f(x)=\underset{x\to 0^+}{\text{Lt}}\ \dfrac{e^{[x]+|x|}-2}{[x]+|x|}$

$=\underset{x\to 0^+}{\text{Lt}}\ \dfrac{e^x-2}{x}\to -\infty$

Clearly none of (a), (b), (c) is correct.

2. **(a)** $F'(x)=\left[f\left(\frac{x}{2}\right).f'\left(\frac{x}{2}\right)+g\left(\frac{x}{2}\right)g'\left(\frac{x}{2}\right)\right]$

Here, $g(x)=f'(x)$
and $g'(x)=f''(x)=-f(x)$

So, $F'(x)=f\left(\frac{x}{2}\right)g\left(\frac{x}{2}\right)-f\left(\frac{x}{2}\right)g\left(\frac{x}{2}\right)=0$

$\Rightarrow$ $F(x)$ is constant function
So, $F(10)=5$

3. **(a)** Given

$f'(a)=\lim\limits_{h\to 0}\dfrac{f(a-h)-f(a)}{-h}=0\ \ldots(1)$

Now $f'(-a^-)=\lim\limits_{h\to 0}\dfrac{f(-a-h)-f(-a)}{-h}$

$=\lim\limits_{h\to 0}\dfrac{-f(a+h)+f(a)}{-h}$

[$\because f(x)$ is odd function]

$=\lim\limits_{h\to 0}\dfrac{-f(a-h)+f(a)}{-h}$

[$\because f(2a-x)=f(x)\Rightarrow f(a+x)=f(a-x)$]

$=\lim\limits_{h\to 0}\dfrac{f(a-h)-f(a)}{h}=0$ [From (1)]

4. **(a)** We have,
$f(x)=\cos x\cos 2x\cos 2^2x\cos 2^3x\ \ldots\ldots\ \cos 2^{n-1}x$

$\Rightarrow\ f(x)=\dfrac{\sin 2^n x}{2^n\sin x}$

$\Rightarrow\ f'(x)=\dfrac{2^n\cos 2^n x\sin x-\sin 2^n x\cos x}{2^n\sin^2 x}$

$\Rightarrow\ f'\left(\frac{\pi}{2}\right)=\dfrac{2^n\cos 2^{n-1}\pi}{2^n}=\cos 2^{n-1}\pi=(-1)2^{n-1}=1$

5. **(c)** We have,
$[f(x)]^n=f(nx)$ for all x
$\Rightarrow\ n[f(x)]^{n-1}f'(x)=nf'(nx)$
$\Rightarrow\ n[f(x)]^n f'(x)=nf(x)f'(nx)$
[Multiplying both sides by $f(x)$]
$\Rightarrow\ f(nx)f'(x)=f(x)f'(nx)$
[$\because [f(x)]^n=f(nx)$]
$\Rightarrow\ f(nx)f'(x)=f(x)f'(nx)$

6. **(b, d)** $\dfrac{d^n}{dx^n}[f(x)]=$

$$\begin{vmatrix}\dfrac{d^n}{dx^n}x^n & \dfrac{d^n}{dx^n}\sin x & -\dfrac{d^n}{dx^n}\cos x\\ n! & \sin(n\pi/2) & \cos(n\pi/2)\\ a & a^2 & a^3\end{vmatrix}$$

$$=\begin{vmatrix}n! & \sin\left(\dfrac{n\pi}{2}+x\right) & \cos\left(\dfrac{n\pi}{2}+x\right)\\ n! & \sin n\pi/2 & \cos n\pi/2\\ a & a^2 & a^3\end{vmatrix}$$

$\therefore$ At $x=0$, $R_1=R_2$

$\therefore\ \dfrac{d^n}{dx^n}[f(x)]=0$

7. **(a, c)** $f(x)=x+|x|+\cos 9x, g(x)=\sin x$

Since both $f(x)$ and $g(x)$ are continuous everywhere, $f(x)+g(x)$ is also continuous everywhere

$f(x)$ is non-differentiable and $x=0$

Hence $f(x)+g(x)$ is non-differentiable at $x=0$

Now $h(x)=f(x)\times g(x)$

$=\begin{cases}(\cos 9x)(\sin x), & x<0\\ (2x+\cos 9x)(\sin x), & x\geq 0\end{cases}$

Clearly, $h(x)$ is continuous at $x=0$

Also

$h'(x)=\begin{cases}\cos x\cos 9x-9\sin x\sin 9x, & x<0\\ (2-9\sin 9x)\sin x+\cos x(2x+\cos 9x), & x>0\end{cases}$

$h'(0^-)=1, h'(0^+)=1$

$\Rightarrow f(x)\times g(x)$ is differentiable everywhere.

8. (a, b, c)

$$g(f(x))=x \Rightarrow g'(f(x))f'(x)=1$$

$$\Rightarrow g'(f(x))=\frac{1}{f'(x)}$$

Now, $f(x)=2$

$$\Rightarrow x^3+3x^2-33x-33=2$$

$$\Rightarrow x^3+3x^2-33x-35=0$$

$$\Rightarrow x^3-5x^2+8x^2-40x+7x-35=0$$

$$\Rightarrow (x-5)(x^2+8x+7)=0$$

$$\Rightarrow (x-5)(x+1)(x+7)=0$$

$\therefore x=-7,-1,5$

Thus, we have

$$k=f'(-1)=3(-1)^2+6(-1)-33$$
$$=3-6-33=-36$$

$$k=f'(-7)=3(-7)^2+6(-7)-33$$
$$=147-63-33=51$$

$$k=f'(5)=3.5^2+6.5-33$$
$$=75+30-33=72$$

9. (a, c) $f(x)=\begin{cases}(\sin^{-1}x)^2\cos\left(\frac{1}{x}\right), & x\neq 0\\ 0, & x=0\end{cases}$

$$\lim_{x\to 0} f(x)=\lim_{x\to 0}(\sin^{-1}x)^2\cos\left(\frac{1}{x}\right)$$

$=0\times$ (any value between -1 to 1) $=0$

Hence $f(x)$ is continuous at $x=0$

$$f'(0^+)=\lim_{h\to 0}\frac{(\sin^{-1}h)^2\cos\left(\frac{1}{h}\right)-0}{h}$$

$$=\left(\lim_{h\to 0}\frac{\sin^{-1}h}{h}\right)\left(\lim_{h\to 0}\sin^{-1}h\right)\left(\lim_{h\to 0}\cos\left(\frac{1}{h}\right)\right)$$

$=1\times(0)\times$ (any value between -1 to 1) $=0$

Similarly, $f'(0^-)=0$

Hence, $f(x)$ is continuous and differentiable in $[-1, 1]$ and $(-1, 1)$, respectively.

10. (3) Here, we know $\sin x$ and $\cos x$ are periodic with period 2π. Thus we could sketch the curve(In the interval 0 to 2π) as

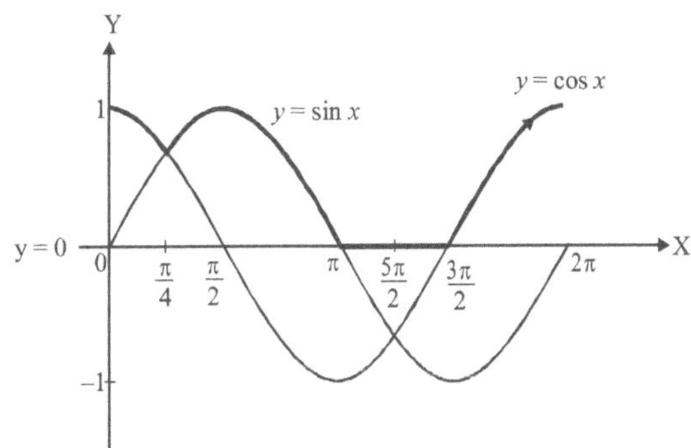

Which shows,

$y=\max\{\sin x, \cos x, 0\}$

$$=\begin{cases}\cos x, & 0<x<\frac{x}{4} \text{ or } \frac{3\pi}{2}<x<2\pi\\ 0, & \pi<x<\frac{3\pi}{2}\\ \sin x, & \frac{\pi}{4}<x<\pi\end{cases}$$

Clearly, $y=\max\{\sin x, \cos x, 0\}$ is not differentiable at 3 points when $x=(0,2\pi)$.

Thus, $y=\max\{\sin x, \cos x, 0\}$ is not differentiable at 3n points. Hence, $p=3$.

11. (0) $\frac{dy}{dx}=\left(\frac{dx}{dy}\right)^{-1}\Rightarrow\frac{d^2y}{dx^2}=-\left(\frac{dx}{dy}\right)^{-2}\left\{\frac{d}{dx}\left(\frac{dx}{dy}\right)\right\}$

$$\Rightarrow \frac{d^2y}{dx^2}=-\left(\frac{dx}{dy}\right)^{-2}\left\{\frac{d}{dy}\left(\frac{dx}{dy}\right)\frac{dy}{dx}\right\}$$

$$=-\left(\frac{dy}{dx}\right)^2\left\{\frac{d^2x}{dy^2}.\frac{dy}{dx}\right\}=-\left(\frac{dy}{dx}\right)^3\frac{d^2x}{dy^2}$$

$$\Rightarrow \frac{d^2y}{dx^2}+\left(\frac{dy}{dx}\right)^3\frac{d^2x}{dy^2}=0$$

12. (8) As, $f(x)$ is continuous at $x=0$.

$\therefore$ We must have

RHL (at $x=0$) = LHL (at $x=0$) $=f(0)$

RHL (at $x=0$) $=\lim_{x\to 0^+}f(x)$

$$=\lim_{x\to 0^+}\frac{\sqrt{x}}{\sqrt{16+\sqrt{x}}-4}$$

Put $x=0+h$

$$=\lim_{h\to 0}\frac{\sqrt{0+h}}{\sqrt{16+\sqrt{0+h}}-4}\times\frac{\sqrt{16+\sqrt{h}}+4}{\sqrt{16+\sqrt{h}}+4}$$

$$=\lim_{h\to 0}\frac{\sqrt{h}\left\{\sqrt{16+\sqrt{h}}+4\right\}}{16+\sqrt{h}-16}$$

$= \lim_{h\to 0}\left\{\sqrt{16+\sqrt{h}}+4\right\} = 8$

Also LHL (at $x = 0$) $= \lim_{x\to 0^-} f(x)$

$= \lim_{x\to 0^-} \frac{1-\cos 4x}{x^2}$

$= \lim_{h\to 0} \frac{1-\cos 4(0-h)}{(0-h^2)}$ [put $x = 0-h$]

$= \lim_{h\to 0} \frac{1-\cos 4}{h^2} = \lim_{h\to 0} \frac{2\sin^2 2h}{h^2}$

$= \lim_{h\to 0} 8\left(\frac{\sin 2h}{2h}\right)^2 = 8$

and $f(x) = a$.

Since $f(x)$ is continuous at $x = 0$

$\Rightarrow$ $f(0) = \text{RHL} = \text{LHL}$

or $f(0) = 8$.

or $a = 8$

13. **(3)** Apply Rolle's theorem to $F(x) = f(x) - 2g(x)$

$F(0) = 0, F(1) = f(1) - 2g(1)$

$\Rightarrow 0 = 6 - 2g(1) \Rightarrow g(1) = 3$.

14. **(c)**

$\because$ $y = e^{3x+7}$

$\therefore$ $y_1 = 3e^{3x+7}, y_2 = 3^2 e^{3x+7} \ldots$

$\therefore$ $y_n(x) = 3^n . e^{3x+7}$

Then $y_n(0) = 3^n . e^7$

15. **(d)**

$\because$ $y = (2-3x)^{-1}$

$\therefore$ $y_1 = (-1)(2-3x)^{-2}(-3)$

$y_2 = (-1)(-2)(2-3x)^{-3}(-3)^2$

$y_3 = (-1)(-2)(-3)(2-3x)^{-4}.(-3)^3$

....

$y_n = (-1)^n . n!\,(2-3x)^{-n-1}(-3)^n$

$\therefore$ $y_n(1) = (-1)^n . n!\,(-1)^{-n-1}(-3)^n$

$= (-1)^{n+1} . 3^n . n!$

16. **(b)** Here $-\frac{1}{2} \le x < 0$ gives $-1 \le 2x < 0$

So that $[2x] = -1$ in $\frac{-1}{2} \le x < 0$

Thus $f(x) = 4x^2 - x$, $\frac{-1}{2} \le x < 0$

$f(x) = ax^2 - bx, 0 \le x < \frac{1}{2}$

The function is differentiable in $\frac{-1}{2} \le x < 0$ and also in $0 < x < \frac{1}{2}$ as it is a polynomial of degree 2 in each of the subinterval.

Since $f(0^-) = f(0) = f(0^+) = 0$. $f(x)$ is continuous at $x = 0$ for all a, b

Now, $f'(0^-) = -1$ and $f'(0^+) = -b$.

It follows that $f'(0)$ exists, if $b = 1$, independent of a.

17. **(a)** Here $f(0) = 0$

So, $f(x)$ will be continuous, if $\lim_{x\to 0} x^p \sin\frac{1}{x} = 0$

This is possible only when $p > 0$ ... (i)

$f'(0) = \lim_{h\to 0} \frac{f(0+h)-f(0)}{h}$

$= \lim_{h\to 0} \frac{h^p \sin\frac{1}{h} - 0}{h} = \lim_{h\to 0} h^{p-1}\sin\frac{1}{h}$

$f'(0)$ will exist only when $p > 1$

$\therefore$ $f(x)$ will not be differentiable if $p \le 1$ ... (ii)

From (i) and (ii), for $f(x)$ to be not differentiable but continuous at $x = 0$, possible values of p are given by $0 < p \le 1$

18. **(d)** $f(x) = \cos\pi(|x| + [x])$

$= \begin{cases} \cos\pi(-x+(-1)), & -1 \le x < 0 \\ \cos\pi(x+0), & 0 \le x < 1 \end{cases}$

$= \begin{cases} -\cos\pi x & -1 \le x < 0 \\ \cos\pi x & 0 \le x < 1 \end{cases}$

Obviously $f(x)$ is discontinuous at $x = 0$ otherwise $f(x)$ is continuous and differentiable in $(-1, 0)$ and $(0, 1)$.

19. **(A)$\to$(q, s); (B)$\to$(p, s); (C)$\to$(p, r); (D)$\to$(q, s)**

(A) $f(x) = \begin{cases} \frac{5e^{1/x}+2}{3-e^{1/x}}, & x \ne 0 \\ 0, & x = 0 \end{cases}$

$f(0^+) = \lim_{h\to 0} \frac{5e^{1/h}+2}{3-e^{1/h}} = \lim_{h\to 0} \frac{5+2e^{-1/h}}{3e^{-1/h}-1} = -5$

Hence, $f(x)$ is discontinuous and non-differentiable at $x = 0$

(B) $g(x) = x\,f(x) = \begin{cases} x\frac{5e^{1/x}+2}{3-e^{1/x}}, & x \ne 0 \\ 0, & x = 0 \end{cases}$

$f(0^+) = \lim_{h\to 0} h\frac{5e^{1/h}+2}{3-e^{1/h}} = \lim_{h\to 0} h\frac{5+2e^{-1/h}}{3e^{-1/h}-1}$

$= 0 \times (-5) = 0$

$f(0^-) = \lim_{h\to 0} h\frac{5e^{-1/h}+2}{3-e^{-1/h}} = 0 \times (2/3) = 0$

Hence, $f(x)$ is continuous at $x = 0$

$Lg'(0) = \lim_{h\to 0} \frac{g(0-h)-g(0)}{-h}$

$$= \lim_{h \to 0} \frac{-hf(-h) - 0}{-h} = \lim_{h \to 0} f(-h)$$

$$= \lim_{h \to 0} \frac{5e^{-1/h} + 2}{3 - e^{-1/h}} = \frac{0+2}{3-0} = \frac{2}{3}$$

$$Rg'(0) = \lim_{h \to 0} \frac{g(0+h) - g(0)}{h}$$

$$= \lim_{h \to 0} \frac{g(h) - 0}{h}$$

$$= \lim_{h \to 0} f(h) = \lim_{h \to 0} \frac{5e^{1/h} + 2}{3 - e^{1/h}}$$

$$= \lim_{h \to 0} \frac{5 + 2e^{-1/h}}{3e^{-1/h} - 1}$$

$$= \frac{5+0}{0-1} = -5$$

$\because LF'(0) = RF'(0)$ hence, $F(x)$ is not differentiable, but continuous at $x = 0$

(C) For $x^2 f(x)$,

Let $F(x) = x^2 f(x)$

$$\therefore \; LF'(0) = \lim_{h \to 0} \frac{F(0-h) - F(0)}{-h}$$

$$= \lim_{h \to 0} \frac{h^2 f(-h) - 0}{-h} = 0$$

$$RF'(0) = \lim_{h \to 0} \frac{F(0+h) - F(0)}{h}$$

$$= \lim_{h \to 0} \frac{h^2 f(h) - 0}{h} = 0$$

$\therefore LF'(0) = RF'(0)$

Hence, $F(x)$ is differentiable at $x = 0$, then it is always continuous at $x = 0$.

20. (A) → (p, q, r); (B) → (p, r, s); (C) → (p, r, s); (D) → (p, r, s)

(A) $f(x) = |x^3| = x(x|x|)$ is continuous and differentiable.

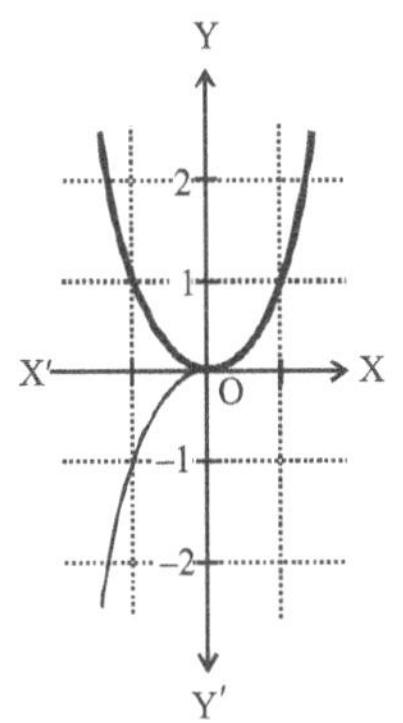

(B) $f(x) = \sqrt{|x|}$ is continuous

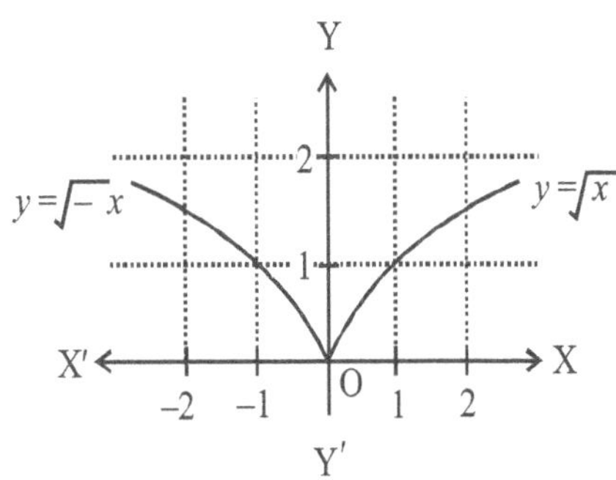

Clearly from the graph, $f(x)$ is non-differentiable at $x = 0$

(C) $f(x) = \left|\sin^{-1} x\right|$ is continuous.

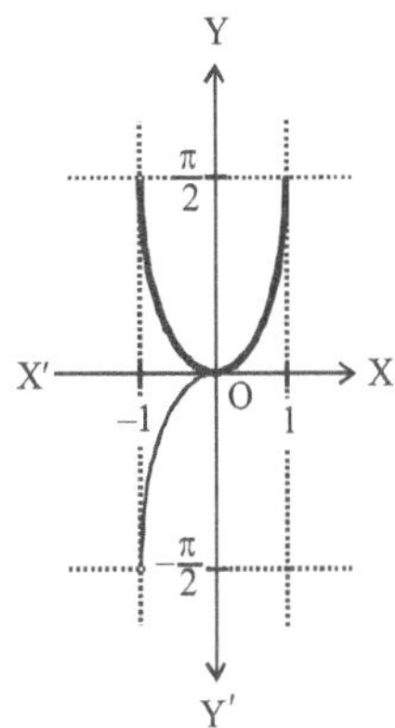

Clearly from the graph, $f(x)$ is non-differentiable at $x = 0$

(D) $f(x) = \cos^{-1}|x|$ is continuous

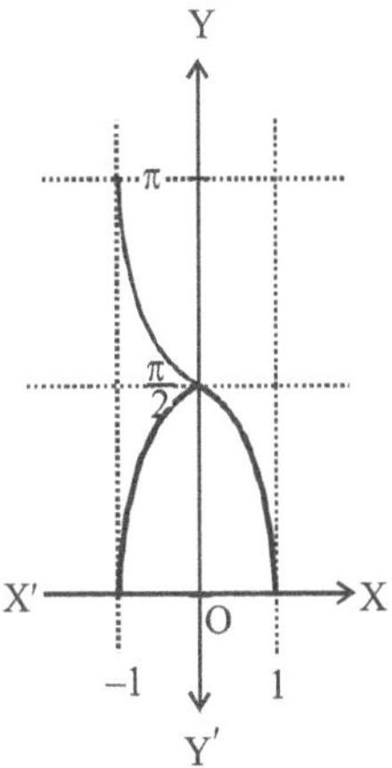

Clearly from the graph, $f(x)$ is non-differentiable at $x = 0$.

1. (a) Here $a^2 = 27, b^2 = 1,$

$a = 3\sqrt{3}$, $b = 1$

The point (a cos θ, b sin θ) is

$(3\sqrt{3}\cos\theta, \sin\theta)$.

Tangent at the above point is

$$\frac{x^3\sqrt{3}\cos\theta}{9} + \frac{y\sin\theta}{1} = 1$$

$\therefore$ Sum of intercepts $= \frac{9}{\sqrt{3}\cos\theta} + \frac{1}{\sin\theta}$

or $s = 3\sqrt{3}\sec\theta + \text{cosec}\,\theta$

$\Rightarrow \frac{ds}{d\theta} = 3\sqrt{3}\sec\theta\tan\theta - \text{cosec}\,\theta\cot\theta = 0$

$\Rightarrow \tan^3\theta = \frac{1}{3\sqrt{3}} \therefore \tan\theta = \frac{1}{\sqrt{3}} \Rightarrow \theta = \frac{\pi}{6}$

$\frac{d^2s}{d\theta^2}$ is positive at $\theta = \frac{\pi}{6}$.

Therefore, sum is minimum at $\theta = \pi/6$.

2. (d) $f'(x) = \frac{\cos x - \sin x}{1 + (\sin x + \cos x)^2}$

$f(x)$ is monotonic increasing when $f'(x) > 0$

$\Rightarrow \frac{\cos x - \sin x}{1 + (\sin x + \cos x)^2} > 0$

$\Rightarrow \cos x - \sin x > 0$

$\Rightarrow \sqrt{2}\cos(x + \pi/4) > 0$

$\Rightarrow -\pi/2 < x + \pi/4 < \pi/2$

($\because \cos\theta$ is positive when $-\pi/2 < \theta < \pi/2$)

$\therefore -3\pi/4 < x < \pi/4$

3. (b) $\frac{dy}{dx} = -\sin(x+y).[1 + dy/dx]$ ...(1)

Since the tangent is parallel to $x + 2y = 0$

therefore, $\frac{dy}{dx} = \text{slope} = -\frac{1}{2}$

Putting in (1), $\sin(x+y) = 1 = \sin(\pi/2)$

$\therefore \cos(x+y) = 0$

$\therefore y = \cos(x+y) = 0$

$\therefore \sin(x+y) = 1 \Rightarrow \sin x = 1, \because y = 0$

$\therefore x = \frac{\pi}{2}, -\frac{3\pi}{2}$ as $-2\pi < x < 2\pi$

Hence the points are $[(-3\pi)/2, 0]$ and $[\pi/2, 0]$, where the tangents are parallel to the line $x + 2y = 0$

$\therefore$ The equation of tangents are

$y - 0 = -\frac{1}{2}(x + 3\pi/2)$ and $y - 0$

$= -\frac{1}{2}(x - \pi/2)$

or $x + 2y + 3\pi/2 = 0$ and $x + 2y - \pi/2 = 0$

4. (a) Let h be the height of the cone and r be its radius.

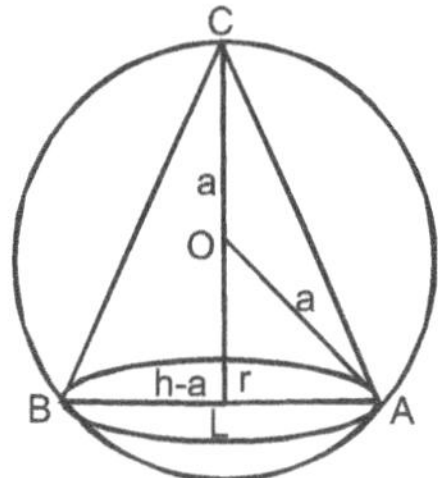

$\therefore h = CL = CO + OL = a + OL$

$\therefore OL = h - a$

$r = LA = \sqrt{(OA^2 - OL^2)}$

or $r = \sqrt{\{a^2 - (h-a)^2\}}$

$= (2ah - h^2)$

$V = \frac{1}{3}\pi r^2 h = \frac{1}{3}\pi(2ah - h^2)h$

$= \frac{1}{3}\pi(2ah^2 - h^3)$

$\frac{dy}{dh} = (\pi/3)(4ah - 3h^2) = 0$

$\therefore h = 0$ or $4a/3$

$h = 0$ is rejected, $\therefore h = 4a/3 = (2/3)(2a)$

$h = \frac{2}{3}$ (diameter)

5. (d) Let $y = ax^2 + bx + c$ be the given parabola. Then, $f(x) = ax^2 + bx + c$

Clearly, $\frac{dy}{dx} = 2ax + b$

It is given that $y = x$ touches the parabola at $x = 1$.

$\therefore \left(\frac{dy}{dx}\right)_{x=1} = $ (Slope of the line $y = x$)

$\Rightarrow 2a + b = 1$ .... (i)

Putting $x = 1$ in $y = x$, we get $y = 1$.
So, the line $y = x$ touches the parabola $y = ax^2 + bx + c$ at (1, 1).

$a + b + c = 1$ .... (ii)

Now,

$f(x) = ax^2 + bx + c \Rightarrow f'(x) = 2ax + b$ and $f''(x) = 2a$

$\therefore$ $f(0) = c, f'(0) = b, f''(0) = 2a$ and $f'(1) = 2a + b$.

From (ii), we have

$a + b + c = 1$

$\Rightarrow$ $2a + 2b + 2c = 2$

$\Rightarrow$ $2a + b + (b + 2c) = 2$

$\Rightarrow$ $1 + (b + 2c) = 2$ [$\because$ $2a + b = 1$ from (i)]

$\Rightarrow$ $b + 2c = 1$

$\Rightarrow$ $2c = 1 - b \Rightarrow 2f(0) = 1 - f'(0)$

Also, $f'(1) = 2a + b = 1$ [using (i)]

6. **(c)** Let $\angle C = \theta$. Then,

$a = b \cos \theta$

$\therefore$ $a + b = 4$

$$\Rightarrow a + b \cos \theta = 4 \Rightarrow b = \frac{4}{1 + \cos \theta}$$

$$\therefore a = b \cos \theta \Rightarrow a = \frac{4 \cos \theta}{1 + \cos \theta}$$

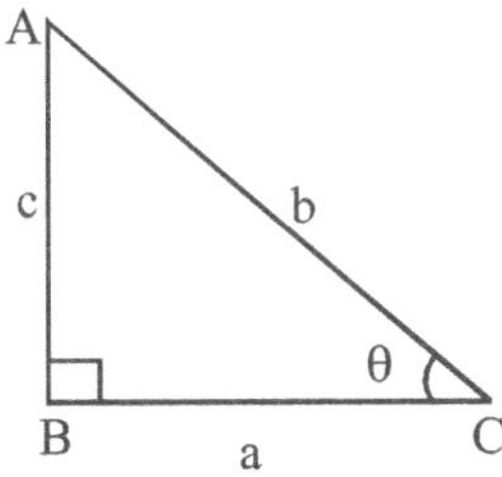

Let Δ be the area of ΔABC. Then,

$$\Delta = \frac{1}{2} ab \sin \theta$$

$$\Rightarrow \Delta = \frac{1}{2} \times \frac{4 \cos \theta}{1 + \cos \theta} \times \frac{4}{1 + \cos \theta} \times \sin \theta$$

$$\Rightarrow \Delta = \frac{8 \sin \theta \cos \theta}{(1 + \cos \theta)^2} = \frac{4 \sin 2\theta}{(1 + \cos \theta)^2}$$

$$\frac{d(\Delta)}{d\theta} = \frac{(1 + \cos 2\theta)^2 \times 8 \cos 2\theta + 8 \sin 2\theta (1 + \cos \theta) \sin \theta}{(1 + \cos \theta)^4}$$

$$\Rightarrow \frac{d(\Delta)}{d(\theta)} = \frac{8 \cos 2\theta + (1 + \cos \theta) 8 \sin 2\theta \sin \theta}{(1 + \cos \theta)^3}$$

$$\Rightarrow \frac{d(\Delta)}{d\theta} = \frac{8 \cos \theta + 8 \cos 2\theta}{(1 + \cos \theta)^2}$$

$$\Rightarrow \frac{d(\Delta)}{d\theta} = \frac{8(2 \cos^2 \theta + \cos \theta - 1)}{(1 + \cos \theta)^2} = 8\left(\frac{2 \cos \theta - 1}{1 + \cos \theta}\right)$$

For Δ to be maximum, we must have

$$\frac{d(\Delta)}{d\theta} = 0 \Rightarrow 2 \cos \theta - 1 = 0 \Rightarrow \cos \theta$$

$$= \frac{1}{2} \Rightarrow \theta = \frac{\pi}{3}$$

Now,

$$\frac{d^2(\Delta)}{d\theta^2} = 8\left\{\frac{-2(1 + \cos \theta) \sin \theta + (2 \cos \theta - 1) \sin \theta}{(1 + \cos \theta)^2}\right\}$$

Clearly, $\frac{d^2(\Delta)}{d\theta^2} < 0$ for $\theta = \frac{\pi}{3}$

Hence, (Δ) is maximum when $\theta = \frac{\pi}{3}$

7. **(a,c)**

We have, $9y^2 = x^3$ .... (1)

Differentiating w.r.t. x, we get

$$18y \frac{dy}{dx} = 3x^2 \Rightarrow \frac{dy}{dx} = \frac{x^2}{6y}$$

$$\text{Slope of the normal} = -\frac{6y^2}{x^2} = \pm 1 \quad \text{........ (2)}$$

($\because$ any line making equal intercepts on axes will have its slope as 1 or – 1)

Now from (2), we have

$$y = -\frac{x^2}{6} \text{ or } y = \frac{x^2}{6}$$

Solving these with the equation (1), we get the points $\left(4, \frac{8}{3}\right), \left(4, -\frac{8}{3}\right)$.

8. **(a,c)**

$y = \sqrt{9 - x^2}$ is the semicircle on the line segment joining (–3, 0) and (3, 0),

$y = \sqrt{1 + x^2}$ is the hyperbola with its transverse axis along the y-axis and one vertex at (0, 1). Points of intersection : A = $(-2, \sqrt{5})$, A′ = $(2, \sqrt{5})$.

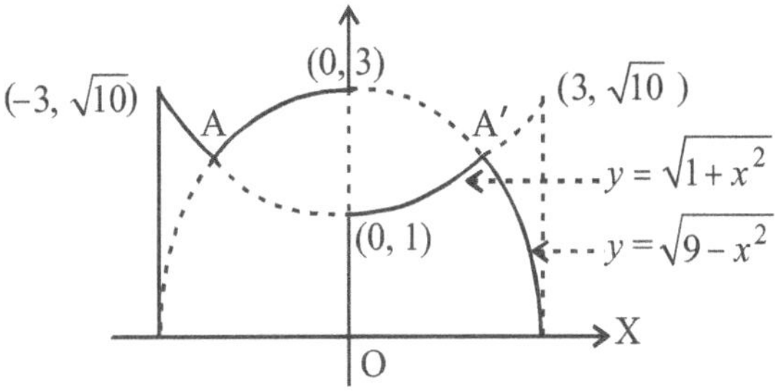

As shown in figure, $f(x)$ consists of the segment of the hyperbola between $(-3, \sqrt{10})$ and $A(-2, \sqrt{5})$, the segment of the semicircle between $(-2, \sqrt{5})$ and $(0, 3)$, the segment of the hyperbola between $(0, 1)$ and $A'(2, \sqrt{5})$ and the segment of the semicircle between $(2, \sqrt{5})$ and $\left(3, \sqrt{10}\right)$.

$x = 0$ is a point of discontinuity of $f(x)$. $(-2, \sqrt{5})$ is a point of minimum and $(2, \sqrt{5})$ is a point of maximum.

9. **(b, c)**

We have, $f(x) = \sin x + \cos x$

$\Rightarrow f'(x) = \cos x - \sin x = \sqrt{2} \cos\left(x + \frac{\pi}{4}\right)$

$f'(x) > 0$, if $0 \le x + \frac{\pi}{4} < \frac{\pi}{2}$

or $\frac{3\pi}{2} < x + \frac{\pi}{4} \le 2\pi$

i.e. $-\frac{\pi}{4} \le x < \frac{\pi}{4}$ or $\frac{5\pi}{4} < x \le \frac{7\pi}{4}$

But $f(x)$ is defined in $[0, 2\pi]$.

$\therefore\ f'(x) > 0$ in $\left[0, \frac{\pi}{4}\right) \cup \left(\frac{5\pi}{4}, \frac{7\pi}{4}\right]$

$\Rightarrow f(x)$ is increasing in $\left[0, \frac{\pi}{4}\right) \cup \left(\frac{5\pi}{4}, \frac{7\pi}{4}\right]$

Also, $f'(x) < 0$, if $\frac{\pi}{2} < x + \frac{\pi}{4} < \frac{3\pi}{2}$

i.e., $\frac{\pi}{4} < x < \frac{5\pi}{4}$.

$\therefore\ f(x)$ is decreasing in $\left(\frac{\pi}{4}, \frac{5\pi}{4}\right)$.

10. **(b, c)**

$\therefore\ x = a(\cos\theta + \theta\sin\theta)$

and $y = a(\sin\theta - \theta\cos\theta)$

$\therefore\ \frac{dx}{d\theta} = a(\theta\cos\theta), \frac{dy}{d\theta} = a(\theta\cos\theta)$

$\therefore\ \frac{dy}{dx} = \frac{\sin\theta}{\cos\theta}$

$\therefore$ Slope of normal $= -\frac{\cos\theta}{\sin\theta}$

Equation of normal at 'θ' is

$y - a(\sin\theta - \theta\cos\theta) = -\frac{\cos\theta}{\sin\theta}(x - a)$ $(\cos\theta + \sin\theta))$

$\Rightarrow\ y\sin\theta - a(\sin^2\theta - \theta\sin\theta\cos\theta)$

$-x\cos\theta + a(\cos^2\theta + \theta\sin\theta\cos\theta)$

$\Rightarrow\ x\cos\theta + y\sin\theta = a$ .... (i)

Distance from origin to (i) $= a =$ constant

Hence, $x\cos\theta + y\sin\theta = a$

touches a fixed circle $x^2 + y^2 = a^2$, whose centre (0, 0) and radius a.

11. **(5)** Let $f(x) = (x-5)^{55}(x-6)^{66}$

$f'(x) = (x-5)^{55}\, 66\,(x-6)^{65} + (x-6)^{66}\, 55\,(x-5)^{54}$

$= (x-5)^{54}(x-6)^{65}(66(x-5) + 55(x-6))$

$f'(x) = 0 \Rightarrow (x-5)^{54}(x-6)^{65}(121x - 660) = 0$

$\Rightarrow\ x = 5, 6, \frac{660}{121}$

Now, applying method of intervals

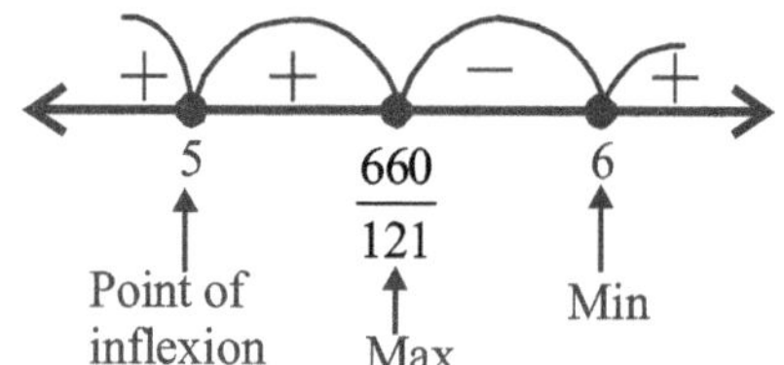

12. **(4)**

(a) We know that, $1 \le |\sin x| + |\cos x| \le \sqrt{2}$, for all real values of x

[Note that $(|\sin x| + |\cos x|)^2 + |\sin 2x| \ge 1$

$\therefore\ y = [|\sin x| + |\cos x|] = 1$

Let P and Q be the points of intersection of given curves

Clearly the given curves meet at points where $y = 1$ so, we get

$x^2 + 1 = 5, x = \pm 2$

Now, $P(2,1)$ and $Q(-2,1)$

Now, $x^2 + y^2 = 5$

Differentiating the above equation with respect to x we get

$2x + 2y\frac{dy}{dx} = 0 \Rightarrow \frac{dy}{dx} = -\frac{x}{y}$

$\therefore\ \left(\frac{dy}{dx}\right)_{(2,1)} = -2$

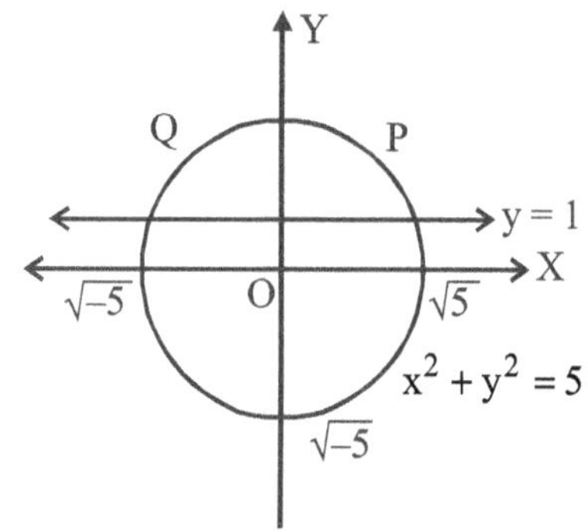

$$\left(\frac{dy}{dx}\right)_{(-2,1)} = 2$$

Clearly the slope of line $y = 1$ is zero and the slope of the tangents at P and Q are (-2) and (2) respectively. Thus, the angle of intersection is $\tan^{-1}(2)$.

13. **(2)** We have, $f(x) = (x+1)^{1/3} - (x-1)^{1/3}$

$$\therefore\ f'(x) = \frac{1}{3}\left[\frac{1}{(x+1)^{1/3}} - \frac{1}{(x-1)^{1/3}}\right]$$

$$= \frac{(x-1)^{2/3} - (x+1)^{2/3}}{3(x^2-1)^{2/3}}$$

Clearly, $f'(x)$ does not exist at $x = \pm 1$
Now, $f'(x) = 0 \Rightarrow (x-1)^{2/3} = (x+1)^{2/3} \Rightarrow x = 0$
Clearly $f'(x) \neq 0$ for any other value of $x \in [0, 1]$ The value of $f(x)$ at $x = 0$ is 2.
Hence, the greatest value of $f(x)$ is 2

14. **(3)** Let θ be the semi-vertical angle and r be the radius of the cone at time t. Then,
$r = 20 \tan\theta$

$$\Rightarrow \frac{dr}{dt} = 20\sec^2\theta \frac{d\theta}{dt}$$

$$\Rightarrow \frac{dr}{dt} = 20\sec^2 30° \times 2$$

$$\left[\because \theta = 30° \text{and} \frac{d\theta}{dt} = 2 \text{(given)}\right]$$

$$\Rightarrow \frac{dr}{dt} = 20 \times \frac{4}{3} \times 2 \text{ cm/sec} = \frac{160}{3} \text{ cm/sec}$$

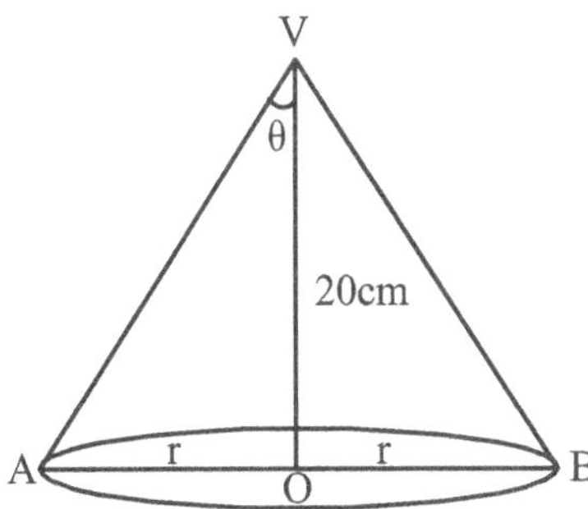

15. **(c)** $\alpha = 2\pi r = \pi \Rightarrow r = 1/2,$

Also, $h = \sqrt{1-r^2} = \frac{\sqrt{3}}{2}$

$$\Rightarrow v = \frac{1}{3}\pi r^2 h \Rightarrow \frac{\sqrt{3}\pi}{24}$$

16. **(c)** $\frac{dV}{d\alpha} = \frac{\pi}{3}\left[2r\frac{dr}{d\alpha}.\sqrt{1-r^2} - \frac{r^3}{\sqrt{1-r^2}}.\frac{dr}{d\alpha}\right]$

$$\Rightarrow \frac{dV}{d\alpha} = \frac{1}{6}\left[\frac{2r-3r^3}{\sqrt{1-r^2}}\right]\left\{\because \frac{dr}{d\alpha} = -\frac{1}{2\pi}\right\}$$

For maximum or minimum values of V, we must have

$$\frac{dV}{d\alpha} = 0 \Rightarrow r = \sqrt{\frac{2}{3}}$$

$$\frac{d^2V}{d\alpha^2} = -\frac{1}{6}\left\{\frac{\sqrt{1-r^2}(2-9r^2)\frac{dr}{d\alpha} + (2r-3r^3)\frac{r}{\sqrt{1-r^2}}.\frac{dr}{d\alpha}}{1-r^2}\right.$$

Putting $r = \sqrt{\frac{2}{3}}$ and $\frac{dr}{d\alpha} = \frac{1}{2\pi}$, we get

$$\frac{d^2V}{d\alpha^2} = -\frac{1}{6} \times \frac{1}{\left(1-\frac{2}{3}\right)}(2-6).\frac{-1}{2\pi} < 0$$

Hence V is maximum, when $r = \sqrt{2/3}$

17. **(b)** $f'(x) \leq 0\ \forall x \in [0, b]$, so $f(x)$ is decreasing function and $f(c) = 0 \Rightarrow f(x)$ cuts x – axis once when $x = c$

18. **(d)** We note that $f(c) = 0, f'(c) = 0$. Also tangent to $f'(x)$ at $x = c$ is $y = 0$. So $f''(c) = 0$

$\therefore$ $x = c$ is repeated root of third order. That is the equation

$f(x) = 0$ has at least three repeated roots.

19. **(A) → (q); (B) → (r); (C) → (p); (D) → (s)**

(A) Point of intersection

$$(0, b), \frac{dy}{dx} = be^{-\frac{x}{a}}\left(-\frac{1}{a}\right);$$

$$m = \left(\frac{dy}{dx}\right)_{(0,\, b)} = -\frac{b}{a}$$

$$\Rightarrow \text{Slope of normal} = \frac{a}{b}$$

(B) $\frac{dy}{dx} = -\frac{y}{x}$, Subnormal $= \left|y\frac{dy}{dx}\right|$

$$= \left| y.\left(\frac{-y}{x}\right) \right| = \left| \frac{y^2}{x} \right| = \left| \frac{y^2}{\frac{a^2b^2}{y}} \right| = \frac{|y^3|}{a^2b^2}$$

(C) $m = \frac{dy}{dx} = \frac{xb^2}{ya^2}$;

Length of subtangent

$$= \left| \frac{y}{\frac{dy}{dx}} \right| = \left| \frac{y}{\frac{xb^2}{ya^2}} \right| = \frac{y^2}{|x|} \frac{a^2}{b^2}$$

(D) $\frac{x^2}{a^2} - \frac{y^2}{b^2} = 1 \Rightarrow \frac{2x}{a^2} - \frac{2y}{b^2}\frac{dy}{dx} = 0$

$$\Rightarrow \frac{dy}{dx} = \frac{b^2x}{a^2y}$$

20. (A) → (q); (B) → (r); (C) → (p); (D) → (s)

(A). r = 6 cm $\delta r = 0.06$

$$A = \pi r^2 \delta A = 2\pi r \delta r = 2\pi(6)(0.06) = 0.72\pi$$

(B). $v = x^3, \delta v = 3x^2 \delta x$

$$\frac{\delta v}{v} \times 100 = 3\frac{\delta x}{x} \times 100 = 3 \times 2 = 6$$

(C) $(x-2)\frac{dx}{dt} = 3\frac{dx}{dt}$

$\Rightarrow x = 5$

(D) $A = \frac{\sqrt{3}}{4}x^2 \Rightarrow \frac{dA}{dt} = \frac{\sqrt{3}}{2}\left(x\frac{dx}{dt}\right)$

$$= \frac{\sqrt{3}}{2} \times 30 \times \frac{1}{10} = \frac{3\sqrt{3}}{2}$$

DAILY PRACTICE PROBLEMS

MATHEMATICS SOLUTIONS

DPP/CM20

1. (c) $\int \frac{dx}{3\sin^2 x + 4\cos^2 x} = \int \frac{\sec^2 x}{3\tan^2 x + 4} dx$

$= \int \frac{dt}{3t^2 + 4}$, where $t = \tan x$

$= \frac{1}{3}\int \frac{dt}{t^2 + (2/\sqrt{3})^2} = \frac{1}{2\sqrt{3}} \tan^{-1}\left(\frac{t}{2/\sqrt{3}}\right) + c$

$= \frac{1}{2\sqrt{3}} \tan^{-1}\left(\frac{\sqrt{3}}{2}\tan x\right) + c$

2. (d) **Case -I :** If $x > 0$, then $|x| = x$

$\therefore \int |x| \ln |x| dx$

$= \int x \ln x \, dx = \ln x . \frac{x^2}{2} - \int \frac{1}{x} . \frac{x^2}{2} dx$

$= \frac{x^2}{2} . \ln x - \frac{x^2}{4} + c$

$= \frac{x^2}{2} . \ln |x| - \frac{x^2}{4} + c$

Case- II : If $x < 0$, then $|x| = -x$

$\int |x| \ln |x| dx = -\int x \ln(-x) dx$

$= -\left\{ \ln(-x) . \frac{x^2}{2} - \frac{x^2}{4} \right\} + c$

$= -\frac{x^2}{2} \ln |x| + \frac{x^2}{4} + c$

Combining both cases, then we get

$\frac{1}{2} x |x| \ln |x| - \frac{1}{4} x |x| + c$

3. (b) Let $I = \int \frac{(\sqrt{x})^5}{(\sqrt{x})^7 + x^6} dx$

$= \int \frac{dx}{(\sqrt{x})^2 + (\sqrt{x})^7}$

$= \int \frac{dx}{(\sqrt{x})^7 \left(\frac{1}{(\sqrt{x})^5} + 1 \right)}$

Put $\frac{1}{(\sqrt{x})^5} + 1 = t$

$\therefore dt = -5/2 \, (x)^{-7/2} dx = -\frac{5}{2} . \frac{1}{(\sqrt{x})^7} dx$

or $\frac{dx}{(\sqrt{x})^7} = -\frac{2}{5} dt$

$\therefore I = -\frac{2}{5} \int \frac{dt}{t} = -\frac{2}{5} \ln |t| + c$

$= -\frac{2}{5} \ln \left| \frac{1}{(\sqrt{x})^5} + 1 \right| + c$

$= \frac{2}{5} \ln \left(\frac{(\sqrt{x})^5}{(\sqrt{x})^5 + 1} \right) + c$

$= \frac{2}{5} \ln \left(\frac{x^{5/2}}{x^{5/2} + 1} \right) + c$

On comparing, we get

$\lambda = \frac{2}{5}$ and $a = \frac{5}{2}$

$\because$ AM > GM

$\therefore \frac{\lambda + a}{2} > \sqrt{\lambda a} = 1$

$\therefore \lambda + a > 2$

4. (a) Let $I = \int_0^\infty \frac{\tan^{-1} x}{\sqrt{x}(1+x)} dx$ ...(i)

put $x = \frac{1}{t} \Rightarrow dx = -\frac{1}{t^2} dt$

$\therefore \int_\infty^0 \frac{\tan^{-1}\left(\frac{1}{t}\right)}{\frac{1}{\sqrt{t}}\left(1 + \frac{1}{t}\right)} \frac{1}{t^2} dt$;

$\int_0^\infty \frac{\tan^{-1}\left(\frac{1}{t}\right)}{\sqrt{t}(1+t)} dt = \int_0^\infty \frac{\tan^{-1}\left(\frac{1}{x}\right)}{\sqrt{x}(1+x)} dx$ ...(ii)

Adding (i) and (ii),

$2I = \frac{\pi}{2} \int_0^\infty - \frac{dx}{\sqrt{x}(x+1)}$

(put $x = y^2$, $dx = 2y \, dy$)

$$2I = \frac{\pi}{2}\int_0^\infty \frac{2y\,dy}{y(1+y^2)}$$

$$\Rightarrow 2I = \left[\pi \cdot \tan^{-1} y\right]_0^\infty = \frac{\pi^2}{2} \Rightarrow I = \frac{\pi^2}{4}$$

Hence, $\frac{502\pi^2}{k} = \frac{\pi^2}{4} \Rightarrow k = 2008$

5. (b) Let

$$l = \lim_{n\to\infty}\left(\tan\frac{\pi}{2n}.\tan\frac{2\pi}{2n}..........\tan\frac{n\pi}{2n}\right)^{\frac{1}{n}}$$

$$\therefore \quad \log l = \lim_{n\to\infty}\frac{1}{n}\sum_{r=1}^{n}\log\left(\tan\frac{r\pi}{2n}\right)$$

$$\log I = \int_0^1 \log\left(\tan\frac{\pi}{2}x\right)dx \qquad ...(i)$$

$$\Rightarrow I = \int_0^1 \log\left(\tan\frac{\pi}{2}(1-x)dx\right)$$

$$\Rightarrow I = \int_0^1 \log\left(\cot\frac{\pi}{2}x\right)dx \qquad ...(ii)$$

Adding equations (i) and (ii), we get

$$2\log l = \int_0^1\left\{\log\tan\frac{\pi}{2}x + \log\cot\frac{\pi}{2}x\right\}dx$$

$$= \int_0^1 \log\left(\tan\frac{\pi}{2}x.\cot\frac{\pi}{2}x\right)dx$$

$$= \int_0^1 0.dx = 0, \ \therefore \qquad l = e^0 = 1.$$

6. (a) Let $q = p+d, r = p+2d, s = p+3d$

$$\therefore f(x) = \begin{vmatrix} p+\sin x & p+d+\sin x & -2d+\sin x \\ p+d+\sin x & p+2d+\sin x & -1+\sin x \\ p+2d+\sin x & p+3d+\sin x & 2d+\sin x \end{vmatrix}$$

Applying $R \to R_1 + R_3 - 2R_2$, we get

$$f(x) = \begin{vmatrix} 0 & 0 & 2 \\ p+d+\sin x & p+2d+\sin x & -1+\sin x \\ p+2d+\sin x & p+3d+\sin x & 2d+\sin x \end{vmatrix}$$

$$= 2[(p+d+\sin x)(p+3d+\sin x) - (p+2d+\sin x)^2$$

$$= -2d^2$$

Given $\int_0^2 f(x)dx = -4$

$$\Rightarrow \int_0^2 (-2d^2)\,dx = -4$$

$$d^2 = 1 \Rightarrow d = \pm 1$$

7. (b,d) $I = \int \frac{\sin(\theta/2)\sin^2(\theta/2)\sin^2(\theta/2)}{(\cos^2\theta/2)\sqrt{\cos^3\theta+\cos^2\theta+\cos\theta}}d\theta$

$$= \frac{1}{2}\int \frac{\sin\theta(1-\cos\theta)}{(1+\cos\theta\sqrt{\cos^3\theta+\cos^2\theta+\cos\theta}}d\theta$$

Put $\cos\theta = x$, so that

$$I = -\frac{1}{2}\int\frac{(1-x)}{(1+x)\sqrt{x^3+x^2+x}}dx$$

$$= \frac{1}{2}\int\frac{x^2-1}{(x+1)^2 x\sqrt{x+\frac{1}{x}+1}}dx$$

$$= \frac{1}{2}\int\frac{x^2-1}{x^2\left(x+\frac{1}{x}+2\right)\sqrt{x+\frac{1}{x}+1}}dx$$

Put $x + \frac{1}{x} + 1 = t^2$

$$\Rightarrow \left(1-\frac{1}{x^2}\right)dx = 2+dt$$

$$\therefore I = \frac{1}{2}\int\frac{2t\,dt}{(t^2+1)t} = \tan^{-1}t + c$$

$$= \tan^{-1}(\cos\theta + \sec\theta + 1) + c$$

8. (b, c) $I = \int \frac{x^2+n(n-1)}{(x\sin x+n\cos x)^2}dx$

Multiplying and dividing by x^{2n-2}

$$I = \int\frac{(x^2+n(n-1)).x^{2n-2}}{(x\sin x+n\cos x)^2.x^{2n-2}}dx$$

$$I = \int\frac{(x^2+n(n-1))x^{2n-2}}{(x^n\sin x+nx^{n-1}\cos x)^2}dx$$

Let $x^n\sin x + nx^{n-1}\cos x = t$

$\Rightarrow$ $(nx^{n-1}\sin x + x^n\cos x + n(n-1))x^{n-2}$
$\cos x - nx^{n-1}\sin x)dx = dt$

$\Rightarrow$ $x^{n-2}\cos x \cdot (x^2 + n(n-1))dx = dt$

$$I=\int\frac{(x^2+n(n-1))\cdot x^{n-2}\cos x}{(x^n\sin x+nx^{n-1}\cos x)^2}\cdot x^n\cdot\sec x\,dx$$

Integrating by parts; we get

$$I=x^n\sec x\cdot\left(-\frac{1}{x^n\sin x+nx^{n-1}\cos x}\right)$$

$$+\int\frac{x^n\sec x\tan x+nx^{n-1}\sec x}{(x^n\sin x+nx^{n-1}\cos x)}dx$$

$$=-\frac{x^n\sec x}{x^n\sin x+nx^{n-1}\cos x}+\tan x+c$$

9. **(a, d)** $\int\sin^{-1}x\cos^{-1}x\,dx$

$$=\left[\frac{\pi}{2}\sin^{-1}x-(\sin^{-1}x)^2\right]dx$$

$$=\frac{\pi}{2}\left(x\sin^{-1}x+\sqrt{1-x^2}\right)$$

$$-\left(x(\sin^{-1}x)^2+\sin^{-1}x\sqrt{1-x^2}-x\right)+c$$

(integrating by parts)

$$=\sin^{-1}x\left[\frac{\pi}{2}x-x\sin^{-1}x-2\sqrt{1-x^2}\right]$$

$$+\frac{\pi}{2}\sqrt{1-x^2}+2x+c$$

$\therefore f^{-1}(x)=\sin^{-1}x, f(x)=\sin x$

10. **(a, d)** The eccentricities of a hyperbola and its conjugate e_1 and e_2 are related by

$$\frac{1}{e_1^2}+\frac{1}{e_2^2}=1\Rightarrow e_2=\frac{e_1}{\sqrt{e_1^2-1}}$$

$$\therefore f(e)=\frac{e}{\sqrt{e^2-1}}\Rightarrow ff(e)=e$$

$$\therefore \underbrace{fff\,.....f}_{n\text{ times}}(e)$$

$$=\begin{cases}\dfrac{e}{\sqrt{e^2-1}}, & \text{if } n \text{ is odd}\\ e, & \text{if } n \text{ is even}\end{cases}$$

$$\therefore \int_1^3 fff....f(e)\,de=\begin{cases}2\sqrt{2}, & \text{if } n \text{ is odd}\\ 4, & \text{if } n \text{ is even}\end{cases}$$

11. **(2)**

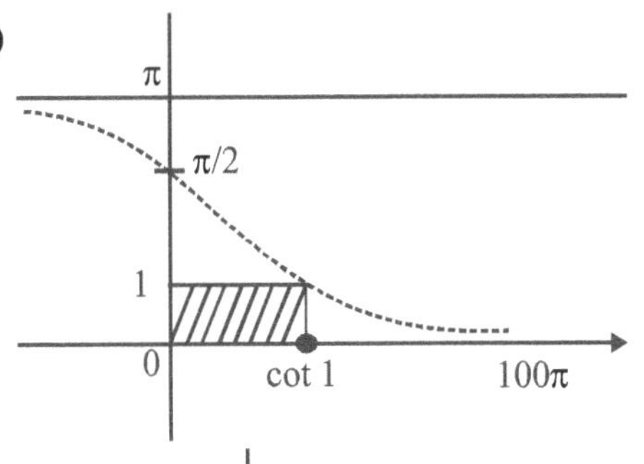

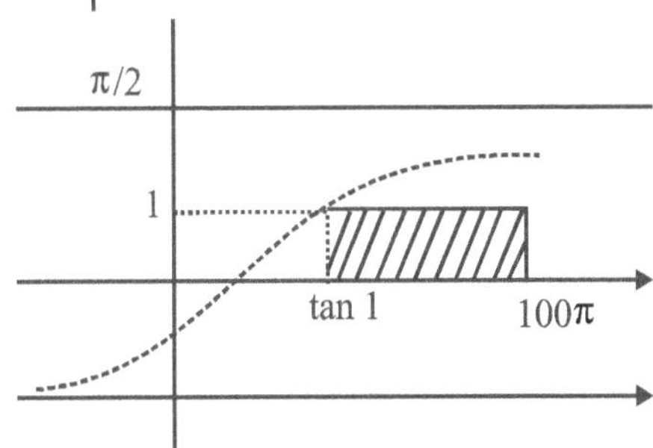

$$\int_0^{100\pi}([\cot^{-1}x]+[\tan^{-1}x])\,dx=\cot 1+(100\pi-\tan 1)$$

$$=100\pi+\frac{1-\tan^2 1}{\tan 1}=100\pi+2\cot 2$$

12. **(0)** We have $x\int_0^x(1-t)f(t)dt=\int_0^x tf(t)dt$

Differentating both sides with respect to x, we get

$$x(1-x)f(x)+\int_0^x(1-t)f(t)dt=x\,f(x)$$

$$\Rightarrow\ x^2f(x)=\int_0^x(1-t)f(t)dt$$

Differentiating again with respect to x on both sides, we get

$$x^2f'(x)+2x\,f(x)=(1-x)\,f(x)$$

$$\Rightarrow\ \frac{f'(x)}{f(x)}=\frac{1-3x}{x^2}$$

Integrating both the sides, we get

$$\ln|f(x)|=-\frac{1}{x}+3\ln x+\lambda$$

$$\Rightarrow\ \ln\left[x^3|f(x)|\right]+\frac{1}{x}=\lambda \text{ and } f(1)=1$$

$$\Rightarrow\ \lambda=1$$

$$\Rightarrow\ |f(x)|=\frac{1}{x^3}e^{\left(1-\frac{1}{x}\right)}.$$

Thus $\lim_{x\to\infty}f(x)=0$

13. **(2)** $I(n)=\int_0^{\pi/2}\theta.\sin^n\theta\,d\theta$

$$\Rightarrow\quad I(n)=\int_0^{\pi/2}\theta.\sin^{n-2}\theta(1-\cos^2\theta)d\theta$$

$$=I(n-2)-\int_0^{\pi/2}(\theta.\cos\theta).\cos\theta.\sin^{n-2}\theta\,d\theta$$

$$=\left[I(n-2)-\theta.\cos\theta.\frac{\sin^{n-1}\theta}{n-1}\right]_0^{\pi/2}$$

$$+\int_0^{\pi/2}[\theta.(-\sin\theta)+\cos\theta].\frac{\sin^{n-1}\theta}{n-1}d\theta$$

$$=I(n-2)-\frac{1}{(n-1)}\int_0^{\pi/2}\theta.\sin^n\theta\,d\theta$$

$$+\frac{1}{n-1}\int_0^{\pi/2}\cos\theta.\ \sin^{n-1}\theta\,d\theta$$

$$=I(n-2)-\frac{1}{(n-1)}.I(n)$$

$$+\frac{1}{(n-1)(n)}.\left[\sin^n\theta\right]_0^{\pi/2}$$

$$\Rightarrow\quad \frac{n}{n-1}I(n)=I(n-2)+\frac{1}{(n-1)(n)}$$

$$\Rightarrow\quad I(n)-I(n-2).\frac{n-1}{n}=\frac{1}{n^2}$$

$$\Rightarrow\quad n\ I(n)-(n-1)\,I(n-2)=\frac{1}{n}$$

Put $n=2010$, then

$$2010\ I(2010)-2009\ I(2008)=\frac{1}{2010}$$

$$\Rightarrow\quad [2010\ \ I(2010)\ -2009\ \ I(2008)]^{-1}$$

$$=2010=1005\times 2$$

14. **(1)**

$$I=\int \text{cosec}^2 x\ ln\left(\cos x+\sqrt{\cos 2x}\right)dx$$

$$=-\cot x.\log_e\left(\cos x+\sqrt{\cos 2x}\right)$$

$$-\int(-\cot x),\frac{1}{\cos x+\sqrt{\cos 2x}}$$

$$\left\{-\sin x+\frac{1}{2}(\cos 2x)^{-1/2}(-\sin 2x\ .2)\right\}dx$$

$$=-\cot x\,ln\left(\cos x+\sqrt{\cos 2x}\right)$$

$$-\int\cot x\frac{\sin x\sqrt{\cos 2x}+\sin 2x}{\sqrt{\cos 2x}\left(\cos x+\sqrt{\cos 2x}\right)}dx$$

$$=-\cot x\,ln\left(\cos x+\sqrt{\cos 2x}\right)$$

$$-\int\frac{\cos x\sqrt{\cos 2x}-\cos^2 x\cos 2x}{\cos 2x\sin^2 x}dx$$

$$=-\cot x\,ln\left(\cos x+\sqrt{\cos 2x}\right)$$

$$-\int\frac{\cos x}{\sqrt{\cos 2x}\sin^2 x}dx+\int\cot^2 x\,dx$$

Now, $I_1=\int\frac{\cos x\,dx}{\sqrt{\cos 2x}\sin^2 x}$

$$=\int\frac{\cos x\ dx}{\sin^2 x\sqrt{1-2\sin^2 x}}=\int\frac{dt}{t^2\sqrt{1-2t^2}}$$

Put $t=\frac{1}{u}\Rightarrow dt=-\frac{1}{u^2}du$

$$\therefore\ I_1=-\int\frac{u\,du}{\sqrt{u^2-2}}=-\sqrt{u^2-2}=-\sqrt{\text{cosec}^2 x-2}$$

Thus $I=-\cot x\,ln\left(\cos x+\sqrt{\cos 2x}\right)$

$$+\sqrt{\text{cosec}^2 x-2}-\cot x-x+c$$

$$\therefore\ f(x)=-\cot x\ and\ g(x)=\sqrt{\text{cosec}^2 x-2}$$

15. **(d)** If $f(x)$ is an even function, then

$$\phi(-x)=-\int_{-a}^{x}f(t)\,dt$$

$$=-\int_{-a}^{a}f(t)\,dt-\int_{a}^{x}f(t)\,dt$$

$$= -2\int_0^a f(t)\,dt - \int_a^x f(t)\,dt$$

(as $f(x)$ is an even function)

Now, $\int_0^a f(t)\,dt = \int_0^a f(a-t)\,dt$

$= -\int_0^a f(t)\,dt$ [using $f(a-x) = -f(x)$]

$\Rightarrow \int_0^a f(t)\,dt = 0$

$\Rightarrow \phi(-x) = -\int_a^x f(t)\,dt = -\phi(x)$

$\Rightarrow \phi(x)$ is an odd function.

16. (d) $g(x+\alpha) + g(x) = 0$

$\Rightarrow g(x) + 2\alpha) + g(x+\alpha) = 0$

$\Rightarrow g(x+2\alpha) = g(x)$

$\Rightarrow g(x)$ is periodic with period 2α

$\Rightarrow \int_b^{2k} g(t)\,dt = \int_b^{b+c} g(x)\,dx$

($\because$ b, k, c are in A. P.)

This is independent of b then c has least value 2α.

For Qs. 17 & 18

$$A = \begin{bmatrix} x & x \\ x & x \end{bmatrix} \Rightarrow A^2 = \begin{bmatrix} 2x^2 & 2x^2 \\ 2x^2 & 2x^2 \end{bmatrix},$$

$A^3 = \begin{bmatrix} 2^2x^2 & 2^2x^2 \\ 2^2x^2 & 2^2x^2 \end{bmatrix}$ and so on

Then $e^A = I + A + \frac{A^2}{2!} + \frac{A^3}{3!} + ... +$

$$= \begin{bmatrix} 1+x+\frac{2x^2}{2!}+\frac{2^2x^3}{3!}+.... & x+\frac{2x^2}{2!}+\frac{2^2x^3}{3!}+... \\ x+\frac{2x^2}{2!}+\frac{2^2x^3}{3!}+... & 1+x+\frac{2x^2}{2!}+\frac{2^2x^3}{3!}+... \end{bmatrix}$$

$$= \begin{bmatrix} \frac{1}{2}\left(1+2x+\frac{2^2x^2}{2!}+\frac{2^3x^3}{3!}+....\right)+\frac{1}{2} & \frac{1}{2}\left(1+2x+\frac{2^2x^2}{2!}+....\right)-\frac{1}{2} \\ \frac{1}{2}\left(1+2x+\frac{2^2x^2}{2!}+\frac{2^3x^3}{3!}+....\right)-\frac{1}{2} & \frac{1}{2}\left(1+2x+\frac{2^2x^2}{2!}+....\right)+\frac{1}{2} \end{bmatrix}$$

$$= \frac{1}{2}\begin{bmatrix} e^{2x}+1 & e^{2x}-1 \\ e^{2x}-1 & e^{2x}+1 \end{bmatrix}$$

$\Rightarrow f(x) = e^{2x} + 1$ and $g(x) = e^{2x} - 1$

17. (a) $\int \frac{e^{2x}-1}{e^{2x}+1}dx = \int \frac{e^x - e^{-x}}{e^x + e^{-x}}dx$

18. (b) $\int (g(x)+1)\sin x dx$

$$= \int e^{2x}\sin x dx = \frac{e^{2x}}{5}(2\sin x - \cos x)$$

19. **(A) → (r); (B) → (p); (C) → (t); (D) → (s)**

$$\int \frac{\ln(x+\sqrt{1+x^2})}{\sqrt{1+x^2}}dx = I$$

Put $\ln(x+\sqrt{1+x^2}) = t \Rightarrow \frac{dx}{\sqrt{1+x^2}} = dt$

So, $I = \int t\,dt = \frac{t^2}{2} + c = \frac{1}{2}\left\{\ln(x+\sqrt{1+x^2}\right\}^2 + c.$

Thus,

(A) $f(x) = \frac{x^2}{2}$

(B) $g(x) = \ln(x+\sqrt{x^2+1})$

(C) Now, $\int \frac{x^2}{2}\ln(x+\sqrt{x^2+1})dx$

$$= \frac{x^3}{6}\ln(x+\sqrt{x^2+1})$$

$$-\frac{1}{2}\int \frac{x^3}{3} \times \frac{1}{x+\sqrt{x^2+1}}\left\{1+\frac{2x}{2\sqrt{x^2+1}}\right\}dx$$

$$= \frac{x^3}{6}\ln(x+\sqrt{x^2+1}) - \frac{1}{6}\int \frac{x^3 dx}{\sqrt{x^2+1}}$$

$$= \frac{x^3}{6}\ln(x+\sqrt{x^2+1}) - \frac{1}{6}\int (t^2-1)\,dt$$

Putting $x^2 + 1 = t^2$

$$= \frac{x^3}{6}\ln(x+\sqrt{x^2+1}) - \frac{1}{18}(1+x^2)^{3/2}$$

$$+\frac{1}{6}(1+x^2)^{1/2} + c$$

(D) $\int e^{g(x)}dx = \int (x+\sqrt{1+x^2})dx$

$$= \frac{x^2}{2} + \frac{x}{2}\sqrt{1+x^2} + \frac{1}{2}\ln(x+\sqrt{1+x^2}) + c$$

$$= \frac{1}{2}x(x+\sqrt{1+x^2}) + \frac{1}{2}g(x) + c$$

20. (A)→(r); (B)→(t); (C)→(q); (D)→(p, q, r, s)

(A) $0 < \frac{3}{x^2+1} \le 3$

$\Rightarrow \frac{3}{x^2+1} = 2$

$\Rightarrow x = \frac{1}{\sqrt{2}}$ and $\frac{3}{x^2+1} = 1$

$\Rightarrow x = \sqrt{2}$

$$I = \int_0^{1/\sqrt{2}} 2dx + \int_{1/\sqrt{2}}^{\sqrt{2}} 1.dx + \int_{\sqrt{2}}^{\infty} 0\,dx = \sqrt{2} + \sqrt{2} - \frac{1}{\sqrt{2}}$$

$$= 2\sqrt{2} - \frac{1}{\sqrt{2}} = \frac{3}{\sqrt{2}}$$

(B) $\int_{-10}^{10} \frac{3}{3^{[x]}}dx = 20\int_0^1 3^{x-[x]}dx = 20\int_0^1 3^x\,dx$

$$= 20\left[\frac{3^x}{\ln 3}\right]_0^1 = \frac{40}{\ln 3}$$

(C) $\int_{-1}^{1} [x[1+\sin\pi x]+1]\,dx$

$$= \int_{-1}^{0} [x[1+\sin\pi x]+1]\,dx + \int_0^1 [x[1+\sin\pi x]+1]dx$$

Now, $-1 < x < 0 \Rightarrow [1+\sin\pi x] = 0$

And $0 < x < 1 \Rightarrow [1+\sin\pi x] = 1$

$\Rightarrow [x[1+\sin\pi x]+1] = 1$

So, $\int_{-1}^{1} [x[1+\sin\pi x]+1]\,dx = 2$

(D) The L.H.S. of given inequality is equal to

$$\left[a^2\left(\frac{\sin 3x}{12} + \frac{3}{4}\sin x\right) - a\cos x - 20\sin x\right]_0^{\pi/2}$$

$$= a^2\left(-\frac{1}{12} + \frac{3}{4}\right) - a(0-1) - 20$$

$$= \frac{2a^2}{3} + a - 20$$

Thus the given inequality is $\frac{2a^2}{3} + a - 20 \le -\frac{a^2}{3}$ i.e.,

$a^2 + a - 20 \le 0$

$\Rightarrow -5 \le a \le 4$

Since 'a' is a positive integer so, $a = 1, 2, 3, 4$.

1. **(a)**

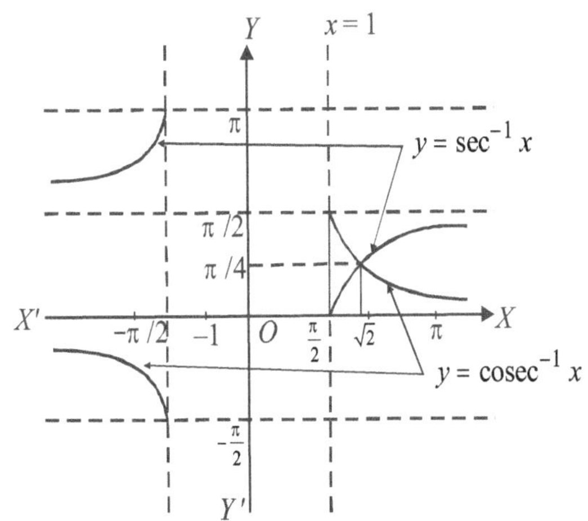

Integrating along x-axis, we get

$$A=\int_{1}^{\sqrt{2}}(\operatorname{cosec}^{-1}x-\sec^{-1}x)\,dx$$

Integrating along y-axis, we get

$$A=2\int_{0}^{\pi/4}(\sec y-1)\,dy$$

$$=2[\log|\sec y+\tan y|-y]_{0}^{\pi/4}$$

$$=2\left[\log|\sqrt{2}+1|-\frac{\pi}{4}\right]=\left(\log(3+2\sqrt{2})-\frac{\pi}{2}\right)\text{ sq.units}$$

2. **(b)** $ay^2=x^2(a-x)\Rightarrow y=\pm x\sqrt{\dfrac{a-x}{a}}$

Curve tracing : $y=x\sqrt{\dfrac{a-x}{a}}$

We must have $x\le a$

For $0<x\le a$, $y>0$ and for $x<0, y<0$

Also $y=0\Rightarrow x=0, a$

Curve is symmetrical about x-axis.

When $x\to-\infty, y\to-\infty$

Also, it can be varified that y has only one point of maxima for $0<x<a$.

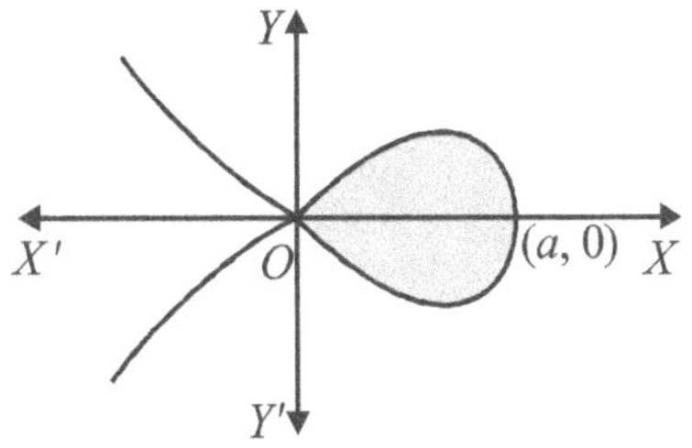

$$\text{Area}=2\int_{0}^{a}x\sqrt{\frac{a-x}{a}}\,dx$$

$$\sqrt{\frac{a-x}{a}}=t\Rightarrow 1-\frac{x}{a}=t^2\Rightarrow x=a(1-t^2)$$

$$\Rightarrow\quad A=2\int_{1}^{0}a(1-t^2)\,t(-2at)dt$$

$$=4a^2\int_{0}^{1}(t^2-t^4)dt$$

$$=4a^2\left[\frac{t^3}{3}-\frac{t^5}{5}\right]_0^1$$

$$=4a^2\left[\frac{1}{3}-\frac{1}{5}\right]=\frac{8a^2}{15}\text{ sq.units}$$

3. **(a)** The two curves are

$$xy^2=a^2(a-x)\Rightarrow x=\frac{a^3}{a^2+y^2}\qquad\ldots\text{(i)}$$

and $(a-x)y^2=a^2x$

$$\Rightarrow\quad x=\frac{ay^2}{a^2+y^2}=\frac{ay^2+a^3-a^3}{a^2+y^2}$$

$$=a-\frac{a^3}{a^2+y^2}\qquad\ldots\text{(ii)}$$

Curve (i) is symmetrical about x-axis and have y-axis as the asymptote.

Curve (ii) is symmetrical about x-axis, tangent at origin as y-axis and the asymptote $x=a$.

The two curve intersect at the point $P(a/2, a)$ and $Q(a/2, -a)$.

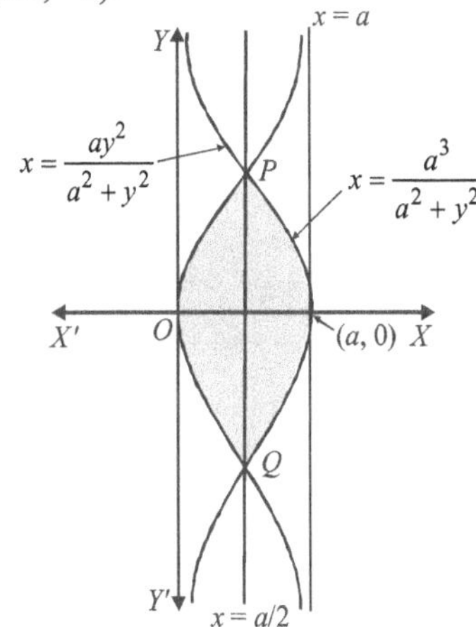

Required area $= 2\int_0^a \left[a - \frac{a^3}{a^2+y^2} - \frac{a^3}{a^2+y^2}\right] dy$

(integrating along y-axis)

$= 2\left[ay - 2a^2 \tan^{-1}\frac{y}{a}\right]_0^a$

$= 2\left[a^2 - 2a^2\frac{\pi}{4}\right]$

$= (\pi - 2)\, a^2$ sq.units

4. (c) As, $f(x) = \begin{cases} \sqrt{\{x\}}, & x \notin z \\ 1, & x \in z \end{cases}$ and $g(x) = \{x\}^2$, where both $f(x)$ and $g(x)$ are periodic with period '1' shown as,

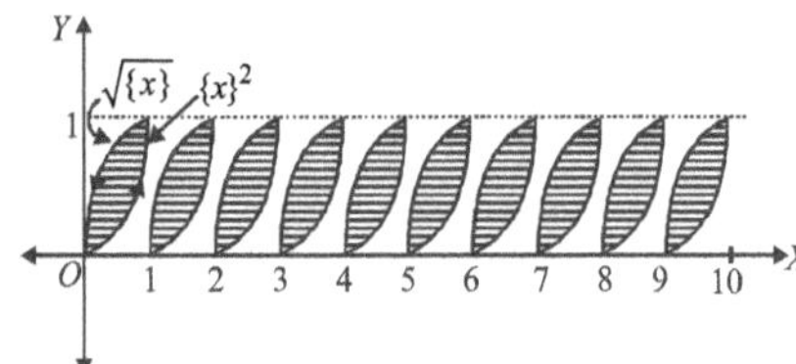

Thus required area $= 10\int_0^1 (\sqrt{\{x\}} - \{x\}^2)\,dx$

$= 10\int_0^1 ((x)^{1/2} - x^2)\,dx = 10\left\{\frac{x^{3/2}}{3/2} - \frac{x^3}{3}\right\}_0^1$

$= 10\left\{\frac{2}{3} - \frac{1}{3}\right\} = \frac{10}{3}$ sq.unit

5. (c) $y = 2 - |2 - x|, y = \frac{3}{|x|}$

$y = \begin{cases} x, & x \le 2 \\ 4 - x, & x \ge 2 \end{cases}; \quad y = \begin{cases} \frac{3}{x}, & x > 0 \\ -\frac{3}{x}, & x < 0 \end{cases}$

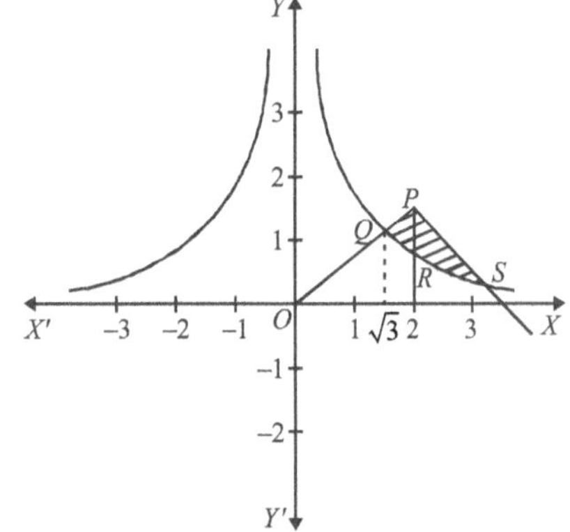

Hence, required area = Area of region $PQRSP$
= area of region $PQRP$ + area of region $PRSP$

$= \left|\int_{\sqrt{3}}^2 \left(x - \frac{3}{x}\right)\right| dx + \left|\int_2^3 \left((4 - x) - \frac{3}{x}\right) dx\right|$

$= \left(\frac{4 - 3\ln 3}{2}\right)$ sq. units

6. (b, c) Area $= \int_0^3 (f(x) - g(x))\,dx + \int_3^5 (g(x) - f(x))\,dx$

$= \int_0^3 f(x)\,dx - \int_0^3 g(x)\,dx + \int_3^5 g(x)\,dx - \int_3^5 f(x)\,dx$

$= (a - c) - (d) + (b - d) - c$

$= a + b - 2c - 2d$

7. (a, c, d)

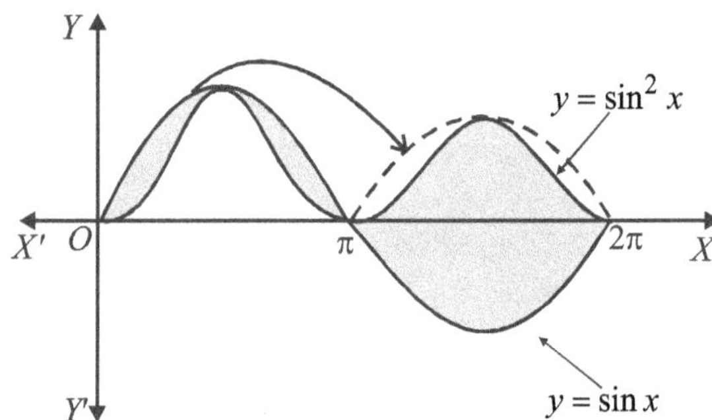

We know that area bounded by $y = \sin x$ and x-axis for $x \in [0, \pi]$ is 2 sq. units.

Then area bounded by $y = \sin x$ and $y = \sin^2 x$ is 4 sq. units for $x \in [0, 2\pi]$.

Then for $x \in [0, 10\pi]$, the area bounded is 20 sq. units.

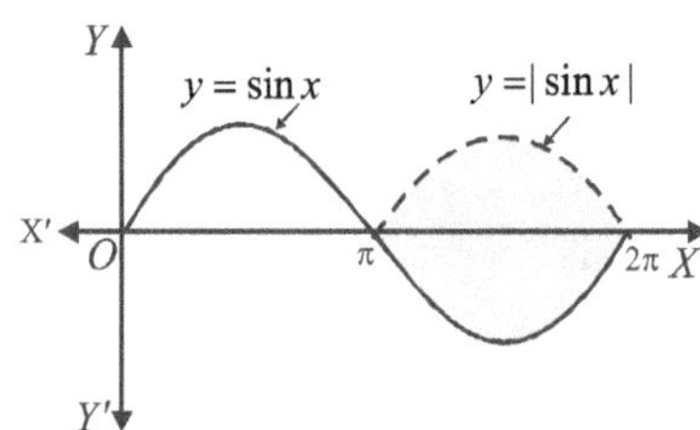

The area bounded by $y = \sin x$ and $y = |\sin x|$ for $x \in [0, 2\pi]$ is 4 sq. units.

Then for $x \in [0, 2\pi]$, the area bounded is 40 sq. units.

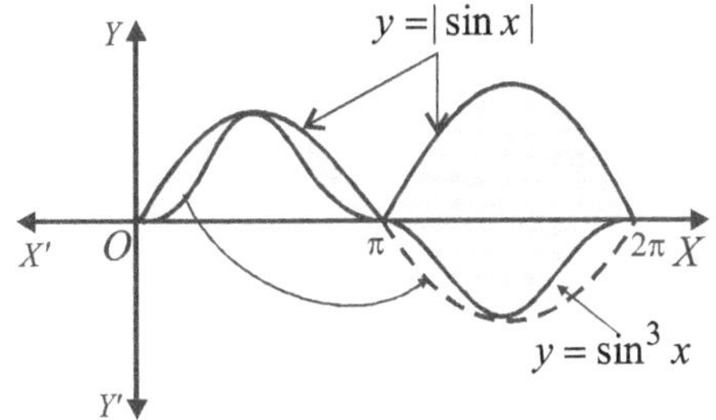

The area bounded by $y = \sin x$ and $y = \sin^3 x$ for $x \in [0, 2\pi]$ is 4 sq. units.

Then for $x \in [0, 10\pi]$, the area bounded is 20 sq. units. Similarly, the area bounded by $y = \sin x$ and $y = \sin^4 x$ for $x \in [0, 10\pi]$ is 20 sq. units.

8. **(c, d)** Here, curve $ABCD$ is max $\{f(x), g(x)\} = p(x)$ and curve $EBCF$ is min $\{f(x), g(x)\} = q(x)$.

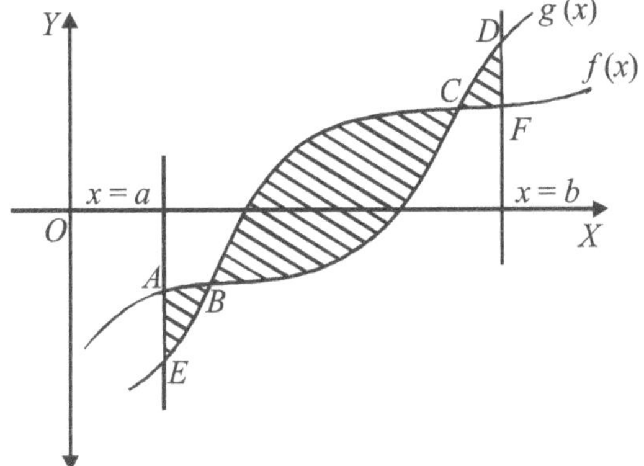

Thus, area can be determine by either (c) or (d).

9. **(a, b, d)** First of all let us draw a rough sketch of $y = e^{-x^2}$.
At $x = 0, y = 1$ and at $x = 1, y = 1/e$

Also $\frac{dy}{dx} = -2xe^{-x^2} < 0 \ \forall \ x \in (0, 1)$

$\therefore y = e^{-x^2}$ is decreasing on (0, 1)
Hence its graph is as shown in figure given below

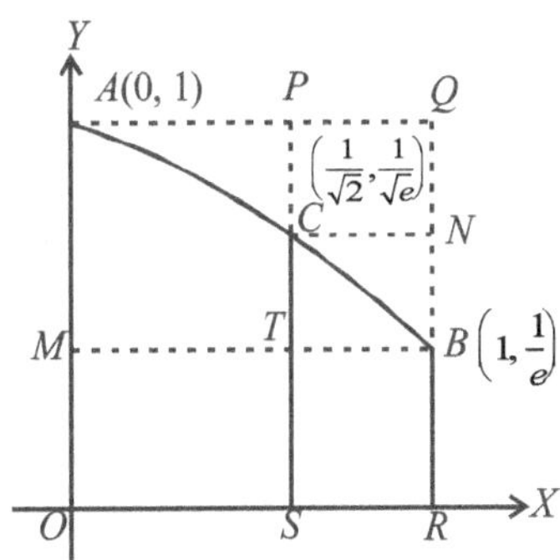

Now, S = area exclosed by curve = ABRO

and area of rectangle ORBM = $\frac{1}{e}$

Clearly $S > \frac{1}{e}$ $\quad \therefore$ A is true.

Also $x^2 < x \quad \forall x \in [0, 1]$

$\Rightarrow -x^2 > -x \quad \Rightarrow e^{-x^2} \geq e^{-x} \ \forall \ x \in [0, 1]$

$\Rightarrow \int_0^1 e^{-x^2} dx > \int_0^1 e^{-x} dx = 1 - \frac{1}{e}$

$\Rightarrow S > 1 - \frac{1}{e} \qquad \therefore$ (b) is true.

Now S < area of rectangle APSO + area of rectangle CSRN

$\Rightarrow \quad S < \frac{1}{\sqrt{2}} \times 1 + \left(1 - \frac{1}{\sqrt{2}}\right) \frac{1}{\sqrt{e}}$

$\therefore \quad S < \frac{1}{\sqrt{2}} + \frac{1}{\sqrt{e}}\left(1 - \frac{1}{\sqrt{2}}\right) \qquad \because$ (d) is true

Also as $\frac{1}{4}\left(1 + \frac{1}{\sqrt{e}}\right) < 1 - \frac{1}{e} \qquad \therefore$ (c) is incorrect.

10. **(8)**

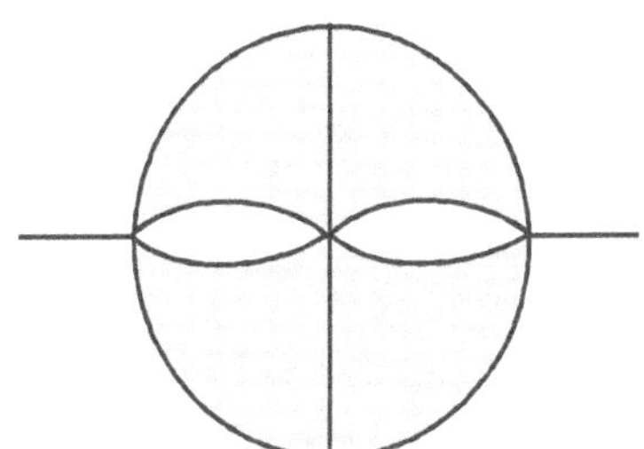

Required area

$$= \pi(\pi^2) - 4\int_0^{\pi} \sin x dx = \pi^3 - 8$$

11. **(7)**

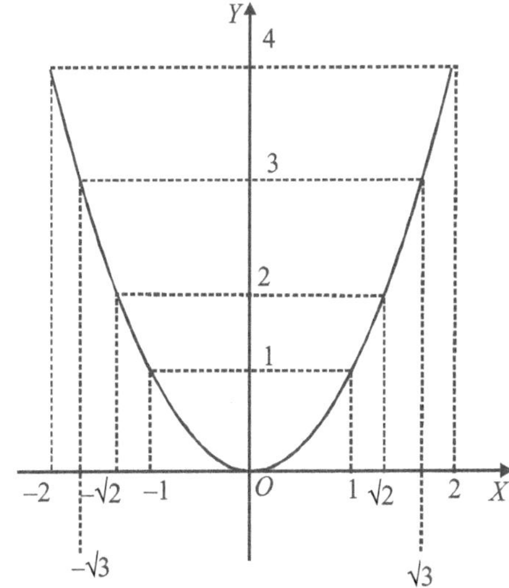

As we know that fractional part of any thing must lie between 0 and 1 thus

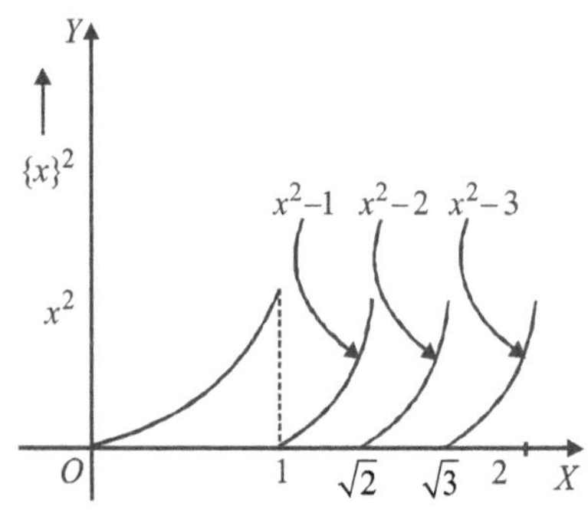

$\therefore$ Area of region bounded by $y = \{x\}^2$ between x-axis for the $x \in [0, 2]$ is

$$= \int_0^1 x^2 dx + \int_1^{\sqrt{2}} (x^2 - 1)\, dx + \int_{\sqrt{2}}^{\sqrt{3}} (x^2 - 2)\, dx + \int_{\sqrt{3}}^{2} (x^2 - 3)\, dx$$

$$A_0 = \sqrt{2} + \sqrt{3} - \frac{7}{3}$$

$\therefore$ Required area $= 2A_0 = 2\left(\sqrt{2} + \sqrt{3} - \frac{7}{3}\right)$

12. (2) $|y + x| \le 1 \Rightarrow -1 \le x + y \le 1$

It represents the region between the lines $x + y = 1$ and $x + y = -1$

Similarly, $|y - x| \le 1$

$\Rightarrow$ $-1 \le y - x \le 1$ represents the region between the lines $x - y = 1$ and $-x + y = 1$

$\Rightarrow$ Both together form a square of side $\sqrt{2}$ units

$3x^2 + 12y^2 = 2$ is an ellipse with

$a = \sqrt{\frac{2}{3}},\ b = \frac{1}{\sqrt{6}}$

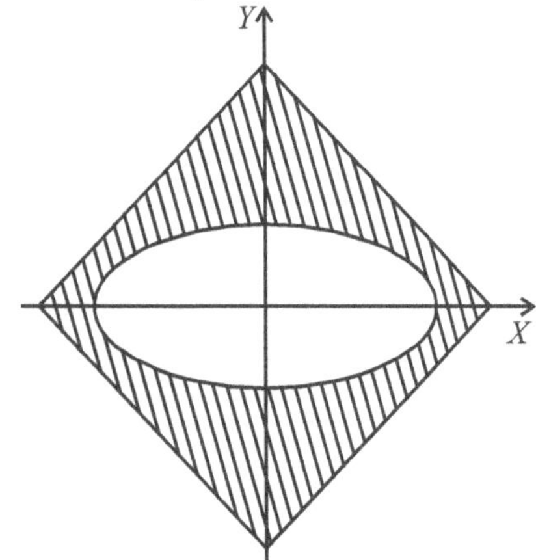

Area of the ellipse $= \pi ab = \frac{\pi}{3}$

Area of the square = 2 sq. units

Required area $= \left(2 - \frac{\pi}{3}\right)$ sq. units.

13. (4) $\frac{|x| + |y|}{2} + \left|\frac{|x| - |y|}{2}\right| \le 2$

$\Rightarrow$ $||x| - |y|| \le 4 - (|x| + |y|)$ (here $|x| + |y| \le 4$)

$\Rightarrow$ $|x| + |y| - 4 \le |x| - |y| \le 4 - (|x| + |y|)$

$\Rightarrow$ $|x| \le 2$ and $|y| \le 2$

So, that the region satisfying

$|x| \le 2, |y| \le 2$ and $|x| + |y| \le 4$ is

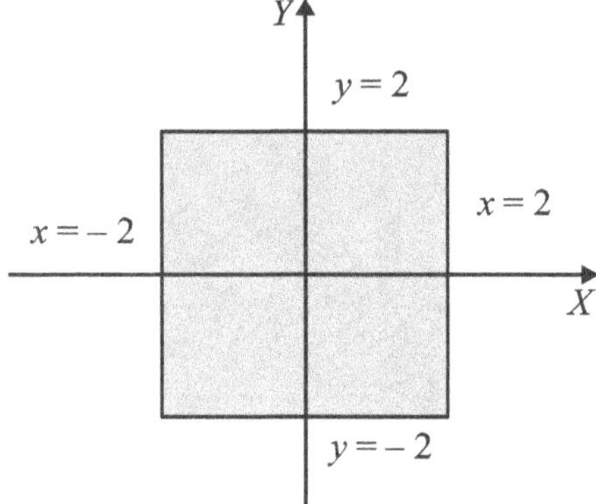

Also curve $|y| = e^{-|x|} - \frac{1}{2}$ is symmetric about both x and y-axis. So that the curve is

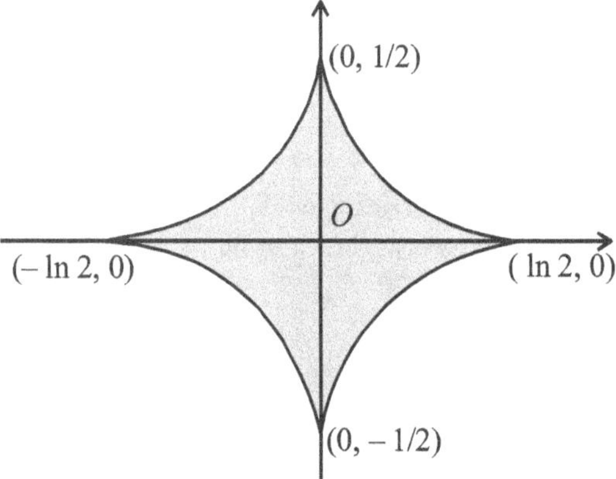

So that the required region is the the shaded region = (area of square $ABCD$) – (area of curve $A'B'C'D'$)

$$= 16 - 4\int_0^{\ln 2} \left(e^{-x} - \frac{1}{2}\right) dx$$

$= 14 + \ln 4$ sq. units

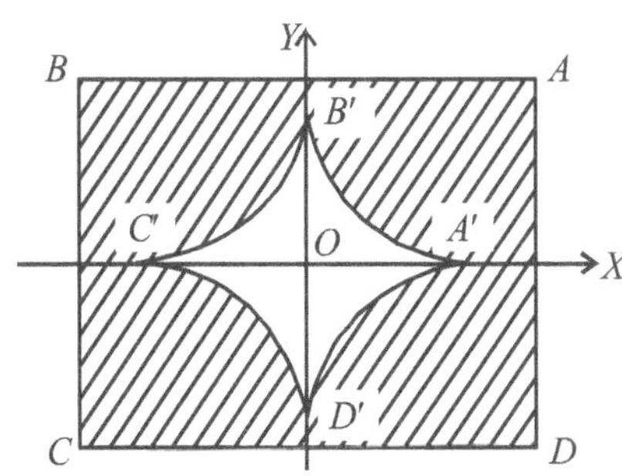

14. (4) $f(x)=\frac{\pi}{2}-\sin^{-1}(\sin x)$; $g(x)=\frac{\pi}{2}-\cos^{-1}(\cos x)$

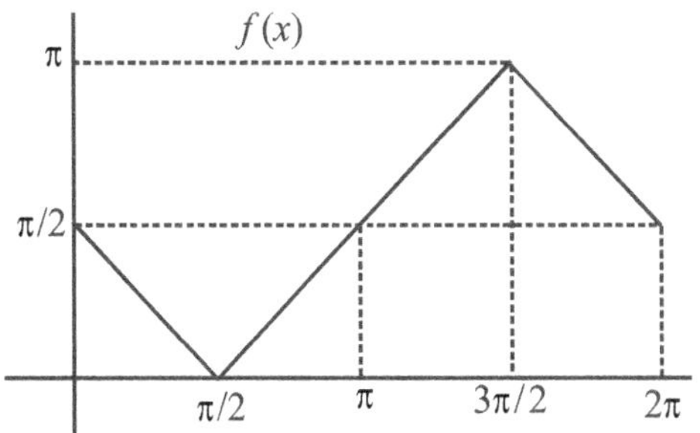

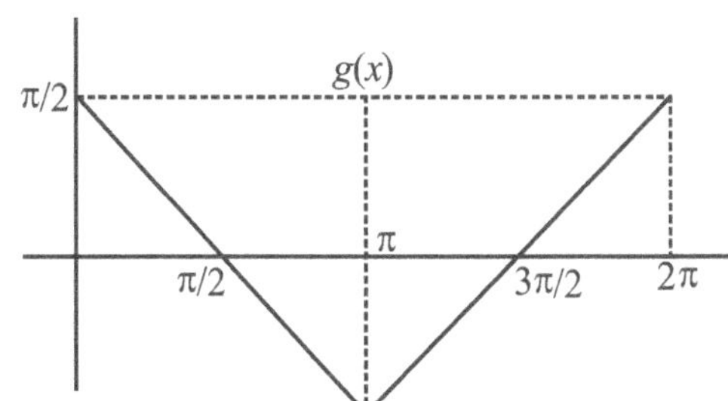

Both $f(x)$ and $g(x)$

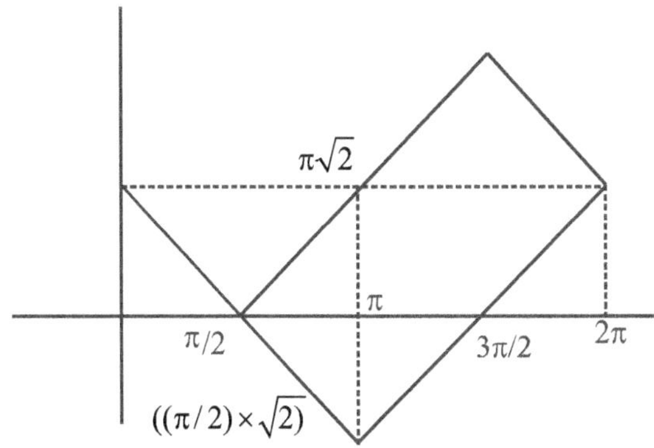

So, area $=\pi\sqrt{2}\times\frac{\pi}{2}\sqrt{2}=\pi^2$

From 0 to 98π, there are 49 period

So, $A=49\pi^2=49\times\frac{22}{7}\times\frac{22}{7}=(22)^2=484$

For Q. 15—16

Since $-1\le\sin x\le 1$, the curve $y=e^{-x}\sin x$ is bounded by the curves $y=e^{-x}$ and $y=e^{-x}$.

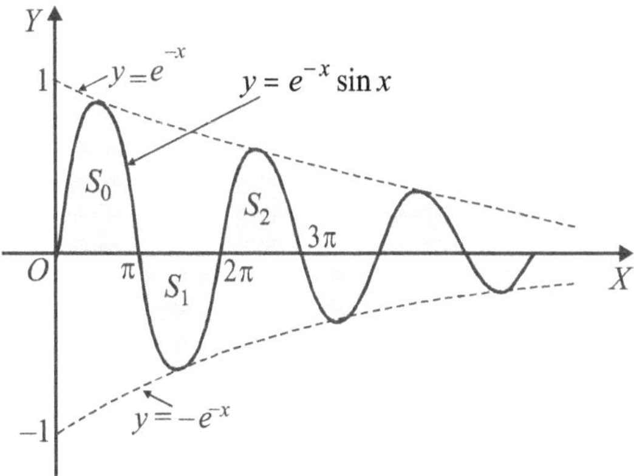

Also, the curve $y=e^{-x}\sin x$ intersects the positive semi-axis OX at the points where $\sin x=0$, where $x_n=n\pi,\ n\in Z$. Also $|y_n|=|y$ coordinate in the half-wave $S_n|=(-1)^n e^{-x}\sin x$, and in S_n, $n\pi\le x\le(n+1)\pi$

$$\therefore\ S_n=(-1)^n\int_{n\pi}^{(n+1)\pi}e^{-x}\sin x\,dx$$

$$=\frac{(-1)^{n+1}}{2}\left[e^{-x}(-\sin x+\cos x)\right]_{n\pi}^{(n+1)\pi}$$

$$=\frac{(-1)^{n+1}}{2}[e^{-(n+1)\pi}(-1)^{n+1}-e^{n\pi}\beta(-1)^n]$$

$$=\frac{e^{-n\pi}}{2}\left(1+e^{\pi}\right)$$

$$\Rightarrow\ \frac{S_{n+1}}{S_n}=e^{-\pi}\text{ and }S_0=\frac{1}{2}(1+e^{\pi})$$

$\therefore$ The sequence $S_0, S_1, S_2, \ldots\ldots$ forms an infinite G.P. with common ratio $e^{-\pi}$

15. (a) **16. (b)**

For Q. 17 - 19

- The graph of $|x-p|+|y-q|=k$ is a square. Area of the region bounded by $|x-p|+|y-q|=k$ is given by $2k^2$ (area is independent of p and q).
- The resultant figure for $a|x-p|+b|y-q|=k$ is a rhombus. Area of the region bounded by $a|x-p|+b|y-q|=k$ is given by $\frac{2k^2}{ab}$ (area is independent of p and q)
- The resultant figure for $|x-p|-|y-q|=k$ is not a closed loop so we cannot find the area bounded by the graph.

- The resultant figure which is bounded by $|x+y|=p$ and $|x-y|=q$ is a rectangle and its area will be $(\sqrt{2}p)(\sqrt{2}q)$ i.e., $2pq$.
  Area of the regions bounded by $|x-p|+|y-q|=k$ and $\left|x-\frac{1}{p}\right|+\left|y-\frac{1}{q}\right|=k$ is same.

17. **(b)**

18. **(a)**

19. **(d)**

20. **(A) → (q) ; (B) → (p); (C) → (s); (D) → (r)**

(A) Area $= 2\left(\frac{1}{2}.1.1\right) = 1$ sq. units. (q)

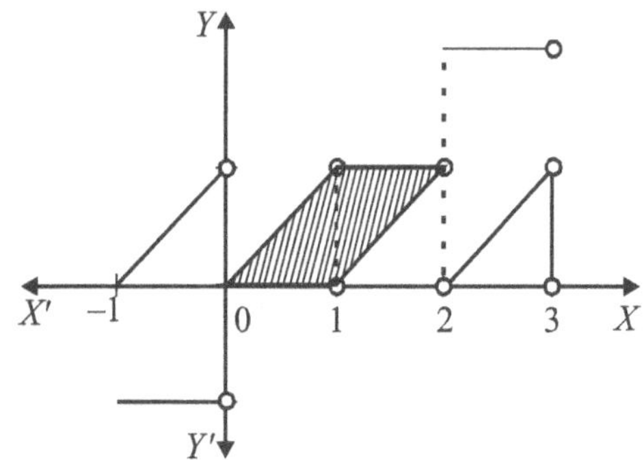

(B) $y^2 = x^3$ and $|y| = 2x$, both the curve are symmetric about y-axis

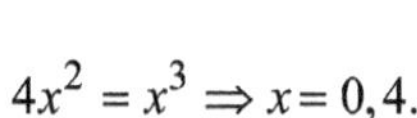

$4x^2 = x^3 \Rightarrow x = 0, 4.$

Required area $= 2\int_0^4 (2x - x^{3/2})dx$

$= \frac{16}{5}$ sq. units. (p)

(C) $\sqrt{x} + \sqrt{|y|} = 1$

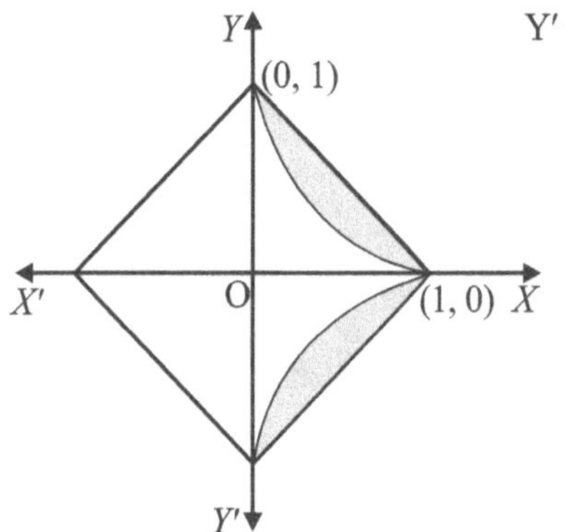

The curve is symmetrical about x-axis, because $\sqrt{|y|} = 1 - \sqrt{x}$ and $\sqrt{x} = 1 - \sqrt{|y|}$

$\Rightarrow$ for $x > 0,\ y > 0,\ \sqrt{y} = 1 - \sqrt{x}$

$$\frac{1}{2\sqrt{y}}\frac{dy}{dx} = -\frac{1}{2\sqrt{x}}$$

$$\frac{dy}{dx} = -\sqrt{\frac{x}{y}}$$

$\frac{dy}{dx} < 0,$ function is decreasing. Required area

$$= 2\int_0^1 (1-x) - (1 - 2\sqrt{x} + x)dx \ = 4\int_0^1 (\sqrt{x} - x)dx$$

$$= 4\left[\frac{x^{3/2}}{3/2} - \frac{x^2}{2}\right]_0^1 = 4\left[\frac{2}{3} - \frac{1}{2}\right]$$

$= \frac{2}{3}$ sq. units **(s)**

(D) If $-8 < x < 8$, then $y = 2$

If $x \in (-8\sqrt{2}, -8] \cup [8, \sqrt{2})$, then $y = 3$, and so on

Intersection of $y = x - 1$ and $y = 2$. We get $x = 3 \in (-8, 8)$.

Intersection of $y = x - 1$ and $y = 3$, we get $x = 4 \notin (-8\sqrt{2}, -8] \cup [8, 8\sqrt{2})$.

Similarly, $y = x - 1$ will not intersect $y = \left[\frac{x^2}{64} + 2\right]$ at any other interval, except in the interval $x \in (-8, 8)$.

The required area (shaded region)

$= 2 \times 3 - \frac{1}{2} \times 2 \times 2 = 4$ sq. units (r)

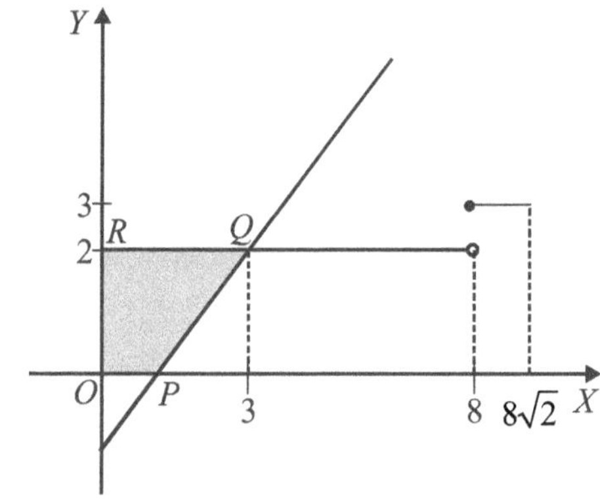

1. (a) $\frac{dy}{dx}-\frac{y}{x}=-\frac{5x}{(x+2)(x-3)}$,

which is linear in y

$$\text{I.F.} = e^{\int -\frac{1}{x}dx} = e^{-\ln x} = \frac{1}{x}$$

So the solution is

$$y.\frac{1}{x}=-\int \frac{5}{(x+2)\,(x+3)}dx+c$$

$$y.\frac{1}{x}=\ln\left(\frac{x+2}{x-3}\right)+c$$

It passes through (4, 0)

$\therefore$ $0=\ln 6+c \Rightarrow c=-\ln 6$

$\therefore$ $\frac{y}{x}=\ln\frac{x+2}{x-3}-\ln 6$

Then point (5, a) lies on it

$\therefore$ $a=5\ln(7/12)$

2. (d) Putting $v=y/x$ so that $x\frac{dv}{dx}+v=\frac{dy}{dx}$

We have $x\frac{dv}{dx}+v=v+\phi(1/v)$

$\Rightarrow$ $\frac{dv}{\phi(1/v)}=\frac{dx}{x}$

$\Rightarrow$ $\log|Cx|=\int\frac{dv}{\phi(1/v)}$

(C being constant of integration)

But $y=\frac{x}{\log|Cx|}$ is the general solution,

So $\frac{x}{y}=\frac{1}{v}=\log|Cx|=\int\frac{dv}{\phi(1/v)}$

$\Rightarrow$ $\phi(1/v)=-1/v^2$

(differentiating w.r.t. v both sides)

$\Rightarrow$ $\phi(x/y)=-y^2/x^2$

3. (a) We have

$dy+\{y\phi'(x)-\phi(x)\phi'(x)\}\,dx=0$

$\Rightarrow$ $\frac{dy}{dx}+\phi'(x).y=\phi(x)\phi'(x)$

This is a linear differential equation with

$\text{I.F.} = e^{\int\phi'(x)dx=e^{\phi(x)}}$.

Multiplying (i) by $\phi(x)$ and integrating we get

$$ye^{\phi(x)}=\int\phi(x)\phi'(x)e^{\phi(x)}dx$$

$\Rightarrow$ $ye^{\phi(x)}=\int e^{\phi(x)}\,\phi(x)\phi'(x)\,dx$

$\Rightarrow$ $ye^{\phi(x)}=\int \underset{\text{I}}{\phi(x)}\;\underset{\text{II}}{e^{\phi(x)}}\phi'(x)dx$

$\Rightarrow$ $ye^{\phi(x)}=\phi(x)e^{\phi(x)}-\int\phi'(x)e^{\phi(x)}\,dx$

$\Rightarrow$ $ye^{\phi(x)}=\phi(x)e^{\phi(x)}-e^{\phi(x)}+c$

$\Rightarrow$ $y=(\phi(x)-1)+ce^{-\phi(x)}$

4. (a)

(a) Order of the differential equation is 2.

(b) $\frac{xdy-ydx}{\sqrt{x^2+y^2}}=dx \Rightarrow \frac{\frac{xdy-ydx}{x^2}}{\sqrt{1+\frac{y^2}{x^2}}}=\frac{dx}{x}$ ...(i)

Put $t=\frac{y}{x}$, $\therefore$ $\frac{dt}{dx}=\frac{x.\frac{dy}{dx}-y}{x^2}$

$\Rightarrow$ $\frac{dt}{dx}=\frac{xdy-ydx}{x^2.dx}\Rightarrow dt=\frac{xdy-ydx}{x^2}$

L.H.S. of equation (i) $=\frac{1}{\sqrt{1-t^2}}dt$

$\therefore$ $\int\frac{1}{\sqrt{1-t^2}}dt=\int\frac{1}{x}dx$

$\therefore$ $\int\frac{1}{\sqrt{1-t^2}}dt=\int\frac{1}{x}dx$

$\Rightarrow$ $\ln\left|\frac{y}{x}+\sqrt{1+\frac{y^2}{x^2}}\right|=\ln|cx|$,

$\Rightarrow$ $\frac{y}{x}+\frac{\sqrt{x^2+y^2}}{x}=cx$

$\Rightarrow$ $y+\sqrt{x^2+y^2}=cx^2$

(c) $y=e^x(A\cos x+B\sin x)$

$$\frac{dy}{dx}=e^x(A\cos x+B\sin x)$$
$$+e^x(-A\sin x+B\cos x)$$

$= y + e^x(-A\sin x + B\cos x)$

$\therefore \quad \frac{d^2y}{dx^2} = \frac{dy}{dx} + e^x(-A\sin x + B\cos x)$

$+ e^x(-A\cos x - B\sin x)$

$\therefore \quad \frac{d^2y}{dx^2} = \frac{dy}{dx} + e^x(-A\sin x + B\cos x) - y$

$= \frac{dy}{dx} + \frac{dy}{dx} - y - y = 2\left(\frac{dy}{dx} - y\right)$

(d) $\frac{dx}{dy} + \frac{x}{1+y^2} = \frac{2e^{\tan^{-1}y}}{1+y^2}$;

I.F. $= e^{\int \frac{1}{1+y^2}} = e^{\tan^{-1}y}$

$\Rightarrow \quad x.e^{\tan^{-1}y} = 2\int e^{\tan^{-1}y}.\frac{e^{\tan^{-1}y}}{1+y^2}dy$

$\Rightarrow \quad x.e^{\tan^{-1}y} = e^{2\tan^{-1}y} + k$

5. **(a)** Taking $x = r\cos\theta$ and $y = r\sin\theta$, so that $x^2 + y^2 = r^2$ and $y/x = \tan\theta$, we have

$xdx + ydx = rdr$ and

$xdy - ydx = x^2\sec^2\theta d\theta = r^2 d\theta$.

The given equation can be transformed into

$\frac{rdr}{r^2 d\theta} = \sqrt{\frac{a^2 - r^2}{r^2}} \Rightarrow \frac{dr}{d\theta} = \sqrt{a^2 - r^2}$

$\Rightarrow \quad c + \sin^{-1} r/a = \theta = \tan^{-1} y/x$

$\Rightarrow \quad y = x\tan\left(c + \sin^{-1}\frac{1}{a}\sqrt{x^2 + y^2}\right)$

or $\quad \sqrt{x^2 + y^2} = a\sin\left(\text{const.} + \tan^{-1}\frac{y}{x}\right)$

6. **(b, c)**

(a): $\quad y = 2 + c_1\cos x + \sqrt{c_2}\sin x$

$\frac{dy}{dx} = -c_1\sin x + \sqrt{c_2}\cos x$

$\frac{d^2y}{dx^2} = -c_1\cos x - \sqrt{c_2}\sin x = 2 - y$

$\frac{d^2y}{dx^2} + y + 2 = 0$

(b): $\quad y = \cos x\ln\left(\tan\frac{x}{2}\right)$

$\frac{dy}{dx} = \cos x\frac{\sec^2(x/2)}{2\tan(x/2)} - \sin x\ln\left(\tan\frac{x}{2}\right)$

$\frac{dy}{dx} = \cot x - \sin x\ln\left(\tan\frac{x}{2}\right)$

$\frac{d^2y}{dx^2} = -\cot^2 x - 2 - \cos x\ln\left(\tan\frac{x}{2}\right)$

$\frac{d^2y}{dx^2} + y + \cot^2 x = 0$

(c): $\quad y = 2 + c_1\cos x + c_2\sin x + \cos x\ln\tan\frac{x}{2}$

$\frac{dy}{dx} = -c_1\sin x + c_2\cos x$

$+\frac{d}{dx}\left(\cos x\ln\left(\tan\frac{x}{2}\right)\right)$

$\frac{d^2y}{dx^2} = -(c_1\cos x + c_2\sin x)$

$+\frac{d^2}{dx^2}\left(\cos x\ln\left(\tan\frac{x}{2}\right)\right)$

$\Rightarrow \quad \frac{d^2y}{dx^2} = -c_1\cos x - c_2\sin x - \cot^2 x$

$-2 - \cos x\ln\left(\tan\frac{x}{2}\right)$

$\Rightarrow \quad \frac{d^2y}{dx^2} + y + \cot^2 x = 0$

7. **(a, d)** Equation of tangent at (x, y),

$Y - y = \frac{dy}{dx}(X - x)$

$\therefore$ Coordinate of A is $\left(x - y\frac{dx}{dy}, 0\right)$

Radius vector $OP = \sqrt{x^2 + y^2}$

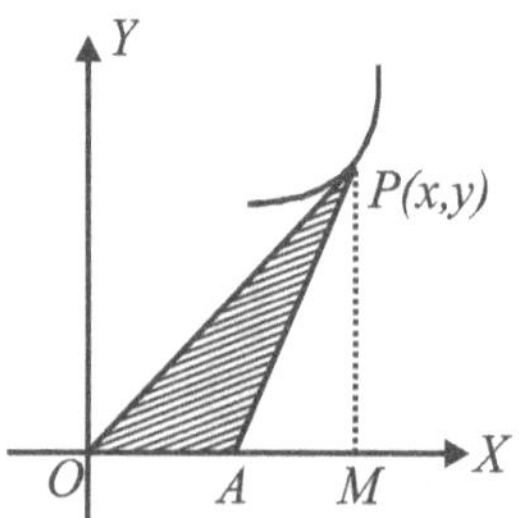

Area of $\Delta OAP = \Delta OPM - \Delta APM$

$$= \frac{1}{2}xy - \frac{1}{2}\left(y\frac{dx}{dy}\right) y = \pm a^2 \text{ (given)}$$

$\Rightarrow$ $$xy - y^2\frac{dx}{dy} = \pm 2a^2$$

$\Rightarrow$ $$y^2\frac{dx}{dy} - xy \pm 2a^2 = 0$$

$\Rightarrow$ $$\frac{dx}{dy} - \frac{x}{y} = \pm\frac{2a^2}{y^2}$$

This is a linear equation and

$$\text{I.F.} = e^{-\ln y} = \frac{1}{y}$$

$\therefore$ Solution is $x\left(\frac{1}{y}\right) = \mp 2a^2\int\frac{1}{y^3}dy + c$

$\Rightarrow$ $$\frac{x}{y} = \pm\frac{a^2}{y^2} + c \Rightarrow x = cy \pm \frac{a^2}{y},$$

where c is an arbitrary constant.

8. (a, b, c)

(a) $$f(\lambda x, \lambda y) = \frac{\lambda(x-y)}{\lambda^2(x^2+y^2)} = \lambda^{-1}f(x,y)$$

$\Rightarrow$ homogeneous of degree (– 1).

(b) $$f(\lambda x, \lambda y) = (\lambda x)^{1/3}(\lambda y)^{-2/3}\tan^{-1}\frac{x}{y}$$

$$= \lambda^{-1/3}x^{1/3}y^{-2/3}\tan^{-1}\frac{x}{y}$$

$$= \lambda^{-\frac{1}{3}}f(x,y)$$

$\Rightarrow$ homogeneous

(c) $$f(\lambda x, \lambda y) = \lambda x(\ln\sqrt{\lambda^2(x^2+y^2)} - \ln \lambda y) + \lambda y e^{x/y}$$

$$= \lambda x\left[\ln\left(\frac{\lambda\sqrt{(x^2+y^2)}}{\lambda y}\right)\right] + \lambda y e^{x/y}$$

$$= \lambda[x(\ln\sqrt{x^2+y^2} - \ln y) + ye^{x/y}]$$

$$= \lambda f(x,y)$$

$\Rightarrow$ homogeneous

(d) $$f(\lambda x, \lambda y) = \lambda x\left[\ln\frac{2\lambda^2x^2+\lambda^2y^2}{\lambda x\lambda(x+y)}\right] + \lambda^2x^2\tan\frac{x+2y}{3x-y}$$

$$= \lambda x\left[\ln\frac{2x^2+y^2}{x(x+y)}\right] + \lambda^2x^2\tan\frac{x+2y}{3x-y}$$

$\Rightarrow$ non homogeneous

9. (a, d) Differentiating the given equation, we have

$$2x + 2y\frac{dy}{dx} + 2g = 0$$

$\Rightarrow$ $$g = -\left(x + y\frac{dy}{dx}\right)$$

Putting this value in

$x^2 + y^2 + 2gx + c = 0$, we have

$$x^2 + y^2 - 2x\left(x + y\frac{dy}{dx}\right) + c = 0$$

Replacing $\frac{dy}{dx}$ by $-\frac{dx}{dy}$, we have the differential equation of orthogonal trajectories as

$$y^2 - x^2 + 2xy\frac{dy}{dx} + c = 0$$

$\Rightarrow$ $$2x\frac{dx}{dy} - \frac{1}{y}x^2 = -\frac{c}{y} - y$$

Putting $x^2 = v$, we have $\frac{dv}{dy} - \frac{1}{y}v = -\frac{c}{y} - y$,

which is linear in v and y whose I.F. is $\frac{1}{y}$. Hence

$$\frac{v}{y} = \int\left(-\frac{c}{y^2} - 1\right)dy + c' = \frac{c}{y} - y + c'$$

$\Rightarrow$ $x^2 + y^2 - c'y - c = 0$, which represent system of circles with center on y-axis.

10. (8) Differentiating both sides of the given equation w.r.t. x, we get

$$x.y(x) + \int_0^x y(t)dt.1 = (x+1)x.y(x) + \int_0^x ty(t)dt$$

or $$\int_0^x y(t)dt = x^2y(x) + \int_0^x ty(t)dt$$

Again differentiating both sides w.r.t. x

$$y(x) = x^2y'(x) + y(x)2x + xy(x)$$

$\Rightarrow$ $$(1-3x)y(x) = x^2y'(x)$$

$\Rightarrow \quad \frac{y'(x)}{y(x)} = \left(\frac{1}{x^2} - \frac{3}{x}\right)$

Integrating, we get

$\ln y(x) = -\frac{1}{x} - 3\ln x + \ln c$

$\Rightarrow \quad \ln\left(\frac{x^3 y(x)}{c}\right) = -\frac{1}{x}$ or $\frac{x^3 y(x)}{c} = e^{-1/x}$

$\Rightarrow \quad y(x) = \frac{ce^{-1/x}}{x^3}$

So, $y(1) = e \Rightarrow c = e^2$

$\therefore \quad y\left(\frac{1}{2}\right) = 8$

11. (8)

Let population $= x$, at time t years

Give $\frac{dx}{dt} \propto x \Rightarrow \frac{dx}{dt} = kx$

Where k is constant of proportionality or $\frac{dx}{x} = kdt$

Integrating, we get $\ln x = kt + \ln c \Rightarrow \frac{x}{c} = e^{kt}$

or $x = ce^{kt}$

If initially i.e., when time $t = 0, x = x_0$ then $x_0 = ce^0 = c$

$\therefore \; x = x_0 e^{kt}$

Given $x = 2x_0$ when $t = 30$ then $2x_0 = x_0 e^{30k}$

$\Rightarrow \quad 2 = e^{30k}$ .... (1)

$\therefore \quad \ln 2 = 30k$

To find t, when it tripples, $x = 3x_0$

$\therefore \quad 3x_0 = x_0 e^{kt} \Rightarrow 3 = e^{kt}$ ....(2)

$\therefore \quad \ln 3 = kt$

Diving (2) by (1) then $\frac{t}{30} = \frac{\ln 3}{\ln 2}$

or $t = 30 \times \frac{\ln 3}{\ln 2} = 30 \times 1.5849 = 48$ years. (approx.)

$\Rightarrow \; 6m = 48$

$\Rightarrow \; m = 8$

12. (6)

Given $y = C_1 e^{m_1 x} + C_2 e^{m_2 x} + C_3 e^{m_3 x}$ ...... (1)

so, $y_1 = C_1 m_1 e^{m_1 x} + C_2 m_2 e^{m_2 x} + C_3 m_3 e^{m_3 x}$

$= m_1 (y - C_2 e^{m_2 x} - C_3 e^{m_3 x}) + C_2 m_2 e^{m_2 x} + C_3 m_3 e^{m_3 x}$ {from (1)}

$= m_1 y + C_2 (m_2 - m_1) e^{m_2} + C_3 (m_3 - m_1) e^{m_3 x}$ ...(2)

Next $y_2 = m_1 y_1 + C_2 m_2 (m_2 - m_1) e^{m_2 x} + C_3 m_3 (m_3 - m_1) e^{m_3 x}$

$= m_1 y_1 + m_2 [y_1 - m_1 y - C_3 (m_3 - m_1) e^{m_3 x}] + C_3 m_3 (m_3 - m_1) e^{m_3 x}$ [from (2)]

$= (m_1 + m_2) y_1 - m_1 m_2 y + C_3 (m_3 - m_1)(m_3 - m_2) e^{m_3 x}$ ......(3)

Further, $y_3 = (m_1 + m_2) y_2 - m_1 m_2 y_1 + C_3 m_3 (m_3 - m_1)(m_3 - m_2) e^{m_2 x}$

$= (m_1 + m_2) y_2 - m_1 m_2 y_1 + m_3 [y_2 - (m_1 + m_2) y_1 + m_1 m_2 y]$ [from (3)]

$= (m_1 + m_2 + m_3) y_2 - (m_1 m_2 + m_1 m_3 + m_2 m_3) y_1 + m_1 m_2 m_3 y$

$= 0.y_2 - (-7) y_1 - 6y \Rightarrow y_3 - 7y_1 + 6y = 0$

13. (2) The given differential equation is in the form of a polynomial in the differential coefficient $\frac{dy}{dx}, \frac{d^2y}{dx^2}$ and $\frac{d^3y}{dx^3}$. The differential coefficient $\frac{d^3y}{dx^3}$ is the highest order differential coefficient out of $\frac{dy}{dx}, \frac{d^2y}{dx^2}$ and $\frac{d^3y}{dx^3}$. The highest exponent of this highest order differential coefficient $\frac{d^3y}{dx^3}$ is 2. Hence degree of the given differential equation is 2.

For Qs.14 – 15

Integrating $\frac{d^2y}{dx^2} = 6x - 4$, we get

$\frac{dy}{dx} = 3x^2 - 4x + A$

When $x = 1, \frac{dy}{dx} = 0$ and hence $A = 1$.

$\therefore \quad \frac{dy}{dx} = 3x^2 - 4x + 1$ ...(i)

Integrating, we get $y = x^3 - 2x^2 + x + B$.

When $x = 1, y = 5$, then $B = 5$.

Thus, we have, $y = x^3 - 2x^2 + x + 5$

From equation (i), we get the critical points $x = 1/3$, $x = 1$

At the critical point $x = \frac{1}{3}, \frac{d^2y}{dx^2}$ is – ve

Therefore, at $x = 1/3$, y has a local maximum.

At $x = 1$, $\frac{d^2y}{dx^2}$ is + ve.

Therefore, at $x = 1$, y has a local minimum.

Also $f(1) = 5$, $f\left(\frac{1}{3}\right) = \frac{157}{27}$, $f(0) = 5$, $f(2) = 7$

Hence the global maximum value = 7 and the global minimum value = 5

14. (c) **15. (a)**

For Qs. 16 – 18

$$(1+x^2)\frac{dy}{dx} + 2xy - 4x^2 = 0$$

$$\text{I.F.} = e^{\int \frac{2x}{1+x^2}dx} = 1+x^2$$

So, $y(1+x^2) = \int \frac{4x^2}{1+x^2}(1+x^2)dx + c$

$$y(1+x^2) = \frac{4}{3}x^3 + c$$

Similarly for, $(x+2y^3)\frac{dy}{dx} = y$

$$\text{I.F.} = \frac{1}{y}$$

So, $x = y^3 + cy$

For, $(1+x)\frac{dy}{dx} - xy = 1 - x$

I.F. $= e^{-x}(1+x)$

So, $y(1+x) = x + ce^x$

For, $\frac{dy}{dx} + \frac{y}{(1-x^2)^{3/2}} = \frac{x+\sqrt{1-x^2}}{(1-x^2)^2}$

$$\text{I.F.} = e^{\frac{x}{\sqrt{1-x^2}}}$$

$$y = \frac{x}{\sqrt{1-x^2}} + ce^{-x/\sqrt{1-x^2}}$$

16. (d)

17. (c)

18. (a)

19. (A) → (q,s) ; (B) → (r) ; (C) → (q,s) ; (D) → (p,t)

We have

$$\frac{dy}{dx} = y + \int_0^1 y\,dx \Rightarrow \frac{d}{dx}\left(\frac{dy}{dx}\right) = \frac{dy}{dx} + 0 \Rightarrow \frac{d}{dx}p = p$$

(where $p = \frac{dy}{dx}$)

Integrating we get $\ln p = x + \ln k \Rightarrow p = ke^x$.

$$\therefore \frac{dy}{dx} = k\,e^x \quad .....(1)$$

Integrating again $y = ke^x + c$ .....(2)

Now $f(0) = 1 \Rightarrow 1 = c + k$ or $c = 1 - k$

Also $\frac{dy}{dx} = y + \int_0^1 y\,dx \Rightarrow ke^x = ke^x + 1 - k + \int_0^1 (ke^x + 1 - k)\,dx$

$$\therefore 0 = 1 - k + ke + 1 - k - k \Rightarrow k = \frac{2}{3-e}$$

Clearly $\left.\frac{dy}{dx}\right|_{x=0} = f'(0) = k = \frac{2}{3-e}$

$$\left.\frac{d^2y}{dx^2}\right|_{x=0} = f''(0) = k = \frac{2}{3-e}$$

Also, $y = f(x) = \frac{2e^x + 1 - e}{3-e} \Rightarrow f(1) = \frac{e+1}{3-e}$

$$\lim_{x\to 0}\frac{f(x)-1}{x} = \lim_{x\to 0}\frac{2e^x + 1 - e - 3 + e}{x(3-e)}$$

$$= \frac{2}{3-e}\lim_{x\to 0}\frac{e^x - 1}{x} = \frac{2}{3-e}$$

20. (A) → (p, q, r); (B) → (p); (C) → (q); (D) → (q, s)

(A) $f(x) = \int_0^x e^t \sin(x-t)\,dt$

$$= \int_0^x e^{x-t}\sin(t)\,dt$$

$$f(x) = e^x\int_0^x e^{-t}\sin t\,dt$$

$$f'(x) = e^x.e^{-x}\sin x + \left(\int_0^x e^{-t}\sin t\,dt\right)e^x$$

$f'(x) = \sin x + f(x)$ ...(i)

$f''(x) = \cos x + f'(x) = \cos x + \sin x + f(x)$ [Using (i)]

$f''(x) - f(x) = \sin x + \cos x$ ...(ii)

$g(x) = \sin x + \cos x \Rightarrow g(x) \in [-\sqrt{2}, \sqrt{2}]$

(B) $x = \tan^{-1} t \Rightarrow \dfrac{dx}{dt} = \dfrac{1}{1+t^2}$

$$\frac{dy}{dx} = \frac{dy}{dt} \cdot \frac{dt}{dx} = \frac{dy}{dt}(1+t^2) \qquad \ldots(i)$$

$$\frac{d^2y}{dx^2} = \frac{d}{dt}\left[\frac{dy}{dt}(1+t^2)\right] \cdot \frac{dt}{dx}$$

$$= \left[\frac{dy}{dt}2t + (1+t^2)\frac{d^2y}{dt^2}\right](1+t^2) \qquad \ldots(ii)$$

Hence the given differential equation

$\dfrac{d^2y}{dx^2} + xy\dfrac{dy}{dx} + \sec^2 x > 0$, becomes

$$(1+t^2)\left[2t\frac{dy}{dt} + (1+t^2)\frac{d^2y}{dt^2}\right]$$

$$+ y\tan^{-1} t\left[\frac{dy}{dt}(1+t^2)\right] + (1+t^2) = 0$$

Cancelling $(1 + t^2)$ throughout we get

$$(1+t^2)\frac{d^2y}{dt^2} + (2t + y\tan^{-1} t)\frac{dy}{dt} = -1$$

$\Rightarrow$ $k = -1$

(C) Let $a = \cos\theta$, $b = \sin\theta$

$\therefore$ $E = ab(a^2 - b^2) = \cos\theta \sin\theta (\cos 2\theta)$

$= \dfrac{1}{2}\sin 2\theta \cos 2\theta = \dfrac{1}{4}\sin 2\theta.$

$\Rightarrow$ $-\dfrac{1}{4} \le E \le \dfrac{1}{4}$; Possible vlaue = 0

(D) Obviously $D_1 = D_2 = D_3 = 0$

$$D = \begin{vmatrix} 1 & -\lambda & -1 \\ \lambda & -1 & -1 \\ 1 & 1 & -1 \end{vmatrix} \ne 0$$

$$= \begin{vmatrix} 0 & -\lambda & -1 \\ \lambda - 1 & -1 & -1 \\ 0 & 1 & -1 \end{vmatrix} = (\lambda - 1)(\lambda + 1) \ne 0$$

$\Rightarrow$ $\lambda \ne 1, -1$

Hence, $\lambda = R - \{-1, 1\}$

1. (d) $\vec{a} = 2\hat{i} + \hat{j} - 2\hat{k}, \vec{b} = \hat{i} + \hat{j}$

$\Rightarrow |\vec{a}| = 3$

and $\vec{a} \times \vec{b} = \begin{vmatrix} \hat{i} & \hat{j} & \hat{k} \\ 2 & 1 & -2 \\ 1 & 1 & 0 \end{vmatrix} = 2\hat{i} - 2\hat{j} + \hat{k}$

$|\vec{a} \times \vec{b}| = \sqrt{4+4+1} = 3$

Now, $|\vec{c} - \vec{a}| = 2\sqrt{2} \Rightarrow |\vec{c} - \vec{a}|^2 = 8$

$\Rightarrow |\vec{c} - \vec{a}|.(\vec{c} - \vec{a}) = 8$

$\Rightarrow |\vec{c}|^2 + |\vec{a}|^2 - 2\vec{c}.\vec{a} = 8$

$\Rightarrow |\vec{c}|^2 + 9 - 2|\vec{c}| = 8$

$\Rightarrow (|\vec{c}| - 1)^2 = 0 \Rightarrow |\vec{c}| = 1$

$\therefore |(\vec{a} \times \vec{b}) \times \vec{c}| = |\vec{a} \times \vec{b}||\vec{c}| \sin 30° = 3 \times 1 \times \frac{1}{2} = \frac{3}{2}$

2. (b) $(\hat{x} + \hat{y} + \hat{z})^2 \geq 0$

$\Rightarrow \quad 3 + 2\Sigma\, \hat{x}.\hat{y} \geq 0$

$\Rightarrow \quad 2\Sigma\, \hat{x}.\hat{y} \geq -3$

Now, $|\hat{x} + \hat{y}|^2 + |\hat{y} + \hat{z}|^2 + |\hat{z} + \hat{x}|^2$

$= 6 + 2\Sigma\, \hat{x}.\hat{y} \geq 6 + (-3)$

$\Rightarrow \quad |\hat{x} + \hat{y}|^2 + |\hat{y} + \hat{z}|^2 + |\hat{z} + \hat{x}|^2 \geq 3$

3. (d)

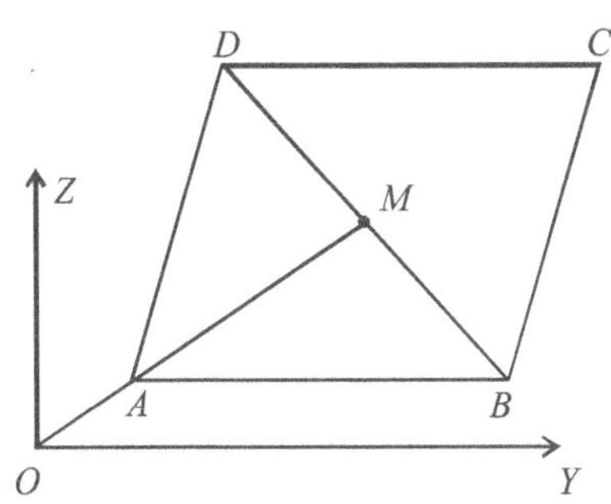

In a parallelogram, diagonals bisect each other. So, mid point of DB is also the mid-point of AC.

Mid-point of $M = 2\hat{i} - \hat{j}$

Direction ratio of $OC = (1, -5, -5)$

Direction ratio of $OM = (2, -1, 0)$

Angle θ between OM and OC is given by

$$\cos\theta = \frac{(1 \times 2) + (-5)(-1) + (-5)(0)}{\sqrt{2^2 + (-1)^2}\sqrt{(1)^2 + (-5)^2 + (-5)^2}}$$

$$= \frac{2+5}{\sqrt{5}\sqrt{51}} = \frac{7}{\sqrt{5}\sqrt{51}}$$

Projection of $\vec{OM}$ on $\vec{OC}$ is given by

$$|OM|.\cos\theta = \sqrt{5} \times \frac{7}{\sqrt{5} \times \sqrt{51}} = \frac{7}{\sqrt{51}}$$

4. (b) $\vec{p}.\vec{q} = ab + bc + ca$

$= \sqrt{a^2 + b^2 + c^2}\sqrt{b^2 + c^2 + a^2} \cos\theta$

$\Rightarrow \quad \cos\theta = \frac{ab + bc + ca}{(a^2 + b^2 + c^2)}$

$\Rightarrow \quad$ Now $(a-b)^2 + (b-c)^2 + (c-a)^2 \geq 0$

$a^2 + b^2 + c^2 \geq ab + bc + ca$

$\Rightarrow \quad \frac{ab + bc + ca}{a^2 + b^2 + c^2} \leq 1$

Also

$(a + b + c)^2 = a^2 + b^2 + c^2 + 2(ab + bc + ca) \geq 0$

$\Rightarrow \quad \frac{ab + bc + ca}{a^2 + b^2 + c^2} \geq -1/2$

$\Rightarrow \quad -\frac{1}{2} \leq \cos\theta \leq 1$

$\Rightarrow \quad \theta \in [0, 2\pi/3].$

5. (d) Suppose that $\vec{a}, \vec{b}, \vec{c}$ are coplanar.

$$\Rightarrow \begin{vmatrix} \cos\alpha & 1 & 1 \\ 1 & \cos\beta & 1 \\ 1 & 1 & \cos\gamma \end{vmatrix} = 0$$

applying $R_2 \longrightarrow R_2 - R_1$ and $R_3 \longrightarrow R_1$

$$\text{or} \begin{vmatrix} \cos\alpha & 1 & 1 \\ 1 - \cos\alpha & \cos\beta - 1 & 1 \\ 1 - \cos\alpha & 0 & \cos\gamma - 1 \end{vmatrix} = 0$$

or $\cos\alpha(\cos\beta - 1)(\cos\gamma - 1)$

$-(1 - \cos\alpha)(\cos\gamma - 1) - (1 - \cos\alpha)(\cos\beta - 1) = 0$

Dividing through out by $(1-\cos\alpha)(1-\cos\beta)(1-\cos\gamma)$; we get

$$\frac{\cos\alpha}{1-\cos\alpha}+\frac{1}{1-\cos\beta}+\frac{1}{1-\cos\gamma}=0$$

$$\Rightarrow \frac{-(1-\cos\alpha)+1}{(1-\cos\alpha)}+\frac{1}{(1-\cos\beta)}+\frac{1}{(1-\cos\gamma)}=0$$

$$\Rightarrow -1+\frac{1}{1-\cos\alpha}+\frac{1}{1-\cos\beta}+\frac{1}{1-\cos\gamma}=0$$

$$\Rightarrow \frac{1}{1-\cos\alpha}+\frac{1}{1-\cos\beta}+\frac{1}{1-\cos\gamma}=1$$

$\Rightarrow \text{cosec}^2\frac{\alpha}{2}+\text{cosec}^2\frac{\beta}{2}+\text{cosec}^2\frac{\gamma}{2}=2$ which is not possible as $\text{cosec}^2\frac{\alpha}{2}\geq 1,\ \text{cosec}^2\frac{\beta}{2}\geq 1,\ \text{cosec}^2\frac{\gamma}{2}\geq 1.$

So the vectors cannot be coplanar.

6. **(a)** $\vec{a}=(1, 3, \sin 2\alpha)$ makes an obtuse angle with the z-axis.

$\therefore\ \sin 2\alpha < 0$

Since $\vec{b}$ and $\vec{c}$ are orthogonal

$\Rightarrow \vec{b}.\vec{c}=0.$ ....(1)

$\therefore \tan^2\alpha-\tan\alpha-6=0 \Rightarrow \tan\alpha=3$ or -2.

If $\tan\alpha=3$, then $\sin 2\alpha=\frac{2\tan\alpha}{1+\tan^2\alpha}=\frac{3}{5}>0$, which is not possible (from (1))

$\therefore\ \tan\alpha=-2.$

Again $\tan 2\alpha=\frac{2\tan\alpha}{1-\tan^2\alpha}=\frac{4}{3}>0$. Also $\sin 2\alpha<0$.

$\therefore 2\alpha$ lies in the third quadrant

$\Rightarrow \frac{\alpha}{2}$ lies in the first quadrant

$\therefore \sqrt{\sin\frac{\alpha}{2}}$ is valid and $\alpha=(4n+1)\pi-\tan^{-1}2.$

7. **(b,d)** The point that divides $5\hat{i}$ and $5\hat{j}$ in the ratio of $k:1$ is $\frac{k(5\hat{j})+(5\hat{i}).1}{k+1}$

$$\therefore \vec{b}=\frac{5\hat{i}+5k\hat{j}}{k+1}$$

also $|\vec{b}|\leq\sqrt{37} \Rightarrow \frac{1}{k+1}\sqrt{25+25k^2}\leq\sqrt{37}$

$$\Rightarrow 5\sqrt{1+k^2}\leq\sqrt{37}(k+1)$$

Squaring both sides

$25(1+k^2)\leq 37(k^2+2k+1)$ or $6k^2+37k+6\geq 0$

$\Rightarrow (6k+1)(k+6)\geq 0$

$$k\in(-\infty,-6)\cup\left[-\frac{1}{6},\ \infty\right)$$

8. **(a, b, c)** $\left\{(\vec{a}\times\vec{b})\times(\vec{b}\times\vec{c})\right\}\times(\vec{c}\times\vec{a})=\vec{0}$

$$\left\{(\vec{a}\cdot\vec{b})\vec{c}-(\vec{b}\cdot\vec{c})\vec{a}\right\}\left[\vec{a}\,\vec{b}\,\vec{c}\right]=0$$

$$(\vec{a}\cdot\vec{b})\vec{c}=(\vec{b}\cdot\vec{c})\vec{a}$$

Leads to $2\alpha^3+10\alpha+12=0,\ \alpha^2+6\alpha=0,$ $6\alpha^2-6\alpha-6=0$ which do not have a common solution.

If $\left[\vec{a}\ \vec{b}\ \vec{c}\right]=0\Rightarrow\alpha=\frac{2}{3}$

$\alpha=0$

then $\left[\vec{a}\ \vec{b}\ \vec{c}\right]=-10$

$\vec{a}.\vec{b}=6$

$\vec{b}.\vec{c}=0$

$\therefore$ The vector product is $-60(2\hat{i}+\hat{k})$.

9. **(a, c, d)**

$\vec{a}+\vec{b}+\vec{c}=\vec{o}$

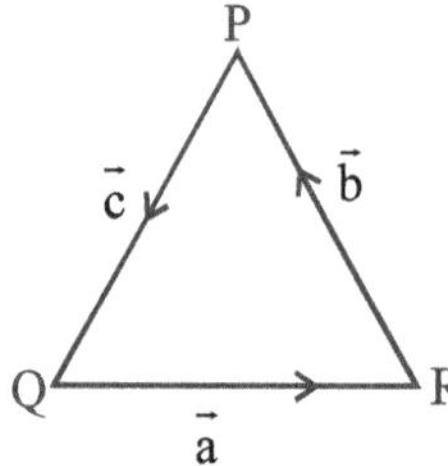

$$\Rightarrow |\vec{b}+\vec{c}|^2=|-\vec{a}|^2$$

$$\Rightarrow |\vec{b}|^2+|\vec{c}|^2+2\vec{b}.\vec{c}=|\vec{a}|^2$$

$$\Rightarrow 48+|\vec{c}|^2+48=144\Rightarrow|\vec{c}|^2=48\Rightarrow|\vec{c}|=4\sqrt{3}$$

$$\therefore \frac{|\vec{c}|^2}{2}-|\vec{a}|=\frac{48}{2}-12=12$$

$$\frac{|\vec{c}|^2}{2}+|\vec{a}|=24\neq 30$$

Also $|\vec{b}|=|\vec{c}| \Rightarrow \angle Q=\angle R$

and $\cos(180-P)=\dfrac{\vec{b}.\vec{c}}{|\vec{b}||\vec{c}|}=\dfrac{1}{2}$

$\Rightarrow \quad \angle P=120° \therefore \angle Q=\angle R=30°$

Again $\vec{a}+\vec{b}+\vec{c}=0 \Rightarrow \vec{a}\times(\vec{a}+\vec{b}+\vec{c})=\vec{0} \Rightarrow \vec{a}\times\vec{b}=\vec{c}\times\vec{a}$

$\therefore \quad |\vec{a}\times\vec{b}+\vec{c}\times\vec{a}|=2|\vec{a}\times\vec{b}|=2\times 12\times 4\sqrt{3}\times\sin 150=48\sqrt{3}$

And $\vec{a}.\vec{b}=12\times 4\sqrt{3}\times\cos 150=-72$

10. (a, b, c) $|\vec{x}|=|\vec{y}|=|\vec{z}|=\sqrt{2}$

Angle between each pair is $\dfrac{\pi}{3}$

$$\vec{a}=\lambda\left[\vec{x}\times\left(\vec{y}\times\vec{z}\right)\right]$$

$$=\lambda\left[\left(\vec{x}\cdot\vec{z}\right)\vec{y}-\left(\vec{x}\cdot\vec{y}\right)\vec{z}\right]$$

$$=\lambda\left[\left(\sqrt{2}.\sqrt{2}\cos\frac{\pi}{3}\right)\vec{y}-\left(\sqrt{2}.\sqrt{2}\cos\frac{\pi}{3}\right)\vec{z}\right]$$

$$=\lambda\left(\vec{y}-\vec{z}\right)$$

$$\vec{b}=\mu\left[\vec{y}\times\left(\vec{z}\times\vec{x}\right)\right]$$

$$=\mu\left[\left(\vec{y}.\vec{x}\right)\vec{z}-\left(\vec{y}.\vec{z}\right)\vec{x}\right]$$

$$=\mu\left[\left(\sqrt{2}.\sqrt{2}.\cos\frac{\pi}{3}\right)\vec{z}-\left(\sqrt{2}.\sqrt{2}.\cos\frac{\pi}{3}\right)\vec{x}\right]$$

$$=\mu\left(\vec{z}-\vec{x}\right)$$

Now $\vec{b}.\vec{z}=\mu\left[\vec{z}.\vec{z}-\vec{x}.\vec{z}\right]$

$=\mu(2-1)=\mu$

$\therefore \vec{b}=\left(\vec{b}.\vec{z}\right)\left(\vec{z}-\vec{x}\right)$ is correct

Also $\vec{a}.\vec{y}=\lambda\left(\vec{y}.\vec{y}-\vec{z}.\vec{y}\right)=\lambda(2-1)=\lambda$

$\therefore \vec{a}=\left(\vec{a}.\vec{y}\right)\left(\vec{y}-\vec{z}\right)$ is also correct

$$\vec{a}.\vec{b}=\lambda\mu\left(\vec{y}.\vec{z}-\vec{y}.\vec{x}-\vec{z}.\vec{z}+\vec{z}.\vec{x}\right)$$

$$=\lambda\mu(1-1-2+1)=-\lambda\mu=-\left(\vec{a}.\vec{y}\right)\left(\vec{b}.\vec{z}\right)$$

$\therefore$ (c) is correct.

$$-\left(\vec{a}.\vec{y}\right)\left(\vec{z}-\vec{y}\right)=\lambda\left(\vec{z}-\vec{y}\right)=-\vec{a}$$

(d) is not correct.

11. (4)

We have $\overrightarrow{AB}=d\hat{i}$. Let $\overrightarrow{AC}=x\hat{i}+y\hat{j}$. Then we have

$AC=d \Rightarrow x^2+y^2=d^2$,

$\overrightarrow{AB}.\overrightarrow{AC}=AB\times AC\times\cos 60°$

[ΔABC in xy plane is equilateral]

$d\hat{i}.(x\hat{i}+y\hat{i})=d.d\dfrac{1}{2}$

$\Rightarrow \; dx=\dfrac{d^2}{2} \Rightarrow x=\dfrac{d}{2}$ and $y=\pm\dfrac{\sqrt{3}}{2}d$

Now, let $\overrightarrow{AD}=p\hat{i}+q\hat{j}+r\hat{k}$. Then

$AD=d \Rightarrow p^2+q^2+r^2=d^2$;

$\overrightarrow{AD}.\overrightarrow{AB}=\overrightarrow{AD}.\overrightarrow{AC}=\dfrac{d^2}{2}$

$\Rightarrow \; pd=px+qy=\dfrac{d^2}{2} \Rightarrow p=\dfrac{d}{2}$

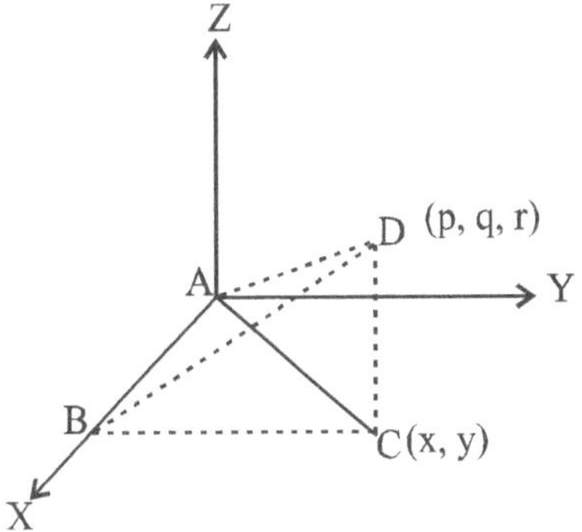

If $y=\dfrac{\sqrt{3}}{2}d$, then $q=\dfrac{pd-px}{q}=\dfrac{d}{2\sqrt{3}}$

and $r^2 = d^2 - p^2 - q^2 = \frac{2d^2}{3} \Rightarrow r = \pm\frac{\sqrt{2}}{\sqrt{3}}d$

If $y = -\frac{\sqrt{3}}{2}d$, then $q = -\frac{d}{2\sqrt{3}}$ and $r = \pm\frac{\sqrt{2}}{\sqrt{3}}d$.

So, $\overrightarrow{AB}, \overrightarrow{AC}$ and $\overrightarrow{AD}$ can be

(i) $d\hat{i}, \frac{d}{2}\hat{i} + \frac{d\sqrt{3}}{2}\hat{j}, \frac{d}{2}\hat{i} + \frac{d}{2\sqrt{3}}\hat{j} + \frac{d\sqrt{2}}{\sqrt{3}}\hat{k}$

(ii) $d\hat{i}, \frac{d}{2}\hat{i} + \frac{d\sqrt{3}}{2}\hat{j}, \frac{d}{2}\hat{i} + \frac{d}{2\sqrt{3}}\hat{j} - \frac{d\sqrt{2}}{\sqrt{3}}\hat{k}$

(iii) $d\hat{i}, \frac{d}{2}\hat{i} - \frac{d\sqrt{3}}{2}\hat{j}, \frac{d}{2}\hat{i} - \frac{d}{2\sqrt{3}}\hat{j} + \frac{d\sqrt{2}}{\sqrt{3}}\hat{k}$

(iv) $d\hat{i}, \frac{d}{2}\hat{i} - \frac{d\sqrt{3}}{2}\hat{j}, \frac{d}{2}\hat{i} - \frac{d}{2\sqrt{3}}\hat{j} - \frac{d\sqrt{2}}{\sqrt{3}}\hat{k}$

Hence, 4 tetrahedra are possible.

12. (2)

$\vec{w} + (\vec{w} \times \vec{u}) = \vec{v}$ ....(i)

$\Rightarrow \vec{w} \times \vec{u} = \vec{v} - \vec{w}$

$\Rightarrow (\vec{w} \times \vec{u})^2 = \vec{v}^2 + \vec{w}^2 - 2\vec{v}.\vec{w}$

$\Rightarrow 2\vec{v}.\vec{w} = 1 + \vec{w}^2 - (\vec{u} \times \vec{w})^2$ ....(ii)

Also taking dot product of (i) with $\vec{v}$ we get

$\vec{w}.\vec{v} + (\vec{w} \times \vec{u}).\vec{v} = \vec{v}.\vec{v}$

$\Rightarrow \vec{v}.(\vec{w} \times \vec{u}) = 1 - \vec{w}.\vec{v}$ ....(iii) $[\vec{v}.\vec{v} = |\vec{v}|^2 = 1]$

Now $\vec{v}.(\vec{w} \times \vec{u}) = 1 - \frac{1}{2}(1 + w^2 - (\vec{u} \times \vec{w})^2)$

(Using (ii) and (iii))

$= \frac{1}{2} - \frac{w^2}{2} + \frac{(\vec{u} \times \vec{w})^2}{2}$ $(\because 0 \le \cos^2\theta \le 1)$

$= \frac{1}{2}(1 - w^2 + w^2 \sin^2\theta) = \frac{1}{2}(1 - w^2\cos^2\theta)$ ....(iv)

as we know $0 \le w^2\cos^2\theta \le w^2$

$\therefore \frac{1}{2} \ge \frac{1 - w^2\cos^2\theta}{2} \ge \frac{1 - w^2}{2}$ .... (v)

$\Rightarrow \frac{1 - w^2\cos^2\theta}{2} \le \frac{1}{2}$

From (iv) and (v) $|\vec{v}.(\vec{w} \times \vec{u})| \le \frac{1}{2}$

$\Rightarrow |\vec{v}.(\vec{w} \times \vec{u})|^{-1} \ge 2$ or $|(\vec{u} \times \vec{v}).\vec{w}|^{-1} \ge 2$

13. (5)

$\vec{a}.\vec{b} = 0 \Rightarrow x_1 + x_2 + x_3 = 0$

We have to obtain the number of integral solution of this equation $\Rightarrow$ Coefficient of

x^0 in $(x^{-3} + x^{-2} + x^{-1} + x^0 + x + x^2)^3$

$=$ Coeff. of x^0 in $\left(\frac{1 + x + x^2 + x^3 + x^4 + x^5}{x^3}\right)^3$

$=$ Coeff. of x^9 in $(1 - x^6)^3(1 - x)^{-3} = {}^{11}C_9 - 3.{}^5C_3 = 25$

14. (5)

Let $P(x_1 y_1)$ and $Q(x_2, y_2)$ be the two points on $y = 2^{x+2}$

$\overrightarrow{OP}.\hat{i} =$ Projection on $\overrightarrow{OP}$ on the x-axis

$\Rightarrow x_1 = -1$ $[\because \overrightarrow{OP}.\hat{i} = -1]$

Also (x_1, y_1) lies on $y = 2^{x+2}$

$\therefore y_1 = 2^{x_1+2} \Rightarrow y_1 = 2$

Also $\overrightarrow{OQ}.\ \hat{i} =$ projection of $\overrightarrow{OQ}$ on x-axis

$\Rightarrow x_2 = 2$ [given $\overrightarrow{OQ}.\hat{i} = 2$]

as (x_2, y_2) lies on $y = 2^{x+2}$

$\therefore y_2 = 2^{x_2+2} \Rightarrow y_2 = 16$

Thus, $\overrightarrow{OP} = x_1\hat{i} + y_1\hat{j} = -\hat{i} + 2\hat{j}$

and $\overrightarrow{OQ} = x_2\hat{i} + y_2\hat{j} = 2\hat{i} + 16\hat{j} \Rightarrow \overrightarrow{OQ} - 4\overrightarrow{OP} = 6\hat{i} + 8\hat{j}$

$\Rightarrow |\overrightarrow{OQ} - 4\overrightarrow{OP}| = \sqrt{36 + 64} = 10 = 2k$

15. (4) $\vec{a}.\vec{b} = \vec{b}.\vec{c} = \vec{c}.\vec{a} = \cos\frac{\pi}{3} = \frac{1}{2}$

Given $p\vec{a} + q\vec{b} + r\vec{c} = \vec{a} \times \vec{b} + \vec{b} \times \vec{c}$

Taking its dot product with $\vec{a}, \vec{b}, \vec{c}$, we get

$$p+\frac{1}{2}q+\frac{1}{2}r=\left[\vec{a}\ \vec{b}\ \vec{c}\right] \quad ...(1)$$

$$\frac{1}{2}p+q+\frac{1}{2}r=0 \quad ...(2)$$

$$\frac{1}{2}p+\frac{1}{2}q+r=\left[\vec{a}\ \vec{b}\ \vec{c}\right] \quad ...(3)$$

From (1) and (3), $p=r$ Using (2) $q=-p$

$$\therefore \frac{p^2+2q^2+r^2}{q^2}=\frac{p^2+2p^2+p^2}{p^2}=4$$

16. (a) Vector equation of CD and BE are

$$\vec{r}=\hat{i}-2\hat{j}+4\hat{k}+\frac{\lambda}{3}(7\hat{j}-7\hat{k}) \quad ....(1)$$

and $\vec{r}=-\hat{i}+\hat{j}+\hat{k}+\frac{\mu}{3}(7\hat{i}-7\hat{j}+7\hat{k}) \quad ....(2)$

At point of intersection P,

$$1=-1+\frac{7\mu}{3}, -2+\frac{7\lambda}{3}=1-\frac{7\mu}{3}, 4-\frac{7\lambda}{3}=1+\frac{7\mu}{3}$$

$$\mu=\frac{6}{7}, \lambda=\frac{3}{7}$$

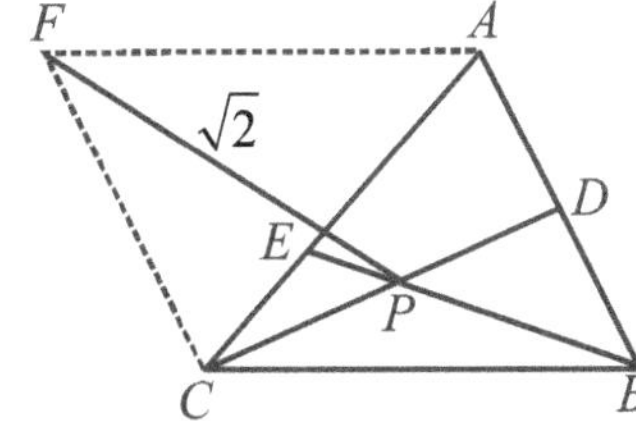

Position vector of P is $\hat{i}-\hat{j}+3\hat{k}$.

17. (a) Area of $\Delta ABC=\frac{1}{2}\left|\overrightarrow{AB}\times\overrightarrow{AC}\right|$

$$=\frac{1}{2}\left|(-3\hat{i}+\hat{j}-\hat{k})\times(-\hat{i}-2\hat{j}+2\hat{k})\right|$$

$$=\frac{1}{2}\left|7\hat{j}+7\hat{k}\right|=\frac{7\sqrt{2}}{2} \text{ sq. units.}$$

Volume of tetrahedron $ABCF$

$$=\frac{1}{3}\times\text{area of base}\times\text{height}=\frac{7}{3} \text{ cubic units.}$$

18. (b) $\vec{a}_1=\left[(2\hat{i}+3\hat{j}-6\hat{k}).\frac{(2\hat{i}-3\hat{j}+6\hat{k})}{7}\right]\frac{2\hat{i}-3\hat{j}+6\hat{k}}{7}$

$$=\frac{-41}{49}(2\hat{i}-3\hat{j}+6\hat{k})$$

$$\vec{a}_2=\frac{-41}{49}\left(2\hat{i}-3\hat{j}+6\hat{k}.\left(\frac{(-2\hat{i}+3\hat{j}+6\hat{k})}{7}\right)\right)\frac{(-2\hat{i}+3\hat{j}+6\hat{k})}{7}$$

$$=\frac{-41}{(49)^2}(-4-9+36)(-2\hat{i}+3\hat{j}+6\hat{k})$$

$$=\frac{943}{49^2}(2\hat{i}-3\hat{j}-6\hat{k})$$

19. (a) $\vec{a}_1.\vec{b}=\frac{-41}{49}(2\hat{i}-3\hat{j}+6\hat{k}).(2\hat{i}-3\hat{j}+6\hat{k})=-41$

20. (A)→(s); (B)→(q, r); (C)→(t); (D)→(p)

(A) $\vec{a}+\vec{b}+\vec{c}+\vec{d}=(\alpha+1)\vec{d}=(\beta+1)\vec{a}$

If $\alpha\neq-1$, then $\vec{d}=\left(\frac{\beta+1}{\alpha+1}\right)\vec{a}$

$$\Rightarrow \vec{a}+\vec{b}+\vec{c}=\alpha\vec{d}=\alpha\left(\frac{\beta+1}{\alpha+1}\right)\vec{a}$$

$$\Rightarrow \left\{1-\alpha\left(\frac{\beta+1}{\alpha+1}\right)\right\}\vec{a}+\vec{b}+\vec{c}=0\Rightarrow\vec{a},\vec{b},\vec{c}$$

are coplanar, which is against the given condition,

so $\alpha=-1$ and hence $\vec{a}+\vec{b}+\vec{c}+\vec{d}=\vec{0}$

(B) $|\vec{a}+\vec{b}|<1\Rightarrow|\vec{a}|^2+|\vec{b}|^2+2|\vec{a}||\vec{b}|\cos\theta<1$

$$\Rightarrow \cos\theta<-\frac{1}{2}$$

So, $\frac{2\pi}{3}<\theta<\pi$

(C) $\vec{a}\times(\vec{a}\times\vec{b})=(\vec{a}.\vec{b})\vec{a}-(\vec{a}.\vec{a})\vec{b}=-\vec{b}$

$$a\times\{\vec{a}\times(\vec{a}\times\vec{b})\}=\vec{a}\times-\vec{b}=-\vec{a}\times\vec{b}$$

$$a\times[\vec{a}\times\{\vec{a}\times(\vec{a}\times\vec{b})\}=\vec{a}\times(-\vec{a}\times\vec{b})$$

$$=(\vec{a}.\vec{a})\vec{b}-(\vec{a}.\vec{b})\vec{a}=\vec{b}$$

(D) $\vec{a}+\vec{b}=-\vec{c}\Rightarrow|\vec{a}+\vec{b}|^2=|\vec{c}|^2=1$

$$\Rightarrow \vec{a}.\vec{b}=-\frac{1}{2}\Rightarrow\theta=\frac{2\pi}{3}$$

1. **(c)**

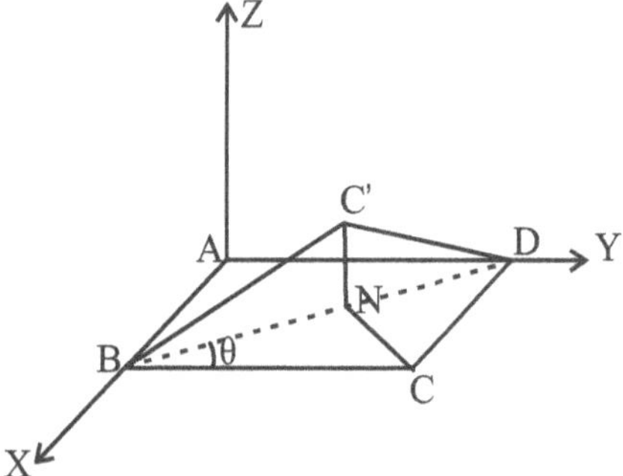

Let AB = CD = r and BC = AD = 2r

then $\tan\theta = \frac{CD}{BC} = \frac{1}{2}$

Also,

$\sin\theta = \frac{CN}{BC} \Rightarrow \frac{1}{\sqrt{5}} = \frac{CN}{2r} \Rightarrow CN = C'N = \frac{2}{\sqrt{5}}r$

In xy plane the equation of BD is $\frac{x}{r} + \frac{y}{2r} = 1$

$\Rightarrow 2x + y - 2r = 0$ and C is $(r, 2r)$

$\therefore$ Coordinates of N are given by

$\frac{x-r}{2} = \frac{y-2r}{1} = \frac{-(2r+2r-2r)}{5}$

$\therefore \quad x = r - \frac{4r}{5} = \frac{r}{5}$ and $y = 2r - \frac{2r}{5} = \frac{8r}{5}$

$\therefore$ Coordinate of C' in three dimensions are

$\left(\frac{r}{5}, \frac{8r}{5}, \frac{2}{\sqrt{5}}r\right)$

$\therefore AC' = \sqrt{\frac{r^2}{25} + \frac{64r^2}{25} + \frac{4r^2}{5}} = \frac{\sqrt{85}r}{5}$

2. **(c)** Let P be the image of O in the given plane.

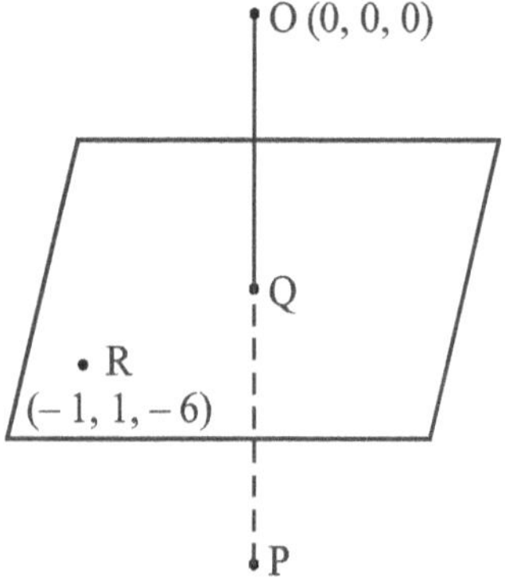

Equation of the plane, $4x - 3y + z + 13 = 0$

OP is normal to the plane, therefore direction ratio of OP are proportional to 4, – 3, 1

Since OP passes through (0, 0, 0) and has direction ratio proportional to 4, –3, 1. Therefore equation of OP is

$\frac{x-0}{4} = \frac{y-0}{-3} = \frac{z-0}{1} = r$ (let)

$\therefore x = 4r, y = -3r, z = r$

Let the coordinate of P be $(4r, -3r, r)$

Since Q be the mid point of OP

$\therefore Q = \left(2r, -\frac{3}{2}r, \frac{r}{2}\right)$

Since Q lies in the given plane

$4x - 3y + z + 13 = 0$

$\therefore 8r + \frac{9}{2}r + \frac{r}{2} + 13 = 0$

$\Rightarrow r = \frac{-13}{8 + \frac{9}{2} + \frac{1}{2}} = \frac{-26}{26} = -1$

$\therefore Q = \left(-2, \frac{3}{2}, -\frac{1}{2}\right)$

$QR = \sqrt{(-1+2)^2 + \left(1 - \frac{3}{2}\right)^2 + \left(-6 + \frac{1}{2}\right)^2}$

$= \sqrt{1 + \frac{1}{4} + \frac{121}{4}} = 3\sqrt{\frac{7}{2}}$

3. **(b)** Let equation of the required line be

$\frac{x-x_1}{a} = \frac{y-y_1}{b} = \frac{z-z_1}{c}$ ...(i)

Given two lines

$\frac{x}{1} = \frac{y}{-1} = \frac{z}{1}$ ...(ii)

and $\frac{x-1}{0} = \frac{y+1}{0} = \frac{z}{1}$ ...(iii)

Since the line (i) is perpendicular to both the lines (ii) and (iii), therefore

$a - b + c = 0$ ...(iv)

$-2b + c = 0$ ...(v)

From (iv) and (v) c = $2b$ and $a + b = 0$, which are not satisfy by options (c) and (d). Hence options (c) and (d) are rejected.

Thus point (x_1, y_1, z_1) on the required line will be either (0, 0, 0) or (1, –1, 0).
Now foot of the perpendicular from point (0, 0, 0) to the line (iii)
= $(1, -2r - 1, r)$

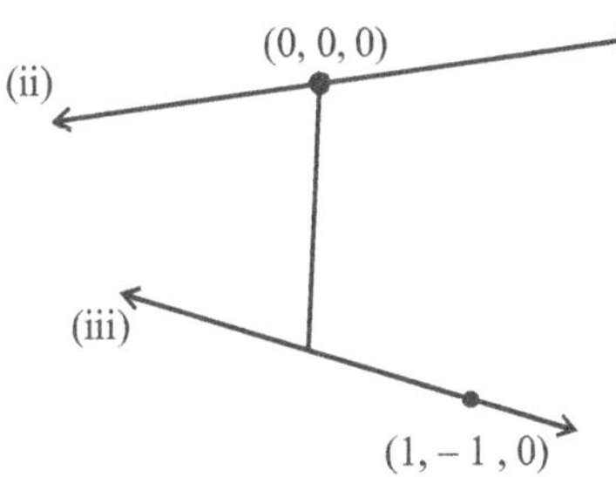

The direction ratios of the line joining the points (0, 0, 0) and $(1, -2r - 1, r)$ are $1, -2r - 1, r$
Since sum of the x and y-coordinate of direction ratio of the required line is 0.
$\therefore\ 1 - 2r - 1 = 0, \Rightarrow r = 0$
Hence direction ratio are 1, – 1, 0
But the z-direction ratio of the required line is twice the y-direction ratio of the required line
i.e. 0 = 2 (–1), which is not true.
Hence the shortest line does not pass through the point (0, 0, 0). Therefore option (a) is also rejected

4. (c)

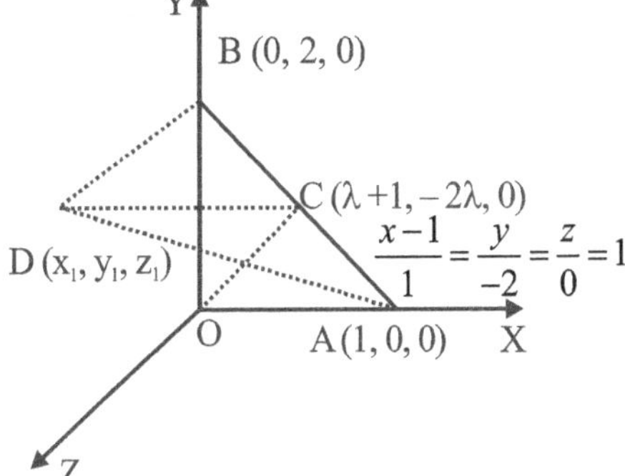

Equation of line AB is $\frac{x-1}{1}=\frac{y}{-2}=\frac{z}{0}=\lambda$

Now $AB \perp OC \Rightarrow 1\,(\lambda+1)+(-2\lambda)(-2)=0 \Rightarrow 5\lambda=-1$

$\Rightarrow \lambda=-\frac{1}{5}$

C is $\left(\frac{4}{5},\frac{2}{5},0\right)$. Now

$x_1^2+(y_1-2)^2+z_1^2=4$

and $(x_1-1)^2+y_1^2+z_1^2=1$

Now $OC \perp CD$

$\Rightarrow \left(x_1-\frac{4}{5}\right)\frac{4}{5}+\left(y_1-\frac{2}{5}\right)\frac{2}{5}+(z_1-0)\,0=0$

Form (i), and (ii), we get

$-4y_1+2x_1=0 \Rightarrow x_1=2y_1$

From (iii), Putting $x_1=2y_1 \Rightarrow 2y_1=\frac{4}{5} \Rightarrow y_1=\frac{2}{5}$

$\Rightarrow x_1=\frac{4}{5}.$

Putting this value of x_1 and y_1 in (i), we get

$= z_1 \pm \frac{2}{\sqrt{5}}$

5. (b.)

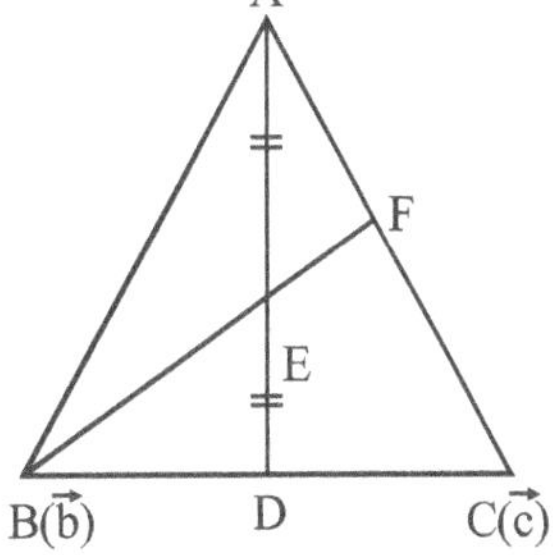

Taking A is the origin, let P.V. of B and C be $\vec{b}$ and $\vec{c}$, respectively.

P.V. of D is $\frac{\vec{b}+\vec{c}}{2}$ and P.V. of E is $\frac{\vec{b}+\vec{c}}{4}$

Equation of line BF is $\vec{r}=\vec{b}+\lambda\left(\frac{\vec{b}+\vec{c}}{4}-\vec{b}\right)$

Equation of line AC is $\vec{r}=0+\mu c$

For the point of intersection, $\vec{b}+\lambda\left(\frac{\vec{b}+\vec{c}}{4}-\vec{b}\right)=\mu\vec{c}$

$\Rightarrow 1-\frac{3\lambda}{4}=0$ and $\frac{\lambda}{4}=\mu\left(\frac{\vec{b}+\vec{c}}{2}\right)$

$\Rightarrow \lambda=\frac{4}{3}$ and $\mu=\frac{1}{3}$. therefore, P.V., of F is

$\vec{r}=\frac{1}{3}\vec{c} \Rightarrow \overline{AF}=\frac{1}{3}\overline{AC} \Rightarrow AF : AC = 1:3$

6. (a, b, c) Let $\overrightarrow{OA}=\vec{a},\ \overrightarrow{OB}=\vec{b},\ \overrightarrow{OC}=\vec{c}$, then we have

$\vec{a}.\vec{a}+(\vec{b}-\vec{c}).(\vec{b}-\vec{c})=\vec{b}.\vec{b}+(\vec{c}-\vec{a}).(\vec{c}-\vec{a})$

$\Rightarrow -2\vec{b}.\vec{c}=-2\vec{c}.\vec{a} \Rightarrow (\vec{a}-\vec{b}).\vec{c}=0$ or $\overrightarrow{BA}.\overrightarrow{OC}=0$

Hence AB is perpendicular to OC. Similarly, BC is perpendicular to OA and CA is perpendicular to OB.

7. (a, d)

The equation of a plane passing through the line of intersection of the x-y and y-z planes is $z+\lambda x=0,\ \lambda\in R$

This plane makes an angle 45° with the x-y plane (z = 0).

$$\Rightarrow \cos 45° = \frac{1}{\sqrt{1}\sqrt{\lambda^2+1}}$$

$$\Rightarrow \lambda = \pm 1$$

8. (a, b) The plane is equally inclined to the lines. Hence, it is perpendicular to the angle bisector of the vectors $2\hat{i}-2\hat{j}-\hat{k}$ and $8\hat{i}+\hat{j}-4\hat{k}$.

Vector along the angle bisectors of the vectors are

$$\frac{2\hat{i}-2\hat{j}-\hat{k}}{3}\pm\frac{8\hat{i}+\hat{j}-4\hat{k}}{9},\text{ or}$$

$$\frac{14\hat{i}-5\hat{j}-7\hat{k}}{9}\text{ and }\frac{-2\hat{i}-7\hat{j}+\hat{k}}{9}.$$

Hence, the equation of the planes is $14x-5y-7z=0$ or $2x+7y-z=0$

9. (a, c, d)

The rod sweeps out the figure which is a cone.

The distance of point A(1, 0, –1) from the plane is

$$\frac{|1-2+4|}{\sqrt{9}}=1\text{ unit.}$$

The slant height l of the cone is 2 units.

Then the radius of the base of the cone is $\sqrt{l^2-1}=\sqrt{4-1}=\sqrt{3}$.

Hence, the volume of the cone is $\pi\left(\sqrt{3}\right)^2(1)=3\pi$ cubic units.

Area of the circle on the plane which the rod traces is 3π.

Also, the centre of the circle is Q(x, y, z). Then

$$\frac{x-1}{1}=\frac{y-0}{-2}=\frac{z+1}{2}=\frac{-(1-0-2+4)}{1^2+(-2)^2+2^2},\text{ or}$$

$$Q(x,y,z)\equiv\left(\frac{4}{3},\frac{-2}{3},-\frac{1}{3}\right).$$

10. (1)

Let P be (x_1, y_1, z_1). Point M is $(x_1, 0, z_1)$ and N is $(x_1, y_1, 0)$

So normal to plane OMN is $\overrightarrow{OM}\times\overrightarrow{ON}=\vec{x}$ (say)

i.e. $$\begin{vmatrix}\hat{i} & \hat{j} & \hat{k}\\ x_1 & 0 & z_1\\ x_1 & y_1 & 0\end{vmatrix}=\hat{i}(-y_1z_1)-\hat{j}(-x_1z_1)+\hat{k}(x_1y_1)$$

therefore, $$\sin\theta=\frac{-x_1y_1z_1+x_1y_1z_1+x_1y_1z}{\sqrt{x_1^2+y_1^2+z_1^2}\sqrt{\sum x_1^2y_1^2}}$$

or $\left(\because \sin=\frac{\vec{n}\times\overrightarrow{OP}}{|n||\overrightarrow{OP}|}\right)$

$$\Rightarrow \operatorname{cosec}^2\theta=\frac{\sum x_1^2\sum x_1^2y_1^2}{(x_1y_1z_1)^2}$$

$$=\frac{\sum x_1^2}{x_1^2}+\frac{\sum x_1^2}{y_1^2}+\frac{\sum x_1^2}{z_1^2}$$

Now, $$\sin\alpha=\frac{\overrightarrow{OP}.\hat{k}}{|\overrightarrow{OP}|}=\frac{z_1}{\sqrt{\sum x_1^2}}$$

$$\sin\beta=\frac{x_1}{\sqrt{\sum x_1^2}}\text{ and }\sin\gamma=\frac{y_1}{\sqrt{\sum x_1^2}}$$

Now, $\operatorname{cosec}^2\alpha+\operatorname{cosec}^2\beta+\operatorname{cosec}^2\gamma$

$$=\frac{x_1^2+y_1^2+z_1^2}{x_1^2}+\frac{\sum x_1^2}{y_1^2}+\frac{\sum x_1^2}{z_1^2}=\operatorname{cosec}^2\theta$$

11 (7) Let the equation of the plane be $\frac{x}{a}+\frac{y}{b}+\frac{z}{c}=1$

$$\Rightarrow \frac{1}{a}+\frac{1}{b}+\frac{1}{c}=1$$

$\Rightarrow$ volume of tetrahedron OABC = V = $\frac{1}{6}$ (a b c)

Now $(abc)^{1/3}\ge\frac{3}{\frac{1}{a}+\frac{1}{b}+\frac{1}{c}}\ge 3$.(G.M. ≥ H.M.)

$$\Rightarrow abc\ge 27\Rightarrow V\ge\frac{9}{2}$$

12. (7) Let the plane $\vec{r}\cdot(\vec{i}-2\vec{j}+3\vec{k})=17$ divide the line joining the points

$-2\vec{i}+4\vec{j}+7\vec{k}$ and $3\vec{i}-5\vec{j}+8\vec{k}$ in the ratio t : 1 at the point P.
Therefore, point P is

$$\frac{3t-2}{t+1}\vec{i}+\frac{-5t+4}{t+1}\vec{j}+\frac{8t+7}{t+1}\vec{k}$$

This lies on the given plane

$$\therefore \frac{3t-2}{t+1}.(1)+\frac{-5t+4}{t+1}(-2)+\frac{8t+7}{t+1}(3)=17$$

Solving, we get

$$t=\frac{3}{10}$$

13. **(6)** Both the lines pass through origin. Line L_1 is parallel to the vector

$$\vec{V}_1=(\cos\theta+\sqrt{3})\hat{i}+\left(\sqrt{2}\sin\theta\right)\hat{j}+(\cos\theta-\sqrt{3})\hat{k}$$

and L_2 is parallel to the vector

$$\vec{V}_2=a\hat{i}+b\hat{j}+c\hat{k}$$

$$\therefore \cos\alpha=\frac{\vec{V}_1\times\vec{V}_2}{|\vec{V}_1||\vec{V}_2|}$$

$$=\frac{a(\cos\theta+\sqrt{3})+(b\sqrt{2})\sin\theta+c(\cos\theta-\sqrt{3})}{\sqrt{a^2+b^2+c^2}\sqrt{(\cos\theta+\sqrt{3})^2+2\sin^2\theta+(\cos\theta-\sqrt{3})^2}}$$

$$=\frac{(a+c)\cos\theta+b\sqrt{3}\sin\theta+(a-c)\sqrt{3}}{\sqrt{a^2+b^2+c^2}\sqrt{2+6}}$$

In order that $\cos\alpha$ is independent of θ, we get $a+c=0$ and $b=0$

$$\therefore \cos\alpha=\frac{2a\sqrt{3}}{a\sqrt{2}\,2\sqrt{2}}=\frac{\sqrt{3}}{2}$$

$$\Rightarrow \alpha=\frac{\pi}{6}$$

14. **(a)** The projection will be an ellipse whose major axis is $AB=2a$.
If its minor axis be b, then $\pi ab=(\cos\theta)\pi a^2$
$\Rightarrow\ b=a\cos\theta.$

$$\therefore\quad e=\sqrt{1-\frac{b^2}{a^2}}=\sin\theta.$$

15. **(b)** Let the positive direction of the normal to the plane ABC from O has direction cosines $\cos\alpha$, $\cos\beta$, $\cos\gamma$. Since ΔOBC is the projection of ΔABC on the plane YOZ, so

$$\cos\alpha.\Delta=\frac{1}{2}bc.$$

Similarly

$$\cos\beta.\Delta=\frac{1}{2}ca,\cos\gamma.\Delta=\frac{1}{2}ab.$$

Using $\cos^2\alpha+\cos^2\beta+\cos^2\gamma=1$, we get

$$\Delta=\frac{1}{2}\sqrt{a^2b^2+b^2c^2+c^2a^2}.$$

16. **(a)**
(I) Any point on L_1 is $(2\lambda+1,-\lambda,\lambda-3)$
and that on L_2 is $(\mu+4,\mu-3,2\mu-3)$
For point of intersection of L_1 and L_2
$2\lambda+1=\mu+4,-\lambda=\mu-3,\lambda-3=2\mu-3$
$\Rightarrow\ \lambda=2,\mu=1$
$\therefore$ Intersection point of L_1 and L_2 is $(5,-2,-1)$
$\because$ $ax+by+cz=d$ is perpendicular to P_1 and P_2
$\therefore$ $7a+b+2c=0$ and $3a+5b-6c=0$

$$\Rightarrow\ \frac{a}{-16}=\frac{b}{48}=\frac{c}{32}\Rightarrow\frac{a}{1}=\frac{b}{-3}=\frac{c}{-2}$$

$\therefore$ Equation of plane is $x-3y-2z=d$
As it passes through $(5,-2,-1)$
$\therefore$ $5+6+2=d=13$
$\therefore$ $a=1,b=-3,c=-2,d=13$
(I) (i) (R) is the correct matching.

17. **(d)** All options (a), (b) and (c) are incorrect combinations.

18. **(c)** (III) Any point on L_1 is $(\lambda+1,0,0)$
and that on L_2 is $(0,\mu+1,0)$
For point of intersection of L_1 and L_2
$\lambda+1=0,\quad 0=\mu+1,\quad 0=0$
$\Rightarrow\ \lambda=-1,\mu=-1$
$\therefore$ Intersection point of L_1 and L_2 is $(0,0,0)$
$\because$ $ax+by+cz=d$ is perpendicular to $x+2y+3z=2$ and $2x+3y+4z=4$
$\therefore$ $a+2b+3c=0$ and $2a+3b+4c=0$

$$\Rightarrow\ \frac{a}{8-9}=\frac{b}{6-4}=\frac{c}{3-4}\Rightarrow\frac{a}{-1}=\frac{b}{2}=\frac{c}{-1}$$

or $\dfrac{a}{1}=\dfrac{b}{-2}=\dfrac{c}{1}$

$\therefore$ Equation of plane is $x-2y+z=d$
As it passes through $(0,0,0)$
$\therefore$ $0-0+0=d=0$
$\therefore$ $a=1,b=-2,c=1,d=0$
(III) (iii) (Q) is the correct matching.

19. **(A) – (r), (B) – (t), (C) – (s), (D) – (p,q)**
(A) Let D, E, F be the mid points then

$$EF^2=\frac{BC^2}{4}\Rightarrow BC^2=4(b^2+c^2)$$

Similarly $AB^2=4(a^2+b^2)$ and $AC^2=4(a^2+c^2)$

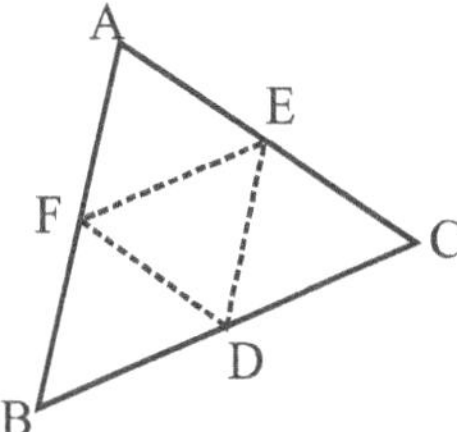

$\therefore \dfrac{AB^2+BC^2+CA^2}{a^2+b^2+c^2}=8$

(B) The image (x_1, y_1, z_1) is given by

$\dfrac{x_1-1}{1}=\dfrac{y_1+2}{-1}=\dfrac{z-3}{1}=-\dfrac{2}{3}(1-2+3-5)$

$\Rightarrow (x_1, y_1, z_1)\equiv(3, -4, 5)$

$\therefore$ desired distance $=\sqrt{50}=5\sqrt{2}$

(C) $D. R.$ of edge OA are 1, 0, 0 and $D. R.$ of diagonal OP are 1, 1, 1.

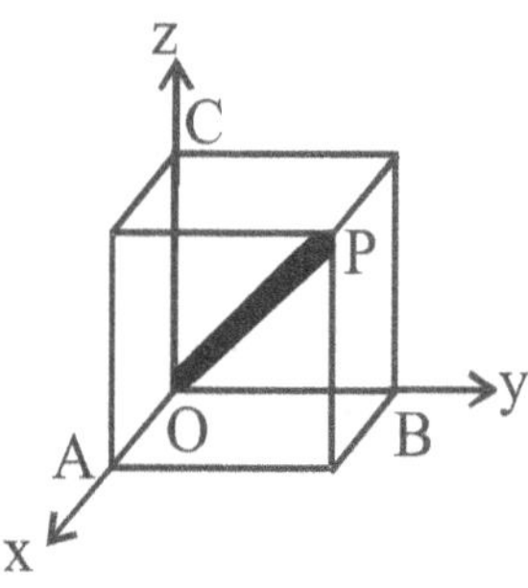

$\therefore \cos\theta=\dfrac{1}{\sqrt{3}}\Rightarrow \tan\theta=\sqrt{2}$

(D) We have $\begin{vmatrix} p & \frac{3}{2} & \frac{1}{2} \\ \frac{3}{2} & 1 & 1 \\ \frac{1}{2} & 1 & q \end{vmatrix}=0$ and $p+1+q=0$.

$\Rightarrow 4pq-4p-5q+5=0$ and $p+1+q=0$

Eliminating p, we get $q=-3, \dfrac{3}{4}$.

20. (A) - r, (B) - q, (C) -p, t, (D) - p, q, s

(A) We have $a^2-b^2+c^2=0$ and $a^2-2bd+c^2=0$

$\Rightarrow b^2=2bd.$ As $b\neq 0\Rightarrow \dfrac{b}{d}=2$.

(B) Equation of line through (1, –2, 3) and parallele to given line is $\dfrac{x-1}{2}=\dfrac{y+2}{3}=\dfrac{z-3}{-6}$.

Any point on it is $(2r+1, 3r-2, -6r+3)$.

This point lies on the plane if $r=\dfrac{1}{7}$. So, the point is $\left(\dfrac{9}{7}, -\dfrac{11}{7}, \dfrac{15}{7}\right)$.

Desired distance

$=\sqrt{\left(\dfrac{9}{7}-1\right)^2+\left(-\dfrac{11}{2}+2\right)^2+\left(\dfrac{15}{7}-3\right)^2}=1$.

(C) General points on two given lines may be written as $(r_1+2, r_1+3, -kr_1+4)$ and $(kr_2+1, 2r_2+4, r_2+5)$. If two lines intersect then for some r_1 and r_2

$r_1+2=kr_2+1, r_1+3=2r_2+4$ and $-kr_1+4=r_2+5$

Eliminating r_1 and r_2, $k^2+3k=0\Rightarrow k=0$ or -3

(D) $\cos^2\theta+\cos^2\theta+\cos^2\gamma=1\Rightarrow \cos^2\gamma=-\cos 2\theta$

$\cos 2\theta\le 0\Rightarrow \theta\in\left[\dfrac{\pi}{4}, \dfrac{\pi}{2}\right]\Rightarrow 0\le\cot\theta\le 1$

DAILY PRACTICE PROBLEMS

MATHEMATICS SOLUTIONS

1. **(c)** This question is based on principle of inclusion and exclusion

Let X, Y and Z be the events that the student passes in Maths, Physics and chemistry.

P(X) = m, P(Y) = p and P(Z) = c and P (passing in at least one) $= P(X \cup B \cup C) = 0.75$ [given]

Now, $1 - P(X^c \cap Y^c \cap Z^c) = 0.75$, $P(X) = 1 - P(X^c)$ and $P(X \cup B \cup C)^c = P(X \cap Y \cap Z)$

$\Rightarrow 1 - P(X^c)P(Y^c)P(Z^c) = 0.75$

X, Y and Z are independent event therefore X^c, Y^c and Z^c are also independent.

$1 - (1 - m)(1 - p)(1 - c) = 0.75$

$(1 - m)(1 - p)(1 - c) = 0.25$ ...(i)

also P(passing exactly in one subject) = 0.4

$\Rightarrow P(X \cap Y \cap Z^c \cup X \cap Y^c \cap Z \cup X^c \cap Y \cap Z) = 0.4$

$\Rightarrow P(XYZ)P(XYZ) \cup P(XYZ) = 0.4$

$pm - pmc + pc - pmc + mc - pmc = 0.4$ ...(ii)

Again P(passing at least in two subjects) = 0.5

$P(XYZ)\,P(XYZ)\,P(XYZ)\,P(XYZ) = 0.5$

$(pm + pc + mc) - pcm = 0.5$ ...(iii)

From (ii) we get

$(pm + pc + mc) - 3pcm = 0.4$ ...(iv)

From (i) we get,

$1 - (m + p + c) + (pm + pc + cm) - pcm = 0.25$ ...(v)

Now from (iii), (iv) and (v) we get,

$p + m + c = 1.35 = 27/20$

and $pmc = 1/10$

2. **(c)** When two dice is thrown then sample space has $6 \times 6 = 36$ elements so n(S) = 36

Now consider the event of getting 9 is (3, 6), (4, 5), (5, 4) and (6, 3)

So probability of getting 9 when two dice is thrown is $4/36 = 1/9$

If Sanchita starts the game then the probability that she wins is

$$\left(\frac{1}{9}\right) + \left(\frac{8}{9}\right)\left(\frac{8}{9}\right)\left(\frac{1}{9}\right) + \ldots\ldots$$

$$= \frac{\frac{1}{9}}{1 - \frac{64}{81}} = \frac{1}{9} \times \frac{81}{17} = \frac{9}{17}$$

And if Raj starts the game then probability that Sanchita wins the game is $1 - 9/17 = 8/17$

3. **(a)** Let X = Number of times A shoots at the target to hit it for the first time.

Y = Number of times B shoots at the target to hit it for the first time.

Then $P(X = m) = \left(\frac{2}{5}\right)^{m-1}\left(\frac{3}{5}\right)$ and

$$P(Y = n) = \left(\frac{2}{7}\right)^{n-1}\left(\frac{5}{7}\right)$$

We have $P(Y > X) = \sum_{m=1}^{\infty} \sum_{n=m+1}^{\infty} P(X = m)P(Y = n)$

[$\because$ X and Y are independent]

$$= \sum_{m=1}^{\infty}\left[\left\{\left(\frac{2}{5}\right)^{m-1}\left(\frac{3}{5}\right)\right\} \sum_{n=m+1}^{\infty}\left\{\left(\frac{2}{7}\right)^{n-1}\left(\frac{5}{7}\right)\right\}\right]$$

$$= \sum_{m=1}^{\infty}\left(\frac{2}{5}\right)^{m-1}\left(\frac{3}{5}\right)\left\{\frac{5}{7} \cdot \frac{\left(\frac{2}{7}\right)^m}{1 - \frac{2}{7}}\right\} =$$

$$\sum_{m=1}^{\infty}\left(\frac{2}{5}\right)^{m-1}\left(\frac{3}{5}\right)\left(\frac{2}{7}\right)^m$$

$$= \frac{6}{35}\sum_{m=1}^{\infty}\left(\frac{4}{35}\right)^{m-1} = \frac{6}{35} \cdot \frac{1}{1 - \frac{4}{35}} = \frac{6}{31}$$

4. **(c)** Let A and B arrive at the place of their meeting 'a' minutes and 'b' minutes after 5 pm. Their meeting is possible only if $|a-b| \le 20$ ...(i)

Clearly, $0 \le a \le 60$ and $0 \le b \le 60$.

$\therefore$ a and b can be selected as an ordered pair (a, b) from the set $[0, 60] \times [0, 60]$.

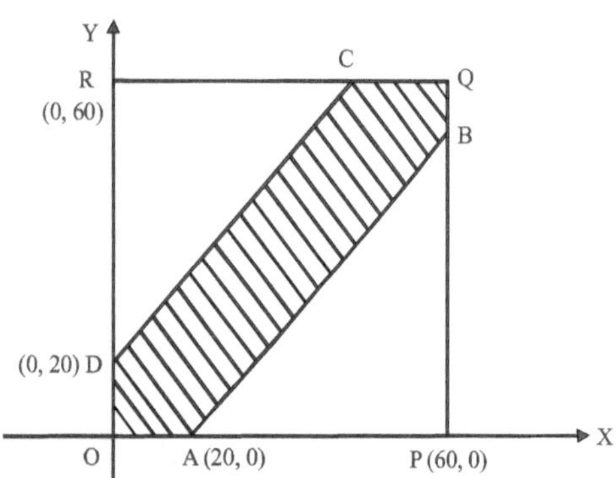

Alternatively, it is equivalent to selecting a point (a, b) from the square $OPQR$, where P is (60, 0) and R is (0, 60) in the cartesian plane.

Now, $|a-b| \le 20 \Rightarrow -20 \le a-b \le 20$

$\therefore$ Points (a, b) satisfy the equation $-20 \le x-y \le 20$

$\therefore$ Favourble condition is equivlent to selecting a point from the region bounded by

$y \le x+20$ and $y \ge x-20$

$$\therefore \text{Required probability} = \frac{\text{Area of } OABQCDO}{\text{Area of square } OPQR}$$

$$= \frac{[Ar(OPQR) - 2Ar(\Delta APB)]}{Ar(OPQR)}$$

$$= \frac{[60\times 60 - \frac{2}{2}\times 40\times 40]}{60\times 60} = \frac{5}{9}$$

5. **(b)** Since X has a binomial distribution, B (n, p)

$\therefore$ P $(X=2) = {}^nC_2\,(p)^2\,(1-p)^{n-2}$

and P $(X=3) = {}^nC_3\,(p)^3\,(1-p)^{n-3}$

Given P $(X=2)$ = P $(X=3)$

$\Rightarrow {}^nC_2\,p^2\,(1-p)^{n-2} = {}^nC_3\,(p)^3\,(1-p)^{n-3}$

$$\Rightarrow \frac{n!}{2!(n-2)!}\cdot\frac{p^2(1-p)^n}{(1-p)^2} = \frac{n!}{3!(n-3)!}\cdot\frac{p^3(1-p)^n}{(1-p)^3}$$

$$\Rightarrow \frac{1}{n-2} = \frac{1}{3}\cdot\frac{p}{1-p}$$

$\Rightarrow 3\,(1-p) = p\,(n-2)$

$\Rightarrow 3 - 3p = np - 2p$

$\Rightarrow np = 3 - p$

$\Rightarrow$ E(X) = mean = $3 - p$

($\because$ mean of B $(n, p) = np$)

6. **(a, b, d)** Note that $P(Z \le m) = P\{X \le m, Y \le m\}$

$= P\{X \le m\}\,P\{Y \le m\}$

But $P\{Y \le m\} = P\{X \le m\}$

$= P(X=0) + P(X=1) + \ldots\ldots\ldots + P(X=m)$

$= p + pq + pq^2 + \ldots\ldots\ldots$

$$+ pq^{m-1} = \frac{p(1-q^m)}{1-q} = 1-q^m$$

$\therefore P(Z \le m) = (1-q^m)^2$

Now, $P(Z=m) = P(Z \le m) - P(Z \le m-1)$

$= (1-q^m)^2 - (1-q^{m-1})^2$

$= 1 - 2q^m + q^{2m} - (1 - 2q^{m-1} + q^{2m-2})$

$= 2pq^{m-1} - p(1+q)\,q^{2m-2}$ $\quad [\because 1-q=p]$

Clearly, $\sum_{m\ge1} P(Z=m)$

$$= \sum_{m\ge1} [2pq^{m-1} - p(1+q)\,q^{2m-2}]$$

$$= \frac{2p}{1-q} - \frac{p(1+q)}{1-q^2} = 2-1 = 1.$$

7. **(a, c)** Let A_i denote the event that the ith letter is placed in the right envelope. Then the required probability is

$P(\overline{A_1} \cap \overline{A_2} \cap \ldots\ldots \cap \overline{A_n})$

$= P(\overline{A_1 \cup A_2 \cup \ldots\ldots A_n})$ [By De-Morgan law]

$= 1 - P(A_1 \cup A_2 \cup \ldots\ldots \cup A_n)$

$= 1 - [\Sigma P(A_i) - \Sigma P(A_i \cap A_j) + \Sigma P(A_i \cap A_j \cap A_k) - \ldots\ldots$

$+(-1)^{n-1} P(A_1 \cap A_2 \cap \ldots\ldots \cap A_n)]$

$i \ne j \ne k$

Now $P(A_i) = \dfrac{(n-1)!}{n!}$ as having placed i^{th} letter in the right envelope, the remaining letters can be placed in $(n-1)!$ ways.

Similarly $P(A_1 \cap A_2 \cap \ldots\ldots \cap A_r)$ = Prob. of r particular letters in right envelopes $= \dfrac{(n-r)!}{n!}$.

$\therefore \quad \Sigma P(A_1 \cap A_2 \cap \ldots\ldots \cap A_r)$

$$= {}^nC_r \cdot \frac{(n-r)!}{n!} = \frac{1}{r!}$$

Where $r = 1, 2, 3, \ldots\ldots, n$.

$\therefore \quad \Sigma(\overline{A_i} \cap \overline{A_2} \cap ..... \cap \overline{A_n})$

$= 1 - \left\{\frac{1}{1!} - \frac{1}{2!} + \frac{1}{3!} - ... + (-1)^{n-1} \cdot \frac{1}{n!}\right\}$

$= \frac{1}{2!} - \frac{1}{3!} + \frac{1}{4!} - ..... + (-1)^n \cdot \frac{1}{n!}$

which is equal to first $n-2$ terms in the expansion of e^{-1}.

8. (b, d) $p(r) = \frac{3}{10}$ so $p(\bar{r}) = \frac{7}{10}$.

The probability of at least one rainy day in 7 days

$P(A) = 1 - \left(\frac{7}{10}\right)^7$

Now the probability that at least two rainy days in 7 days.

$P(B) = 1 - \left(\frac{7}{10}\right)^7 - {}^7C_1\left(\frac{3}{10}\right)\left(\frac{7}{10}\right)^6$

Hence $P(B/A) = \frac{P(B \cap A)}{P(A)}$

$= \frac{1 - \left(\frac{7}{10}\right)^7 - {}^7C_1\left(\frac{3}{10}\right)\left(\frac{7}{10}\right)^6}{1 - \left(\frac{7}{10}\right)^7}$

$= \left\{\frac{1 - \left(\frac{7}{10}\right)^7 - 7\left(\frac{3}{10}\right)\left(\frac{7}{10}\right)^6}{1 - \left(\frac{7}{10}\right)^7}\right\}$

9. (a, b, c, d) We have

$P(A_1) = \frac{2}{4} = \frac{1}{2} = P(A_2) = P(A_3)$.

[Note that $P(A_1)$ is the probability of the event that the first digit is 1 and since there are two numbers having 1 at the first place out of four, we have $P(A_1) = \frac{2}{4} = \frac{1}{2}$. Similarly for $P(A_2)$ and $P(A_3)$].

$A_1 \cap A_2$ is the event that the first two digits in the numbers drawn are each equal to 1 and so $P(A_1 \cap A_2)$

$= \frac{1}{4} = \frac{1}{2} = P(A_1)P(A_2)$

Similarly $P(A_2 \cap A_3) = P(A_2)(A_3)$

and $P(A_3 \cap A_1) = P(A_3)P(A_1)$.

Thus the events A_1, A_2 and A_3 are equal to 1 and since there is no such number, we have

$P(A_1 \cap A_2 \cap A_3) = 0.$

$\neq P(A_1)P(A_2)P(A_3).$

Hence the events A_1, A_2, A_3 are the not mutually independent although they are pairwise independent.

10. (1) Lets define the events as

Probability of getting project copy (A) = p

Probability of getting blue pen (B) = q

Probability of getting black pen (C) =1/2

Then $P(AB\bar{C}) + p(AC\bar{B}) + p(ABC) = \frac{1}{2}$

$p \cdot q \cdot \frac{1}{2} + p \cdot \frac{1}{2}(1-q) + p \cdot q \cdot \frac{1}{2} = \frac{1}{2}$

$= pq + p - pq + pq = 1 \;\therefore\; p(1+q) = 1$

11. (3) Let $A_i(i = 1, 2, 3, 4)$ be the event that the urn contains 2, 3, 4 or 5 white balls and B the event that two white balls are drawn.

We have to find $P(A_4/B)$.

Since the four events A_1, A_2, A_3, A_4 are equally likely, we have

$P(A_1) = P(A_2) = P(A_3) = P(A_4) = \frac{1}{4}$.

$P(B/A_1)$ is the probability of event that the urn contains 2 white balls and both have been drawn.

Hence $P(B/A_1) = \frac{{}^2C_2}{{}^5C_2} = \frac{1}{10}$.

Similarly $P(B/A_2) = \frac{{}^3C_2}{{}^5C_2} = \frac{3}{10}$.

$P(B/A_3) = \frac{{}^4C_2}{{}^5C_2} = \frac{6}{10} = \frac{3}{5}$.

and $P(B/A_4) = \frac{{}^5C_2}{{}^5C_2} = 1$.

$\therefore$ by Baye's theorem

$P(A_4/B) = \frac{P(A_4)P(B/A_4)}{\sum_{i+1}^{4} P(A_i)P(B/A_i)}$

$$= \frac{\frac{1}{4}\cdot 1}{\frac{1}{4}(\frac{1}{10}+\frac{3}{10}+\frac{3}{5}+1)} = \frac{1}{2}$$

12. (7) Since the coin is fair,

$$P(H) = P(T) = \frac{1}{2}$$

By binomial distribution,

$$P(X=K) = {}^nC_k\left(\frac{1}{2}\right)^{n-k}\left(\frac{1}{2}\right)^k$$

$$= {}^nC_k\left(\frac{1}{2}\right)^n$$

By hypothesis

$2P(X=5) = P(X=4) + P(X=6)$

Therefore, $2\left({}^nC_5\right) = {}^nC_4 + {}^nC_6$

$n^2 - 21n + 98 = 0$

$n = 7, 14$

Therefore, $n = 7$ (smaller value).

13. (6) Let x shell are fixed at point I. Define the following events

E_1 : The target is at point I $\Rightarrow P(E_1) = \frac{8}{9}$

E_2 : The target is at point II $\Rightarrow P(E_2) = \frac{1}{9}$

A : The target is hit

The target will be hit if at least one shell hits the target.

$P(A/E_1) = 1 -$ None of the shells hit when the target is at point I $= 1-\left(\frac{1}{2}\right)^x$ and $P(A/E_2) = 1-\left(\frac{1}{2}\right)^{21-x}$

$$\therefore\ P(A) = \frac{8}{9}\left[1-\left(\frac{1}{2}\right)^x\right]+\frac{1}{9}\left[1-\left(\frac{1}{2}\right)^{21-x}\right]$$

$$= 1-\frac{1}{9}\left[\left(\frac{1}{2}\right)^{x-3}+\left(\frac{1}{2}\right)^{21-x}\right]$$

For maximum probability; $\frac{dP(A)}{dx} = 0$

$$\Rightarrow -\frac{1}{9}\left[\left(\frac{1}{2}\right)^{21-x} ln2 - \left(\frac{1}{2}\right)^{x-3} ln2\right] = 0 \Rightarrow x = 12$$

Also,

$$\frac{d^2P(A)}{dx^2} = -\frac{1}{9}\left[\left(\frac{1}{2}\right)^{x-3}(ln2)^2+\left(\frac{1}{2}\right)^{21-x}(ln2)^2\right] < 0$$

$\therefore P(A)$ is maximum when $x = 12$.

$\Rightarrow k = 6$

14. (b) Let $A_i (i = 1, 2, 3)$ be the event that ith urn is chosen and B the event that a white ball is drawn.

Since all the urns are equally likely to be selected, we have

$$P(A_1) = P(A_2) = P(A_3) = \frac{1}{3}$$

and $P(B/A_1) = \frac{2}{5}$, $P(B/A_2) = \frac{3}{5}$

$P(B/A_3) = \frac{4}{5}$.

Hence $P(B) = P(A_1)\,P(B/A_2) = \frac{3}{5}$, $P(B/A_2) = \frac{4}{5}$,

Hence $P(B) = P(A_1)\,P(B/A_1) + P(A_2)\,P(B/A_2) + P(A_3)\,P(B/A_3)$

$$= \frac{1}{3}\cdot\frac{2}{5}+\frac{1}{3}\cdot\frac{3}{5}+\frac{1}{3}\cdot\frac{4}{5} = \frac{9}{15} = \frac{3}{5}.$$

15. (c) Here we have to find $P(A_1/B)$

By Baye's theorem required probability

$$= \frac{\frac{1}{3}\cdot\frac{2}{5}}{\frac{3}{5}} = \frac{2}{9}.$$

16. (a) $P(A^C) = 0.3$, $P(b) = 0.4$ and $P(A \cap B^C) = 0.5$

$$P[B/(A \cap B^C)] = \frac{P[B \cap (A \cup B^C)]}{P(A \cup B^C)}$$

$$= \frac{P((B \cap A) \cup (B \cap B^C))}{P(A \cup B^C)}$$

$$= \frac{P(A \cap B)}{P(A) + P(B^C) - P(A \cap B^C)}$$

$$= \frac{P(A) - P(A \cap B^C)}{1 - P(A^C) + 1 - P(B) - P(A \cap B^C)}$$

$$= \frac{1 - 0.3 - 0.5}{1 - 0.3 + 1 - 0.4 - 0.5} = \frac{0.2}{0.8} = \frac{1}{4}$$

17. (d) $P(A) = \frac{1}{5}$, $P(B) = \frac{4}{5}$, $P(C) = \frac{7}{100}$

$$P\left(\frac{B}{\bar{C}}\right) = \frac{P\left(\frac{\bar{C}}{B}\right)P(B)}{P\left(\frac{\bar{C}}{A}\right)P(A) + P\left(\frac{\bar{C}}{B}\right)P(B)}$$

$$= \frac{\frac{80}{100} \times \frac{39}{40}}{\frac{20}{100} \times \frac{30}{40} + \frac{80}{100} \times \frac{39}{40}}$$

$$\left[\because P\left(\frac{\bar{C}}{A}\right) = \frac{30}{40}, P\left(\frac{\bar{C}}{B}\right) = \frac{39}{40}\right]$$

$$= \frac{156}{186} = \frac{26}{31}$$

18. **(b)** $P(A) = \frac{1}{2} \cdot P(B) = \frac{1}{4} = P(C)$

$$P(A \cap B \cap C^C) + P(A \cap B^C \cap C) + P(A^C \cap B \cap C) + P(A \cap B \cap C)$$

$$= \frac{1}{2} \times \frac{1}{4} \times \frac{3}{4} + \frac{1}{2} \times \frac{3}{4} \times \frac{1}{4} + \frac{1}{2} \times \frac{1}{4} \times \frac{1}{4} + \frac{1}{2} \times \frac{1}{4} \times \frac{1}{4}$$

$$= \frac{1}{4}$$

19. **A → (r); B → (s); C → (q); D → (p)**

(A) Probability that Aman will hit the target is P(A) = 4/5 and probability that Aman will not hit the target is P(A') = 1 – 4/5 = 1/5.

Probability that Binay will hit the target is P(A) = 3/4 and probability that Binay will not hit the target is P(A') = 1 – 3/4 = 1/4

Probability that none of them will hit the target is P(A'∩B')

= 1/5 × ¼ = 1/20

So probability that at least one of them will hit the target is 1 – 1/20 =19/20

(B) Let P(A) probability of getting a prime number = 3/6 = 1/2 then P(A') = 1/2

And P(B) = probability of getting a composite number 2/6 = 1/3 then P(B') = 2/3

Now consider Kushal wins the game it is possible in following cases-

Case (1) in one throw- if kushal gets a prime = P(A) = 1/2

Case (2) in three throws- If kushal fails to get a prime in 1st throw, Karina fails to get composite in 2nd throw and Kushal gets a prime in 3rd throw, in this case probability is P(A') × P(B') × P(A) = 1/2 × 2/3 × 1/2 = 1/6

Case (3) in 5 throw then similar to above case probability is (1/2) × (2/3) × (1/2) × (2/3) × (1/2) = 1/18

And this process will continue and the required probability is (1/2) + (1/6) + (1/18) +.....∞

Or required probability $\frac{\frac{1}{2}}{1-\frac{1}{3}} = \frac{3}{4}$

(C) Probability that Karina will win the game is 1 – 3/4 = 1/4

(D) Probability of getting a six is 1/6

If Sanchita starts the game then the probability that she wins is

$$\left(\frac{1}{6}\right) + \left(\frac{5}{6}\right)\left(\frac{5}{6}\right)\left(\frac{1}{6}\right) + ...\infty = \frac{\frac{1}{6}}{1-\frac{25}{56}} = \frac{6}{11}$$

And if Raj starts the game then probability that Sanchita wins the game is 1 – 6/11 = 5/11

20. **(A) → r; (B) → s; (C) → p; (D) → q**

(A) $\frac{^{11}C_5}{^{12}C_6} = \frac{1}{2}.$

(B) Let E_1 be the event that S_3 and S_4 are in same group

Let E_2 be the event that S_3 and S_4 are in different group.

$$P(E_1) = \frac{1}{11}$$

$$P(E_2) = \frac{10}{11}$$

Ler E be the event that exactly one of S_3 and S_4 is among the losers, then

$$P(E) = P(E_1)P(E/E_1) + P(E_2)\ P(E/E_2)$$

$$= \frac{1}{11} \times 1 + \frac{10}{11} \times \left(\frac{1}{2}.\frac{1}{2} + \frac{1}{2}.\frac{1}{2}\right) = \frac{6}{11}.$$

(C) S_2 and S_4 should be in different groups for both winner

Required probability $= \frac{10}{11}\left(\frac{1}{2}.\frac{1}{2}\right) = \frac{5}{22}$

or $\frac{^{10}C_4}{^{12}C_6} = \frac{5}{22}.$

(D) S_4 and S_5 will not play against each other if they are paired together whose probability $= \frac{10}{11}$

1. **(a)** Given $\cot\theta = \cot A + \cot B + \cot C$

$\Rightarrow \cot\theta - \cot A = \cot B + \cot C$

$$\Rightarrow \frac{\cos\theta\sin A - \sin\theta\cos A}{\sin\theta\sin A} = \frac{\cos B\sin C + \sin B\cos C}{\sin B\sin C}$$

$$\Rightarrow \sin(A-\theta) = \frac{\sin A\sin\theta\sin(B+C)}{\sin B\sin C} = \frac{\sin^2 A\sin\theta}{\sin B\sin C}$$

$[\because A+B+C=\pi]$

Similarly, $\sin(B-\theta) = \dfrac{\sin^2 B\sin\theta}{\sin A\sin C}$ and

$$\sin(C-\theta) = \frac{\sin^2 C\sin\theta}{\sin A\sin B}$$

$\therefore\ \sin(A-\theta)\sin(B-\theta)\sin(C-\theta) = \sin^3\theta$

2. **(c)** $\cos A + \cos B + \cos C$

$$= 2\cos\frac{A+B}{2}\cos\frac{A-B}{2} + 1 - 2\sin^2\frac{C}{2}$$

$$= 2\sin\frac{C}{2}.\left(\cos\frac{A-B}{2} - \sin\frac{C}{2}\right) + 1\ (\therefore A+B=\pi-C)$$

$$\le 2\sin\frac{C}{2}\left(1-\sin\frac{C}{2}\right)+1$$

$\left(\therefore \text{ the greatest value of } \cos\dfrac{A-B}{2} \text{ is } 1\right)$

and equality holds when $\cos\dfrac{A-B}{2} = 1$ ...(1)

$$\therefore\ \cos A + \cos B + \cos C \le 1 - 2\left(\sin^2\frac{C}{2} - \sin\frac{C}{2}\right)$$

$$= 1 - 2\left(\sin^2\frac{C}{2} - \sin\frac{C}{2} + \frac{1}{4}\right) + 2.\frac{1}{4}$$

$$= \frac{3}{2} - 2\left(\sin\frac{C}{2} - \frac{1}{2}\right)^2 \le \frac{3}{2}$$

equality holding when $\sin\dfrac{C}{2} = \dfrac{1}{2}$

Thus, $\cos A + \cos B + \cos C \le \dfrac{3}{2}$

equality holding when (1) and (2) both hold, i.e., when

$A = B = C = \dfrac{\pi}{3}$

3. **(b)** a, b, c are sides of a triangle

$\therefore\ a+b>c,\ b+c>a,\ c+a>b$

$\therefore\ a>|b-c|,\ b>|c-a|,\ c>|a-b|$ square and add

$a^2+b^2+c^2 < 2(ab+bc+ca)$

$\Rightarrow a^2+b^2+c^2+2(ab+bc+ac) < 4(ab+bc+ca)$

$$\Rightarrow \frac{(a+b+c)^2}{ab+bc+ca} < 4 \Rightarrow P < 4$$

Again $(a-b)^2+(b-c)^2+(c-a)^2 \ge 0$

$$\Rightarrow \frac{(a+b+c)^2}{ab+bc+ca} \ge 3 \Rightarrow P \ge 3$$

$\therefore\ 3 \le P < 4$ or $P \in [3, 4)$

4. **(b)** $\dfrac{a^2+b^2}{a^2-b^2}\sin(A-B) = 1$

$$\Rightarrow \frac{\sin^2 A + \sin^2 B}{\sin^2 A - \sin^2 B}.\sin(A-B) = 1$$

$$\Rightarrow \frac{\sin^2 A + \sin^2 B}{\sin(A+B)\sin(A-B)} \times \sin(A-B) = 1$$

$\Rightarrow \sin^2 A + \sin^2 B = \sin(A+B) = \sin C$

$\Rightarrow 1 - \cos 2A + 1 - \cos 2B = 2\sin C$

$\Rightarrow \cos 2A + \cos 2B = 2(1-\sin C)$

$\Rightarrow 2\cos(A+B)\cos(A-B) = 2(1-\sin C)$

$$\Rightarrow \cos(A-B) = \frac{1-\sin C}{-\cos C} \qquad \left(\text{if } C \ne \frac{\pi}{2}\right)$$

$$\Rightarrow \cos(A-B) = \frac{\left(\sin\frac{C}{2} - \cos\frac{C}{2}\right)^2}{\sin^2\frac{C}{2} - \cos^2\frac{C}{2}} = \frac{\sin\frac{C}{2} - \cos\frac{C}{2}}{\sin\frac{C}{2} + \cos\frac{C}{2}}$$

$$= \frac{\tan(C/2)-1}{\tan(C/2)+1} = \tan\left(\frac{C}{2} - \frac{\pi}{4}\right)$$

5. **(a)** Let OP be the tower of height h, A be a point due south of it such that $\angle OAP = \alpha$ and B, a point due east of it such that $\angle OBP = \beta$. (see figure)

It is given that $\tan\alpha = 0.6 = \frac{3}{5}$ and $\tan\beta = 0.75 = \frac{3}{4}$

Now, $OA = h\cot\alpha = \frac{5h}{3}$ and $OB = h\cot\beta = \frac{4h}{3}$. So that from right angled triangle AOB

$(AB)^2 = (OA)^2 + (OB)^2 = \frac{41}{9}h^2$

$\Rightarrow AB = \lambda h$, where $\lambda^2 = 41/9$

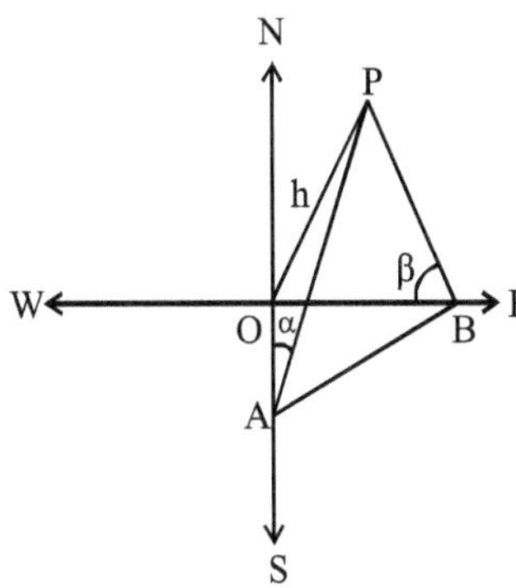

6. **(c)** We have

$\angle CAD = 45°, \angle BAD = 30°, \angle CBH = 60°$ (see figure)

$\Rightarrow \angle ACD = 45°, \angle BCH = 30°,$

so that $\angle ACB = 15°$ and

$\angle CAB = 45° - 30° = 15° \Rightarrow \angle ABC = 150°$

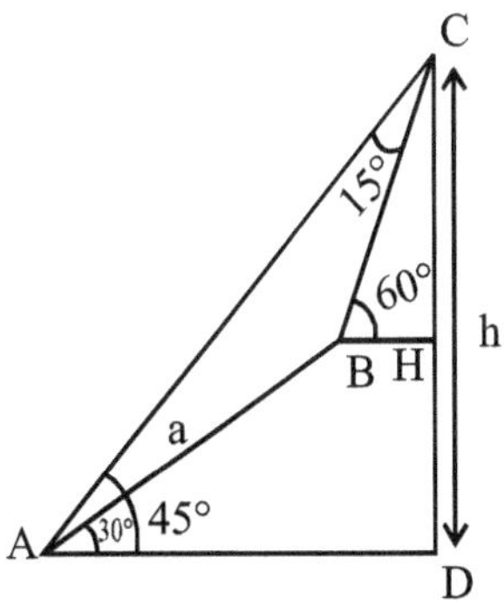

From ΔADC, $AC^2 = h^2 + h^2 = 2h^2$ [$\because$ AD=CD=h]
and from ΔABC

$$\frac{AB}{\sin 15°} = \frac{AC}{\sin 150°} \Rightarrow \frac{a}{\sin 15°} = \frac{\sqrt{2}h}{\sin 150°}$$

$$\therefore a = \left(\frac{\sqrt{2}\sin 15°}{\sin 30°}\right)h, \quad [\therefore \sin 150° = \sin 30°]$$

$$= \frac{\sqrt{2}\left(\frac{\sqrt{3}-1}{2\sqrt{2}}\right)}{\frac{1}{2}}h = h\left(\sqrt{3}-1\right)$$

7. **(a,b,d)** $b\cos^2\frac{A}{2} + a\cos^2\frac{B}{2} = \frac{3c}{2}$

$\Rightarrow \frac{b}{2}(1+\cos A) + \frac{a}{2}(1+\cos B) = \frac{3c}{2}$

$\Rightarrow b + a + (b\cos A + a\cos B) = 3c$

$\Rightarrow b + a + c = 3c \Rightarrow a + b = 2c$

Thus, $a + b \ge 2\sqrt{ab}$

$\Rightarrow 2c \ge 2\sqrt{ab} > \sqrt{ab}$

Also $2c \ge 2\sqrt{ab} \Rightarrow c^2 \ge ab$

Moreover, $\frac{a+c}{2c-a} + \frac{b+c}{2c-b} = \frac{a+c}{b} + \frac{b+c}{a}$

$= \frac{a}{b} + \frac{c}{b} + \frac{b}{a} + \frac{c}{a} \ge 4\left(\frac{c^2 ab}{a^2 b^2}\right)^{1/4} \ge 4$ and

$\frac{a}{c} + \frac{c}{b} + \frac{b}{a} \ge 3\left(\frac{acb}{cba}\right)^{1/3} = 3$

8. **(a,b,d)** Let the sides of a triangle be a, ar, ar^2

$\because ar^2$ is the greater side ($r > 1$).

$\therefore a + ar > ar^2$

$\because r^2 - r - 1 < 0 \Rightarrow \frac{1-\sqrt{5}}{2} < r < \frac{1+\sqrt{5}}{2}$

$\Rightarrow 1 < r < \frac{1+\sqrt{5}}{2}$

Therefore (a) is correct.

Also $r^2 < \frac{1}{4}(6+2\sqrt{5}) = \frac{1}{2}(3+\sqrt{5})$

and $r^4 < \frac{1}{4}(14+6\sqrt{5}) = \frac{1}{2}(7+3\sqrt{5})$

$\therefore 1 + r^2 - r^4 < 1 + \frac{1}{2}(3+\sqrt{5}) - \frac{1}{2}(7+3\sqrt{5})$

$= -1 - \sqrt{5} < r$

$\cos C = \frac{a^2 + a^2r^2 - a^2r^4}{2a^2r} = \frac{1 + r^2 - r^4}{2r} < \frac{1}{2}$

$\therefore \cos C < \cos\frac{\pi}{3} \Rightarrow C > \frac{\pi}{3}$

Therefore (d) is correct.

Also, $\cos B = \frac{a^2 + a^2r^4 - a^2r^2}{2a^2r^2} = \frac{1 + r^4 - r^2}{2r^2}$

$$=\frac{1}{2}\left[r^2+\frac{1}{r^2}-1\right]=\frac{1}{2}\left[\left(r-\frac{1}{2}\right)^2+1\right]>\frac{1}{2}$$

$\therefore \cos B>\cos\frac{\pi}{3}\Rightarrow B<\frac{\pi}{3}$

Also,

$a<ar<ar^2\Rightarrow A<B<C\Rightarrow A<B<\frac{\pi}{3}<C$

Hence (b) is also correct and (c) is incorrect.

9. (a,b,c) Let $BP=n, CQ=n+1, AR=n+2$

Then $BP=BR=n$

$CQ=CP=n+1$ and $AR=AQ=n+2$

$\therefore\ BC=2n+1, CA=2n+3, AB=2n+2$ and

$S=\frac{1}{2}[2n+1+2n+3+2n+2]=3n+3$

$\Delta=\sqrt{(3n+3)(n+2)(n)(n+1)}$ and inradius

$=\frac{\Delta}{s}=4$

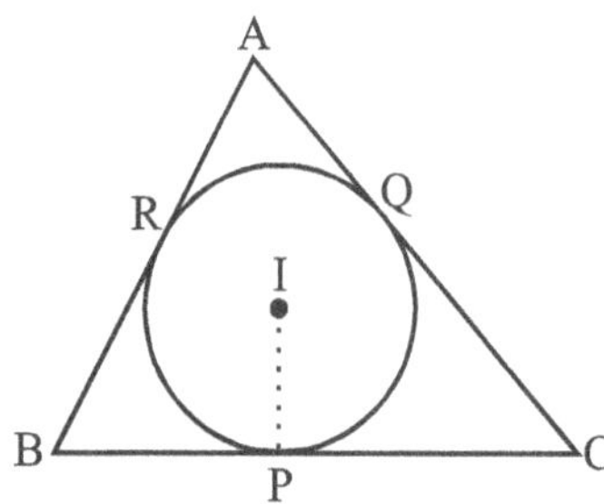

$\therefore\ \sqrt{\frac{n(n+2)}{3}}=4\Rightarrow n^2+2n-48=0\Rightarrow n=6$

So, the sides are 13, 14, 15. and perimeter $=2s=42$ unit

$\Delta=\sqrt{31\times8\times6\times7}=7\times3\times4=84$ unit

$\therefore$ radius of circumcircle

$R=\frac{13\times14\times15}{4\times84}=\frac{65}{8}$ cm

10. (b, c) Here $\cos A$, $\cos B$, $\cos C$ are in A.P.

$\Rightarrow 2\cos B=\cos A+\cos C$

$$=2\cos\frac{A+C}{2}\cos\frac{A-C}{2}$$

$$\Rightarrow\left(1-2\sin^2\frac{B}{2}\right)=\sin\frac{B}{2}\cos\frac{A-C}{2}$$

or $\cos^2\frac{B}{2}=\sin\frac{B}{2}\left[\sin\frac{B}{2}+\cos\frac{A-C}{2}\right]$

$$=\sin\frac{B}{2}\left[\cos\frac{A+C}{2}+\cos\frac{A-C}{2}\right]$$

$$=2\sin\frac{B}{2}\cos\frac{A}{2}\cos\frac{C}{2}.$$

$$\Rightarrow\cot\frac{B}{2}=\frac{2\cos\frac{A}{2}\cos\frac{C}{2}}{\sin\left(\frac{A+C}{2}\right)}$$

$$=\frac{2\cos\frac{A}{2}\cos\frac{C}{2}}{\sin\frac{A}{2}\cos\frac{C}{2}+\cos\frac{A}{2}\sin\frac{C}{2}}$$

$$\Rightarrow\cot\frac{B}{2}=\frac{2}{\tan\frac{A}{2}+\tan\frac{C}{2}}$$

$$\Rightarrow\tan\frac{A}{2}+\tan\frac{C}{2}=2\tan\frac{B}{2}$$

$\Rightarrow\tan\frac{A}{2},\tan\frac{B}{2},\tan\frac{C}{2}$ are in A.P.

$$\Rightarrow\sqrt{\frac{(s-b)(s-c)}{s(s-a)}}+\sqrt{\frac{(s-a)(s-b)}{s(s-c)}}$$

$$=2\sqrt{\frac{(s-a)(s-c)}{s(s-b)}}$$

or $\frac{\Delta}{s(s-a)}+\frac{\Delta}{s(s-c)}=2\frac{\Delta}{s(s-b)}$

or $r_1+r_2=2r_2\Rightarrow r_1,r_2,r_3$ are in A.P.

11. (6) We have $\frac{1}{2}ah_1=\Delta=rs$

$$\Rightarrow\frac{h_1}{r}=\frac{2s}{a}=\frac{a+b+c}{a}$$

$$\Rightarrow\frac{h_1+r}{h_1-r}=\frac{2a+b+c}{b+c}=\frac{2(a+b+c)}{b+c}-1$$

Hence $\sum\frac{h_1+r}{h_1-r}=2(a+b+c)\left[\frac{1}{b+c}+\frac{1}{c+a}+\frac{1}{a+b}\right]-3$

$$\geq2(a+b+c).3\frac{3}{(b+c)+(c+a)+(a+b)}-3$$

(A.M. $\geq$ H.M.)

i.e., $\sum\frac{h_1+r}{h_1-r}\geq6$.

12. **(3)** Given $A+B+C=\pi$

$$\Rightarrow \cot\frac{A}{2}\cot\frac{B}{2}\cot\frac{C}{2}=\cot\frac{A}{2}+\cot\frac{B}{2}+\cot\frac{C}{2} \quad \ldots(i)$$

But $\tan\frac{A}{2}, \tan\frac{B}{2}, \tan\frac{C}{2}$ are in H.P.

$$\Rightarrow \cot\frac{A}{2},\cot\frac{B}{2},\cot\frac{C}{2} \text{ are in A.P.}$$

$$\Rightarrow \cot\frac{A}{2}+\cot\frac{C}{2}=2\cot\frac{B}{2} \quad \ldots(ii)$$

From (i) and (ii), we get $\cot\frac{A}{2}.\cot\frac{B}{2}.\cot\frac{C}{2}=3\cot\frac{B}{2}$

$$\therefore \cot\frac{A}{2}.\cot\frac{C}{2}=3$$

Now, $\dfrac{\cot\frac{A}{2}+\cot\frac{C}{2}}{2}\geq\sqrt{\cot\frac{A}{2}\cot\frac{C}{2}}$

$$\Rightarrow \frac{2\cot\frac{B}{2}}{2}\geq\sqrt{3} \quad \text{[From (ii) an (iii)]}$$

$$\therefore \cot\frac{B}{2}\geq\sqrt{3}$$

13. **(5)** Let h_a, h_b, h_c be sides of $\Delta A'B'C'$ and h_a', h_b', h_c' be sides of $A''B''C''$

Then $\frac{1}{2}ah_a=\frac{1}{2}bh_b=\frac{1}{2}ch_c=\Delta$ ....(1)

Also, $\frac{1}{2}h_ah'_a=\frac{1}{2}h_bh'_b=\frac{1}{2}h_ch'_c=\Delta'$ ...(2)

$$\therefore h'_a=\frac{2\Delta'}{h_a}=\frac{2\Delta'}{\frac{2\Delta}{a}}=\frac{a\Delta'}{\Delta} \quad \text{from (1)}$$

Now $\Delta''^2=\left(\dfrac{h'_a+h'_b+h'_c}{2}\right)\left(\dfrac{h'_a+h'_b-h'_c}{2}\right)$

$$\left(\frac{h'_a-h'_b+h'_c}{2}\right)\left(\frac{-h'_a+h'_b+h'_c}{2}\right)$$

$$=\frac{1}{2^4}\left[\frac{a\Delta'}{\Delta}+\frac{b\Delta'}{\Delta}+\frac{c\Delta'}{\Delta}\right]\left[\frac{a\Delta'}{\Delta}+\frac{b\Delta'}{\Delta}-\frac{c\Delta'}{\Delta}\right]$$

$$\left[\frac{a\Delta'}{\Delta}-\frac{b\Delta'}{\Delta}+\frac{c\Delta'}{\Delta}\right]\left[-\frac{a\Delta'}{\Delta}+\frac{b\Delta'}{\Delta}+\frac{c\Delta'}{\Delta}\right]$$

$$=\frac{(\Delta')^4}{2^4\Delta^4}(a+b+c)(a+b-c)(a-b+c)$$

$$(-a+b+c)=\frac{(\Delta')^4\Delta^2}{\Delta^4}$$

$$\therefore \Delta^2=\frac{(\Delta')^4}{(\Delta'')^2}=\frac{(30)^4}{(20)^2}=\frac{3^4\times10^2}{2^2}$$

$$\therefore \Delta=\frac{3^2\times10}{2}=45 \Rightarrow \frac{\Delta}{9}=5$$

14. **(6)** $p_1=\frac{2\Delta}{a}, p_2=\frac{2\Delta}{b}, p_3=\frac{2\Delta}{c}$

$$\therefore p_1+p_2+p_3\geq3(p_1p_2p_3)^{1/3}$$

$$=3\left\{\frac{(2\Delta)^3}{abc}\right\}^{1/3}=6\Delta\left(\frac{1}{abc}\right)^{1/3}$$

$$=6rs\left(\frac{1}{abc}\right)^{1/3}=6r\frac{a+b+c}{2}\left(\frac{1}{abc}\right)^{1/3}$$

$$=9r\left(\frac{a+b+c}{3}\right)\left(\frac{1}{abc}\right)^{1/3}\geq9r \quad (AM/GM\geq1)$$

(Equality occurs when $p_1=p_2=p_3$ and $a=b=c$, i.e. when ΔABC is equilateral)

$$\therefore p_1+p_2+p_3\geq9\times\frac{2}{3}=6$$

15. **(c)** $r_1+r_2+r_3-r=\Delta\left[\frac{1}{s-a}+\frac{1}{s-b}+\frac{1}{s-c}-\frac{1}{s}\right]$

$$=\Delta\left[\frac{2s-a-b}{(s-a)(s-b)}+\frac{s-s+c}{s(s-c)}\right]$$

$$=\Delta c\left[\frac{s(s-c)+(s-a)(s-b)}{s(s-a)(s-b)(s-c)}\right]$$

$$=\frac{\Delta c}{\Delta^2}\left[2s^2-s(a+b+c)+ab\right]=\frac{abc}{\Delta}=4R$$

$\therefore r_1+r_2+r_3=r+4R$

$r_1r_2+r_2r_3+r_3r_1$

$$=\Delta^2\left[\frac{1}{(s-a)(s-b)}+\frac{1}{(s-b)(s-c)}+\frac{1}{(s-c)(s-a)}\right]$$

$$=\frac{\Delta^2(s-c+s-a+s-b)}{(s-a)(s-b)(s-c)}=s^2$$

$$r_1r_2r_3=\frac{\Delta^2}{(s-a)(s-b)(s-c)}=\Delta s=rs^2$$

$\therefore r_1, r_2, r_3$ are roots of the equations

$x^3-x^2(r_1+r_2+r_3)+x(r_1r_2+r_2r_3+r_3r_1)-r_1r_2r_3=0$

$\Rightarrow x^3-x^2(4R+r)+x(s^2)-rs^2=0$

16. **(a)** We have

$x^3-(4R+r)x^2+s^2x-rs^2=(x-r_1)(x-r_2)(x-r_3)$

$\Rightarrow(-s)^3-(4R+r)(-s)^2+s^2(-s)-rs^2$

$=(-s-r_1)(-s-r_2)(-s-r_3)$

$\therefore (s+r_1)(s+r_2)(s+r_3)=2s^2(s+r+2R)$

17. **(b)** For real roots c_1 and c_2, $D>0$, i.e., $a>b\sin A$

Consider the smaller root, say

$c_1=b\cos A-\sqrt{a^2-b^2\sin^2 A}$

$c_1>0$ if $b\cos A>\sqrt{a^2-b^2\sin^2 A}$, i.e., if

$b^2\cos^2 A>a^2-b^2\sin^2 A$ and $\cos A>0$

or if $b^2>a^2$ and $\cos A>0$.

Hence, two different triangles are possible if $a>b\sin A$, $b>a$ and A is acute.

ALTERNATIVELY

The equation $c^2-(2b\cos A)c+b^2-a^2=0$ has two distinct positive roots c_1 and c_2 if and only if discriminant >0, $c_1+c_2>0$ and $c_1c_2>0$

$\Rightarrow a>b\sin A$, $2b\cos A>0$ and $b^2-a^2>0$

$\Rightarrow a>b\sin A$ and $b>a$

18. **(b)** If $a=b$, then $a^2=b^2(\cos^2 A+\sin^2 A)$

$\Rightarrow a^2-b^2\sin^2 A=b^2\cos^2 A$

$\therefore \sqrt{a^2-b^2\sin^2 A}=b\cos A\Rightarrow G=0$

but $c_2>0$. So, only one triangle is possible.

19. **(A)→(p); (B)→(s); (C)→(p, q); (D)→(q)**

(A) We have,

$$\frac{r}{r_1}=\frac{4R\sin\frac{A}{2}\sin\frac{B}{2}\sin\frac{C}{2}}{4R\sin\frac{A}{2}\cos\frac{B}{2}\cos\frac{C}{2}}=\tan\frac{B}{2}\tan\frac{C}{2}=\frac{1}{4}$$

$$\therefore \tan\frac{A}{2}\left(\tan\frac{B}{2}+\tan\frac{C}{2}\right)$$

$$=1-\tan\frac{B}{2}\tan\frac{C}{2}=1-\frac{1}{4}=\frac{3}{4}$$

(B) We have, $(r_1r_2r_3)^{1/3}\ge\dfrac{3}{\frac{1}{r_1}+\frac{1}{r_2}+\frac{1}{r_3}}=3r$

$$\therefore \frac{r_1r_2r_3}{r^3}\ge 27$$

(C) $a+b>c\Rightarrow 2b-c+b>c\Rightarrow\dfrac{b}{c}>\dfrac{2}{3}$

Also, $b+c>a\Rightarrow b+c>2b-c\Rightarrow\dfrac{b}{c}<2$

Again, $c+a>b\Rightarrow 2b>b\ \therefore\ \dfrac{b}{c}\in\left(\dfrac{2}{3},2\right)$

(D) We have, $\dfrac{PD}{AD}=\dfrac{ar(\Delta BPC)}{ar(\Delta BAC)}$,........*etc.*

$$\therefore \frac{PD}{AD}+\frac{PE}{BE}+\frac{PF}{CF}$$

$$=\frac{ar(\Delta BPC)+ar(\Delta CPA)+ar(\Delta APB)}{ar(\Delta ABC)}=1$$

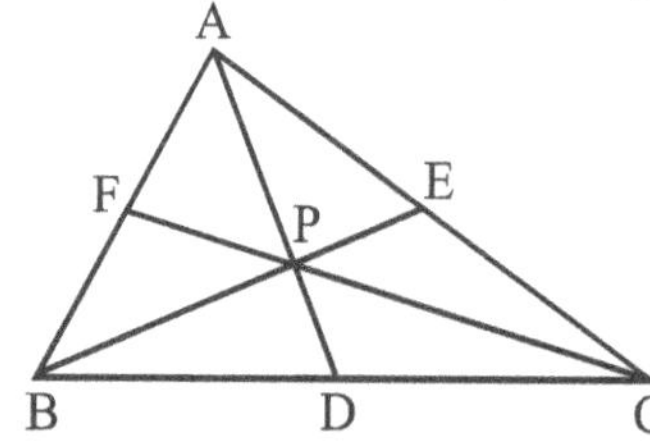

20. **(A)→(r); (B)→(q); (C)→(p); (D)→(s)**

(A) $\alpha=\dfrac{1}{2}\sqrt{2b^2+2c^2-a^2}$, $\beta=\dfrac{1}{2}\sqrt{2c^2+2a^2-b^2}$,

$$=\frac{1}{2}\sqrt{2a^2+2b^2-c^2}$$

$$\therefore \alpha^2+\beta^2+\gamma^2=\frac{1}{4}(3a^2+3b^2+3c^2)$$

$$\Rightarrow\frac{\alpha^2+\beta^2+\gamma^2}{a^2+b^2+c^2}=\frac{3}{4}$$

(B) $ar(\Delta ABC)=ar(\Delta PBC)+ar(\Delta CPA)+ar(\Delta APB)$

$$\frac{\sqrt{3}}{4}\times 4=\frac{1}{2}[x\times 2+y\times 2+z\times 2]$$

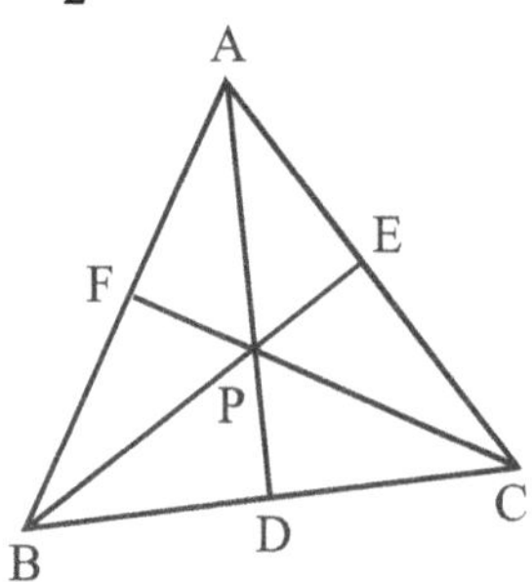

$\therefore x+y+z=\sqrt{3}$

(C) $2B=A+C\Rightarrow B=\dfrac{\pi}{3}$ and $A+C=\dfrac{2\pi}{3}$

$b^2=ac\Rightarrow\sin^2 B=\sin A\sin C\Rightarrow\sin A\sin C=\dfrac{3}{4}$

$\therefore \cos(A-C)-\cos(A+C)=\dfrac{3}{2}\Rightarrow\cos(A-C)=1$

$\therefore A=C\Rightarrow A=B=C=\dfrac{\pi}{3}$

so the triangle is equilateral.

(D) $\dfrac{\sqrt{abc(a+b+c)}}{\Delta}=\dfrac{1}{\Delta}\sqrt{4R\Delta\,.\,2s}$

$$=\sqrt{\frac{8Rs}{\Delta}}=\sqrt{\frac{8R}{r}}\ge\sqrt{8\times 2}=4$$

Mock Test Full Syllabus Mathematics

Paper -1

SECTION – I - Multiple Correct Choice Type

This section contains 7 multiple choice questions. Each question has 4 choices (a), (b), (c) and (d) for its answer, out of which ONE OR MORE is/are correct.

1. Two sides of a triangle are lies along the lines (a + b)x + (a – b)y – 2ab=0 and (a – b) x + (a + b) y – 2ab = 0. If the triangle is isosceles and the third side passes through the point (b – a, a – b), then the equation of third side can be

(a) $x+y=0$ (b) $x=y+2(b-a)$

(c) $x-b+a=0$ (d) $y-a+b=0$

2. With the usual notation for the greatest integer function $f(x)=[x]^3-[x^3]$ is discontinuous at all

(a) integers n

(b) integers $n \neq 1$

(c) integers $n \neq 1$ since $f(n^-) \neq f(n)$

(d) integers $n \neq 1$ since $f(n^+) \neq f(n)$

3. If [x] denotes the greatest integer less than or equal to x then $\lim\limits_{n\to\infty} \sum\limits_{k=1}^{n} [kx]$ is not equal to

(a) x/2 (b) x/3 (c) x (d) 0

4. $f(x)=\dfrac{[x]+1}{\{x\}+1}$ for $f:[0,\frac{5}{2}) \to (\frac{1}{2},3]$, where [.] represents greatest integer function and { . } represents fractional part of x, then which of the following is/are true?

(a) f(x) is injective discontinuous function

(b) f(x) is surjective non differentiable function

(c) $\min\left(\lim\limits_{x\to 1^-} f(x), \lim\limits_{x\to 1^+} f(x)\right) = f(1)$

(d) max (x values of point of discontinuity)= f(1)

5. A function f (x) satisfies the relation $f(x+y)$ $=f(x)+f(y)+xy(x+y)\ \forall\ x, y \in R$. If $f'(0)=-1$, then

(a) f(x) is a polynomial function

(b) f(x) is an exponential function

(c) f(x) is twice differentiable for all $x \in R$

(d) $f'(3)=8$

6. Let $P(X=r)=pq^r$ and $P(Y=r)=pq^r$, where $r=1, 2, \ldots\ldots\ldots\ldots\ldots$, $0<p<1, q=1-p$. Suppose X and Y are independent. Let $Z=\max(X, Y)$. Then

(a) $P(Z \leq m)=(1-q^m)^2$

(b) $P(Z=m)= 2pq^{m-1} - p(1+q)\,q^{2m-2}$

(c) $\sum\limits_{m\geq 1} P(Z=m)=\dfrac{1}{p}$

(d) $P(X \leq m)=1-q^m$

7. If the conics whose equations are

$$S_1:(\sin^2\theta)x^2+(2h\tan\theta)xy+(\cos^2\theta)y^2 +32x+16y+19=0$$

$$S_2:(\cos^2\theta)x^2-(2h'\cot\theta)xy+(\sin^2\theta)y^2 +16x+32y+19=0$$

intersect in four concyclic point, where $\theta \in \left(0, \frac{\pi}{2}\right)$, then the correct statement(s) can be

(a) $h+h'=0$ (b) $h-h'=0$

(c) $\theta=\dfrac{\pi}{4}$ (d) $\theta=\dfrac{\pi}{6}$

SECTION – II - Integer Answer Type

This section contains 5 questions. The answer to each of the questions is a single-digit integer, ranging from 0 to 9. The appropriate bubbles below the respective question numbers in the ORS have to be darkened. For example, if the correct answers to question numbers X, Y, Z and W (say) are 6, 0, 9 and 2, respectively, then the correct darkening of bubbles will look like the following:

X	Y	Z	W
0	0	0	0
1	1	1	1
2	2	2	2
3	3	3	3
4	4	4	4
5	5	5	5
6	6	6	6
7	7	7	7
8	8	8	8
9	9	9	9

8. If $2\tan^{-1}(2x+1)=\cos^{-1}x$, then find the value of x.

9. Consider the curve $C_1: y=\sin 2x-\sqrt{3}\,|\sin x|$, C_1 cuts the x - axis at (a, 0), $a \in (-\pi, \pi)$. A_1: The area bounded by the curve C_1 and the positive x-axis between the origin and the ordinate x = a,

A_2: The area bounded by the curve C_1 and the negative x-axis between the ordinate x = a and the origin. Find the value of $A_1+A_2+8A_1A_2$.

10. Find the value of $\lim\limits_{x\to\frac{\pi}{2}} \sqrt{\dfrac{\tan x-\sin(\tan^{-1}(\tan x))}{\tan x+\cos^2(\tan x)}}$.

11. Find the value of $\int_2^4 \left(\log_x 2 - \frac{(\log_x 2)^2}{\ln 2} \right) dx$.

12. Let $f(x), x \geq 0$ be a non-negative continuous function and let $F(x) = \int_0^x f(t)dt, x \geq 0$.

If for some $c > 0, f(x) \leq c\,F(x)$, then find the value of $f(c)$.

SECTION – III - Matching Type

This section contains 6 questions of Matching Type, contains two tables each having 3 columns and 4 rows. Based on each table, there are three questions. Each question has four options (a), (b), (c) and (d) ONLY ONE of these four options is correct.

(Qs. 13–15): By appropriately matching the information given in the three columns of the following table, give the answer of the question that follows.

Column 1 gives information about first order non-linear differential equations.

Column 2 gives information about general solutions of the given differential equations.

Column 3 gives information about singular solutions of the given differential equations.

Column 1	Column 2	Column 3
(I) $1 + \left(\frac{dy}{dx}\right)^2 = \frac{1}{y^2}$	(i) $y = Cx + C^2 + x^2$	(P) $y = 2$
(II) $y = x\frac{dy}{dx} + \left(\frac{dy}{dx}\right)^2$	(ii) $(x + C)^2 + y^2 = 1$	(Q) $y = -\frac{1}{4}x^2$
(III) $y = \left(\frac{dy}{dx}\right)^2 - 3x\frac{dy}{dx} + 3x^2$	(iii) $4(2 - y)(y + 1)^2 = 9(x + C)^2$	(R) $y = 1$
(IV) $\left(\frac{dy}{dx}\right)^2 (1 - y)^2 = 2 - y$	(iv) $y = Cx + C^2$	(S) $y = \frac{3}{4}x^2$

[Note : Singular solution of a differential equation does not have any arbitrary constant.]

13. Which of the following options is the only correct combination?

(a) (I) (ii) (R) (b) (II) (iii) (P) (c) (III) (iv) (S) (d) (IV) (i) (Q)

14. Which of the following options is the only correct combination?

(a) (I) (ii) (P) (b) (IV) (iii) (P) (c) (III) (iv) (S) (d) (II) (i) (S)

15. Which of the following is the only incorrect combination?

(a) (I) (ii) (R) (b) (IV) (iii) (P) (c) (III) (i) (S) (d) (III) (iv) (Q)

(Qs. 16–18): By appropriately matching the information given in the three columns of the following table, give the answer of the questions that follows.

Columns 1 and 2 gives information about inequalities.

Column 3 gives information about the solutions of given system of inequalities.

Column 1	Column 2	Column 3
(I) $2(x - 1) < x + 5$	(i) $x - \frac{5x}{3} < -8$	(P) $(-7, 11)$
(II) $3x - 7 > 2(x - 6)$	(ii) $2x + 19 < 6x + 47$	(Q) $(-1, 7)$
(III) $\frac{3x}{2} + 5 < \frac{x}{2}$	(iii) $3(x + 2) > 2 - x$	(R) $(5, \infty)$
(IV) $5(2x - 7) - 3(2x + 3) < 0$	(iv) $6 - x > 11 - 2x$	(S) No solution

16. Which of the following options is the only correct combination?
(a) (I) (ii) (Q) (b) (II) (i) (S)
(c) (III) (iv) (R) (d) (IV) (ii) (P)

17. Which of the following options is the only correct combination?
(a) (IV) (ii) (R) (b) (II) (iv) (Q)
(c) (III) (i) (S) (d) (I) (iii) (P)

18. Which of the following options is the only incorrect combination?
(a) (II) (iv) (Q) (b) (III) (i) (S)
(c) (IV) (ii) (P) (d) (I) (iii) (Q)

Paper -2

SECTION – I - Single Correct Choice Type

This section contains 7 multiple choice questions. Each question has 4 choices (a), (b), (c) and (d) for its answer, out of which ONLY ONE is correct.

1. A ray of light travels along a line $y = 4$ and strikes the surface of a curve $y^2 = 4(x + y)$ then equation of the line along reflected ray travel
(a) $x = 0$ (b) $x = 2$
(c) $x + y = 4$ (d) $2x + y = 4$

2. The conic represented by
$x = 2(\cos t + \sin t), y = 5(\cos t - \sin t)$ is
(a) a circle (b) a parabola
(c) an ellipse (d) a hyperbola

3. If the straight line $ax + by = 2$; $a, b \neq 0$ touches the circle $x^2 + y^2 - 2x = 3$ and is normal to the circle $x^2 + y^2 - 4y = 6$, then the values of a and b are respectively
(a) $1, -1$ (b) $1, 2$
(c) $-4/3, 1$ (d) $2, 1$

4. The exponent of 7 in ${}^{100}C_{50}$ is
(a) 0 (b) 2
(c) 4 (d) None of these

5. The equation $3\sin^2 x + 10\cos x - 6 = 0$ is satisfied if $(n \in I)$
(a) $x = n\pi + \cos^{-1}(1/3)$ (b) $x = n\pi - \cos^{-1}(1/3)$
(c) $x = 2n\pi \pm \cos^{-1}(1/3)$ (d) $x = \frac{n\pi}{2} - \cos^{-1}(1/3)$

6. Let the coordinates of the two points A and B be (1, 2) and (7, 5) respectively. The line AB is rotated through 45° in anti clockwise direction about the point of trisection of AB which is nearer to B. The equation of the line in new position is
(a) $2x - y - 6 = 0$ (b) $x - y - 1 = 0$
(c) $3x - y - 11 = 0$ (d) None of these

7. A line intersects the straight lines $5x - y - 4 = 0$ and $3x - 4y - 4 = 0$ at A and B respectively. If a point P (1, 5) on the line AB is such that AP : PB = 2 : 1 (internally), find the point A.
(a) $\left(\frac{75}{17}, \frac{307}{17}\right)$ (b) $\left(\frac{65}{17}, \frac{304}{17}\right)$
(c) $\left(\frac{75}{17}, \frac{104}{17}\right)$ (d) $\left(\frac{75}{17}, \frac{180}{17}\right)$

SECTION – II - Multiple Correct Choice Type

This section contains 7 multiple choice questions. Each question has 4 choices (a), (b), (c) and (d) for its answer, out of which ONE OR MORE is/are correct.

8. Let $\Delta(x) = \begin{vmatrix} 3 & 3x & 3x^2 + 2a^2 \\ 3x & 3x^2 + 2a^2 & 3x^3 + 6a^2 x \\ 3x^2 + 2a^2 & 3x^3 + 6a^2 x & 3x^4 + 12a^2 x^2 + 2a^4 \end{vmatrix}$

then
(a) $\Delta'(x) = 0$
(b) $\Delta(x)$ is independent of x
(c) $\int_0^1 \Delta(x)\, dx = 16a^6$
(d) $y = \Delta(x)$ is a straight line of infinite slope

9. Indicate the relation which is/are true?
(a) $\tan|\tan^{-1} x| = |x|$ (b) $\cot|\cot^{-1} x| = x$
(c) $\tan^{-1}|\tan x| = |x|$ (d) $\sin|\sin^{-1} x| = |x|$

10. Choose the correct statements
(a) The largest term in the sequence $a_n = \frac{n^2}{n^3 + 200}$ is a_7.
(b) log y lies between $\frac{2(y-1)}{y+1}$ and $\frac{y^2 - 1}{y}$ for all $y > 0$.
(c) If $a, b > 0$; $0 \leq p < 1$ then $(a + b)^p \leq a^p + b^p$.
(d) The radius of the right circular cylinder of greatest curved surface which can be inscribed in a given cone is half that of the cone.

11. Choose the correct statements
(a) If $f(x) = x^3 - x^2 + x + 1$ and
$$g(x) = \begin{cases} \max. f(t); & 0 \leq t \leq x \text{ for } 0 \leq x \leq 1 \\ 3 - x; & 1 < x \leq 2 \end{cases}$$
then g(x) is not differentiable at $x = 1$.
(b) If $y = f(x)$ where $x = 2t - |t|$, $y = t^2 + t|t|$, $t \in R$ then it is differentiable in $[-1, 1]$.
(c) A function f is defined by $f(x^2) = x^3$ for all $x > 0$ then f is not differentiable at 4.
(d) Every differentiable function is continuous, but the converse is not true.

12. The solution of $x^2 y_1^2 + x y y_1 - 6y^2 = 0$ are (y_1 means $\frac{dy}{dx}$)
(a) $y = cx^2$ (b) $x^2 y = c$
(c) $\frac{1}{2}\log y = c + \log x$ (d) $x^3 y = c$

13. The graph of the function $\cos x\cos(x+2)-\cos^2(x+1)$ is

(a) A straight line passing through (0, 0)

(b) A straight line passing through $\left(\frac{\pi}{2},-\sin^2 1\right)$ and paralles to x-axis

(c) A straight line passing through $(0, -\sin^2 1)$

(d) Not a straight line

14. Let ω be a complex cube root of unity with $\omega \neq 1$ and $P=[p_{ij}]$ be a $n \times n$ matrix with $p_{ij}=\omega^{i+j}$. Then $p^2 \neq 0$, when n =

(a) 57 (b) 55

(c) 58 (d) 56

SECTION – III - Comprehension Type

This section contains 2 paragraphs. Each paragraph has 2 multiple choice questions based on a paragraph. Each question has 4 choices (a), (b), (c) and (d) for its answer, out of which ONLY ONE is correct.

PARAGRAPH - 1

Let f be an even function integrable everywhere and periodic with period 2. Let $g(x)=\int_0^x f(t)dt$ and $g(1)=\alpha$

15. Function g(x) is

(a) odd (b) even

(c) neither even nor odd (d) none of these

16. Which of the following statement is correct for all x?

(a) $g(x+2)+g(x)=g(2)$ (b) $g(x+2)-g(x)=g(2)$

(c) $g(x+2)-g(x)=2g(2)$ (d) none of these

PARAGRAPH - 2

Three concepts related to lines are :

(a) Let equation of the line be

$$\frac{x-a}{\ell}=\frac{y-b}{m}=\frac{z-c}{n}=r \quad \text{(say)} \quad ....(1)$$

and (α, β, γ) be the point, Let ℓ,m,n, denote the actual d.c.'s of the line. Any point on the line (1) is

$P(\ell r+a, mr+b, nr+c)$ ....(2)

If it is the foot of the perpendicular, from A on the line, then AP is ⊥ to the line, so

$\ell(\ell r+a-\alpha)+m(mr+b-\beta)+n(nr+c-\gamma)=0$

i.e. $r=(\alpha-a)\ell+(\beta-b)m+(\gamma-c)n$

Since $\ell^2+m^2+n^2=1$

Putting this value of r in (2), we get the foot of the perpendicular from point A to the line

Since foot of perpendicular P is known, length of perpendicular,

$$AP=\sqrt{[(\ell r+a-\alpha)^2(mr+b-\beta)^2+(nr+c-\gamma)^2]}$$

(b) Shortest distance between the lines $\vec{r}=\vec{a}_1-\lambda\vec{b}_1$ and $\vec{r}=\vec{a}_2-\lambda\vec{b}_2$ is given by S.D. $=\left|\frac{(\vec{a}_2-\vec{a}_1).(\vec{b}_1\times\vec{b}_2)}{|\vec{b}_1\times\vec{b}_2|}\right|$

(c) To find image of a line in a plane consider the line

$$\frac{x-\alpha}{\ell}=\frac{y-\beta}{m}=\frac{z-\gamma}{n}=r.$$

A variable point on this line be taken as

$Q(\ell r+\alpha, mr+\beta, nr+\gamma)$.

If this lies on the plane, then

$a(\ell r+\alpha)+b(mr+\beta)+c(nr+\gamma)+d=0$

or $r=-\frac{a\alpha+b\beta+c\gamma+d}{a\ell+bm+cn}$

The co-ordinates of Q can be obtained by the substituting the value of r.

Now, find the image R of (α,β,γ) in the plane. Find the equation of the line RQ which is the image of the PQ.

17. A line with direction cosines proportional to (2, 7, –5) is drawn to intersect the lines $\frac{x-5}{3}=\frac{y-7}{-1}=\frac{z+2}{1}$ and $\frac{x+3}{-3}=\frac{y-3}{2}=\frac{z-6}{4}$. The intercepted length is

(a) $\sqrt{58}$ (b) $\sqrt{78}$

(c) $\sqrt{65}$ (d) $\sqrt{62}$

18. Let A, B, C be points with position vectors $\vec{r}_1=2\hat{i}-\hat{j}+\hat{k}$, $\vec{r}_2=\hat{i}+2\hat{j}+3\hat{k}$ and $\vec{r}_3=3\hat{i}+\hat{j}+2\hat{k}$ relative to the origin O. The shortest distance between point B and plane OAC is

(a) 10 (b) 5

(c) $\sqrt{5/7}$ (d) $2\sqrt{5/7}$

SOLUTIONS

ANSWER KEY - PAPER 1							
1	(a, b)	6	(a, b, d)	11	(0)	16	(d)
2	(b, c)	7	(b, c)	12	(0)	17	(c)
3	(b, c, d)	8	(0)	13	(a)	18	(a)
4	(a, b, d)	9	(4)	14	(b)		
5	(a, c, d)	10	(1)	15	(d)		
ANSWER KEY - PAPER 2							
1	(a)	6	(c)	11	(a, b, d)		
2	(c)	7	(a)	12	(a, c, d)	16	(b)
3	(c)	8	(a, b, c)	13	(b,c)	17	(b)
4	(a)	9	(a, b, d)	14	(b, c, d)	18	(d)
5	(c)	10	(a, b, c, d)	15	(a)		

EXPLANATORY NOTES

PAPER - 1

1. **(a,b)**

$(a+b)x + (a-b)y - 2ab = 0$

and $(a-b)x + (a+b)y - 2ab = 0$

Equation of the angle bisectors are

$(a+b)x + (a-b)y - 2ab = 0 = \pm((a-b)x + (a+b)y - 2ab)$

$2bx - 2by = 0$ i.e., $x = y$

and $2ax + 2ay - 4ab = 0$ i.e., $x + y = 2b$

$\therefore$ Equation of third side is given by

(i) $x - y = k$ satisfying the point $(b-a, a-b)$

$\therefore$ $k = 2b - 2a$

$\therefore$ the line is $x - y = 2(b-a)$

(ii) $x + y - 2b = k$ passing through the point $(b-a, a-b)$

$\therefore$ $k = -2b$

$\therefore$ the line is $x + y = 0$

2. **(b, c)** $f(n) = [n]^3 - [n^3] = n^3 - n^3 = 0$

$$f(n^+) = \lim_{h\to 0}\{[n+h]^3 - [(n+h)^3]\}$$

$$= \lim_{h\to 0}\{n^3 - [n^3 + h(h^2 + 3n^2 + 3nh)]\}$$

$$= n^3 - n^3 = 0 = f(n)$$

$$f(n^-) = \lim_{h\to 0}\{[n-h]^3 - [(n-h)^3]\}$$

$$= \lim_{h\to 0}\{(n-1)^3 - [n^3 - h(h^2 + 3n^2 - 3nh)]\}$$

$= (n-1)^3 - (n^3 - 1) \neq f(n)$ except when $n = 1$.

3. **(b, c, d)** For any integer k,

$kx - 1 < [kx] < kx + 1$

$$\Rightarrow \sum_{k=1}^{n}(kx-1) < \sum_{k=1}^{n}[kx] < \sum_{k=1}^{n}(kx+1)$$

$$\frac{xn(n+1)}{2} - n < \sum_{k=1}^{n}[kx] < \frac{xn(n+1)}{2} + n$$

$$\frac{x}{2}\left(1+\frac{1}{n}\right) - \frac{1}{n} < \frac{1}{n^2}\sum_{k=1}^{n}[kx] < \frac{x}{2}\left(1+\frac{1}{n}\right) + \frac{1}{n}$$

Taking limit as $n \to \infty$, we have

$$\lim_{n\to\infty}\sum_{k=1}^{n}[kx] = \frac{x}{2}$$

4. **(a,b,d)**

$$f(x) = \begin{cases} \dfrac{1}{x+1}, & 0 \le x < 1 \\ \dfrac{2}{x}, & 1 \le x < 2 \\ \dfrac{3}{x-1}, & 2 \le x < 5/2 \end{cases}$$

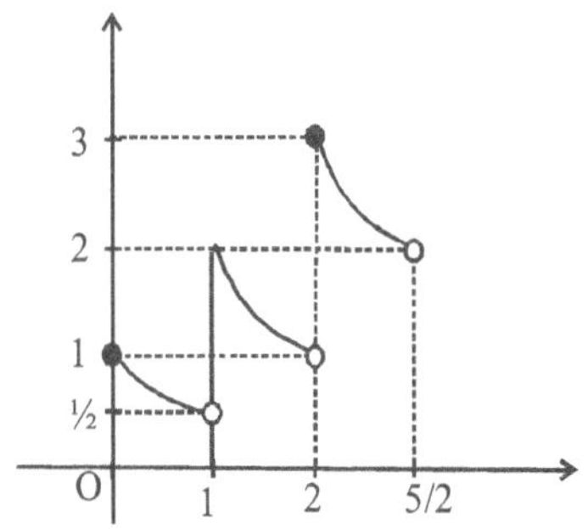

Clearly f (x) is discontinuous and bijective (both injective and surjective) function $\lim_{x\to1^-} f(x)=\frac{1}{2}$; $\lim_{x\to1^+} f(x)=2$

$$\min\left(\lim_{x\to1^-} f(x), \lim_{x\to1^+} f(x)\right)=\frac{1}{2}\neq f(1)$$

max (1, 2) = 2 = f(1).

5. **(a, c, d)**

$f(x+y)=f(x)+f(y)+xy(x+y)$

$$f(0)=0 \quad \therefore \lim_{h\to0}\frac{f(h)}{h}=-1$$

$$\therefore \lim_{h\to0}\frac{f(x+h)-f(x)}{h}=\lim_{h\to0}\frac{f(x)+f(h)+xh(x+h)-f(x)}{h}$$

$$=\lim_{h\to0}\frac{f(h)}{h}+\lim_{h\to0}x(x+h)=-1+x^2$$

$$\therefore f'(x)=-1+x^2 \qquad \therefore f(x)=\frac{x^3}{3}-x+c$$

$\therefore$ f (x) is a polynomial function, f (x) is twice differentiable for all $x\in R$ and $f'(3)=3^2-1=8$

6. **(a, b, d)** Note that $P(Z\le m)=P\{X\le m, Y\le m\}$

$$=P\{X\le m\}\,P\{Y\le m\}$$

But $P\{Y\le m\}=P\{X\le m\}$

$$=P(X=0)+P(X=1)+\ldots\ldots\ldots\ldots+P(X=m)$$

$$=p+pq+pq^2+\ldots\ldots\ldots\ldots$$

$$+pq^{m-1}=\frac{p(1-q^m)}{1-q}=1-q^m$$

$$\therefore P(Z\le m)=(1-q^m)^2$$

Now, $P(Z=m)=P(Z\le m)-P(Z\le m-1)$

$$=(1-q^m)^2-(1-q^{m-1})^2$$

$$=1-2q^m+q^{2m}-(1-2q^{m-1}+q^{2m-2})$$

$$=2pq^{m-1}-p(1+q)q^{2m-2} \quad [\because 1-q=p]$$

Clearly, $\sum_{m\ge1} P(Z=m)$

$$=\sum_{m\ge1}[2pq^{m-1}-p(1+q)q^{2m-2}]$$

$$=\frac{2p}{1-q}-\frac{p(1+q)}{1-q^2}=2-1=1.$$

7. **(b, c)** Curve through the intersection of S_1 and S_2 is given by $S_1+\lambda S_2=0$

$$\Rightarrow x^2(\sin^2\theta+\lambda\cos^2\theta)+2(h\tan\theta-\lambda h'\cot\theta)xy$$

$$+(\cos^2\theta+\lambda\sin^2\theta)y^2+(32+16\lambda)x+(16+32\lambda)y$$

$$+19(1+\lambda)=0$$

The above equation will represent a circle if

$$\sin^2\theta+\lambda\cos^2\theta=\cos^2\theta+\lambda\sin^2\theta$$

$$\Rightarrow (1-\lambda)(\sin^2\theta-\cos^2\theta)=0$$

$$\Rightarrow \lambda=1 \text{ or } \theta=\frac{\pi}{4}$$

Also $h\tan\theta-\lambda h'\cot\theta=0$

$\Rightarrow$ $h\tan\theta=\lambda h'\cot\theta$ which is satisfied if $\lambda=1 \text{ and } \theta=\frac{\pi}{4}$

$$\Rightarrow h=h'$$

8. **Ans : 0**

$$2\tan^{-1}(2x+1)=\cos^{-1}x$$

$$\Rightarrow \cos\left[2\tan^{-1}(2x+1)\right]=x$$

or $\frac{1-(2x+1^2)}{1+(2x+1)}=x$, or $\frac{4x^2+4x}{4x^2+4x+2}=x$

$$\Rightarrow 2x^3-x=0 \text{ or } x=0,\frac{1}{\sqrt{2}},-\frac{1}{\sqrt{2}}$$

Let us verify whether these roots satisfy the parent equation.

$x=0 \Rightarrow$ L. H. S. $=\frac{\pi}{2}$; R. H. S. $=\frac{\pi}{2}$ x is a root ...(1)

$x=\frac{1}{\sqrt{2}}\Rightarrow$ L. H. S. $=2\tan^{-1}\left(\sqrt{2}+1\right)$

$$=\pi+\tan^{-1}\left(\frac{2\sqrt{2}+2}{1-(2+2\sqrt{2}+1}\right)$$

$$=\pi+\tan^{-1}\left(\frac{2(\sqrt{2}+1)}{-2-2\sqrt{2}}\right)=\pi-\frac{\pi}{4}=\frac{3\pi}{4}$$

$$\text{R. H. S.}=\cos^{-1}\left(\frac{1}{\sqrt{2}}\right)=\frac{\pi}{4}$$

$x = \frac{1}{\sqrt{2}}$ is not a root ...(2)

$x = -\frac{1}{\sqrt{2}} \Rightarrow \text{L. H. S.} = 2\tan^{-1}\left(2-\sqrt{2}\right)$

$= -2\tan^{-1}\left(\sqrt{2}-1\right) < 0$

$\text{R. H. S.} = \cos^{-1}\left(-\frac{1}{\sqrt{2}}\right) = \frac{3\pi}{4}$

$\therefore x = -\frac{1}{\sqrt{2}}$ is not a root. ...(3)

Thus from (1), (2) and (3), x = 0 is the required solution.

9. Ans : 4

The given curve is $C_1 : y = \sin 2x - \sqrt{3}\,|\sin x|$

Now, C_1 cuts the x-axis i.e, when y = 0 at $x = -\frac{5\pi}{6}$ and $x = \frac{\pi}{6}$ for $x \in (-\pi, \pi)$ i.e.

We have two values of a .

$a = -\frac{5\pi}{6}$ and $a = \frac{\pi}{6}$

$[y = \sin 2x - \sqrt{3}\sin x$ for $x \in (0, \pi)$

and $y = \sin 2x + \sqrt{3}\sin x$ for $x \in (-\pi, 0)]$

Thus,

$$A_1 = \int_0^{\pi/6}\left(\sin 2x - \sqrt{3}\sin x\right)dx = \left[-\frac{\cos 2x}{2} + \sqrt{3}\cos x\right]_0^{\pi/6}$$

$$= \left[-\frac{1/2}{2} + \sqrt{3}\left(\frac{\sqrt{3}}{2}\right)\right] - \left[-\frac{1}{2} + \sqrt{3}(1)\right]$$

$$= -\frac{1}{4} + \frac{3}{2} + \frac{1}{2} - \sqrt{3} = \frac{7}{4} - \sqrt{3}$$

$$A_2 = \left|\int_{-\frac{5\pi}{6}}^{0}\left(\sin 2x + \sqrt{3}\sin x\right)dx\right|$$

$$= \left|\left[-\frac{\cos 2x}{2} - \sqrt{3}\cos x\right]_{-\frac{5\pi}{6}}^{0}\right|$$

$$= \left|\left[-\frac{1}{2} - \sqrt{3}\right] - \left\{-\frac{1/2}{2} - \sqrt{3}\left(-\frac{\sqrt{3}}{2}\right)\right\}\right|$$

$$= \left|-\frac{1}{2} - \sqrt{3} + \frac{1}{4} - \frac{3}{2}\right| = \frac{7}{4} + \sqrt{3}$$

Thus, $A_1 + A_2 + 8A_1A_2 = \frac{7}{2} + 8\left(\frac{49}{16} - 3\right) = \frac{7}{2} + \frac{1}{2} = 4$

10. Ans : 1

We have

$$\text{LHL} = \lim_{x \to \frac{\pi}{2}^-}\sqrt{\frac{\tan x - \sin\tan^{-1}(\tan x)}{\tan x + \cos^2(\tan x)}}$$

$$= \lim_{x \to \pi/2^-}\sqrt{\frac{\tan x - \sin x}{\tan x + \cos^2(\tan x)}}$$

$$= \lim_{x \to \pi/2^-}\sqrt{\frac{1 - \frac{\sin x}{\tan x}}{1 + \frac{\cos^2(\tan x)}{\tan x}}} = \sqrt{\frac{1-0}{1+0}} = 1$$

(As $x \to \frac{\pi}{2}^-$, $0 < x < \frac{\pi}{2}$ $\therefore \tan^{-1}(\tan x) = x$

Further as , $x \to \frac{\pi}{2}-$, $\tan x \to \infty$ and $\cos^2(\tan x)$ is a real number between 0 and 1)

$$\text{RHL} = \lim_{x \to \frac{\pi}{2}^+}\sqrt{\frac{\tan x - \sin\tan^{-1}(\tan x)}{\tan x + \cos^2(\tan x)}}$$

$$= \lim_{x \to \frac{\pi}{2}^+}\sqrt{\frac{\tan x + \sin x}{\tan x + \cos^2 x(\tan x)}}$$

$$= \lim_{x \to \frac{\pi}{2}^+}\sqrt{\frac{1 + \frac{\sin x}{\tan x}}{1 + \frac{\cos^2(\tan x)}{\tan x}}} = \sqrt{\frac{1+0}{1-0}} = 1$$

(As $x \to \frac{\pi}{2}^+$, $x > \frac{\pi}{2} \Rightarrow \tan^{-1}\tan x$

$= \tan^{-1}\tan(x-\pi) = x - \pi$

$\therefore \sin\tan^{-1}(\tan x) = \sin(x-\pi) = -\sin x$

Further as $x \to \frac{\pi}{2}+; \tan x \to -\infty$ and $\cos^2(\tan x)$ is a real number between 0 and 1)

LHL = RHL = 1 $\therefore$ required limit = 1.

11. Ans : 0

$$I = \int_2^4 \left[\frac{ln2}{ln\,x} - \frac{(ln\,2)^2}{(ln\,2)\,(ln\,x)^2}\right]$$

$$dx = (ln\,2)\int_2^4\left[\frac{1}{ln\,x} - \frac{1}{(ln\,x)^2}\right]dx$$

Put $ln\,x = t \Rightarrow x = e^t \Rightarrow dx = e^t dt$

For $x = 2, t = ln\,2$, $x = 4, t = ln\,4 = 2\,ln\,2$

$$\therefore I = (ln\,2)\int_{ln2}^{2ln2}\left[\frac{1}{t} - \frac{1}{t^2}\right]e^t dt = (ln\,2)\left[\frac{e^t}{t}\right]_{ln2}^{2ln2}$$

$$= (ln\,2)\left[\frac{4}{2\,ln\,2} - \frac{2}{ln\,2}\right] = 0.$$

12. Ans : 0

Given that, for $x \geq 0$,

$$F(x) = \int_0^x f(t)dt \Rightarrow F(0) = \int_0^0 f(t)dt = 0$$

As $f(x) \leq cF(x) \forall x \geq 0$, we get $f(0) \leq cF(0) \Rightarrow f(0) \leq 0$

Since $f(x) \geq 0\ \forall x \geq 0$, we get

$f(0) \geq 0 \quad \therefore f(0) = 0$

Since, f is continuous on $[0,\infty]$, F is differentiable on $[0,\infty]$, and $F'(x) = f(x)\ \forall\ x \geq 0$.

Since $f(x) \leq c\,F(x) \leq 0\ \forall\ x \geq 0$, Multiplying both sides by e^{-cx} (the integrating factor) we get

$$e^{-cx}F'(x) - ce^{-cx}F(x) \leq 0 \Rightarrow \frac{d}{dx}[e^{-cx}F(x)] \leq 0$$

So, $g(x) = e^{-cx}F(x)$ is a decreasing function on $[0,\infty)$ i.e., $g(x) \leq g(0)$ for each $x \geq 0$.

But $g(0) = e^{\circ}F(0) = 0$

$\therefore \quad g(x) \leq 0 \forall x \geq 0$

$\Rightarrow \quad e^{-cx}F(x) \leq 0\ \forall\ x \geq 0 \Rightarrow F(x) \leq 0\ \forall\ x \geq 0$

But it is given that $f(x) \geq 0\ \ \forall x \geq 0$.

Hence, $f(x) = 0\ \forall x \geq 0$. So, $f(c) = 0$

13. (a) Since, $1 + (y')^2 = \frac{1}{y^2}$ ...(1)

Differentiating above equation with respect to y' gives,

$2y' = 0 \quad \Rightarrow y' = 0$

Putting $y' = 0$ in equation (1), we get

$$1 + 0 = \frac{1}{y^2}$$

$\Rightarrow \quad y = \pm 1$

which will be a singular solution. To find general solution of differential equation.

$$(y')^2 = \frac{1}{y^2} - 1 = \frac{1-y^2}{y^2}$$

$$\Rightarrow \quad y' = \pm\frac{\sqrt{1-y^2}}{y}$$

$$\Rightarrow \quad \frac{y\,dy}{\sqrt{1-y^2}} = \pm dx$$

After integrating, on both sides, we get

$$\sqrt{1-y^2} = \pm(x + C)$$

where C is an arbitrary constant.

Hence, $(x + C)^2 + y^2 = 1$

14. (b) Since, $y'(1-y^2) = 2 - y$... (B)

Differentiating with respect to x, we get

$2y'(1-y)^2 = 0$ ... (C)

Eliminating y' from (B) and (C), we get

$$(y')^2 = \frac{2-y}{(1-y)^2}$$

$$\Rightarrow \quad \frac{2-y}{(1-y)^2}\cdot(1-y)^4 = 0$$

$$\Rightarrow \quad (1-y)^2(2-y) = 0$$

$$\text{Here, } \left(\frac{dy}{dx}\right)^2 = \frac{2-y}{(1-y)^2}$$

$$\Rightarrow \quad \frac{dy}{dx} = \pm\frac{\sqrt{2-y}}{1-y}$$

$$\Rightarrow \quad \frac{(1-y)\,dy}{\sqrt{2-y}} = \pm dx$$

On integrating both sides, we get

$$\int \frac{(1-y)\,dy}{\sqrt{2-y}} = \pm \int dx + C$$

$$\Rightarrow \frac{2}{3}\sqrt{2-y}\,(2-y-3) = \mp x - C$$

$$\Rightarrow \frac{4}{9}(2-y)(y+1)^2 = (x+C)^2$$

$$\Rightarrow 4(2-y)(y+1)^2 = 9(x+C)^2$$

Differentiating with respect to C, we get

$0 = 18(x+C)$

$x + C = 0$

So, $(y+1)^2(2-y) = 0$

$\Rightarrow y = 2$

which will be the singular solution.

15. (d) Since, $y = (y')^2 - 3xy' + 3x^2$ ... (A)

The general solution of above differential equation is given by

$y = Cx + C^2 + x^2$

Differentiating with respect to x, we get

$-x - 2C = 0$

$\Rightarrow C = \frac{-x}{2}$

Putting $C = \frac{-x}{2}$ in the equation (A), we get

$$y = \left(-\frac{x}{2}\right)\cdot x - \left(\frac{-x}{2}\right)^2 - x^2 = \frac{3}{4}x^2$$

16. (d) Since, $5(2x-7) - 3(2x+3) < 0$

$\Rightarrow 4x - 44 < 0$

$\Rightarrow x < 11$

and $2x + 19 < 6x + 47$

$-4x < 28$

$x > -7$

Hence, $x \in (-7, 11)$

17. (c) Since, $\frac{3x}{2} + 5 < \frac{x}{2}$

$\frac{3x}{2} - \frac{x}{2} + 5 < 0$

$2x < -10$

$x < -5$

and, $x - \frac{5x}{3} < -8$

$3x - 5x < -24$

$-2x < -24$

$x > 12$

Hence, there is no solution of the given system of inequalities.

18. (a) Since, $3x - 7 > 2(x-6)$

$3x - 2x > -12 + 7$

$x > -5$

and $6 - x > 11 - 2x$

$-x + 2x > 11 - 6$

$x > 5$

Hence, $x \in (5, \infty)$

PAPER - 2

1. **(a)** Given curve is

$y^2 - 4y = 4x$

$(y-2)^2 = 4(x+1)$

Focus : $x + 1 = 1$

$\Rightarrow x = 0$

$y - 2 = 0$

$\Rightarrow y = 2$

Point of intersection of the curve and y = 4 is (0, 4) from the reflection property of parabola reflected ray passes through the focus.

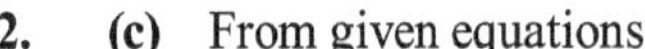

2. **(c)** From given equations

$x/2 = \cos t + \sin t$; $y/5 = \cos t - \sin t$

Eliminating t from (1) and (2), we have

$$\frac{x^2}{4} + \frac{y^2}{25} = 2 \Rightarrow \frac{x^2}{8} + \frac{y^2}{50} = 1, \text{ which is an ellipse.}$$

3. **(c)** Given $x^2 + y^2 - 2x = 3$

$\therefore$ Centre is (1, 0) and radius is 2 and $x^2 + y^2 - 4y = 6$

$\therefore$ Centre is (0, 2) and radius is $\sqrt{10}$.

Since line $ax + by = 2$ touches the first circle.

$$\therefore \frac{a(1) + b(0) - 2}{\sqrt{a^2 + b^2}} = 2 \text{ or } (a-2) = [2\sqrt{a^2 + b^2}\,] \quad ...(i)$$

Also the given line is normal to the second circle. Hence it will pass through the centre of the second circle.

$\therefore$ $a(0) + b(2) = 2$ or $2b = 2 \Rightarrow b = 1$

Putting this value in equation (i), we get

$a - 2 = 2\sqrt{a^2 + 1}$, or $(a-2)^2 = 4(a^2 + 1)$

or $a^2+4-4a=4a^2+4$, or $3a^2+4a=0$

or $a(3a+4)=0$, or $a=0,-4/3$

$\therefore$ values of a and b are $-4/3$ and 1 respectively according to the given choices.

4. **(a)** We have $^{100}C_{50}=\frac{100!}{50!50!}$

The exponent of 7 in 50! is

$$\left[\frac{50}{7}\right]+\left[\frac{50}{7^2}\right]=7+1=8,$$

and the exponent of 7 in 100! is

$$\left[\frac{100}{7}\right]+\left[\frac{100}{7^2}\right]=14+2=16$$

Thus, exponent of 7 in $^{100}C_{50}$ is $16-2(8)=0$

5. **(c)** The given equation is equivalent to

$3(1-\cos^2x)+10\cos x-6=0$

$\Rightarrow$ $3\cos^2x-10\cos x+3=0$

$\Rightarrow$ $(3\cos x-1)(\cos x-3)=0$

Therefore $\cos x=1/3$ (because $\cos x\neq 3$).

Hence $x=2n\pi\pm\cos^{-1}(1/3), n\in I$.

6. **(c)** $\tan\theta=\frac{m_1-m_2}{1+m_1m_2}$

$$\frac{m-(1/2)}{1+(m/2)}=1$$

$\Rightarrow$ $m-\frac{1}{2}=\frac{m}{2}+1$

$\Rightarrow$ $\frac{m}{2}=\frac{3}{2}\Rightarrow m=3$

Trisection point (5, 4)

So, equation of line in new position will be

$y-4=3(x-5)$ or $3x-y-11=0$

7. **(a)** Any point A on the first line is $(t, 5t-4)$. Any point B on the second line is $\left(r,\frac{3r-4}{4}\right)$.

Hence, $1=\frac{2r+t}{3}$ and $5=\frac{\frac{3r-4}{2}+5t-4}{3}$

$\Rightarrow$ $2r+t=3$ and $3r+10t=42$.

On solving, we get $t=\frac{75}{17}$.

Hence A is $\left(\frac{75}{17},\frac{307}{17}\right)$

8. **(a, b, c)** Applying $C_3\to C_3-xC_2, C_2\to C_2-xC_1$ we obtain

$$\Delta(x)=\begin{vmatrix}3 & 0 & 2a^2\\ 3x & 2a^2 & 4a^2x\\ 3x^2+2a^2 & 4a^2x & 6a^2x^2+2a^4\end{vmatrix}$$

Apply $C_3\to C_3-xC_2$, we get

$$\Delta(x)=4a^4\begin{vmatrix}3 & 0 & 1\\ 3x & 1 & x\\ 3x^2+2a^2 & 2x & x^2+2a^2\end{vmatrix}$$

Apply $C_1\to C_1-3C_3$, we get

$$\Delta(x)=4a^4\begin{vmatrix}0 & 0 & 1\\ 0 & 1 & x\\ -4a^2 & 2x & x^2+2a^2\end{vmatrix}=16a^6$$

$\therefore$ $\Delta'(x)=0$, Δx is independent of x,

$\int_0^1\Delta(x)\,dx=16a^6$, $y=16a^6$ is a straight line of zero slope.

9. **(a, b, d)**

Since $|\tan^{-1}x|=\begin{cases}\tan^{-1}x, & \text{if } 0\le\tan^{-1}x<\pi/2\\ -\tan^{-1}x, & \text{if } -\pi/2<\tan^{-1}x<0\end{cases}$

$\begin{cases}\tan^{-1}x, & \text{if } x\ge 0\\ -\tan^{-1}x, & \text{if } x<0\end{cases}\Rightarrow|\tan^{-1}x|=\tan^{-1}|x|\quad\forall x\in R$

$\Rightarrow$ $\tan|\tan^{-1}x|=\tan\tan^{-1}|x|=|x|$

Likewise $\sin|\sin^{-1}x|=\sin\sin^{-1}|x|=|x|\quad\forall|x|\le 1$

$\cot|\cot^{-1}x|$ as $0<|\cot^{-1}x|<\pi,\ \forall x\in R$

$\Rightarrow\cot|\cot^{-1}x|=\cot\cot^{-1}x=x$

$|\tan x|$ is not necessarily always equal to $\tan|x|$

10. **(a, b, c, d)**

(a) Consider the function $f(x)=\frac{x^2}{x^3+200}$ in the interval $[1,\infty)$.

Since the derivative $f'(x)=\frac{x(400-x^3)}{(x^3+200)^2}$ is positive for $0<x<\sqrt[3]{400}$ and negative for $x>\sqrt[3]{400}$, the function f(x) increases in $0<x<\sqrt[3]{400}<8$. It follows that the largest term in the sequence can be either a_7 or a_8. Since $a_7=49/543>a_8=8/89$, the largest term in the given sequence is $a_7=\frac{49}{543}$.

(b) If $f_1(y)=\frac{2(y-1)}{y+1}-\log y$,

$f'_1(y)=-\frac{(y-1)^2}{y(y+1)^2}<0$ for all $y>0$

Thus $f_1(y)$ is a decreasing function for all $y>0$ and as

$f(1) = 0,\ f_1(y) < 0$ for all $y > 1$.

If $f_2(y) = \dfrac{y^2-1}{y} - \log y$,

$f'_2(y) = 1 - \dfrac{1}{y} + \dfrac{1}{y^2} > 0$ for all $y > 1$.

$f_2(1) = 0$ and $f_2(y)$ is increasing for all $y > 1$ so that $f_2(y) > 0,\ y > 1$.

$\therefore$ for all $y > 1$, $\dfrac{2(y-1)}{y+1} < \log y < \dfrac{y^2-1}{y}$

(c) We have to check if $(a + b)^p \le a^p + b^p$
By dividing both sides by b^p, we have to prove

$$\left(1+\frac{a}{b}\right)^p \le \left(\frac{a}{b}\right)^p + 1 \text{ i.e., } (1+x)^p \le x^p + 1,$$

where $x = \dfrac{a}{b} > 0$

Let $f(x) = x^p + 1 - (1+x)^p,\ x > 0$
$\therefore\ f'(x) = px^{p-1} - p(1+x)^{p-1}$

$$= p\left\{\frac{1}{x^{1-p}} - \frac{1}{(1+x)^{1-p}}\right\} > 0 \text{ always as } 1 - p > 0 \text{ and}$$

$x > 0$
Hence the function increases in $(0, \infty)$
$\therefore\ f(x) = 1 + x^p - (1+x)^p > f(0) = 0$, which proves the proposition.

(d) Let 'b' be the height of the cone and α be its semivertical angle.
$LD = x$ = radius of the inscribed cylinder and $LM = h$ be its height, $LM = OM - OL = b - x \cot\alpha$

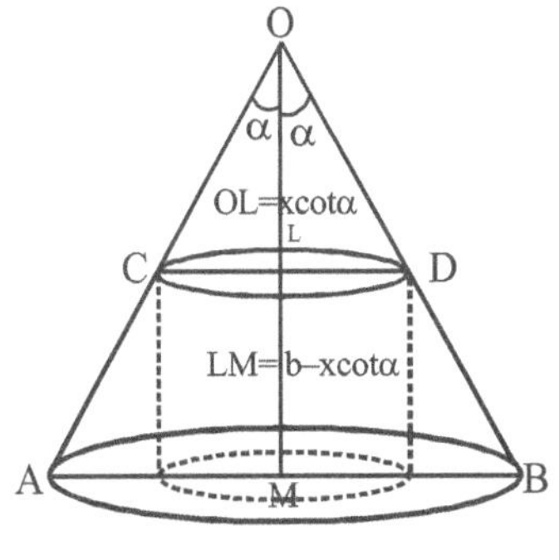

Now, $S = 2\pi rh$ = curved surface
$S = 2\pi x\,(b - x\cot\alpha)$ or $S = 2\pi\,(bx - x^2\cot\alpha)$
$\therefore\ dS/dx = 2\pi\,(b - 2x\cot\alpha) = 0$

$\therefore\ x = (b/2)\tan\alpha$ or $x = \dfrac{1}{2}(b\tan\alpha) = \dfrac{1}{2}(r_1)$

or radius of cylinder $= \left(\dfrac{1}{2}\right)$. (radius of cone)

Thus all statements (a, b, c, d) are correct.

11. (a, b, d)
(a) Here $f(x) = x^3 - x^2 + x + 1$
$\Rightarrow f'(x) = 3x^2 - 2x + 1$, which is strictly increasing in $(0, 2)$

$\therefore\ g(x) = \begin{cases} f(x); & 0 \le x \le 1 \\ 3 - x; & 1 < x \le 2 \end{cases}$ [as $f(x)$ is increasing so, $f(x)$ is maximum, when $0 \le t \le x$]

So, $g(x) = \begin{cases} x^3 - x^2 + x + 1; & 0 \le x \le 1 \\ 3 - x; & 1 < x \le 2 \end{cases}$

also, $g'(x) = \begin{cases} 3x^2 - 2x + 1; & 0 \le x \le 1 \\ -1; & 1 < x \le 2 \end{cases}$

which clearly shows $g(x)$ is not differentiable at $x = 1$.

(b) When $t \ge 0$; $|t| = t$
$\therefore\ x = 2t - t = t \Rightarrow x \ge 0$
and $y = t^2 + t^2 = 2t^2$
i.e. $y = 2x^2$, when $x \ge 0$
When $t < 0$; $|t| = -t$
$\therefore\ x = 2t - (-t) = 3t \Rightarrow x < 0$
and $y = t^2 + t(-t) = 0$
i.e. $y = 0$, when $x < 0$

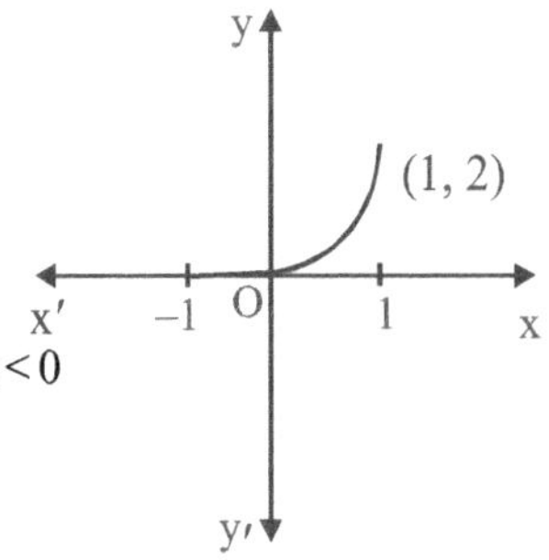

Thus $f(x) = \begin{cases} 2x^2; x \ge 0 \Rightarrow 0 \le x \le 1 \\ 0; x < 0 \Rightarrow -1 \le x < 0 \end{cases}$

Hence, the function is differentiable in $[-1, 1]$.

(c) We have

$$f'(4) = \lim_{h\to 0}\frac{f(4+h) - f(4)}{h}$$

$$= \lim_{h\to 0}\frac{f\left((\sqrt{4+h})^2\right) - f(2^2)}{h}$$

$$= \lim_{h\to 0}\frac{(4+h)^{3/2} - 8}{h} = \lim_{h\to 0}\frac{8[(1+h/4)^{3/2} - 1]}{h}$$

$$= \lim_{h\to 0}\frac{8\left[1 + \frac{3}{2}\frac{h}{4} + \dots - 1\right]}{h}$$

$$= \lim_{h\to 0}\frac{8\left[\frac{3}{8}h + \frac{3}{8}\left(\frac{h^2}{16}\right) + \dots\right]}{h}$$

$$= \lim_{h\to 0}[3 + 0 + \dots] = 3,$$

which is a finite number.
Hence f is differentiable at 4.
Hence option (c) is not correct.
Option (d) is obviously correct.

12. (a, c, d) $x^2y_1^2 + xyy_1 - 6y^2 = 0$

$$y_1 = \frac{-xy \pm \sqrt{x^2y^2 + 24x^2y^2}}{2x^2} = \frac{-xy \pm 5xy}{2x^2} = \frac{2y}{x}, -\frac{3y}{x}$$

$$\frac{dy}{dx}=\frac{2y}{x} \text{ or } \frac{dy}{dx}=-\frac{3y}{x}$$

i.e., $\frac{1}{2}\frac{dy}{y}=\frac{dx}{x}$ or $\int\frac{dy}{y}=-3\int\frac{dx}{x}$

i.e., $\ln y=\ln cx^2$ or $\ln y=-\ln cx^3$

or $y=cx^2$ or $x^3y=c$

13. (b, c) $y=\cos x\cos(x+2)-\cos^2(x+1)$

$$=\frac{1}{2}[\cos(2x+2)+\cos 2-(1+\cos(2x+2))]$$

$$=\frac{1}{2}(\cos 2-1)=-\sin^2 1$$

$\therefore$ Graph is a straight line $y=-\sin^2 1$, which is parallel to x-axis

14. (b, c, d) For $n=3$, $P=\begin{bmatrix} w^2 & w^3 & w^4 \\ w^3 & w^4 & w^5 \\ w^4 & w^5 & w^6 \end{bmatrix}$

and $P^2=\begin{bmatrix} 0 & 0 & 0 \\ 0 & 0 & 0 \\ 0 & 0 & 0 \end{bmatrix}$

It shows $P^2=0$ if n is a multiple of 3.
So for $P^2\neq 0$, n should not be a multiple of 3 i.e. n can take values 55, 58, 56

15. (a) $g(-x)=\int_0^{-x} f(t)dt=-\int_0^{x} f(-y)dy$ (where $t=-y$)

$$=-\int_0^x f(y)dy=-g(x)$$

so g (x) is an odd function.

16. (b) $g(x+2)-g(2)=\int_0^{x+2} f(t)dt-\int_0^{2} f(t)dt$

$$=\int_0^x f(y+2)dy \quad (\text{where } t=y+2)$$

$$=\int_0^x f(y)dy=g(x) \Rightarrow g(x+2)-g(x)=g(2) \text{ for all x.}$$

17. (b) The given equations

$$\frac{x-5}{3}=\frac{y-7}{-1}=\frac{z+2}{1} \quad \text{..........(1)}$$

$$\frac{x+3}{-3}=\frac{y-3}{2}=\frac{z-6}{4} \quad \text{..........(2)}$$

Any point P on (1) is $(3r_1+5,-r_1+7,r_1-2)$ and any point Q on (2) is $(-3r_2-3, 2r_2+3, 4r_2+6)$

The direction ratios of PQ are

$(3r_1+3r_2+8,-r_1-2r_2+4,r_1-4r_2-8)$ ....(3)

The line with d.r's 2, 7, -5 will be proportional to the d.r's given by (3)

$$\therefore \frac{3r_1+3r_2+8}{2}=\frac{-r_1-2r_2+4}{7}=\frac{r_1-4r_2-8}{-5} \quad \text{..........(4)}$$

Solving (4), we get $r_1=r_2=-1$

So point of intersection are P (2, 8, – 3) and Q (0, 1, 2) and intercepted length

$$=PQ=\sqrt{(2-0)^2+(8-1)^2+(-3-2)^2}=\sqrt{78}$$

18. (d) Shortest distance between B and plane OAC is

$$h=\frac{\overrightarrow{OA}\times\overrightarrow{OC}\cdot\overrightarrow{OB}}{|\overrightarrow{OA}\times\overrightarrow{OC}|}$$

Here, $\overrightarrow{OA}\times\overrightarrow{OC}\cdot\overrightarrow{OB}=\begin{vmatrix} 1 & 2 & 3 \\ 2 & -1 & 1 \\ 3 & 1 & 2 \end{vmatrix}$

$$=1(-2-1)+2(3-4)+3(2+3)=10$$

$$\overrightarrow{OA}\times\overrightarrow{OC}=\begin{vmatrix} \hat{i} & \hat{j} & \hat{k} \\ 2 & -1 & 1 \\ 3 & 1 & 2 \end{vmatrix}$$

$$=\hat{i}(-2-1)+\hat{j}(3-4)+\hat{k}(2+3)=-3\hat{i}-\hat{j}+5\hat{k}$$

$$|\overrightarrow{OA}\times\overrightarrow{OC}|=\sqrt{35} \;;\; h=\frac{10}{\sqrt{35}}=2\sqrt{\frac{5}{7}}$$

www.ingramcontent.com/pod-product-compliance
Lightning Source LLC
LaVergne TN
LVHW060821170826
845678LV00010B/1861

* 9 7 8 9 3 8 8 2 4 0 0 2 4 *